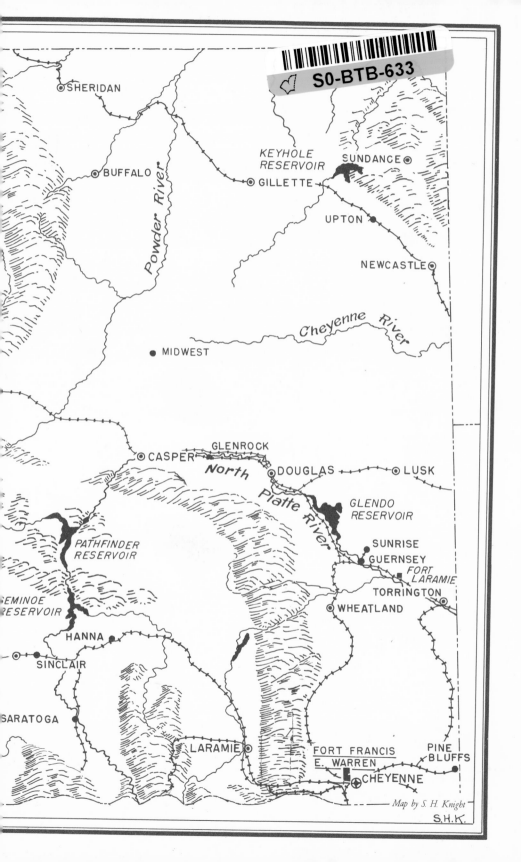

Map by S. H. Knight

S.H.K.

History of Wyoming

UNIVERSITY OF NEBRASKA PRESS

LINCOLN AND LONDON · 1978

History of Wyoming

Second Edition, Revised

By T. A. Larson

LINE DRAWINGS BY JACK BRODIE

Publishers on the Plains

UNP

COPYRIGHT © 1965, 1978 BY THE UNIVERSITY OF NEBRASKA PRESS
ALL RIGHTS RESERVED
MANUFACTURED IN THE UNITED STATES OF AMERICA

First printing 1978

LIBRARY OF CONGRESS CATALOGING IN PUBLICATION DATA

Larson, Taft Alfred, 1910–
History of Wyoming.

Bibliography: p. 623
Includes index.
1. Wyoming—History. I. Title.
F761.L3   1978   978.7   78–5653
ISBN 0–8032–2851–1

Dedicated TO GENE HARDY, A COURAGEOUS COLLEAGUE

Preface to the First Edition

HERE IN WYOMING, in an area of almost 100,000 square miles, a proud and enterprising people have labored mightily to come up with adequate responses to a host of tough challenges. In 1965, as they pause to contemplate seventy-five years of statehood, may this volume be a help and a stimulus to their reflections.

Until now, there has been no attempt to prepare a critical history of Wyoming for adult readers. In order to treat in detail territorial and state developments, I have excluded all but brief mention of the explorers, fur traders, and travelers on the Oregon, Mormon, and California trails—the people who came and went many years before there was a Wyoming. Since excellent studies of these interesting transients already are in print, perhaps I can be forgiven for slighting them.

During the writing of this volume, as well as during many hours of research scattered over a quarter of a century, I have incurred numerous debts. In addition to the persons listed in the "Sources" section, I wish to thank Wilson O. Clough and my wife, Mary, for reading the manuscript critically. I also wish to thank my wife and my daughter, Mary Lou, for having endured several years of neglect with patience and understanding.

Preface to the Second Edition

REVISING THE *History of Wyoming* has involved mainly the post–World War II chapters. The first sixteen chapters remain much as they were in the first edition except for forty-two pages where new information has been incorporated or interpretations have been modified.

Chapter 17 ("The Postwar Economy"), Chapter 18 ("Postwar Politics and Government"), and Chapter 19 ("Postwar Society and Culture") are at least 80 per cent new. In addition, the "Sources" discussion at the end of the volume has been revised and extended.

T. A. LARSON

Contents

List of Illustrations

Following page 306 there is a 32-page pictorial review.

History of Wyoming

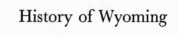

The Natural Setting and First Visitors

"HERE IS AMERICA high, naked and exposed," observed John Gunther in *Inside U.S.A.* A mean elevation of 6,700 feet makes Wyoming second highest among the fifty states, just below Colorado, its neighbor on the south. The altitude varies from 3,125 feet in the northeast to 13,804 feet at the summit of Gannett Peak in the Wind River Range. Mountain ranges lie oriented in various directions, the general trend, however, being from northwest to southeast. The Continental Divide crosses the state from the northwest corner to a point near the middle of the southern boundary, leaving three-fourths of the state on the eastern

1

side of the Divide. While several of the mountain ranges are strikingly beautiful, countless observers have pronounced the Teton Range most spectacular in the United States. The Tetons are remarkable, not for their altitude, which is only 13,766 feet, but because they rise, almost perpendicularly, 7,000 feet above the floor of Jackson Hole with no foothills in front of them.

Wyoming ranks ninth among the states in size, its area being 97,914 square miles, of which about 600 square miles is water. The state is situated between 41° and 45° north latitude, and between 104° 03′ and 111° 03′ west longitude. The United States acquired the area which eventually came to be known as Wyoming by the Louisiana Purchase (1803) and by treaties with Spain (1819), Great Britain (1846), and Mexico (1848).[1]

The state has exceptionally favorable conditions for the study of geology and paleontology. Ages ago, folding of the earth's crust caused mountains to be formed. Thereafter, gradual erosion of the mountains filled the basins, a second series of uplifts raised new mountains, and another period of erosion ensued. Great seas advanced and receded, leaving behind them sediments rich in fossils. At one time there were many dinosaurs, some of whose skeletons have been excavated and placed on display in major museums throughout the nation. There are valuable oil-bearing horizons in the state, and forests of semitropical trees once flourished there, to be turned eventually into rich coal deposits. Near Kemmerer are found fossils of fish that once swam in a great fresh-water lake covering all of southwestern Wyoming. In the northwest are to be seen hot-water phenomena and evidences of volcanic activity.

The great ice sheets that pushed into the Middle West from Canada failed to reach Wyoming, but ice caps formed on the mountain ranges. They fed glaciers which formed many beautiful mountain lakes in their progress down the slopes and pushed morainal deposits into the adjacent plains.

From a naked hill in the northeast, the poet Wilson Clough surveyed another typical Wyoming scene:

> . . . *Looking sunward on leagues of gaunt, marginal land,*
> *With strange buttes rising, apart, far distant, mysterious,*
> *Against the glistening afternoon sky,*
> *Like great ship-bulks, forever stranded on a static sea . . . .*

[1] See L. Milton Woods, *The Wyoming Country before Statehood* (Cheyenne: Wyoming State Archives and Historical Department, 1971) for maps showing political changes affecting Wyoming from earliest times to the present.

SOILS

Wyoming's sixty-two million acres of soils are remarkably variegated. Professor T. J. Dunnewald has listed seven major soil groups found in the state: shallow, stony mountain soils; limey valley alluvial soils; tight gray clays and loams on salty marine shales; friable grayish-brown loams from fresh-water shale; reddish-brown loams on red shale, sandstone, limestone, and scoria; brown sandy loams on loess, limestone, and sandstone; and dune sands. Each of the seven groups is divided into from eight to thirty soil series. The mainstay of irrigators has been the four million acres of alluvial soils laid down in river valleys by the erosion of mountains and hills. Salt accumulations reduce the value of perhaps one million acres of alluvial soils. Generally, the other soils listed, because they lack water or have other deficiencies, can sustain only one cow for every thirty to forty acres.

VEGETATION ZONES

Not more than 5 per cent of Wyoming's soil has been subjected to the plow. As was the case a century ago, most of the state—58,201 square miles—is still dotted with sagebrush. No other state has quite that much sagebrush.

Professor C. L. Porter has described six major vegetation zones of Wyoming: alpine zone; timbered mountain slopes; foothills scrub; grassland; desert and basin; and river bottoms. On the timbered mountain slopes the chief trees found at high elevations are Englemann spruce and subalpine fir; at middle elevations, lodgepole pine; at low elevations, ponderosa pine and Douglas fir. Chief constituents of the foothills scrub are mountain mahogany, sagebrush, and juniper. The broad belt of grassland along the eastern border includes tall grasses, such as needle grass and bluestem; shorter grasses, such as buffalo grass and blue grama; soapweed; prickly pear; and showy forbs, such as lupines, purple loco, and white-flowered beardtongue. The interior grassland plains have short grasses, such as blue grama, blue grass, June grass, needle grass, and wheat grass; they also have low species of vetch and rabbit brush, as well as greasewood, saltsage, and alkali spike grass. In the arid lands of the Great Basin in the south and the Big Horn and Powder River basins in the north occur prickly pear, hop sage, saltbrush, low sagebrush, rabbit brush, and greasewood. The wooded bottoms along the rivers have Plains cottonwood, box elder, and peach-leaved willow, while in the low northeastern corner of the state are found bur oak, elm, and green ash.

WILDLIFE

Wyoming's wildlife varies with elevation and vegetation zones. In the alpine zone one finds cony and mountain sheep. On timbered mountain slopes there are mule deer, elk, moose, bear, mountain lion, snowshoe rabbit, beaver, marmot, and porcupine. In desert and basin there are mule deer, pronghorn, white-tailed jack rabbit, white-tailed prairie dog, sage grouse, and golden eagle. On the plains are pronghorn, black-tailed prairie dog, ground squirrel, pocket gopher (at all elevations), badger, prairie falcon, golden eagle, and, rarely, bald eagle.

Mountain sheep and elk are no longer on the plains, where white men first found them. Mule deer were and still are in foothills scrub, as well as on timbered mountain slopes. Several thousand elk migrate from their summer range in the forested mountains to a federal-state elk refuge in Jackson Hole where they are fed hay in winter. Bison are raised for meat and hides on a large private ranch south of Gillette. Many coyotes and a few bobcats can still be found in the plains, desert-basin, and foothills regions despite private, state, and federal predator-control efforts.

Reptiles and amphibians are not common except on the plains and in river bottoms at the lowest elevations. Rattlesnakes occur in desert-basin and foothills zones, and a few boreal amphibians range into the mountains, even as far as the alpine zone.

Pheasants have been introduced in farming areas, as have wild turkeys around Laramie Peak and in the Black Hills. Many species of ducks frequent rivers and lakes.

The native cutthroat trout was present, except in the North Platte drainage, when white men first came, and several additional species of trout and other game fish have been introduced.

CLIMATE AND WEATHER

Wyoming enjoys great variety in climate because of the wide range in altitude. Semiarid is, however, an appropriate designation for all except the higher altitudes, since the average annual precipitation is about 14.31 inches. Mountain areas in the northwest receive more than 40 inches of precipitation a year, while substantial areas outside the mountains, notably the Red Desert west of Rawlins, the northern part of the Big Horn Basin, and the area around Shoshoni, receive less than 8 inches. Along the eastern border, where most of the state's dry farming is attempted, precipitation in some places exceeds 16 inches annually. Although rains are normally so light and of such short duration that many natives do not own umbrellas, torrential downpours and flash floods are not unknown.

Snow falls frequently from November through May, but rarely in large amounts except in the high mountains. Snowfall varies from 15 or 20 inches a year in the Big Horn Basin to more than 200 inches in the high mountains. The mountain snowpack, which accumulates in winter, supplies precious runoff in summer for irrigation, hydroelectric power, recreation, and other uses.

The average frost-free period in agricultural areas of Wyoming is about 125 days. Hardy plants which can stand a temperature of 28°F. enjoy a growing season of about 145 days in the eastern part of the state.

Severe winter storms are not common but can be terrifying when they do come. The blizzard which began January 2, 1949, raged furiously for three days in southeastern Wyoming and adjacent states. Many persons froze to death, and thousands were marooned for a few days in stalled trains or at isolated filling stations along blocked highways.

The heaviest snows are apt to come in March, April, or May, when they are least expected by newcomers. Five persons froze to death in a blizzard that struck most of eastern Wyoming on May 8, 1927. Tornadoes are rare, and do comparatively little damage, but to bolster a common opinion that anything can happen, a twister in July, 1960, cut a swath through timberland high in the Medicine Bow Mountains, uprooting large trees on the shore of Towner Lake. Another tornado felled trees near Union Pass in the Wind River Mountains in June, 1977. Hailstorms are quite common in eastern counties.

Evaporation is high because of the low relative humidity, high percentage of sunshine, and considerable wind. Evaporation and wind explain the observation sometimes heard that snow does not melt but blows back and forth until it wears out. Similarly, the wind is responsible for the rather common assertion that not much snow falls but a lot blows through. A phenomenon which astonishes and frightens visitors from lower altitudes is the ground blizzard, in which one cannot see the highway because of blowing snow, even though blue sky may be seen overhead.

Natives joke about the wind but become defensive when visitors complain about it. The average wind velocity is 13.8 miles per hour at Casper, 12.3 at Cheyenne, 12.0 at Rock Springs, 9.6 at Laramie, 8.3 at Sheridan, and 7.0 at Lander. These figures may be compared with

AVERAGE NUMBER OF DAYS WITHOUT KILLING FROST

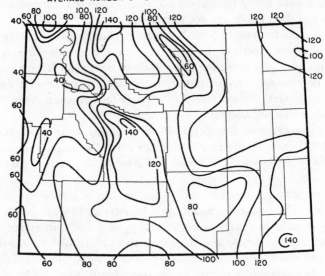

AVERAGE ANNUAL PRECIPITATION (INCHES)

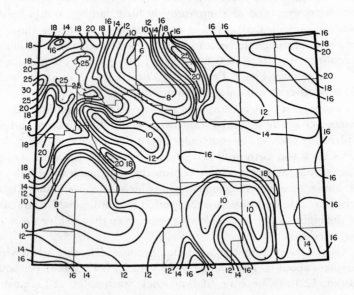

WYOMING WEATHER

14.0 at Oklahoma City, 11.3 at Omaha, 10.1 at Chicago, 9.7 at New York City, 9.6 at Denver, and 6.9 at New Orleans.

Temperatures sometimes reach 100° F at lower elevations in summer, and −50° F in winter at higher elevations. However, the low humidity has a cooling effect in summer and makes the cold less penetrating in winter.

FIRST HUMAN OCCUPANTS

More than 20,000 years ago ancestors of the American Indians crossed the Bering Strait from Asia to Alaska and moved south by various routes into what is now the United States. Some of these ancient people of the Clovis Complex stalked and killed ice-age mammoths in the Wyoming country about 11,500 years ago. Southwest of present-day Rawlins they butchered a mammoth whose skull was excavated in 1961 and placed on display in the University of Wyoming Geology Museum. A team of archeologists led by Dr. George C. Frison of the University of Wyoming in 1975 excavated the Colby Clovis site near Worland, where six immature mammoths had been killed and butchered. Many Folsom sites, about 10,500 years old, have also been found.

Teams led by Frison have excavated traps in which ancient hunters butchered herds of *bison antiquus*. These bison, larger than modern buffalo, were extant 9,000 to 10,000 years ago. They were trapped in arroyos or deep sand. Projectile points, knives, bone tools, and stacked piles of bison bones were found at the trap sites.

Other ancient people lived at the Jimmy Allen site near Laramie 7,900 years ago and at the Horner site near Cody 6,800 years ago. Many paleo-Indians, transients from the Midwest, dug quartzite for artifacts north of present Guernsey in a large area erroneously named "Spanish" Diggings.

About 6,000 years ago much of the region became desert, causing most of the people to leave. Then about 4,500 years ago, as the climate improved, foragers arrived with a marginal mixed economy of wild-vegetable products and rodent-size animals. Various Middle Period sites, dating from 2,500 B.C. to A.D. 500, have been found, notably along the Belle Fourche and North Platte rivers and in the Shoshone Basin. About A.D. 500, with further climatic improvements, the Middle Period gave way to the Late Period as more people moved in and established a prosperous buffalo economy. Late Prehistoric artifacts have been found in large quantities.

Among the Middle and Late Period relics are many stone circles or "tipi rings." Some of these anchored tipis or served as foundations for log lodges and brush wickiups. Professors George C. Frison and William T. Mulloy of the University of Wyoming and other anthropologists believe that a number of them were probably used for ceremonial purposes—perhaps as shrines or dance areas. They argue that many circles are located at very poor campsites, away from shelter, wood, and water; that there is too large a range in the size of the circles for them to have been used as tipi rings; and that the absence of charcoal and artifacts rules out habitation.

One of the best-known relics of the Late Period is the Great Medicine Wheel, a circle of stones measuring about seventy-five feet in diameter, with twenty-eight "spokes," located in the Big Horn Mountains east of Lovell. The Wyoming Archaeological Society has concluded that the Great Medicine Wheel was probably laid down about the year 1770 as a monument to some chief.

First White Visitors

A blade found in 1961 near the Tongue River at Dayton has been identified by the Curator of Arms and Armor at the Metropolitan Museum of Art, New York City, as "probably" part of a seventeenth-century Spanish rapier. Other Spanish articles discovered in Wyoming may have been brought by Spanish traders or by Indians who had stolen or traded for them. Coronado visited Kansas in 1541, Villasur was in Nebraska in 1720, and Escalante explored Utah in 1776, but there is no evidence indicating that any Spanish expedition came into Wyoming.

The Verendrye brothers, François and Louis-Joseph, and two other Frenchmen in 1742 traveled southwest from the Mandan villages in North Dakota and may have come as far as the Big Horn Mountains near Sheridan in January, 1743. The French trader Larocque came up the Powder River and Clear Creek in 1805. Virginian John Colter, veteran of the Lewis and Clark Expedition, almost certainly visited the Cody area, Jackson Hole, and Yellowstone Park during the winter of 1807–1808, and in August and September, 1811, Wilson Price Hunt led a party of sixty westward through northern Wyoming. During the winter of 1812–1813 Robert Stuart and six other Astor partners and employees traveled eastward across Wyoming, either through or just south of South Pass. They spent a few weeks in a cabin they built on the North Platte River west of Casper. Then, frightened by twenty-three Arapaho Indians who paid them a visit, they moved on to a second winter quarters, just east of present-day Torrington, where they remained until March, 1813, before advancing eastward.

After Colter, Hunt, and Stuart came more and more men of the fur trade, so that in the early 1830's there may have been as many as two hundred of them in Wyoming at one time. The story of these "mountain men" has been told in great detail in hundreds of volumes and will not be repeated here. They explored the area thoroughly, skinned thousands of beaver, lived virtually as savages, and for the most part vanished from history without leaving an imprint, except for a few place names, on modern Wyoming.

TRAILS

As the fur trade dwindled in the late 1830's, people with other interests entered Wyoming. First came a few scientists, missionaries, and sportsmen, then emigrants bound for Oregon, California, or Utah. Dale L. Morgan, the eminent historian of the trails, dates the era of emigration from 1840, when Joel Walker, the "first avowed home-seeker," went west. For many years thereafter the traffic was heavy every summer. The principal route lay up the North Platte River to Fort Laramie, situated at the junction of the Laramie and North Platte rivers, which was a fur-trade post and supply depot from 1834 to 1849 and an army post from 1849 to 1890.[2] From Fort Laramie the route followed the North Platte to present-day Casper, then the Sweet-water River to the Continental Divide at South Pass. West of South Pass the trail became frayed. Some travelers went southwest to Fort Bridger, built in 1842–1843 on Black's Fork of the Green by the old mountain man Jim Bridger and his partner Louis Vásquez. Beginning in 1844, more people used the Greenwood Cutoff, later known as the Sublette Cutoff or Sublette Road, and in 1859 the new Lander Road drew part of the traffic. There were several variations from these three major routes west of South Pass.[3]

Because nine-tenths of the travelers who used the central-Wyoming route were headed for California or Utah rather than Oregon, it seems appropriate to use the term Oregon-California-Utah Trail instead of Oregon Trail. A more southerly route, the Overland Trail, was used by many emigrants, especially in the years 1862–1868, but also, to some extent, as late as 1900. It led northwest across the Laramie Plains,

---

[2] Fort Laramie lies ninety miles (as the crow flies) northeast of the present university city of Laramie, where most easterners think it is located.

[3] Since writing this sentence, I have read in the Henry E. Huntington Library more than fifty unpublished diaries kept by travelers along the Wyoming trails, and I have become more impressed than ever with the complexity of the trail pattern from one end of Wyoming to the other.

around Elk Mountain, across the Platte north of present-day Saratoga, and over the Continental Divide at Bridger Pass.[4]

Even more books have been written about the trails and the people who followed them than about the mountain men. The story of emigrant experiences is a national epic which cannot be told well in a state history and will not be repeated here. The travelers spent less than thirty days in Wyoming and left little besides ruts, names and dates on

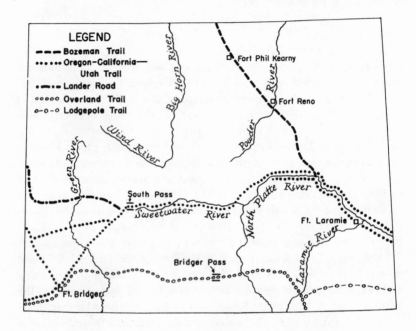

LEGEND
— —— Bozeman Trail
• • • • • • Oregon–California–
         Utah Trail
• —• — Lander Road
o o o o o Overland Trail
o–o–o Lodgepole Trail

Fort Phil Kearny
Fort Reno
Big Horn River
Powder River
Wind River
Green River
South Pass
Sweetwater River
North Platte River
Ft. Laramie
Laramie River
Bridger Pass
Ft. Bridger

WYOMING'S HISTORIC TRAILS

trailside cliffs, a few place names, and some graves. Indeed, exfoliation removed the early names from Independence Rock a long time ago. Like the mountain men, the emigrants left no significant imprint on modern Wyoming.

Mingling with the emigrants in the 1840's and 1850's were many unusual persons—such as John Charles Frémont, Stephen W. Kearny, Francis Parkman, Brigham Young, Howard Stansbury, F. T. Bryan, Frederick W. Lander, and W. F. Raynolds—who contributed to the

---

[4] To protect the Overland Trail, Fort Halleck was established at the north end of the Medicine Bow Range in July, 1862. It was abandoned in 1866.

opening of the West. Francis Parkman, for instance, visited Fort Laramie and the Laramie Plains in 1846 and wrote vivid descriptions of his experiences in his famous book entitled *The Oregon Trail.*

In the 1850's stagecoaches careened along the trails, to be followed by the Pony Express in 1860 and the first transcontinental telegraph line in October, 1861. Already the area which would soon be given the name Wyoming was quite well known to many people. Scarcely anyone, however, had shown any interest in making Wyoming his home— except the Indians.[5]

[5] See the "Sources" section at the end of this volume for a discussion of the sources which have been found most valuable in gathering information used in preparing this chapter and the chapters which follow.

CHAPTER 2

The Indians

THE FIRST WHITE VISITORS to Wyoming found roving bands of Indians: Shoshonis in the west, Crows in the north, and Cheyennes and Arapahos in the southeast. Sometimes, also, Blackfeet entered from the north and Utes from the south. The Oglala and Brulé Sioux moved to eastern Wyoming from South Dakota in the 1830's to complete the pattern of Indian settlement.

The Shoshonis and the Crows welcomed the whites and made friends with them, although the Crows continued to steal horses from both red men and white men without discrimination. The Sioux, with occasional help from the Cheyennes and Arapahos, caused endless grief in the period 1853–1877.

12

While the Shoshonis and Utes had entered Wyoming from the Great Basin before 1700, all of the other tribes had moved this way from Minnesota—the Crows, Cheyennes, and Arapahos in the eighteenth century, the Sioux in the nineteenth. The Oglalas and Brulés were the first Sioux to cross the Missouri from Minnesota, doing so after 1780. They drifted westward to settle in western South Dakota, the Oglalas in the Black Hills, the Brulés in the White River country south of the Black Hills. In 1834 the Oglalas accepted an invitation from traders Robert Campbell and William Sublette to move down to the vicinity of Fort Laramie, where they were soon joined by the Brulés.

Cheyennes and Arapahos who had preceded the Sioux into southeastern Wyoming had already shown a preference for the area to the south, between the North Platte and the Arkansas, and so did not resent the Sioux encroachment. Other Sioux tribes who followed the Oglalas and Brulés across the Missouri around 1800—Miniconjous, Hunkpapas, and Sans Arcs—would hunt and fight in Wyoming in later years, but they would never become as prominent in Wyoming affairs as the Oglala and Brulé Sioux, Cheyennes, Arapahos, Crows, and Shoshonis.

As the number of white travelers along the Platte increased in the 1840's, minor incidents suggested that serious trouble might develop at any time. The Indians persisted in begging and stealing, and they were not above killing stray whites. Some of the Sioux chiefs warned Lieutenant John Charles Frémont at Fort Laramie in 1842 that young warriors along the road west of the fort might make further travel dangerous for him. The chiefs explained that they had no control over their young men. The whites were to hear this statement from chiefs again and again during the next thirty years. There was much truth in it. Frémont proceeded in spite of the warning and was not harmed, but later travelers were not so fortunate. Although there was no large-scale assault on the emigrants, there was enough trouble to persuade the government of the need for a council with the Indians. Traffic on the Platte was increasing each year, and the Indians felt growing uneasiness about what might happen to their country. Perhaps a peace treaty would halt the erosion of remaining good will.

Thomas Fitzpatrick, first United States agent for the High Plains Indians, and D. D. Mitchell, Superintendent of Indian Affairs at St. Louis, worked out the details and obtained a congressional appropriation of $100,000 for expenses. They were named commissioners to represent the government. Runners were sent out to invite the High

Plains Indians to a treaty council at Fort Laramie beginning on September 1, 1851.[1]

Perhaps ten thousand Indians appeared at Fort Laramie in response to the government's invitations. The tribes represented at the council were the Sioux, Cheyennes, Arapahos, Crows, Assiniboins, Gros Ventres, Mandans, Arikaras, and Shoshonis. The Brulé and Oglala Sioux were most numerous, and there were quite a few Cheyennes and Arapahos. There were about two hundred Shoshonis, including eighty men, but since they were from west of the Rockies and were therefore not High Plains Indians, they were excluded from the treaty.

Colonel A. B. Chambers, editor of the *Missouri Republican* (St. Louis), and one of his reporters, B. Gratz Brown, attended the council and served as secretary and assistant secretary, respectively. The St. Louis editor was disappointed that there were not enough soldiers—only about two hundred—to impress the Indians with the power of the United States. And there seems to have been some concern lest traditionally hostile tribes might fall upon one another. Nothing of this kind happened, except for the scalping of two Shoshonis by some Cheyennes just east of South Pass on the way to the council.

The shortage of grass around the fort made it necessary to move the council thirty-six miles down the Platte, to the mouth of Horse Creek in Nebraska. Here D. D. Mitchell, the Superintendent of Indian Affairs at St. Louis, addressed the assembly through interpreters. He assured the Indians that the Great Father "has heard and is aware that your buffalo and game are driven off, and your grass and timber consumed by the opening of roads and the passing of emigrants through your country." He promised that there would be compensation. He explained that the Great Father wanted peace "between nations and bands as well as with the whites." The discussion continued for several days, terminating in a treaty on September 17. The Indians promised "to abstain in future from all hostilities whatever against each other" and to "recognize the right of the United States Government to establish roads, military and other posts, within their respective territories." The Indians promised, further, "to make restitution or satisfaction for any wrongs committed . . . on the people of the United States" and to

---

[1] Major source for the account which follows concerning the 1851 council is the report of the Commissioner of Indian Affairs for 1851 in *House Executive Document 2* (Serial 636), 32 Cong., 1 Sess., pp. 265–582. There are many secondary accounts, some of which are listed in the "Sources" section at the end of this volume. The treaty appears in Charles J. Kappler (ed.), *Indian Affairs: Laws and Treaties* (Washington: U.S. Government Printing Office, 1904), II, pp. 594–595.

sustain head chiefs, "through whom all national business will hereafter be conducted." The Indians accepted national boundaries: the Sioux north of the North Platte as far west as Red Buttes (just west of present-day Casper), their western boundary to be a diagonal line from Red Buttes to the western side of the Black Hills and beyond; the Crows from Powder River west to the Wind River Mountains; the Cheyennes and the Arapahos between the North Platte and Arkansas rivers. The other tribes were assigned territories north of Wyoming. These tribal boundaries, however, were virtually obliterated by the insertion of a qualifying sentence: "It is, however, understood that . . . the aforesaid Indian nations do not hereby abandon or prejudice any rights or claims they have to other lands; and further, that they do not surrender the privilege of hunting, fishing, or passing over any of the tracts of country heretofore described."

In return for the Indians' concessions, the United States government promised to protect them against "the commission of all depredations by the people of the said United States" and also promised an annuity of $50,000 in goods for fifty years. Twenty-one chiefs made their marks at the end of the treaty, and fifteen whites signed as witnesses.

The United States soon modified the treaty unilaterally in that the Senate reduced the fifty years to ten years and granted the President the right to continue the annuity for another five years. Some color of legality for the change was achieved when Thomas Fitzpatrick later obtained the approval of twenty-one chiefs for the amendment.

The supply train arrived at Horse Creek on September 20, bringing $50,000 worth of presents for immediate distribution. After he returned to St. Louis, Superintendent Mitchell wrote to the Commissioner of Indian Affairs that the presents were considered as full payment for past injuries to the Indians in the form of destruction of buffalo, timber, and grass.

Mitchell thought that fifty years was time enough in which to learn whether the Indians could be civilized. The annuities, he hoped, could be used to turn their attention gradually to agriculture. He estimated that while only ten thousand Indians were at the council, they represented at least fifty thousand.

As the heavy migration along the Platte continued in the 1850's, a new grievance developed among the Indians. The Indian agent at Fort Pierre reported in 1853 "the great loss of so many of their friends and relatives by the distressing ravages made by the introduction amongst them of the smallpox, measles, and cholera, which they attribute solely to the emigrants passing through their country." Thomas Fitzpatrick, Indian agent for Upper Platte and Arkansas, touched on another sore spot the same year when he reported that "great numbers" of traders bound for Oregon and California "pay no regard to . . . restrictions, traffic without license, furnish liquor to the Indians, and render all efforts to regulate intercourse a mere farce."[2]

Rash actions by officers at Fort Laramie brought needless bloodshed and hard feelings in 1853 and 1854. In June, 1853, three Miniconjou Sioux were killed and three wounded in a battle which ensued when a lieutenant with twenty-three men and an interpreter entered an Indian camp to arrest a brave who had fired a shot at a sergeant.

A far worse tragedy occurred in August, 1854. A Miniconjou Sioux, visiting in a Brulé Sioux village near the fort, killed a cow belonging to a Mormon emigrant. Lieutenant Hugh B. Fleming, commanding officer, sent Lieutenant John Lawrence Grattan with 29 soldiers and an interpreter to arrest an accused Indian. The Indian refused to surrender, and many young Brulés sustained their Miniconjou guest. Someone started shooting, and when the smoke cleared, the whole detachment from the fort had been killed except one soldier, who lingered three days before he, too, died. There was one Indian killed, Chief Brave Bear of the Brulés.[3]

Lieutenant Grattan evidently had not been able to accept the alternative of returning to the fort empty handed. His interpreter hated Indians, had lost two cattle to them a few days before, and fortified himself with a few drinks before entering the Sioux village. Several officials investigated the affair; Congress and the press discussed it heatedly. Indian Agent Whitfield's conclusions are as good as any: "No doubt Lieutenant Grattan's want of knowledge of the Indian character, and the rash language used by a drunken interpreter, was the cause of the unfortunate affair." There was no resident agent at the fort at the time. Upper Platte Agent Whitfield arrived from the south about one week later. Had he been in residence near Fort Laramie, it seems probable that there would have been no massacre, for the Brulé chiefs had been willing to pay for the cow, and he could have arranged for compensation in one form or another.

[2] For further discussion of 1853 events, see the report of the Commissioner of Indian Affairs for 1853 in *Senate Executive Document 1* (Serial 690), 33 Cong., 1 Sess., pp. 241–481.

[3] The major report on the Grattan Massacre appears in *House Executive Document 63* (Serial 788), 33 Cong., 2 Sess., pp. 1–27. Other important material is found in Government Documents, Serials 746, 747, and 777.

When Whitfield arrived on his yearly visit to distribute annuity goods, he found part of his work already done for him. After the massacre, the Sioux had broken into storehouses and helped themselves. In fact, they had even considered attacking the fort before traders dissuaded them. Whitfield reported that there were only ten soldiers in the fort, the rest of the small garrison being off some distance on hay detail. After raiding the storehouses, the Sioux divided and moved north and south of the Platte. Most of the North Platte Cheyennes and half of the North Platte Arapahos were still near the fort, however, and Whitfield found them in a foul mood. He called the Cheyennes into council, where their spokesman made some extraordinary proposals: "He commenced by stating that the travel over the Platte road by emigrants should be stopped; that next year I must bring four thousand dollars in money, balance of their annuity in guns and ammunition, and one thousand white women for wives." Whitfield found "this band of Cheyennes the sauciest Indians I have ever seen."

Fort Laramie got a resident Indian agent in 1855 in the person of the remarkable Thomas S. Twiss, who had been graduated from West Point second in his class in 1826 but resigned his commission in 1829. His first official report, dated August 20, 1855, said: "There is not, as I can find, within this agency, a single hostile Indian; on the contrary, they are all friendly." [4] Nevertheless, for a time Twiss cooperated with General W. S. Harney—who was on his way up the Platte with 600 men to punish the Sioux—to the extent that he warned all the Indians he could find to move south of the Platte. Those who remained north of the Platte would be regarded as hostile and treated accordingly. General Harney found Little Thunder's band of Brulé Sioux north of the Platte near Ash Hollow in Nebraska in September. Harney killed 86, wounded 5, and captured 70 women and children. For his own forces, Harney reported 4 killed, 7 wounded, and one missing. And so the deaths that can be traced to the killing of a ten-dollar cow piled up: 32 in the Grattan Massacre, 90 in the Harney retribution for the Grattan Massacre. After chastising the Brulé Sioux, General Harney summoned all the Sioux of the Platte and Missouri to a council at Fort Pierre in March, 1856. The character of the Indian was undergoing great modifications, he reported; they now desired to work to live, he optimistically advised the Secretary of War.

Alfred Cumming, Superintendent of Indian Affairs at St. Louis, in

[4] Twiss's first report as Upper Platte agent appears in *House Executive Document 1* (Serial 840), 34 Cong., 1 Sess., pp. 398–405.

his August 20, 1857, report to the Commissioner of Indian Affairs, noted "a growing spirit of insubordination . . . among the wild tribes of the prairies." [5] He suggested that the War Department take control of the Indian Service, which had been placed in the new Interior Department in 1849.

Twiss reported in September, 1858, that the "insolent, audacious, and lawless" Crows and Blackfeet "are constantly sending war parties against the Sioux, Arapahoes, and Cheyennes, of this agency." [6] George E. Hyde states that by this time Twiss was living with an Oglala girl and a pet bear at Deer Creek (present-day Glenrock). Twiss said that he was "with much difficulty" able to restrain his tribes from striking back. The Sioux were in fact busy driving the Crows north and west of the Big Horn Mountains.

Gold discoveries brought thousands of people and a plateful of Indian troubles to Colorado in 1859. Major John Sedgwick, stationed at Fort Wise in southeastern Colorado, characterized the participants in the Pikes Peak gold rush: "I hope there never was a viler set of men in the world than is congregated about these mines; no man's life is safe. . . . They have established a vigilance committee, and it may get rid of some of the scoundrels, but it would depopulate the country to kill them all." [7]

The Cheyennes and Arapahos of the Upper Platte and Arkansas agencies in particular were affected by the gold rush across their tribal lands. They found it harder to locate buffalo and harder to resist the temptation to prey on white travelers and settlers. In April, 1861, Governor Gilpin of Colorado asked for the transfer to his superintendency of the Cheyennes and Arapahos between the Plattes who were attached to Twiss's agency. Twiss was not around to protest because he had just been removed from office. He chose to move up into the Powder River country with his Sioux in-laws.

The area between the North Platte and the Arkansas had been assigned to the Cheyennes and Arapahos by the Fort Laramie Treaty of 1851, but the great changes incidental to the Pikes Peak gold rush prompted federal authorities to force the Arapahos and Cheyennes upon a small reserve in southeastern Colorado. Such volatile spirits could not easily be compressed. Many of both tribes refused to stay on

[5] Cumming's report for 1857 is in Government Documents, Serial 919.

[6] Twiss's 1858 report appears in Government Documents, Serial 974, pp. 94–96.

[7] In a letter to his sister. See p. 271 of LeRoy R. Hafen and Ann W. Hafen (eds.), *Relations with the Indians of the Plains, 1857–1861* (Glendale: Arthur H. Clark Co., 1959).

the land assigned to them, preferring to attack ranches and raid along the trails. When they tired of such activity, they would go hunting in Kansas or Nebraska or up in Wyoming's Powder River country.

Preoccupation of federal authorities with the Civil War permitted relations with the Indians to worsen all along the frontiers. There were lots of people moving around in the West and few troops to protect them. In 1862, Ben Holladay moved his stage line from the Oregon Trail to the Overland Trail in southern Wyoming to avoid Indian harassment but found just as much trouble along the new route. Indeed, his move complicated the problem of defense because heavy travel continued on the central route, making it necessary to protect two routes instead of one. The telegraph line completed across central Wyoming in 1861 also required protection.

The worst Indian trouble of the war years occurred in August, 1862, in Minnesota, far from the Wyoming frontier. Tired of being pushed around, the eastern (or Santee) Sioux, in a series of attacks, killed more than seven hundred whites. In subsequent months, Minnesota militiamen under General H. H. Sibley repaid the Indians with interest. Many of the Minnesota Indians fled westward, spreading the infection of hatred for the whites wherever they went.

Even the Shoshoni reputation for magnanimity toward the whites was tarnished in 1862 when hostile Shoshoni and Bannock warriors raided the trails in Idaho and Wyoming. The following January, Brigadier General Patrick E. Connor surprised their camp on Bear River in southern Idaho, killing more than 250 of them. Connor's success gave him great stature as a western hero, and many westerners began to demand that Indian fighting be turned over to him. Here, they said, was an efficient Indian exterminator!

Governor John Evans of Colorado had trouble in trying to separate the friendlies from the hostiles. In June, 1864, he instructed the Indian agent on the Arkansas to feed all friendly Cheyennes and Arapahos who would come in and establish their credentials. Late in September, Black Kettle brought his Cheyenne band in to make peace. Governor Evans wondered what the Cheyennes had been doing all summer and told Black Kettle that he would have to negotiate with the military authorities. Colonel John M. Chivington, in command of the Colorado militia, was equally cold. Both Evans and Chivington advised the Cheyennes to go to Fort Lyon on the Arkansas for a conference with the commanding officer there. The officer at Fort Lyon refused to feed the Indians, explaining that his supplies were inadequate. He sent them away with instructions to stay within thirty-five miles of the fort and to report their location regularly. Black Kettle assumed that he was under military protection.

Meanwhile, Colonel Chivington was smarting under public sneers. His Third Colorado Cavalry, consisting of 100-day volunteers, had seen little action in its first seventy days and was known as the "Bloodless Third." Pushed to fury by public pressure, Chivington decided that he must have action. He chose Black Kettle's band at Sand Creek for his target. There were 550 Indians, Cheyennes except for a few Arapahos; Chivington had 825 men and the benefit of surprise. The cavalrymen struck the village early on the morning of November 29, slaughtering men, women, and children. First reports indicated 500 victims, but a later, more accurate tally placed the Indians' losses at 150 dead, compared with only 7 for the Third Cavalry. While it is true that some westerners applauded, most easterners condemned the slaughter, and Indian warriors were infuriated. A congressional investigation reached the conclusion that the Indians were under the protection of the army at the time of the attack. Chivington countered that all battles produce some excesses. An army court of inquiry, like Congress, criticized Chivington.

Inevitably, High Plains Indians became more hostile. Cheyenne survivors retaliated by attacking Julesburg, Colorado, and several other places. They pounced on a party of former soldiers headed east on the South Platte. With their traditional associates, the Arapahos and Sioux, the Cheyenne warriors laid plans for a large-scale campaign of terror. They would place their families out of harm's way in northern Wyoming and the Black Hills. Upper Platte Indians—Brulés, Oglalas, Cheyennes, and Arapahos—were drawn into the struggle. Some docile friendlies who were known as "Laramie Loafers" stayed close to Fort Laramie, while others fell into the familiar pattern of friendly today, hostile tomorrow.

A soldier of fortune with a good military record in the Civil War, Colonel Thomas Moonlight first inherited the responsibilities of keeping peace in Colorado and was then transferred to Fort Laramie. In the spring of 1865, this was the chain of command in the Wyoming country: Major General Grenville M. Dodge, commander, Division of the Missouri; Brigadier General Patrick E. Connor, commander, District of the Plains; Colonel Thomas Moonlight, commander, North Sub-District of the Plains.

Dodge at Leavenworth and Connor at Julesburg planned to strike at the roots of hostile power in the Powder River–Tongue River area.[8] The termination of the Civil War, it was thought, would free large numbers of troops for action. As Connor tried to round up 4,500 men, the Indians were not idle. They put relentless pressure on all trails in the region and soon squandered what good will had accrued to them from sympathy over mistreatment at Sand Creek.

While Connor fumed over delays in the delivery of men and matériel, Moonlight became restless and took the initiative. He left Fort Laramie on May 3, 1865, hopeful that, under the able guidance of Jim Bridger, he and his five hundred cavalrymen could surprise a band of Cheyennes reported to be in the Wind River Valley. En route he advised Connor on May 9: "Have positive information that large village of Cheyennes are on Wind River and Big Horns. Will strike that village by rapid night marches and while this moon lasts." His men suffered from the cold, his horses from inadequate feed on the snow-covered prairie. He found no Indians in 450 miles of search and returned, chagrined, to Fort Laramie on May 21. A few days later Moonlight hanged, without trial, two Oglala Sioux chiefs, Two Face and Black Foot. There has been much controversy over these hangings, and some would have it that the victims were really friends of the whites mistaken for enemies.

In June, Generals Dodge and Connor, with approval from Washington, decided to move the friendly Brulés and Oglalas, including the Laramie Loafers, from Fort Laramie eastward to Fort Kearny, Nebraska. The purpose was to prevent any of them from joining the hostiles who were soon to be placed under the hammer in the Powder River country. Not desiring to move into enemy Pawnee country, the Sioux, en route on Horse Creek, rebelled and killed Captain W. D. Fouts and four other members of the military escort, then fled northward. On an expedition to intercept the fleeing Indians, Colonel Moonlight had most of his horses run off by them. He was promptly relieved of his command. General Connor considered him responsible for "a series of blunders" during his brief administration at Fort Laramie. In baseball one is permitted three strikes before he goes out; Moonlight missed four times: a fruitless search for Indians in the Wind River country; the hasty execution of the two chiefs, without trial, for which there was criticism; the revolt and flight of the friendly Sioux

[8] Principal sources for the 1865 campaigns which are discussed here are gathered together in LeRoy R. Hafen and Ann W. Hafen (eds.), *Powder River Campaigns and Sawyers Expedition of 1865* (Glendale: Arthur H. Clark Co., 1961). See also H. D. Hampton, "The Powder River Expedition 1865," *Montana, The Magazine of Western History*, XIV, 4 (Autumn 1964), pp. 2–15.

(Moonlight should have dismounted them before starting them on their way to Fort Kearny, said Connor); and the loss of the horses (California horses, the best in the District of the Plains, said Connor). The District Commander was in bad humor anyway, for he was under considerable pressure to get moving on his Powder River campaign, and everything seemed to be working against him.

The 4,500 men promised to Connor for the Powder River campaign were not forthcoming. Civil War volunteers expected to be mustered out and sent home, even though their enlistment periods had not expired. They did not relish the prospect of an Indian campaign. Instead of 4,500 men, Connor got 2,500, and among these were some who had to be threatened "with grape and canister" before they would go.[9]

Had Connor been able to get organized more quickly, he might have been able to save 26 lives lost in central Wyoming that summer. A large number—the figure 3,000 is often given—of Sioux, Cheyennes, and Arapahos focused their attention on Platte Bridge Station in late July.[10] The hostiles destroyed a government wagon train approaching the army post from the west and also killed several men sent out from the post to succor the wagon train. Among the dead was Lieutenant Caspar W. Collins, whose given name was soon applied to the military

[9] At Fort Laramie on June 29, 1865, Private Cyrus C. Scofield, Company K, Sixteenth Kansas, wrote to his wife: "I understand it is the talk among some of the leading Officers that we will go to Powder river, build a Fort and garrison it next winter.... If the report in regard to this plan on Powder river is correct it was probably concocted by the Col. and General, in order to give them a fat office a while longer, for I suppose they have not sucked Uncle Sam's paps long enough to satisfy them yet; I rather think they will fail of their plan, for wherever I go from one end of camp to the other the talk is the same, nearly everyone believes that our Officers are going against orders. It is said that Capt. Ames and Co. will go no farther. And if he goes back it is my candid opinion that a majority of the Regt. will follow him. It is bad to be driven to desperation, but I do believe that our highest authorities in the War Department do not intend to have volunteers kept in the service after they can possibly be relieved by regulars, and regulars can certainly be sent here to relieve us some time this summer. I believe some things are too bad to be endured, and if they cannot be cured in one way they will in another. If we are kept here much longer, and it is known that we are kept against orders, then in that case, vengeance is sworn on many an officer if we ever get into a fight, from all I can learn I would not be in some of their places for all the world." The excerpt is from a letter preserved in the University of Wyoming Library.

[10] Platte Bridge Station was so named because it was located at the south end of a bridge built across the North Platte in 1858–1859 by a trader, Louis Guinard. Several years earlier (1851–1853) another trader, John Richard (Reshaw), had built a bridge over the North Platte five miles down river at present Evansville. The Richard bridge was dismantled in 1865–1866.

post and eventually to the city established nearby. General Connor was still at Fort Laramie during the troubles at Platte Bridge Station, but he was able to put his men into the field a few days later. At last the agonizing delays were over.

The Powder River campaigns of 1865 involved the poorly coordinated activities of three columns of troops. Colonel J. H. Kidd's column, which was accompanied by General Connor, comprised 475 officers and men. Among them were 95 Pawnee scouts under Captain Frank North and 84 Winnebago and Omaha scouts under Captain W. W. Nash. This column left Fort Laramie and generally followed the Bozeman Trail into the area east of the Big Horns. Connor paused to build Fort Connor, a supply base on the Powder some twenty miles east of present-day Kaycee—"nothing but a collection of cottonwood shacks," said a visitor. Two companies under Captain Albert Brown swung west past Platte Bridge Station before rejoining the column in northern Wyoming.

The second column, led by Colonel Samuel Walker, consisted of six hundred officers and men and moved north from Fort Laramie past modern Lusk and Newcastle into Dakota and Montana. Meanwhile, the third column, fourteen hundred men under Colonel Nelson Cole, was on its way through Nebraska, having left Omaha on July 1. This third column crossed Dakota along the east side of the Black Hills and entered southeastern Montana before turning south to follow up the Powder into Wyoming. All three columns were supposed to get together in southeastern Montana and northeastern Wyoming for energetic harassment of the hostiles known to be there.

Several forces conspired to leave results far short of expectations. The late start, terrible weather in late August and early September (extremes of temperature, sleet, and snow), poor guide service, inability to get together in a strange, vast country, and clever hit-and-run tactics by the Indians contributed to endless confusion and frustration.

While Connor was building his fort, his Pawnee scouts jumped a party of 24 Cheyennes, consisting of 23 men and one woman, and after a sixty-mile chase managed to kill and scalp all of them without loss to themselves. The other principal achievement was destruction of the Arapaho village of Black Bear and Old David in the Battle of Tongue River, fought at what is now Ranchester. The village of perhaps 500 persons was surprised by Connor and Kidd as preparations were under way for moving early on the morning of August 29. Connor reported 35 warriors killed, the lodges and all their contents destroyed, and 500 horses captured. Connor lost 8 men in this engagement. In a subsequent report, General Dodge described the battle as "chastising one tribe of Indians in a manner seldom before equaled and never excelled."

After punishing the Arapahos, Connor moved down the Tongue into Montana before returning to Fort Connor on the Powder. While in Montana he received word that a wagon-road survey crew was under attack by some of these same Arapahos at a point on Tongue River only three miles from the site of recent battle. This was the Sawyers Expedition, numbering about one hundred men at this time. Sawyers was laying out a road from Sioux City, Iowa, west along the Niobrara and on to the gold fields in southwestern Montana, and the party had crossed Wyoming south of present-day Newcastle and Gillette. The Arapahos struck the survey group on September 1 and kept it corralled for several days. Sawyers had decided to abandon the survey and had started slowly back toward Fort Connor when a relief party arrived from Connor to escort the surveyors to their Montana goal.

While Kidd's column (with Connor) was enjoying moderate success, the two thousand men with Walker and Cole were less fortunate. Walker and Cole met just north of the Black Hills and moved into Montana, where they were on the Powder early in September at the time Connor was sixty miles west on the Tongue. They were harried for several days by thousands of Indians (Walker estimated three thousand, others six thousand), so many that Walker and Cole were constantly on the defensive. The weather was vile, first hot, then cold. The troops lost more than six hundred horses and mules, most of them frozen to death when left picketed in the open in a sleet storm. The men suffered terribly. They burned their saddles and walked, many of them barefooted. With rations exhausted, they were reduced to eating horse and mule meat. Worst of all, they were lost and on the point of complete demoralization and collapse. The Pawnee scouts found them just in time and directed them to Fort Connor. When they straggled into the post, they were manifestly the sorriest army ever seen in Wyoming, reminiscent of Napoleon's veterans returning from Moscow.

Analysis of the reports which followed the Powder River campaigns leads to the conclusion that the net damage done to the hostiles was approximately as follows: 100 Indians killed, an Arapaho village of perhaps 200 lodges and all their contents destroyed, and 1,100 horses captured, although many of them were later lost to the Indians. Only twenty of the troops were killed, a remarkably small total considering the circumstances.

Already before the battle on the Tongue, orders were on the way recalling Connor and sending him to Utah.

General William Tecumseh Sherman of Civil War fame replaced General John Pope in command of the West while the Powder River campaigns were under way. He soon had to yield to the wishes of easterners and economy-minded congressmen who felt that the army was too large for peacetime needs. His western forces of twenty-five thousand men were cut in half before the end of 1866.[11]

Recognizing that there were still thousands of Sioux, Cheyennes, and Arapahos whom Connor had disturbed but not destroyed in the Powder River country, the government sent five Indian messengers out in October, 1865, to invite some of the hostiles in for treaty-making purposes in June, 1866. In March, 1866, Colonel Maynadier of Fort Laramie reported a promising augury to the Commissioner of Indian Affairs: Spotted Tail, head chief of the Brulés, had just brought his daughter's body in for burial in the white man's cemetery at the fort. Colonel Maynadier was right in thinking that Spotted Tail had made up his mind to be friendly toward the whites, but wrong in supposing that this would mean "a certain and lasting peace." Red Cloud and other hostiles were not influenced much by Spotted Tail thereafter.

Many hostiles joined the friendlies at Fort Laramie for the conference in June, 1866. Two thousand Brulés and Oglalas met with the commissioners. After considerable argument, most of them signed a treaty and agreed to behave in return for liberal annuity goods to be distributed twice a year, spring and fall, not just once a year as in the past.[12]

The major concession extracted from the reluctant Sioux at Fort Laramie in June, 1866, was their promise that they would not interfere with travel on the Bozeman Trail. John Bozeman had pioneered this cutoff route to the Montana gold fields in 1863. It passed through the highly regarded last hunting grounds of the Sioux, Cheyennes, and Arapahos. Some of the Cheyennes came in and signed a similar treaty late in the year, but not enough Arapahos gathered to justify a treaty.

In their report the commissioners expressed guarded optimism, neglecting to mention the most significant occurrence during the negotiations with the Sioux. Colonel Henry B. Carrington marched past Fort Laramie with seven hundred infantrymen, headed for the

[11] Robert G. Athearn, *William Tecumseh Sherman and the Settlement of the West* (Norman: University of Oklahoma Press, 1956), p. 29. Anyone who would understand the Indian problem of the 1860's and 1870's needs to read this volume.

[12] The treaty making of 1866 is covered in the report of the Commissioner of Indian Affairs for that year in Government Documents, Serial 1284.

Powder River country, while discussions were still in progress. This caused Red Cloud and Man-Afraid-of-His-Horse to withhold their signatures. To them it seemed hypocritical and underhanded to send troops into the disputed area during the negotiations. Carrington had received his orders in April. Clearly the War Department and Interior Department were working at cross-purposes, as was the case most of the time during the years of the Indian wars. Red Cloud of the Oglalas was now the recognized leader of the hostile warriors in the Powder River country. His refusal to treat spelled much more trouble than the commissioners and their superiors imagined.

People today who do not know the Powder River country (and some who do) may wonder why the Indians loved the region with such a passion. The late T. J. Gatchell of Buffalo explained it thus: "From the Indians' standpoint, the country was all that could be desired—plenty of shelter, mild winters, sufficient food for their ponies, and an abundance of game in the broken country surrounding them for their own subsistence. It was an Indian paradise."

Carrington left some men on the left bank of the Powder at the site of abandoned Fort Connor. They built a new fort, which was named Fort Reno, while he marched on to the Big Horns, where he began the construction of Fort Phil Kearny on Little Piney Creek between present-day Buffalo and Sheridan. The hostiles ran off some of his horses on his second day on Piney Creek, and they kept up the pressure as long as troops remained there. In August, Carrington sent two companies ninety miles northwest into Montana to build Fort C. F. Smith. Carrington and his men were constantly on the defensive, barely able to protect themselves, and quite unable to keep the Bozeman Trail open. From Fort Laramie, General Sherman wrote in August that the Indians had killed twenty-five persons on the Bozeman Trail during the summer, mostly civilians.

The favorite tactic of the Sioux, tried over and over again during the Indian-war period, was to assign a small, bold decoy party the task of leading troops into a trap in which they could be surrounded and destroyed by an overwhelming number of hidden warriors. Such a trap was sprung December 21, 1866, on a detachment sent out from Fort Phil Kearny to relieve a wood train under attack. Captain (brevet Lieutenant Colonel) W. J. Fetterman and 81 officers and men, including 2 civilians, were slain.[13] Participating in the slaughter were

[13] Much has been published about the Fetterman disaster. The basic federal-government documents are *Senate Executive Document 33* in Serial 2504 and *Senate*

Red Cloud, recognized war chief of the Oglalas; Crazy Horse, who in his early thirties was gaining stature as a war leader of the Oglalas; and High-Back-Bone, Miniconjou war leader. Crazy Horse has been credited with leading the decoy party, which retired slowly before Fetterman's advance until the most successful trap in Sioux history could be sprung. Normally, overeager young men showed themselves and gave the trap away, but not this time. Historians have guessed that from 100 to 300 Indians were killed, but the Indians later argued, plausibly, that their loss was less than that of the whites.

Although he still had more than 300 men, Colonel Carrington was afraid that Indians might storm the fort and overwhelm them. So he sent two civilian volunteers, John "Portugee" Phillips and Daniel Dixon, to Fort Laramie, 235 miles away, for reinforcements. It is not known whether they rested and changed horses at Fort Reno and Bridger's Crossing of the Platte. They sent a telegram from Horseshoe Station to Fort Laramie, after which Phillips covered the remaining 40 miles alone. He arrived at Fort Laramie about 10:00 P.M. Christmas night, four days and nights out of Fort Phil Kearny. Phillips and Dixon received three hundred dollars apiece for their mission. It was the most remarkable ride in Wyoming history, whether we accept Grace R. Hebard's statement that "Red Cloud's warriors watched every mile of the way." Reinforcements reached Fort Phil Kearny in mid-January.

Colonel Carrington was at first blamed for the Fetterman disaster. General Sherman wrote to General Augur that Carrington was "better qualified for a safe place than one of danger." Carrington eventually managed to shift most of the blame to Captain Fetterman by claiming that he had disobeyed explicit orders not to go beyond Lodge Trail Ridge. Scholars, however, divide the responsibility between Colonel Carrington and Captain Fetterman. Part of the blame was for a while attributed to General Philip St. George Cooke, Carrington's immediate superior, who had failed to respond to Carrington's pleas for reinforcements and more ammunition.

With the arrival of spring, Red Cloud renewed his raids on soldiers and civilians in the Powder River country. Emigrants and freighters gave up trying to use the Bozeman Trail, and the garrisons at the forts along the trail remained strictly on the defensive.

Report 563 in Serial 3620. Scholars disagree on the spelling of the fort near which the battle occurred. Usage in the 1860's favored *Kearney*, although the man for whom the fort was named spelled his name without the *e*, and *Kearny* is usually favored in Wyoming.

The War Department and army were not happy to see the northern Sioux go unwhipped. General Sherman, at the head of the western military forces, wished to send General Augur with cavalry to catch Red Cloud. Before this design for a northern campaign could jell, a pervasive fear of Indians spread over Kansas, Nebraska, Montana, and Colorado. General Grenville M. Dodge, who was now chief engineer of Union Pacific construction, became infected with the epidemic dread of Indians. In May, 1867, he wrote Sherman that to send Augur into the Powder River country would leave the Union Pacific unprotected and "play h–ll [*sic*] with our completed road." [14] In short, in view of the limited military forces available, few people other than General Sherman wanted troops diverted to the Big Horns. Who would protect the heavily traveled trails and the frontiers of settlement? Who would buy produce from hard-working pioneers?

On July 20, 1867, Congress passed an act authorizing the President to appoint a commission to make a general settlement with the Indians of the Plains. At the same time Congress was preparing for a new peace offensive, two new forts were established in the Wyoming country. On July 19, 1867, troops began to build Fort Fetterman on the south side of the North Platte at the mouth of La Prele Creek a few miles northwest of modern Douglas. On August 16, 1867, other troops began to build Fort D. A. Russell (renamed Fort F. E. Warren in 1929) on Crow Creek at Cheyenne. Both forts would be useful in future operations against Indians. Both were strategically located, one on the Oregon Trail, the other on the route selected for the rapidly approaching Union Pacific Railroad. In the previous year, Fort Buford, soon to be renamed Sanders, had been started near present-day Laramie, like Fort Russell, for the purpose of protecting the railroad. A short-lived Fort Halleck at Elk Mountain was torn down when Fort Buford (Sanders) was built.

Before they could be told about the new peace policy, Red Cloud, Crazy Horse, and High-Back-Bone, on August 2, 1867, collaborated in an enterprise which turned out to be far less successful than their trapping of Fetterman. In considerable force they descended on the area around Fort Phil Kearny. After running off some horses near the fort, they pounced on the wood train five miles to the northwest. Then they surrounded the military escort for the woodcutters and became involved in what has become known as the Wagon Box Fight. Captain J. N. Powell, in command of the military escort, lifted fourteen wagon

14 Athearn, *William Tecumseh Sherman*, p. 149.

boxes from their running gears and arranged them on the ground to form an oval corral. Contrary to some published reports, it seems that the wagon boxes were standard wooden ones, not covered with metal plate. Within this fragile fortification, Powell's thirty-two men, including four civilians, defended themselves capably against tremendous odds. The Indians besieged the defenders for three or four hours, but they had no stomach for rushing the barricades against the withering fire of new breech-loading rifles. Early in the afternoon a relief detachment arrived from the fort, and the Indians withdrew.

There were 3 dead whites in the corral; the Indians later admitted 6 dead. The Indians probably lost more than 6, but some of the tales of slaughter on that day must be discounted. Powell placed the number of dead Indians at 60. Others have said 300 and even 1,500. C. G. Coutant wrote in his *History of Wyoming*: "The ground on three sides of the wagon beds was covered with the dead and wounded."

Meanwhile, the peacemakers were at work. The Indian peace commission authorized on July 20, 1867, included three generals, W. T. Sherman, Alfred H. Terry, and W. S. Harney, and four civilians, N. G. Taylor, Commissioner of Indian Affairs, Senator John B. Henderson, chairman of the Senate Committee on Indian Affairs, Samuel F. Tappan, and John B. Sanborn. The commissioners first steamed up the Missouri into Dakota Territory for interviews with small groups of friendly Sioux. Then, in September, they went to North Platte, Nebraska, for a preliminary conference with the Brulés and Oglalas. Friendlies like Spotted Tail were not hard to deal with, but other chiefs, such as Pawnee Killer, were not interested in reservation talk. Pawnee Killer wanted only arms and ammunition and managed to get some before the conference broke up. Crucial decisions were postponed until a later date. The commissioners then went to Kansas, where, in October, they appeared to be more successful. They got some of the Arapahos, Cheyennes, Comanches, Kiowas, and Katakas to agree, in two Medicine Lodge treaties, to settle down on Indian Territory reservations.

The commissioners then turned north again to have another talk with the Sioux. They found that very few of those whom they had met in September kept their appointment for a second North Platte session in November. They continued on to Fort Laramie, hoping to find enough Indians for a conference, but Red Cloud and the northern hostiles had ignored the invitation to be there. The commissioners departed without a treaty after conferring on November 12 and 13 with a Crow delegation and a few Arapahos.[15]

By this time there were perhaps ten thousand people in southern Wyoming and in the South Pass gold-mining area. Before July, 1867, Wyoming had been virtually unoccupied Indian country except for transient travel on the trails. However, as railroad construction gangs, miners, and people with assorted commercial interests flocked in, they caused new problems in Indian relations. Generally they wanted to get rid of the Indians as quickly as possible.

Cheyenne was Wyoming's first substantial settlement. Its early history will be chronicled in the next chapter, but its Indian relations will be described here. At a large public gathering in October, 1867, Cheyenne's first mayor, H. M. Hook (who had recently come from Colorado), offered this toast: "Here is to the city of Cheyenne: May she ever prosper, and the tribe of Indians after whom she is named be completely exterminated." The *Cheyenne Leader* reported that "this sentiment was met with resounding applause." The Mayor's toast led to public discussion of the Indian question. General John D. Stevenson of Fort Russell stated that "there was the slight difficulty of catching the red skins before executing this decree." The citizens, according to the *Leader*, let the General know that they considered the army deficient.

The Cheyenne Indians had caused no trouble for the people of Cheyenne, but obviously these pioneers (many of them from Colorado) despised Indians. When the railroad tracks arrived in Cheyenne a month later, the *Leader* heralded the event with this prophecy: "The grave of the Lo family is dug, and the eastern Lo sentiment shall be buried in it, and the poisonous arrow, and treacherous tomahawk, shall henceforth be harmlessly shelved in the alcoves of the museum."

Peace commissioners were scoffed at in Cheyenne. On January 28, 1868, the *Leader* reported that in recent months "seven white men have been killed by Indians. They are simply trying the guns presented to them by the Commission, so as to be sure that Lo wasn't swindled! That's all!" The editor did not list these killings; they were certainly not in or around Cheyenne. On March 5, 1868, the *Leader* quieted

[15] An excellent account of the futile peace conference held at Fort Laramie in November, 1867, appears in Louis Laurent Simonin, *Le Grand-Ouest des Etats Unis* (Paris: Charpentier, 1869). A translation by Professor W. O. Clough was published in 1966. After visiting for a week in Cheyenne and at Fort Russell, Simonin traveled east with the military escort of eighty men sent out to meet the peace commissioners, who got off a Union Pacific train at Hillsdale on November 8 to be escorted overland to Fort Laramie.

rumors that Fort Russell troops were going out after Indians and at the same time changed hats and sounded almost eastern: "Doubtless there are lean and hungry contractors who improve every opportunity to get up a scare about the Indians. The benefits of idle rumors accrue to the telegraph and sensation papers. The evils result in hindering immigration to our enterprising city, and keep old ladies awake o' nights." March was, of course, the wrong month for Indian excitement, but, in April, Indian scares and Indian commissioners visited Cheyenne almost simultaneously. The *Leader* reported on April 3 that the Indian commissioners headed for Fort Laramie were expected that evening, and reported also that there was "intense excitement" in town because five Indians had fired on a small party of herders, wounding one, on Lone Tree Creek, twenty-five miles west of town. The five were supposed to be part of a larger band, said the *Leader*. The next day, the commissioners had not arrived, but the Indian question was given much attention in the *Leader*. The shooting the previous day had been the work of whites, not Indians. There was, however, a report of another Indian fight which may have been genuine. Thirteen white men were said to have been engaged in a skirmish with seventy-five Indians at Rock Creek. One Indian was reported killed. On the strength of this remote threat, the *Leader* suggested the organization of companies of volunteers to drive back the Indians in view of the fact that "assistance from government may not be hoped for."

On April 6 the peace commissioners arrived in Cheyenne on their way to Fort Laramie. The party included twenty-three men and nine women. Among them were Generals Sheridan, Augur, Harney, Terry, and Gibbon. A great crowd of curiosity seekers escorted them as they marched from the depot to their hotel. The *Leader* said that the crowd accompanied their march "by long and numerous cries and shouts of hi, hi, hi's yeou, yeou, yeou's and whoo, whoo, whoo's. . . . In short the Big Injuns were hustled around in a very unceremonious manner."

This time the commissioners found enough Indians at Fort Laramie to warrant making a treaty, one of the most important in the history of the region, to be known as the "Treaty with the Sioux—Brule, Oglala, Miniconjou, Yanktonai, Hunkpapa, Blackfeet, Cuthead, Two Kettle, Sans Arcs, and Santee—and Arapaho, 1868." [16] The treaty stipulated, first, that "from this day forward all war between the parties to this agreement shall forever cease." Bad white men and bad Indians should be punished. The Indians should have a reservation with substantially

[16] Kappler (ed.), *Indian Affairs*, II, pp. 998–1007.

the boundaries of the western half of present South Dakota—everything west of the Missouri River to the Wyoming line. On this reservation they should receive help to become farmers. Each Indian over the age of four who settled on the reservation was to receive one pound of meat and one pound of flour per day for the next four years. Certain articles of clothing were to be supplied each year for thirty years. Physicians, teachers, carpenters, millers, engineers, farmers, and blacksmiths would be placed on the reservation to instruct and guide the Indians. The Indians promised to withdraw all opposition to railroads being built on the Plains and to military posts or roads south of the North Platte River.

Generally these provisions were unexceptionable. Major difficulties were to stem, however, from the inclusion of the following provision in Article 11:

The tribes . . . will relinquish all right to occupy permanently the territory outside their reservation as herein defined, but yet reserve the right to hunt on any lands north of North Platte, and on the Republican Fork of the Smoky Hill River, so long as the buffalo may range thereon in such numbers as to justify the chase.

Further difficulties inhered in Article 16:

The United States hereby agrees and stipulates that the country north of the North Platte River and east of the summits of the Big Horn Mountains shall be held and considered to be unceded Indian territory, and also stipulates and agrees that no white person or persons shall be permitted to settle upon or occupy any portion of the same; or without consent of the Indians . . . to pass through the same.

To place the Indians on reservations in one breath and then authorize them to hunt off those reservations in the next was asking for future trouble and the commissioners were afraid of it, but they yielded the hunting privilege when it appeared that they could get the treaty in no other way. Some of the commissioners wanted to force the Indians onto reservations without the escape clause. In answer to a question from General Sherman, General Augur, commander of the Department of the Platte, said he would require twenty thousand men to protect the Union Pacific Railroad and the frontiers of his department and at the same time carry on a campaign against the Indians. General A. H. Terry stated that he would need another twenty thousand men for similar purposes in his Department of Dakota. When General Sherman declared that forty thousand men were not available, the commissioners dropped their plan to place all the Indians on reservations at once. It was hoped that the difficulty would solve itself within a few years: with the disappearance of game, the Indians would go to the reservation voluntarily, before the hunting grounds were needed for white settlement.

On April 18, 1868, some of the commissioners returned to Cheyenne on their way east. They were greeted with *Cheyenne Leader* headlines: "Lo indicates the terms on which peace will be granted," "A reservation for the whites!" "Ammunition for the red man!" John B. Sanborn remained at Fort Laramie to obtain treaty approval from various chiefs in April and May and then departed, authorizing the commanding officer to take other signatures. Meanwhile, during the month of April the *Leader* reported four Indian raids between Sidney, Nebraska, and the Laramie Plains, resulting in the slaying of two whites and the wounding of six others. While some of the Indians were accepting the treaty, others clearly were still at large south of the North Platte. Their forays into Union Pacific country caused the summoning of two well-attended mass meetings in Cheyenne on April 30 and May 1. Out of the second meeting, "an immense assemblage" at the Big Tent, came a memorial to Congress, the sentiments of which may be summarized as follows: murders have been repeated "with fearful regularity" for years; Cheyenne people have no confidence in the regular troops; volunteers can be found who will donate their time if the government will mount and arm them, allowing the regular troops to guard the railroad; the only method by which the war can be ended speedily and permanently is "to find their villages, and capture their women and children and hold them as hostages until a satisfactory treaty is obtained."

The *Leader* soon ceased trying to solve the Indian question. When a band of two hundred Indians camped for a while three miles south of Cheyenne in July, 1868, their presence was announced without any sign of alarm. They were not even identified in an article which related that they were selling bows, arrows, quivers, and moccasins.

Meanwhile, in southwestern Wyoming the Shoshonis, under that great friend of the whites Chief Washakie, had earned a much better reputation than the Sioux, Cheyennes, and Arapahos of eastern Wyoming. Some Shoshonis, it is true, had broken with Washakie, had raided the trails in 1862, and had been severely punished by General Connor in the Battle of Bear River in January, 1863. Thereafter, however, there was no serious difficulty with the Shoshonis. In a treaty made at Fort Bridger on July 2, 1863, the Shoshonis promised not to molest whites on the trails and were promised $10,000 in goods annually for twenty years. Then at Fort Bridger on July 3, 1868, General Augur, representing the Indian peace commissioners, signed another treaty with Washakie's band. The Shoshonis were assigned a large reservation east of the Wind River Mountains.[17]

In Cheyenne, the *Leader's* Indian pot boiled over once again in late August, 1868. Reports of raids in Kansas led the editor to write that the "brutal, filthy savages" were on the rampage again. On August 27, it was reported, five Indians killed and scalped a herder one and one-half miles east of Cheyenne. On the same day, a Denver dispatch indicated that the Arapahos and Cheyennes were on the war path in eastern and central Colorado, and reports came in that there were Indians somewhere north of Cheyenne. The *Leader* promptly published an extra dealing with Indian outrages, calling for volunteers, and asking for a mass meeting to take precautionary measures. Two meetings were held. There was much speech making, but no substantial action, except that Mayor Luke Murrin detailed twenty or twenty-five citizens for picket duty around the city for a few nights.

The citizens could not be stirred up for long. Some of them almost immediately began to berate the editor for retarding immigration by his emphasis on Indian troubles. In disgust, the editor reported August 29 a "Change of Temperature": "Two days ago the town was hot for Indian hunting. . . . Two days ago the Indian race was exterminated—by proclamation. . . . The boiling blood of Thursday cooled to sluggish indifference on Friday, and on Saturday the bare existence of Indians is apparently doubted."

The editor of the *Leader* showed little concern when four men were reported killed by Indians near Elk Mountain on October 25, 1868, and even less concern when dispatches a few days later suggested that the Indians involved might have been led by the notorious white horse thief Musgrove.

Red Cloud and many of the northern hostiles had not attended the

[17] *Ibid.*, pp. 1020–1024. The Bannocks were included in the Fort Bridger Treaty of 1868, but they chose not to join the Shoshonis on the Wind River Reservation, settling instead in Idaho. To serve the Shoshonis, Camp Augur was established on the site of present Lander in July, 1869. Camp Augur was renamed Camp Brown in March 1870. In 1871, Camp (or Fort) Brown was moved sixteen miles northwest and was renamed Fort Washakie, which name was retained until the present time, although the post was abandoned in 1909. Meanwhile, another small military post, Camp (or Fort) Stambaugh, was in existence from 1870 to 1878 on the Oregon-California-Utah Trail three and one-half miles southeast of Atlantic City.

treaty making in April and May, 1868. They were waiting to see whether the hated forts in the north—C. F. Smith, Phil Kearny, and Reno—would really be abandoned. After these forts were given up and the troops withdrawn, Red Cloud and his followers turned up at Fort Laramie in November, 1868, and signed the treaty.

In his November, 1868, report to the Secretary of the Interior, Commissioner of Indian Affairs N. G. Taylor wrote a scathing attack on current proposals for turning Indian affairs over to the War Department. He argued that successful management of Indian affairs was too large a burden for the Secretary of War. In one flight of rhetoric, Taylor calculated that in the light of past experience it would take the army 25,000 years to exterminate the 300,000 Indians at a total cost of 7,500,000 white lives and $300,000,000,000 in money. "Extermination by arms is simply an absurdity, unless we could get the Indians under the protection of the flag in large masses, surround and butcher them as at Sand Creek."

The government's purpose in the late 1860's was to confine the High Plains Indians to two reservations, one in Indian Territory (later Oklahoma) and the other in what is now the western half of South Dakota. The Medicine Lodge Treaties of 1867 and the Fort Laramie Treaty of 1868 did not achieve what was desired by the government. The Indians of the Southern Plains were not really ready to settle down on small reservations where there was virtually no game. While the commissioners waited for the northern hostiles to come to Fort Laramie, there was raid after raid on the Southern Plains. These raids provoked a winter campaign in which Lieutenant Colonel George A. Custer and the Seventh Cavalry killed more than one hundred Indians of Black Kettle's Cheyenne village in the Battle of the Washita on November 27, 1868.

In the north, whites were specifically barred from the area north of the Platte by the Fort Laramie Treaty of 1868. Yet there was much travel along the Oregon Trail on the north side of the river (as well as the south side) between Fort Laramie and Red Buttes. Red Cloud properly complained about this. He also complained, with less reason, about the presence of Fort Fetterman in white territory on the south side of the river. All of his complaints were rejected. Meanwhile, construction of the Union Pacific brought closer a final showdown with the High Plains Indians.

CHAPTER 3

The Coming of the Union Pacific

THE MOST EXCITING YEARS in Wyoming history were 1867, 1868, and 1869. Major cause of the commotion was the coming of the Union Pacific Railroad. In his inaugural address to the first Wyoming legislature in 1869, Governor John A. Campbell focused attention on a unique aspect of the Wyoming situation: "In one particular our situation as a territory is entirely new and somewhat anomalous for pioneers. For the first time in the history of our country, the organization of a territorial government was rendered necessary by the building of a railroad. Heretofore the railroad has been the follower instead of the pioneer of civilization." In Wyoming many people who considered themselves pioneers rode to their frontier homes, not in covered wagons drawn by oxen, but in railway coaches and Pullman cars.

36

Governor Campbell did not say, as is often reported, that the railroad ran far ahead of settlement, and indeed it did not. Wyoming towns, as will be seen, sprang up many miles ahead of the rails, but settlement and railroad may be said to have arrived at virtually the same time, and there is no doubt about which caused the other to come.

A transcontinental railroad had been discussed interminably since the 1840's. In the period 1853–1856 government explorations and surveys were made of five main routes, and many variations, under the general supervision of Secretary of War Jefferson Davis. These studies established that transcontinental railroads could be built along several routes between Canada and Mexico, although, ironically, little attention was paid to the route which would be used first.

The construction of a transcontinental railroad was impossible in the 1850's for both political and financial reasons. One impediment was the deepening chasm between the North and the South. Neither section would approve a route serving the other. Nevertheless, the talk continued. At its convention in Chicago in 1860, the Republican party adopted a plank stating "that a railroad to the Pacific Ocean is imperatively demanded by the interests of the whole country." Both branches of the Democratic party that year adopted similar planks. Then when the southerners withdrew from Congress at the beginning of the Civil War in 1861, it became possible for northern congressmen to pass an act authorizing the long-discussed railroad.

Some persons felt that the government should build the road, thinking that it was too big a task for private enterprise. Instead, a mixed-enterprise arrangement was adopted in the Pacific Railway Act of July 1, 1862, which called for construction by two subsidized corporations, the Union Pacific to build west from the Missouri River and the Central Pacific to build east from Sacramento, California. President Lincoln, to whom the decision was left, chose Council Bluffs, Iowa, as the eastern terminus.

The Pacific Railway Act of 1862 provided for land grants to the two companies—ten sections of public land for each mile of track laid—and first-mortgage loans in the form of government bonds, the first bonds to be transferred after the first forty miles of track had been laid. The promoters soon concluded that they must have additional assistance, and this they were able to obtain in a second Pacific railway act adopted by Congress in 1864. The bill, which was drawn up by a Union Pacific attorney, doubled the land grant, making it twenty sections of land for each mile of track. These sections would be the odd-numbered ones in a strip forty miles wide, twenty miles on each side of the track. The subsidy was further sweetened by the inclusion of mineral rights.

The Pacific Railway Act of 1864 contained another major concession, one which meant more to the promoters at the time than did the doubled land grant. The promised government loan was changed from first-mortgage to second-mortgage status, and bonds authorized for issue by the railroad were permitted first-mortgage status. This change would much enhance the attractiveness of the railroad bonds.

All told, the Union Pacific received government loans totalling $27,000,000, enough to cover one-half of the legitimate costs of construction. The government loans (which were eventually paid back) were for thirty years at 6 per cent interest and were based on a formula which allowed $16,000 or $32,000 or $48,000 per mile, depending on the terrain. The Union Pacific received $16,000 per mile to a point six miles west of Cheyenne, $48,000 for the next 150 miles, and $32,000 thereafter.

Little was accomplished during the confused, small-subsidy years of 1863 and 1864, and not much more in 1865. Only forty miles of track, beginning at Omaha, had been laid by the end of 1865. During that winter, however, preparations were made for rapid acceleration. Private investors had to be impressed in one way or another, and the best way to stimulate their enthusiasm was to show some spectacular progress. Observers were electrified by the speed of the advance: 260 miles of track were laid in 1866, 240 in 1867, and almost 500 in 1868. In part the speed was due to the Central Pacific, which was building eastward to meet the Union Pacific. Each company wanted to outdo the other, and so uncertainty and delay gave way to pell-mell haste.

Meanwhile, the route through the Rocky Mountains had to be chosen. The government surveys of 1853–1856 had brought no consensus regarding the best route, and many more surveys followed. Four engineering parties that were in the field in 1864 supplied reports on the basis of which it was concluded that a route by way of Denver was impracticable but that a route by way of the Cache la Poudre River and another by way of Lodgepole Creek (north of Cheyenne) were feasible.[1]

The route finally decided upon in November, 1866, via Crow Creek,

[1] *Senate Executive Document 69* (Serial 2336), 49 Cong., 1 Sess., *Reports Made by the Government Directors of the Union Pacific Railroad Company, 1864–1886*, p. 6. This document is a gold mine. The five government directors did not control the railroad, since they were outnumbered and sometimes ignored by the fifteen directors chosen by the company, but they had much to say about policies and operation.

was one which General Grenville M. Dodge had found in 1865, the year before he became chief engineer of the Union Pacific. In his essay *How We Built the Union Pacific Railway*, he relates that he took advantage of his location in the West as a military commander to search for possible crossings of the Rockies. Once while examining the east slope of the Laramie Mountains (then known as the Black Hills), he found a ridge which "led down to the plains without a break." Dodge offered different versions of the discovery at different times. The traditional story, based on Dodge's statements in his old age and on J. R. Perkins' *Trails, Rails and War*, is that Indians on the horizon frightened Dodge and sent him, by lucky chance, down the natural gangplank, which he might not have noticed otherwise. In his official biography, Perkins relates that Dodge and thirteen men fought off three hundred Crow Indians. Professor Wallace D. Farnham, however, has stripped the discovery of its romantic embroidery by directing attention to Dodge's diary, in which there is no mention of Indians but only of "Indian signs" on the day the gangplank was found.[2]

The North Platte–Sweetwater–South Pass route, which had served the emigrants well, was recognized by General Dodge to be the best from an engineering point of view. There is quite a climb on the eastern slope of South Pass, but the summit is only 7,550 feet, while the Sherman Pass (also called Evans Pass) route, which was followed instead, was 8,236 feet (subsequent relocations have lowered this somewhat). The southern-Wyoming route was given the nod because it had better coal deposits, was forty miles shorter, and was closer to Denver.

In early July, 1867, when the tracklayers were seventy-five miles or so west of North Platte, Nebraska, General Dodge came out to locate the division point at Cheyenne. General C. C. Augur, who was with General Dodge, located Fort D. A. Russell nearby. At Cheyenne and at many other places the army proved to be the indispensable ally of the Union Pacific. The army smoothed the way by keeping order among both Indians and whites. Army cooperation, which was provided for by Congress, was further facilitated by General Dodge's close personal acquaintance with many army officers, such as U. S. Grant, W. T. Sherman, and C. C. Augur.

At one time—at the peak in the summer of 1868—perhaps as many as six thousand men were employed in building the Union Pacific Railroad. No accurate breakdown is possible, but workers at various

[2] Wallace D. Farnham, "Grenville Dodge and the Union Pacific: A Study of Historical Legends," *Journal of American History*, LI, 4 (March 1965), pp. 638–639.

tasks were scattered over hundreds of miles. More or less in order along the route from front to rear were surveyors, graders, bridge gangs, tracklayers, track-ballasting crews, and train crews. In the Laramie and Medicine Bow Mountains and along the headwaters of the Green and Bear rivers swarmed hundreds of tie hacks employed by various tie contractors. Other hundreds of workers were engaged in operating sawmills and in quarrying and hauling stone. In the railroad boom towns and along the newly laid tracks, many company employees directed a mighty stream of supplies to the workers ahead.

Most prominent among the construction personnel were Samuel B. Reed, superintendent of construction, and the Casement brothers, Jack and Dan, who were the contractors for laying track. General Dodge wrote that he thought that "every chief of the different units of the [track] force had been an officer of the army." Likewise, most of the laborers were army veterans. While it is generally agreed that many of the construction workers were Irish, other nationalities participated. J. R. Perkins, who evidently got the information from Dodge's papers, wrote that General Jack Casement had one thousand men, "a mixed crowd of ex-Confederate, and Federal soldiers, mule-skinners, Mexicans, New York Irish, bush whackers, and ex-convicts from the old prisons of the East."

Among the higher-ups, Thomas C. Durant, vice-president and general manager, and Grenville M. Dodge, chief engineer, were outstanding for their energy and drive, as well as for their inability to get along with one another. Other major figures in the Union Pacific story during the construction period were Oliver Ames, Cornelius Bushnell, Sidney Dillon, and (somewhat less important) Oakes Ames. General Dodge really had less to do with the construction of the railroad than his account, *How We Built the Union Pacific Railway*, indicates. Professor Wallace D. Farnham has shown that Dodge, in his capacity as chief engineer, was mainly an organizer, administrator, and public-relations man, while the actual construction was handled by the superintendent of construction, Samuel B. Reed, working under Thomas C. Durant. For the spectacular construction feats, more credit must be assigned to Reed and Durant than to Dodge. Professor Farnham credits Dodge with being the "balance wheel and trouble shooter." [3]

Troops stationed at the four forts along the route in Wyoming—Russell (1867), Sanders (1866), Steele (1868), and Bridger (built by Jim Bridger in 1842–1843 and taken over by the government in 1858)—

[3] *Ibid.*, p. 648.

helped to keep both red men and white men in line. Indians caused the most trouble for surveying crews in 1867. They killed two chiefs of survey crews, L. L. Hills east of Cheyenne and Percy T. Browne on Bitter Creek. Browne's party was attacked three times and lost two other men before Browne was killed. General Dodge reported that much of the surveying in west-central Wyoming had to be done twice as a result of Browne's death. As the construction crews advanced in 1868, protected by troops, Indians caused very little trouble.

No doubt the new forts along the Union Pacific route were helpful to the corporation. For example, when graders at Green River struck for more pay, troops backed Samuel B. Reed's threat to starve them out, and the strike collapsed. The records of the forts in the National Archives, however, show that the commanding officers spent more time worrying about internal problems of their commands than they did about the Union Pacific. The guardhouse was usually full.

People were "excessively prone to aid and abet deserters," reported Captain Henry R. Mizner, commanding officer at Fort John Buford (temporary name of Fort Sanders) in July, 1866.[4] "Road ranchers" on the Laramie Plains were a constant irritation. He raided several of them to seize liquor. "Without such action I cannot preserve my command from demoralization." "An old offender" near the Big Laramie stage station was a ranchman named Gelm (Jelm), who is commemorated by Jelm Mountain. "Ranchmen upon the Plains with few exceptions are unscrupulous, dangerous men whose chief traffic is whiskey. It is a notorious fact that a large portion of the revolvers, guns and ammunition now in the hands of Indians were obtained from Ranchmen for immunity from danger." These ranchmen, Mizner asserted, concealed deserters and bought horses, mules, arms, clothing, and other government property from them. Mizner's successor as commanding officer at Fort Sanders, Colonel John Gibbon, continued Mizner's campaign against the road ranchers, whom he described as "miserable leaches [*sic*]." He reported in December, 1867, that of six deaths in the vicinity since he took command, five had been the result of liquor and one had been attributed to Indians.

The Union Pacific brought a dozen towns to Wyoming where there had been none before. Half a dozen of them were large enough to rate classification as cities: Cheyenne, Laramie City, Benton, Green River City, Bryan, and Bear River City. Three of the larger communities—

---

[4] In a letter dated July 23, 1866, in Post Letters Sent, July, 1866–May, 1882, Film Roll No. 2, Fort Sanders Microfilm, University of Wyoming Library.

Benton, Bryan, and Bear River City—survived only a short time, while smaller communities—Rawlins, Rock Springs, and Evanston—put down strong roots.

Cheyenne's first settlers followed close on the heels of Generals Dodge and Augur in July, 1867. Six men and three women arrived where the new town was to be on July 9. They were Mr. and Mrs. James Masterson, Mr. and Mrs. John Bachtold, a Mr. and Mrs. Hammond, James R. Whitehead, Thomas E. McLeland, and Robert M. Beers. General Dodge's crew immediately began the survey of the townsite, four miles square, with blocks, lots, streets, and alleys. Three days later, James R. Whitehead opened an office for the sale of Union Pacific lots, the first one going for $150. On the twenty-fifth, a small frame house, the town's first, rose among the tents on the corner of Sixteenth and Ferguson (Carey).[5]

Every day brought more people, until some of them agreed it was time for a provisional, or people's, city government. It is assumed that the impetus came from the Union Pacific, since General Dodge later asserted that "we . . . organized the local government." A mass meeting in a store on the evening of August 7, with James R. Whitehead in the chair, chose a committee to draft a city charter. The people met again the following evening to adopt the charter. The committee had examined the territorial laws of Colorado and Dakota and the ordinances of Omaha and Denver. They adopted the city ordinances of Denver. Two days later an election was held, at which a livery-stable proprietor, H. M. Hook, was chosen mayor. He was thirty-six years old, had been born in Pennsylvania, and had been in the West several years, most recently at Laporte, Colorado. Six other businessmen were chosen councilmen, and others were named clerk and recorder, city attorney, police magistrate, and marshal. The city attorney was the ubiquitous Whitehead.

On August 20, W. W. Corlett, a young lawyer from Ohio who had spent a month in Denver, came to Cheyenne on his way home. Whitehead persuaded Corlett to become his law partner and to take over the job of prosecuting attorney. In his manuscript "The Founding of Cheyenne" (1885), Corlett recalled that when he arrived in Cheyenne, "five or six hundred people were scattered around the prairie living mostly under wagons or in tents. I had my office with Whitehead in a

[5] The information in this paragraph was taken from an anniversary article in the *Cheyenne Leader*, July 9, 1868. Professor Wallace D. Farnham has called my attention to the fact that on July 15, 1867, Dodge wrote in his diary that he had appointed two men named Talpey and Glenn as Cheyenne agents for selling lots and that on the same day, Dodge wrote to Sidney Dillon: "People are flocking in here to settle."

tent, and slept under a wagon myself for two or three months." Corlett recalled that "most everybody here had come from Denver or other portions of Colorado." The people who had organized the provisional government, said Corlett, "were all of the better class, the business people of the town who had come here for business purposes." Very soon, however, came the advance guard of railroad builders and camp followers from Julesburg and points east.

A second mass meeting on September 27 began the effective organization of Laramie County, which had been created by the Dakota Legislature the previous January with Fort Sanders as county seat. For the time being, all of the Wyoming country comprised just one county of Dakota Territory. Since the Dakota government at Yankton had not supplied commissioners, provisional ones were chosen in the Cheyenne mass meeting of September 27. These temporary commissioners arranged for an October 8 election at which a full set of county officials were named. Not surprisingly, James R. Whitehead was chosen representative to the Dakota Legislature, and 1,645 voters indicated a preference for Cheyenne as county seat rather than Fort Sanders, which received 439 votes. The change of county seat would have to wait for action by the Dakota Legislature; and, of course, the county government established was of the provisional, or people's, variety, like the city government, for the election had not been authorized in Yankton. The Laramie County officials provided only minimal services in subsequent months. The principal governing body for Cheyenne was the extralegal people's government established by the August mass meeting. The city government had to have revenue, which it proceeded to get from two sources: business licenses and fines.

Fortunately for the historian, a triweekly tabloid, the *Cheyenne Leader*, began publication on September 19, 1867, with Nathan A. Baker as editor. This enterprising pioneer editor and politician later recalled how he had hauled his hand press and "shirt-tailful of type" up from Denver by ox team. He put out an initial edition of three hundred copies, which he sold for fifteen cents per copy.

For a few months Cheyenne was largely a city of tents, but in September high winds and a few snowflakes suggested that it was time for more substantial shelters. Any man who could drive a nail could get plenty of work, said the *Leader*. Ninety per cent of the homes and stores were built of pine lumber (often prefabricated), but adobe, stone, brick, grout, and concrete were also used. At Fort Russell, as well, frame barracks and log structures supplanted tents.

On November 2, 1867, the *Leader* noted that "Julesburg continues to arrive by ox train" and estimated that there were two hundred business houses and four thousand people in Cheyenne. When tracks were laid to the city on November 13, the *Leader* reported that "there was no shouting and cheering; our citizens swarmed along the grade and watched . . . the magic work. . . . The hearty greeting we gave this gigantic enterprise was too deep and full for expression." That night, James McDaniels displayed a large transparency over his saloon with the legends "Honor to Casement, to whom honor is due" and "The Iron Horse snorts defiance at the Rocky Mountains." The following night, "Our Jack" Casement, boss of the tracklayers, was observed perched on the bar in McDaniels' place, "treating everybody" while the crowd cheered, sang, drank, and danced. Two nights later, there was an official reception for Casement at City Hall.

A few weeks after the railroad reached Cheyenne, the town's population had grown to perhaps 6,000, among whom there may have been about 400 women and 200 children. By February, 1868, the city had 114 children enrolled in school, with a daily attendance of 86.

A French writer, Louis Laurent Simonin, visited Cheyenne just before the railroad reached the city. He described the men he found: "How rough and crude in appearance they are . . . with their long hair . . . their ill-kept beards, their clothing of nondescript color, their great leather boots engulfing their pantaloons. But what virile characters, proud, fearless! What dignity, what patience! No one complains here."

The first paper read at the newly formed Young Men's Literary Association in December, 1867—presented by Dr. E. H. Russell, a medical doctor—was entitled "Have an Aim in Life" and argued: "We are all in search of wealth. . . . It is the main spring of life." Few except the two clergymen in town would have quarreled with Dr. Russell's materialistic philosophy, which, to be sure, was widespread in post–Civil War America.

The *Leader* found all too few solid homemakers. In August, 1868, long after the flotsam of railroad-construction days was gone, the editor sized up the westbound folks as follows: "Half the people who start west are home-sick, love-sick, or some kind of sick, before they are out of sight of their native village. They firmly resolve to go west, strip the country . . . and with their booty retreat home. . . . Such people are an injury instead of a benefit to the West."

Maintenance of law and order was a major problem both before and after the arrival of the rails. One aspect of the problem was settled quite early. The Union Pacific, with the aid of the army, established its authority on October 27, 1867, when soldiers from Fort Russell demolished shanties erected by squatters on railroad lots. Beyond protecting its own property, however, the Union Pacific did not go, leaving normal police protection to the city government. C. G. Coutant reported the brief existence of a special organization to help the city authorities in pre-track days. He wrote that fifty-eight leading citizens volunteered to serve as special officers in emergencies.

The *Leader* never pretended to give complete coverage of violence, but its columns carry enough items to suggest that disorderly behavior was already common two months before the railroad reached the city. The September 19, 1867, issue of the newspaper reported that a sergeant who had been trying to subdue an intoxicated soldier had fractured the soldier's skull and had accidentally shot himself, that there had been an exchange of shots in a robbery attempt at a gunshop, that a man had been knocked down and robbed, and that there had been much stealing of revolvers and blankets from tents and wagons. In the next issue of the newspaper (September 24) it was reported that there had been a street fight, that a man who had fired a shot at a policeman had been placed on the chain gang at the fort, and that a hundred men had gathered on the street to bet on a dogfight. The September 26 issue said that the city marshal had reported two neighbors fined for abusing each other, a drunk fined, a fight, a man mauled by an inebriated "friend," and another man fined for trying "to run things at a saloon." The September 28 issue reported that a drunk had been fined, a man in a camp above town had been cut in a fight, a man had been fined for drawing a gun on a newsman, and a gang had created a "muss" at a house of ill fame.

Undismayed, the *Leader* editor commented on September 28 that it was gratifying "that Cheyenne remains so free of crime and rowdyism in comparison with towns below." No doubt there was more violence a few months later, but after October 22 the editor obviously ignored much that was going on. He noted on November 2 that many matters of interest were omitted for want of space, and between October 22 and November 12 his only crime report concerned theft from the editor's woodpile. Later comments indicate that the editor thought conscientious crime reporting would bring the wrong kind of people to Cheyenne.

"Western" movies and television shows mislead in implying that the West was generally lawless for long periods of time. On the other hand, no one should imagine that Wyoming towns were orderly and law abiding in 1867 and 1868. The editor of the *Leader* left much unsaid, but he said enough to give a pretty fair picture of the situation in Cheyenne. On December 10 he advised citizens to carry and use arms at night for self-protection, in view of "frequent occurrences of garroting." On January 2, 1868, he noted that "the police court does a vast amount of business each week." On February 15 he inveighed against dance houses: "The jades who coy with intoxicated teamsters, or miners, or laborers and clean them out of every cent in their pockets, and then have their dupes set upon and maltreated by the pet roughs whom they subsist, are a terrible reproach and infliction on any community." On February 26 he noted that "wife beating and man bruising" are common in justice of the peace court. On August 11, 1868, when the head of track was 225 miles west of Cheyenne, and presumably most of the scum had floated by, the editor wrote:

There are a number of low doggery proprietors of hellish rum holes in this town that . . . entice a customer within their dens, by the aid of an accomplice . . . and serve out a glass of drugged liquor . . . shove him into a convenient place . . . and rob him at their leisure. They then kick him out to recover his senses as best he may. Let all who follow the practice of indiscriminate drinking take heed where they go, and who their companions are.

And on October 13, 1868, after reporting two killings, the editor declared: "Pistols are almost as numerous as men. It is no longer thought to be an affair of any importance to take the life of a fellow being."

During 1868 the police force was cut (not counting the chief) from twelve men to eight and then to six, suggesting declines in both population and crime. The adoption of ordinances against disreputable houses, carrying weapons, dance houses, and vagrants indicates that forces were at work to ameliorate vice and crime conditions, but enforcement amounted only to small fines, except in the case of vagrants, who were sometimes floated out of town.

The editor felt that as long as there were houses of ill fame there would be brawls, but the city did little about such places except to collect small fines now and then. Many were still in Cheyenne, judging by the news item on September 10, 1868: "Today the police court levied an assessment of five dollars and costs on each one of forty women in this town."

The provisional city government established in August, 1867, was replaced in January, 1868, by a government elected under a new charter provided by the Dakota Legislature. In an election on January

23, 1868, Luke Murrin defeated W. W. Corlett in the mayoralty race, 593 votes to 345. Six aldermen were elected at the same time.

No attention seems to have been paid to party affiliation in the August, 1867, election, but party lines were drawn in the January, 1868, election, and the Democrats won the day. It was not, however, a victory for southerners. The mayor and all six aldermen were northerners. The mayor and four of the aldermen had fought in the Union army, and this clearly helped them get elected.

Vigilante organizations were common in the pioneer West, particularly in California in 1851 and Montana in 1864. Wyoming's first vigilante activity appeared at Cheyenne in January, 1868, during the last days of the provisional government. Three men who had been arrested for theft were released on bond. The next morning, the three men were found tied together, but otherwise unharmed, with a sign which read: "$900 Stole . . . $500 Recovered. . . . Next case goes up a tree. Beware of Vigilance Committee." Then, on the following morning, the Cheyenne vigilantes struck more savagely at Dale City, a community of perhaps six hundred people on Sherman Hill thirty miles west of Cheyenne. There they caught and lynched three ruffians who had recently left Cheyenne. Perhaps there was help from Dale City, but the Cheyenne vigilantes are usually given credit for these lynchings. A few days later the vigilantes rounded out the week's activities by driving five undesirables out of Cheyenne with threats.

These incidents created much excitement. The *Leader* insisted that there was little need for vigilantes. Mayor Luke Murrin, on January 30, the day he was sworn into office, announced that his regime would not tolerate vigilance committees. A few days later when the police were directed by the Mayor "to call to account" all members of the vigilance committee "if now existing," the *Leader* reported that the committee had already disbanded. Either their retirement was only temporary or substitutes appeared, for a group of masked men in March, 1868, lynched two men named Charles Martin and Charles Morgan. Martin, a saloonkeeper with an appalling reputation, had just been acquitted in United States District Court of a charge of murdering a partner in crime. Evidently, the vigilantes did not think much of his successful self-defense plea or of his threats to kill the respected attorney W. W. Corlett, who had assisted in the prosecution. Corlett himself thought the jury was packed. The other victim, Morgan, had just been arrested on a charge of stealing mules. It is assumed that the vigilantes thought he would not be punished by the courts. Charles

Martin, one may judge, died not for his most recent crime only but rather for an accumulation of grievances. No one was arrested for lynching Martin and Morgan.

About two weeks later, a respectable brewer was killed in a midnight altercation when a gang called on him at his home to collect money owed to a saloonkeeper. Corlett thought that the debt collectors were members of the vigilante organization and that it consequently lost the respect of the community, although no one was punished for the murder. Cheyenne thereafter forgot about local vigilantes, though taking note now and then of others who operated in other Wyoming communities. Thus Cheyenne vigilantes probably lynched just two men in Cheyenne and three at Dale City.[6] It seems fair to say that the record of popular justice in Cheyenne was neither very extensive nor very creditable. But it may well be that vigilantes in Cheyenne and elsewhere had a positive deterrent value which is hard to measure.

One of the most difficult early problems facing the Cheyenne city government was the danger of fire. The *Leader* described the situation accurately: "A ruinous fire is the danger we, in this town, of tinder like tenements live under at all times." One of the first officials named was the fire warden, whose duties included the inspection of chimneys, flues, and stovepipes. Dozens of buildings burned down despite his best efforts. The *Leader* regularly suspected incendiarism, but never mentioned any proof. Usually only one building went at a time, until early on the morning of October 8, 1868, when a half-block was destroyed with more than $50,000 damage. A prairie fire north of town invaded the city in October, 1867. Embattled citizens with wet gunny sacks were able to avert catastrophe.

An ordinance adopted in November, 1867, authorized a volunteer hook-and-ladder company. Mayor Murrin promised to donate uniform hats. Red flannel shirts, ornamented belts, and blue cloth caps arrived in June, after which the hook-and-ladder boys received plenty of exercise. Often, however, buckets proved to be more useful than hooks and ladders. The fire-fighting equipment was supplemented in January, 1869, with the purchase of a steam fire engine.

[6] C. G. Coutant credited the Cheyenne vigilantes with twenty or more lynchings (unnamed except for the five above) and with driving hundreds of people from the city. He also asserted that they never hanged an innocent man. Few persons have been as enthusiastic as Coutant in appraising the achievements of the Cheyenne vigilantes. The long-time Cheyenne editor John Charles Thompson, Jr., scoffed at the figure of twenty lynchings, suggesting that Coutant jumped to the conclusion that a turbulent town like Cheyenne must have had that many.

The pioneer fire fighters in Cheyenne were constantly handicapped by lack of water. Indeed, this caused much grief for everyone, whether there was a fire or not. Crow Creek, which the *Leader* said was ten feet wide and a foot deep in September, ran past the southwest side of the city, but it could be of little use in winter. In the autumn of 1867, three public wells were dug on Sixteenth Street. The *Leader* frequently deplored their inadequacy.[7] In October, 1868, all property holders were asked to have two barrels of water on their premises for use in case of fire.

Crow Creek water was used for some purposes. Young's Bath House advertised creek-water bathing, hot and cold. The *Leader* campaigned for a ditch which would lead water to town from Crow Creek or Lodgepole Creek. Not until the spring of 1871 was a Crow Creek ditch to the city realized. With rare prescience, the editor implored in February, 1868: "Give us water, if we have to tunnel the Black Hills [Sherman Hill] and bring the Big Laramie down this way." Such a project was undertaken with an $11,000,000 bond issue in 1961 to bring Douglas Creek water by pipeline.

Meanwhile, in October, 1868, the city began construction of a cistern at the corner of Seventeenth and Pioneer for use with the hoped-for steam engine. Early in 1869 the new fire engine from New York was assembled and given several trials. Its one thousand feet of hose and two-inch nozzle could play water from the cistern on almost every structure in town. Getting up steam on a cold day took time, however, and all too often the new engine served only to cool the ashes. The long-expected holocaust finally came on January 11, 1870, wiping out two city blocks of buildings, with only two or three of the eighty-odd properties having any insurance.

There was much grumbling about the inadequacies of local government in the new city. Abuse was heaped on the mayor and aldermen both before and after the change that came with the legal charter in January, 1868. There were complaints about the water problem; hogs running at large; the condition of the streets—muddy and filthy, with

[7] In December, 1867, the editor complained about the well at Sixteenth and Carey: "Persons are induced to rush there with their water buckets by the curb and wheel and rope; and after letting down and letting up for half an hour, cannot obtain as much water as an infant would run in the same time." The following month he noted that "there are three or four public holes in the ground, with curbs thrown around them . . . but very little water in them, and that little not available." One well was dug deeper in February, and another well was provided with a pump. A potential auxiliary supply was lost when a Union Pacific water tank with windmills burned down.

dead animals lying around for days; the dearth of sidewalks; failure to keep law and order; police brutality, corruption, and inefficiency; "fast driving by fast women"; defaulting on city debts; nonenforcement of city ordinances; inequities of the business license-fee system; and extravagance.

Dakota Territory's District Judge Ara Bartlett undermined the city's revenue structure when he ruled in March, 1868, in the case of *The City* v. *Preshaw*, that only those few businesses specifically named in the charter had to pay license fees. Thereafter, most of the merchants and professional men paid no fees. The city debts mounted. City warrants were discounted, or not paid at all. An ordinance was adopted making city warrants negotiable at par for all fines, licenses, or debts due the city government; this brought more warrants than cash into the till. During one quarter, about half the fines and almost all of the license fees were paid in warrants. When Luke Murrin retired from the mayor's chair in January, 1869, he left the city in debt $9,965.47.

The debt of almost $10,000 was not outrageous, considering that the city's main prop, license fees, had been knocked out by the district court and considering, too, that almost $6,000 had been obligated for a jail, hospital, school, and three wells. The two-room schoolhouse, opened in January, 1868, cost $2,235, of which $1,335 was raised by private subscription. For the balance of $900, the city issued bonds bearing 5 per cent interest per month, a commentary on the city's credit rating.

Looking ahead, the city did not extricate itself from the financial mire without default. In November, 1869, the Union Pacific obtained a judgment against the city, and the county sheriff sold desks, tables, chairs, stoves, and "the city bell" to satisfy the judgment. Even the jail was scheduled to go under the gavel, but the necessary sixty-eight dollars was raised after the sale. In December, 1869, the first Wyoming legislature dropped the Dakota charter and provided a new one for the city. Among the first actions of the new city trustees in 1870 was to declare illegal the warrants issued under the Dakota charter; so the outstanding scrip appeared to be worthless. Later the trustees undertook to redeem the scrip at fifty cents on the dollar by a bond issue. Stories that some of the warrants had been distributed among saloonkeepers by city officials in return for bar bills reconciled most citizens to the default.

The Dakota Legislature and Dakota judges have been criticized for neglecting the Wyoming country. A Cheyenne lawyer observed in

February, 1868, that "what may be very wholesome law among the Norwegians at Yankton, is far from meeting the lightning like necessities of a people whose every movement is made at the rate of 'twenty-five miles an hour.'" The Dakota officials could not keep up with the rapid changes in Wyoming, but they seem to have done just about as well as could have been expected. Part of the failures usually attributed to Dakota officials should be assigned instead to James R. Whitehead, prominent pioneer lawyer and Laramie County's only representative in the 1868 legislature. For some reason he did not go to Yankton until about ten days before the end of the forty-day session. He was refused a seat. Had he been there for the full forty days, he might have obtained some redress for grievances.[8]

Dakota Judge Ara Bartlett held district court in Cheyenne in spring and fall, 1868. For Cheyenne's transient population, these regular terms were probably not adequate, but Laramie County taxpayers did not want any extra sessions. In February, 1869, the county commissioners asked Judge Bartlett not to hold the regular spring term of district court. He complied with the request, which was made, presumably, for financial reasons and in anticipation of the arrival of Wyoming territorial judges later in the spring.

In the days of Dakota's jurisdiction, the county commissioners provided no jail, but they built a courthouse, levied a five-mill school tax, and with some reluctance agreed to share the expense of a city-county hospital in which indigents were cared for. The county was evidently hard up, for the commissioners decided to rent the lower floor of the courthouse to a clothing store for $1,800 a year. The district-court sessions in 1868 were held in cheaper rented quarters. In retrospect, the seams stand out in the fabric of Cheyenne's early government. Towns to the west would fare no better.

Business was good in Cheyenne during the winter of 1867–1868. The city was lucky that Sherman Hill and winter weather posed construction difficulties. General Dodge's natural ramp, which "led down to the plains without a break," was not quite the perfect crossing over the

---

[8] In reply to later complaints from Cheyenne, the *Yankton Dakotian* declared that Whitehead "asked for no legislation except such as would undo work already completed. Cheyenne got all it asked for." That the Dakota Legislature was not unsympathetic toward Wyoming people is indicated by the fact that in the absence of Whitehead, his seat was given to Archie J. Turner, whom South Pass miners had sent to make a plea for quartz-mining laws and a new county, Carter. The legislature certainly did not need to seat Turner, who was merely an unofficial spokesman, but evidently it was felt that Wyoming should be represented.

Laramie Mountains that one could wish. There was much work to do, even in the days when only the absolute minimum was undertaken. As a result, Cheyenne was an end-of-track community for six months, a much longer period than was allowed to any other Wyoming town. All through that winter, Cheyenne merchants were busy forwarding goods to railroad camps on Sherman Hill and to communities in Colorado. The Kansas Pacific was still in Kansas and would not reach Denver until August, 1870.

Beginning in January, 1868, people who were headed for the Sweetwater mines began to gather in Cheyenne, where they outfitted and waited until the weather would permit travel. The city was full of transients looking for opportunities of one kind or another, but all requiring food, drink, and a place to sleep.

Entertainment was big business. Union Pacific construction workers, tie hacks, teamsters, and soldiers had money to spend. A theatrical troupe from Julesburg and a "jolly band of hurdy-gurdy performers fresh from the east" beat the rails to the city by almost two months. They were followed closely by an equally jolly throng of other entertainers. The *Leader* editor saw so many dancing girls that their charms palled on him. He wrote of Seventeenth Street "hurdy gurdy dance houses, where the buxom Teuton girls trip the light fantastic toe, and sweat and stink by turns." "Here's another bawdy house coming," he noted in January, 1868. "We think if there ever was a city on the face of this sinful sphere, that was well supplied with bawdy houses, that village is ours . . . don't afflict us with any more." *Chicago Tribune* reporter James Chisholm, who, like many others, was waiting for the weather to permit travel to the Sweetwater mines, counted about a score of dance houses in March, 1868. He described them as follows:

They are generally crowded to the door all night long, and the sound of fiddles and banjoes, mingled with the voice of the master of ceremonies. "Only two more gentlemen wanted for the next dance," as you hear it from the various halls, conveys the idea of a whole city being one huge rustic festival—an impression which is by no means sustained on entering the halls of mirth. A space in the centre is devoted to the terpsichorean art, where females of the lowest type may be secured as partners in the dance, while faro tables, keno, and all imaginable games constitute the side dishes.[9]

The city's music was by no means confined to the indoors. In January, 1868, the Cheyenne City Council declared the bagpipe playing each

[9] Lola M. Homsher (ed.), *South Pass, 1868* (Lincoln: University of Nebraska Press, 1960), p. 19.

night at the corner of Seventeenth and Pioneer a nuisance. James McDaniels' forty-horsepower Brussels organ, when it opened up on *Listen to the Mocking Bird*, probably frightened magpies and sparrows on the outskirts of the city.

James McDaniels, whose bar on Pioneer Avenue was a popular resort, was without question the nonpareil showman. With reason he was known as the "Barnum of the West": he offered a free museum for the enjoyment of his bar patrons. As he prospered, he expanded his operations; in 1868 he added a live theater. At his showhouse and others during 1868, the playbills offered such attractions as *Rip Van Winkle*, *Still Water Runs Deep*, *The Drunkard*, *The Old Guard*, *Morning Call*, *Lend Me Five Shillings*, *Richard III*, *Othello*, *Lucretia Borgia*, *Cinderella*, and *Our American Cousin*. Also in 1868, the enterprising McDaniels added a zoo which included porcupines, parrots, monkeys, apes, snakes, and bears. Perhaps McDaniels' greatest coup occurred in January, 1869, when he returned from the East with "the world renowned Circassian girl who is but nineteen years of age, and a beauty of the rarest description." This oval-faced charmer was indeed a sensation.

Places where one could buy a drink numbered as many as seventy at one time. These varied from mere holes in the wall to "The Old Green-back Rooms," 100 by 112 feet, containing two bars and billed as the "largest saloon in the western country." In April, 1868, a 40 by 100-foot wall tent was erected for use as combination saloon and gambling house. This evidence of spring was apparently the same tent that appeared a short time later as the center of entertainment in Laramie City and then in other new towns to the west.

Undoubtedly, entertainment meant far more to most of the first citizens of Cheyenne than going to church, but the faithful few made significant beginnings in Christian endeavor. The Reverend W. W. Baldwin of Burlington, Iowa, preached to seventy persons on "The Efficacy of Prayer" in City Hall on September 29, 1867, in what was described as "the second occurrence of divine worship." He helped to organize the Methodist Episcopal church on that day. It appears that a Dr. Scott of the Methodist Episcopal church had preached the first sermon at some earlier date. In October, 1867, a few members of the Protestant Episcopal church were "out with a subscription paper for the erection of a church edifice." Their efforts were not crowned with immediate success, but on August 23, 1868, a 25 by 50-foot frame church was consecrated for them by Bishop Randall of Colorado. A strawberry festival, with strawberries, ice cream, and dancing, raised money for an organ for the new church. The Methodists also raised money with a strawberry festival, although they omitted the dancing.

Cheyenne's St. Mark's Episcopal Church was reputed to be the first church consecrated in Wyoming. The Roman Catholics, however, had previously erected a small chapel which they began using in June, 1868. The Union Pacific shipped the prefabricated chapel from Omaha without charge. The Union Pacific also began with the Episcopalians its practice of donating lots to many churches across southern Wyoming. General John D. Stevenson of Fort Russell had anticipated the Union Pacific, with respect to the Catholics, by giving them four lots in November, 1867.

The Reverend Joseph W. Cook, first Episcopal missionary in Cheyenne, in his contemporary diary and letters, has left a record of his experiences in the city, beginning in January, 1868. In March he noted that "our congregation depends very much on the state of the wind. On calm days we have about one hundred worshippers, and on windy days the number varies with the force of the wind." When Reverend Cook mentioned communion, he usually had only five communicants, which was a considerable disappointment to him.

Three churches, Methodist, Episcopal, and Roman Catholic, were established in Cheyenne before the rails moved over Sherman Hill. No other congregation joined them during end-of-track days, and no church structures rose until after trains were running over the hill to Laramie City. Church folk were not legion in Cheyenne's end-of-track days.

In the fall of 1867, few of Cheyenne's gamblers would have wagered much money without favorable odds on the city's chances of prolonged survival. A glance eastward would confirm the opinion that railroad boom towns had a short life expectancy. The first city council's decision to license businesses by the quarter rather than by the year was not accidental. "Bubble, is it?" asked the first issue of the *Leader*. "There are some among the recent newcomers that seem to imagine that Cheyenne will begin to decline in a few months, with a rapidity equal to its rise." "Croakers" were suggesting that Cheyenne was "a butterfly place; that it has wings and will fly over to the Laramie Plains or somewhere else in the spring." Although he obviously had nagging worries, the editor, along with a minority of the citizens, thought that Cheyenne's future might be assured by its location at the east face of the mountains, making it a logical junction for branch railroads south to Denver and north to Montana. There were expectations also of railroad shops and a roundhouse.

Citizens expected mining to become important in the area, but would it develop in time to save Cheyenne? Grazing and agricultural opportunities were scarcely noticed in the hectic end-of-track months. Cheyenne was not yet a cow town, although John Iliff and others had cattle on the range. The city was still almost entirely dependent upon the Union Pacific. In keeping with the spirit of the times, the first man arrested for riding his horse into a saloon was not a cowboy but a railroader.

In early March, 1868, the Union Pacific agent in Cheyenne informed the *Leader* that the Union Pacific's board of directors in New York had recently adopted the following: "Resolved, That Cheyenne was located under the sanction of the Union Pacific Railroad Company, with the intention of making it the location of their repair and other shops, and it is their intention to make *there* the principal depot and repair shops of the company for the eastern base of the Rocky Mountains." This was good news to Cheyenne people, but it was still too vague to suit some of them. The Cheyenne Board of Trade drew up a set of resolutions on May 7, 1868, asking the directors "when said improvements (if ever) will be made." The improvements they had in mind were permanent machine shops and a branch line to Denver.

Not all Cheyenne citizens were eager for the Denver railroad. Many of them believed that such a railroad would hurt Cheyenne business in that it would divert to Denver the business which Cheyenne was enjoying with Central City, Golden, Blackhawk, and other mining towns in Colorado. The *Leader* maintained that the branch railroad was inevitable and that therefore the Cheyenne merchants would be wise to assist Denver in getting the road. By helping in the project, they might earn Denver's good will. Cheyenne aldermen were feted in Denver in March, 1868, and John Evans, president of the Denver Pacific, returned the visit in April; but there is no evidence that Cheyenne people took any of the $100,000 of Denver Pacific stock that Denver interests thought they should buy.

Anxiety about Union Pacific intentions coincided with the establishment of a new railhead, Laramie City, just over the Laramie Mountains. On May 9, 1868, the *Leader* used the headline "Hour of Trial" for its statement that "at no time since the founding of Cheyenne has there been more universal gloom and doubt pervading the minds of our citizens. . . . It is useless to disguise the peculiarities of our situation any longer. . . . Cheyenne is a creation of the Union Pacific Railroad, and by the acts of that corporation does she stand or fall."

Meanwhile, Cheyenne could not hold many of its people. They were

Laramie bound, beginning in February, 1868. For a few months the *Leader* followed a policy of ignoring or ridiculing Laramie. Then on April 27 the editor jibed: "Vive le Laramie City! Vive le humbug!" But Laramie was no humbug; Union Pacific agents had begun laying out the town in February. Agent W. B. Bent wrote to General Dodge's assistant, J. E. House, on February 28 that "a few tents are up and are ocupied [*sic*] by parties wating [*sic*] to purchase lots. . . . Lumber for a dozen or more buildings is also upon the ground." On May 4, Agent Bent wrote to Thomas C. Durant that lots worth $34,440 had been sold for $7,315, with credit extended for the balance. On May 8 the *Leader* reported that "a heavy train, with two locomotives, went over the mountain this morning. There were seven platform cars crowded with men, seven cars of freight." Westbound Wells Fargo stages began running out of Laramie instead of Cheyenne.

Less than two weeks later, there appeared a break in the clouds which had gathered over Cheyenne. An agent sent to New York by the Cheyenne Board of Trade reported that the Union Pacific directors had given assurances of a roundhouse and machine shops for Cheyenne and a Denver branch railroad. At the edge of Denver, ground was broken for the Denver Pacific on May 20, 1868—an independent road, not a branch of the Union Pacific at the outset. There remained some lingering doubt whether Cheyenne, or some place like Pine Bluffs, would be the junction, but this was finally dispelled in mid-July. Also in July began the construction of roundhouse and shops in Cheyenne. During that same summer the city received a railroad hotel, which augured continuing Union Pacific interest in Cheyenne. All of these items served as stakes to fasten Cheyenne down permanently. The city was not to be a "butterfly place."

Business slowed down in Cheyenne, but not as drastically as had been feared. Summer brought lots of visitors, among them businessmen bound for Colorado, Utah, Idaho, Montana, Nevada, and California. "A trip to the Rocky Mountains is the fashion now," said the *Leader*. Long lists of prominent easterners who were in town or passing through can be found in the Cheyenne newspapers of the summers of 1868 and 1869. Meanwhile, much of the old business remained. For the next year, Cheyenne merchants would be engaged as much as ever in forwarding goods to Colorado. They also retained some of their forwarding business for Union Pacific construction camps and for Forts Laramie and Fetterman to the north. Instead of moving, as it was feared they would, some Cheyenne firms simply opened temporary branches in new railroad towns.

Fort Russell was a stabilizing force in the Cheyenne economy. With some justice, C. G. Coutant rates it from 1869 forward as the most important fort in the Rocky Mountain country. It became more important than Fort Laramie as a depot for the distribution of troops.

Working in Cheyenne's favor was the precarious status of all the new towns. They offered less security than Cheyenne. Once over the Laramie Mountains, the Union Pacific construction crews broke all speed records. No town could hope to stay within fifty miles of the tracklayers for as much as a month.

It is sometimes supposed that there was an orderly procession of towns across Wyoming, like beads being strung one after another. On the contrary, new towns arose almost simultaneously, owing partly to the way in which the various work gangs were spread out, partly to the speed of advance, and partly to speculative enterprise. One correspondent aptly described the railroad towns as being engaged in a game of leapfrog. Some camp followers seem to have stopped in every town, many others evidently jumped over a few, and there was some shuttling back and forth. Legh R. and Fred K. Freeman, publishers of that famous newspaper on wheels the *Frontier Index*, paused successively at Fort Sanders, Laramie City, Benton, Green River City, and Bear River City. It was a difficult period for merchants who were trying to assess the relative opportunities in several new towns. Small wonder that more cautious merchants chose to stay in Cheyenne or to go no farther than Laramie, the division headquarters for construction throughout 1868. In their early histories, Laramie City, Benton, Green River City, Bryan, Bear River City, and Evanston had much in common with their prototype, Cheyenne, although none of them flourished to the same extent.

Many squatters learned the hard way that the Union Pacific, backed by the army, was calling the tune. At Brownsville and Green River City, the first settlers failed to profit from the embarrassment of Cheyenne squatters who had been driven off railroad lots by the army. At the North Platte crossing, Lieutenant Colonel R. I. Dodge of Fort Steele drove the squatters from the old town, Brownsville, to the new town, Benton, which had been platted two miles away by the Union Pacific. It was reported in the press that the railroad company collected more than $17,000 for lots in Benton before the fly-by-night city vanished. The $17,000 figure is suspect because Albany County records show that the Union Pacific realized less than this in Laramie, where sales should have been better than in Benton. In all of 1868 the Union Pacific deeded only 78 lots to 41 buyers. The usual price was

$200, and 15 of the deeded lots went to 3 churches at the token price of a dollar. Apparently, many of the original lot "buyers" were speculators who never completed their payments. The $7,315 mentioned earlier as having been collected for Laramie lots by May 4, 1868, was probably more than one-half of the total lot revenue collected in all of the year 1868.

H. M. Hook, who was mayor of Cheyenne when the army drove the squatters off the railroad lots, was leader of the squatters at Green River City. He and his partners claimed that they had obtained the right to go on the land from the Overland Mail Company. They said that the mail contractors had secured from Congress a land grant which antedated the Pacific railway acts. Spokesmen for the railroad nevertheless demanded from $70 to $250 for each lot. After ten days of fruitless discussions, the Green River citizens offered to pay the prices demanded for the lots if they could be assured that Green River City would be the winter terminus for passenger and freight trains. The Union Pacific wired in reply: "We cannot accept the proposition of the citizens, as we cannot state where the winter terminus will be." Although the company could not say where the winter terminus would be, it proceeded at once to bypass Green River by laying out a new town, Bryan (for a while also known as Corinne), on Black's Fork twelve miles west of Green River. The tracks were laid through Green River City, and through Bryan as well, in mid-October. By early November, Green River City was virtually extinct and Bryan was sinking fast, although with the Union Pacific's blessing the latter would do better than Green River City for a few years. Neither could really flourish more than a few months after the tracklayers had passed by on their way to Bear River. The *Cheyenne Leader* reported that "there will be no halt at Bear River, as that is an opposition town. The railroad will rush on to Evansville [Evanston]," and so it did, the first train arriving there December 16, 1868. It appears that the Union Pacific did not pause to argue with the squatters at Bear River City (twelve miles southeast of present Evanston) and did not even place a switch there.

Thus Cheyenne's history foretold the pattern which would prevail in other towns along the railroad, although details and circumstances varied. The basic principle did not change: the Union Pacific would have its way, falling back on troops as needed.

As in Cheyenne, provisional governments were instituted in the other railroad boom towns. Had any of them besides Cheyenne been in existence in December, 1867, they no doubt would have received charters, as Cheyenne did, but failing this, they had to get along with extralegal substitutes. Previous experience in Cheyenne helped some leaders in the new towns. The same problems were faced again and again by those who joined the westward movement, with only a few weeks or months separating the successive experiences.

The maintenance of law and order was most difficult. C. G. Coutant considered Benton to be "the one bad town along the Union Pacific." This tends to overrate the virtue of its competitors, but no doubt Benton was bad. The *Cheyenne Leader* was of the opinion that "there is more whiskey walking about in that community than in any other of the same size in the world." Benton had another distinction, which was a function of its soil and its aridity. J. H. Beadle, visiting journalist, found that "the streets were eight inches deep in white dust . . .; the suburbs appeared as banks of white lime, and a new arrival with black clothes looked like nothing so much as a cockroach struggling through a flour barrel."

If Benton was most turbulent for a few weeks, Laramie City offset its slightly better behavior by maintaining a pretty high level of turmoil for a few months. Laramie's first provisional government was elected on May 12, 1868. M. C. Brown, a lawyer who had lived in Cheyenne for some months, was elected mayor. Thus Laramie, unlike Cheyenne, did not get a provisional government until the place was at its peak, several days after the first trains arrived. Mayor Brown threw up his hands a month later, and according to J. H. Triggs, in his *History and Directory of Laramie City, Wyoming Territory*, "a weak government at best, soon degenerated into no government at all. . . . Robbery and garroting were daily occurrences." The "no government at all" statement is an exaggeration because provisional governments carried on after a fashion, aided or hindered eventually by vigilantes.[10]

Laramie's vigilance committee, unlike Cheyenne's, was not organized until the next railhead had been established. Some of the scum had moved on to Benton or other places, but what might be described as the dregs remained in Laramie. Laramie's vigilantes must have been better organized than Cheyenne's; at least one gets that impression from the *Cheyenne Leader*, J. H. Triggs, H. H. Bancroft, and other accounts. In August they hanged a desperado who was charged with

[10] M. C. Brown's letter of resignation, dated June 12, appeared in the June 16 issue of the *Frontier Index*: "In consideration of the fact of the incompetency of many of the officers elected . . . in conjunction with myself, and the incapacity and laxity of said officers in the discharge of their duties, I find it impossible for me to administer the city government in accordance with my views of the necessities of the case."

drugging and robbing. In October they unleashed most of their energies, hanging four men and driving other hoodlums out of town. Two of their victims were partners in a saloon who were accused of drugging, robbing, and sometimes murdering their victims. Their behavior was particularly heinous because they had wangled positions as marshal and justice of the peace and had used these positions to give the color of legality to their wrongdoings. Such "working both sides of the street" was one of the most insidious aspects of local government in early Wyoming. Men got positions in law enforcement before their character could be established.

To round out their work, a delegation of Laramie vigilantes then went to Cheyenne in an effort to apprehend certain refugee hoodlums. They received no cooperation from Cheyenne authorities, who installed special police to prevent violence. The Laramie vigilantes may have extended their influence westward as well as eastward. When vigilantes appeared for the first time in Bear River City and lynched five men in late October, 1868, the *Cheyenne Leader* reported that they were supposed to be a branch of the Laramie organization. Hubert Howe Bancroft, in his *Popular Tribunals*, agreed that the operations of the Laramie vigilantes "extended as far as the western end of the Union Pacific Railroad."

With hoodlums moving back and forth among the railroad towns, it would not be surprising if vigilantes did the same. Moreover, railroad men were said to be prominent in the Laramie vigilante organization. With Laramie the division headquarters of the railroad throughout 1868 and with some of the railroaders moving back and forth in connection with their jobs, intercity vigilante activity probably occurred as reported. The Union Pacific seems not to have frowned on it.

Leaders of the Laramie vigilantes have not been identified with certainty, although N. K. Boswell and L. P. Griswold have been mentioned. In time, Boswell achieved a great reputation as sheriff and stock detective. Griswold, on the other hand, was jailed in Denver in 1872 for getting up a hanging party there and was shot to death trying to escape.

In Bear River City on November 3, 1868, the *Frontier Index* carried a notice, signed "All Good Citizens," ordering garroters to "vacate this city or hang within sixty hours from this noon." Five days later, three young men were arrested for garroting citizens, and on November 10 they were taken from jail and lynched. This affair led to a riotous aftermath, the precise details of which are shrouded in obscurity. According to Bancroft, one of the victims had a brother working on the railroad grade who "succeeded in rousing the rough element in retaliation." After a preliminary encounter, several graders were jailed. Then a throng of "shovel men" from a neighboring grading camp descended on the city, staged a jail delivery, burned the jail, and destroyed the *Frontier Index* office with everything in it.[11] Thus they ended the days of that famous "Press on Wheels." A spectator is often quoted as saying that the proprietor of the *Index*, Legh Freeman, left town so fast bound for Fort Bridger that one could have played checkers on his coattail.

Confronted by the mob, the police of Bear River City took refuge in a store. When someone fired into the store, the police came out with guns blazing, and with the help of citizens drove the mob out of town. From a rendezvous in the neighboring hills the mobsmen summoned a doctor from town to patch up their wounds and then sent word back with the doctor that the town would be burned that night. The mayor called for troops from Fort Bridger, who arrived the following day, after the mob's midnight attack had been repulsed by citizens. The army established martial law for a few weeks, quartering troops in private homes at the expense of the citizens.

First reports stated that 25 of the mob were dead and 50 or 60 wounded in the first phase of the fracas. Two more invaders, it was reported, died that night. Legh Freeman reported 40 dead to the *Salt Lake Telegraph*. A later report indicated that only 11 members of the mob were killed. The *Sweetwater Mines* at Bryan said not more than 9 died. H. H. Bancroft accepted the figure of 14 dead rioters. Most of the later accounts agree that whatever the death toll may have been among the attacking mob, only 1 defending citizen was killed. The modern student, however, must ponder C. G. Coutant's statement: "In this riot no one was killed but several persons were badly injured." Wyoming's pioneer historian rarely overlooked any bloodshed or minimized its quantity.

Many actions against individuals which were loosely called vigilante activity in early Wyoming probably did not deserve the name. All too often vigilante action was hardly distinguishable from mob action. If

[11] On November 13 the *Frontier Index* warned "ring leaders" of the garroters who remained in town to leave or expect further action. In the same issue, Legh Freeman (Fred was apparently in Laramie) stated that, contrary to rumors, "we have never been connected with the vigilantes at any time, though we do heartily endorse their action in ridding the community of a set of creatures who are not worthy of the name of men." The last issue of the *Index* came out on the seventeenth, three days before the riot.

anyone lynched in this period of railroad construction was privileged to have a hearing and some semblance of a trial, the details have not come down to us. It was simply grab him and destroy him. J. H. Triggs conceded that one innocent man was lynched in Laramie; probably there were others.

"Bubble, is it?" the *Cheyenne Leader* had asked in 1867. A look at the results of the special census taken in June and July, 1869, just after the two gold and two silver spikes were driven at Promontory Summit, Utah, on May 10, 1869, shows that in a sense it really was a bubble after all. Even bellwether Cheyenne had shrunk to 2,305. Laramie was smaller, for all of Albany County totaled only 2,027. "Bryan Vicinity and Sweetwater Settlement" totaled 1,932; the "Rawlins district" had 460; Green River City had 101. The whole of Wyoming Territory retained, after the construction workers had gone, only 8,104 people. There was building to be done, but optimism was not lacking. In October, 1869, the *Leader* was boosting Cheyenne as future national capital, citing its central location, climate, and transportation facilities.

Before we dismiss the coming of the Union Pacific, the company's achievements and procedures should be given a summary review. After the work was done, there were many post mortems all over the country. The financial operations of the promoters came under scrutiny in 1872 and 1873. It was found that the promoters had profiteered by setting up a dummy construction company, Credit Mobilier, and contracting with themselves at inflated rates. The Wilson Committee in the House of Representatives estimated that on a personal investment of less than $4,000,000, the Credit Mobilier profit was about $44,000,000 figured at the face value of the securities received by the promoters or about $23,000,000 figured at the cash value of the securities at the time. A modern study of the financial operations of the promoters reduces their net profit to a figure somewhere between $13,000,000 and $16,500,000.[12] In either case, they profited handsomely without having to wait upon uncertain future profits of the road. Congress censured the promoters, particularly the two brothers Oakes and Oliver Ames, for milking the Union Pacific Company and for jeopardizing the investments of the government and the public. Oakes Ames, who was in Congress, was further censured for permitting some of his colleagues in Congress to share in the Credit Mobilier bonanza. This smelled like bribery. The Union Pacific later set up a $75,000 monument to Oakes

[12] Robert W. Fogel, *The Union Pacific Railroad* (Baltimore: Johns Hopkins Press, 1960), pp. 66–71.

and Oliver Ames, a granite pyramid sixty feet high, on the summit between Cheyenne and Laramie, which has helped the history books in keeping alive the memory of the Credit Mobilier scandals.[13]

While the financial shenanigans of the Union Pacific promoters have been frowned upon rather consistently by American scholars, there has been less consensus with respect to the land grants. The Union Pacific received 11,141,114 acres of land, of which 4,582,520 acres lay in Wyoming. Was this land grant necessary and desirable? Or was it, as is sometimes asserted, a case of throwing away the national heritage? There has been much argument over this, but it does appear that substantial subsidies were necessary if there was to be a transcontinental railroad at that time. Most observers doubted that the Union Pacific would ever repay the government loan it had received, but ultimately it did so, with interest. Besides, as a land-grant railroad, the Union Pacific for many years (until the arrangement was terminated by an act of Congress in 1946) transported government freight and passengers at reduced rates.

While most students agree that the Union Pacific promoters were greedy and unethical, they admire their ability and energy. And most of them have recognized that, considering the problems, the quality of work done was about as good as could be expected. As an engineering achievement, the completion of the railroad in such a short time was spectacular.

The first transcontinental railroad has been called a catalyst in American life, and so it was, opening the West and linking West to East. It has also been said that the first transcontinental railroad solved the Indian problem by facilitating the movement of troops and bringing settlers, who helped push the Indians onto reservations. Yet some phases of the Indian problem stubbornly defied solution, as will be seen in Chapter 5.

[13] Commissioned by the Ames family, two renowned artists, the architect H. H. Richardson and the sculptor Augustus Saint-Gaudens, participated in the planning and execution of the Ames monument in 1881–1882. Originally it stood beside the Union Pacific tracks at the highest point on the transcontinental railroad twenty miles east of Laramie. Later the tracks were moved southward a few miles, but motorists have easy access to the monument from U.S. Interstate Highway 80.

CHAPTER 4

Organization of Wyoming Territory and Adoption of Woman Suffrage

CONSTRUCTION OF THE UNION PACIFIC Railroad brought organization of Wyoming Territory. President Andrew Johnson approved the organic act on July 25, 1868, when the tracklayers were near present-day Rawlins in central Wyoming. Most of the area making up Wyoming was detached from huge Dakota Territory, of which it had been a part since 1864. To square the western part of the new Wyoming Territory, small portions were taken from Utah and Idaho territories.

Congress had been toying with the idea of establishing such a territory since 1865. On January 5 of that year, James M. Ashley of Ohio introduced in the House of Representatives a bill which would have included in Wyoming Territory the present panhandle of Nebraska and the Black Hills of South Dakota. It would have omitted the parts eventually taken from Utah and Idaho. The Ashley bill, however, died in committee. Another Ohio congressman, William Lawrence, introduced similar bills in 1866 and 1867, using the name Lincoln instead of Wyoming, but they, too, failed of passage. Congressman Ashley was back with his Wyoming bill in January, 1868, but again his bill died in committee. In the following month the scene of action moved to the Senate. Senator Richard Yates of Illinois introduced a bill for the Territory of Wyoming, which, after various amendments, received the approval of Congress and the President.

In its very infancy Cheyenne had pleaded for severance from Dakota Territory. "Dakota is a slow coach; we travel by steam," said the *Leader* in October, 1867. Not to be outdone, Governor A. J. Faulk, in his opening message to the Dakota Legislature in December, 1867, said that if Dakota efforts to satisfy the needs of the westerners were "not sufficient in their opinion, I know of no good reason why they may not be clothed with all the blessings and protection of a separate organization." In short, let them go. The legislature took the Governor's advice, without a dissenting vote, and petitioned Congress to make a separate territory out of southwestern Dakota. Rarely in history has a government given up control over so large an area with such unanimous approval.

The Dakota memorial to Congress spelled out the reasons for separation. The western, or Wyoming, part of Dakota Territory was remote from the rest of the territory. Dakota Territory was a huge area, destined to be divided sooner or later. The two parts, eastern and western, were separated by Indian lands, there were no direct lines of communication between the two parts, and the western part already had populous settlements.[1]

The farmers and small-town folks in eastern Dakota had problems of their own without having to cope with those of an alien world several hundred miles away. They knew little and cared less about the needs of hell-on-wheels communities and South Pass mining camps. They knew that already there were more people in the western part than in

---

[1] The text of the memorial appears in Marie H. Erwin, *Wyoming Historical Blue Book* (Denver: Bradford-Robinson Printing Co., 1946), p. 142, as well as in *The Laws of Dakota, 1867–68*. Mrs. Erwin discusses the creation of Wyoming Territory on pp. 127–128.

the eastern part of Dakota Territory. How long could the westerners be allowed only one representative in the legislature? In time the westerners might even dominate territorial affairs, to the inconvenience of the easterners.

Two Cheyenne men, J. B. Wolff and Dr. Hiram Latham, were in Washington lobbying for Wyoming territorial organization in June, 1868, the latter with part of his expenses paid by business and professional men who chose him to represent them. The *Leader* and C. G. Coutant considered Wolff to be a long-winded bore and perhaps he was, but Dr. Latham made up for Wolff's shortcoming. Latham no doubt represented the Union Pacific as well as Cheyenne in his lobbying efforts. The talented promoter and Union Pacific surgeon, as part of his campaign for territorial organization, distributed among congressmen a circular which claimed 35,000 American citizens for Wyoming and promised 60,000 within a year. After gaining Senate approval easily by voice vote, the Wyoming bill passed the House, 106 to 54, on July 22. Dr. Latham jubilantly dispatched a telegram to Cheyenne: "Hurrah for the land of blue skies and golden sunshine."

The Dakota Legislature hitherto had paid slight attention to the Wyoming country, except for efforts to get rid of it. In January, 1867, all of the Wyoming country had been organized as Laramie County, with Fort Sanders as the county seat. All told, there might have been 1,500 whites in January, 1867, most of them at Forts Laramie, Sanders, Phil Kearny, Reno, and Bridger. By election time in October, 1867, the Wyoming population had burgeoned. Cheyenne alone had 3,000, and many more were on the plains to the east and in the hills to the west. Several hundred people also had materialized in the South Pass area, looking for gold. In the Dakota election, James R. Whitehead of Cheyenne won the county's single seat in the legislature.

Unhappily, Whitehead, for some unknown reason, did not reach Yankton until the December 1867–January 1868 session was almost over. When he arrived, he found that his seat had been given to Archie J. Turner of South Pass City, who had been sent to Yankton by South Pass miners to lobby for a quartz-mining law and a separate county of Carter. Whitehead was not seated, and had little opportunity to do much for his constituents. Turner was able to obtain a new Carter County, but failed to get satisfactory mining laws from legislators who knew nothing about mining problems, since the Black Hills were not yet open to settlement.

The Dakota Legislature placed both Laramie and Carter counties in one judicial district. Judge Ara Bartlett, chief justice of Dakota Territory, came to hold court for both counties at Cheyenne in March, 1868. He found not nearly as much business as Wyoming's reputation might lead one to expect. Most of the business that normally would go into district court was settled, if settled at all, in other ways in the spring of 1868—in the mayor's or justice of the peace courts, by private vengeance, or by the vigilantes.

In an excess of zeal, Laramie County, in the October, 1867, Dakota election, chose J. S. Casement, the Union Pacific tracklaying chief, as Wyoming delegate to Congress. There was no election that year for Dakota territorial delegate, or the Wyoming people might have been able to capture that position. It is doubtful that Casement expected to qualify for a seat in Congress, but he went to Washington, where he learned definitely that an unorganized territory could not have a seat. Nevertheless, during his brief stay in Washington he helped push for the separate territorial organization.

In debating the bill for the new territory, the United States Senate gave considerable time to a discussion of what name to use.[2] The names of Indian tribes—Cheyenne, Shoshoni, Arapaho, Sioux, and Pawnee— were suggested. The names of rivers were also proposed—Platte, Big Horn, Yellowstone, and Sweetwater. Most favored were Lincoln and Wyoming. The people in Wyoming were not polled and showed no strong preference, although the name Wyoming was certainly already in common use. As a place name in northeastern Pennsylvania, the word seems to have come originally from the Delaware Indians. James M. Ashley had first proposed the name in 1865, possibly because he was born in Pennsylvania. The name gained support after it was pointed out that it meant "at the big plains" or "on the great plain," appropriate for the territory under consideration. The Senate was also swayed by arguments that it was beautiful, euphonious, and easy to spell.

In the final stages of the debate in the House of Representatives, James M. Ashley, who had championed Wyoming territorial organization since 1865, surprisingly announced that he had changed his mind about Wyoming. He explained that his proposals for organization had been based on insufficient knowledge of the region. Now he had been through the territory twice and had learned that "in this proposed Territory . . . there was not fertility enough in the soil to subsist a

[2] *Congressional Globe*, 40 Cong., 2 Sess., June 3, 1868, Part 3, pp. 2792–2802.

population sufficient for a single congressional district. Not one acre in a thousand can be irrigated."[3]

Like organic acts for other territories, Wyoming's was rooted in the Ordinance of 1787, which, in providing a government for the Ohio country, set a pattern to be followed, with minor changes, time after time. Wyoming was given a simple government designed to serve a small population temporarily until conditions would warrant statehood.

The organic act provided the same boundaries as would later be given to the state in 1890.[4] The President of the United States was to appoint the governor, with the consent of the Senate, for a four-year term. Similarly, he was to appoint a secretary, comparable in some respects to a secretary of state or a lieutenant governor. The secretary would be second in command, filling in for the governor in case of death, removal, resignation, or other absence.

Legislative power was given to a council of nine members and a house of representatives of thirteen members, with provision for later enlargement of these bodies.

The highest judicial authority was vested in three judges, to be appointed for four-year terms by the President with the approval of the Senate. They would sit together as a supreme court and separately as district judges. One would be chief justice and the other two, associate justices. An attorney and a marshal were also to be appointed by the President for four-year terms.

The highest position for which territorial citizens could vote was that of delegate to the United States House of Representatives. The delegate was elected to a two-year term, was privileged to discuss and debate, but was not permitted to vote.

President Andrew Johnson nominated A. S. Paddock of Nebraska for governor and Omar F. Roberts of Indiana for secretary of Wyoming on the same day he signed the organic act, but the Senate recessed without confirming them.[5] There was much confusion as a result. Paddock finally withdrew from consideration for the governorship in December, 1868. In January, President Johnson presented new nominations to the Senate (Mathew F. Pleasants of Kentucky for governor, Henry M. Slade of Ohio for secretary, Dr. Hiram Latham of

[3] *Ibid.*, June 22, 1868, Part 5, p. 4344.

[4] Erwin, *Wyoming Historical Blue Book*, pp. 151–156, has the text of the organic act.

[5] Information about appointments was taken from the National Archives, Wyoming Territory Appointment Files. The Department of State handled territorial affairs until an act of Congress, March 1, 1873, transferred them to the Department of the Interior.

Wyoming for surveyor general, etc.), but these received no more attention than his first set. The Senate would wait until U. S. Grant, who
had been elected to the presidency in November, 1868, could supply
nominations after he assumed office on March 4, 1869.

In the meantime there were many complaints about turbulence and
lack of government in Wyoming, though it is erroneous to say that
there was no government. The organic act expressly provided the
Dakota laws should continue in force until repealed by the Wyoming
Legislature, and Dakota officials, although inclined to look the other
way, did not turn their heads completely. They supplied county
officials for the two Wyoming counties, the United States marshal
made occasional visits, and Judge Ara Bartlett came back to hold district court in October, 1868, as he had in March.

Wyoming voters participated halfheartedly in Dakota politics in
1868. Dennis Toohey, a lawyer from Bryan, was an unsuccessful candidate for Dakota delegate to Congress. Local contests concerned the
Wyoming voters more. Three tickets appeared in a Cheyenne municipal
election: Democratic, People's, and Independent. Republicans led by
J. H. Hayford, editor of the *Cheyenne Star*, were behind the People's
party, believing that there were not enough Republicans to win without fusion. Through fusion, a few Republicans were elected. The
Wyoming part of Dakota Territory was represented in the December
1868–January 1869 session of the legislature by one man, Charles D.
Bradley of Laramie County. Bradley secured the passage of a bill which
formed two new counties, Albany and Carbon, from the western part
of Laramie County.

As was noted earlier, Judge Ara Bartlett did not come to Wyoming
for the normal spring term of district court in March, 1869. The
Laramie County commissioners asked him not to come, no doubt
because they expected quick organization of Wyoming Territory once
President Grant assumed office. They were not disappointed. President
Grant's appointments were announced on April 3, 1869: John A.
Campbell of Ohio, governor; Edward M. Lee of Connecticut, secretary;
Joseph M. Carey of Pennsylvania, United States attorney; John H.
Howe of Illinois, chief justice; W. T. Jones of Indiana and John W.
Kingman of New Hampshire, associate justices; and Church Howe of
Massachusetts, United States marshal. Confirmations came quickly.

In general surveys of the history of western territories, harsh things
are said about the over-all quality of the men who received appointments. While some of the men who received Wyoming appointments in

1869 soon became involved in bitter controversy, there can be no question about the superior competence of the group as a whole. The two young men who were to head Wyoming's government in 1869 had both risen to the rank of brigadier general in the Civil War.[6] Governor Campbell had served on General John M. Schofield's staff. Secretary Lee had been a cavalry officer under Kilpatrick, Custer, and Sheridan and had spent more than a year, 1863–1864, in Libby Prison at Richmond before being exchanged. Lee had practiced law and had been in the Connecticut Legislature in 1866–1867. He had lectured throughout the East in the postwar period under the auspices of the American Literary Bureau, winning the plaudits of New York, Boston, and Indianapolis newspapers.

The new officers came to Wyoming in May to set up the new government. A group of Cheyenne dignitaries went down to Potter, Nebraska, to meet Campbell, Lee, and John H. Howe on May 7. That afternoon at five o'clock, the party got off the train in Cheyenne in a violent rain squall. More rain the following day dampened the public reception, which featured a parade by the fire companies and a twenty-piece band from Fort Russell. Then the crowd gathered in a hall to hear speeches: "All of us spoke—Lee twice as much as Howe and me," Campbell noted in his diary. Campbell and Lee entrained again the next day to go to Promontory Summit, Utah, to help celebrate the completion of the transcontinental railroad on May 10. After they returned, there were further receptions in Laramie and Cheyenne.

Both Campbell, thirty-three, and Lee, thirty-one, were bachelors when they came to Wyoming. They took hold of their work with gusto, and were able to work together on friendly terms. Both became active in the campaign to organize a Presbyterian church in Cheyenne, Campbell serving on the committee to obtain a lot, Lee on the committee to raise money. Lee hung out his shingle and soon had a good law practice while waiting for the legislature to convene. He spoke in public at every opportunity, and made friends quickly. Said the *Rocky Mountain News* (Denver): "He is a lively, rollicking fellow, full of music and, we should judge, possessing a fair show of ability."

The judges lost no time in opening district courts in Cheyenne in May and in Laramie and South Pass City in June.

The Sioux Indians saluted the new government by killing three men and running off stock in the Wind River country. A telegram to

[6] Much of the information about territorial officials, presented here and below, was taken from the National Archives, Wyoming Territory Appointment Files.

Governor Campbell from Carter County commissioners at South Pass City on May 18 said in part: "Send us troops if possible. We are surrounded by Indians." Campbell sent a telegram to General Augur, commanding the district, who sent two companies to the affected area from Fort Bridger. Later, in response to another request, Augur sent one hundred Springfield rifles and six thousand rounds of ammunition to be distributed among the settlers for self-defense. The Sioux were troublesome all summer long in the Wind River Valley.

Governor Campbell designated Cheyenne as the temporary capital. He also arranged to house persons convicted of crimes in the Detroit (Michigan) House of Correction at $1.25 per week, since there were only local jails available in Wyoming. He set Marshal Howe and 16 assistants to work taking a census as required by the organic act for purposes of apportionment before the first election in September. Marshal Howe reported in July that the total population of Wyoming was 8,014, divided as follows: Laramie County, 2,665; Albany County, 2,027; Carbon County, 460; and Carter County, 2,862 (including the unorganized part of the territory). On the basis of the population returns, Governor Campbell assigned the 13 House seats as follows: Laramie County, 4; Albany County, 3; Carbon County, 1; Carter County, 3; the portion detached from Utah and Idaho territories, 1; and the territory at large, 1. He divided the territory into 3 Council districts, assigning 3 members to each: Laramie County; Albany and Carbon counties; and Carter County and the unorganized area.

Republican and Democratic party conventions chose the candidates for the legislature and the office of delegate to Congress to be voted on September 2, 1869. The campaign was a bitter one, but at least factionalism within the parties was temporarily subdued. In Cheyenne the *Leader* had bought out the *Star* in June, so there was only one paper for each party there, the *Leader* and the *Argus*. J. H. Hayford of the defunct *Star*, who had regularly crossed swords with his fellow Republican of the *Leader*, moved to Laramie City, where he began publishing the *Sentinel* on May 1, 1869, with money supplied mainly by Nathan A. Baker. The latter shipped the *Star* equipment to South Pass City, where he began publication of the *South Pass News*. Thus Baker had a hand in the publication of all three of the territory's Republican newspapers during the campaign. Appropriately, he was chosen chairman of the territorial Republican Central Committee.

The candidates for the office of delegate, W. W. Corlett and Stephen

F. Nuckolls, were men of ability and prominence in the territory. Both arrived in Cheyenne in 1867. Corlett was a lawyer, aged twenty-seven, born in Ohio, a veteran of the Union army, trained in law, and admitted to the bar in Cleveland in 1866, the year before he joined the westward movement. He nailed up his shingle in Cheyenne when it was still a tent town in August, 1867, entering a partnership with James R. Whitehead. He was a natural orator who often spoke in community meetings.

Stephen F. Nuckolls was a prosperous merchant, aged forty-five, born in Virginia. He had lived successively in Missouri, Nebraska, Colorado, and New York before moving to Cheyenne in 1867. His advertisements in the *Leader* offered "Dry Goods, also Liquors, Tobacco and Cigars and Outfitting goods generally." Nuckolls had avoided the Civil War, being in Colorado, 1860–1864, but perhaps he had owned slaves in Missouri and Nebraska, as was asserted by the *Leader*. This was used by the Republicans in an effort to win the votes of workingmen and Negroes. There were perhaps one hundred Negroes in Cheyenne, and it was argued that they should all vote Republican in gratitude for the vote recently received from a Republican Congress.

There were no serious disturbances, only the usual drinking and rowdyism, on election day. United States Marshal Howe distinguished himself at South Pass City by leading a march of fifteen or twenty Negroes up to the polls in defiance of Democrats who had tried to keep the Negroes away.

Nuckolls won by a vote of 3,331 to 1,963. The Democrats also took all seats in both houses of the legislature.[7] Disgruntled Republicans complained that there was too much Democratic whiskey in Evanston, that there should have been a registry law, and that the Democrats polled nearly 2,000 fraudulent votes. The *Leader* was "forced to admit that barbarism and rebelism . . . yet exists in Wyoming."

Secretary Edward M. Lee called the two houses to order at noon on October 12, 1869. Only seven members of each house were present to

---

[7] Elected to the Council were T. D. Murrin, T. W. Poole, and J. R. Whitehead of Laramie County; James W. Brady and Fred Laycock of Albany County; George Wilson, Jr., of Carbon County; and W. H. Bright, W. S. Rockwell, and George Wardman of Carter County. Elected to the House of Representatives were J. C. Abney, Herman Haas, Howard Sebree, and Posey S. Wilson of Laramie County; J. N. Douglas, William Herrick, and Louis Miller of Albany County; S. M. Curran of Carbon County; John Holbrook, J. W. Menefee, and Ben Sheeks of Carter County; J. M. Freeman of the unorganized area; and J. C. Strong at large (he was from Albany County). The only member known to have had previous legislative experience was S. M. Curran.

be sworn in.[8] William H. Bright of South Pass City, Carter County, was chosen president of the Council, and S. M. Curran of Carbon County was chosen speaker of the House of Representatives. To complete its membership, W. S. Rockwell joined the Council on October 15 and George Wilson, Jr., on October 27. Five members of the House who were not present for the opening session straggled in, the fifth, John Holbrook, on November 23. One member elected to the House, J. M. Freeman, never appeared. The Council met 50 days, the House of Representatives 51, of the 60 days permitted by the organic act.

Governor Campbell's opening message included passages which encouraged the legislators to take a long view of their responsibilities:

The duties devolving upon you are arduous and of the most important character that will probably fall to any Legislative Assembly convened during our Territorial organization. Coming together as the pioneers of the future State, I trust that this initial point in our history will be marked by no personal dissensions, no mere partisan schemes and no local jealousies, but that we may work unitedly for the common good of the whole Territory, and through it for the good of our whole country. In this way, and in this way alone, can we secure our own self-respect, the esteem of our contemporaries and the regard of posterity.

After reviewing difficulties with Sioux Indians in the Wind River Valley, the Governor recommended the passage of a militia law providing for the formation of volunteer companies. He urged wise laws for the regulation of mining and the protection of miners, with provisions which would "prevent an ignorant, wasteful and destructive system of mining." He recommended the establishment of a bureau of statistics charged with the responsibility of gathering information of interest to prospective immigrants, because the "encouragement of immigration is of the greatest importance to us." He remarked that for the first time in the nation's history the railroad in Wyoming had gone ahead of settlement. He paid tribute to the vision and ability of the Union Pacific railroad builders, but also emphasized the need for low freight and passenger rates. While he looked forward to the collection of Indians on reservations and reduction in the size of the Shoshonis' reservation, he cautioned that changes should come honorably and legally: "Honorable men, respecting the laws of the land, cannot be induced to break the faith of the government."

Since there was no capitol building, two rooms were rented in

[8] Much of the information offered in the next several pages was gleaned from the House and Council journals and *The Laws of Wyoming, 1869.*

buildings about one and one-half blocks apart on Sixteenth and Seventeenth streets for use by the two houses of the legislature. The Council chamber was within half a block, and the House chamber within a block and a half, of Luke Murrin's wholesale liquor house, which had a convenient sample room in the back. Tradition has it that Murrin's place was the favorite rendezvous for legislators in territorial days when social drinking among men was almost universal. Murrin had been described by the *Leader* in 1868, when elected first Democratic mayor, as "a stoutly built gentleman, about five feet ten . . . a bachelor in the prime of life . . . reliable and energetic business man . . . very popular." Murrin later lost the support of the Republican paper, but he always had a large following among Democrats.

A chaplain, the Reverend W. C. Poole, opened all meetings of each house of the legislature with prayer. The House even adopted a rule prohibiting smoking while in session. Most of the legislators took their responsibilities seriously. They worked hard, and their achievements would seem to compare favorably with those of other "first" territorial legislatures on the frontier.

Secretary Lee worked remarkably well with the Democratic legislators, Governor Campbell tolerably so. Lee obtained for them copies of the laws of Nevada, Colorado, and Nebraska, and copies of the legislative journals of Colorado and Nebraska. They probably had other models as well. The Wyoming laws of 1869 run to more than 700 pages in a 6 by 9-inch volume. It may be conjectured that more than 90 per cent of them were copied, as had been the practice in other new territories, from available models. Details were changed to meet local needs.

Evidence in the legislative journals shows that the Democratic legislators used Governor Campbell's message as a guide for matters to consider, but were only slightly influenced by his opinions. A few of the things he specifically recommended, they did: they adopted various laws for the regulation of mining and the protection of miners; they protected game; they appropriated money for increasing the pay of the three federal judges; they selected a site (Laramie) for a penitentiary. Although the Governor did not specifically ask for action to locate the capital, they approved his tentative choice, naming Cheyenne. While the Governor recommended "the most rigid economy," they were alternately extravagant and penurious. Besides legalizing 1869 property taxes already levied, they adopted a general property-tax law which provided a two-mill limit for the territory and thirteen for the counties.

They adopted a two-dollar poll tax for persons under sixty, for county purposes. Their game law is interesting for what it left out. They forbade the sale of elk, deer, antelope, and mountain sheep during breeding season, but they did not mention buffalo. The next legislature, meeting in 1871, added buffalo to the protected list.

Governor Campbell was wary of the all-Democratic legislature. He noted in his diary on November 19: "Find that Legislature intends not

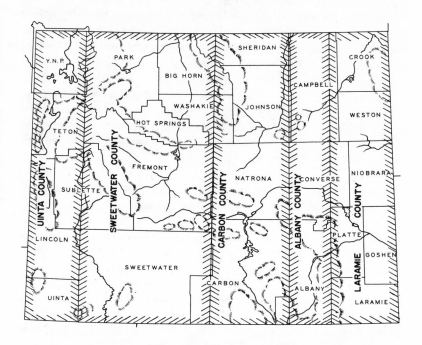

WYOMING, FIVE-COUNTY MAP, 1869

to send me any bills until last week of session in order that I cannot veto."[9] His information was incorrect. The legislature sent bills to him early enough for his careful consideration, then overrode several of his vetoes. Unhappy with their pay of only four dollars per day, the legislators appropriated an additional six dollars per day for each member and twelve dollars for the presiding officers. Governor Campbell pointed out that this violated the spirit and letter of the organic act and

[9] *Annals of Wyoming*, X, 2 (April 1938), 68.

jeopardized the territory's solvency, but the legislature quickly found the necessary two-thirds vote to override. To look ahead, Judge W. T. Jones nullified this law and thus saved the territory $7,920.

When the legislature met, there were four counties, Laramie, Albany, Carbon, and Carter, and an unorganized strip along the western border of the territory. The legislature formed Uinta County from the unorganized area, altered the boundaries of the other four counties, and changed the name of Carter County to Sweetwater. They evidently thought the change in boundaries justified their legislative appointment of fifty-seven new officials for Laramie, Albany, Carbon, and Sweetwater counties, who should hold office until the following September, when there would be a general election. Governor Campbell objected that the appointive power belonged to the executive branch of government and vetoed the four bills, one for each of the counties. The legislature overrode the vetoes, but after the end of the session, Campbell took the matter into court, where he succeeded in making his point, and the fifty-seven legislative appointees were thrown out.

The legislature voted, over the Governor's veto, to license gambling. The act was named "an act to restrict gaming." Campbell's veto message stated that he would prefer to make keeping a gambling house a criminal offense.

The legislature also overrode the Governor's veto of "an act to prevent intermarriage between white persons and those of Negro or Mongolian blood." Said the Governor:

How far it may be expedient or well to attempt to govern social life and taste by legislative prohibitions and restrictions is not easily answered; but there can be no doubt that any bill of this character should be formed so as to bear equally upon all races of men. If it be a wise policy to prohibit intermarriage between persons of different races . . . I can see no reason for excepting any race from the operations of the law . . . it is well known that there have been and probably will be, more marriages in this territory between Indians and whites, than between persons of all other races combined.

The legislature submitted to Washington two memorials dealing with Indians. One to President Grant asked that the Shoshoni Indians be moved somewhere else and that their Wind River reservation be opened to white settlement. The other, to Congress, asked for vigorous measures against Sioux who had been violating the Fort Laramie

Treaty of 1868 and demanded that the Sioux be compelled to remain on their Dakota reservation and that the Powder River route to Montana be opened once again.

The lawmakers did not establish, as requested, a bureau of statistics, although they seriously considered the matter.

The legislators did not adopt a voter-registration law. A Council committee report stated that "the population is so migratory that if a man registers in one point, from one to three weeks before a general election, his business would in every fourth case take him to another point; then to vote he must return to the place of registry."

The legislature did not make representations, as suggested, for lower Union Pacific freight and passenger tariffs, but this may have been an oversight, since several laws adopted were definitely anti–Union Pacific. Chapter 65 provided that the widow or heirs of a railroad employee killed by a train or other company property, "whether in the performance of his duty or otherwise," should have the same right of action for damages against the company as if the person killed were not employed by the company, and "any agreement he may have made . . . to hold such company harmless or free from an action for damages . . . shall be null and void." Similarly, any employee injured was assured of the right to sue the railroad for damages. This was designed to outlaw "yellow dog" contracts, common in that era, by which persons signed away their rights in order to get employment. Chapter 55 was also anti-railroad. It authorized county tax collectors to seize and sell corporation property, except for mining and milling companies, to satisfy 1869 tax claims. It further forbade the use of a court injunction to restrain the collection of such taxes. The Union Pacific had refused to pay $17,000 in Laramie County property taxes, advancing, among others, the interesting argument that since the United States had aided in building the road, had a lien on the property, and made use of it in transporting troops and the mails, this should remove the liability of taxation. These two anti–Union Pacific measures and one other measure were debated in the United States Senate with a view to possible disallowance in 1870. Delegate Nuckolls and lawyers representing Union Pacific creditors argued for letting the anti–Union Pacific measures stand. In the end, the Senate permitted Wyoming to outlaw the yellow-dog contracts, but the other anti–Union Pacific legislation was disallowed.

A new Republican weekly newspaper, the *Wyoming Tribune*, was started by Secretary Edward M. Lee and his brother-in-law S. Allan Bristol on November 20, 1869. In its opening issue the *Tribune* called the legislature "painfully Democratic," but added that up to that time the members "have been attentive to their duties and . . . have seemed to legislate only for the public interests." The *Leader* was much less kind in its post-session commentary, calling the members of the legislature "reckless copperheads . . . characterized by neglect and selfishness."

WOMAN SUFFRAGE

The 1869 legislators showed much interest in women's rights. They adopted an "act to protect Married Women in their separate property, and the enjoyment of the fruits of their labor." They borrowed this law from Colorado, one of the first territories or states that had such a law. They adopted a school law which provided that "in the employment of teachers, no discrimination shall be made in the question of pay on account of sex when the persons are equally qualified." At the beginning of the session, the House adopted a resolution directing the sergeant at arms to assign seats within the bar of the House "to ladies who may desire to attend the deliberations of this body." This was a privilege otherwise allowed only to members of the Council, federal officers, and a few distinguished male visitors. Most important of all, however, the first legislature gave women the right to vote and hold office.

In the preface to the volume *The Laws of Wyoming, 1869*, Secretary Edward M. Lee singled out one law for special mention: "Among other acts, a law was passed enfranchising women; thus, by a single step, placing the youngest territory on earth in the vanguard of civilization and progress." Lee was right, of course, in focusing attention on this act. No other Wyoming law has received so much favorable attention down through the years. Susan B. Anthony, great national suffrage leader, said at Laramie in 1871: "Wyoming is the first place on God's green earth which could consistently claim to be the land of the Free!" Subsequently, Wyoming became the first state to have woman suffrage in 1890. The call to the annual national suffrage convention in 1891 included the tribute: "Wyoming, all hail; the first true republic the world has ever seen!" Wyoming promptly became known as "The Equality State."

The suffrage act is one of the shorter acts passed by the 1869 legislature:

FEMALE SUFFRAGE

Chapter 31

AN ACT TO GRANT TO THE WOMEN OF WYOMING TERRITORY THE RIGHT OF SUFFRAGE, AND TO HOLD OFFICE

Be it enacted by the Council and House of Representatives of the Territory of Wyoming:

Sec. 1. That every woman of the age of twenty-one years, residing in this territory, may at every election to be holden under the laws thereof, cast her vote. And her rights to the elective franchise and to hold office shall be the same under the election laws of the territory, as those of electors.

Sec. 2. This act shall take effect and be in force from and after its passage.

Approved, December 10th, 1869.

First mention of the bill came on Friday, November 12, the twenty-seventh day of the session, when William H. Bright, president of the Council, called another member temporarily to the chair and "gave notice that on Monday or some subsequent day, he would introduce a bill for woman's rights." Fifteen days later, Bright introduced the bill. It was read the first and second times, then referred to the committee of the whole. As introduced, the bill would have given women the right to vote at the age of eighteen. On November 30 the bill was passed, without change, on the third reading by a vote of 6–2, with one member of the Council absent. The bill encountered more opposition in the House of Representatives, where Ben Sheeks, an able young lawyer from South Pass City, fought it vigorously. He offered two amendments, one giving "all colored women and squaws" the franchise and the other substituting age twenty-one for age eighteen. His second amendment was adopted, and the bill passed the House by a vote of 7 to 4. After the Council had accepted the amendment, the bill was transmitted to Governor Campbell on December 6. On the evening of the tenth, the last day of the session, the Governor signed the bill and made Wyoming the first territory or state to grant women full rights to vote and hold office.

The question is often asked, why did woman suffrage come first in Wyoming? As usual, causation was complex, and the answer, if it is to be worth much, cannot be made in a few words. It was certainly not a bolt from the blue. Limited suffrage rights—for example, in school elections—had been given to women from time to time in some parts of the United States ever since a few women voted in New Jersey in 1776. Since the 1840's, suffragists had been campaigning strenuously in the East. A woman-suffrage weekly, *The Revolution*, began publication in New York City in 1868. The *Cheyenne Leader* said in October, 1868: "There are few of our weekly exchanges that we peruse with more interest than we do the *Revolution . . . . The Revolution* is bound to win."

In 1868 also, constitutional amendments admitting suffrage were proposed in both houses of Congress, and in 1869 the American Woman Suffrage Association was organized to promote legislation in the states. Woman-suffrage bills had been introduced in several state and territorial legislatures. One house of the Nebraska Territorial Legislature had passed such a bill in 1856, and the Dakota Territorial Legislature had failed by just one vote to pass another in January, 1869. Clearly, conditions were ripe for a legislative victory somewhere. The Wyoming legislators had the option of jumping in at the head of the parade or of watching it pass by. Had they failed to act as they did in December, 1869, the honors would have gone to Utah Territory, whose legislators were right on their heels, adopting woman suffrage in February, 1870.

Apart from the pressures which promised a breakthrough somewhere very soon, certain conditions made it probable that victory would come first in a western territory. One factor was the scarcity of women. With only one woman in Wyoming over twenty-one years of age for every six men over twenty-one (1870 census), adoption of woman suffrage was less revolutionary than it would have been in a state or territory where there were as many women as men.

Western territories were desperately eager for publicity which might attract population. Free advertising was a common explanation in the 1870's and 1880's for Wyoming's action. The *Cheyenne Leader*, for instance, said when the act was adopted, "We now expect at once quite an immigration of ladies to Wyoming," and added in March, 1870, that it was "nothing more or less than a shrewd advertising dodge. A cunning device to obtain for Wyoming a widespread notoriety."

Historian C. G. Coutant in the 1890's interviewed surviving members of the 1869 legislature and reported: "One man told me that he thought it right and just to give women the right to vote. Another man said he thought it would be a good advertisement for the territory. Still another said that he voted to please someone else, and so on." [10]

---

[10] Letter from Coutant to Frank W. Mondell, no date, on file in the Wyoming State Archives and Historical Department, Cheyenne. The reasons given on various occasions by Colonel Bright, who introduced the bill, were that he thought it right and just and that if Negroes had the vote, as they did, women like his (Bright's) wife and mother should also have the right.

It was often said in the early days that the whole thing was done as a joke. Strongest support for this interpretation lies in an editorial in the *Wyoming Tribune*, October 8, 1870, apparently written by Edward M. Lee, who had been secretary of the territory in 1869:

Once, during the session, amid the greatest hilarity, and after the presentation of various funny amendments and in the full expectation of a gubernatorial veto, an act was passed Enfranchising the Women of Wyoming. The bill however, was approved, became a law, and the youngest territory placed in the van of progress. . . . How strange that a movement destined to purify the muddy pool of politics . . . should have originated in a joke. . . . All honor to them, say we, to Wyoming's first legislature!

Since Lee had worked closely with the legislators, his testimony is important, although he did not say that everyone involved was joking, and William H. Bright later denied that he had introduced the bill as a joke.[11]

Governor John A. Campbell was reported to have said in 1871 that "no public discussion preceded passage." While the bill may not have been discussed much, the subject of woman suffrage was treated often in the Cheyenne newspapers in the months preceding the legislature's

---

[11] Edward M. Lee had more to say about the woman-suffrage bill in an article, "The Woman Movement in Wyoming," *The Galaxy*, XIII (June 1872), 755–760, available in the Henry E. Huntington Library: "The first Legislature, composed of elements common in border communities, assembled in the autumn of 1869, and proceeded to enact a code of laws, among which was a statute enfranchising women. The law in question was not adopted in obedience to public sentiment, but because the Territorial lawgivers believed it would operate as a 'first-class advertisement'; that their action on the premises would be telegraphed throughout the civilized world, and public interest thereby aroused, resulting in increased immigration and large accretions of capital to their new and comparatively unknown Territory. I am sure that up to that time not a score of suffrage disciples could be found within the Territorial limits. Even the women themselves did not appear as petitioners; no pungent satire, or unanswerable argument, or impassioned platform harangue fell from their lips in advocacy of political equality; but the suffrage was conferred, as has been said, solely for advertising purposes. The Council originated and adopted the measure, believing that the House of Representatives would disagree; but the last named body ultimately concurred, in anticipation of an Executive veto."
Territorial Justice E. A. Thomas (1873–1877) was not a firsthand observer, but he certainly had ample opportunity to talk to many pioneers. He wrote an article, "Female Suffrage in Wyoming," *Potter's American Monthly*, XVIII (May 1882), 492–495, in which he stated that the first legislature was "instigated partly by a desire to make their infant territory famous, partly to annoy the young Republican governor." The members of the legislature, he added, felt very much as if they had "caught a Tartar" when, to their astonishment, the Governor approved the bill.

action. Much of the newspaper comment concerned the activities of
Anna Dickinson, a nationally known suffragist. After reading about
her in an Omaha paper, Nathan A. Baker, in his *Cheyenne Leader*, proposed in June, 1869: "Let's try to get her here." Ten days later, on
June 17, Miss Dickinson passed through Cheyenne on her way to fulfill
speaking engagements in California. The *Leader* reported that when the
"celebrated lady" stepped out on the platform for a breath of air, she
was "surrounded by a crowd of staring mortals. She sought refuge in a
passenger coach. She was then subjected to an enfilading fire from the
eyes of those who succeeded in flattening their noses against the car
windows. . . . Anna is good looking." [12]

After it had been arranged for Miss Dickinson to lecture in Cheyenne
on her way east, the *Leader* hailed her approaching visit as "quite an
event in our city" and as "an opportunity to listen to one of the most
entertaining and graceful of female orators." On September 24, 1869,
Territorial Secretary Lee introduced Miss Dickinson to "some 250
people whom curiosity had attracted," according to the *Leader* next day.
Governor Campbell was in the audience, but out-of-town legislators
probably were not present, since the legislature would not meet until
three weeks later. The *Leader* said little about Miss Dickinson's message,
but noted that "in person she is rather below medium height, and well
formed; her face is rather of the oval type."

Another woman-suffrage lecturer, Miss Redelia Bates, spoke in
Cheyenne on November 5, 1869, just a week before William H. Bright
announced that he intended to introduce a woman-suffrage bill. The
House of Representatives had voted to let Miss Bates use its hall, which
she did. The *Leader* had made only a few comments about woman
suffrage since Miss Dickinson's visit in September, but in anticipation
of Miss Bates's arrival, it reported that she had enjoyed a successful
tour through Colorado and that she was beautiful and talented. Just
how many paid the advertised price of fifty cents to hear Miss Bates is
in doubt, the *Wyoming Tribune* reporting "a large and appreciative
audience," the *Leader* an audience "though not large . . . select and
appreciative." The *Leader* praised the lecturer's charm, asserting that
"her presence would make any home a Heaven," but did not yet
accept her argument. The *Tribune*, on the other hand, found her both

[12] In several other articles in subsequent weeks the *Leader* called Anna "the female
humbug," one who lectured for the love of money and notoriety, and "the pepper"
of the woman's-rights movement in contrast to "the vinegar," Susan B. Anthony.

charming and persuasive: "Miss Bates is exceedingly prepossessing in personal appearance. . . . Her arguments were unanswerable, except upon the basis of prejudice." The *Tribune* review was probably written by Edward M. Lee, for he was financial backer of the paper and often wrote for it.

After Miss Bates's visit to Cheyenne one finds no more ridicule of woman suffrage in the *Leader* during the legislative session. When Bright introduced his bill, the *Leader*, under the heading "Interesting Question," assumed a position of neutrality: "It will be up for consideration tonight, at the evening session, on which occasion many of our citizens will doubtless find it convenient to attend." When the bill passed both houses, the *Leader*'s comment was noncommittal: "Ladies prepare your ballots." While awaiting the Governor's decision, the *Leader* indicated qualified approval: "Although we have not yet been fully convinced of the wisdom or necessity of the measure, yet we have something of a curiosity to witness its practical operation and results, and we hope, as we believe that Governor Campbell will approve the bill." Editor Baker was never an ardent supporter, but he had come a long way since Anna Dickinson first visited Cheyenne in June. And when the Governor signed the bill, Baker showed that while he had been carried away temporarily by the charm of Redelia Bates, he was still loyal to Miss Dickinson: "Won't the irrepressible 'Anne D' come out here and make her home? We'll even give her more than the right to vote—she can run for Congress!"

Unlike the *Leader*, the *Wyoming Tribune* needed no conversion. It greeted passage of the bill with the accurate judgment that it "is likely to be THE measure of the session, and we are glad our Legislature has taken the initiative in this movement, which is destined to become universal. Better appear to lead than hinder when a movement is inevitable." A week later the *Tribune* hailed the Governor's signature with the headlines: "WOMAN SUFFRAGE, Wyoming in the Van, All Honor to the Youngest Territorial Sister!"

Manifestly, Nathan A. Baker, who was young (twenty-seven) like most Wyoming men of the period, was attracted to Anna Dickinson (twenty-six) and Redelia Bates (age unknown but young), but he was repelled by Susan B. Anthony (forty-nine), whom he described in February, 1870, as "the old maid whom celibacy has dried, and blasted, and mildewed, until nothing is left but a half crazy virago." One must conclude that it was fortunate that Miss Dickinson and Miss

Bates, and not Miss Anthony, came to Wyoming to promote woman suffrage in the autumn of 1869.[13]

EXPERIMENTING WITH WOMAN SUFFRAGE

Woman suffrage was adopted by Wyoming's first legislature in December, 1869. Many questions remained to be answered during the next few years. Would women go to the polls? Should they participate in the selection of candidates for office? Should they aspire to office? Would they make good officeholders? Should they be summoned for jury service? Would they be willing to serve on juries? Would they be satisfactory jurors? How would woman suffrage affect politics, government, and public morality?

Two months after the suffrage measure was adopted, three women were commissioned justices of the peace.[14] Only one of them, Mrs. Esther Morris, is definitely known to have served, and she held office for only eight and one-half months, but the consensus at the time and in later years was that a Wyoming woman met the test of public office.

A second test of woman suffrage occurred in March and April, 1870, when women began service on grand and petit juries in Laramie. Enemies of women's rights may have had a hand in getting women

[13] For more about Anna Dickinson, see Giraud Chester, *Embattled Maiden: The Life of Anna Dickinson* (New York: Putnam, 1951). Probably the greatest moment of glory for this "Queen of the Lyceum" was in 1864 when at the age of twenty-one she addressed the Congress of the United States, at its invitation, with President and Mrs. Abraham Lincoln present. On that occasion she talked for more than an hour on the conduct of the war, abolition, and in praise of the President. Redelia Bates, on the other hand, missed fame, not even being mentioned in the six-volume *History of Woman Suffrage* of Elizabeth Cady Stanton, Susan B. Anthony, Mathilda Joslyn Gage, and Ida Husted Harper. Although the *Cheyenne Leader* said Miss Bates was "of St. Louis," Mrs. Fred C. Harrington, Librarian, Missouri Historical Society, at my request, searched the society's collections in January, 1965, without finding any trace of her.

[14] The *Letterpress Book, Secretary of State, Wyoming, May 25, 1869–October 11, 1872*, preserved in the Wyoming State Archives, Cheyenne, shows that Secretary Edward M. Lee transmitted commissions to Mrs. Caroline Neil, Point of Rocks, and Mrs. Esther Morris, South Pass City, on February 17, 1870. Both had been recommended by Judge J. W. Kingman, and each was congratulated by Lee "upon holding the first Judicial position ever held by woman." The copy of Mrs. Neil's letter precedes that of Mrs. Morris in the *Letterpress Book*, but Mrs. Neil was delayed in qualifying, first because of her English citizenship and then because of some question about her bond. Mrs. Neil's docket has never been found, and she may not have served, although the 1870 census listed her as "Justice of the Peace" and she was mentioned as a justice at least once in the *Wyoming Tribune* and once again in *Frank Leslie's Illustrated Newspaper* (June 25, 1870). Secretary Lee transmitted a third commission to Mrs. Francis C. Gallagher, South Pass City, on February 28, 1870, but her service, if any, has left no trace.

summoned for jury service, on the assumption that they would refuse
to serve, or prove unsatisfactory, and thus discredit the experiment.
Two of the territorial judges, Howe and Kingman, spoke persuasively
to the first six women summoned and were able to overcome their
reluctance to serve. Women participated with men on both grand and
petit juries in Laramie in 1870 and 1871 and in Cheyenne in 1871.
Previously, Wyoming's male jurors had interrupted their deliberations
with drinking and gambling. Such practices were dropped, and so were
smoking and chewing tobacco while on duty. The female jurors were
more ready than the men to enforce the law requiring the closing of
saloons on Sunday. It was noticed further that the female jurors were
more disposed than the men to convict and to impose heavy sentences.
In particular, they were not quite so ready to accept at face value pleas
of self-defense in murder cases. The women on juries, then, contributed,
as Mrs. Morris had done, to the success and reputation of the Wyoming
experiment. Opinion in the territory, nevertheless, was divided on the
subject of woman jury service, as objections were raised to the disrup-
tion of home life and to the added expense of providing two bailiffs and
two sets of overnight accommodations. New judges in 1871 stopped the
use of women on juries on grounds that jury service was not an adjunct
of suffrage.

Doubts about whether many of the one thousand eligible women
would go to the polls were dispelled when most of them turned out at
their first opportunity in September, 1870. Editors argued over the
impact of female participation. The *Cheyenne Leader* said that the women
divided their votes evenly between the two parties, increasing the
aggregate vote but not affecting the final outcome. On the other hand,
the *Laramie Sentinel* and the *Wyoming Tribune* (Cheyenne) reported that
most of the women voted Republican. J. H. Hayford of the *Sentinel*
thought the women had tipped the scales in favor of Judge W. T.
Jones, Republican candidate for delegate to Congress. Hayford said he
had observed most of them selecting Republican ballots—which he
could do, since this was twenty years before the secret ballot was
adopted. The *Tribune* attributed Jones's popularity to his youthful good
looks. All of the editors agreed that the presence of women at the polling places inhibited drunkenness and rowdyism. "There was plenty of
drinking and noise at the saloons," noted one observer, "but the men
would not remain, after voting, around the polls. It seemed more like
Sunday than election day." [15] And so the women of Wyoming provided

[15] Elizabeth Cady Stanton, Susan B. Anthony, Mathilda Joslyn Gage (eds.), *History of Woman Suffrage* (Rochester: Susan B. Anthony, 1887), III, 736.

encouraging answers to questions about the experiment in woman suffrage.

Meanwhile, the bonanza of free advertising was smaller than expected. Eastern dailies and weeklies took passing notice but, except for the woman-suffrage weekly *The Revolution*, never displayed any excitement. *The Revolution* used the headline "The Deed is Done" over its report of the passage of the woman-suffrage act, quoted the text of the act in full, and concluded with this statement: "It is said [accurately] there is not one republican in the Legislature of the Territory!"[16] The *New York Times* carried brief front-page mention of the first employment of women on a jury in Laramie. *Frank Leslie's Illustrated Newspaper* on April 2, 1870, reported that "Mrs. Esther Morris, one of the new justices of the peace in Wyoming, is fifty-seven years old. On the first court day she wore a calico gown, worsted breakfast-shawl, green ribbons in her hair, and a green neck-tie." The same weekly reported on June 25, 1870, that "Mrs. Morris and Mrs. Neil continue to exercise their functions as Justices of the Peace in Wyoming. They are the terror of all rogues, and afford infinite delight to all lovers of peace and virtue."[17]

W. F. Poole's comprehensive *Index to Periodical Literature*, Volumes I and II, which cover the period from before 1869 down through 1881, lists only six articles under the heading "Wyoming," two of which discuss the territory generally, two its botany, and two its geology. The same two volumes list sixty-seven articles on Colorado, sixteen articles on Utah, and about one hundred articles on Mormons or Mormonism. Two reasons which help explain eastern neglect of Wyoming woman suffrage are suggested in a brief comment by *The Nation*, March 3, 1870: "The experiment is also being made in Wyoming Territory; but the women there are but a handful, and, it is said, leave much to be desired, to use a very safe and convenient Gallicism, on the score of character, so that their use of the franchise will hardly shed much light on the general question." The few easterners who thought about the Wyoming experiment realized that not many women were involved and that prostitutes were common on the frontier. *Scribner's Monthly* seems to have mentioned the Wyoming experiment only once in its first twenty volumes (November, 1870, through October, 1880): in the

[16] *The Revolution*, IV, 24 (December 16, 1869), 377. This volume has been used in the Henry E. Huntington Library.

[17] *Frank Leslie's Illustrated Newspaper* has been searched in the Henry E. Huntington Library.

"Topics of the Times" column, February, 1875, discussion of the defeat of a woman-suffrage amendment in Michigan and of a letter from "a public man" in Wyoming was followed by the comment that "it seems far more likely to us that within ten years Wyoming will 'go back' on her woman suffrage record, than that any State of the Union will follow her present example."

Since census takers in 1870 were less ready than those of 1880 would be to call Wyoming women prostitutes, we can only guess how many of the women who were designated as waitresses, seamstresses, dressmakers, laundresses, and chambermaids were accurately identified. Probably, however, most of the one thousand women in Wyoming in 1870 were respectable housewives. Yet by enforcing Sunday closing and by voting for the Republican candidate for delegate to Congress the newly enfranchised women exasperated influential Democratic leaders. In June, 1871, Mrs. Elizabeth Cady Stanton and Susan B. Anthony lectured in Cheyenne (the latter twice). "Neither is handsome, Susan less so," reported the *Cheyenne Leader*. Although after Miss Anthony's second address the *Leader* conceded that her arguments were "well put and forceful," she seems not to have overcome the Democrats' growing disillusionment with woman suffrage. In December, 1871, the second territorial legislature almost terminated the experiment. Only one vote was lacking to override Governor John A. Campbell's veto of the repeal measure. Whereas the 1869 legislature had been composed entirely of Democrats, a few Republicans had turned up in 1871—just enough to keep the Democrats from overriding the veto.[18] Except for a petition from Laramie, women made no attempt to influence the legislature.

After their rights had been saved in 1871, the women soon learned that most of the men were not interested in having them engage in political activity beyond exercise of the franchise. After she had completed the partial term for which she had been appointed, Mrs. Morris was not nominated for another term. Only Edward M. Lee publicly expressed regret, writing in his *Wyoming Tribune* that he was sorry "that the people of Sweetwater county [new name for Carter

---

[18] Only one member of the 1869 legislature was returned in 1871, but that one was Ben Sheeks, South Pass City attorney, who had led the opposition to woman suffrage in 1869. Sheeks now became speaker of the House of Representatives, and spearheaded the drive to end the experiment. Only two of the 1869 legislators had stood for re-election in 1871. Without naming anyone, Governor Campbell noted in his diary: "Am offered $2,000 and favorable report of Committee if I will sign Woman Suffrage [repeal] Act." See *Annals of Wyoming*, X, 3 (July 1938), 127.

County] had not the good sense and judgment to nominate and elect her for the ensuing term."

After 1871 there was never any serious threat to women's right to vote in the territory, as virtually all substantial citizens rallied to the cause. E. A. Curley, roving correspondent for the *London Field*, noticed in 1874, as others had, that woman suffrage tended to weaken the influence of the numerous young, transient, male "irresponsibles" because "the married man who has come here for permanent residence has, practically speaking, two votes against the one which the roving man is able to cast." [19]

Getting the right to vote did not mean immediate economic equality. Herman Glafcke, new editor of the *Cheyenne Leader*, complained in March, 1874, that despite the law about equal pay adopted in 1869, "for the same work much less is paid (even here in Cheyenne, where woman's labor is scarce) to women than is paid to men; and this too, when the work is as well done by women as by men." He said that women teachers were paid barely more than half what men were paid. Furthermore, Governor John M. Thayer in 1875 told the legislature that the 1869 statute which permitted the wife to acquire and hold real estate did not permit her to convey property without her husband's concurrence. Yet not until 1882 did the legislature enable wives to convey their separate property without their husbands' consent.

Meanwhile, the women had abandoned attempts to organize with a view to nominating members of their sex for public office, after they had learned that neither men nor women would vote for female candidates for positions other than county superintendent of schools. Only two women ran for the territorial legislature in twenty years; one received eight votes, the other five, when at least five hundred votes were needed for election. Although three women were nominated, none was elected to the constitutional convention in 1889.

Thus while Wyoming men gave women the right to vote and hold office in 1869, they moved most slowly in the direction of sharing political and economic affairs with their better halves. Probably it was not merely an oversight when Hubert Howe Bancroft's agents, who visited the territory in 1885 to collect information for use in compiling

[19] Curley visited Wyoming from August 15 to October 30, 1874. The comment quoted here is taken from p. 74 of a booklet entitled *The Territory of Wyoming: Its History, Soil, Climate, Resources, Etc.* (Laramie City: Board of Immigration, December, 1874), in the Appendix of which are reprinted Curley's *London Field* articles. Copies of the booklet are in the University of Wyoming Library and the Henry E. Huntington Library.

a history of Wyoming, interviewed more than one hundred prominent male citizens but not a single woman.

WHO DESERVES THE CREDIT FOR WOMAN SUFFRAGE IN WYOMING?

Among those who formed the woman-suffrage parade in Wyoming, William H. Bright is the neglected central figure. A Virginian, he had served in the Union army (not the Confederate army, as is usually said) as a major in the office of the Chief Quartermaster in Washington, D.C., in 1864. After the war he worked for a time at a federal job in Salt Lake City, and then in 1868 he took his family to South Pass City, Wyoming, where he opened a saloon, and later worked as a miner. In Wyoming he was known as "Colonel," although his promotion beyond the rank of major cannot be verified. After his September, 1869, election to the Council of the territorial legislature, his colleagues elected him president of that body, and he proved to be a conscientious, unassuming presiding officer. Late in the legislative session he left the chair to introduce the woman-suffrage bill.

One who introduces a bill normally gets credit for it, and this was true for Bright as long as he was around to defend himself. Two months after the act was adopted, the *Cheyenne Leader* gave him full credit for it and remarked that "Bright, of Wyoming, is already immortal." For the next twenty years he was generally recognized as the person mainly responsible for establishing woman suffrage in Wyoming.[20] Beginning in 1889, however, long after Bright had left the territory, Mrs. Esther Morris moved from a place in the wings and began to nudge Bright from the center of the stage. Before Mrs. Morris' partisans were through, Colonel Bright was in the wings, barely visible, and Mrs. Morris was sole occupant of the center of the stage. Thanks to the successful upstaging, Mrs. Morris was chosen in 1955 as Wyoming's outstanding deceased citizen, and statues of her were placed in Statuary Hall in Washington, D.C., and in front of the state capitol.

[20] J. H. Hayford, editor of the *Laramie Sentinel*, in his newspaper columns in January, 1871, and again in January, 1876, claimed major credit. Somehow, Colonel Bright, who resided in Denver in 1876, came across Hayford's latest claim and denied it in a letter to the *Denver Tribune*, January 15, 1876. Bright dismissed Hayford's claim by directing attention to the Council journal of 1869 and stating that "the record speaks for itself." Thereupon, Denver, Cheyenne, and Laramie editors criticized Hayford and accorded to Bright the credit he deserved. Then, in his weekly of January 31, 1876, Hayford joined in conceding the honor and credit to Bright. John W. Kingman, associate justice of the Wyoming Supreme Court, 1869–1873, wrote in 1885 that Bright "was the author of the woman suffrage bill, and did more than all others to secure its passage."

Esther Hobart McQuigg was born in New York State in 1812. Orphaned at fourteen, she worked as a milliner until at twenty-eight she married Artemus Slack, a civil engineer. Slack soon died, leaving an infant son, Archibald. Mrs. Slack moved to Peru, Illinois, where she married a merchant, John Morris. Twin sons, Robert and Edward, were born to them. In 1868 John Morris and young Slack moved to South Pass City, Wyoming, where he opened a saloon. Mrs. Morris and the twins joined the rest of the family in June 1869. At this time she was fifty-six, weighed 180 pounds, and stood almost six feet tall— "heroic in size, masculine in mind," said historian Grace R. Hebard.

On February 17, 1870, Mrs. Morris was appointed justice of the peace to replace a man who had resigned. Her bailiwick was the little town of South Pass City (1870 population, 460), eighty miles from a railroad. She served only eight and one-half months and handled only twenty-six cases, but the novelty of having a woman judge attracted national attention. Son Robert, age eighteen, was her clerk.

After Mrs. Morris' retirement from the bench there were domestic difficulties, causing her to leave her husband.[21] She went to live with her editor son (Edward A. Slack), who had moved to Laramie, where he published a newspaper from 1871 to 1876. While living in Laramie, Mrs. Morris attended a few national suffrage conventions. She was reported to have made a few remarks but "no attempt at a speech" at a meeting in San Francisco. In 1873, Laramie women nominated her and another woman for the legislature, but Mrs. Morris withdrew her name two weeks later.

Mrs. Morris followed her editor son to Cheyenne in 1876, and thereafter she lived part of the time with him and his family, and part of the time with Robert Morris, one of her twin sons, who was a bachelor living in Cheyenne as a court reporter.

The first public suggestion that Mrs. Morris had any other claim to fame than that of having been first woman justice of the peace occurred in 1889 when M. C. Brown, while discussing woman suffrage in the constitutional convention, declared that Mrs. Morris had presented a

[21] Less is known about John Morris than about his wife. The 1870 census listed him as a native of Poland, a miner, who had property worth three hundred dollars. Evidently he had left the saloon business by 1870. The 1870 census also credited Mrs. Morris with property worth one thousand dollars. In June, 1871, Mrs. Morris swore out a warrant for her husband's arrest on a charge of assault and battery. The Carter County court record (Wyoming State Archives and Historical Department, Cheyenne) states: "Warrant issued, but not served, the matter being settled between the parties." Morris was elected Sweetwater County coroner in 1872. He died in South Pass City in 1877.

bill and had asked favorable action of the legislature. No one previously had said that she had presented a bill, and there is no evidence to support Brown's statement.[22]

In 1890, Edward A. Slack, in his *Cheyenne Sun*, began to refer to his mother as "Mother of Woman Suffrage." Subsequently, at the University of Wyoming, Grace Raymond Hebard took the lead in proclaiming the achievements of Mrs. Morris. For some years Miss Hebard permitted Colonel Bright to share the credit for bringing woman suffrage to Wyoming. In October, 1913, for example, she wrote in the *Laramie Republican* that woman suffrage "owed its existence to Colonel William H. Bright and Mrs. Esther Morris, who thus became respectively the father and the mother of equal suffrage. . . . These two minds acting upon each other were the flint and the steel which produced the spark that lighted the torch of real democracy." In the same year, Miss Hebard wrote in the *Journal of American History* that Bright believed that mothers and wives were better qualified than Negroes "but, most of all, he was helped in his convictions and fortified for the battle he expected to fight by the opinions of his wife and the acquaintance of one of his townspeople, Mrs. Esther Morris, who has since earned the unchallenged right to the title of 'The Mother of Woman Suffrage.'"

One can only guess how Colonel Bright would have reacted had he been told that Mrs. Morris (who had died in 1902) was beginning to receive major credit for instituting woman suffrage in Wyoming. Bright had left the territory in the early 1870's, was heard from in Denver in 1876, and then faded from view, although his death in 1912 in Washington, D.C., was reported in Wyoming.

In February, 1919, the *Wyoming State Journal* (Lander) published a letter from a Lander citizen, H. G. Nickerson, stating that he and Colonel Bright had attended a tea party at Mrs. Morris' home in South Pass City just before the election in 1869. After tea had been served, Mrs. Morris asked of Nickerson and Bright, both of whom were candidates for the legislature, that whoever was elected would introduce a woman-suffrage bill. Both promised, and Bright later, "true to his promise, introduced the bill and it became a law, passed in a jocular manner as an experiment, as Col. Bright informed me after he returned home."[23] Nickerson's story might have fallen on deaf ears but for the

22 Mrs. Morris and M. C. Brown were friends, and possibly she told him that she had handed Colonel Bright a bill, but she never claimed this publicly.

23 *Wyoming State Journal*, February 14, 1919. Why Nickerson waited so long before publishing the tea-party story is puzzling. Moreover, the story is inconsistent with

fact that it soon received the imprimatur of his good friend Grace
Raymond Hebard. In an attempt to corroborate the tea-party story,
Miss Hebard wrote to Mrs. Bright on October 15, 1919, asking her to
"say exactly why Mr. Bright introduced the bill and why he stood for
suffrage." The letter was returned with the notation "Mrs. Julia A.
Bright died Nov. 18, 1915."

Deciding that Bright's explanation of his actions in early-day newspapers—that he had introduced the bill because he thought that if
Negroes had the right to vote, women like his wife and mother should
also—was inadequate,[24] Miss Hebard in 1920 published a pamphlet,
How Suffrage Came to Wyoming, in which major emphasis was placed
on the tea-party story. The pamphlet was read in all the schools of
the state, and rapidly reduced Bright to the role of a puppet manipu-
lated by Mrs. Morris. Annoyed by a few unreconstructed skeptics,
Nickerson arranged in 1923 to have a joint resolution introduced in the
Wyoming Legislature "recognizing the services of Mrs. Esther Morris
as the originator of woman's suffrage as a principle of law." The tea-
party story was included in the resolution. It sailed through the House
by a lopsided football score of 50 to 0. Something happened in the
Senate, however, and the resolution did not become a part of the
statutes of Wyoming.

On the basis of verifiable evidence, Colonel Bright must still be
regarded as the leading actor in the drama, and the chief supporting
actor may well have been Edward M. Lee, secretary of the territory.
As a member of the Connecticut Legislature in 1867, he had introduced
a woman-suffrage amendment to the Connecticut Constitution, but it
failed to pass. In Wyoming his dedication to women's rights was
unexcelled. His daily contact with the legislators and the respect with
which they regarded him are matters of public record, as are several
enthusiastic suffrage articles he published in the *Wyoming Tribune*.

---

what he had written in an earlier letter. The *Laramie Republican*, October 10, 1914,
quoted a Nickerson letter to the *Cheyenne Leader* in which he said that the Democrats
had adopted woman suffrage in 1869 because they believed it would aid their party.
In that letter he did not mention Mrs. Morris.

[24] A remarkable document in the Hebard "Woman Suffrage" file in the University
of Wyoming Library is the Bright statement that he thought women like his wife and
mother should have the vote, with the names Esther Morris and Susan B. Anthony
interpolated in Miss Hebard's hand. For many years Miss Hebard and others had used
the shorter version, which is evidently as Bright said it, but in later years Miss Hebard
used the extended version.

Possibly he wrote Bright's bill, as his relatives insisted later,[25] since Bright was poorly educated and lacked experience in writing bills.

A recently discovered letter is very damaging to the tea-party story. The letter, which was written by Robert Morris and was published in the suffrage paper, *The Revolution*, makes it appear that Mrs. Morris first met Bright *after* the 1869 legislature had ended.

Another person who might have been influential was Bright's attractive young wife, who was twenty-five in 1869 when he was forty-six. Contemporaries said that she was a firm believer in woman suffrage and that the Colonel adored her. In his old age, Ben Sheeks, who had been a member of the 1869 legislature, wrote Miss Hebard that "Mrs. Bright was a very womanly suffragist and I always understood and still believe, that it was through her influence that the bill was introduced. I know that I supposed at the time that she was the author of the bill. What reason, if any, I had for thinking so I do not remember. Possibly it was only that she seemed intellectually and in education superior to Mr. Bright." Sheeks, who wrote this in 1920, also declared that he thought Esther Morris "too mannish to influence Bright."[26]

Although Mrs. Morris was, no doubt, in her quiet way an advocate of woman suffrage, it cannot be established that she influenced Bright or anyone else. She was not the usual type of reformer, since she campaigned for no public office for herself or others, wrote nothing for publication, and made no public addresses except for very brief remarks on a few occasions.[27] There is nothing to indicate that she was in

[25] Lee's sister, Mrs. Mary Lee Stark, and his niece, Mrs. Sadie Bristol Jensen, were certain that Lee persuaded Bright to introduce the suffrage bill, but they could not get Wyoming newspapers to print their heresy in the 1920's, so Mrs. Stark aired her opinion in the *Denver Post* in January, 1923. Mrs. Stark's story, as she had received it from her brother, was that in several conversations, Lee had persuaded Bright, not without difficulty, to introduce the bill. Lee had argued, she recalled, that "the act will give you a lasting place in history, advertise the territory and promote immigration of people with capital." Lee, she contended, drew up the bill and used his influence to get it passed in the legislature. Mrs. Jensen, Lee's niece, wrote: "General E. M. Lee recounted the drafting of the bill to me a number of times during his late years." (For details of the Stark-Jensen story, see Miriam Gantz Chapman, "The Story of Woman Suffrage in Wyoming, 1869–1890," a 1952 University of Wyoming M.A. thesis.) Lee was not available for comment, since he had died in New York City on January 1, 1913.

[26] Miss Hebard's "Woman Suffrage" file in the University of Wyoming Library.

[27] Apparently in an attempt to improve Mrs. Morris' woman-suffrage record, Miss Hebard sometimes wrote that she had done much work for the cause in Illinois during the twenty-five years she lived there before coming to Wyoming. However, her name is not even mentioned among the hundreds of women who are recognized in Stanton,

Cheyenne during the 1869 legislative session.

Hubert Howe Bancroft sent agents into Wyoming who interviewed more than one hundred leading citizens in 1885. With the aid of these interviews and other material gathered from various sources, Bancroft in 1890 published 148 pages of Wyoming history.[28] He did not mention Esther Morris.

At the turn of the century, however, suffragists were looking everywhere for heroines. With good reason they resented the fact that women had been neglected in history books. Needing a heroine for Wyoming, they turned to Esther Morris. She was the inevitable choice for glorification because hers was the best public record ("first woman judge") of any woman in Wyoming before Esther Reel was elected state superintendent of public instruction in 1894. Yet Esther Morris's judicial work was not enough. It was essential that she be identified as the one who had brought woman suffrage to Wyoming, had made Wyoming "the first true republic," the first state with woman suffrage. She looked the part—"heroic in size, masculine in mind," as Grace Raymond Hebard said.

The evidence, however, requires giving major credit to William H. Bright and the other legislators who voted for woman suffrage in 1869 and 1871, to Governor John A. Campbell, and to Edward M. Lee. Lesser roles were played by Esther Morris, Mrs. Bright, Mrs. M. E. Post, Mrs. Seth Paine, Mrs. M. B. Arnold, Judge J. W. Kingman, Anna Dickinson, Redelia Bates, and James H. Hayford. Moreover, many men and women in the East had set the stage, without which there would have been no woman's rights drama in Wyoming in 1869.

Anthony, Gage (eds.), *History of Woman Suffrage*, III, 559–593, the section devoted to activities in Illinois.

[28] *Bancroft's Works* (San Francisco: The History Co., 1883–1890). Vol. XXV contains the histories of Nevada, Colorado, and Wyoming.

CHAPTER 5

The 1870's—A Troubled Decade

DURING THE 1870's it was touch and go whether Wyoming could survive as a separate entity, as one problem after another defied solution. The Indians, who occupied much of the north, infuriated the pioneers; Union Pacific officials behaved more like enemies than friends; precious metals rarely could be found in paying quantities except in the Black Hills, over the Dakota border; and attempts to promote immigration failed. In short, it borders on understatement to describe the 1870's as a troubled decade.

"THE BLOOD-SEEKING BRAVE"

During the winter of 1869–1870 there was much excitement over the affairs of the Big Horn and Black Hills Mining Association, which was

95

organized in Cheyenne for the purpose of sending an armed mining
expedition north of the Platte into the area barred to the whites by the
Fort Laramie Treaty of 1868. Promoters talked of enlisting 10,000 men
through a national recruiting campaign. At first the government discouraged the project, afraid that it would ignite an Indian war. Later
the expedition was permitted, on condition that it stay west of the Big
Horn Mountains and east of the Shoshoni Reservation. Only 127 men
were found who would go. Led by W. L. Kuykendall, the expedition

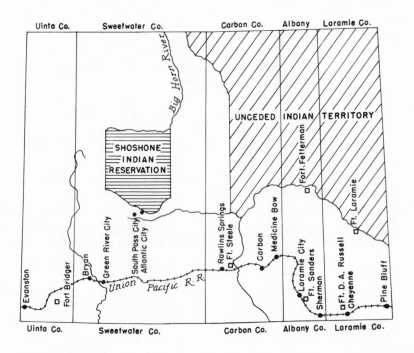

WYOMING, 1870

went north in May, 1870, encountered no Indians, found no gold, and
bitterly blamed government restrictions for its failure.

As antagonism toward the Indians increased in the West, there was a
corresponding increase in sympathy for the Indians among eastern
people, who talked much about past injustices and advocated a gentle,

patient policy. President U. S. Grant instituted his "Quaker Policy," one phase of which involved letting church groups, rather than politicians, nominate Indian agents. The Congregational minister in Cheyenne, the Reverend J. D. Davis, was one of the few westerners who approved the Quaker Policy. In a sermon on the "Indian Question" in June, 1870, Davis maintained that the Indians as a whole had been "more sinned against than sinning." He advocated treating and punishing the Indians as individuals rather than as communities. In its commentary, the *Wyoming Tribune* rejected Davis' faith that the Indians could be civilized. Edward M. Lee was writing many of the *Tribune* editorials that year. Here was an easterner, with strong egalitarian principles and liberal attitudes on many subjects, who after a year in the West accepted the prevailing hostility toward the Indians. He wrote that "no lasting peace can be enjoyed until these accursed savages have been thoroughly whipped."

General Sherman had long been a believer in the efficacy of a "big stick" policy in dealing with Indians. He had often objected to division of Indian responsibilities between the Interior Department and the War Department. When he became general of the army in 1869, he hoped to have his way in these matters, but he was doomed to further frustration. There were too many friends of the Indians in the East. They could not forgive Custer's slaughter of friendlies in the Battle of the Washita. They were revolted even more by Colonel E. M. Baker's destruction of a Piegan camp (173 Indians dead) on the Marias River in Montana on January 3, 1870. Baker, who was under orders from General Sheridan, killed men, women, and children, as was normal when an Indian village was struck. He reported only one of his men killed and one wounded. To easterners, this was another Sand Creek. A bill in Congress transferring the Indian Bureau to the War Department seems to have had a good chance until the slaughter of the Piegans, but it died with them.

Red Cloud, Spotted Tail, and other Sioux chiefs visited the nation's capital in June, 1870, at the invitation of the government. Red Cloud asked President Grant to remove Fort Fetterman. The President replied that the fort was needed to keep whites off the reservation and to protect whites against bad Indians. Red Cloud also asked Grant for arms and ammunition (for buffalo hunting), but he got little encouragement. Grant advised the chiefs to begin farming and raising cattle. Red Cloud dismissed his numerous western critics: "My Father has a great many

children out West with no ears, brains, or heart."[1] The Sioux chiefs
also appeared before a packed house of sympathizers in Cooper Institute, New York City. Their interpreter was an eloquent speaker, which
perhaps contributed to the tremendous ovation accorded them. The
rotund Chief Red Dog was quoted as saying: "When the Great Father
first sent out men to our people, I was poor and thin; now I am large,
and stout, and fat. It is because so many liars have been sent out there,
and I have been stuffed full with their lies."

The eastern press was kind to the visitors. The *New York Times*
declared that Red Cloud never understood the true nature of the Fort
Laramie Treaty of 1868 until it was properly explained to him in
Washington and asked: "Is this the way the business of a great government should be carried on . . . ?" After the Cooper Institute session the
Times observed that "the truth is that the Indians spoke far better than
ninety-nine out of a hundred members of Congress." The *New York
Tribune* was equally laudatory, and concluded: "We learn . . . that our
military leaders may sometimes be mistaken in regard to Indian
matters; we learn that newspapers of Cheyenne and Laramie are not
always to be trusted in their reports about the Sioux." Horace Greeley
infuriated Cheyenne people who read in their own *Tribune* a quotation
from his *New York Tribune* in which he said: "The drinking saloons, the
gamblers, and the prostitutes out there want a war . . . speculators want
hay, beef, and grain contracts."

When the Sioux delegation returned to Wyoming, there was interminable wrangling with the arrogant, stubborn Red Cloud over his
proposal that the Oregon Trail on the north side of the Platte be
closed and over his desire to have the Oglala agency near Fort Laramie.
This was too close to the emigrant road to suit the government, whose
representatives tried vainly to gain acceptance of a location at Rawhide
Buttes, forty miles northeast of Fort Laramie. Finally, after threats that
his rations would be cut off if he persisted in his demands to be near
the fort, Red Cloud agreed on a location on the north side of the Platte,
thirty miles downstream at the Nebraska line. Meanwhile, the first
Spotted Tail agency had been established on White River in northwestern Nebraska. The Red Cloud agency was moved to White River
in 1873, taking all Sioux except blanket Indians outside Wyoming.

In the early 1870's both the Red Cloud and Spotted Tail agencies

---

[1] This quotation and the one which follows are taken from the *Second Annual Report
of the Board of Indian Commissioners for the Year 1870* (*Executive Document 39* [Serial 1440],
41 Cong., 3 Sess.). The first three quotations in the following paragraph are taken
from the same report.

were lively places, with trouble bordering on war from time to time. Oglalas and Brulés alike hunted on the Republican River, against their agents' wishes, taking time out to raid Pawnees. Many Indians from the Powder River country joined the friendlies as winter approached, eager to eat white man's rations until spring. Some of them were supposed to be at agencies on the Missouri River. The 1868 treaty called for "a full and exact census" by the agent each year, but for several years the Indians thwarted efforts to count them, and the agents had to deal with constantly fluctuating numbers.

In 1874 and 1875, what to do with the Black Hills was the principal problem in relations with the Sioux. The Hills were a part of the reservation under the 1868 treaty, except for the western fringe, which lay in the "unceded Indian country." Mining interests suspected the presence of gold in the Hills, but when exploration was suggested from time to time in the late sixties and early seventies, military authorities warned against trespassing on Indian lands. In 1874, however, Lieutenant Colonel George A. Custer, in direct violation of the 1868 treaty, was sent with one thousand men into the Hills for a reconnaissance. He was supposed to look for places where military posts might be located in case of further troubles with the nonagency Indians. With Custer were assorted civilians, including miners, scientists, newspaper correspondents, and a photographer. When the miners found traces of gold in French Creek, soldiers and civilians alike joined the search. Custer's subsequent reports of discoveries brought the inevitable gold rush.

For a time army patrols tried to bar trespassers. One small party was escorted to Cheyenne in April, 1875. Others were caught before they reached the Hills and were turned back, but the area to be patrolled was extensive, and hundreds managed to escape the military net.

Government officials were embarrassed. Some of them contemplated eventual removal of the Sioux from the Hills, but they had counted on more time for negotiations. Instead, the situation quickly became critical in 1875, with pressures on all sides for official opening of the area, while excitement spread among the resentful Sioux.

Three delegations of Sioux chiefs (Brulés, Oglalas, and Miniconjous) were brought to Washington in May, 1875, to discuss the problem. Spotted Tail confided to the Commissioner of Indian Affairs: "I don't brag about the Black Hills country when I am talking to white men but I love it and don't want to leave." The Commissioner told Spotted Tail, Red Cloud, and other chiefs that Congress would give $25,000 for their rights in the Hills. The Secretary of the Interior explained that if this was unacceptable, the government might terminate Sioux aid, which amounted to $1,200,000 a year. Saying that they were not authorized to act, the chiefs went home in June to talk with their people.

While the chiefs were in Washington, the government sent a group of geologists into the Black Hills with a military escort to check on the gold prospects. Walter P. Jenney of the New York School of Mines led the experts. He was accompanied by George Bird Grinnell, who was to achieve fame later as a historian of the Indians. The geologists confirmed earlier reports of gold. This meant an even greater rush of prospectors, many of them coming from Sidney and Cheyenne on the Union Pacific. In his 1875 report the Commissioner of Indian Affairs conceded that events of that year "proved the utter impracticability of keeping American citizens out of a country where gold exists, by any fear of a cavalry patrol, or by any consideration of the rights of Indians."

United States commissioners visited the Sioux at Red Cloud Agency south of the Black Hills in September, 1875. They planned to purchase the Hills and at the same time acquire rights to the "unceded Indian lands" in Wyoming and Montana. This was easier said than done. The Indian attachment for the country in question was much stronger than the whites realized.

As the discussions proceeded, it became evident that the Indians would not part with their Wyoming and Montana rights for any small price. The Indians quarreled violently among themselves. Red Cloud is said to have been willing to give up the Hills if the government would pay $600,000,000 and feed the Sioux for seven generations. The commissioners offered to pay $400,000 a year for the mining rights or to purchase the Black Hills outright for $6,000,000. With offers and demands so far apart and with the Indians becoming more and more excited, the commissioners gave up and went home.

In Cheyenne the pioneers, to whom exclusion from the region north of the North Platte had been a source of constant annoyance since 1868, renewed their clamor for action. In his address to the legislature on November 4, 1875, Governor John M. Thayer gave more attention to the Indian question than to any other. He claimed to have reliable documentary evidence showing that since July, 1868, seventy-three citizens "engaged in lawful callings" had been killed by Indians and stock valued at more than $600,000 had been stolen by them—all on land from which the Indians were supposed to have been excluded. During the same period, he said, only four Indians, who had stolen horses, had been killed by the whites. The Black Hills were of no use to the Indians, he said, since they rarely went there and did nothing to develop the area. Upon the Governor's recommendation, the 1875 legislature submitted a memorial asking the federal government to confine the Sioux on their reservations and protect the whites. The memorial described the Indians as "the blood-seeking brave . . . and his filthy squaw."

Before the Wyoming petition could reach Washington, President Grant and his cabinet decided, in November, 1875, that the Indians must give up the Black Hills and the Powder River country. To implement the new policy, Grant issued a proclamation that all Sioux Indians must come in to their various agencies by January 31, 1876, or be subject to military action. To justify the proclamation, a few depredations were mentioned. More than one thousand Indians came in to Red Cloud Agency. Many others who either did not learn of the January deadline until it had passed or chose to ignore it were classed as hostiles, subject to punishment. In an enforcement measure, General George Crook and Colonel J. J. Reynolds left Fort Fetterman in February, 1876, with ten companies of cavalry and two companies of infantry. After spending the month of March in the Powder River country amid ice, snow, and bitter cold, they returned, with little to show for their enterprise beyond the destruction of one hundred Sioux and Cheyenne lodges. Colonel Reynolds incurred the wrath of General Crook for inefficiency in this campaign; he was tried by court-martial in Cheyenne in January, 1877, for his shortcomings and found guilty, but President Grant remitted the sentence of suspension.

With the approach of summer in 1876, three armies were sent into the "unceded Indian country" of northern Wyoming and southern Montana to complete the project of herding the "hostiles" to the agencies. Information indicated that there was a concentration of non-agency Indians between the Big Horns and the Yellowstone River. General George Crook was to approach the hostile concentration from the south, Colonel John Gibbon from the west, and General Alfred H. Terry from the east. With Terry was Lieutenant Colonel George A. Custer and his Seventh Cavalry Regiment.

General Crook went up the Bozeman Trail in late May. He camped for a few weeks on Big Goose Creek at present-day Sheridan. Here Indian allies, consisting of 176 Crows and 86 Shoshonis, joined the forces to bring the grand total of men under Crook to 1,325.

At the Big Goose campground occurred a spectacular incident which may be compared with the less exciting wild-horse race offered as entertainment at the annual Cheyenne Frontier Days show: Crook ordered two hundred infantrymen mounted on work mules from the wagon train. "I never saw so much fun in all my life," said Crook's head scout, Frank Grouard. "Many of the infantry . . . had never been in a saddle in their lives, while none of the mules had ever had a saddle on their backs." [2] Cavalrymen gathered for advice and applause. In due time, mules and infantrymen were reconciled, and Crook was ready to ride north.

On June 17 as Crook looked for hostiles along the Rosebud in Montana, forty miles north of Sheridan, they came to meet him head on. The Indians, under Crazy Horse and Sitting Bull, apparently outnumbered Crook's forces slightly, there being perhaps 1,400 Sioux and 100 Cheyennes. The figure 6,000 is sometimes given. In this Battle of the Rosebud, the two armies fought on even terms for several hours until the Indians suddenly decided to withdraw. Thus Crook held the field and claimed the victory, but few students of the battle give him better than a draw.

General Crook reported only 10 of his men killed and 21 wounded. Others who were present said as many as 28 were killed and 56 wounded. Crazy Horse is said to have admitted that 36 of his men were killed and 63 wounded. No doubt the battle was hard fought. Crook is said to have expended 25,000 rounds of ammunition. It is amazing that 3,000 men could fight for several hours at close quarters, as apparently they did, without more casualties than were reported. In his volume on the Rosebud battle, J. W. Vaughn compares it with the much better known Battle of the Little Big Horn: "The Battle of the Rosebud . . . virtually unknown except to a few students—involved more troops, had fewer casualties, lasted for most of a day, and was of far greater historical significance." [3]

Fearful of a trap in Rosebud Canyon which may or may not have been there and short of ammunition, Crook decided not to follow the departing Indians. Instead, he retired to his wagon train on Big Goose Creek and called for reinforcements. His overconfidence had vanished.

While Crook rested on Big Goose Creek and hunted less dangerous game in the Big Horns, Lieutenant Colonel George Custer attacked a large Sioux camp on the Little Big Horn River in Montana on June 25. The dashing cavalry leader must have believed that no force could stop

    [2] Joe DeBarthe, *Life and Adventures of Frank Grouard*, ed. Edgar I. Stewart (Norman: University of Oklahoma Press, 1958), p. 115.
    [3] J. W. Vaughn, *With Crook at the Rosebud* (Harrisburg: The Stackpole Co., 1956), Preface.

his Seventh Cavalry, numbering some 630 men. General Terry had sent the Seventh Cavalry ahead to locate the hostiles and prepare the way for concerted action by the forces of Gibbon and Terry. Although Custer has been accused of disobeying orders, he was not specifically forbidden to do battle if he thought circumstances warranted. He chose to gamble on winning undying fame for himself and the Seventh Cavalry. It appears that he paid little attention to his Crow scouts, who warned that 2,000 warriors were expecting him. Presumably, Custer doubted that there were so many Indians and hoped that he could, by pushing his men hard for two days and a night, surprise an unsuspecting village. When the battle was joined, there turned out to be 3,000 or more warriors, better equipped and better disciplined than Plains Indians had ever been before. Custer divided his command of 630 into four parts, which weakened his already inferior force. Within an hour, all of the 220 men that he led personally were dead, and other casualties brought the total dead in the Seventh on that ill-starred day to 254 (some say a few more).

The victors were largely Sioux, with the aid of some Cheyennes. Their leaders were Sitting Bull, Crazy Horse, Gall, Rain-in-the-Face, and Two Moon. The Indians fought well in the Battle of the Little Big Horn, as was the case the week before against Crook on the Rosebud, but they were in no condition to continue the contest. They had spent most of their ammunition; they must thereafter flee or surrender to determined armies advancing against them.

Early in July, Crook sent a scouting party of thirty men into the Big Horns. They were led by Lieutenant F. W. Sibley and guided by Frank Grouard and Baptiste (Big Bat) Pourier. They encountered many hostiles, yet were able to escape without loss of life. The Sibley Scout is a famous expedition, partly because a *Chicago Times* reporter, John F. Finerty, participated in it and wrote about it in *Warpath and Bivouac* (1890).

Colonel Wesley Merritt joined Crook in August with ten companies of the Fifth Cavalry, bringing the total in Crook's command to two thousand men. In the previous month, Merritt's men had blocked a large band of Cheyennes headed northwest from Red Cloud Agency. Merritt intercepted the runaways at Hat Creek Crossing in northwestern Nebraska and turned them back. The incident received unusual publicity because at the confrontation of whites and Indians, the great showman Buffalo Bill Cody advanced to kill and scalp a young Cheyenne chief, Yellow Hand, who had challenged him to a duel.

General of the Army William T. Sherman had clucked at Crook's retreat from the Rosebud and did not like his practice of taking newspaper correspondents on his campaigns, but he authorized Crook to enter Montana for a second effort in what is known as the Big Horn and Yellowstone Expedition. Crook left his tents in Wyoming, expecting to find his quarry in four or five days. Once he thought he had the elusive Sioux when he spied a great dust cloud on the horizon, indicating a moving host. It turned out to be General Terry, who had seen Crook's dust and thought that he, too, was in luck.

Together the two armies pushed their search. Then they separated, Terry going north of the Yellowstone River, Crook going east into Dakota Territory. They found a few Indians, but not many, for most of them had scattered in small bands. Some of the Indians made their way to the agencies, and others, under Sitting Bull, sought refuge in Canada. On September 8, Crook's advance column north of the Black Hills stumbled upon and destroyed the small camp of American Horse. Crazy Horse lashed back, and for the next few days there was sporadic fighting, but no large-scale combat. As it normally happened when armies spent much time on the High Plains, Crook's men suffered from exposure to extremes of weather and from lack of food. The army novelist Charles King, who was with the expedition as a lieutenant, later recalled hugging campfires in the rain until ragged garments were scorched, gnawing at tough horse meat, and trying to sleep under a soggy blanket and overcoat without benefit of tents.[4]

Crook reached Deadwood on September 16, turned his men over to Colonel Merritt, and hurried to Fort Laramie, where General Phil Sheridan gave him fresh troops for another venture into Powder River country. Crook and Colonel R. S. Mackenzie left Fort Fetterman in November with more than two thousand men, including about four hundred Indian scouts (Pawnees, Shoshonis, Bannocks, Sioux, Arapahos, and a few Cheyennes). To keep intruders out of the battle arena, agency Indians in Dakota had been deprived of arms and horses and two Sioux villages in northwestern Nebraska (Red Cloud's and Swift Bear's) were moved to Fort Robinson, where they were left under guard. As a further precaution, horses of the Nebraska Sioux were taken to Fort Laramie and sold.

As the expedition advanced to Old Fort Reno, the Indian scouts scoured the countryside. Arapaho scouts found Dull Knife's Cheyenne

---

[4] Charles King, *Campaigning with Crook and Stories of Army Life* (New York: Harper, 1890), *passim.*

village of 175 lodges on Red Fork twenty-three miles west of present Kaycee. Early on November 26, 1876, Colonel Mackenzie charged the village with 1,100 cavalrymen, including the Indian scouts. According to George Bird Grinnell, the Cheyennes had received warning of approaching troops but could not make up their minds to flee. They were not prepared for battle when the cavalry attacked at dawn, and put up only a token defense as they took to the hills. Major North's Pawnees burned the lodges and their contents. Grinnell states that they found many Seventh Cavalry articles in the village, while George E. Hyde maintains that Dull Knife's band was not in the Battle of the Little Big Horn. Whether they deserved such treatment or not, they were speedily made aware of the advantages of life at the agencies. Grinnell writes: "In the dead of winter, without food or shelter of any sort, they sat or stood on the mountainside and saw all that they owned —their subsistence and their homes—disappear."[5] After making virtually no effort to kill the Indians, Mackenzie's men withdrew the next day, aware that the Wyoming winter would round out the punishment. The Cheyennes were able to find some of their ponies, so they had horse meat to eat and green hides for warmth. Slowly they made their way to Crazy Horse's village on Beaver Creek in Montana, where they received shelter until spring. There were still many hostiles off the reservation during that winter of 1876–1877, but with the exception of Dull Knife's band, Crook did not find any of them. They were in Montana, beyond his reach.

Meanwhile, in the fall of 1876 a government peace commission visited the Sioux agencies and managed to obtain the X marks of some of the chiefs on an agreement ceding the Black Hills and all rights to the land west of them. No attempt was made to respect the provision in the 1868 treaty which stipulated that any future cession of Sioux lands must first have the signatures of three-fourths of the adult males. The 1876 agreement carries the signatures of only 241 Indians, all Sioux except for 6 Arapahos and 5 Cheyennes. To the chiefs who "touched the pen," it was clear that the alternative to giving up their rights was starvation. The Sioux bill passed by Congress in August, 1876, contained a provision that there would be no further appropriations for the Sioux unless they yielded the territory in question.

How little the commissioners enjoyed their work that fall may be judged from a long letter they signed and sent to the Commissioner of

[5] George Bird Grinnell, *The Fighting Cheyennes* (Norman: University of Oklahoma Press, 1956), p. 368.

Indian Affairs under date of December 18, 1876. After reciting various past injustices to the Sioux, they added: "We hardly know how to frame in words the feelings of shame and sorrow which fill our hearts as we recall the long record of the broken faith of our Government."[6]

With regard to the mood in which the Sioux touched the pen, the commissioners wrote that "we were painfully impressed with their lack of confidence in the pledges of the Government." One chief spoke wryly: "Tell your people that since the Great Father promised that we should never be removed we have been moved five times. . . . I think you had better put the Indians on wheels and you can run them about wherever you wish." By spring, all of the blanket Indians who had not already gone to the agencies were ready to do so, except Sitting Bull's band in Canada, where it remained until 1881. Crazy Horse, one of the bitterest of the blanket Indians, surrendered on May 6, 1877. Thus by the spring of 1877 the hostile bands were all cleared out of Wyoming and Montana. In August of that year, it is true, those who worried about possible flare-ups among the agency Indians watched closely as the press excitedly followed the remarkable retreat of Chief Joseph and his Nez Percés through Idaho, Yellowstone Park, and Montana. Dodging one trap after another, the refugees were finally cornered in northern Montana in October, 1877, without having attracted any help from the reservation Sioux.

Late in 1877, almost a thousand Arapahos from Dakota Territory were placed "temporarily" on the Shoshonis' Wind River reservation. The Arapahos and Shoshonis were traditional enemies. As recently as July 4, 1874, they had fought each other in the Bates Battle near the head of Nowood Creek in the Big Horn Basin. In 1877, Washakie accepted his old enemies reluctantly and asked repeatedly in 1878 that they be removed, but he was required to share his reservation with the unwelcome guests permanently.[7]

In September, 1879, there was great excitement along the Union Pacific when Ute Indians at White River Agency in Colorado, south of Rawlins, Wyoming, rebelled. The agent there, Nathan C. Meeker, had tried to discourage their summer wanderings and had frowned on their preference for horse racing over farming. He had plowed up their race track and their favorite pony pasture, and was threatening to institute a work-or-starve policy. A subchief assaulted Meeker, who called for

[6] *Senate Executive Document 9* (Serial 1718), 44 Cong., 2 Sess.

[7] The Wind River Reservation was reduced in size in 1872, 1896, and 1905. In 1939 the Shoshonis netted about four million dollars from an award in the United States Court of Claims. Other awards by the Court of Claims were made to the Shoshonis and Arapahos in later years.

troops. Major Thomas T. Thornburgh and 190 men, hurrying south from Fort Steele, were ambushed on the Milk Creek branch of the Yampa. Thornburgh and 13 of his men died, but the rest dug trenches in which they were able to defend themselves until relieved by Colonel Merritt with 500 men from Fort Russell. The relief expedition had been summoned by a scout with Thornburgh, Joe Rankin, who had slipped through the Indian lines to make a remarkable ride to Rawlins: 170 miles in 28 hours. During the siege, some of the Utes visited the agency, where they killed Meeker and other white men and carried off a few white women and children. One of the Ute leaders, known as Captain Jack, while on a visit to friends on the Wind River Reservation in 1882, killed a soldier and was in turn killed by a shell from a howitzer. His death inspired an obituary by Laramie editor Bill Nye:

Many of our people have been pained to hear of the sudden death of Captain Jack, of the Ute nation, and none more so than the writer of this. He was sick but a short time, and even he hardly realized that he was going to die. It is said that five minutes before his demise he was strong and well. In fact, he was a man of unusually strong physique and had a digestion like a cornsheller. He never felt a pain and rarely employed a physician.

On Saturday last he retired to his tepee, little dreaming that he would be carried out of it in a salt bag. It seems that he had defied the paleface at the post and in a moment of irritability had killed one of the soldiers. The officer in charge then procured a howitzer and fired a shell into the warrior's tent. This shell, owing to some fault in its construction, no doubt, burst with great havoc near Captain Jack's bosom and a few inches north of his liver. . . .

While the post surgeon was changing the remains from the salt bag to a baking powder can, Captain Jack breathed his last. . . . Jack was not educated, but he was great in some respects. He was a self-made man, starting out with no money, no clothes and no friends. He soon, however, acquired distinction as a warrior and a liar which was the envy and admiration of the Ute nation. Now his active brain is still. It has ceased to act. It is congested and scattered over four acres of sage brush.

Still it were better, if he were to die, that he should die in such a manner that we would have no doubts about it. We feel more secure when we know that an Indian has passed away in this manner. . . . Those who saw his remains will always feel certain that death was instantaneous and painless. His body will lie in state in a cigar box, until the time set for his burial, when he will be interred with proper ceremonies and a corn-planter. We believe that the mountain howitzer is destined at no distant day to become an important factor in the civilization of the Indian and the amelioration of mankind.[8]

[8] From the *Laramie Sentinel*, May 6, 1882. No doubt the obituary appeared first in Nye's *Boomerang*, but the files of that famous newspaper were lost in a fire many years ago.

Bill Nye's sentiments were cruel, but typical of those held by frontiersmen in Wyoming and surrounding territories and states. No doubt the Indians troubled the pioneers in the 1870's, yet other problems gave the pioneers even more concern.

ECONOMIC STAGNATION

The departure of Union Pacific construction workers in the winter of 1868–1869 meant declining population and depression in Wyoming. The special census of June and July, 1869, showed a population of only 8,014, perhaps half of what it had been the year before. The decennial census of 1870 showed 9,118, and only small additions were made in the next few years. By 1880 the population was only 20,789, of which one-half was concentrated in seven towns along the Union Pacific. Cheyenne had 3,456; Laramie, 2,696; Rawlins, 1,451; Evanston, 1,277; Rock Springs, 763; Carbon, 365; and Green River City, 327.

In a moment of candor the *Cheyenne Leader* stated in September, 1869, that business was anything but good, mining was not what it had been, public improvements were almost at a standstill, capital was timid and hesitating, and opportunities for laborers, clerks, and mechanics were scarce. The *Wyoming Tribune* said eight months later that "our merchants are laboring under the most depressed season of trade ever known in Cheyenne." Conditions improved little in 1871 and 1872. Joseph M. Carey did some writing for the *Leader* in 1873. The man who was to become one of Wyoming's outstanding business and political leaders wrote: "Be not discouraged. . . . Much labor, toil and privation must be endured to make a new and unpopulated country wealthy and populous."

High interest rates smothered enterprise. The going rate on cattle loans was 3 per cent per month in the 1870's, 2 per cent per month in the 1880's, though merchants could sometimes obtain better terms.

The business panic of 1873, touched off by the failure of the investment house of Jay Cooke and Company in New York, brought depression to all parts of the nation, but it could add little to the woes of Wyoming. Few Wyoming people owned securities. Falling agricultural prices did little harm to Wyoming agriculture, since there were few farmers and not many ranchers. Grasshoppers that compounded the distress of Great Plains farmers in 1874, 1875, and 1876 visited Wyoming but found few people to complain about them. People simply were not coming to Wyoming except as sight-seers or tramps. The tramps rode freight trains to California and back again. Some of them who dropped off in Wyoming towns were set to work on the streets and later floated out of town.

The *Cheyenne Leader* observed in 1875 that "it has been the practice of a number of our people to cry aloud to the railroad gods, military gods, and the political gods to lift the wheels of progress out of the ruts." The editor thus named three props supporting the ramshackle economy: the railroad, the army, and the federal government. Or perhaps one should say two props, since the army was part of the federal government.

The railroad failed to live up to expectations. Census reports show that there were 848 railroad employees in Wyoming in 1870 and 693 in 1880. Reports of the railroad's five government directors show that the company was making money, its surplus (net) earnings rising steadily from $2,329,790.94 in the year ending June 30, 1870, to $8,317,091.58 in the year ending June 30, 1877 (averaging $5,119,235.91 in the eight years). These net earnings were after expenses which averaged $4,985,594.67 in the eight years.[9] Most of the money mentioned did not reach Wyoming pockets.

Citizens often abused the management of the Union Pacific for its town-lot policies, high freight and passenger rates, high coal prices, introduction of Chinese labor, resistance to local taxation, and failure to build and improve shops and passenger stations. In keeping with the accepted business philosophy of the period, the railroad paid as low wages as possible and charged as high rates as the traffic would bear. The *Cheyenne Leader* typically declared on June 18, 1873, that the railroad so far had been "a curse to the community" for its "outrageous and discriminating freight and passenger tariffs west of this city."

Cheyenne was better situated in the 1870's than the rest of Wyoming. The Denver Pacific, which connected Cheyenne with the Kansas Pacific at Denver, permitted Cheyenne to enjoy the fruits of competition as long as the Denver Pacific and Kansas Pacific remained independent.

The partial relief which Cheyenne enjoyed as a result of competition between the Kansas Pacific and the Union Pacific vanished in 1878 when men in control of the Union Pacific acquired control of the Kansas Pacific.

[9] The figures for expenditures and earnings have been taken from the 1876 and 1877 reports of the government directors in *Senate Executive Document 69* (Serial 2336), 49 Cong., 1 Sess., *Reports Made by the Government Directors of the Union Pacific Railroad Company, 1864–1886.*

Wyoming people in the late 1870's were briefly under the illusion that a railroad, the Colorado Central, which was being built north from Fort Collins, would lower their freight rates. The Colorado Central joined the Union Pacific four miles west of Cheyenne in November, 1877. During the promotional stage of the Colorado Central, people in Wyoming were led to believe that the new railroad would be more than just a connecting link for the Union Pacific system and that it would be extended north into central Wyoming. On the strength of such assurances the 1877 legislature authorized Laramie County to issue bonds in the amount of $150,000 to aid the Colorado Central. To their chagrin, Wyoming people soon learned that the Colorado Central would not build north of Cheyenne and that it was in reality a satellite of the Union Pacific.

The June, 1870, announcement that the Union Pacific had decided to employ Chinese on their sections caused public indignation and a few threats from displaced white employees. There were 63,199 Chinese in the United States in 1870, most of them on the West Coast. The Union Pacific found the Chinese to be docile and willing to work for very little. Railroad officials explained that they had experienced difficulty in finding enough white workers. The *Cheyenne Leader* conceded that not all white men were eager to work on the section in all kinds of weather and in danger of Indian attack for $52 a month when they had to pay a dollar a day out of that for board. The Chinese were put to work on sections at $32.50 per month. It "looks bad—narrow— ill-advised and fogyish. It is penny wise and pound foolish," said the *Leader*. Soon Chinese were given work also in the coal mines at Almy (three miles west of Evanston).

The Cheyenne Literary Association debated the "Chinese Question," and many editorials were written on the subject. Editor Hayford in Laramie wrote: "We are not disposed to yield up this country to a horde of half civilized Pagans without a struggle." Edward M. Lee frequently ventilated the subject in the columns of his *Wyoming Tribune*. Before the literary association he advocated the doctrine of civil and political equality without regard to race or sex. Lee believed in welcoming Chinese if they were treated as men, but opposed contract labor at low wages.

The Union Pacific contended that it was exempt from taxation by state and territorial governments because it was chartered to perform duties of a public character, such as the transport of government troops, mail, and freight. In 1873, in a case in which the state of Nebraska and the Union Pacific were the litigants, the United States Supreme Court decided that railroad property was taxable. In consequence of this Nebraska victory, Wyoming was able to collect about one-third of its property taxes from Union Pacific right of way, track, and rolling stock.

The Union Pacific likewise fought attempts to tax its land grant. In 1875 the United States Supreme Court ruled that the railroad's patented land was subject to property taxes. This decision did not mean much to Wyoming in the 1870's because the corporation postponed patenting the land until buyers appeared. Most of its land grant in Wyoming escaped taxation until 1887, partly, to be sure, because of slow surveying.

In 1873 and 1874, Cheyenne, Laramie, and Evanston competed for the privilege of having a Union Pacific rolling mill in which old rails would be rerolled. In September, 1874, the Union Pacific agreed to locate the mill in Laramie and to pipe water into the city from a nearby spring. The *Cheyenne Leader* at the time estimated that Laramie paid $68,000 "for a very cheap whistle." Probably the *Leader*'s sour-grapes estimate was excessive, but no doubt Albany County and Laramie paid generously for the rolling mill. Documents in the Albany County Library show that the Union Pacific asked that the mill be exempt from taxes for ten years, that taxes on other railroad property be reduced, and that the county pay the company $18,000. Urged on by a petition from 250 taxpayers, the county paid the company $18,000 "for making an aqueduct," refunded $3,876 in taxes, and cut the company's assessed valuation for 1875 by $90,997.

The rolling mill, which was completed in 1875 at a cost of $188,293.93, was operated by private parties on lease. It consumed old rails and assorted scrap and produced rails and other railroad equipment. For many years it stood as one of Wyoming's leading industrial plants, employing on the average about one hundred men. Until the plant was destroyed by fire in 1910, and not replaced, it was cherished by Laramie citizens as the acorn which someday might grow into an industrial oak and make Laramie the "Pittsburgh of the West."

Wyoming's second economic prop in the 1870's, government, was at least as strong as the railroad prop most of the time. The Census of 1870 showed 1,534 men in service and 1,139 civilians at forts in the territory. Ten years later the count was 1,287 servicemen and 1,135 civilians at the forts. Soldier payday was a red-letter day for civilians close to the forts. Many other persons besides those identified as servicemen and civilians at the forts were dependent on government contracts for providing hay, wood, and coal and for hauling Indian annuity goods.

Moreover, the federal officials spent most of their income in the territory.

Wyoming's economic story in the early years is one of trying to add new props to the two furnished by the railroad and the government. South Pass gold was expected to provide employment for thousands of people. There had been rumors of gold discoveries there ever since 1842, but Indians frightened some prospectors away and at the same time gave boomers a plausible excuse with which to explain slow development. The area's first mining district, the Lincoln, was organized in November, 1865. In June, 1867, the Carissa lode was discovered by a party of Mormons whose success became known in Salt Lake City, whereupon two hundred Mormons and Gentiles rushed to South Pass. During the winter of 1867–1868 exaggerated stories circulated, with the result that perhaps two thousand people gathered in the summer of 1868. They came from the west by way of Fort Bridger and from the east by way of Cheyenne and other points on the Union Pacific. Freighters hauled in several stamp mills, the first in operation being one powered by an overshot water wheel in Hermit Gulch. Saloonkeepers, such as William H. Bright and John Morris, and other entrepreneurs catered to the desires of the miners. For a time the "Sweetwater fever" raged, but the rush was small compared to those in earlier years to California, Colorado, Nevada, Idaho, and Montana. There wasn't much gold, too many skeptical stories were published, and too many visitors soon left talking about "humbug."

James Chisholm, a reporter for the *Chicago Tribune*, came to Wyoming ostensibly to file stories about the South Pass mines, but he found other phases of Wyoming life far more interesting and spent the six months from March to September, 1868, in the end-of-track towns. Finally he went to the mining country in September and found, as he must have suspected, that there was nothing much doing there. Three small villages—South Pass City, Atlantic City, and Hamilton City (also known as Miner's Delight)—each had fifty or sixty people. Scores of deserted cabins indicated that the population recently had been considerably larger. The miners, according to Chisholm, were mostly old Californians, and few of them were making more than wages. After sojourning with the miners for several weeks, Chisholm set down the observation that westerners generally "would have done better (and they know it) to remain where they came from." [10]

[10] Lola M. Homsher (ed.), *South Pass, 1868* (Lincoln: University of Nebraska Press, 1960), p. 75.

There may have been, as noted, 2,000 people in the South Pass area briefly in the summers of 1868 and 1869, but the population dwindled each winter and dropped off sharply after 1870. The special census of June and July, 1869, showed 1,517 in the mining area; the regular census of 1870 showed 1,166.

S. H. Knight, head of the Geology Department at the University of Wyoming, after a study of the area in later years, reached the conclusion that not more than $2,000,000 in gold was taken from the South Pass mines in the years 1867–1873. At the peak of production, 12 mills were operating with a total of 161 stamps, but their yield clearly was disappointing. Gold was sought in other parts of the territory as well, particularly in the Medicine Bow Mountains, but nowhere did the search prove worth while.[11]

Iron Mountain in the Laramie Mountains was known to have vast reserves of iron ore. Surveyor General Silas Reed arranged to send ten tons of the Iron Mountain ore to St. Louis in 1870 for a practical test of its possibilities. The Kansas Pacific cooperated by charging no freight, but results were not published. Men of Cheyenne and Laramie hauled many samples to town for display purposes. Each town feared that the other might gain the major advantage from its development. None would have believed it if told that Iron Mountain would still rest undeveloped in the 1960's.

From the outset, coal was expected to become the territory's leading source of wealth. In time it became important, but the growth of its production came slowly. The presence of coal had been an important factor in the Union Pacific's decision to locate in southern Wyoming. Mines were opened at Carbon and Rock Springs in 1868 and at Almy, near Evanston, in 1869. Production increased from 6,925 tons in 1868 to 208,222 tons in 1875 and 527,811 tons in 1880. There were 581 men employed in coal mining in 1870 but only 330 in 1880. The early mining was done by the Wyoming Coal and Mining Company, which contracted to sell coal to the railroad at artificially high prices. Nine-tenths of the Wyoming Coal and Mining Company's stock was held by President Oliver Ames and five Union Pacific directors, so they managed to renew milking the railroad, the activity which they had

[11] Wyoming writers have exaggerated the importance of the South Pass gold rush, while others who have written general histories of western gold rushes have paid almost too little attention to it. Rodman W. Paul, *Mining Frontiers of the Far West, 1848–1880* (New York: Holt, Rinehart and Winston, 1963), devotes five lines to the South Pass rush, and William S. Greever, *The Bonanza West: The Story of the Western Mining Rushes, 1848–1900* (Norman: University of Oklahoma Press, 1963), ignores it.

first enjoyed in the days of the Credit Mobilier Company. After government criticism, the Wyoming Coal and Mining Company contract was terminated in 1874 and the Union Pacific established its own coal department. No doubt the Union Pacific profited handsomely from its coal, using it as fuel, selling it at high prices, and preventing competition by charging outrageous freight rates.[12] Union Pacific President Charles Francis Adams, Jr., testified in 1887 that coal mines were "the salvation of the Union Pacific; those mines saved it. Otherwise the Union Pacific would not have been worth picking up."[13]

The Union Pacific's labor policies in the mines were similar to those of other employers at that time. In 1871, Thomas Wardell of the Wyoming Coal and Mining Company fired all men who had gone out on strike and replaced them with Scandinavians at two dollars per day, considerably less than the wages paid previously. Federal troops were sent from Fort Steele to maintain order at Carbon and Rock Springs. When the Union Pacific took over the mines, it continued the Wardell practices. In the summer of 1875 the pay for mining coal was cut from five cents per bushel to four cents.[14] That fall, the miners at Rock Springs and Carbon walked out because they had not received a reduction in the cost of provisions and clothing, which they had understood they were to get as an offset to the wage cut. The striking miners, who asked for restoration of the five-cent rate, were promptly discharged and replaced by Chinese. The strikers then offered to go back to work at four cents, but they could get nothing more than an offer of free transportation to Omaha, where it was thought they might have a better chance for other employment. The Union Pacific, expecting trouble, asked Governor John M. Thayer for troops. Having no

[12] In their December 2, 1874, report to the Secretary of the Interior, the government directors said that the railroad's policy of charging other producers of coal discriminatory rates was "without justification or excuse, injurious to true interest of the company, and obstructs the development of the country." The directors said that the Union Pacific charged nine dollars a ton for its coal in Omaha, and charged other producers ten dollars a ton to transport their coal to Omaha. The Union Pacific charged seven dollars a ton for its coal in Cheyenne, and charged other producers six dollars a ton for transportation to Cheyenne. *Senate Executive Document 69* (Serial 2336), 49 Cong., 1 Sess., *Reports Made by the Government Directors of the Union Pacific Railroad Company, 1864–1886*, pp. 93–94.

[13] *Senate Executive Document 51*, 50 Cong., 1 Sess., *U.S. Pacific Railway Commission Testimony*, p. 82. Coal was certainly the Union Pacific's most important single item of freight in the territorial period. In each of the years 1874 and 1875, for example, about one-fourth of the one billion pounds of freight carried by the railroad was coal. *Union Pacific Annual Report, 1875.*

[14] A comparable wage cut had been imposed on the anthracite miners in Pennsylvania after the failure of their long strike, January–June, 1875.

territorial militia, Thayer appealed to General George Crook, who sent four companies, two to Carbon and two to Rock Springs, to protect company property. The troops found no trouble and did not have to stay long. This use of federal troops in Wyoming was contrary to practices in the East, where Pinkerton detectives restrained strikers.

As in earlier years, many whites in Wyoming had misgivings about the Union Pacific's employment of Chinese. The territory's Republicans, no radical mob, resolved in their convention at Rawlins in October, 1876, that "the introduction of Chinese labor into this country is fraught with serious and dangerous consequences." Nevertheless, finding the Chinese easier to deal with, the Union Pacific thereafter brought in more of them until they outnumbered whites in the Wyoming mines.

THE GREAT DIAMOND HOAX

For a brief period in 1872, hopes flickered that Rawlins or Rock Springs might become the diamond capital of the world. Two gold prospectors, Philip Arnold and John Slack, who had made their money in some place other than Wyoming, invested their earnings, perhaps $35,000, in a scheme which netted them $600,000. They bought in London and Amsterdam a few quarts of rough, uncut, but brilliant-looking stones, mainly diamonds. These they planted just across the Colorado line southeast of Rock Springs, distributing most of them in mounds of dirt resembling anthills.[15] They organized a company and began to sell stock, but in November, 1872, before much of the stock had been sold, Clarence King, a geologist and engineer in the service of the United States government, revealed the fraud.

Fortunately, Wyoming pioneers had no part in what has become known as the Great Diamond Hoax. The territory's reputation was bad enough without having some of its people identified as swindlers. On the other hand, the economy, badly in need of buttressing, got no support from the hoax.

THE PATTEE SWINDLE

James M. Pattee, an engaging rascal, gave a minor, temporary boost to the territory's economy, particularly in Laramie, when he opened a lottery there in March, 1875, as he was entitled to do under a law passed by the 1869 legislature. Pattee was soon flooding the country

---

[15] Peter Farquhar, "Site of the Diamond Swindle of 1872," *Pacific Historical Society Quarterly*, XLII, 1 (March 1963), 49–53, has located the fake diamond field less than five miles south of the Wyoming line and less than ten miles west of Highway 430.

with circulars which advertised tickets at a dollar each and promised monthly drawings for a first prize of fifty thousand dollars and other lesser prizes. The Laramie post office soon attained first-class rank. Drawings were never held. The *Laramie Sentinel* and the *Laramie Sun* were profiting too much from printing lottery circulars to permit editors Hayford and Slack to crusade against the lottery, as their normal instincts in other circumstances might have prompted them to do. Pattee contributed liberally to all worthy causes in the community and wisely refrained from selling lottery tickets locally. In 1876, Congress terminated Pattee's lottery by making it a felony to use the mails to swindle the public. After he was no longer profiting from the Pattee swindle, Hayford [16] of the *Sentinel* warned that thieving swindles could soon give the territory a bad reputation and frighten away prospective investors.

One can, nevertheless, find some balm in Gilead. Without the prosperity that Pattee brought him, editor Hayford could not have employed Edgar Wilson Nye, better known as Bill Nye, [17] who was to win great fame as a humorist in Laramie from 1876 to 1883.

[16] James H. Hayford, whose name appears often in this volume, merits recognition as Wyoming Territory's ablest editorial writer and one of its most colorful characters. A competitor once conceded that "Doc Hayford can throw more mud with a teaspoon than I can with a scoopshovel." Born in Potsdam, New York, in 1828, he taught school in Ohio and Indiana before enrolling in the University of Michigan Medical School, from which he was graduated in 1855. He then studied law in a lawyer's office in Fon du Lac, Wisconsin, where he was admitted to the bar and practiced for three years. During the Civil War he moved to Colorado, where he practiced law and became involved in mining ventures. He went to Cheyenne in 1867 to edit the *Rocky Mountain Star*, then on May 1, 1869, began publication of the *Laramie Sentinel*, which he continued until 1895. At various times he served as territorial auditor and ex officio superintendent of public instruction, postmaster at Laramie, secretary of the first board of trustees of the University of Wyoming, and district judge of the state. He was justice of the peace and police judge in Laramie at the time of his death in 1902. He was survived by the second of his two wives and by nine of his eighteen children.

[17] Not as able a newspaperman as Hayford, but nevertheless the most famous of all Wyoming editors, was Edgar Wilson Nye, better known as Bill Nye. Born in Maine in 1850 and brought up in Wisconsin, he was twenty-five when Hayford hired him at twelve dollars a week. Nye's amusing paragraphs soon brought him widespread fame. In 1881 he started his own paper, the *Laramie Boomerang*, which attracted further attention, as did two humorous books published in Laramie, *Bill Nye and Boomerang* and *Forty Liars and Other Lies*. He left Laramie in 1883 to become columnist for the *New York World*. He also delivered humorous lectures all over the country and published eighteen books in addition to the two published in Laramie. His best-selling burlesque *History of the United States* sold more than 500,000 copies. It is fair to say that he was the country's best-known humorist in the late 1880's and early 1890's. He died in 1896 at the age of forty-five and was buried at Fletcher, North Carolina.

PROMOTION OF IMMIGRATION

When people did not come to the territory, promoters went to work to attract them. One phase of promotion was handled by agents of the Union Pacific Railroad. Most noteworthy among them was Dr. Hiram Latham, who served in Cheyenne and Laramie as railroad surgeon but who certainly spent more time in promotional work than he did in surgery. In November, 1870, the *Wyoming Tribune* said that "Latham has done more to attract attention to Wyoming than any man who ever lived in it." He traveled a good deal, gave speeches, and wrote articles and letters to newspapers. The company provided him with an experimental irrigated farm (two acres) near the Fort Sanders buildings south of Laramie, where, to hear him tell it, he raised the best small grain and vegetables in the world.

The *Tribune* suggested that the Union Pacific establish colonies based on agriculture and stock raising. The Laramie Plains and Fort Bridger were named as promising locations for such colonies. "Put Dr. Latham at the head of the scheme," said the *Tribune*. "A suitable man should be sent to Europe, and another appointed to remain in New York to attend to these immigrants as they arrive."

Union Pacific officials were aware of the obstacles confronting agriculture in southern Wyoming. They knew also that hundreds of thousands of people had seen Wyoming from train windows and were spreading the word that the territory looked like a barren wasteland. The company was not prepared to spend any large sums of money on promoting the settlement of farmers in Wyoming. Dr. Latham was a remarkable booster, but he got very few results.

Although he was unable to bring many people to Wyoming, Dr. Latham was nevertheless more persuasive than almost anyone else because he put his own money into the open-range cattle and sheep business. He had sold himself. He went bankrupt in 1873, largely, it seems, because he suffered losses in the severe winter of 1871–1872.

A second phase of promotion was handled by federal officials in the territory and by the legislatures. There is nothing in the organic act to suggest that promoting immigration was one of the responsibilities of federal officials, but they were usually interested in advancing the economy of the territory. Governors and secretaries made speeches in the East extolling the virtues of Wyoming. In 1871, the *New York Sun* discussed Surveyor General Reed's report to Congress, in which he stated that alkalies are great fertilizers. Wyoming gardeners, said the report, were able to raise larger vegetables than gardeners east of Wyoming because of the prevalence of alkali. Wyoming cabbages were said to weigh as much as fifty pounds and turnips fifteen pounds.

Judge John W. Kingman published four columns on irrigation in 1871 in the *Omaha Herald*. He maintained that the cost of irrigation was "very trifling, and its results very profitable." Irrigated lands never wear out, he said; on the contrary, they always grow better. Judge Kingman was a Harvard graduate who had learned his law in the office of Daniel Webster. He was, nevertheless, not a reclamation expert. He had seen Cheyenne and Laramie bring water into town by ditches from nearby streams. Naïvely, he thought that this was all there was to it.

In his opening message to the first legislature, Governor Campbell recommended the establishment of a bureau of statistics to collect information about the territory's resources for distribution to prospective settlers. Because the two houses could not agree on appropriate legislation, they took no action. Campbell persisted, however, and in 1873 he obtained an appropriation of four thousand dollars, of which one half was to cover the expenses of a board of immigration and the other half was to pay the salary of a commissioner of immigration. The immigration board published a promotional booklet entitled *The Territory of Wyoming: Its History, Soil, Climate, Resources, Etc.* (Laramie, December 1874).

In 1875, Governor Thayer asked for the repeal of the act which had set up the Board of Immigration in view of "the present state of our agricultural department, and the uncertainty of the market for labor amongst us." The *Laramie Sentinel* defended the Board of Immigration but could not, when challenged by the *Cheyenne Leader*, name a single person who had moved to Wyoming as a consequence of the board's work. Governor Thayer's request for repeal was granted, and not until 1888 did the legislature appropriate any more money for the encouragement of immigration. In the meantime, the annual reports of the governors provided a stopgap. These reports, which were required in Washington after 1878, included information about the territory's resources and progress. A few thousand extra copies were printed for mailing when inquiries about the territory came to the governor's office.

A third phase of immigration promotion was the domain of assorted newspapermen. Among the enthusiastic newspaper promoters was Hayford of the *Laramie Sentinel*. He had picked up the idea that plowing the soil would bring rain. Perhaps he got it from Samuel Aughey, professor of natural sciences at the University of Nebraska, who propagated the notion that plowing the ground would increase rainfall because, instead of running off, rain would be absorbed by the broken soil and would be returned to the air by evaporation for the production of more rainfall. Hayford also passed on the notion that iron railroad tracks attracted rain. In short, the country was getting "more seasonable" all the time. Other Wyoming newspapers, the *Cheyenne Leader* in particular, carried much promotional matter but rarely approached the extremes to which Hayford was addicted. Sometimes, newspapermen turned out promotional booklets, such as J. H. Triggs's *History and Directory of Laramie City* (Laramie, 1875) and Robert E. Strahorn's *Handbook of Wyoming* (Cheyenne, 1877). Both put Wyoming's best foot forward.

The immigration promotion in Wyoming during the 1870's bore little fruit for several reasons. The Union Pacific offered a discouraging show window to a vast number of excursionists. Also, the winter of 1871–1872 hurt because newspapers reported that trains were stalled amid great snowdrifts for weeks at a time. Trains were blocked, off and on, from December to April. When a man out looking for cattle was reported frozen to death, a New York farmer wrote to Governor Campbell asking how this was possible when he had read previously about the mild, equable climate. Wyoming received entirely too much news coverage for the terrible winter of 1871–1872. For years afterward, promotional stories about the mild climate were discounted. Similarly, the easterners detected inconsistencies in stories, on the one hand, about millions of unoccupied acres to the north and, on the other, hair-raising reports about Indian raids on isolated settlers. Editors were prone to use exaggerated stories about the Indian dangers in order to get the government to clear all Indians out of Wyoming. Many unchecked rumors of terrible deeds, all too often untrue, were given currency. Overstressing the Indian dangers boomeranged and made it more difficult to attract settlers.

ANNEXATION TO COLORADO

Wyoming's disappointing economic progress led some people to favor the dismemberment of Wyoming and the annexation of the southeastern part, including the Union Pacific, to Colorado. This would add enough wealth to Colorado, it was thought, to make possible its admission to statehood in the early 1870's. The proposal was aired in

Congress occasionally, and whenever it was, the pros and cons were argued in Wyoming.

In December, 1872, President Grant discussed a Colorado statehood bill with the House Committee on Territories. He said he would approve attaching southeastern Wyoming to the new state. He favored abolishing Wyoming Territory and dividing the land into four parts, to be given to Utah, Montana, Idaho, and Colorado. He said that Wyoming's population did not exceed ten thousand and that the territory would not within the lives of those present have enough people for statehood. The House Committee on Territories was reported to be in favor of the bill, and the people of Cheyenne gathered at a mass meeting to adopt resolutions expressing uncompromising opposition to the scheme.

The proposition was up for further discussion in December, 1873. By this time Wyoming people were about equally divided on the subject. "While much may be said in opposition to dismemberment," said the *Cheyenne Leader*, "a great many prospective advantages may be pointed to in becoming part of a sovereign state." Late in January, 1874, Delegate W. R. Steele gained a "Hurrah" from the *Leader* when he wrote that dismemberment was once again a failure. Thereafter, Colorado made enough progress to warrant statehood in 1876 without Wyoming assistance.

POLITICAL FIREWORKS

During the session of the first legislature, Secretary Lee fell out with the chairman of the Republican Central Committee of the territory, Nathan A. Baker, 26-year-old editor of the territory's leading newspaper, the *Cheyenne Leader*. One of the Secretary's responsibilities was to assign the public printing, particularly the printing of the proceedings of the legislature and the session laws. Naturally, the city's only Republican editor, Baker of the *Leader*, assumed that he would get the printing, particularly since he was head of the Republican Central Committee. Nevertheless, Lee made other plans. He brought his brother-in-law S. Allan Bristol from Colorado to Cheyenne and supplied him with financial backing for starting a second Republican newspaper, the *Wyoming Tribune*. The *Tribune* opened shop just in time to take on the task of printing the legislative proceedings and the session laws.

Lee's decision to ignore the claims of Nathan A. Baker to the territory's printing led to a terrible factional battle in the Republican party which endured for years. First inkling of the course to be followed by Lee's enemies was a letter, dated December 8, 1869, from Connecticut's United States Senator W. A. Buckingham to Secretary of State Hamilton Fish: "I am credibly informed that E. M. Lee . . . has disgraced his position by intemperance. I knew him in Connecticut as a public advocate of the principles of temperance and feel chagrined that I could have been so much deceived in his character." [18] Apparently, United States Marshal Church Howe was Senator Buckingham's informant.

The anti-Lee campaign picked up steam in January, 1870. Two petitions were forwarded to Washington. One received at the State Department on January 25 said that "he [Lee] has been beastly drunk on several occasions in public, and . . . has been living publicly with a notorious prostitute known as the 'Circassian Girl' and with her has taken his meals at the public table at the Ford House in Cheyenne." He had been so brazen, asserted the petition, as to introduce the "Circassian Girl" to one of his two sisters who were in Cheyenne. The wording of this petition closely resembled the wording of a letter which Church Howe sent to Senator Patterson at about the same time. Among the twenty-seven signatures on this petition were those of two county commissioners, the sheriff, the clerk of the Wyoming Supreme Court, the superintendent of the Union Pacific Railroad, the rector of St. Mark's Episcopal Church, and three lawyers. Attached to this petition was another one signed by nine women (one of them was Mrs. Church Howe) which said substantially the same thing and likewise asked for Lee's removal.

Baker of the *Leader* dispatched a long letter to President Grant elaborating on Lee's "drunken revelries and licentious debaucheries." Baker did not mention the printing business, but alleged that he was yielding reluctantly to unanimous demand of the people. The Mayor of Cheyenne and a few others signed a statement stating that Lee "on Saturday eve last January twenty ninth . . . appeared at McDaniels' Museum and publicly played cards with a woman whose name to us is unknown but who is attached to a troupe known as the Can Can Troupe now giving exhibitions in this city." They further charged that Lee was living with a prostitute and paying her rent.

When Lee and his friends finally learned of these activities, there was such an accumulation of incriminating testimony in Washington that the task of clearing his name was a formidable one. Lee probably did not know, until it was too late, how active his foes had been and what an overwhelming barrage they had laid against his honor.

Judging by the files in the National Archives, fifteen women of

[18] This quotation and other material which follows is taken from the National Archives, Department of State Appointment File for Edward M. Lee.

Cheyenne struck the first blow for Lee. On February 5 they wrote President Grant that they had just learned of a petition by other women against Lee and they "hasten to contradict it." Except for one "Miss," they all signed themselves "Mrs." Their longhand petition to the President included not a few misspelled words—for example, they called Lee's enemies "a few degreaded women and some few miserable Rebble traitors hoo ar a curse to the community." Their semiliterate defense of Lee seems to have been the only friendly statement Grant had before him when, on February 18, he nominated Major Herman Glafcke of Connecticut to replace General Lee from the same state. On the very next day, Governor Campbell, who was in Washington, forwarded to Secretary of State Hamilton Fish three affidavits in defense of Lee which he had just received from Cheyenne.

To climax the belated defense, on February 26 a petition bearing the signatures of 222 Cheyenne men reached the State Department, asserting that Lee's character was above reproach and that "the few persons" who sought his removal were moved solely by personal spite and vindictiveness. Many prominent citizens of both political parties were among the petitioners for Lee.

Lee might have been able to hold his office had documents defending him reached Washington sooner and had he been free to go to Washington when he first learned about the campaign against him. But Governor Campbell was in Washington, and Lee was compelled to remain in Cheyenne as acting governor. Finally, after Campbell had returned to Cheyenne, Lee went to Washington to try to vindicate himself. This he may have done in part, but he could not retrieve his office. Governor Campbell, had he been so disposed, could probably have saved Lee's job for him. It appears that he made no fight for Lee.

When Lee left Cheyenne for Washington in March, he was given a tremendous ovation by his friends. When he returned in April, without having been reinstated, there was a public reception at the courthouse. Lee remained in Cheyenne most of the time during the following year, practicing law and writing for his newspaper, the *Wyoming Tribune*. In February, 1871, he sold his interest in the *Tribune*. He returned to the lecture platform in the East, then practiced law in New York City until his death on January 1, 1913. He never married the "Circassian Girl" or anyone else.

As to Lee's behavior in Wyoming, it seems likely that his political enemies indulged in considerable exaggeration, though some of the allegations presumably were true. Considering the level of morality in frontier Wyoming, Lee probably could have done all the things they said he did and still have kept his job, if he had just given the printing to Nathan A. Baker. The Lee affair is in some respects typical of Wyoming political behavior in the territorial period. Outrageously libelous statements, supported by long lists of signatures, were often dispatched to Washington.

REPUBLICANS AT WAR

Until Governor Campbell resigned in 1875, two groups of Republican leaders in the territory were at loggerheads constantly. The Republican editor of the *Laramie Sentinel*, J. H. Hayford, later described the war between federal officials as one "which rapidly spread among the citizens of the territory and grew into the most bitter feud ever known in the west." On one side were Governor Campbell; United States Attorney and later Associate Justice Joseph M. Carey; Receiver Frank Wolcott of the United States Land Office; Dr. Hiram Latham; and editor Hayford. On the other side were editor Baker; United States Marshal Church Howe; Herman Glafcke, who replaced Lee as secretary; and Surveyor General Silas Reed. The Democrats no doubt enjoyed watching the strife, and it may have helped them in winning most of the elective positions in the territory, although all federal positions remained in the hands of Republicans.

Only a few items can be selected to illustrate the course of the factional struggle among the Republicans. In a chaotic convention in August, 1870, the Campbell faction nominated Judge W. T. Jones for delegate to Congress in preference to Church Howe. Editor Baker claimed that two votes were purchased to achieve the convention victory. In the following May, at the instigation of Governor Campbell, Grant's ax fell on Church Howe's neck. Campbell had a personal interest in getting Howe ousted because the latter had been criticizing him in Washington. Petitions against Howe, and some letters in his defense, began piling up in Washington as early as February, 1870.[19] The *Cheyenne Leader* was by this time referring to the Governor as "Little Johnny." It called him "quarrelsome, crochety, spiteful and venomous . . . he has proved himself an imbecile." As Church Howe's replacement, Grant sent out an Indiana man, Major General Robert H. Gilroy, who brought his brother as deputy but concluded after a few days that there was not enough opportunity for profit in the marshal's

---

[19] Appointment files in the National Archives have supplied most of the information on which the discussion in the next few pages is based.

job and went east again. Then Church Howe was restored to office, to the consternation of the Campbellites. A Washington dispatch—perhaps sent by Delegate Jones—to the *Chicago Tribune* related that Gilroy had been bought off by Church Howe. Editor Baker, who had been bested by the Campbell clique and admitted as much, gave up the battle in April, 1872, and moved to Denver. He turned the *Leader* over to Herman Glafcke, secretary of Wyoming Territory. Editor Glafcke promised to be "gentlemanly in politics" and to keep his columns "aloof from petty cliques and factions." For a while he was gentle with Governor Campbell and Delegate Jones, but eventually he was unable to separate the Governor and the Delegate from their friends.

Just a month after Glafcke took charge of the *Leader*, the Campbell faction won control of the Cheyenne convention and named the six delegates to the territorial convention to meet at Rawlins. If we can believe the *Leader*, John W. Corey, territorial Republican Central Committee chairman and by this time editor of the *Tribune*, was drunk at the Cheyenne convention and "every barroom in town had been bought up to send its delegation." The seventy "honest Republicans" were outnumbered. At the Rawlins convention the *Wyoming Tribune* and the *Laramie Sentinel* were designated as official organs of the Republican party. A few weeks later, President Grant's ax fell a second time on United States Marshal Church Howe, and Frank Wolcott, Campbell man, who was known thereafter to his enemies as the "Jack of Spades," assumed the office of United States marshal. Frank Wolcott had become well known as receiver of the United States Land Office. He had been United States marshal only a short time before letters and petitions began to flow to Washington. He was, they said, "obnoxious and hateful to us," "overbearing and abusive," "insolent and dishonest." His private life was said to be "corrupt and disgraceful." Such terms were, of course, mild in comparison with those which Johnson County people would apply to him twenty years later when he was a leader of the big cattlemen's invasion of their county.

The anti-Campbell faction may have been ready to buy Democratic help, judging by this June 22, 1872, entry in Governor Campbell's diary: "Posey Wilson tells me . . . that Kingman and Reed sent Nuckolls to Murrin with promise of $500 cash and $500 or $1,000 after election if M. would support Reed for Congress, and waited behind Presbyterian Church for answer. Murrin refused." [20]

Territorial citizens could not vote in national elections. Nevertheless,

[20] *Annals of Wyoming*, X, 3 (July 1938), 137.

they paid some attention to the growth of anti-Grant feeling in the East, and there was much newspaper discussion of the Liberal Republican opposition which nominated and supported Horace Greeley against Grant in 1872. There was even a small Liberal convention in Laramie in June, 1872, at which Greeley was applauded. After Grant had vanquished Greeley, Wyoming politicians began to use charges of Liberal Republicanism against any Republican whom they desired to disgrace in Washington. Justice Kingman's term ran out in March, 1873, and the taint of Liberalism was used to prevent his reappointment. The things said about Kingman were almost complimentary compared to what was to be said later about several other judges in the territory, but there was enough criticism of Kingman to prevent his reappointment.

In March, 1873, Secretary Glafcke and Surveyor General Reed were notified that they had been removed from office. Glafcke wired Delegate Jones to learn the cause of his removal and received this reply: "You were removed because you were in the Laramie Liberal convention." The hatchet work in the case of Glafcke and Reed had been done by John W. Corey, chairman of the territorial Republican Central Committee. He had written to President Grant, submitting a newspaper clipping from Edward A. Slack's *Laramie Independent* of June 27, 1872, which listed Glafcke and Reed among those who attended the Liberal, or "People's," convention.

Glafcke sent wires asking Secretary of State Hamilton Fish and Secretary of the Interior Columbus Delano "to interfere" in his behalf. He wrote a letter to President Grant insisting that he had attended the gathering only as a newspaper reporter. He pointed out that his son, born on election day, 1868, was named Grant Glafcke. He offered to send the Secretary of the Interior a bound file of the *Cheyenne Leader* of 1872, "not knowing a more effectual method to meet my accusers." Evidently, Glafcke was able to make his point because a few months later Grant appointed him postmaster of Cheyenne.

Surveyor General Reed, who, like Glafcke, was falsely tainted with Liberalism, rushed to Washington in person, fought harder than Glafcke, and was able to win reinstatement. The Campbell wheel horse, J. H. Hayford, commented in his *Laramie Sentinel* that the Republicans of the territory "feel like cursing Grant." Grant was, wrote Hayford, "the most consummate ass that ever disgraced the presidential chair."

Glafcke had written in 1872 that "the pioneers of the far west love fair play even in political warfare." The record does not bear him out. Of course, President Grant and his corrupt administration must be blamed for some of the political troubles in Wyoming. Samuel E. Morison and Henry S. Commager, in their well-known textbook on American history, are unfair to Spotted Tail and Red Cloud when they write that Grant's "political sense was as primitive as that of a Sioux Indian." Fortunately, the Republican factional strife in Wyoming showed signs of diminishing when Campbell left the territory in the spring of 1875. He resigned the governorship in the middle of his second term to go to Basel, Switzerland, as United States consul.

Soon after Campbell's departure, his good friend Judge Joseph M. Carey had to fight removal efforts. One of Carey's enemies was the Laramie banker Edward Ivinson, who wrote the United States Attorney General in Washington that "Judge Carey is not a man of learning in the law or anything else and is completely blinded by his likes and dislikes to such an extent that he cannot decide any question fairly. He always tries to protect his political friends and *punish* his political enemies." Ivinson may have weakened his attack by scattering his fire. He had worse things to say about the other two judges. His spelling was atrocious, but his meaning was unmistakable: "Judge Fisher is a week old man, feble in health and more feble in intellect." Judge Thomas, he added, was a "vulgar whisky drinker . . . hostile and abusive," and the district attorney was "an ignorant petifogger." Ivinson reported that he would be compelled to leave the country unless there was a change of officers.

In June, 1875, at the Attorney General's request, Gilbert Adams, new United States marshal, interviewed ten leading citizens about Carey's reputation. All liked him personally; all questioned his ability as lawyer and judge. Francis E. Warren liked Carey as an honorable and energetic gentleman "but as a lawyer thinks he does not know anything about it and very much prejudiced." Luke Murrin "thinks Judge Carey a nice clever fellow, highly honorable, does not know any more about law than a hog . . . full of prejudice and owned and run by the Campbell clique." [21] All three judges survived the onslaught, although when their terms ended, Carey and Thomas were not reappointed. As always, they did not lack supporters who wrote to Washington in their defense. Carey was able to get seventeen of the twenty lawyers practicing in the territory to petition in his favor.

[21] The quotations in this paragraph have all been taken from appointment files in the National Archives.

The war between the two Republican factions dominated the scene in the early years of Wyoming Territory, but it was not the only political phenomenon of the period. The Democrats also had their troubles, but the Republican newspapers were too busy fighting each other to dwell on them, and they held no offices under Grant, so less is known of their difficulties.

After watching Wyoming political-convention behavior in August, 1874, "our own correspondent" wrote in the *New York Times* that the

average convention is ostentatious, stormy and exciting. While party lines are usually drawn, local questions are made to serve their purpose, sectional feeling is strong, and a man's place of residence and his nearness to being an "old timer" have much to do with his success at the polls. . . .

The gamblers are a strong element and of course can always be "bought with a price." They have the best organization and mass their men. They pack primaries, scuttle conventions and stuff ballot boxes with impunity.

Political crosscurrents were at work in the legislatures in keeping with sectional interests. The Democrats were in the majority in both houses in 1869 and 1871. The Republicans had a majority of one in each house in 1873. In the sessions of 1871 and 1873, capital location was a burning issue, with Laramie and Evanston being the strongest contenders with Cheyenne. The assignment of judges caused other conflicts in which party affiliation was forgotten.

The 1873 legislature ended in chaos. Fear of a bill to move the capital to Laramie, which had passed the House, 7 to 6, evidently caused Cheyenne members of the Council to absent themselves with the expectation that there would not be a quorum. Another explanation for the absences, current at the time, was that Judge Joseph M. Carey's party for the legislators the night before had left some of them in no condition to conduct legislative business. Whatever the reasons for the absences, six members did appear, and they passed a bill declaring vacant the seats of the absent members, including President Francis E. Warren. They also replaced the absent secretary, Warren Richardson. The rump session then passed the capital-removal bill and sent it back to the House. Governor Campbell did not approve the bill. Had he done so, there would undoubtedly have been a lawsuit over the legality of the rump session's actions. Editor Hayford recalled ten years later that panic seized the Cheyenne members over the capital-removal proposition "and the exact history of the transaction will probably never be known, though it would form a most comic and ludicrous chapter in the history of Wyoming politics."

GOVERNOR JOHN M. THAYER

Another brigadier general, John M. Thayer, replaced Campbell in 1875. He understood western problems, having lived in Nebraska for many years and having represented that state in the United States Senate. He had kept in touch with Wyoming affairs ever since he had placed cattle on Rock Creek in 1871. He was Herman Glafcke's house guest on his arrival as governor, foretelling that the *Cheyenne Leader* would henceforth be on the inside rather than the outside, that it would get the public printing, and that it would support the new governor vigorously. Naturally, the Laramie newspapers found occasion to criticize Thayer during his first year as governor. He was absent from the territory too much, they said; his efforts to extinguish the Indian title in the north were unavailing. Hayford finally lost his position as auditor. That he should call Thayer "grossly ignorant and incompetent" is not surprising, though his pique was short-lived. By 1876 he had buried the hatchet and was working with Thayer. Another Campbell crony, Frank Wolcott, was removed from office as United States Marshal. Thayer wrote that Wolcott was "offensive to almost the whole people."

Governor Thayer was more effective in dealing with legislators than Governor Campbell had been. Both the 1875 and 1877 legislatures were overwhelmingly Democratic, which threatened trouble for Thayer, but he adroitly avoided most of it. He seems to have ascertained accurately what he could and could not do, and did not try the impossible. Unlike Campbell, he did not preach to the legislature in veto messages. Indeed, he vetoed nothing that came before him. Were it not for the fact that he had a few appointments turned down by the Council, one might be tempted to conclude that Republican governor and Democratic legislature were consistently cheek by jowl.

Governor Thayer urged legislation to eliminate wanton destruction of wild game animals by hide hunters. He reported that more than three thousand elk hides had been shipped from Union Pacific stations between Laramie and Green River in the past six months. "The meat of course was left to waste." In line with his recommendation, the legislature forbade big-game hunting except for food. With the needs of the settlers in mind, Thayer also wanted to begin the planting of trout in streams, since the North Platte drainage did not have the trout which were present in the South Platte, Yellowstone, and Green River drainages, but not until 1879 did the legislature inaugurate fish propagation.

The 1875 legislature once again tried unsuccessfully to move the capital from Cheyenne to Evanston. Two new counties were added, Pease and Crook in the northeastern part of the territory, but for lack of population they were not organized until the 1880's. Pease came in as the sixth county, under the name of Johnson, in 1881, and Crook was organized as the seventh in 1885.

Helping Thayer to restore unity in the Republican party was the election of President Rutherford B. Hayes, who was more shrewd politically than Grant. Helping also was the enlistment of Colonel E. A. Slack in the Republican cause. J. M. Carey wrote to M. C. Brown in February, 1876, asking the Laramie attorney to talk to Slack about moving his *Laramie Sun* to Cheyenne and making it Republican. Slack moved to Cheyenne in March, 1876, and no doubt added strength to the Republican party.

The affair of William Ware Peck likewise contributed to Republican unity.[22] Peck was practicing law in New York City when, at the age of fifty-eight, he wangled appointment as associate justice of Wyoming Territory. He came west highly recommended by members of bench and bar in New York and in his native Vermont. He was assigned to Sweetwater and Uinta counties. Almost as soon as he opened the July, 1877, term of district court in Evanston, people in Evanston and Green River began to take sides for or against him. Judge Peck was too deliberate for many people who were accustomed to having court business wrapped up in a hurry. A movement was organized to prevent Judge Peck's confirmation by the United States Senate. He had been appointed during a Senate recess and had gone to work without confirmation.

All of the legislators from Uinta and Sweetwater counties went to Cheyenne in November, 1877, with their minds made up to oust Peck. They got legislators from the eastern counties to join them in petitioning President Hayes to withdraw Peck's nomination. Their memorial attributed "incompetency and gross extravagance" to Judge Peck. His court expenses were "enormous and unprecedented." When, nevertheless, President Hayes let the appointment stand and the Senate confirmed it, the legislature chose another weapon from its arsenal. With only one dissenting vote it passed a redistricting bill by which Peck was transferred to a new district made up of the two as yet unorganized counties, Pease and Crook. The legislature appropriated $1,000 for

[22] For further details and documentation for the Peck story which follows, see T. A. Larson, "Exiling a Wyoming Judge," *Wyoming Law Journal*, X, 3 (Spring 1956), 171–179. Most of the story is based on appointment-file material in the National Archives.

Judge Blair and $800 for Judge Fisher as additional compensation for extra work they would have to do in the settled areas along the Union Pacific. Governor Thayer reluctantly signed the redistricting bill, offering the rationalization that if he tried to block it, there were plenty of votes to pass it over his veto. The *New York Times* called it "legislative persecution of Judge Peck."

Since there were very few people in northeastern Wyoming in 1876, the legislature's action was recognized at once as a method of exiling Peck—"sagebrushing" him, it was called. Other western legislatures had treated judges in similar fashion. The legislators believed that they were within their rights, since the organic act merely provided that there should be three districts and left the definition of district boundaries to the legislature.

The United States Senate quickly voted to disallow the Wyoming redistricting act, but the repeal measure stuck in the Judiciary Committee of the House of Representatives. Wyoming's delegate to Congress, W. W. Corlett, was able to persuade state's-rights southerners on the committee that virtually all the people of Wyoming were against Peck and that the rights of the territory should be upheld.

When Peck's hopes for congressional intervention were not realized, he thought of getting another job. Some of his enemies were willing to write in praise of him until it was discovered that he was trying to use these testimonials in Wyoming instead of abroad. Failing to get another job, Peck decided to make the most of what he had. During the next three years he did supreme-court work in Cheyenne. Since Peck had no district chores, the other two judges were pleased to permit him to write almost all of the supreme-court opinions. Gradually, Peck's friends came to the realization that it was hopeless to try to get him restored to his old district.

Judge Peck was a Republican, but opposition to him was bipartisan. He could find scarcely any friends, even in his own party.[23] One of the few Republicans with a kind word for Peck was J. H. Hayford, who wrote that he was "an honorable, upright, Christian" who was handicapped because he was "a little too old fogyish and puritanic for this latitude, and he let these traits manifest themselves in a way that excited prejudice and hostility in the minds of the free and easy western people." Predictably, Peck was not reappointed when his term expired.

[23] Nine of the ten Republicans in the legislature voted against Peck, as did all the Democrats.

Meanwhile, in May, 1878, Governor Thayer lost his job because of the Peck affair; President Hayes and the United States Senate were provoked by his failure to veto the sagebrushing act. When President Hayes removed Thayer, Wyoming newspaper editors generally thought the territory had lost a good governor. That he had not satisfied everyone is apparent, however, in a letter which the prominent Cheyenne Republican Francis E. Warren wrote to Delegate Corlett stating that, apart from Thayer's failure to veto the sagebrushing act, there were "numberless other grounds upon which his dismissal could, with perfect propriety, be asked for." [24]

THE BLACK HILLS GOLD RUSH

One factor which tended to dispel Wyoming's gloom after 1875 and which, as much as anything, made it possible for Governor Thayer to say in 1877 that Wyoming did not feel the national depression was the Black Hills gold rush. As was mentioned earlier, discovery of gold in the Black Hills led to an invasion of that area by prospectors, which in turn led to the removal of the Indians from northeastern Wyoming as well as from Dakota's Black Hills. Cheyenne was one gateway to the Hills. The *Cheyenne Leader* printed fifty thousand copies of a special Black Hills edition for national distribution in May, 1875. Such advertising brought more people to Cheyenne on their way to the Hills. "Cheyenne resembles ancient Rome—all roads lead to it," crowed the *Leader*.

What Frances Beard has called "the redemption of the Powder River country" stands out as the most significant event of Governor Thayer's administration in Wyoming. At last, in 1877, the coveted area was thrown open, though no rush to occupy it followed. People were more interested in the Black Hills.

The completion of a military bridge over the North Platte at Fort Laramie in December, 1875, helped Cheyenne in its efforts to share in the profits of Black Hills development. Cheyenne vied with Sioux City, Yankton, and Sidney for Black Hills business. The new mines proved to be far richer than those in South Pass, and heavy traffic flowed back and forth from Cheyenne for several years. Perhaps ten thousand people had reached the Hills by March 1, 1876. A Chicago reporter

[24] Warren Letterbooks, University of Wyoming Library, March 25, 1878. Warren did not like the sagebrushing act, not because he had any interest in Peck, whom he had never met, but because he was afraid it might prejudice the administration and Congress against Wyoming Territory. He wrote that Thayer's signing the bill "was a direct 'swap' the consideration being legislation advantageous to the Governor."

wrote in late 1876 that on a Deadwood Street he had seen "half of the population that I met in Cheyenne last May." Agnes Wright Spring, in her volume *The Cheyenne and Black Hills Stage and Express Routes*, has written a detailed history of Cheyenne and eastern Wyoming during the years when the stage line was in operation. No doubt the pace of life quickened in the capital city and along the stage and freighting routes to the north.

The Black Hills gold rush reached its peak in the spring of 1877. There was not, however, the sharp decline thereafter that characterized many other gold-mining communities. Annual gold production in the Black Hills in the late 1870's and in the 1880's exceeded three million dollars. Cheyenne and eastern Wyoming continued to benefit from the Black Hills activity for several years,[25] but the territory, if it were to flourish, needed something more stimulating than Dakota gold.

YELLOWSTONE NATIONAL PARK

Wyoming in 1872 acquired one asset which in time would contribute much to the enjoyment of its people. This was Yellowstone Park, the first national park in the United States, created by Act of Congress. Located in the mountainous northwest corner of the territory, the park, which would become famous for its hot springs, geysers, and bears, would remain inaccessible to all but a few thousand people for half a century. Narrow strips along the west and north sides of the park are in Idaho and Montana.

[25] Completion of a Chicago and North Western railroad line from Chadron, Nebraska, to Rapid City, Dakota Territory, in 1886 ended most of the Cheyenne–Black Hills traffic.

CHAPTER 6

Progress Under Diverse Leaders, 1879–1889

A REMARKABLY ODD ASSORTMENT of men governed Wyoming Territory beginning with John W. Hoyt,[1] whom President Hayes appointed on April 10, 1878, as a replacement for John M. Thayer, whom he had removed. Hoyt, who, like his predecessor, was a Republican, was a

[1] Born in Ohio in 1831, Hoyt was brought up on an Ohio farm. After graduation from Ohio Wesleyan University he pursued further education in both medicine and law. Thereafter he practiced medicine briefly, taught chemistry and natural history at Antioch College, edited the *Wisconsin Farmer and Northern Cultivator*, and served as United States and Wisconsin commissioner to the World Exhibition in London in 1862 and the Universal Exposition in Paris in 1867. At the request of Secretary of

133

highly educated world traveler with the soul of a poet and the mind of a reformer and conservationist. Generally respected and even admired, he would nevertheless find himself all too often dismissed as an impractical dreamer, blessed with good ideas which politicians thought would not work.

Hoyt was accorded a warmer welcome in Wyoming than he expected in view of the popularity of the man he replaced. The knowledge that he had not sought the job was in his favor. Newspaper editors soon praised him for his energy, intelligence, and enthusiasm. He made a series of horseback rides around the territory, to acquaint himself with its resources, and after six months knew his bailiwick as well as any native. His October, 1878, report to the Secretary of the Interior was fifty-six printed pages long and gave an excellent overview of the territory. He told of "vast and varied" mineral resources awaiting development. The South Pass mines had been largely abandoned; the Centennial District, opened in 1876, had petered out; small gold and silver mines were being worked in the Medicine Bow Mountains; the Rawlins Metallic Paint Company had opened mines and built paint works, but was temporarily inactive; there were outcrops of coal all over the territory.

The Governor estimated that a thousand men were engaged in producing lumber, shingles, lath, railroad ties, and charcoal[2] in parts of the forest areas, which he calculated amounted to between five and fifteen million acres.

The Governor's love of wild life was unmistakable: "Here that noble beast . . . the elk, is still found in great herds. . . . Here the buffalo still lingers, loth to leave the haunts so long enjoyed by him from time immemorial. . . . Thousands of them are slain every year for either hide or flesh, and too often for neither."

Governor Hoyt directed attention to intangible, nonmaterial re-

---

State William H. Seward, he prepared a 398-page volume on European and American education. He became chairman of the Wisconsin State Railway Commission from 1874 to 1876. According to Hoyt's autobiography, President Hayes, for whom he campaigned in 1876, sent his nomination for the governorship of Wyoming to the United States Senate without previous consultation about the position. For more about Hoyt, see Henry J. Peterson, "John Wesley Hoyt," *Annals of Wyoming*, XXII, 1 (January 1950), 3–68.

[2] At Hilliard, near Evanston, in the 1860's and 1870's, great quantities of charcoal were prepared in pits for use in smelters in Utah and elsewhere. The output approached 100,000 bushels per month. At one time the charcoal brought twenty-seven cents a bushel, but the substitution of coke in the smelters soon drove the price down to seven cents, and another local industry disappeared.

sources: "A pure and invigorating atmosphere, equability of temperature . . . a cheerful sky, and attractive scenery, can one of them be
weighed in the balance or measured in the bushel; but yet each of them
has a very important bearing on the health, happiness, and prosperity
of a people." Wyoming was in his opinion "one of the most healthful
portions of the world." He based this opinion on army records, inquiries
among medical men, and observation of the vigorous health of the
people.

Hoyt reported to the Secretary of the Interior that agriculture was
not possible without irrigation, although he noted that there had been
a few dry-farming successes when there had been more than normal
precipitation. The "present great resource" he recognized to be livestock: "The stock business in Wyoming, for security and the magnitude
of its profits, is to-day unequalled by any other of which I have knowledge in this part of the world and in these times."

Governor Hoyt spent most of the summer of 1879 as he had spent the
previous summer, traveling over the territory. No doubt he was well
acquainted with the land and its people when he met his first legislature
in November, 1879. In a message more than an hour in length he
offered a comprehensive analysis of the territory's problems.

The legislature, which was made up of a Democratic Council and a
Republican House, turned down his recommendations for reform in the
assessment of livestock, organization of a militia regiment better to protect life and property, and a voter-registration law. He proposed that
something be done about big outfits that engrossed great areas and
denied others access to streams and lakes, but he got action only in the
form of a joint resolution passing the problem on to Congress.

To encourage prospecting and mining, Hoyt proposed the employment of a geologist and mining engineer whose responsibility it would
be to help demonstrate that precious metals were available in quantities worth developing. The 1877 legislature had authorized a territorial
assayer. Hoyt had employed J. G. Murphy, an experienced graduate of
the Columbia School of Mines, but more than an assayer was needed.
The legislature provided for the new officer.

As in his report of 1878, Hoyt deplored the great losses of timber
through forest fires. He wanted stricter laws with severe penalties for
those who carelessly started fires. The legislature obliged by passing an
act fixing a penalty of up to five hundred dollars' fine and up to six
months' imprisonment for anyone willfully or negligently setting on fire
any woods or grasslands.

Also in his report of 1878, Hoyt urged the planting of trout. A law was passed for the "Culture and Propagation of Fish," by which the Governor was authorized to appoint a fish commissioner who should plant suitable fish.

Hoyt, who had already shown special interest in Yellowstone National Park, asked for the establishment of "a good highway" to it from the Union Pacific. The legislature passed this on to Congress in the form of a joint memorial.

Governor Thayer's 1877 request for action to reduce the number of elections in the territory was renewed by Hoyt. He wanted to save expense and to avoid "that perpetual ferment of political excitement in which our people are kept from the beginning to the end of their lives." The legislature complied by providing that the next legislature and county officers would be elected in November, 1880, at the same time as the delegate to Congress. The legislature elected in 1880 would not meet until January, 1882. There was, throughout the 1880's, an unfortunate gap of fourteen months between the election of legislators and their session.

The usual attempts to move the capital did not reach the Governor in the form of an act. Laramie and Rawlins wanted the capital but could not muster a majority.

Governor Hoyt had less than the usual quota of partisan political trouble in his first legislature, but was criticized elsewhere. Either by design or accident he did not make adequate arrangements for entertaining former President Grant when the latter visited Cheyenne just before the legislature met in 1879. Since he abominated the scandals of the Grant Administration, Hoyt could not be expected to prostrate himself before the visiting former President. By telegram he excused himself from meeting Grant at the Utah line, "owing to the rapidity of your movements, illness, and the pressure of duties." Instead, he promised to meet Grant at the station in Cheyenne and to give him lunch in his home. Grant arrived in a huff, nothing went right, and Grant's friends never forgave Hoyt.

Hovering in the background was A. Worth Spates, disgruntled secretary of the territory, who wanted to be governor in place of Hoyt. Spates appears to have been quite unprincipled. He was involved in a fraudulent mining venture and an illegal lottery scheme. Bill Nye described him as "the champion intellectual light weight of his time." His association with editor Glafcke in the lottery business gave him strong support from the *Cheyenne Leader*, but other editors backed Hoyt and helped him to gain Spates's removal.

The federal census of 1880 revealed that Hoyt's estimate of 25,000 population had been too high, for there were only 20,789 people, barely more than twice as many as the 9,118 of 1870. Most of the people still lived, as in 1870, along the Union Pacific. The two new and as yet unorganized counties in the northeast had only a few people—Johnson, 637, and Crook, 239. Laramie County with 6,400 and Albany with 4,625 were still dominant, but not to the same extent as in 1870. Carbon County had 3,438; Sweetwater, 2,561; and Uinta, 2,879.

Wyoming's delegates to Congress rarely attracted attention, but one did so in 1880 when Colonel Stephen W. Downey, Laramie attorney, introduced a bill providing for certain paintings on the walls of the national capitol. The bill called for an appropriation of $500,000 to commemorate "in suitable paintings by great living artists . . . the birth, life, death and resurrection of Jesus Christ." Downey asked for routine permission to extend his remarks in the *Congressional Record*. To the consternation of congressmen and to the delight of his friends, Downey thereupon published in the *Record* more than 2,500 lines of free verse entitled "The Immortals." The poem shows considerable debt to Homer, Vergil, and Dante and is heavily freighted with mythology, allegory, and moral instruction.

The *New York Times* thought Downey's lines "well constructed and pleasing to the ear," but could find little connection between the bill and this supporting "argument." The incident illustrated to the *Times* the extremes to which could be carried Congress' bad practice of allowing members to print undelivered speeches. Bill Nye and other Wyoming and Denver editors had much fun with Downey's poem.[3] Downey's bill did not pass the House, but his extraordinary argument was not expunged from the *Congressional Record*, as some congressmen thought it should be.

Hoyt's efforts to find another productive industry with which to supplement livestock proved unavailing. In his 1881 report to the Secretary of the Interior, he could write, as before, of all sorts of promising potentialities, but not of any profitable production.

[3] Bill Nye commented as follows: "Now it came to pass during the reign of one Hoyt, surnamed 'The Snubber of Ulysses' and in the days when Stephen, the son of his father, and who played upon the harp, went forth even unto the gates wherein the rulers, and the law givers, and the wise men and maidens sat, and did play upon his harp and did warble even unto the law givers and wise men a psalm which extended even unto fifteen pages of the book wherein the deeds of the great men were writ; and even in these days came the judges of the land to judge. The wise men arise and say, after it is too late, 'This is indeed the work of one who laugheth at us and putteth up a job on us of the size of a Presbyterian church.' And no man wotteth why it is so."

Similarly, Hoyt's 1881 report had to deal with manufacturing "advantages" rather than actual manufacturing plants. But he felt certain that in time there would be "activity that will astonish the most sanguine."

Governor Hoyt visited Yellowstone National Park on horseback in the summer of 1881. His party of sixteen men included an army escort of seven men headed by Major Julius W. Mason, two Shoshoni guides, two packers, and four civilians. They entered the park by way of Togwotee Pass and left by way of Jones's Pass and the North Fork of the Shoshone. Hoyt concluded that the wonders of the park far exceeded his expectations and "are certainly destined to attract a constantly increasing number of visitors from all parts of the world." He urged, as before, the establishment of a good wagon road from Fort Washakie to the park.

One of Governor Hoyt's constant endeavors was to persuade the Union Pacific to reduce its freight rates for Wyoming raw materials. Both the company and the territory would prosper, he suggested, if the railroad would accord "actual cost rates" for a term of years, until undeveloped industries could become established.

In January, 1882, Governor Hoyt met his second legislature. Both houses were Democratic, the Council 8 to 4 and the House 13 to 10 (nine Republicans and one People's party). As in 1879, Hoyt's address was well received but did not lead to much legislation. He tried, as before, to increase tax collections on livestock. Although he was friendly to the stock business and had been made an honorary member of the Wyoming Stock Growers Association, he could not reconcile himself to the common knowledge that one-half of the livestock animals in the territory were not reported to assessors. An act was passed for assessment of herds that came into counties after the time of the annual assessment, but this did not solve the basic problem that was troubling Hoyt. He also renewed, without getting any satisfaction, his earlier plea for legislative action to open roads through fences in order to give all stock access to water. Still distressed by waste of timber and deterioration of forest assets, he warned that the current rate of depletion would soon bring the forests to an end; yet no legislation concerning the forests emerged from the 1882 session.

The Governor got no action on his proposal that a strong public library be established at the chief center of population in each county. On the other hand, his suggestion that counties be made directly responsible for the support of their insane was adopted.

Hoyt's message included praise for woman suffrage, which accorded with the views of virtually all leaders of the territory at the time.

When rumors reached Cheyenne that Hoyt would not be reappointed by Chester A. Arthur, who had assumed the presidency upon the assassination of James A. Garfield, both houses, by unanimous vote, adopted a resolution urging reappointment. Nevertheless, President Arthur appointed William Hale, an Iowa lawyer, on July 18, 1882, at the end of Hoyt's four-year term. In Republican politics, Hoyt was identified with the "half-breed" reform faction rather than the "stalwart" faction to which U. S. Grant and Chester A. Arthur belonged. For instance, the Department of the Interior Appointment File in the National Archives includes an April, 1882, appeal from Wyoming territorial geologist Fred J. Stanton to Senator John A. Logan of Illinois: "For God's sake my dear Sir, tell the President, we want a *man*—a stalwart, prompt and representative specimen of the genus *homo* who won't take dancing lessons in the daytime, frequent negro dives at night, and be the most loud mouthed and demonstrative in his responses at the Church. . . . We want a man—a stalwart—and no canting, whining hypocrite."

Governor William Hale turned out to be a capable and conscientious man, within the limitations of his health. He was familiar with at least one western problem because he had been president of a Colorado mining company. His ill health, however, made him a poor substitute for Hoyt. Suffering from Addison's disease, he was under the care of a "water cure physician" who sent him to take mineral baths in many places. He obtained one sixty-day leave after another as he sought relief from his disease in Iowa, New York, Southern California, and Colorado. The search for health failed, and he died in Cheyenne on January 13, 1885, at the age of forty-seven.

Wyoming was fortunate that during Hale's administration an unusually able secretary of the territory, Elliott S. N. Morgan, was on hand to become acting governor regularly. He had the confidence of Governor Hale, people generally in Wyoming, and his superiors in Washington.

After many years of talk about the desirability of having a governor chosen from Wyoming residents, Francis E. Warren, Cheyenne resident since 1868, was appointed by President Arthur to replace the deceased William Hale. The Democrat Grover Cleveland had been elected President in November, 1884, and would take office on March 4, 1885. In appointing the Republican Warren less than a week before he left office, President Arthur calculated that the Republican Senate would make it difficult for Cleveland to make a change. Warren received appointment on February 27 and took his oath of office on the following day.

The new governor was forty-one. Born and brought up in Massachusetts and educated briefly in an academy there, he had served as a

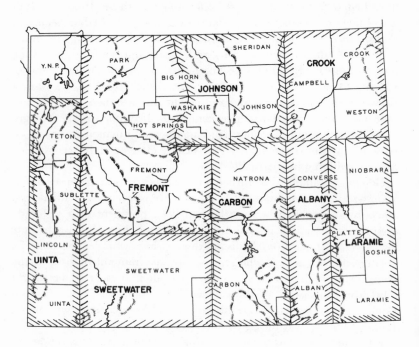

WYOMING, EIGHT-COUNTY MAP, 1884

private and a corporal in the Civil War. After the war he engaged in farming and stock raising in Massachusetts until 1868, when he moved west. After working briefly in railroad construction in Iowa, he went to Cheyenne to take employment as a clerk in the crockery and hardware store of A. R. Converse, a man he had known in Massachusetts. After a few years he became Converse's partner and then sole proprietor of the Warren Mercantile Company. He quickly prospered and expanded his interests until, by 1885, he was or had been president of the Warren Livestock Company, president of the Cheyenne Electric Light Company, vice-president of the First National Bank, treasurer of the territory, secretary of the Cheyenne and Montana Railroad Company, and mayor of Cheyenne. In 1884, the Republican Central Committee offered him nomination as territorial delegate. After he declined, the honor went to Joseph M. Carey, who was elected.

The appointment of Warren to the governorship received widespread support from the people of the territory. The Republicans, of course, were jubilant. Delegate-elect Carey had written to the Secretary of the Interior in January, 1885, that "while the Territory has had many good officers sent here, so many miserable fellows have, from time to time, crept in that the people are sick at heart. They do not want a sick man or a politician sent from elsewhere." Carey said that Warren was so well and favorably known that were he appointed, the Democrats would make small effort to have him removed.

Not until he had served more than twenty months was Governor Warren removed by President Cleveland. During his term a major crisis developed at Rock Springs.

THE ROCK SPRINGS MASSACRE

White men at Rock Springs on September 2, 1885, killed twenty-eight Chinese, wounded fifteen others, chased several hundred other Chinese out of town, and destroyed property valued at more than $147,000 in what has come to be known as the Rock Springs Massacre.[4]

In the background of the riot were bitterness against the Union Pacific Coal Department and smoldering racial prejudice. The Union Pacific's coal mines at Rock Springs had been worked exclusively by whites until 1875, when a strike occurred and Chinese were brought in as strikebreakers. The strikers were fired less than two weeks after they left their work, and mining resumed with 150 Chinese and 50 white miners. The whites disliked the Chinese from their first appearance in Rock Springs, and liked them less as more of them were brought in. At the time of the massacre there were 150 whites and 331 Chinese employed in the mines at Rock Springs.

Governor Warren made a personal investigation at Rock Springs on

---

[4] The full story, with source citations, is told in Paul Crane and T. A. Larson, "The Chinese Massacre," *Annals of Wyoming*, XII, 1 (January 1940), 47–55, and 2 (April 1940), 153–161. See also A. R. Wilson's M.A. thesis, University of Wyoming, 1967.

September 3 and then moved on to Evanston, whence he sent a telegram to President Cleveland asking for federal troops. The troops
finally arrived from Camp Murray, Utah Territory, and escorted the
Chinese fugitives back to Rock Springs, just a week after the massacre.
Sixteen men, including Isaiah Whitehouse, a member-elect of the
legislature, were arrested by the Sweetwater County sheriff and lodged
in the Green River jail, but they were not held long because a county
grand jury brought in no indictments.

Wyoming newspapers generally disapproved of the massacre but
sympathized with the white workers, thought no one could be punished,
and had little good to say for Chinese labor.

White miners at Rock Springs received support from other white
workers along the Union Pacific, particularly in the mining towns
of Almy and Carbon. Heading the opposition to employment of
Chinese was the Knights of Labor Association, but it cannot be established that this labor union directed the use of violence against the
Chinese.

Governor Warren showed unmistakable leadership ability during the
critical days following the massacre. His forceful stand gave him stature
with propertied interests, but it made him unpopular with white
workers, who sometimes thereafter referred to him as "Chinese"
Warren.

After the Chinese fugitives were brought back to Rock Springs and
lodged in boxcars near the mines, the company discharged forty-five
white miners, and reopened the mines. For a time the issue remained in
doubt, the presence of the army being all that prevented another outbreak. The *Rock Springs Independent* insisted repeatedly that "The
Chinese Must Go." Other editors added their voices to the clamor
against the company's policy. Gradually, as leaders of the opposition
left town, the spirit of revolt was dissipated. Troops, however, remained
at Camp Pilot Butte at Rock Springs for thirteen years, until the
Spanish-American War.

In protest against the continued use of Chinese miners, the white
miners at Carbon, said to number five hundred, went out on strike
September 30, 1885. They were mainly Finns who belonged to the
Knights of Labor. After two months passed without success, the strikers
went back to work.

Who were the leaders of the massacre? Governor Warren did not
blame the Knights of Labor nor most of the white miners. He told a
St. Louis Republican reporter two weeks after the massacre:

It is the most damnable and brutal outrage that ever occurred in any country. The men who did murder, arson and robbery were tramps and outlaws, who wouldn't work under any circumstances at anything but crime and some of them were fugitives from justice. They were the original assailants of the Chinese, and they were followed by some miners, who are the dregs of the lowest order of immigrants, ignorant and brutal by nature, never having had an opportunity to learn any better than to be led into such performances. . . .

The grand jury, as mentioned above, failed to bring in any indictments, but blamed the massacre on unspecified abuses which the Union Pacific had failed to adjust. What were these abuses? The *Rock Springs Independent* said that hundreds of resident white men could not get work, while Chinese were shipped in by the carload and given jobs. Thomas Neasham, chairman of the Knights of Labor executive committee of Union Pacific employees, charged that white miners had been replaced by Chinese who paid mine bosses as much as one hundred dollars for their places. He said that the whites had been required to work where Chinese would not work, had been robbed by the use of false weights, had been discharged for not voting "right" in a school election, and had been compelled to patronize the company store. These "abuses" were denied by company officials, and there is not enough evidence to prove them true or false.

Although the Chinese were put back to work, it was soon evident that they could get no compensation in Wyoming for property losses. The Chinese consul at New York, who had joined the Chinese consul at San Francisco in an investigation of the massacre, prepared a list of losses totaling $147,748.74, which Congress voted to pay upon President Cleveland's recommendation.

Although the Union Pacific won its battle to keep Chinese at work, the fears expressed in 1885, that Rock Springs would become a "Chinatown," were not realized. Chinese workers were harder to find after Congress had suspended their immigration in 1882. Possibly, the Union Pacific was also influenced by strong sentiment in the territory against further employment of Chinese. Governor Warren, who had done all he could for the Chinese in 1885, conceded to the legislature in January, 1886, that "the Chinese do not assimilate with our people, and therefore are not to be regarded as a desirable element in our civilization." Gradually, most of the Chinese left Wyoming.

The Rock Springs Massacre may well have been a principal factor in making it possible for Republican Governor Warren to remain in office for twenty months after Democratic President Cleveland took office. Not a few Democrats were clamoring for his removal. Since organization of the territory, all Presidents had been Republican, and they had sent only Republican governors to Wyoming. Now that a Democrat was in the White House, Democrats could not understand his failure to act. In June, 1885, Cheyenne banker Posey S. Wilson filed several charges against Warren, among them being one that "Warren has himself fenced in vast areas of the U.S. public lands, to the injury of his fellow citizens and in disregard of law." [5] In January, 1886, Carbon County Democrats lamented that soon Warren would appoint twenty-five persons to offices becoming vacant March 1, and then "the [Democratic] party will be too dead to bury." Nevertheless, Cleveland did not act.

Having to deal with a Republican United States Senate no doubt contributed to Cleveland's delay, but another factor was the prestige attained by Warren through his handling of the Rock Springs affair. This gained him influential friends. Three government directors of the Union Pacific, James W. Savage, M. A. Hanna, and E. P. Alexander, wrote to President Cleveland on October 14, 1885, suggesting that petitions for Warren's removal should be ignored, since "his dismissal at this time would be regarded as a triumph for those who sympathize with the Rock Springs rioters." Moreover, Union Pacific President Charles F. Adams, Jr., wrote to Secretary of the Interior Lucius Lamar on October 17, 1885: "I should regard his removal, therefore, at this time as little less than a public calamity." The cautious Cleveland was not prepared to assume responsibility for visiting calamity upon the powerful Union Pacific Railroad. Not until November, 1886, did he remove Warren.

GOVERNOR WARREN AND THE LEGISLATURE OF 1886

In 1886, for the second time in history, both houses of the legislature were Republican, the first time occurring in 1873. In the Council of 1886 there were eight Republicans and four Democrats, while in the House of Representatives there were fourteen Republicans, ten Democrats, and one member of the People's party.

Governor Warren, with his long experience in the territory and acquaintance with most of the legislators, took charge more effectively than had been possible for past governors. His suggestions for legislation

---

[5] The communications quoted in this paragraph and the one following are all taken from the National Archives, Department of the Interior Appointment Files, Governor, Wyoming, Box 239.

were generally carried out. At the end of the session the *Cheyenne Democratic Leader* scored the legislators: "Like the wooden performers of a play, they have danced to the music from the executive office."

In his 45-minute message to the legislature, Warren said that wealth and population had tripled in the past six years. The 1885 assessed valuation was $30,717,249.81, and this figure, thought Warren, represented no more than one-third of the actual valuation. Fifty-seven per cent of the valuation was attributed to livestock. As the valuation had increased, the property-tax rate had declined, from four mills in 1881 to one mill in 1885.

Warren recommended the establishment of two institutions, an insane asylum and a school for the deaf and dumb. Counties had been sending their insane, numbering about twenty, to a private asylum at Jacksonville, Illinois. It was estimated that there were fifteen deaf and dumb who needed attention. The legislature provided for these two institutions, and also provided for a capitol building and a university, neither of which had been asked for by the Governor.

Wyoming legend has it that in the distribution of institutions, Cheyenne, Rawlins, Evanston, and Laramie made selections in that order and chose the capitol, penitentiary, insane asylum, and university. There is no truth in the legend because Laramie had more influence than Rawlins and Evanston. Cheyenne and Laramie together controlled a majority of the legislators in 1886. In the upper house there were twelve senators, four of them from Laramie County and three from Albany County. In the lower house there were twenty-four representatives, eight of them from Laramie County and five from Albany County.

In one act, approved by the Governor on March 4, 1886, provision was made for the construction of a capitol building at Cheyenne, at a cost not exceeding $150,000, and for the establishment of the University of Wyoming at Laramie, with a building to cost not more than $50,000.

As the bill advanced, E. A. Slack exulted in his *Cheyenne Sun* that for the first time in the history of the territory, Laramie and Albany counties were pulling together. Indeed, the two counties normally had fought each other. Representative Stephen W. Downey of Albany County asked: "Why should we sit supinely and wait for people to come and populate the northern part of the territory?" The veteran J. H. Hayford wrote unabashedly in his *Laramie Sentinel*:

We are among those who have struggled amid poverty and privation through the pioneer days, and now if there are any advantages to be had, any harvest to be gathered, we have no scruples at all against appropriating our share of what we can get of it. Nobody need fancy us standing in meek humility and holding out the capitol and university with a pair of sugar tongs waiting for generations yet unborn or ragamuffins from over the seas to follow a railroad into the northern portion of the territory and reap whatever of benefits and advantages there are to be had. We aint "built that way!"

Later the irrepressible Hayford observed that he would rather have the university than ten capitols.

Five days after Warren approved the capitol-university measure, he approved a bill establishing an insane asylum at Evanston, at a cost not to exceed $30,000. This brought the bond authorization up to $230,000 ($150,000 for the capitol, $50,000 for the university, and $30,000 for the insane asylum).

The second institution recommended by Governor Warren was provided for in an act locating at Cheyenne an institute for the education of the blind, deaf, and dumb as soon as there would be twelve pupils ready to enter such a school. With an appropriation of $8,000, a building was erected, but for various reasons the institute was never opened.

With fourth choice, Rawlins tried to wangle a $75,000 appropriation for a penitentiary in 1886, but had to wait two years before it could win approval for the institution and many years before it was built.[6]

The Rock Springs Massacre of 1885 was not forgotten for many years. It had repercussions in the 1886 legislature. House member

[6] Until 1872, Wyoming sent its convicted felons to the Detroit House of Correction. Then the federal government built a 42-cell penitentiary at Laramie. The institution thereafter became involved in politics and litigation because of the high rates charged for housing territorial prisoners—usually one dollar a day. The Detroit House of Correction, the state prison at Lincoln, Nebraska, and the state prison at Joliet, Illinois, accepted Wyoming prisoners for considerably less than this, so the territorial legislature at times preferred to send prisoners out of Wyoming. In 1878 the territorial penitentiary commissioners made a five-year contract with Nebraska, agreeing to pay forty cents a day for each prisoner. The Wyoming Supreme Court ruled in 1880 that territorial prisoners must be kept in Wyoming, but the United States Congress reversed this decision. In 1882 the Wyoming penitentiary commissioners signed a five-year contract with Illinois under which prisoners would be kept without charge at Joliet in exchange for their labor. Until the expiration of this contract, the Laramie institution had few inmates. In December, 1884, a Justice Department investigator, whose report is preserved in the National Archives, Department of Justice Appointment File for Gustave Schnitger, found only ten prisoners, some of whom were permitted to go into Laramie in civilian clothes and without guard on Saturday nights. A few years later, even after another wing had been added, the penitentiary was overcrowded.

Isaiah Whitehouse, a coal miner who had been jailed after the riot, felt that the federal troops should not have been used, and sought unsuccessfully to get a legislative investigation. Whitehouse also introduced a bill to require employers to credit miners with the weight of coal before screening rather than after. Governor Warren said that coal miners were already better off than other workers. He vetoed the measure, arguing that "class legislation which only affects the civil standing or income of a particular class of laborers should be avoided unless it benefits all classes of laboring men alike."

Another coal miners' grievance, company-store practices, was aired in the legislature. Rejected was a bill which would have required payment of coal miners' wages in United States money and would have prohibited the withholding of wages to pay store bills.

The miners, though generally rebuffed, gained approval for one important measure which provided for a territorial coal-mine inspector, prohibited boys under the age of fourteen and women from working in the mines, required coal mines to have at least two openings, established ventilation regulations, and required other safety regulations. Small mines, employing fewer than ten persons, were exempt from the new rules. An explosion which had killed thirteen Mormon miners at Almy just as the legislative session opened dramatized the need for safety regulations. Representative Stephen W. Downey vainly urged the legislature to provide compensation for the widows and orphans at Almy, charging that the past eight territorial legislatures were partly to blame for the deaths in failing to establish safety regulations.

In response to a recommendation from Governor Warren, the 1886 legislature adopted a comprehensive law establishing procedures for the appropriation of water for irrigation. Hitherto, an 1875 statute, maintaining the common-law principle of riparian rights, had been in effect. In the 1886 law, eight irrigation districts were defined, each to have a water commissioner appointed by the Governor. The commissioners would divide available water according to the principle of prior appropriation for beneficial use. District courts were to settle questions concerning the priority of appropriation. Parties claiming water rights were to file records of their claims with district-court clerks.

The 1886 legislature passed a revised revenue law which, beginning in 1887, subjected to taxation much land, such as railroad-grant land, which had previously escaped on the technicality that the final patent had not been issued. The new law said that "all lands entered by pre-emption, final or commuted homestead, or as desert land, or at private or public sale, or under any act of congress, when final proof therefore has been issued, shall be subject to taxation whether patent for the same has been issued or not." A law of Congress, July 10, 1886, made possible the taxation of railroad-grant land. Aside from towns, only 394,789 acres of Wyoming land was on the assessment rolls in 1886. This figure rose fifteen-fold, to 5,868,370 acres, by 1889.

Warren could look back on the 1886 session with satisfaction. He had managed very well indeed, considering that earlier he had expressed the private opinion that he had to deal with "the most trifling body, taken collectively, that ever assembled to make laws for our Territory."[7] His favorite paper, the *Cheyenne Sun*, praised the legislature for its "good and substantial work." Of course not everyone was pleased. The *Cheyenne Leader* charged sycophancy and extravagance.

GOVERNOR GEORGE W. BAXTER

Cleveland's replacement for Governor Warren was George W. Baxter, who took the oath of office on November 11, 1886. Baxter, aged thirty-one in 1886, the son of a Tennessee judge, had come west after graduation from West Point in 1877. He served with the United States Cavalry at several Wyoming and Dakota posts until 1881, when the

[7] Warren wrote to J. M. Carey, Wyoming's delegate to Congress, on February 3, 1886 (Warren Letterbooks, University of Wyoming Library): "Individually, there are [among the legislators] many nice men, perhaps able men; and they may brace up and do some good later on; but up to the present writing they are a heterogeneous mob of discordant spirits:—Working men, dudes, asses, fools, etc. represent the comments made upon the streets, and I confess with shame, quite deservedly." Concerning fellow Republican Stephen W. Downey, former delegate to Congress and now a member of the lower house of the legislature from Laramie, Warren wrote: "So far as Downey is concerned I trust you may hereafter leave him out of any 'count' where my name, or that of any other decent, respectable citizen may figure. I have always contended that D. was an infernal fool, and an unmitigated scoundrel. . . . Unless we knock him down with a club, he will oppose the irrigation bill, the railroad bill, and everything else that this county has any interest in. . . . Out of forty odd bills introduced in the House Downey has prepared four-fifths of them, getting his friends to introduce all that were not too strong for their stomachs, introducing the 'stomach turners' himself. Among these is a bill providing that the *Territory* pay for every man killed in mining, no matter whom he works for, to his wife one thousand dollars, to every child five hundred dollars, and if the man be injured in ever so slight a manner (in or about the mines) he shall receive from the Territory *fifty* dollars *per week* until he is again at work. . . . You will of course understand that I write you this confidentially that I have had no trouble with Mr. Downey and all is as pleasant and serene as ever." One can scan many of Warren's letterbooks without finding comparable vituperation, and Warren appropriately assured Carey: "Permit me to say in writing the above I am neither drunk, crazy, nor especially disgusted; but I wish to give you, for your private use, the cold hard facts."

attractions of the open-range cattle business lured him out of the army. He invested $150,000 in cattle, which he placed first on the open range on Grass and Cottonwood creeks in Fremont County and later on land purchased from the Union Pacific east of Cheyenne.

Immediately after his appointment, Baxter was accused of having government land under fence. The federal government, without much success, had been trying to restrain unlawful fencing of the public domain in Wyoming since 1883. On November 10, the day before Baxter took the oath of office, Secretary of the Interior Lamar sent a telegram to Baxter: "The President, relying entirely upon your honor, accepts your declaration that you have no connection with illegal wire fencing and that you are unconscious of any proper reason why your Commission should be returned."

It soon developed that Baxter actually did have government land under fence, but it was Baxter's contention that his fence was legal. In 1884 he had become frightened by the spread of pleuropneumonia from the east. He decided to remove his cattle from the open range and to isolate them inside a fence; and so he bought from the Union Pacific more than thirty thousand acres of land east of Cheyenne. This land, lying in alternate sections with intervening government sections, he calculated, would be valuable to him only if he could enclose both government sections and Union Pacific sections in one great pasture. Before buying the Union Pacific land, he consulted three leading attorneys in the territory and his father, who was, as mentioned earlier, a Tennessee judge. All four said that he had the undoubted right to enclose an equal amount of government land. So he bought the Union Pacific land and in the spring of 1885 erected his fence.

President Cleveland, when he learned, to his chagrin, that Baxter really did have government land inside his fence, felt compelled to remove him. Secretary of the Interior Lamar asked for Baxter's resignation on December 8, 1886, and obtained it. Thus Baxter, who left office officially on December 20, is credited with only forty-five days of service.

Baxter continued to maintain that he was treated unjustly. Seventeen months later, in May, 1888, Wyoming District Judge Micah Saufley, in the case of *United States* v. *The Douglas-Willan, Sartoris Company*, ruled that it was legal to include government land within a fence as long as the fence posts were erected on private land. Had this decision been rendered in 1886, Baxter might not have been removed. Baxter accepted Saufley's decision as a complete vindication of himself and used it in an unsuccessful effort to get Cleveland to restore him to the governorship in June, 1888.[8]

THE ADMINISTRATION OF THOMAS MOONLIGHT

Discouraged by his failure to find a satisfactory home-grown governor, Cleveland turned to the state of Kansas and rewarded a faithful worker in the Democratic party, Thomas Moonlight, who had just been defeated in the election for the Kansas governorship. Wyoming, of course, had candidates, particularly W. H. Holliday of Laramie and George T. Beck of Beckton, but Cleveland chose to pass over them.

Moonlight, born in Scotland in 1833, emigrated as a boy to New Jersey, where he worked in a glass factory. He enlisted in the regular army in 1853, serving in Florida against the Seminole Indians and at various places in the West. He then married a New York girl and settled in Kansas, even farming briefly, until the Civil War returned him to uniform. He led the Eleventh Kansas Infantry and later the Eleventh Kansas Cavalry. In 1865, as has been described in Chapter 2, he served in Colorado and Wyoming. He was a controversial figure until he was finally mustered out of service in semidisgrace for losing his horses to the Indians. Returning to Kansas, he became active in the Republican party, being elected secretary of state in 1868. He switched to the Democratic party in 1870 in protest against the prohibitionist views of the Kansas Republicans.

Moonlight took the oath of office as governor in Cheyenne on January 24, 1887, and was indoctrinated by E. S. N. Morgan, secretary of the territory, who had been serving as acting governor since Baxter's removal. The *Cheyenne Sun* described Moonlight as six feet tall, sturdily built, broad shouldered, erect, and with his face covered with a short brown beard.

Energetic and forthright, Moonlight made a good first impression on most people—except the cattlemen. Indeed, for a year he enjoyed a remarkably good press. Even the outspoken Hayford, who wore the Republican brand but often acted like a maverick, described the new governor as "a man of inflexible integrity, of sterling sense [who] will undoubtedly perform the duties . . . honestly and faithfully without fear or favor." Gradually, there came to light certain characteristics which would make it difficult for him later: self-righteousness, tactlessness,

[8] An 1895 court decision in Colorado was contrary to Saufley's opinion in the Douglas-Willan, Sartoris Company case.

stubbornness, and unwillingness to accept the definition of politics as the science of the possible.

Moonlight came to Wyoming with firm prejudices against the big cattlemen. President Cleveland had instructed him to prevent land monopoly and to keep the public domain open for settlers. Fond of the familiar pattern of small farms in eastern Kansas, he sought to transfer a modified version of that pattern to Wyoming.

To what extent the middle western pattern of 160-acre farms was appropriate in Wyoming was being debated violently in the territory during the very week in which Moonlight took his oath of office. Professor Charles E. Lowery of the University of Michigan had recently published a three-column letter in the *Buffalo* (New York) *Express* in which he discussed the agricultural possibilities of eastern Wyoming around the headwaters of the North Platte and the Niobrara. Lowery wrote that he was thoroughly familiar with the area, and

I can safely say that not one fiftieth part of the section mentioned above is capable of entry under any one or all of the agricultural land acts applicable to this territory—homestead, pre-emption, timber culture and desert land acts combined. . . . I venture to say that a man with 1,000 acres of the choicest of this land in his own right would starve to death upon it, but for its usefulness for its connection with the range-cattle business. It is a fact that actual settlers who had come with any other purpose . . . have been compelled to engage in some other business, and as a rule are dependent for their very bread upon the charity of stock men. It is nothing but an act of humanity to warn honest laboring men against coming to Wyoming, especially to this part of it—and I am told that this is representative—for the purpose of agriculture. . . .

The *Cheyenne Sun* printed the Lowery letter, and, according to the *Laramie Sentinel*, "Cheyenne cattle kings" were distributing thousands of copies of the letter in pamphlet form. In his *Sentinel*, Hayford called the letter "slanderous." He condemned the *Sun* for giving space to the letter and the cattlemen for using it. Hayford was a promoter of agriculture, which helps to explain why he found the new governor a man of "sterling sense."

Certainly Moonlight was influenced little, if at all, by the Lowery letter, for he began a campaign to weaken the cattlemen's hold on the territory. He soon learned that he had a hard fight on his hands. Even though the cattlemen had been hurt terribly by the winter of 1886–1887, they were still in the saddle and their influence was pervasive.

Characteristically, Moonlight wanted to get out and see how the country people lived. In the summer of 1887 he traveled twelve hundred miles in a buggy, accompanied by Judge (former Probate Judge) Charles F. Miller. The people loaded him with complaints, which he forwarded to Washington. The settlers in northern Johnson County must have the right to reasonable use of timber. The Indians from the Pine Ridge and Shoshoni reservations were killing game out of season. Mail service was almost nonexistent in the Big Horn Basin. The postmaster at Sweetwater, six miles east of Independence Rock, was "a most disreputable character keeping a doggery of a saloon, and a disreputable woman," according to "gentlemen" at Devil's Gate. Moonlight had not met the postmaster, but his name, he learned, was James Averell.

Moonlight needed to appoint a coal-mine inspector in September, 1887, but the two candidates with the strongest support from Democrats in mining towns were both reputed to be polygamists. He appealed to Judge Corn in Evanston for advice: "Would an appointment of this nature be the thing? I can't understand some things." He finally found someone who was not a polygamist.

Moonlight was disturbed to find that the board of trustees at the new University of Wyoming was not required to report to him. The board, without consulting him, named John W. Hoyt, former governor of the territory, president of the institution. This displeased Moonlight, who expressed the opinion that Hoyt was "a mere theorist," and relations with Hoyt thereafter were cool.

Moonlight thought so much of a *Laramie Sentinel* editorial that advocated farming as a substitute for cattle raising in Wyoming that he included it in his 1887 report to the Secretary of the Interior. Among other things, the *Sentinel* editorial said: "At no period of the world's history had any nation or people who devoted themselves exclusively to stock-raising ever risen much above semi-barbarism in science, progress, and general intelligence, and we regard it as a fortunate thing that in the first contest, Cain the tiller of the soil, killed Abel, the stock-grower."

Governor Moonlight, however, was not so stupid as to think that all of Wyoming should be cut up into 160-acre farms. His 1887 and 1888 reports to the Secretary of the Interior show clearly what he had in mind. He wanted more small irrigated farms, it is true, but he wanted most of Wyoming to be in good-sized farming-ranching combination units. He wanted family ranches based on 1,120 acres of patented land and dependent on adjacent public-domain grazing privileges held in common.

Moonlight came by his sympathies for small settlers honestly, for he was himself a poor man with a wife and five children. His financial woes were compounded because Congress appropriated only $2,600 of the $3,500 salary authorized by statute.

In January, 1888, Moonlight met the legislature elected in November, 1886. The Republicans controlled the Council, 9 to 3, the Democrats the House, 14 to 10. As usual, the livestock interest was well represented, although not by many leaders of the industry. Had he been an astute politician, Moonlight might have been able to establish control of the Democratic House. It was to be expected that the Republican Council would give him trouble. "We fought him day and night," recalled Senator Charles A. Guernsey later.

Moonlight's message was the longest in territorial history. Its length, however, was due mainly to the inclusion of generous excerpts from reports submitted by several territorial officials. Newspaper editors generally approved the message as able and exhaustive. Moonlight placed special stress on the need for economy: taxpayers were grumbling about high taxes, there must be strict economy "so that not one dollar may be appropriated where it can possibly be saved." Yet the Governor urged the addition of new counties to save time and distance, without specifying how many more than the existing eight he wanted. He had an ingenious proposal for getting more property on the tax rolls, suggesting that the assessors should compel everyone to "swear to his statement with uplifted hand, so that a charge of perjury could be established."

Outwardly, the legislators and Moonlight appeared to be on good terms until Valentine's Day, when Moonlight began a parade of seven vetoes, sending one to each House. The rejected Council bill dealt with the issue of preferred stock by corporations, while the House bill, introduced by Willis Van Devanter, dealt with the appointment of receivers for corporations. The House sustained both vetoes.

On February 21, Moonlight vetoed a bill prepared by Thomas B. Adams, secretary of the Wyoming Stock Growers Association, and approved by the association's executive committee, to allay hard feelings against the Maverick Law of 1884. Moved by criticism, the stockmen had made minor concessions in 1886. They went into the 1888 legislature prepared to make further concessions, for the changes of 1886 had not quieted the critics. The *Carbon County Journal* asserted that the association was "persistently stealing and appropriating the poor man's stock." The *Laramie Boomerang* charged that "the crimson

handed stock monopoly has more to answer for before heaven than all
the pirates that ever sailed the seas," and the *Cheyenne Leader* reported
that in the legislature, "no one tried to uphold the present maverick
law."

Moonlight had no quarrel with the basic change introduced by the
association's measure, which involved transferring control of the roundups from the association to a territorial board of livestock commissioners. His five-page veto message stated that the bill was "in many
respects a great improvement upon the so called Maverick law." Montana and Colorado had such boards, and Adams had borrowed the
Montana plan for introduction in Wyoming. Some of the details
bothered Moonlight, however, and in discussing them he permitted
pent-up feelings of resentment and suspicion to erupt. He objected to
the not unusual provision that the commissioners, who were to be
appointed by the governor for two years, should hold office "until their
successors shall have been nominated and confirmed, and shall have
qualified." This, said Moonlight, was a direct challenge to gubernatorial appointive power. To him, it seemed to place the Council over
the governor in appointments, permitting the Council to dictate the
nominations after the first two years. He conjured up all kinds of dire
possibilities. The commissioners "may ride rough-shod over the rights
of others and there is no remedy save in the courts. They can appoint
an unlimited number of subordinates, and pay them out of the
maverick fund." He imagined "as another important point" that the
commissioners and their numerous employees would enter politics in
order to control the Council, which could keep them in office simply
by refusing to confirm new appointments.

He angered T. B. Adams, secretary of the association and a member
of the House, by asserting that the board of commissioners might
appoint "a Secretary who is at this moment a member of the Tenth
Legislative Assembly, and who had a voice in creating the office."
This, he said, would be illegal, but "who shall bring the commissioners
to judgment should they do this illegal act? They are beyond all
authority."

Moonlight objected further to giving stock inspectors authority to
make arrests. He suggested that they might instead be permitted to
make complaints before a justice of the peace, or possibly make arrangements to work under county sheriffs with responsibility to them.
Clothed with the power of sheriffs, he charged, "they may summon
their fellow citizens and drag them out of bed to assist in rounding up

a maverick, and may arrest and imprison the citizen." He said that while the secretary of the commission was accountable annually to the treasurer of the territory, he might have in his hands between accountings large sums which he could lend out at 15 per cent "and convert it to his own use."

The language and suspicions of this message were too much for most of the legislators. Three cattlemen, two of them association members, were placed on a four-man House committee to study the veto. They reported that some of the suggestions were reasonable but that the House should override because the veto message was based on "unjust and unwarranted" assumptions regarding the motives of the legislators. The House voted, 11–7, to override, with five members absent, not quite the two-thirds vote needed. Five Democrats (four of them connected with the livestock industry) joined six Republicans on the affirmative side. Another bill was then prepared which was more palatable to Moonlight. He signed this version, but in the meantime, resentments had built up which would make it easier for Democrats to defect in the next crisis.

The legislature followed up on 1886 institutional beginnings by authorizing the expenditure of $215,000: $125,000 for adding wings to the capitol building at Cheyenne; $30,000 (from bond issues) with which to begin a penitentiary at Rawlins; $25,000 (from bond issues) for completing the university building at Laramie; $30,000 (from bond issues) for completing the insane asylum at Evanston; and $5,000 (from bond issues) with which to begin a poor asylum at Lander. The bill stated that the penitentiary should cost no more than $100,000 and the poor asylum no more than $25,000, the assumption being that $70,000 for the penitentiary and $20,000 for the poor asylum would have to be provided for by later legislatures. The bond-issue authorization of $90,000, added to the 1886 authorization of $230,000, brought the territory's bonded debts up to $320,000, the legal limit.

The legislature stepped on the Governor's tenderest toe when it provided that the present capitol-building commission would continue in office if he failed to nominate acceptable replacements. Moonlight vetoed the bill. The passage about perpetuating the present capitol-building commission was a red flag which caused him to declare that "I shall at all times vigorously defend [the appointive power] without fear or favor." Most of the six-page veto message dealt with the need for economy at a time when "poverty [was] staring many a good man and woman in the face." He thought, quite reasonably, that the capitol building, without wings, would be adequate for at least six more years. He thought the insane-asylum building was already adequate: "Will any sane man say it is not sufficient for the insane of Wyoming for many years to come?" He thought $5,000 rather than $25,000 was enough to finish the university building. By way of peroration he concluded that "the bill was rushed through both houses under a suspension of the rules, without debate or amendment being allowed. . . . The bill was called up in the dusk of the evening. . . . The whole surroundings of the bill are dark and mysterious." There was really little mystery about it—legislators were dividing up the institutions, with Cheyenne getting most of the money.[9] The legislature overrode the veto, 16–6 and 10–2.

Newspapers outside Cheyenne, such as the *Boomerang* and *Sentinel* in Laramie, the *Green River News*, the *Lusk Herald*, the *Lander Mountaineer*, the *Big Horn Sentinel*, and the *Carbon County Journal*, thought the Governor was right. They objected most to the $125,000 item for adding wings to the capitol. In a post-mortem discussion the *Cheyenne Leader* contrasted the styles of behavior displayed by Cheyenne and Laramie at the public trough: "Cheyenne is willing to get what it can and makes no bones about it. Laramie is willing to take whatever is in sight . . . but with a singular manifestation of hypocrisy it endeavors at the same time to make people believe it is laboring only for the general good."

Next Moonlight vetoed a measure providing for the organization of three new counties, Converse, Sheridan, and Natrona. He had urged the establishment of new counties in his opening message, and he now stated in his veto that new counties were desirable but that he thought the divisions worked out were unfair. He enclosed, for example, a protest from the county commissioners of Laramie County in which it was argued that the boundaries of Converse County would combine a small number of former Albany County residents with a large number of former Laramie County people and would lead to the taxation of the former Albany County residents for the payment of Laramie County railroad bonds.

The bill for new counties was passed by the Council over the veto and sent to the House, where bill and veto were stolen. When they could not be found, a new bill was prepared and attached as a rider to

---

[9] With the university already in operation, Albany County men tried to curb the free spenders. Francis E. Warren wrote to Thomas Sturgis on February 23, 1888 (Warren Letterbooks, University of Wyoming Library): "Albany county 'fell out of bed with us' on the building proposition and combination is made with Carbon, Uinta, and Fremont."

the general-appropriation bill. Moonlight vetoed the combination, but it was passed over the veto, 14–2 and 9–2, despite the Governor's charge that it was "perhaps the most wonderful piece of legislation ever presented to any executive for approval."

Moonlight found other measures more to his taste. He approved a bill for Sunday closing of saloons, cigar stores, barbershops, and most mercantile establishments. After many disappointments, temperance forces were making progress. A few months earlier, the *Cheyenne Sun* had reported that the city had only 28 places where liquor was sold, compared to 66 thirteen years earlier, when the population was smaller. Cheyenne church workers lobbied vigorously for Sunday closing. Meanwhile, Senator W. H. Holliday of Laramie fought a spectacular but losing battle to outlaw gambling.

Governor Moonlight's last set-to with the legislature occurred in the Council, where the 9–3 ratio of Republicans to Democrats permitted him very little influence. In one of his veto messages he had referred to the possibility of the Council's riding "roughshod" over the executive, and he now received a demonstration. His nominations for assorted appointive positions were scrutinized and ruthlessly rejected. In some cases he had to submit third choices before acceptance. When finally he could not advance acceptable candidates for four positions, he waited until the end of the session and made ad interim appointments. Among the prominent men rejected for various positions were E. Amoretti, Noyes Baldwin, George W. Baxter, Gibson Clark, William Daley, J. C. Friend, and J. H. Hayford.

After the legislative session, Moonlight published and distributed three hundred copies of a pamphlet, *Seven Vetoes by Thomas Moonlight, Governor of Wyoming Territory, Tenth Legislative Assembly, 1888* (Cheyenne, 1888). At least Editor Hayford was impressed, for he wrote in his *Laramie Sentinel* that "the messages are clear, logical and able state papers, and there is no doubt what the judgment of the people will be when they ever get a chance to express it." No doubt, since his Fourth of July visit to Buffalo in 1887, Moonlight's best friends were in Johnson County. At a mass meeting in Buffalo on March 22, 1888, resolutions were adopted praising him as "a man of unswerving integrity, ready at all times to protect the people from the burdens attempted to be placed upon them for the benefit of a few individuals and a few locations." The *Buffalo Echo* concluded that "the Tenth Legislative Assembly goes into history with the proud distinction of having perpetrated more deviltry in less time than any set of men out of the penitentiary."

Even so, Moonlight's behavior during the legislative session made him as many enemies as friends. And his handling of the details for organizing Sheridan and Converse counties cost him more friends. People in Buffalo who did not want Sheridan County organized were made unhappy when Moonlight would not let the Johnson County clerk scrutinize the list of names (three hundred electors who were payers of property tax were required) on the petition initiating organization of the new county. Douglas people, particularly M. C. Barrow of the *Douglas Budget*, were angry because Moonlight had, at the end of the session, tried to block the creation of Converse County. Then in 1889 the Governor became involved in a bitter wrangle over the creation of Natrona County because he doubted that many of the three hundred names on the list of petitioners represented residents. In short, Moonlight was finding it hard to keep from antagonizing most of the people in the territory, including a good many Democrats. With Benjamin Harrison's defeat of Grover Cleveland in November, 1888, most Wyoming people looked forward with pleasure to having a new governor, who turned out to be Francis E. Warren, appointed to his second term on March 29, 1889.

THE ECONOMY

Governor Moonlight was not indulging his imagination when he cried depression and poverty during the 1888 legislative session. In September, 1887, the *Cheyenne Leader* had complained of dullness of business and had charged that "there has been less public enterprise and less public spirit shown in Cheyenne during the past year than during any other year in our history." The *Leader* remained gloomy throughout 1888. The winter of 1886–1887 caused a severe setback for the overexpanded cattle business. The huge Swan Land and Cattle Company in 1887, and the Union Cattle Company in early 1888, went bankrupt. Morton E. Post's bank in Cheyenne, the Maverick Bank in Douglas, and James France's bank in Rawlins closed their doors. Francis E. Warren wrote to Thomas Sturgis in November, 1888: "It has been very 'rocky' traveling in Cheyenne in any business for a long time." Census figures for 1880 and 1890 show the pattern of economic growth:

	1880	*1890*
Total population	20,789	62,555
Total employment, all occupations	8,884	30,630

Industrial Groups

	1880	1890
Laborers	1,549	4,794
General and crop agriculture	1,364	3,784
Stock raising	275	4,147
Military servicemen	1,287	871
Domestic and personal services	932	2,693
Manufacturing	829	2,795
Railroads	700	2,196
Wagon and other road transportation	385	934
Wholesale and retail trade	341	1,330
Coal mining	330	1,893
Metal mining	—	1,160
Building trades and construction	316	1,800
Professional and related services	199	980
Government officials and employees	198	180
Forestry	112	229
Finance and clerical	13	594
Other	154	250

RAILROADS

Railroad construction was of considerable importance in the 1880's. First, the Oregon Short Line was built northwest of Granger ninety-two miles into Idaho in 1881–1882. Then the completion of the Northern Pacific through Montana from St. Paul to Portland in 1883 helped in the opening up of northern Wyoming. The Wyoming Central (which soon became a part of the Chicago and North Western system) came out of Nebraska to reach Lusk and Douglas in 1886, Glenrock in 1887, and Casper in 1888. People are "Coming in Swarms" said the *Cheyenne Sun* in March, 1886. Immigrants came from Iowa, Wisconsin, and Minnesota, mostly in "regulation schooners," to take up land near Lusk.

The Cheyenne and Northern, aided by $400,000 in bonds voted by Laramie County in 1886, bridged the Big Laramie River at Uva, north of Wheatland, in October, 1887, and moved on to Wendover, on the north bank of the North Platte. Aid for a railroad from Cheyenne northward had first been authorized by the legislature in 1879. After renewed authorization by the 1886 legislature, the people of Laramie County voted overwhelming approval.[10]

[10] According to a member of the 1886 legislature, Charles A. Guernsey, thirty unnecessary miles of track had to be agreed upon before the bond authorization could be obtained in the legislature. Guernsey stated in his book *Wyoming Cowboy Days* (New York: Putnam, 1936) that two influential ranch owners threatened to block the bond issue unless the road passed close to their ranch headquarters.

The Burlington tracks reached Cheyenne from Sterling, Colorado, in December, 1887. All of this railroad construction suggested prosperity, but it was actually thin and insubstantial. Colonel E. H. Kimball, in his *Rowdy West* (Douglas) on April 17, 1887, distilled central Wyoming's disillusionment:

We had great confidence in the future of Douglas, and showed our faith by our works, and we are sorry to say the present state of affairs here does not justify our expectations. Douglas made a wonderful growth for three or four months, but the expected spring boom has not become visible to the naked eye. . . . Another thing: The action of our people is not such as inspires public confidence and helps a town. As long as three fourths of them stand upon the street corners and public places and openly deride, berate and curse the town and country and assert that "the town has gone to hell and never will amount to anything," they can scarcely expect strangers to invest and locate here. But this is the exact state of affairs and there is no use denying it.

Later that same year, Colonel E. H. Kimball's son, W. S., complained in his *Glenrock Graphic* about the North Western's freight rates: "Of all highway robbers, this line of railroad stands at the head."

The *Lusk Herald*, in June, 1889, commented on another phase of railroad construction as follows:

The Cheyenne and Northern Railroad, which is costing the people of Laramie and Converse counties so much, is a bird without wings. It doesn't fly to any large and unlimited extent. It is about as invaluable to our growing industries as the trail of an angle-worm in the sands of a duck pond at low water mark. It has now reduced its regular service to three trains a week. The Herald would like to see it sink to the lowest depths of hell—bonds and all.

Lusk, Douglas, Glenrock, and Casper suffered through vest-pocket editions of the boom-and-bust experience so painful to Union Pacific towns of the late 1860's. They had their tent towns and their miniature hells on wheels (without vigilantes), and they suffered from the shrinkage that followed the construction period. Casper's boom was a mild one in comparison with that in Douglas two years earlier. Casper's first buildings were temporary ones erected in June, 1888, from green lumber cut in a sawmill on Casper Mountain. Corrugated iron was used for roofing material. A few tents stood among the frame buildings. The railroad's townsite company surveyed the permanent townsite in the fall of 1888, just west of temporary "old town." In this newly platted town the railroad and J. M. Carey & Brother (original owners of the land) had alternate lots, which they offered at private sale. Even though the lots were offered at low prices, purchasers were scarce, for as A. J.

Mokler has written, "the prospects for Casper in the early days to grow beyond a shambling, temporary frontier village were anything but inviting."

The newspapers of the 1880's were full of promotional statements about mining ventures. Little came of most of these enterprises. Only the old standby, coal, was produced in significant quantity, exceeding 1,000,000 tons in 1887 and attaining a production of 1,870,366 tons in 1890. The Silver Crown mines twenty miles west of Cheyenne inspired glowing accounts of rich gold, silver, and copper ores that were never followed by profitable production. Governor Warren admitted in his report to the Secretary of the Interior in 1889 that "with the exception of coal . . . the mineral wealth of Wyoming can hardly be said to be developed."

Laramie in 1887 showed the promise of greatest industrial development with its rolling mills; glass factory; tannery; flour mill; a chemical works producing lye, caustic soda, soda ash, and salt cake from soda lakes thirteen miles west of the city; and a cigar factory turning out "Woman's Rights" perfectos. Also, the Laramie Board of Trade was trying to get someone to start a woolen mill and an electric street railway. Woolen mill and street railway were not realized, although an electric street-railway company was incorporated in April, 1888.

Laramie's flour mill, built in 1887, was not the first in the territory, having been preceded by one at Beckton on Big Goose Creek. Other flour mills were opened at Buffalo and Lander in 1888.

The Laramie glassworks illustrates the difficulties of pioneer manufacturing enterprise. Local people led by Colonel S. W. Downey and J. W. Donnellan in April, 1887, subscribed $25,000 to match a similar sum to be put up by an eastern glass company. They had ample quantities of sand, lime, soda, and coal. They built a plant to make window glass and imported thirty-seven skilled glassmakers from Illinois. Their melting furnaces proved a failure in October, 1887, and had to be replaced. Then glass prices nationally were depressed during 1888. Next, a railroad rate war reduced the freight on glass shipped from Chicago to Denver so that Laramie glass could not compete in Colorado markets. From time to time there were difficulties over patents for machinery. In 1889 the glassworkers organized a cooperative and took over the unprofitable enterprise, with aid from citizens who contributed $4,000 to make needed repairs. Everything seemed promising until October, 1889, when the plant shut down again. Various explanations were published: the cost of coal was too high; the local glassblowers were unable to come up to national production norms; the eastern glass manufacturers' monopoly was too strong. The plant was not reopened, and the *Laramie Sentinel* claimed that Laramie people had invested, and lost, more than $100,000 in the glassmaking venture.

Wyoming shared only infinitesimally in the vast expansion of farming on the Great Plains during the 1880's, although there was much promotion of farming in the newspapers. It is noteworthy that people swarmed into western Nebraska in the years 1885–1890, but only a few thousand crossed into Wyoming. It is true that the contraction of the cattle industry after 1886 opened the way for competing users of the land. Mostly, however, sheepmen rather than dirt farmers occupied the land relinquished by cattlemen. Thomas Moonlight reported in 1887 that "sheepmen are happy, buoyant, and hopeful."

The 1888 legislature prepared the way for expansion of reclamation by revamping and improving 1886 legislation and by creating the office of territorial engineer. By a vote of 7 to 5 the 1888 Council confirmed Moonlight's nominee, Elwood Mead, of the College of Agriculture at Fort Collins, Colorado. No doubt Mead's support from Francis E. Warren and Charles A. Guernsey meant more than that from Moonlight. Mead was a good choice who was to go far in the realm of reclamation.

As to opportunities for the laboring man in the late 1880's, there is no denying that they were very limited. Transient workers—"tramps," they were called—flooded the Union Pacific towns in the summers of 1887 and 1888, as they had in 1876 and 1877. In his 1889 and 1890 reports to the Secretary of the Interior, Governor Warren could list shortages in only two categories of labor: skilled mechanics and household servants.

Ever hopeful, some promoters kept trying in the 1880's to get legislative support for advertising the territory and boosting immigration. An immigration bureau had failed to achieve demonstrable results in the years 1873–1875, and legislatures thereafter rejected similar proposals until 1888. Then an act was passed making the secretary of the territory ex officio immigration commissioner and placing a small sum of money at his disposal. Secretary Samuel D. Shannon arranged for the publication of ten thousand copies of a pamphlet entitled *Wyoming Resources*, which he and his successor, John W. Meldrum, distributed. The pamphlet's message was not compelling, and only a trickle of immigration resulted.

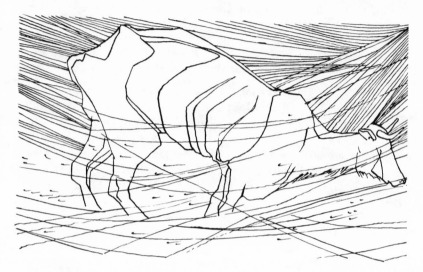

CHAPTER 7

Boom and Bust in Cattle

THE 1880's WITNESSED a spectacular boom in the Wyoming cattle business and an equally spectacular bust. More than fifty years before the climactic developments of the 1880's, mountain men had brought the first cattle to Wyoming. Captain William Sublette and other fur men took five cattle, including one milch cow, to the Wind River rendezvous in 1830. These animals were taken back to the States that fall. Then in the 1840's and 1850's, tens of thousands of cattle were driven along the Oregon-California-Utah Trail. Like Sublette's first quintet, they did not remain in Wyoming, except for a few that were left at Fort Laramie and Fort Bridger. Some of the animals at the forts were sold to emigrants or exchanged for worn-out ones. Trader Seth E. Ward

163

wintered a few hundred work cattle on Chugwater Creek in 1852–1853, and Alexander Majors did likewise in 1854–1855. After delivering more than fifty tons of government stores to Fort Laramie in late November, 1854, Majors decided to turn his sorefooted animals out on the range rather than try to drive them back to Missouri. He wrote on April 15, 1884, to the *Cheyenne Sun*:

We did not turn the cattle out without sending some herders along with them . . . they came out in the spring in the very finest working condition. . . . I wintered cattle upon the same grounds for the following ten years and did not lose one-half of one per cent per winter. Knowing the facts above, I started the first breeding herd in Wyoming which was in 1862. . . .

Mormons may have had small breeding herds in what is now southwestern Wyoming before Majors. They started a colony at Camp Supply near Fort Bridger in 1853. Russell Thorp has identified as the oldest brand in Wyoming the "character open nine," or "Yoke 9," which was adopted by J. W. Myers on Bear River in 1857 and has remained in the Myers family for more than a century. Horace Greeley reported seeing herds of cattle along Black's Fork and Ham's Fork in 1859.

It is not certain that any of the animals discussed so far were left entirely to their own devices. Nevertheless, it was but a short step to the adoption of open-range practices—turning cattle loose in the fall, with no supervision whatever, and hoping that they could find feed and water until they could be gathered in the spring.[1] Soon great herds of Texas cattle would be so treated.

Nelson Story drove a herd of Texas cattle through eastern Wyoming to Montana in 1866. The *Cheyenne Leader*, founded in September, 1867, mentioned cattle for the first time on February 7, 1868: "We guess the 'cattle upon a thousand hills' round about Cheyenne must have the

---

[1] A story often told (with varying details) is one about the accidental discovery that cattle could rustle for themselves in Wyoming winters. In the famous 1885 report of Joseph Nimmo, Jr., chief of the Bureau of Statistics, Treasury Department, Washington, D.C., entitled *Range and Ranch Cattle Traffic* (*House Executive Document 267* [Serial 2304], 48 Cong., 2 Sess.), one Theodore J. McMinn of St. Louis testified that early in December, 1864, a government trader on his way to Camp Douglas, Utah Territory, was caught in a severe snowstorm on the Laramie Plains and was compelled to turn his oxen adrift. To his surprise, he found them four months later "in even better condition than when turned out to die." Robert H. Burns, "Beefmakers of the Laramie Plains," *Annals of Wyoming*, XXXVI, 2 (October 1964), 186, says that it was Tom Alsop, freighting for Edward Creighton, who left between two hundred and three hundred oxen on Sherman Hill in December, 1863, and found them in good condition on Sand Creek near Chimney Rock the following spring.

remaining grass pretty well gnawed off by this time, from the numbers of them we see made to depend upon this mode of sustaining existence." The following July the *Leader* reported that "cattle, horses and mules which were turned upon these prairies last fall . . . came out fat in February, March and April." John W. Iliff brought longhorns to the vicinity of Cheyenne in February, 1868, and Hutton and Creighton placed 3,000 Texas cattle on the Laramie Plains in 1869. These longhorns represented a small stream that swelled to a flood in subsequent years. Meanwhile, W. G. Bullock and B. B. Mills brought 250 cows and a few bulls from the Middle West to the vicinity of Fort Laramie in October, 1868.

The assessment rolls of Wyoming Territory listed 8,143 cattle in 1870. The *Cheyenne Leader* perhaps exaggerated a trifle when it announced on September 12, 1871, that "immense herds of cattle are constantly arriving from the east to be placed on the rich grazing fields adjacent to Cheyenne." Yet no doubt the cattle business was soon recognized as the territory's most promising economic activity.

Editor J. H. Hayford in Laramie seems to have been the first in the region to use the term "cattle king." He applied it in praise to Charles Hutton of the Laramie Plains in April, 1871. Not until the 1880's did the term become derogatory. John W. Iliff was recognized as the cattle king around Cheyenne for several years. He had the beef contract for all military posts along the Union Pacific between Fort Kearny and Fort Steele in 1868. "Cheyenne is the headquarters of the 'cattle kings' of Wyoming," said the *Omaha Herald* in 1875. At that time the *Herald* and the *Cheyenne Leader* (September 20) published a list of nineteen Wyoming outfits with one thousand or more cattle, and fifty-one smaller cattlemen. Heading the list, which had been prepared by J. H. Triggs, was "J. M. Carey & Bro." with six thousand head on Crow Creek and "Creighton & Co." with five thousand on Horse Creek.[2]

---

[2] Not listed among the major cattlemen was W. A. Carter of Fort Bridger, although he may have deserved such recognition. The Board of Immigration's publication *The Territory of Wyoming: Its History, Soil, Climate, Resources, Etc.* (Laramie City: Daily Sentinel print, 1874) included this description of Judge Carter by E. A. Curley, an English correspondent: "[He is] the great man of Fort Bridger, and of all western Wyoming for that matter. He is the post trader, and a general wholesale and retail merchant; he is a lumberman, with several sawmills running in the mountains; he is a stockman, with some 2,000 head of cattle; he contracts for forage, fuel, meat, &c., for the government; he builds roads and bridges on his own account; and he drills through the Wyoming rock for oil." The Bancroft Library at the University of California, Berkeley, has most of the W. A. Carter correspondence, papers, and accounts books.

Dr. Hiram Latham, Union Pacific surgeon, who invested in cattle, was undoubtedly the most enthusiastic promoter of the open-range cattle business. He was ably seconded by editor Hayford of the *Laramie Sentinel*. Judge John W. Kingman was an enthusiastic investor in sheep. During the severe winter of 1871–1872, the *Cheyenne Leader* said in December: "The stock of the country has been subsisting on Latham's letters on winter grazing, and Kingman's essay on sheep culture for a fortnight past."

The hard winter of 1871–1872, in which there were heavy losses, was dismissed as abnormal. Governors Campbell and Thayer invested in the cattle business and took the lead in promoting its development. A newspaperman with considerable experience in the West, Robert Strahorn, included in his 1877 *Handbook of Wyoming* a glowing account of the opportunities in cattle.

Wyoming's third governor, John W. Hoyt, did not invest in Wyoming cattle as his predecessors had done, but he stated in his 1878 report to the Secretary of the Interior that the stock business was unequaled for its opportunities for profits.[3] He explained that the 250,000 or 300,000 cattle in the territory left much of the range unoccupied. He had traveled whole days without seeing a cow or sheep. No doubt these days of the late 1870's were happy ones for the early birds; although prices received at Chicago were not high, costs were so low that good profits were possible.

Most of the cattle in the 1870's were concentrated in southeastern Wyoming. As soon as the Indian threat was eliminated, herds were pushed into the northeastern part of the territory. Then in 1879 the Big Horn Basin was invaded. Charles Carter first brought three thousand or more Oregon cattle, by way of Fort Bridger, to the junction of the North and South forks of the Stinking Water (Shoshone). Another herd belonging to an Englishman, Captain Henry Belknap, was brought from Montana to the South Fork of the Stinking Water in 1880. In the same year, Otto Franc brought a herd from Montana to the Greybull River, and a Kansan, Henry T. Lovell, trailed two herds to the west side of the Big Horn River, just above the mouth of Nowood Creek. Carter's Bug Ranch, Franc's Pitchfork, and Lovell's Home Ranch became famous in later years.

John Luman trailed cattle from Idaho to Paint Rock Creek in 1881. That year or the next, George W. Baxter established the LU Ranch on

[3] Governor Hoyt's report may be found in Government Documents, Serial 1850, pp. 1130–1185.

Grass Creek, and Joseph M. Carey sent a herd to the Greybull country in 1883. Meanwhile, many others had been scrambling to acquire choice locations in the Big Horn Basin, so that the area was quite well stocked by 1884. Other pioneers occupied the upper Green River Valley. Among the first were Daniel B. Budd and Hugh McKay, who brought 750 Nevada cattle to the Piney country in late 1879.

A. H. Swan and J. M. Carey brought Herefords to Cheyenne in 1878, to the delight of editor Hayford, who predicted that many others would follow their example until the Texas drives of common cattle would cease.

In his report to the Secretary of the Interior in 1883, Governor Hale described the activities of the Wyoming Hereford Association, owned by the Swan brothers and Boulter & Morgan.[4] In the summer of 1883 they imported from England four hundred Hereford bulls and cows valued at almost $200,000. Their manager claimed that it was "the largest and most valuable herd of thoroughbred cattle in the world." These animals were provided with hay, water, and shelter at the headquarters on Crow Creek six miles east of Cheyenne. Besides the Texas cattle there were many from the Middle West, called "Americans" or "pilgrims," and others from Oregon, Washington, and Utah. Mrs. Agnes Wright Spring, in *Seventy Years*, has summarized the history of drives from Oregon.

Governor Hale was so impressed by the cattle industry in 1883 that he reported to the Secretary of the Interior: "Stock raising is the chief industry, comparing with all others about as 90 per cent to 10. . . . The business has grown . . . from small beginnings, until cattle by the thousand roam in every valley and drink from every stream in the territory."

In 1885, 894,788 cattle were assessed at $15,388,503; in 1886, 889,121 cattle were assessed at $14,654,125. Thomas Sturgis, secretary of the Wyoming Stock Growers Association, told the organization's convention in 1885 that its members had 2,000,000 cattle valued at $100,000,000 (including horses, plant, and real estate). Perhaps 500,000 cattle belonging to association members in 1885 grazed outside Wyoming. The evidence warrants an estimate of 1,500,000 cattle in Wyoming Territory in 1885 and 1886. In a few short years, 1878–1885, the Wyoming range had filled to overflowing.

Cattle prices in 1882 were the highest they had been since 1870 and

[4] *Ibid.*, Serial 2191, p. 584. In his long report (pp. 559–625), Hale included much about the cattle business.

higher than they would ever be again in the territorial period. That fall at Chicago, Wyoming cattlemen sold "American" cattle at $63.50 per head, Texans at $50, and half-breeds at $52.50. Governor Hale reported that pioneers who sold at that time "were then richly rewarded for their enterprise."

Troubles began to pile up thereafter. The big companies excited resentment and alarm. The *Cheyenne Sun* said in June, 1883: "That sentence 'sold to a syndicate' is becoming dangerous. Gentlemen, there is danger in all this. It means the power of the few over the many." The *Laramie Sentinel* quoted the *Sun* editorial and said that in it were "mutterings of a distant storm." The *Sentinel* returned to the subject in October, 1883: "The tendency has been, in the past few years, to aggregate and consolidate the cattle business into the hands of heavy capitalists and gigantic corporations." Hayford of the *Sentinel* wanted more small operators. "It is men—not steers—which make a state," he said.

In late November, 1883, small stock owners of Johnson County met at Fort McKinney and organized a "Small Dealers' Association." The group passed resolutions charging that the Wyoming Stock Growers Association oppressed small owners, stole their stock, and was trying to drive them out of the country. The "Small Dealers" vowed to resist encroachments of "the cattle kings." "This may prove the beginning of a serious war," said Hayford.

W. Turrentine Jackson has traced the history of British investments in the American cattle business.[5] Scots and Englishmen came as individuals and, more importantly, as investors in heavily capitalized corporations. Jackson has estimated that the British put $45,000,000 into the American cattle business in the 1880's. In 1885 the giant Scottish-owned Swan Land and Cattle Company listed 123,460 head. No other company had that many, although not a few had ten thousand or more.

ORGANIZATION

Pioneer stockmen soon realized that they must organize if they would solve common problems. On May 30, 1871, the Wyoming Stock and

---

[5] See "British Interests in the Range Cattle Industry," in Maurice Frink, W. Turrentine Jackson, and Agnes Wright Spring, *When Grass Was King* (Boulder: University of Colorado Press, 1956), pp. 135–330. In the same volume, Frink reviews developments in the industry north of Texas, 1865–1895, and Mrs. Spring discusses the part played by John W. Iliff.

Wool Growers Association at a meeting in Laramie organized, adopted a constitution and bylaws, and elected the following officers: Governor John A. Campbell, president; Dr. Hiram Latham, secretary; Luther Fillmore, treasurer; and a vice-president for each county—Thomas Alsop for Albany, J. W. Iliff for Laramie, E. Hunt for Carbon, S. I. Field for Sweetwater and W. A. Carter for Uinta.

In discussing this first organization of Wyoming stockmen, the *Wyoming Tribune* said on April 15, 1871: "The object of the Association is for the general advancement of cattle and sheep growing in this Territory. The Association will have a general fund to be expended in the detection, arrest and conviction of stock thieves, and in the purchase of rope with which to hang them." Later references to this organization use the name Wyoming Stock Graziers Association instead of Wyoming Stock and Wool Growers Association. What was called the "annual meeting" of the association occurred in Cheyenne, November 14, 1871. This was a memorable occasion with all the earmarks of spectacular success. The Union Pacific provided half-fare rates. At Dr. Latham's invitation, the House of Representatives joined the stock raisers for the meeting in the House of Representatives hall. The president of the association (and governor of the territory), John A. Campbell, presided. Campbell, Latham, and Fillmore were re-elected president, secretary, and treasurer, respectively. Among the speakers were Governor Campbell, Dr. Latham, John M. Thayer, Judge Kingman, J. M. Carey, William R. Steele, Stephen F. Nuckolls, Stephen W. Downey, and W. W. Corlett.

Soon thereafter the legislature passed a law against theft of "any neat cattle, horse, goat, sheep, mule, ass or swine" and authorized punishment of up to ten years in prison and a fine up to but not exceeding $5,000. The 1871 legislature also authorized a fine not exceeding $500 or imprisonment not exceeding five years, or both, for altering brands. Newspapers in the next year, nevertheless, reported an increase in stock stealing and the virtual impossibility of getting convictions.

Curiously, there is no report of any meeting of the Wyoming Stock Graziers Association in 1872, but on January 21, 1873, the *Cheyenne Leader* named sixteen delegates whom "the executive committee of the Wyoming Stock Growers Association" had designated to attend the Colorado Stock Growers meeting. The Wyoming Stock Graziers Association disintegrated and was not mentioned again after January, 1873. Three factors probably contributed to the death of the pioneer organization: heavy losses in the winter of 1871–1872; the bitter political quarrels which divided some of the leading members; and the 1873 bankruptcy of that remarkable promoter Dr. Hiram Latham and his departure from the territory under a cloud.

Wyoming's first organization of stock raisers was noteworthy for its inclusion of both cattlemen and sheepmen, two classes of stockmen who would later be at each other's throats. The next effort at organization originated in Cheyenne. While some men who were interested in both cattle and sheep were involved, the Laramie County Stock Growers Association, organized on November 29, 1873, was definitely a cattlemen's association. The eleven men who attended the organization meeting chose M. V. Boughton as chairman and W. L. Kuykendall as secretary of the "Stock Association of Laramie County."

No doubt members of the new association inspired the passage by the 1873 legislature of a law forbidding anyone to adopt the mark or brand of another and forbidding county clerks to record the same brand to more than one person. "Laws and regulations" were adopted at a second meeting of the association on February 23, 1874. The admission fee was set at five dollars, the dues at fifty cents per month. In his *Cow Country Cavalcade*, Maurice Frink lists the members in attendance at the meetings thereafter during the 1870's. Emerging as major concerns were the organization of roundups, supervision of branding, legislation, freight rates, and theft. Later, in the 1880's, the control of disease would receive attention.

The 1875 legislature recognized the growing power of the cattlemen by passing a law making railroad companies liable to the owner for killing or injuring stock. The corporation was made responsible for notifying the owner within ten days and was to pay two-thirds of the sworn value. The best way to improve stock, said a pioneer, was to cross a longhorn cow with a railroad locomotive. If the corporation failed to notify within ten days, it was liable for double damages. This legislation raises a question about the common assumption that the Union Pacific was all-powerful in the 1870's and did not yield its position of dominance to the cattlemen until the 1880's. Trains killed 976 cattle in Wyoming from April 1, 1882, to March 31, 1883. In the next four years the death toll was 655, 601, 343, and 205, respectively.[6] The worst slaughter occurred in cuts and snowsheds during blizzards.

[6] These figures are taken from reports of the Wyoming Stock Growers Association secretary preserved in the records of the association in the University of Wyoming Library.

The *Laramie Sentinel* in February, 1880, reported two derailments resulting from collisions with cattle.

Meanwhile, Albany County cattlemen and sheepmen, who had been unorganized since 1873, formed the Albany County Stock Growers Association in April, 1877. The Wind River Valley Stock Growers Association was incorporated by act of the legislature in 1877. Why the Wind River stock raisers should seek incorporation from the legislature, and the Laramie and Albany County stock raisers should not, is puzzling. Also puzzling is the use of the term "rodair" for "roundup" in the Wind River country. Uinta, Carbon, and Johnson counties also formed associations.

At the annual meeting of the Laramie County association on March 29, 1879, it was decided to change the name to Wyoming Stock Growers Association. Two years later the organization invited other associations in Wyoming, western Dakota, western Nebraska, and northern Colorado to merge with it. The Albany County association promptly did so, and others followed in the next few years until in 1885 the Wyoming Stock Growers Association executive committee included five members from Laramie County, three from Albany, two from Carbon, one from Sweetwater, two from Fremont, two from Uinta, two from Johnson, and two from Crook, Wyoming Territory; two from Cheyenne County, Nebraska, one from eastern Nebraska, and one from southern Nebraska; one from Deadwood, Dakota Territory; and one from Miles City, Montana Territory.

The association's influence was so extensive in 1885 that consideration was given to changing the name to Northwestern Stockgrowers Association. The proposal was rejected, said the *Cheyenne Sun*, because it would "involve confusion and confer no benefits." Indeed, the association was already too large. In 1885, Montana members withdrew to form their own association. In April, 1886, the Nebraskans announced their intention to organize their own association, and that year only two non-Wyoming men were elected to the executive committee: T. A. Gage from northern Colorado and Joseph Scott from Montana.

A committee on admissions had the responsibility of investigating applicants for membership and reporting to the executive committee. Three blackballs in the executive committee caused an applicant to be rejected. The committee also prepared a black list, regularly revised, on which were the names of all men whom members of the association were forbidden to employ because they were believed to be of bad character.

CREST OF THE WAVE

Wyoming Territory's cattle boom crested in 1884, 1885, and 1886, when there were 1,500,000 head of cattle worth thirty dollars or more per head. The annual meetings in Cheyenne assumed awesome proportions. In 1884 as many as 500 persons attended the public meetings. In his opening address that year, President Joseph M. Carey greeted the 145 members who answered the first roll call and welcomed special guests: cowboys, representatives of transportation interests, representatives of Chicago commission houses, and Texas suppliers of longhorns. There were 271 active members, compared to 187 a year earlier. Eighty-nine members were admitted, making 360. Thirty-one roundup districts were agreed upon, and confidence in the officers was indicated by their re-election.

The attendance at the 1885 convention was about the same as that in 1884. New members admitted at the convention brought the total to 416, and made the association the largest of its kind in the world, according to Secretary Thomas Sturgis. Thereafter, however, the association began to move downhill. Public resentment mounted. There was a flurry of bad publicity in January, 1886, when prominent member H. E. Teschemacher introduced in the legislature a bill to divert liquor- and gambling-license revenues from the city of Cheyenne to the county. E. A. Slack, usually a friend of the association, blasted the proposal in a *Cheyenne Sun* editorial. He said that most of the territorial taxes already were going for the maintenance of the cattle interest. The *Cheyenne Leader* and *Laramie Boomerang* likewise criticized the association. Upset by the editorials, the executive committee adopted a motion that Slack "be requested to appear before the Executive Committee at once," and committees of two were delegated "to see" the editors of the *Leader* and the *Boomerang*. Editor Slack did not respond to the summons, whereupon the executive committee went to see him. Two days later Slack said editorially that Teschemacher's bill was "an orphan" and "worse off than a maverick." The bill got nowhere. Although Slack was gentle with the association thereafter, other editors did not hold back. Slack had contributed to the public image of the association as a selfish monopoly trying to run the territory for its own ends.

Evidences of association weakness appeared in the 1886 convention. "About 100" members responded to the opening roll call. Secretary Sturgis reported that the list of unpaid dues assessments was unusually long, with 109 names on it. The association was $10,000 in arrears.

Nevertheless, the greatest membership of the territorial period was attained at the end of the 1886 convention when 38 members were admitted and 11 were dropped, leaving a net of 443. Eighty members were lost during the ensuing year, leaving at the 1887 convention a membership of 313. At the close of that convention, 24 new members were added, making a total of 387.

Membership in the association dropped rapidly after 1887 to only 68 in 1890. Only small assessments could be levied, and the annual dues were cut from ten dollars to five dollars in 1889. There was even talk of disbanding altogether in the 1889 and 1890 conventions. J. M. Carey told the 1889 convention: "We must take steps to promote this business in which we are engaged, and the best thing is to open the doors and get in all the small ones who want to join the association. We need them and their help." Others were less eager to welcome small cattlemen, and the latter did not come forward with applications for membership.

The problem of protection against theft persisted. W. C. Irvine told the convention in 1889: "When it comes to protection, we will have to put our hands in our pockets and protect ourselves."

Getting the Land

Usually about forty acres of land per cow is needed for a Wyoming ranch, since the grass is sparse except in irrigated hay meadows. Five-thousand-acre units may be satisfactory; 160-acre units are hopeless.

In the 1870's, pioneer cattlemen depended almost entirely on free use of government land. Only one-seventh of Wyoming's land had been surveyed by June 30, 1880. The territory had only the Cheyenne Land Office, 1870–1877. Other offices were opened at Evanston in 1877, Buffalo in 1888, and Lander and Douglas in 1890. At these offices, under various laws, pioneer cattlemen acquired title to small amounts of land along streams where they established their headquarters.

The Pre-emption Act of 1841 and its later amendments entitled citizens, or those who had expressed their intention to become citizens, to squat on public land, surveyed or unsurveyed, until it was put up for sale, when they had first chance to buy up to 160 acres at $1.25 per acre ($2.50 within a railroad land grant). The patent was issued under the Land Purchase Act of 1820, not under the Pre-emption Act.

Under the Homestead Act of 1862, any person who was the head of a family or had arrived at the age of twenty-one, was a citizen of the United States or had filed his first papers, and who had never borne arms against the United States government or given aid and comfort to its enemies, was entitled to enter up to 160 acres of unappropriated public lands. He had to make affidavit that his entry was made for the purpose of actual settlement and cultivation, and not directly or indirectly for the use or benefit of anyone else. He had to maintain residence for five years. Commutation was possible after six months (later changed to fourteen months)—that is, he could buy for $1.25 per acre ($2.50 if within a railroad grant) and thus avoid further residence and cultivation requirements. An amendment in 1872 gave honorably discharged Civil War Union veterans the privilege of deducting their months of service from the five years of residence. Fees had to be paid for homesteads, but they were trifling, varying from $18 to $34. More onerous for some settlers was the necessity of bringing two witnesses at the time of final proof.

Under the Timber Culture Act of 1873 a person could get 160 acres free, paying the same fees as under the Homestead Act. To get 160 acres under the Timber Culture Act, one had to plant and keep growing forty acres of trees for eight years. In 1878 the required acreage of trees was cut from forty to ten acres. Joseph M. Carey in 1883 filed on a 160-acre timber claim twenty-five miles north of Cheyenne. In 1885 he planted 30,000 white ash, white elm, and box elder trees, which, according to his testimony, all died despite cultivation and irrigation. He blamed drought and hail. He then replanted with 27,000 cottonwood trees, virtually all of which died. After other replantings, he testified in 1896 that he had from 1,000 to 1,200 trees growing, of which not more than 400 were in healthy condition. On the strength of his claim that he had made every reasonable effort to comply with the law, and his claim that on the basis of his own experience and the experience of many others it was impossible to comply with the law "as the conditions exist in the arid region," he was given the patent in 1896.[7]

In getting his timber claim patented, Carey was one of the lucky few. Of the 3,123 original Timber Culture Act filings in Wyoming, only 333 led to final entries under the law, and 125 were commuted. Often in Wyoming and elsewhere, filings were made with no intention of ever planting the trees required. A common practice was to file on a homestead and a timber claim side by side. Sometimes the homestead was

---

[7] Carey's timber-claim experience is recorded in detail on Film Roll No. 1, NIS 156, in the University of Wyoming Library, copied from General Land Office records in the National Archives.

later commuted for cash and the timber claim converted to a homestead.

Another act under which Wyoming land could be acquired was the Desert Land Act of 1877. Under this act one could buy up to 640 acres of desert land (land that could not be cultivated without irrigation). For twenty-five cents an acre, the land could be occupied for three years, after which an additional one dollar per acre had to be paid to gain title. Meanwhile, water must be delivered to the desert-land filing and part of it irrigated before patent could be obtained. Unavailability of water partly explains why only 4,148 of the 15,898 Desert Land Act filings in Wyoming resulted in patents.

These were the principal acts under which Wyoming ranchers obtained title to public land in the territorial period. Land scrip issued under various laws was rarely used in Wyoming. The rancher could obtain title to as much as 1,120 acres by combining his various privileges (pre-emption, homestead, timber-culture entry, and desert-land entry) but 1,120 acres was far short of what was required for a successful cattle ranch.

The Union Pacific received in its land grant 4,582,520 acres of Wyoming land, but little of this was patented or put up for sale in the 1870's. The railroad land consisted of the odd-numbered sections in a strip forty miles wide. A cattleman desiring a large block of land probably would have preferred to buy a solid block rather than one interspersed with equal quantities of government land.[8]

The Union Pacific first tried to collect rent from users of its lands and then in 1884 began selling large quantities at prices averaging one dollar per acre. George W. Baxter bought more than 30,000 acres; Francis E. Warren, 125,000 acres; the Wyoming Central Land and Improvement Company, more than 500,000 acres; and the Swan Land and Cattle Company, 549,423 acres. Others bought until most of the Union Pacific land in the eastern half of the territory was in private hands.

Some people in Washington recognized that existing land laws were not satisfactory for livestock men. S. S. Burdett, Commissioner of the

[8] The government directors of the Union Pacific in 1878 recommended an exchange within the forty-mile strip, the government to cede to the company its even-numbered sections on one side of the track in return for the railroad's odd-numbered sections on the other side (Government Documents, Serial 2336, p. 150). This would have left the company with a solid strip twenty miles wide, all on one side of the track. The following year, the government directors reversed themselves, saying that such an exchange "would create endless confusion" (*ibid.*, p. 157).

General Land Office, in his 1875 report to the Secretary of the Interior, urged that grazing lands west of the one-hundredth meridian be offered for sale in large acreages. Leasing large areas, he said, had also been discussed, but he preferred outright sale. He warned that unless livestock men could obtain some kind of tenure, there would be conflict over the public lands.

Historians have paid much attention to Major John Wesley Powell's 1878 report on the arid regions of the United States, in which the famous one-armed student of the West said that arid-region grazing lands are of value only in large quantities. He thought that the ranch unit should be not less than 2,560 acres. He followed up his report by drawing up a bill which would have permitted free 2,560-acre grazing homesteads. He included provision for abandonment of the rectangular system of surveys because he wanted each rancher to have access to water. He also suggested that an irrigated hay meadow should be attached to the dry-land grazing unit. Unfortunately, Congress did not pass Powell's bill.

The United States Public Lands Commission held extensive hearings in the West in 1879 and 1880. The five members of the commission were J. A. Williamson, Clarence King, A. T. Britton, Thomas Donaldson, and Major Powell. They obtained testimony from more than three hundred individuals located all the way from Nebraska to California and from Montana to Texas. The only large organization that supplied testimony was the Wyoming Stock Growers Association. The association met in Cheyenne on November 18 and 19, 1879, to consider a series of questions submitted by the commission. The special meeting was attended by twenty-four members. F. E. Warren, W. C. Irvine, and A. T. Babbitt led off the discussion by favoring maintenance of the status quo. Many members of the legislature also participated in the discussion. All but three of the men present voted against a proposition that occupants of the public lands be allowed to buy the land they were using at five cents an acre, with the proviso that land not bought by the present users within one year would be thrown open to entry by anyone.[9] Unanimously the men present voted against a proposal that occupants be permitted to lease the land they were using for twenty years at the rate of one-half cent per acre per year, and to have the

[9] The minute book says that this resolution lost by unanimous vote, whereas the commission reported that all but three voted against it. In the discussion, Frank Wolcott and N. R. Davis favored cash sale.

option to buy the land at five cents an acre at any time during the twenty-year period. They adopted unanimously a resolution "that in our judgment the interests of stock owners would be best subserved by the continuance of the present system, which permits only the securing of title to small tracts of land."

Wyoming stockmen in 1879 preferred to use free land without paying taxes or spending money for fences. Other westerners interviewed that year by the Public Lands Commission differed about sale and leasing of grazing lands. About one-half of them approved of sale or lease of large tracts, and a similar fraction favored Powell's idea of enlarged homesteads.

In short, except for the Wyoming Stock Growers Association, westerners in 1879 were divided, perhaps about equally, on the question of whether substantial changes should be made in land policies. Many complained that existing land laws were inapplicable to western conditions, but at the same time many others asked the government to leave things as they were. When westerners themselves disagreed so sharply, it is not surprising that Congress took the path favored by the Wyoming Stock Growers Association and let existing laws stand.

Conditions changed rapidly after 1879. Where there had been 450,000 cattle in 1879, there were 1,500,000 in 1885. As the range became overcrowded, the cattlemen realized that they must acquire title to more of the land they used to protect themselves against competitors. Some bought from the Union Pacific or from speculating pre-emptioners. Some exhausted their individual rights under the land laws, then exhausted their ingenuity in seeking ways to get around the laws. Some arranged for their cowboys to acquire land and then transfer title to their employers. The cowboys rarely obeyed the law—they did not reside on the land and cultivate it, but swore falsely that they did so. Fraudulent desert-land filings were made in the names of non-residents for the benefit of the cattlemen. Choice meadowlands along streams were filed on as desert. This could be done because there had been no classification of lands; so land-office clerks often did not know whether the land was desert or under water, mineral, or forest. Much desert land was taken for grazing without irrigating it as required by the law. Sometimes the 25-cents-per-acre down payment was made with no intention of paying the final dollar at the end of the three years. The twenty-five cents provided "a color of title" and so permitted fencing, and the odds were that the land could be used for many years without any questions being asked. There was wholesale perjury, particularly with respect to the fulfillment of residence requirements.[10]

Many of the cattlemen who had opposed change in the land laws now made an about-face. In convention in 1885, the Wyoming Stock Growers Association adopted by unanimous vote a resolution welcoming "any legislation which would lead to a fair and equitable adjustment of this question and which would secure to all stockmen a legal tenure of the lands they use." They made no specific suggestions and probably could not have agreed on what would be fair and equitable.

While land was valuable, water was much more so. Ernest S. Osgood, in *The Day of the Cattleman*, has reproduced a 1904 map showing Swan Land and Cattle Company land holdings running in a narrow strip along Chugwater Creek through six townships in such a way that the company could control much public land on both sides of the stream. Fortunately, however, the company's example was not followed everywhere. Albany County land records, for instance, show that filings from 1871 to 1890 tended to be concentrated along streams, all right, but no strip extended for more than two miles without a break.

That the 1880's brought a revolution in land acquisition practices is evident in the reports of the General Land Office. Only 365 filings were made on Wyoming public lands in the 1870's, as compared with 10,962 in the 1880's. More land was filed on in 1884 than in all the previous fourteen years taken together, and there were many entries in 1885 and 1886 as well. Most of the entries, however, did not lead to patents. At the time of statehood in 1890, not more than 10 per cent of Wyoming land had been patented.

LAND ENTRIES IN WYOMING UNDER THE VARIOUS APPLICABLE LAND LAWS, 1881–1889

(Figures Taken from General Land Office Reports of the Secretary of the Interior, House Executive Documents for Appropriate Years)

YEAR	HOMESTEAD		PRE-EMPTION		DESERT LAND		TIMBER CULTURE	
	Number	Acres	Number	Acres	Number	Acres	Number	Acres
1881	64	9,216	13	1,781	107	34,282	5	784
1882	123	17,387	26	3,067	102	33,294	20	2,284
1883	189	27,748	31	4,609	324	139,155	98	14,204
1884	296	44,153	90	14,158	1,109	489,001	321	46,027
1885	298	46,195	179	33,794	1,000	402,000	460	67,243
1886	386	50,477	214	32,598	660	256,450	663	100,167
1887	412	62,334	310	47,646	267	94,490	505	74,989
1888	420	65,959	279	42,244	220	73,782	360	53,260
1889	468	74,712	320	48,408	146	46,638	320	46,985

[10] All kinds of frauds were reported by various special agents who were operating in Wyoming in 1884, 1885, and 1886. Some of their reports are available on Film Roll

FENCING

Bothered by too many competitors and worried about cattle diseases, the cattlemen in Wyoming and elsewhere in the early 1880's began to erect barbed-wire fences. They included much public land within their fences. Those who bought Union Pacific land often included much government land rather than fence alternate sections.

The federal government instituted proceedings against unlawful fences in 1883, even before it began canceling fraudulent land entries. M. C. Brown, United States attorney for Wyoming, received instructions in January, 1883, to proceed against ranchers who were unlawfully fencing government land. He brought suit against Alexander H. Swan and won the suit before Chief Justice J. B. Sener. He then brought suit in December, 1883, against John Hunton and H. B. Kelly. However, influential cattlemen and Cheyenne attorney W. W. Corlett blocked Sener's reappointment in 1884. Before the fencers could enjoy their respite, they learned that the federal government meant business. The Commissioner of the General Land Office reported on March 14, 1884, to the United States Senate that "in Wyoming one hundred and twenty-five large cattle companies are reported having fences on the public lands." Then in November, 1884, Grover Cleveland was elected President, and he was more interested than Hayes had been in regulating fencing and enforcing land laws. His hand was strengthened by an act of Congress of February 25, 1885, before he took office, forbidding fencing the public domain. Brown and Sener had been dependent on the common law.

More important than the new law was Cleveland's appointment of a crusading Commissioner of the General Land Office, William A. J. Sparks, who opened war on all fronts. His publicity releases were so damning that the eastern press lashed the cattlemen till they cried in pain. A. S. Mercer, editor of the *Northwestern Live Stock Journal* in Cheyenne and cattlemen's mouthpiece, said in April, 1885: "Every Jim Crow paper from New York to San Francisco is . . . branding us bulldozers and thieves." For the next three years, Wyoming newspapers were full of controversy, since Sparks had both friends and enemies.

Investigators gathered evidence, orders were issued for the removal of fences, and suits were instituted. Many fences went down in 1886 after or in anticipation of court orders. Alexander H. Swan, H. B.

Nos. 1 and 2, NIS 156, University of Wyoming Library, copied from General Land Office records in the National Archives.

Kelly, and John Hunton finally, in response to court orders, took down their extensive fences. Special Agent Henry R. Fry reported to Commissioner Sparks on July 7, 1886, that much remained to be done:

Outside of the R.R. limits there are enclosures of public land in all directions from Cheyenne. *Delegate Carey, Gov. Warren* and many others. To enumerate would be to make a directory of the Territory. Some considerable fence has been removed. The largest cattle dealers are in favor of the fences being removed. The Swan Land and Cattle Co. have removed theirs, probably 130 or 140 miles. . . .[11]

In June, 1887, a popular topic of conversation was the arrival at Camp Carlin of forty-six Negro troops from Fort Robinson for employment by Special Agent Edward A. Bowers in the removal of unlawful fences. Although much was said about the Negro troops, it is not known that they ever actually destroyed any fences.

Despite the best efforts of Sparks and his special agents, government land remained under fence in Wyoming for many years. The fencing activities of Francis E. Warren, for example, would be placed under the spotlight in 1906 and 1912 (see Chapter 12). Sparks and his men found that enforcing the 1885 fencing law was simpler than gaining compliance with land laws. He held up final proofs on land filings until his investigators could determine their legality. The hard-working agents certainly earned their $1,500 salaries. Traveling over vast areas of unfamiliar country in all kinds of weather, confused by imperfect surveys, dealing with disappearing witnesses on the one hand and clever lawyers on the other, making occasional mistakes, being subjected to much abuse, getting involved in misunderstandings on all sides, the investigators found life in Wyoming well-nigh intolerable. Special Agent James A. George complained from Cheyenne in January, 1886, that "it is getting to be too much of a practice for men to file complaints, get an investigation started and then for a fee take back all they may have said."[12]

The General Land Office was handicapped by lack of funds. Only a few of many charges were made to stick in the courts. In his 1886 report, Sparks said it appeared that Wyoming cattlemen had hit upon a new device by which they could control large areas along streams. They were diverting whole streams, "ostensibly for irrigation purposes," and cutting off the water supply for settlers. The Pratt and Ferris

[11] *Ibid.*, Film Roll No. 2.
[12] *Ibid.*

Cattle Company was said to have gained control of forty-five miles of land along Rawhide Creek in this way.

The most publicized case was one in 1887 in which Thomas Sturgis, the Union Cattle Company, and the Goshen Hole Ditching Company were charged with having had fifty-five desert claims filed for them by other parties, mostly residents in New York, New Jersey, and Massachusetts. Only seven of the fifty-five entrymen had ever seen the lands on which they filed. The claims covered a strip of land thirty-five miles long. A single furrow was plowed the length of the strip to establish a pretense of irrigation. Thomas Sturgis, secretary of the Wyoming Stock Growers Association until June 30, 1887, was president of both companies.

While the cancellation case was pending, Special Agent Henry R. Fry visited the lands in dispute in November, 1887, and found that although there had been no irrigation before final proof (as required by law), $25,000 had been spent afterward, and some of the land could be irrigated after all. The explanation was given him that the first contractor had been at fault, not the companies. Fry felt that cancellation was still in order, and in December, 1888, the Cheyenne Land Office recommended cancellation in fifty-one of the fifty-five cases. Three years later, in 1891, with both Cleveland and Sparks out of office, the many desert-land filings of the Union Cattle Company and the Goshen Hole Ditching Company were approved for patent. In instances such as this, where large-scale irrigation was honestly intended, the promoters were driven to the use of dummy entries to prevent speculators from filing in the area to be reclaimed.

Among the many Wyoming land-fraud cases, the last to gain extensive publicity in the territorial period was one involving Francis E. Warren. In November, 1881, he had pre-empted a parcel of land at his ranch headquarters eighteen miles northeast of Cheyenne on Lodgepole Creek. He made final proofs on his pre-emption in November, 1884, swearing that he had lived continuously on the land from November, 1882, to January, 1884. He paid $2.50 per acre, the double minimum required within the area of the railroad land grant. On March 25, 1889, two days before Warren was appointed governor for his second term, William Ware Peck, Cheyenne lawyer and former territorial associate justice, wrote a letter to Washington pointing out that Warren had been living in Cheyenne and serving on the city council there during the time, 1882–1884, he claimed to have been living on his pre-emption filing. Peck's letter led to much discussion in subsequent months, but there was no cancellation.

Several Wyoming editors and a good many citizens supported Sparks in 1885 and 1886, but some of them gradually lost their enthusiasm for him. They were pleased to see him strike down the big "land grabbers," but did not like to see him apply all the rules impartially to small settlers.

Two powerful men who had little use for Sparks were Joseph M. Carey and Francis E. Warren. On June 29, 1886, Delegate to Congress Carey spoke in the House of Representatives to defend the cattlemen, who were receiving more abuse in the eastern press than Sparks was getting in the press west of the Missouri River. He insisted that cattlemen "are just as honorable and upright, have as much business honor, love their country just as well as the members of this House." He called "liars and perjurers" those who said that cattlemen and their cowboys were preventing men from settling where they had the right to settle. He admitted that there were land frauds but maintained that there were not enough of them to warrant so much attention. There had always been land frauds, and more frauds had been committed, he said, under the Swamp Land Act in Indiana than were being committed under other land laws in the West. Two months later, Governor Warren, in his annual report to the Secretary of the Interior, scored the administration's policies. He thought rigid enforcement of the residence requirements particularly objectionable and asked for "leniency and liberality."

Commissioner Sparks persisted in his crusade. Although he was thwarted in many ways and sorely frustrated, he caused such a stir before he resigned in November, 1887, that his name was anathema to many westerners, especially Wyoming cattlemen. He canceled so many filings and held up so many patents that the *Cheyenne Sun* concluded that cattlemen had made a serious mistake in attempting to acquire land under existing laws. However, with Sparks retired and with Cleveland replaced by Benjamin Harrison in 1889, land entrymen and fencers enjoyed a period of more sympathetic treatment.

THE MAVERICK LAW

While Wyoming cattlemen were criticized for many things in the 1880's, the Maverick Law of 1884 brought them more abuse on the home front than anything else. In the early years, unbranded animals (mavericks) on the open range were fair game for anyone with a branding iron. Bill Nye wrote of a man who came up from Texas leading a one-eyed steer with one hand and carrying a branding iron in the other. Within a short time he had a herd of three hundred, "the ostensible progeny" of the old steer.

On cooperative roundups, cattlemen often divided mavericks in proportion to the size of the herds owned by men participating in the roundup, except for calves following branded cows, which were given the brand of their mothers.

Dissatisfied with promiscuous use of branding irons and diversity of roundup procedures, the Wyoming Stock Growers Association met in Cheyenne on November 9, 1883, to resolve their difficulties. Afraid of no one, J. H. Hayford commented in his *Laramie Sentinel*:

As nearly as we are able to get at the objects of the meeting it was called for the purpose of devising ways and means by which the "big thieves" could head off the "small thieves."

The bone of contention is the "maverick." Everybody knows just what this means. It has become the custom of the stock men and companies, at each spring roundup to gather up all the cattle they could find which had no brand upon them and divide them up among themselves and put their brands upon them. To such an extent has this been carried on that small stock men have been completely frozen out.

For a good while the big bugs have had this little game all to themselves. "But," says the *Sun*, "a new enemy has arisen." Upon the very natural aphorism of "Like master like man," the cowboys who have long been in the employ of the wholesale thieves and thus learned the profits of this maverick business concluded to avail themselves of this opportunity to "make a stake" and so got brands of their own, and took in their share of the unbranded cattle. This audacious piece of presumption calls the association together. Like the silversmiths of Diana, their craft is in danger, and something must be done. After grave deliberation they resolved to blackball and discharge any employee who shall hereafter presume to go into the stock business on his own account.

Outsiders will probably care but little about this quarrel between the "big thieves" and the "little thieves" further than that it is natural for people to sympathize with the under dog in a fight. Actuated by that feeling we suggest to the small thieves to also organize an alliance offensive and defensive, to stand by each other, and if the big thieves refuse to share alike in the stealing business to come out and tell what they know about the past history of the stock men in these transactions. . . .

As reported in the *Sentinel*, the association resolved to create a black list of suspected stock thieves, who should be discharged and not hired again by association members. The association adopted a resolution advocating that "all rustlers' brands and all stray brands for which there are no known owners be treated as maverick cattle."

Following up on their November, 1883, meeting, the big cattlemen obtained from the 1884 legislature the notorious Maverick Law, which gave the Wyoming Stock Growers Association full control of roundups in the territory and set up procedures for dealing with mavericks.[13] To justify the law, it was said that association members owned 80 per cent of the cattle in the territory.

Accordingly, the Wyoming Stock Growers Association set up thirty-two roundup districts, worked the whole territory, sold the mavericks, and used the proceeds for hiring detectives. In its April, 1885, convention the association surveyed the results. Secretary Sturgis told the convention that "the legislature, in its attempt to make the law universally applicable and popular, made it cumbersome and some of its provisions can be wisely amended at another session." There was much discussion of the law on the convention floor. Secretary Sturgis explained that the legislature had changed the association's bill so that when "the child came forth . . . many members of the association and even of the executive committee who had indicated willingness to be regarded as its parents denied it in toto. They didn't want anything to do with that bastard." In spite of Sturgis' statement, the Maverick Law of 1884 seems to have been acceptable to most members. In that year the association had received $26,074.15 from the sale of 1,971 mavericks, an average of $13.23 each.

Small cattlemen who were not members of the association despised the Maverick Law. As a concession to criticism, C. A. Guernsey obtained adoption in the 1886 legislature of an amendment, approved by the executive committee of the association, which permitted the sale of mavericks by the roundup foreman, either singly or in lots, at his discretion. It was explained in the April, 1886, convention that the object of the change was to allow every man to buy once on his own range, and to buy only one maverick if he was unable to buy more. The roundup practice since 1884 had been to sell mavericks in large lots to big cattlemen.

The change in the Maverick Law seems to have been a concession

[13] In its original form, the association's bill was too much for the legislature to swallow. A clause in the original bill prohibiting all branding or handling of cattle between December 1 and the spring roundups was changed to read "between February 1 and the spring roundups." Eliminated also were provisions placing the burden of proof on the accused, and a provision that a $3,000 certified check must be deposited in advance by anyone intending to bid at the sale of mavericks. After these obnoxious features were deleted, the bill passed the House 17 to 5 and the Council without a dissenting vote. Governor Hale and editor Hayford were among those who said at the time that the bill was fair as passed.

to the smaller members of the association rather than to nonmembers. Very few small stock raisers who were not association members participated in the official roundups. Normally they were not welcome, and they were not eager to give a few weeks of their time to gathering other people's stock on the chance that they might be able to recover one of their own animals.

The 1886 legislature also put into the Maverick Law a provision that had been knocked out in 1884. It was declared unlawful for any person at any time to brand any maverick except on the official roundup under the supervision of the roundup foreman. The association had construed the 1884 law to mean this, but had no specific statutory statement for such an interpretation before 1886.

Discussion in the April, 1887, convention of the Wyoming Stock Growers Association indicated that the Maverick Law had not worked very well. During the past year, 3,446 mavericks had been sold at an average price of ten dollars, the prices varying from one dollar to thirty dollars. More mavericks had been sold than in either 1885 or 1884, but Thomas B. Adams, assistant secretary, reporting for the absent Thomas Sturgis, complained that many mavericks had been left unsold and "allowed to fall into dishonest hands" and that roundup foremen had been careless in performing their duties except in working the range in which their outfits were particularly interested.

Scarcely anyone has ever maintained that in the 1880's the Wyoming Stock Growers Association was solicitous of the rights of small stockmen who were not members. How many cattle the big cattlemen lost to the little cattlemen and vice versa cannot be ascertained. It is doubtful that any non-association cattlemen ever bought mavericks at the official roundups under the Maverick Law. In looking back at the operation of the law, Jack Flagg wrote in the *Buffalo Bulletin* in May, 1892, that cowboys sometimes thought that they could buy mavericks at the official roundups. They were always outbid, said Flagg, but no matter how high the bid had been, no more than ten dollars would be collected from the "baron" or his foreman.

In 1888 the association got the legislature to do what perhaps should have been done in 1884: give the supervision of roundups to a territorial board of live stock commissioners. This had been done in Colorado since 1879 and in Montana since 1884. By 1888 the Maverick Law had scarcely any friends. Only the *Northwestern Live Stock Journal* had a kind word for the law in its expiring days.

Repeal of the Maverick Law and transfer of roundup supervision from the association to the Board of Live Stock Commissioners unfortunately did not work out as well as many had expected. The big cattlemen continued to run the roundups because the board consisted of eight prominent cattlemen, one from each county. The 1888 legislature appropriated no money for the board, making it necessary for the association to provide expense money until the maverick money came in. The commissioners met in April, at the association's convention time, and accepted bids for mavericks to be taken later in the spring roundups. Each bidder offered a per-head price that he would pay for all mavericks in his roundup district. It was hoped that the territory could take in enough money from the sale of mavericks to support the activities of the Board of Live Stock Commissioners and pay inspectors and detectives. Very little money actually came in, however, because the cattle industry was in terrible shape after the winter of 1886–1887. The 1890 legislature then appropriated $10,000 to maintain the Board of Live Stock Commissioners with the understanding that proceeds from the sale of mavericks would be turned in to the general fund as an offset to the $10,000 appropriation. The proceeds from the sale of mavericks in 1890, however, approached the vanishing point. Apparently, there was virtually no competition among the bidders, who, as a courtesy to one another, agreed to take most of the mavericks at prices of one and two dollars. This prompted the *Laramie Sentinel* to quip: "As the Stock Association has fixed the value of mavericks at from one to two dollars, stealing them will hereafter scarcely be a misdemeanor. Get your branding iron quick."

Prices and Marketing

It is often said that enterprising individuals could gather thousands of unbranded cattle in southeastern Texas at the end of the Civil War and become owners of great herds at virtually no cost. Nevertheless, most Wyoming cattlemen bought their Texas cattle at ten to fifteen dollars per head in the 1870's and often for more than that in the 1880's. Contractors attended meetings of the Wyoming Stock Growers Association and offered to deliver animals in Texas or Wyoming. Usually the cost was about five dollars more per head in Wyoming. Oregon and Washington cattle and "American" cattle from the Middle West cost somewhat more than the Texans. Once in Wyoming, these stockers from outside became foundation herds, and their descendants, after crossbreeding, became known as "natives." "Wintered" Texans brought better prices than Texans direct from Texas.

The great boom of the 1880's might have come sooner had Chicago prices been better in the 1870's, but they were never exciting in that decade. Then in 1881 and 1882, prices improved markedly and remained high in 1883 and 1884. It was this improved price level of 1882–1884 that brought Tom, Dick, and Harry into the Wyoming cattle business. Then, as might be expected, prices declined until in 1887 they were little more than half what they had been five years earlier.

Cheyenne newspaper files supply information about the prices received by individual shippers, as well as summaries of Chicago quotations. The pattern is not simple because Wyoming cattle marketed in the 1880's were variously classified as Americans, Wyoming Texans, wintered Texans, half-breeds, Wyoming natives, stockers and feeders, Oregons, cows, and tailings. Generally the Texas cattle shipped from Wyoming averaged about 1,000 pounds, while non-Texans averaged 1,200. Non-Texas cattle usually brought slightly more per pound than Texas stock. Virtually all Wyoming cattle were marketed in August, September, and October. The prices received for carload lots of Wyoming cattle from August 15 to November 1 varied from year to year as follows:

Year	Extreme Price Range per Cwt.	Price Received per Cwt. for Bulk of Cattle Sold
1882	$3.25–$5.75	$4.00–$5.00
1883	3.60—5.00	4.00—5.00
1884	3.00—5.40	4.00—5.00
1885	2.25—5.15	3.00—4.00
1886	2.25—4.40	2.75—3.25
1887	1.00—3.90	2.00—3.00

Chicago was the great livestock market in the territorial period, although South Omaha began to attract many Wyoming shippers after its yards were opened for business in August, 1884, and St. Paul took a smaller portion. In one exceptional year, 1888, Wyoming cattlemen shipped 126,355 head to South Omaha, 114,490 to Chicago, and 102,209 to St. Paul, but otherwise Chicago led.

DETECTIVES AND INSPECTORS

One of the main reasons for organizing and maintaining the Wyoming Stock Growers Association was to protect members against theft. Beginning in 1874 with one detective, T. M. Overfelt, the force gradually grew until there were twenty-one inspector-detectives in 1885. Laramie, Albany, Uinta, Johnson, and Crook counties paid part of the salaries of some of these men. N. K. Boswell, former sheriff of Albany County, became chief of detectives in November, 1883, at $200 per month plus expenses. It was claimed that no lawbreaker ever got away from this relentless, shotgun-carrying officer. Equally formidable, more feared than respected, was the cold-eyed killer Frank Canton, who served two terms as sheriff of Johnson County, 1883–1887, and worked for the association before and after those years. On April 1, 1887, he became the chief detective for all of northern Wyoming at a yearly salary of $2,500 plus expenses. Other detectives and inspectors received $100 to $150 per month.

The work of association inspectors and detectives overlapped, and the terms were often used interchangeably. No doubt the inspectors at shipping terminals saved more cattle for association members than did the detectives seeking evidence out on the range or in saloons and poolrooms. Strays found in shipments were sold separately and the proceeds remitted to the association, to be credited to the owner, if a member, or otherwise to be added to the association's general fund. Inspectors were regularly told: "It is not expected that our inspectors will do work for or give the benefits of the Association to any but members of the *Association*."

Grangers began to cause trouble in the 1880's. In Wyoming they were less often farmers than small cattlemen trying to become big cattlemen. Inspector Frank Canton, who was running for sheriff of Johnson County, intending to resign from his association job, wrote in 1882: "I expect to have a very heavy race to run, as my opponent is a granger and that element has the majority in this county." He won a contested election and watched the small settlers closely thereafter.

Another granger community developed around Lander. Inspector A. M. Sparhawk wrote from there in 1885: "My reasons for asking for this [more pay] are these, first this country is settled with farmers and small stockmen and when I stop with them, I am compelled to pay for my accommodations."

In the fall of 1886 there was sharp retrenchment after the executive committee at its October, 1886, meeting learned from Acting Secretary Adams that the association's bank account was overdrawn. It was decided to discharge most of the inspectors not working at shipping points. Then in August, 1887, because of a material decrease in the maverick fund, it was decided to cut back the salaries of Boswell and Canton to $150 per month. Other association salaries were cut at the same time. When Boswell resigned, effective November 1, 1887, giving poor health as his public reason, the association's detective bureau was well on the road to collapse.

In December, 1887, the executive committee instructed Secretary Adams to discharge all employees connected with the detective bureau as soon as pending cases had been tried. Two months later the 1888 legislature repealed the statute providing that county commissioners, on recommendation of the county stock growers associations, might appoint one or more detectives, and also repealed the law requiring counties to pay a $250 reward for an arrest leading to the conviction of a stock thief. The detective bureau was dead.

Had the detective bureau been an asset or a liability? A bad man named Middleton is reported to have said that "if the Wyoming Stock Growers Association would let up on him, he did not care for all the sheriffs in Nebraska." The association detectives were not as good as this statement suggests, nor the Nebraska sheriffs as bad. Boswell and Canton had impressive credentials. On the other hand, one detective wrote of another: "He don't know as much about cattle as a hog does of the Bible." The association's correspondence shows unmistakably that some of the detectives were inept, lazy, or not very bright. From time to time such men were discharged. Others were almost too efficient.

Goateed Detective Ben Morrison submitted this laconic report in 1880: "Febr. 13: Left to arrest J. J. McGinnis, captured him at Fort Laramie. On the trip to Cheyenne he attempted to make his escape and met his death. Arrived in Cheyenne February 20." A coroner's jury decided that McGinnis really had been trying to escape when he was shot. After two soldiers who had been close by, though not eyewitnesses, said they thought it was murder, the widow accused Morrison of murder but was unable to convince a grand jury.

No doubt judges and juries were unpredictable in dealing with stock thieves. Punishment was not neatly tailored to the crime. Quipped the *Lander Mountaineer* in August, 1886: "The question now is: if a man for stealing a six dollar pony gets six years at Joliet; one for stealing a $75 horse, three years; and another for stealing a carload of horses, gets but three years; How many would it be necessary for a man to steal in order to escape punishment entirely?"

The "granger" Governor Thomas Moonlight, who might have been expected to be lenient with rustlers, was, on the contrary, an advocate of strict enforcement. In 1888, Louis Peterson and his wife, Anna, were indicted at Lander for stealing "one head of neat cattle." Louis was acquitted, but Anna was found guilty by the jury, which recommended mercy. District Judge Corn sentenced Anna to six months' imprisonment in the penitentiary and imposed a fine of three hundred dollars and costs of the trial. When Anna's attorney appealed to Moonlight for a pardon, the Governor replied that he thought in this case "justice was tempered with mercy," since the maximum penalty was ten years and a fine of five hundred dollars. He wrote: "The Executive cannot allow the sympathy for a woman and a mother to stand between him and lawful, just and merciful punishment." After serving three months in jail, however, Anna was pardoned by Moonlight when two physicians submitted affidavits stating that she was in such poor health that she could not bear a longer confinement.

Anna Peterson's conviction seems to have been an exception. In August, 1888, Wyoming Stock Growers Association Secretary Adams wrote: "Circumstances have forced cattlemen to look to themselves for protection." In the following month he added that "while I would be sorry to see the return of the old days, when it was necessary to defend your property at the expense of human life I am inclined to believe that we shall come to this unless the community insist upon the punishment of cattle thieves through the regular channels of the courts of law." District Judge Saufley said in July, 1889, that it seemed impossible to convict cattle thieves. Editor Hayford, who treated the association with alternate kicks and caresses, was for the moment favorably disposed: "If the courts refuse to protect the property of the stock men they will take the matter into their own hands." Implementation of the do-it-yourself "at the expense of human life" policy will be discussed in Chapter 10.

THE WINTER OF 1886–1887 AND ITS REPERCUSSIONS

Winter losses were a regular part of the open-range cattle business. In every year, the cattlemen were thankful when winter gave way to spring without leaving a scene of great destruction. The common view, said Laramie editor Hayford in May, 1876, was that it is cheaper to lose three or four head out of a hundred than to cut and put up hay, provide shelter, and hire herders. "Laying aside the humanitarian view of the question," he added, "this is probably true." In January, 1880, Hayford reported a rancher's opinion that cattle were suffering from lack of water because no one was keeping the Big Laramie River cut open. Hundreds of cattle were dying because of this "most inhuman act of cruelty." Later reports that winter indicated that cattle in other areas also lacked water.

Townspeople did not have to venture out on the prairie in winter to appreciate the plight of cattle. On February 19, 1881, Hayford described a common winter scene that disturbed him:

There is not a more painful sight in Laramie than the poor starving cattle which are driven into the city from the surrounding country, by the storms and cold, in a vain search for something to eat. They seem to have a sort of instinctive idea, that if they can get where man is their wants will be supplied; and we have seen even the wildest Texas steers with their heads high in the air, their eyes flashing, every look exhibiting terror, yet venturing into the very heart of the city in search of food.

They get little to eat here, but do a great deal of damage, tearing down gates and fences, browsing on our shade trees, etc., and finally lie down and die in the streets. Annoying as it is one can hardly have the heart to throw a stone at one of the poor, starving creatures, even when he sees them destroying his favorite shade trees, which he has been raising for years.

There is we believe, a law which would authorize any person to take up these cattle and feed and care for them and advertise and sell them for the charge, if the owner did not pay for it, and we wish, for humanity's sake as well as the damage they do, some one would do it.

Many accounts of the winter of 1886–1887 have been published. Representative is Professor Louis Pelzer's generalization that "the repeated hurricane blizzards, the heavy falls of snow, and the blood-chilling rains had combined to kill off about one-third of all the northern range cattle." Montana and Dakota suffered more than Wyoming.

A major cause of cattle losses has rarely been mentioned: the inability of open-range cattle to find water. Yet editor Hayford pointed to it in 1880, and Governor Warren reported in 1885 that "probably four times as many cattle die for want of water as for want of food." Governor Moonlight, in his 1887 report, supplied further testimony: "I am convinced from conversations with practical cattlemen and what I have seen that the losses from a want of a sufficiency of water are greater than from a [want of a] sufficiency of food."

In Wyoming the losses probably were not far above 15 per cent. The assessors cut cattle numbers only 15 per cent in 1887, although they reduced the valuation of Wyoming cattle by 30 per cent. Assessors in the major cattle counties cut cattle numbers as follows: Crook, 45 per cent; Carbon, 23 per cent; Albany, 15 per cent; Johnson, 10 per cent; Laramie, 5 per cent. Whatever the death toll may have been, the cattle that survived were in very poor condition and brought little when sold. And certainly the 1887 calf crop was very small.

Had Wyoming, Montana, and Dakota been the only producers of beef in 1887, one could imagine a favorable supply-and-demand situation and high prices at the markets. This was not the case. A combination of debt and despondency on the northern plains and drought in the Southwest and Middle West caused the market to be flooded with thin cattle. A Chicago news release dated October 8, 1887, said: "Never before was so much common stock put upon the market, and at no time within the memory of living man have prices for that class been lower than now." Nevertheless, prices dropped still lower during the two weeks following. Many Wyoming cattlemen who had held their stock the autumn before, because of low prices, could do so no longer, with creditors demanding settlement. They had to unload at giveaway prices. "This was the turning point in the history of Wyoming," Governor Moonlight reported to the Secretary of the Interior in 1888. No small part of the loss was taken by British investors. W. Turrentine Jackson concludes that English investors in the range-cattle industry lost approximately ten million dollars and Scots between seven and eight million, although some of these losses were recovered in the twentieth century.

Thomas Sturgis had urged in 1884 that the cattlemen introduce "system, economy and judgment." Very few of them had done so. Reminiscing in 1923 for *Live Stock Notes*, a Chicago publication, pioneer cattleman John Clay observed that the early cattle business "had a hollow foundation." The crowd at the Cheyenne Club was a cosmopolitan one, he said, "brilliant, resourceful, courageous, but they were deficient in business ability." In their desire to make money fast, they pushed things too hard, took too long chances, and became inextricably entangled in the age-old cycle of boom and bust.

Picking up the pieces afterward took time. An interesting attempt at rehabilitation was the American Cattle Trust, which was organized in 1887 with headquarters in New York. Thomas Sturgis was chairman of the board of directors; Francis E. Warren was the energetic Wyoming manager. The trust, which for a time included many herds, tried to combine various ranges which would not all suffer alike from the vagaries of the weather, hoped to provide economies in range handling, operated feed lots in Nebraska, and aspired to control a substantial part of the market.

Gene M. Gressley has published a full account of the history of the trust.[14] It bought a packing plant for $2,000,000, made contracts for delivery of canned beef to Europe, and worked out involved financial arrangements with cattle companies and individual cattlemen, who were asked to exchange title to their properties in return for trust certificates. At one time the trust controlled 218,934 cattle and total resources of $7,959,071.61. Besides a Wyoming department, there were Colorado, Texas, and New Mexico departments.

Already in July, 1887, Wyoming manager Warren could summarize in a letter to Sturgis the reasons why the growth of the trust was circumscribed: many companies were in too shaky a financial condition to be acceptable; a second group of prospects, expecting a rise in the market, preferred to go it alone; a third group was biased in favor of individual ownership; and finally there were those "who are afraid of change and stay out until they see; those who are suspicious of every thing (and this is an exceedingly large number) and still others who are jealous because they were not first and failed to get prominent positions." He could have added opposition from packers. By 1889 the trust controlled only 164,472 cattle and total assets of only $4,984,762.18. The packing plant was given up that year and returned to its former owner at a loss. In Wyoming the troubles of the trust were exacerbated by a struggle for control between those two old political rivals, Francis E. Warren and George W. Baxter. In 1889, Baxter replaced Warren as trustee. In 1890 the American Cattle Trust failed and was liquidated. As an effort to rehabilitate the western cattle industry, it was a total flop.

Genuine rehabilitation would take many years, and it would be achieved by many men working as individuals. Two years after the debacle, Governor Warren, in his October 15, 1889, report to the Secretary of the Interior, said that the cattle business had "changed quite a little." It represented less than one-half of the territory's wealth as compared to more than three-fourths five years earlier. There were more herds, but of smaller size. Greater care was taken to provide shelter and feed. Management had improved. It would be too much, however, to expect that all abuses had been eliminated. Forty years later, Wyoming's outstanding cattleman and United States Senator

[14] Gene M. Gressley, "The American Cattle Trust—A Study in Protest," *Pacific Historical Review*, XXX, 1 (February 1961), 61–77.

John B. Kendrick, as good an authority as one can find on the subject, said: "We must abandon once and for all the custom at present employed by too many ranchmen, of growing our cattle a part of the year and shrinking them the balance of the year." [15]

ORIGINS OF CATTLEMEN AND COWBOYS

The fact that John B. Kendrick and many of the cattle on the Wyoming range had come from Texas should not be taken to mean that many of the Wyoming cattlemen and cowboys were Texans. The U.S. Census of 1880 (manuscript) for Wyoming lists 311 "stock growers" and "ranchmen," of whom only 2 were natives of Texas. Most of the cattlemen had been born in these states: Ohio (33), New York (29), Pennsylvania (26), Missouri (18), Illinois (14), Indiana (10), Maine (10), Maryland (8), Kentucky (8), and Iowa (7). Most of the 101 who were foreign-born came from these countries: England (29), Canada (19), Ireland (14), Germany (10), and Scotland (9).

Similarly, only 25 of the 669 cowboys who were in Wyoming in 1880 had been born in Texas. Sixty-six of the cowboys were born in Ohio, 58 in Illinois, 58 in New York, 53 in Missouri, 48 in Iowa, 38 in Pennsylvania, 25 in Texas, 23 in Massachusetts, 22 in England, and 21 in Indiana. Smaller numbers of cowboys came from 27 other states, 4 territories, and 13 foreign countries. There were 9 Indian and 2 black cowboys in 1880.[16] The census data give support to Owen Wister's diary entry, July 10, 1885, during his first visit to Wyoming: "Every man, woman, and cowboy I see comes from the East." Most of them probably had grown up on farms.

Many of the cattlemen lived in cities or towns, rarely meeting their hired hands. In 1880, 35 per cent, or 109 out of 311, of the cattlemen lived in cities or towns, 51 of them in Cheyenne.

---

[15] John B. Kendrick file, Western History Research Center, University of Wyoming Library.

[16] George C. Scott, graduate student in history at the University of Wyoming, compiled these data from a typescript copy of the manuscript census preserved in the Western History Research Center. Scattered bits of evidence suggest that the percentages of cowboys from Texas and black cowboys increased slightly after 1880, but accurate data are unavailable because the manuscript census for 1890 was destroyed by fire.

CHAPTER 8

Territorial Life

WYOMING'S CATTLE BOOM did not bring hundreds of thousands of people as did the farming boom just east of the territory. Indeed, the most striking feature of Wyoming development in the 1870's and 1880's was its lack of vigor. By 1890, Kansas had, in round numbers, 1,400,000 people; Nebraska, 1,000,000; Colorado, 400,000; South Dakota, 350,000. Even the laggard Montana picked up more than 100,000 people in the 1880's, while Wyoming added a mere 40,000 to the 20,000 it had at the beginning of the decade. Idaho and Utah also were growing faster than Wyoming.

It was indubitably a hard life in Wyoming—"hell on women and horses" and death on cattle. Governor John W. Hoyt asserted in his

195

1878 report that "Wyoming scenery is a subject for poet and painter" and wrote about "the indescribable charms of a frontier life under sunny skies and in the midst of sublime surroundings," but these charms were not edible.

The young towns in the 1870's were eyesores. In a Congregational Church sermon in November, 1870, the Reverend J. D. Davis gave his impression of Cheyenne (reported in the *Cheyenne Leader*):

> We ought to mourn and languish at the barrenness of our city and its surroundings. . . . We are all mourning that Cheyenne grows no faster, but what is there to bring people here, or to keep them after they are here? A bare, brown, sere, desolate town, with hardly any beauty in it . . . a cemetery which is the picture of the abomination of desolation standing where it ought not, all the dirt and garbage of the city hauled out on the windward side, and left in ugly heaps to be blown back in our faces. . . . I found in my recent visit to the east, that no music in the world had ever been so sweet to my ear as the music of the wind rustling again in the leaves above me.

The shabby, unpainted frame structures (with a few of adobe, logs, or brick) gave way very slowly to more attractive homes. The Chinatowns in Evanston and Rock Springs continued to be shamefully ugly for many years. Old boards, packing boxes, and building paper were basic construction materials, and flattened tin cans were used as roofing. Rows of uniformly ugly company houses in some of the small towns were attractive only when compared with the Chinatowns.

Even in Cheyenne and Laramie the streets remained more or less filthy throughout the territorial period. Hogs and cows had the run of the dirt streets, which were alternately dusty and muddy. Citizens erected board fences to confine their own livestock and to exclude the animals of others. A woman wrote to the *Cheyenne Leader* in March, 1872, complaining that every family had three to five dogs. She often thought she was in an Indian village, as the beasts yapped and tore at her clothes. Rusting tin cans and empty bottles littered vacant lots, alleys, and streets.

In time, cottonwoods and a few evergreens, transplanted from stream banks and mountain slopes, took hold in the recalcitrant soil. In its thirty-odd years of life the coal town of Carbon never acquired trees to shade its sagebrush, greasewood, and prickly pear.

Governor Campbell's diary, 1869–1875, gives many details of the life of a Wyoming man of means and social standing. In July, 1869, he fished for trout on the Little Popo Agie one day and on the Big Popo Agie the next, both days "without success." Like most other Wyoming pioneers, he was not an accomplished fisherman. He had better luck with rattlesnakes, killing four on the road to Fort Laramie. In January, 1872, he went back east to claim a bride in Washington, D.C. He brought her to Cheyenne and installed her in a house which he rented for thirty-two dollars a month until he could build a home of his own. He traveled much on his railroad pass, especially to visit his ranch at Red Buttes, near Laramie. When in Cheyenne, he often worked around the house, once even doing washing all day, and at other times mending fences, varnishing furniture, cleaning house, making a chicken coop, setting a hen, and gardening. A servant helped with some of these things. Campbell's favorite indoor game was whist; favorite outdoor game, croquet. Occasionally he would "ride out" with his wife or friends on summer evenings.

As some of the Cheyenne cattlemen and merchants prospered in the early 1880's, they changed the city's skyline by erecting about forty elaborate mansions. Carey Avenue (originally Ferguson) came to be known as "Millionaires' Row," although not all of the large, expensive homes ($30,000 to $50,000) were placed there. Some of the ostentatious houses were of the heavy Romanesque style of architecture so popular all over the country in the 1880's. A few were mansard style, others were "scroll saw Gothic." A local architect, George Rainsford, drew the plans for many of the Cheyenne structures. There were few novelties and no attempt to adjust the architecture to the Wyoming landscape. Stone, brick, and wood materials were all used, often in combination. Large barns or carriage houses of the same architecture were placed behind the houses. Inside the homes were paneled walls, cut-glass chandeliers, and several fireplaces. The territory's leading merchant, Francis E. Warren, supplied most of the new mansions with carpet, sewing machines, works of art, pianos, and other furniture. The owners planted grass, lilac bushes, cottonwood trees, and evergreens inside wooden fences they erected to keep out livestock and other intruders. The cattlemen built their famous clubhouse in 1880, mainly of brick, at the corner of Seventeenth and Warren. It had a mansard roof, two full-length verandas, and, out front, nineteen hitching posts.

Cheyenne people spent money on churches as well as homes and clubs in the 1880's. In his 1889 report, Governor Warren credited the community with a $25,000 Congregational church, constructed with bricks and equipped with electric lights; a $30,000 Presbyterian church, also of brick, with a pipe organ and three hundred opera chairs, and lighted with gas; a $30,000 Episcopal church, built of stone, with upholstered pews and lighted with gas; and several less expensive places of worship.

As in Cheyenne, homes in other Wyoming towns improved in appearance in the eighties, but only in Cheyenne were many large mansions built in that decade. Laramie cattlemen aped their Cheyenne counterparts by erecting a clubhouse in 1886, but they did not follow them in building great houses in that decade—except for one mansion erected by Ora Haley in 1885. Thanks to an able brickmaker named Pugmire, Evanston was able to use more brick than most other Wyoming towns, though Laramie had a successful brickyard in 1871, and later, in the 1880's, penitentiary prisoners there were put to work making bricks. Native sandstone was quarried near Rawlins and Laramie. Newcastle built permanently of brick and stone in 1889.

With a few exceptions, prosperous cattlemen built small log ranch houses and spent little time at their ranch headquarters. They preferred to live in town, particularly in Cheyenne. In summer, in buggies or buckboards, they visited their ranch properties, leaving their families in town. Mining promoters also lived in towns most of the time. There was, then, little upper-class social life in the Wyoming countryside during the territorial period. Harry Oelrichs was exceptional in that he had a show-place ranch seven miles up Crow Creek from Cheyenne, to which he carried prominent guests, such as Lily Langtry, in a four-in-hand tallyho.

Impecunious homesteaders and prospectors spent more time in the country, although even some of them moved to town in winter in order to earn enough money to hold their claims. Mrs. George Harry Cross has recalled that at the Cross ranch in the 1880's, "life was terribly lonely." Begging squaws abandoned by their white husbands and a few gypsies were her only visitors. Another Douglas-area pioneer remembered that in the mid-1880's when his father made weekly trips to Fort Fetterman (seven miles away) for the mail, "Mother cried until he returned. She was afraid he would be killed."

In her two-volume *Women of Wyoming* (Casper, 1927–1929), Mrs. Cora M. Beach included many biographies and a few autobiographies. Mrs. Henry T. Gray, who lived in a "black shack" seven miles from Lusk, wrote: "My story is the story of perhaps more than one-half of the women on the ranches in those early days. . . . I fought bedbugs and flies all summer, scrubbed rough plank floors and mingled my tears with the suds. I learned to make butter and raised chickens." In time, she learned to love Wyoming.

Town life was modified in the 1880's with the introduction of the telephone, electric lights, the phonograph, free mail delivery, and even a street railway in Cheyenne in 1888 (every thirty minutes, drawn by one horse). Telephones came to Cheyenne and Laramie in 1882. J. H. Hayford described the proper procedure: "You ring your bell and it is answered from the central office. You tell him who to connect you with and ring your bell to notify the party and when they answer you tell them what you have to say, and again ring your bell twice to notify the central office you are through."

FOOD

Most of the pioneers in Wyoming ate simple food. In 1862, Lieutenant Caspar Collins was amused to see Jim Bridger cooking his supper. Old Gabe placed a whole jack rabbit and an eighteen-inch trout on two sticks before the fire. When they were done, he devoured them both without benefit of salt or other seasoning, washing them down with a quart of strong coffee. Bridger's fare may be representative for mountain men, but a decade or two later there was greater variety. W. O. Owen recalled a typical meal of the 1870's: boiled potatoes, boiled pickled pork, hot baking-powder biscuits, Crosse and Blackwell's chowchow, molasses, and coffee. While out surveying, he enjoyed hot biscuits and syrup, frying pans full of antelope steak, canned corn and tomatoes, stewed peaches with Gail Borden's Eagle Brand condensed milk, and pie. Roast beef and browned potatoes were popular. People ate much wild game—elk, deer, and, especially, antelope. The pioneer cattleman A. S. "Bud" Gillespie has recalled that his father went out every Sunday to kill an antelope, which he cleaned, covered with cloth, and pulled up to the top of the meat pole in the ranch yard for regular reference during the following week. The Colorado State Historical Society has published *Pioneer Potluck*, which gives 115 pioneer recipes, as valid for Wyoming as for Colorado. Included are recipes for beaver tail, son-of-a-gun stew, and Rocky Mountain oysters.

For the few who could afford such luxuries, markets in winter offered such "fresh" items as salmon from California, codfish from Boston, oysters from Baltimore, lake trout from Chicago, turkeys and chickens from Nebraska, and vegetables and fruits from California. In summer they had home-grown vegetables. Mrs. E. A. Stone remembered that Chinese trotted through the streets of Evanston offering "lettucie, cabbage and ladishee," as well as peas and root vegetables.

Exceptions to the general rule of plain food can be found on a few special occasions. At the grand opening of the Inter-Ocean Hotel in Cheyenne in September, 1875, not a few poorly spelled French words had crept into the long menu. Yet local foods were not neglected, for several Wyoming game items were included, and other items appear to have been old stand-bys in disguise.

MEDICINE

The territory had thirty physicians and surgeons and four dentists in 1880. After a survey, a Cheyenne physician reported in January, 1884, that there were about fifty healers in the territory—thirty of the regular school, fifteen homeopaths, and five eclectics. His questionnaire sent to Rawhide Buttes elicited the following response: "No balm in Rawhide. No physician here. An occasional suicide seems to be the only exit hence." From Sherman he got the reply: "Jesus Christ is all the physicians in this camp. Old school."

Many small children died of scarlet fever and diphtheria. Counties provided care for indigent transients, many of whom were described as suffering from the intemperate use of alcohol.

Year in and year out in territorial Wyoming a major destroyer of human life was the Union Pacific Railroad. Locomotive boilers exploded. Low-roofed snowsheds, known as "man traps," cracked the skulls or broke the necks of many brakemen. Trains often collided head on; less often there were rear-end collisions. Paying passengers as well as tramps bumming rides fell between the cars.

HOLIDAYS AND SPECIAL DAYS

Citizens of the territory observed the holidays they had been accustomed to celebrating in the states whence they came. On Memorial Day, Grand Army of the Republic veterans marched to the cemetery for a program featuring an oration. In the fall, celebration of Halloween seems to have been limited to harmless fun until the 1880's, when hoodlums began destroying property. The *Cheyenne Leader* noted in 1887 that front wheels on vehicles had been exchanged with back wheels, "and what a confusion of gates." In 1888 the *Leader* reported sidewalks torn up, ash barrels misplaced, and butchers' hooks decorated with dead cats.

Christmas seems to have been observed much as in recent years, with special programs in churches, exchange of gifts, and dinner parties.

Firemen sometimes sponsored Christmas Eve dances. New Year's Eve, too, was celebrated in modern fashion.

The Fourth of July was the great secular holiday, requiring elaborate plans, although certain features appeared again and again. Citizens were usually awakened between three and four in the morning by cannon, small-arms fire, firecrackers, and torpedoes, after which steam-locomotive whistles and bells greeted the dawn. Soldiers sometimes fired artillery salutes at sunrise and at noon. Two indispensable ingredients of a proper Fourth of July celebration were the display of flags and bunting and the reading of the Declaration of Independence. Prominent citizens, nearly always men, were chosen as readers.

The oratory flowed almost as freely as the whiskey. Editors had little to say about the oratory except on rare occasions. In 1870 the *Cheyenne Leader* noted that Judge Howe's address was "out of the usual line of Fourth of July buncombe and grandiloquent rhetoric," and in 1890 the *Leader* observed that the "Fourth of July has been made of late years the excuse for so many tiresome oratorical efforts of fervid patriots . . . that any attempts to draw new lessons from the day are often put down as buncombe."

Regular parts of the festivities were parades, band music, patriotic songs, barbecues, rainstorms, shooting matches, horse races, and a great variety of athletic contests: sack, foot, wheelbarrow, and hurdle races; jumping; putting the stone; vaulting; and throwing the hammer. Commonly, men and boys tried to climb a greased pole to win a reward resting on top. Often a shaved and greased pig was released and a reward offered to anyone who could capture it. There were a few baseball games. South Pass City and Atlantic City clashed at South Pass City in 1870. Fort Russell and Fort Sanders offered baseball competition for Cheyenne and Laramie teams, with scores in the thirties not unusual.

Beginning in the late 1870's, firemen's tournaments became a regular feature of the celebrations, there being straightaway races and more complicated hook-and-ladder and water-test contests. A town of any size had a hundred or more volunteer firemen in two or more companies. At Cheyenne in 1880 the Denver firemen claimed that when they competed in the water test the pressure was much less for them than it had been for the Cheyenne team, making it necessary for them to wait four seconds for water. They objected, furthermore, to having all judges from Cheyenne.

Of course there were accidents. At Laramie in 1876 a whirlwind struck the ladies' stand, brought down the awning and its supports, and inflicted several scalp wounds.

Certain features which would be introduced in Wyoming celebrations of the Fourth in the 1890's were strangely absent in the territorial period: cowboys and cowgirls on horseback, "Wild West" events, bicycle races. There were many horses and a few dozen bicycles, and many riders for them, but they were not incorporated into the parades. Clifford P. Westermeier has noted that Cheyenne had steer riding on the Fourth in 1872, but this was certainly an exception in the territorial period.

Invariably there was a dance in the evening, sometimes lasting till morning. The volunteer firemen, who dominated the celebrations more than any other group, usually sponsored these dances, making some money for their organizations. Occasionally there were fireworks displays in the evenings.

For adults there was much unpleasantness associated with the annual Fourth of July observances. "The celebration . . . is over—Thank heaven," wrote Editor Hayford in 1879. In 1885 he commented at somewhat greater length:

It was about like all Fourths of July. Small boys whooped and yelled, exploded firecrackers and torpedoes, and grown people stood around, wishing it was over. . . . The Fourth of July is the hardest day in the whole year, and everybody except boys—children—dreads it for months ahead, and looks back to it with horror for months afterwards. . . . As it is, the Fourth of July is a "holy-terror," and ought to be abolished.

Hayford recommended "more sensible" observations—go into the country, he said, ride, row, picnic, hunt, fish, get together in families, have a nice dinner, play croquet, swing in hammocks.

A Man's World

The scarcity of women was a striking characteristic of territorial Wyoming. In 1870 there were six men aged twenty-one or over for every woman aged twenty-one or over. In 1880 the ratio of males to females of all ages was 2.56 to 1; in 1890, 2.59 to 1. George B. McClellan, pioneer cattleman from Big Trails, Washakie County, in his later years was wont to say that from 1877 to 1883 he never saw a white woman and that "barbed wire and women are the two greatest civilizing agents in the world." No doubt women are greater civilizing agents than barbed wire. The dearth of wives and children affected Wyoming social life in many ways. Single men paid the piper and called the tune for most of the forms of relaxation.

PROSTITUTION

There were many prostitutes and not a few pimps in the territory. The hell-on-wheels towns were full of them in 1867 and 1868, and new towns that sprang up along the Chicago and North Western in 1886, 1887, and 1888 had their full quotas, as did Newcastle on the new Burlington line in 1889. With the continuing preponderance of single men, it was to be expected that many "soiled doves" could be found in Wyoming towns and at rural "hog ranches." A widely read author, J. H. Beadle, in the 1881 edition of his book *Western Wilds and the Men Who Redeem Them*, stated that Wyoming had three hundred prostitutes. Beadle's count may have been high, yet affairs of the prostitutes, and frequent brawls in their houses, provided much newspaper copy.

A few editors and ministers of the Gospel objected publicly to the licensing of prostitution. Editor Bristol of the *Wyoming Tribune*, asked in March, 1870, two years after the hell-on-wheels days: "Why is it that we can look about us and see so many of noble, talented young men ... apparently rushing headlong to ruin?" Prostitution, he said, "is the gate to Hell."

Opposition to licensed prostitution gradually grew stronger. In 1884 the legislature passed a law making it a misdemeanor to keep a house of prostitution. This statute may have given a few landlords pause, but it certainly did not eliminate the vice.

Hayford of the *Laramie Sentinel*, a Presbyterian deacon, never let up on prostitution and other forms of vice, but quite consistently found the majority of voters in opposition to his views. Merchants normally took the view that there would always be prostitution, especially in a society with so many single men. They thought, too, that they would lose business to other towns if their own city failed to provide prostitutes for cowboys, timber workers, and freighters.

In the late 1880's Cheyenne's "row" was no longer in the heart of town. In Laramie and Casper, the prostitutes were driven off the principal streets in 1889.

Most famous of Wyoming's prostitutes was Martha Jane Canary (or Cannary), better known as Calamity Jane. Some people assert that there were three Calamity Janes, because the name appears so often in the press, and over such a wide area, that there must have been more than one girl so designated. The best-known Calamity Jane was the one who died and was buried in Deadwood, South Dakota, in 1903. There are those who think she was a beautiful and romantic heroine. On the other hand, several scholars who have looked closely at the facts of her career have concluded that she was a mannish, hard-bitten prostitute whose sordid life has been glamorized beyond recognition. In *Burs Under the Saddle*, Ramon F. Adams labels fictional much of the history written about Calamity Jane.

DRINKING

Social drinking was the rule among men of the territory, as elsewhere in the country. Said the *Cheyenne Leader* in October, 1871: "The social use of the intoxicating glass, so universally practiced by the American people, is the one damning characteristic of the age in which we live." Wyoming Stock Growers Association President (1890–1895) John Clay, who came to Wyoming in 1884, later recalled: "Looking back it seems worse than wicked to think of the amount of bad whiskey and very poor beer that we managed to drink and digest in those days."

At the end of the hell-on-wheels era the number of saloons declined briefly. The Census of 1870, however, shows that selling drinks remained the major service industry. In Cheyenne's population of 1,450, there were 27 saloonkeepers, 4 brewers, 7 wholesale liquor merchants, 9 barkeepers, 3 liquor-store clerks, and 2 "tobacco and liquor merchants." Even South Pass City's 460 people included 7 retail liquor dealers, 3 brewers, and one wholesale liquor dealer.

What did the men drink? Bourbon whiskey at ten or fifteen cents a drink or beer, for the most part, and some gin, wine, and brandy. Christmas brought eggnog and Tom and Jerries; society weddings required champagne. Many people consumed widely advertised alcoholic bitters and tonics. Dr. Thomas Maghee of Fort Washakie complained in his 1871 diary that "this habit officers have of drinking hospital liquors is the most trying that I have to meet." Cheyenne Club records show that the cattle barons and their guests consumed vast quantities of Geisler champagne, St. Cruz rum, Zinfandel claret, Old Tom gin, and Red Dog whiskey.

The first legislature in 1869 provided for Sunday closing of saloons, but the 1871 legislature repealed the poorly enforced statute. The 1882 legislature ordered the saloons closed from 10 A.M. to 2 P.M. on Sunday in towns of five hundred or more people and made it unlawful to sell or give away liquor between sunup and sundown on election day. City governments on rare occasions tried to extend the closing to all

day Sunday. When cattle were loaded, shipping points such as Pine
Bluffs, Cheyenne, Laramie, and Lusk resounded night after night with
the drunken revelries of cowboys. Cheyenne prostitutes regularly
migrated to Pine Bluffs for the fall shipping festival.

Railroad workers, coal miners, and soldiers apparently drank just as
hard as the cowboys, and more regularly. Mingling with them were
assorted transients and men of the town. Hardbitten freighters hauled
liquor to communities away from the railroad. In his "In Old Wyoming" column in the *Wyoming Tribune* on May 4, 1940, editor John
Charles Thompson recalled:

Wherever white men went in the pioneer period whisky went with them or soon
followed after. . . . A very considerable volume of the freight which was dragged
from Cheyenne to the [Black Hills] gold fields by mules and "bulls" consisted
of "liquid goods," much of it "rotgut." . . . The fluid shipments suffered considerable shrinkage. . . . Mule-skinners and bull-whackers equipped themselves
with an implement known as a "Freighter's corkscrew." This was simply an
ordinary gimlet but its utilitarianism was perverted to a usage the inventor of
the gadget thought not of when he conceived it. When the pilot of a consign-
ment of whisky craved alcoholic beverage to wet a throat coated with the
heavy dust of the trail he used his "corkscrew" to bore a hole in a barrel,
inserted a straw in the opening and sucked. Between sucks the hole was sealed
with a wooden plug. Just before journey's end this plug would be driven in
firmly, cut off flush and the exposed end smeared with dirt until it was the
color of the wood of the barrel. . . . Reasonable violation of a whisky cargo was
not regarded by the freighting ilk as dishonest but as a legitimate levy by those
who took the risks of transporting merchandise through a region infested with
Indian hostiles and road agents. . . . Consignors and consignees tolerated
shrinkage of the contents of a barrel as a necessary evil so long as it wasn't
overdone.

Several saloonkeepers became leading citizens of the territory. Luke
Murrin served as mayor of Cheyenne. J. W. Connor was elected mayor
of Laramie. Most successful and most esteemed of the pioneer saloonkeepers, however, was Harry P. Hynds, who came to Cheyenne from
Illinois as a young blacksmith in 1882. He was a prize fighter on the
side, and soon started a gambling saloon, the famous Capital. Later he
opened other gambling houses in Laramie, Rawlins, Rock Springs, and
Salt Lake City. In 1896 he killed a socially prominent Salt Lake City
man whom he found with Mrs. Hynds in the Utah city. In his statement for the defense, Hynds's lawyer said that Hynds had married
Maude Peet, "who had entered upon a sporting life at Denver. He
loved her, married her, and made a woman of her." Hynds was

acquitted, obtained a divorce, and remarried. In later years he switched his investments into real estate, the hotel business, and oil. He died in 1933 worth more than one million dollars. The *Wyoming State Tribune* declared after his death that "the career of no other Wyomingite of the last 50 years was more colorful or romantic." Forty-two honorary pallbearers at his funeral included a United States senator, congressman, state governor, chief justice of the state, a federal judge, and the mayor of Cheyenne. Hynds obviously had been a man of rare affability, generosity, and courage.

Temperance workers first attracted attention in Laramie, where the Sons of Temperance established a division with thirty-two members in 1875 and a branch of the Murphy Temperance Union was organized in April, 1877, with thirty-three members taking the pledge. Frances Willard, national temperance leader, came to Cheyenne in April, 1880, to organize a chapter of the Woman's Christian Temperance Union. Later that year, chapters were organized in Laramie and Evanston. Territorial conventions were held alternately in Cheyenne and Laramie beginning in 1883. Children's temperance organizations, known as "Bands of Hope," were formed in Evanston and Laramie. In 1884, 125 Band of Hope boys and girls marched in the Fourth of July parade in Laramie wearing red, white, and blue sashes and carrying flags and banners.

Temperance workers in the 1886 legislature tried but failed to extend Sunday closing beyond the four-hour period set in 1882. It was argued that incorporated towns and cities already had the authority for Sunday closing, which was true, and Laramie for brief periods had enjoyed complete closing on Sundays. The *Cheyenne Leader* reported in 1888 that prohibition sentiment was strongest in Laramie and Evanston. Other cities—Rawlins, Carbon, Rock Springs, Green River City—were wide open and so were the new towns in central Wyoming. The Kilpatrick brothers, who in the northeast founded and controlled the coal-mining town of Cambria, allowed no saloons. In short-lived Tubb Town, less than ten miles away, the people in 1889 passed and enforced an ordinance requiring all passers-by to pay "sufficent toll to set 'em up to the bunch."

Legislators were no different from the rank and file of their male constituents. On April 13, 1884, when a temperance lecture was scheduled for the evening, the legislators entrained at 4 P.M. for Salt Lake City to enjoy their biennial excursion at the expense of the Union Pacific. The *Cheyenne Sun* noted that "the excursionists . . . provided

themselves with large quantities of internal caloric before starting."
While as a rule the legislators liked a nip now and then, they passed a
law in 1886 requiring the instruction of physiology and hygiene in the
public elementary schools, with "special reference to the effects of
alcohol and narcotics upon the human system." It must be noted,
however, that this law did not originate in Wyoming. The U.S.
Congress required all territories to adopt such a law.

OTHER ENTERTAINMENT

Rodeos, which have become such an important form of entertainment in the twentieth century, were rare and unimportant in territorial days. Informal riding and roping contests, it is true, were held
on the range and at scattered ranches and constituted an important
part of cowboy amusement, but in the entertainment world of the great
majority of people, they were negligible.

Baseball was more important. True, the playing season was short,
free time was limited, towns were far apart, and no attempt was made
to organize leagues, yet many communities had Sunday baseball.
Church members objected to Sunday baseball but they could not prevent it, and most people accepted the 1887 view of editor John F.
Carroll of the *Cheyenne Leader*: "The enlightened public sentiment of
this country is not inclined to approve of blue laws of any kind."

Football received only slight attention, beginning in the later 1880's.
Rock Springs pioneered in organizing public support for this new game,
raising seventy-five dollars to outfit one of its teams in August, 1888.

The Cheyenne Gun Club enjoyed matches with the Fort Russell
Gun Club, using live and clay pigeons and sometimes glass balls.
Johnson County staged the territory's first fair at Big Horn City in 1885
and held others thereafter at Buffalo. Governor Warren listed Johnson
County products exhibited at the second fair: "In addition to the
excellent showing of domestic animals . . . good sound corn, common
leaf tobacco, hemp, sugar cane, sweet potatoes, wheat, barley, oats . . .
turnips, ten inches in diameter, cabbages as large as a tub, with water-
melons, pumpkins and squashes of equal size . . . crab apples, grapes
and apples over ten inches in circumference."

Cheyenne introduced its first "Territorial Fair" in September, 1886,
on an eighty-acre fairground just west of the city. In livestock exhibits,
which were outstanding, nearly three hundred horses were entered,
including twenty-one Percheron stallions. In 1886 and 1887 the greatest
attraction at the Territorial Fair seems to have been the program of

horse races—trotting, pacing, and running. Competing with livestock and farm produce for attention were exhibits of breads, cakes, textiles, needlework, and art work. Nineteen babies were entered in the 1887 baby show. Close by, athletes worked their way up a 25-foot greased pole while others pursued a greased pig.

SHOWS

There were many variety shows in Cheyenne, especially in the hell-on-wheels days and in 1876–1877 during the Black Hills rush. Seventeen variety halls have been identified in Cheyenne during the fifteen years from 1867 to 1882. The performances normally included dancing, singing, and acrobatic acts and resembled low-grade vaudeville or burlesque. The typical variety theater had entertainment, drinks, and gambling, all in one large room. Over the bar was a gallery where barmaids served select customers. Said the *Cheyenne Leader* in December, 1872: "One half the drunkenness in this town, and Holy God of the Prophets what an amount that one-half is, can be accounted for by the fact that both the Theaters [are poorly ventilated]." Saloonkeeper Chris Fletcher had a variety theater in the little town of Hartville during its copper-boom days in the 1880's. He advertised "Men Only" except on Sunday evenings, when women were admitted to a cleaner performance.

Legitimate drama and operatic music were offered at times but never drew the crowds of the variety theaters. The Richings-Bernard Opera Company offered a repertoire of *Martha, The Bohemian Girl, Il Trovatore, Maritana,* and *Fra Diavola* in Cheyenne in 1877. Otherwise, opera was generally postponed until the 1880's.

As people took root and became less predominantly transient, some of them built "opera houses." The name did not mean, however, that only operas were offered, for in fact other types of entertainment—plays, concerts, and lectures—were far more common. Cheyenne's splendid opera house (built by Francis E. Warren) opened in May, 1882, and became the center of the capital city's theatrical life for the next twenty years. The opening performance by the Comly-Barton Opera Company attracted many leading citizens of Laramie, who came in a special train, and more than fifty special guests from Fort Collins and Denver.

In Laramie, Blackburn Hall, Ivinson Hall, and Männerchor Hall presented traveling companies of various kinds. Blackburn Hall, completed in 1880, had a stage sixteen by twenty-seven feet and an "unbroken floor 45' by 59' capable of comfortably seating 600 persons or allowing room for 80 dancing couples." A new opera house on the third floor of W. H. Holliday's great mercantile store was prepared in 1887, but it proved a failure, both acoustically and structurally, and was soon condemned and closed. Evanston celebrated the erection of a twelve-thousand-dollar opera house on Front Street in 1885.

Theatrical troupes traveling to or from the West Coast stopped off for one-night or two-night stands. Buffalo Bill appeared in Cheyenne two nights in August, 1879, with the play *Maj. Cody, or Lost and Won*, written by Major A. S. Burt. Cody was back in Wyoming in February, 1886, with the drama *The Prairie Waif*.

J. H. Hayford, in his *Laramie Sentinel* in December, 1879, found the musical entertainment too "highfalutin" for his taste: "The music is all 'operatic'—whatever that is—and it sits upon our ears and stomach about as delightfully as the midnight singing of a jackass." But musical professionals, he said, could usually be persuaded to sing as an encore a "good, touching home ballad," such as *The Last Rose of Summer, Way Down upon the Suwannee River*, or *The Old Log Cabin in the Lane*. "Then it is that one's ears begin to sing," he added, and "the electricity goes tingling up and down his back." The *Cheyenne Sun* reported that the high point of an evening's operatic entertainment by Mme Emma Nevada in 1885 came when she sang, in response to repeated requests, *Home Sweet Home*.

Bill Nye was Wyoming's most widely read music and drama critic, though hardly its best. When *The Bohemian Girl* played in Laramie, Nye concluded his review as follows: "Emma Abbott certainly warbles first-rate. . . . But Brignoli is no singer. . . . He sings like a man who hasn't taken out his second papers yet, and his stomach is too large." At other times Nye grumbled about the ramshackle stage machinery and the grimy wigs worn by the stage baldheads.

No doubt Wyoming's Union Pacific towns caught many down-at-the-heel traveling shows which barely made expenses in the territory. The small towns off the railroad—Lander, Buffalo, and Sheridan—had to forego traveling shows, although a troupe offered *Lucretia Borgia* in South Pass City in June, 1868. Lusk, Douglas, Glenrock, and Casper were on the Chicago and North Western in the late 1880's, but this dead-end railroad (ending at Casper in 1888) did not carry the shows which were so common along the transcontinental Union Pacific.

Perhaps the territory's most memorable theatrical performance was in March, 1890, when the Emma Juch Grand Opera Company presented

Gounod's *Faust* in English in Cheyenne. The company of 125 (including orchestra) traveled in a seven-car special train. Said the *Cheyenne Leader*: "Miss Juch . . . is a small woman of shapely form and of healthy appearance, with a sweet face and beautiful hands. Her stage manner is not graceful, but her acting is superb and the voice enchanting as angel whisperings." With respect to the audience, the *Leader* reported that many ladies appeared in "elaborate toilettes," but "only half a dozen men were in the regulation spike tail."

Circuses visited Wyoming towns occasionally. The 1887 Robinson circus was notable for a "thimble riggin" game (the old shell game) by which suckers were swindled at every stop. If the *Cheyenne Leader* can be believed, the nutshell man robbed Laramie residents of more than one thousand dollars, and this led to such a spirited fight between townspeople and circus men that "the sidewalks in the business portion of the town resembled a slaughter house."

ROLLER SKATING

A favorite pastime for the young and a few grownups was roller skating. Cheyenne had a rink in February, 1872, at which time the *Leader* described roller skating as a "moral and exhilarating diversion." Thirteen years later, in March and April, 1885, the sport aroused the ire of editor Hayford in Laramie. He observed that "the skating rink craze has become such a mania throughout the country that the voice of the press, the pulpit and of the medical faculty has been raised in warning." Among other things, Hayford charged that "it brings the virtuous and the innocent into contact with, and under the influence of the rake and the libertine, and scores of virtuous women have fallen by these influences." He was unable to stop the sport, which persisted into the days of statehood, indoors and out, though never again with the enthusiasm of the winter of 1884–1885. Buffalo in 1885 had two busy rinks where soldiers and Crow Indians mingled with the townspeople.

CYCLING

Cheyenne and Laramie argued in the 1890's about which had the older bicycle club. Evidently, Cheyenne won the dispute, since its club was organized in April, 1882, and Laramie's in August of the same year. Cheyenne's club was heralded as the oldest club of its kind west of the Missouri River.

Cheyenne's first velocipede (1869) was described as having two wheels "about the size of those of a buggy, the larger being in front," and having two pedals on the forward wheel. Everybody tried to ride the novelty, and there was much excitement in its wake. Said the *Leader*: "The untamed velocipede continues to travel about town, with one man on its back, and a dozen holding him there."

Laramie's first bicycle was displayed at that city's Fourth of July celebration in 1876. It was "a wooden affair—two carriage wheels, one about four feet, the other eighteen inches in diameter, with iron tires."

By 1882 there were ten or twelve wheels in Cheyenne and a similar number in Laramie. The bicycle clubs organized excursions and races, treasured trophies in their club rooms, and sponsored dances and other entertainments. Rides between Cheyenne and Laramie were common. In October, 1883, three young men from Laramie returned from a bicycle tour of Yellowstone Park "full of exultation and covered with glory and alkali dust." They had traveled by rail to Beaver Canyon, Idaho, close to the western boundary of the park, and then had mounted their wheels to visit major points of interest.

By 1890 bicycle races appeared on Fourth of July programs, and according to the *Laramie Sentinel*, "bicycling is the popular rage here now and everybody including children, ladies and old grey-headed men, has the disease."

DANCING

The men of the territory loved to dance when they could find female partners. Down in Nebraska, according to Louise Pound, the "best families" in the small towns and rural communities never danced in pioneer days. This was not true for Wyoming, where E. E. Dale's generalization for the cow country as a whole is more appropriate. Dale suggested that dancing was at the two extremes of cow-country society, the primitive and the sophisticated, and that the churches tabooed dancing. Even Dale's statement does not really fit Wyoming, where most people had no scruples about dancing. Most of them had no church affiliation, and among the church members the Catholics, Episcopalians, and Mormons danced, while Baptists, Methodists, Presbyterians, and Congregationalists normally did not.

In Laramie and Cheyenne the Conductors' Brotherhood sponsored dances which were not soon forgotten. On Sunday night, March 4, 1878, nearly two hundred couples attended the Conductors' Brotherhood grand ball at Laramie. A special train brought guests from points as far east as North Platte. Division officers of the brotherhood were in "richly embroidered regalia." Not all could dance at once—there was room for only thirty-six sets of quadrilles at a time. The last dance, a waltz, *Home Sweet Home*, ended at 4:45 A.M. Said the press: "The ladies' toilets were, without exception, the most elegant and tasteful ever seen at a ball in Laramie. The gentlemen dressed in the height of Eastern fashion."

Mont Hawthorne, who was in Carbon from 1881 to 1883, has recalled lying in bed and listening to the "Lankies" (coal miners from Lancashire, England) dancing Saturday nights till daylight to fiddle music.

There is no evidence to suggest that cowboys took part in the "society" balls of the territorial railroad cities, although they undoubtedly appeared quite often in the honky-tonk dance halls connected with saloons and variety shows.

In his autobiography, Congressman Frank Mondell described the party he attended at Christmas, 1887, at Cambria in northeastern Wyoming:

It was a merry party, and after a bountiful dinner the tables were moved back, and to stirring strains from the harmonica of Hans and Old Bill Jones' fiddle, we danced good old fashioned square dances on the rough, unplaned floor. There were only seven women, so to make two "fours," Big Mike, his strong right arm bedecked with a red bandanna as a distinguishing mark, became the extra "lady." And thus the dance went on, until breakfast was served and our party came to an end as, in the clear cold of the early morning, we bade our guests good-bye.

Mrs. Mary Merritt, who came to Douglas as a bride in 1888, has recalled that in her dancing club the men wore swallow-tailed coats and white gloves; the ladies, full evening dress (home made). She remembered also Colonial dance parties and masquerades.

J. K. Howard, in *Montana, High, Wide, and Handsome*, wrote that in that state "dances invariably lasted all night, as they still do in the mountain country." This was not, and is not, true for dances in Wyoming towns and cities, where territorial dances usually ended between 1 A.M. and 3 A.M. On the other hand, country dances at barns, schoolhouses, and homes often continued all night in Wyoming, as elsewhere. The guests preferred to hitch up their teams and depart by daylight, after a bite of breakfast. Some slept for a while in any unoccupied space they could find—the men in haymows and bunkhouses, the women in the house—until noon or later before taking their departure.

Jack Flagg, *Buffalo Bulletin* editor, in June, 1892, recalled the earlier practice of holding weekly all-night dances at Johnson County ranches to break the monotony of the long winters. Everyone came, the women bringing baked meats, cakes, pies, and other food, the men chipping in to pay the musicians, who were usually three in number.

The amount of drinking at dances varied with the community. Certainly exceptional was an incident in March, 1884, when six armed and "liquored up" men crashed a dance on Little Popo Agie in Fremont County, causing an affray in which several shots were fired, the floor manager was struck on the head with a revolver, and three men were stabbed.

An English youth, John J. Fox, who danced to a fiddler's *Arkansas Traveler* and *Turkey in the Straw* at the Elk Mountain schoolhouse in 1885, remembered the experience vividly all his life, partly, perhaps, because there weren't enough girls and he took the part of one. Many years later he recalled that one of his cowboy friends at the dance said that a rancher's daughter present "put on more airs than a stud-horse."

GAMBLING

A favorite pastime for men was gambling, the most common forms of which were poker, keno, faro, wheel of fortune, roulette, and dice. Once in a while special opportunities were offered outside the halls at boxing matches, foot races, and horse races. "Considerable money changed hands," noted the *Cheyenne Leader* in August, 1868, in reporting a horse race between an Omaha horse and a Denver mare. In Laramie in November, 1874, more than twenty thousand dollars was reported to have changed hands at another horse race when miners from Carbon came down in force to support a Carbon horse against a Laramie mare. "The Carbon boys bet everything they could raise . . . and they went home broke." Mont Hawthorne reported that the Lankies of Carbon "never looked ahead to nothing beyond Sunday morning and horse racing and shooting live pigeons on the wing." The Wyoming Stock Growers Association in convention in 1885 adopted a resolution forbidding horse racing and gambling at the roundups, "whereas the racing of horses destroys the usefulness of these animals and also consumes much valuable time."

Although the *Cheyenne Sun* and the *Wyoming Tribune* in 1885 joined the *Laramie Sentinel* in a crusade to curb gambling excesses, progress was slow. An abortive attempt to prohibit gambling was a major issue in the 1888 legislature. "Blue laws will hurt business," argued the

Cheyenne Leader; and Representative Tom Hooper of Crook County shocked the ladies who were listening to the debate when he asserted: "Gambling is an inherent attribute of the human heart. . . . Show me the man who will not gamble in some way and I will show you an imbecile."

In October, 1888, it was reported that Douglas had six monte games, which supplied a monthly revenue of three hundred dollars, besides several poker games. No doubt poker was a popular game in many places besides gambling halls. John Charles Thompson summed it up in his "In Old Wyoming" column: "There have been some gosh-almighty poker games played in Wyoming. Whole herds of cattle, complete ranches, changed hands at the flip of a 'hole card' at a stud table back in the 'good old days' when some very sporty chaps were rated among the 'cattle kings.'"

Gambling indirectly caused Wyoming's most famous congressman, Frank Mondell, to carry a .45-caliber bullet near his spine for most of his life. As mayor of Newcastle in the winter of 1889–1890, he governed what he described as "the banner wide-open frontier town of all the Northwest." By spring, however, when the boom was declining, there were too many gamblers and other undesirables for the needs of the community. Mondell and city council gave the marshal a list of twenty men who must leave town within twenty-four hours, whereupon a hotelkeeper, who had extended credit to some of the undesirables and wanted them to stay until he could collect, shot Mayor Mondell.

PICNICKING AND CAMPING OUT

Picnics in the mountains have always been important in Wyoming recreation. People in all communities of the territory went picnicking in the summer, although slow transportation, or, for many, complete lack of it, limited the possibilities of reaching many areas which later became popular resorts. Bill Nye wrote that he preferred camping out to picnicking:

The picnic is an aggravation. It has just enough civilization to be a nuisance, and not enough barbarism to make life seem a luxury. . . . But to those who wish to forget the past and live only in the booming present, to get careless of gain and breathe brand-new air that has never been used, to appease an irritated liver, or straighten out a torpid lung, let me say, pick out a high dry clime, where there are trout enough to give you an excuse for going there, take what is absolutely necessary and no more and then stay there long enough to have some fun. . . .

It was already getting difficult in the 1880's to find virgin country. Nye noted that "on all sides the rusty, neglected and humiliated empty tin can stares at you with its monotonous, dude-like stare."

HUNTING AND FISHING

For the most part, the pioneers did not hunt and fish, mainly because they lived in towns and cities far from the places where game and fish could be taken and because they had neither the time nor the means of transportation. Evanston was better situated than other pioneer towns, judging by Mrs. Elizabeth Arnold Stone's comment that "poor was considered the marksman who returned from a few hours' ride in any direction with less than a dozen sage chickens. On holidays parties were formed and the buckboards on the homeward trip were piled high with grouse and sage hens to be distributed about the town."

Men who did hunt were often able to take more meat than they could use. Nonhunting townsmen could buy wild meat at reasonable prices in the markets, and sometimes from wagons on the streets. Pat Flannery has published pioneer rancher John Hunton's description of a December, 1875, elk hunt on Deer Creek in which he and Little Bat Garnier killed ninety-seven elk in one day. Most of the animals were brought in and much of the meat was cut up and dried, to be distributed among Hunton's friends at Fort Fetterman and elsewhere. There were many game hogs and hide hunters, judging by newspaper reports of excesses. Game was especially plentiful in northern Wyoming for several years after the Indians were driven out of that area in 1876 and 1877. Thousands of hides were reported sold to the post trader at Fort McKinney and to stores on the Powder River in 1881. In the early 1880's, hide hunters appear to have been active all over the territory, despite an 1875 law making it illegal to kill elk, deer, mountain sheep, or antelope except for food. In 1886 the legislature forbade the shipment of green hides from the territory and declared it unlawful for any person to kill more than two game animals in any one day. Although stock detectives were asked to aid other peace officers in the enforcement of game laws, hide hunting persisted.

Native trout were found in abundance in many parts of Wyoming, but not in the North Platte drainage, where, for instance, Laramie citizens in 1868 thought suckers from the Laramie River were a delicacy. In western Wyoming, the Bear River gained an early reputation for its splendid native trout. In central Wyoming, Dr. Thomas Maghee, who was stationed at Fort Washakie, made this entry in his diary for

July 10, 1874: "Dr. Page was down and got tight and made a fool of himself. He broke my rod, cut my line and lost my flies. Confound him." The heaviest assault upon the native trout occurred in July, 1876, when Crook's army, loafing on Big Goose Creek, caught fifteen thousand, mainly on grasshoppers. Under an 1879 law, a fish commissioner in 1880 began planting eastern brook trout' (and carp) in many streams and lakes, to the delight (and disgust) of future citizens.

CLUBS

In the 1870's a surprising number of business, professional, and political leaders were members of the Masonic fraternity. Governors Campbell, Thayer, and Hoyt; Secretaries Lee and Glafcke; lawyers M. C. Brown, Joseph M. Carey, W. W. Corlett, and S. W. Downey; editors Nathan A. Baker, J. H. Hayford, and Edward A. Slack; merchant prince Francis E. Warren; and perhaps one-half of the legislators were Masons. After lodges had been organized in Cheyenne in 1868, South Pass City in 1869, and Laramie in 1870, the Grand Lodge of Wyoming was founded in 1874 with 214 Masons. Other Masonic lodges were soon organized in Evanston and Rawlins.[1]

Odd Fellows, Good Templars, Knights of Pythias, and national groups of Germans, Scots, Irishmen, and Swedes were also prominent, and the Grand Army of the Republic became so in the 1880's. When a new lodge was proposed in Laramie in May, 1883, editor Hayford thought it might be time to call a halt: "A man of ordinary means can easily join enough to bankrupt himself in paying fees, dues and initiations, and take all his time—night and day—to attend lodges." On January 16, 1885, Governor William Hale's funeral procession in Cheyenne included, besides two bands, several Masonic lodges, AOUW lodge, Odd Fellows, Grand Army of the Republic Post, Sons of Union Veterans, Knights of Pythias, Irish Benevolent Society, and a Pioneer Association.

Cheyenne cattlemen organized their famous Cheyenne Club (first briefly known as the Cactus Club) in 1880, and in the following year built their clubhouse. The membership was first limited to fifty men, the initiation fee was set at fifty dollars, and dues were set at thirty dollars a year. Military personnel were welcome without initiation fee upon payment of thirty dollars in dues each six months. The clubhouse

[1] For the Masonic story, see Julius J. Humphrey, "The Political and Social Influences of Freemasonry in Territorial Wyoming, 1870–1885" (Unpublished M.A. thesis, University of Wyoming, 1964).

had a restaurant, bar, billiard room, reading room, and six upstairs sleeping rooms for permanent or transient guests. By a close vote the members decided not to have a separate dining room for ladies.

Rules adopted to govern the conduct of members suggest what problems the members expected. Grounds for expulsion, as listed, were drunkenness, if "offensive," profanity or obscenity, a blow struck in a quarrel, cheating at cards or other games, commission of a criminal act, and other dishonorable behavior unbecoming to a gentleman. John C. Coble, member from Albany County, resigned after suspension for shooting holes with his .45 in an oil painting hanging in the club. The Cheyenne Club's reading room was supplied with *Harper's Weekly* and *Monthly*, the *New York World*, the *Spirit of the Times* (New York), the *Boston Sunday Herald*, and the *New York Daily Graphic*.

Dress suits, nicknamed "Herefords" for the white fronts, were often worn when ladies were guests at dinners and other evening parties. The annual reception and dance given by the club for Fort Russell and Cheyenne society on June 30, 1887, was described in the *Cheyenne Leader* as "the biggest social event of the season, and in many respects the most notable in the history of the town." This affair was climactic in that the club was about to lose its identity as a cattlemen's club. The building was first taken over by the Club of Cheyenne, then by the Cheyenne Industrial Club, and finally by the Cheyenne Chamber of Commerce, which used it until it was razed in 1936. The cattlemen could not maintain the club after their 1886–1887 losses, and bondholders on the $15,000 building had to accept twenty cents on the dollar.

Laramie cattlemen in October, 1883, organized a club along the lines of the Cheyenne Club. In November, 1885, editor Norman B. Dresser of the *Rock Springs Independent*, after a visit to Laramie, wrote about Laramie's "English lords, who are unmistakably English, but not so unmistakably lordly. They drink plenty of imported liquors, drive fast horses and sport loud cravats, clothes, canes and eyeglasses. We know no reason why these lucky fellows should not enjoy life." In July, 1886, editor Hayford branded the Laramie Club "the lowest and most disgraceful den of infamy in the city." He scored the "carousing, drunkenness and gambling" and was particularly outraged by behavior on the Sabbath.

Possibly the Laramie Club members were noisier than usual on that July day in 1886 because they had just completed plans to build a new clubhouse and may have been celebrating that achievement. The completion of their new clubhouse unfortunately coincided with the collapse of the cattle business, and much of the gaiety noted by Hayford soon vanished. Even hard times, however, could not destroy the peculiar tastes of the few Englishmen who remained on the Laramie Plains after 1887. In 1890 some of them introduced (from Colorado) the sport of "coursing," riding to the hounds in pursuit of jack rabbits, coyotes, and antelope.

In Cheyenne the Young Men's Literary Association was organized in December, 1867. How long the club could maintain the early pace of weekly sessions is not known, but it clearly represented an island of sanity in a pretty mad hell-on-wheels world.

WOMEN'S CLUBS

In the man's world of Wyoming Territory, women's clubs were rare. The *Cheyenne Daily Leader* reported on February 2, 1890, that "one year ago there was but one woman's club in Cheyenne. Now there are five." Thus conditions were changing rapidly as statehood approached. The number of women had increased, and more of them found time for club activity. Among the women's clubs were the Alpha Club, the Beta Club, and the Queen Anne Club. The Alpha and Beta clubs were busy discussing William Cullen Bryant, while the Queen Anne Club ladies were studying Browning.

Cheyenne had its mixed clubs also, such as the Twenty-one, the Pedro Club, and the Social Swim Club. Whist, forerunner of bridge, was becoming popular. Besides the card parties there were high teas, dinners, and dances to keep the ladies busy.

LIBRARIES

In Laramie in September, 1870, lawyer M. C. Brown presided at an organizational meeting for the Wyoming Literary and Library Association. This club, which remained a strictly Laramie organization despite its name, thereafter sponsored occasional debates open to the public, but its major achievement was the assembling of a library, which included one thousand volumes in 1880 and fifteen hundred in 1887.

The territorial library in Cheyenne was primarily for the judges of the supreme court. The 1871 legislature authorized the expenditure of $250 a year for the purchase of books under the direction of the judges. By 1889 the library had more than fourteen thousand volumes.

In 1876, Evanston claimed a "healthy and flourishing" public library which was augmented by Judge W. W. Peck's contribution of a large collection.

The 1886 legislature authorized the setting up of free county libraries. When the county commissioners of any county had received guarantees from citizens, associations, or corporations that a suitable place would be furnished for a public library, they could levy up to one-half mill on all taxable property for the establishment and maintenance of a public library in the county seat. Since the legislators were mainly interested in books "to inform the mind and improve the character of the reader," they stipulated that not more than 25 per cent of library funds could be spent for works of fiction. Local groups accordingly sponsored free public libraries with tax aid. In Laramie, for example, the Wyoming Literary and Library Association turned over to the county library trustees its fifteen hundred volumes and more than seven hundred dollars in cash.

Meanwhile, a popular book agent from Denver, Charles Westley, regularly had been making the rounds of Wyoming towns selling subscription books to citizens. In 1887 he offered the *Encyclopaedia Britannica* at $2.50 per volume on monthly installments. Ashley Bancroft spent much time in the territory selling sets of H. H. Bancroft's works—in calf for $390.[2]

Governor Hoyt tried to stimulate the development of Wyoming culture by organizing a historical association in 1879 and the Wyoming Academy of Sciences, Arts and Letters in 1881. Neither could win much support.

Traveling lectures rounded out the territorial cultural opportunities, though rarely could they draw more than a handful of listeners. Cheyenne public-lecture offerings ran the gamut, from one on a new way to make butter (which no one attended) to one by Henry Ward Beecher on the wastes and burdens of society (attended by a full house, $1.50 per ticket, in 1878).

[2] George A. Morrison, who helped Ashley Bancroft interview Wyoming pioneers in 1885 and helped take orders in advance for the 39-volume set, in which 148 pages of Volume XXV would be assigned to Wyoming, perhaps encouraged the pioneers to think that they would receive better treatment from the historian if they ordered the books. In his report of an interview with Hiram S. Manville, Morrison wrote: "while it requires all the ability I am in possession of, to make them see that they ought to put $264.50 or 312 or 390/00 in Bancroft's works instead of into steers yet when they do see it I am inclined to say we should if possible look upon that as an evidence of more soul than the man who having the money, and being a part of the history of the country won't do it and give them a better place in the country's history." In his report of an interview with another pioneer, Orin C. Waid, said to be worth $200,000, Morrison wrote: "*Note* he is a pinheaded stubborn donkey with small ideas based on coin and refuses to subscribe to the work on the ground that he has no use for it and when he wants it he can go and purchase it." Even so, Waid's biography was included in a four-line footnote in Bancroft's *Works*.

THE CHARIVARI

The ancient French custom of the charivari, or "shivaree," came to the United States by way of French Canada and Louisiana. In Wyoming, as elsewhere on the American frontier, young men serenaded newly married couples with tin pans, whistles, bells, horns, drums, and other improvised noisemaking equipment. The racket' continued until the groom emerged to treat the crowd, usually by tendering money for refreshments.

After such a celebration in January, 1871, the *Cheyenne Leader* clucked that the charivari was "now regarded as a relic of barbarous times." In November, 1879, Hayford in Laramie, after two recent examples, called it a "disgusting practice" engaged in by "so-called men and boys." In July, 1885, he labeled it "a low, disgraceful nuisance . . . now principally confined to two classes—whisky bums, who improve the opportunity to get a drink at someone else's expense, and hoodlums and street gamins." Mrs. Mary Merritt, 1888 bride in Douglas, remembered the charivari as "very disturbing."

CHINESE DRAGONS AND THE JOSS HOUSE

The Chinese in Evanston and Rock Springs celebrated their new year in February by parading dragons through the streets. Mrs. E. A. Stone has described the Evanston dragon as about 200 feet long and "made of gaudy embroidery, which hung down to within two feet of the ground on both sides, and revealed only the legs of the fifty or sixty men who carried the writhing reptile through the streets with its massive head swaying from side to side." A Rock Springs dragon was 130 feet long and cost three thousand dollars in China. An earlier version of the Rock Springs dragon was slightly less than 100 feet in length and was carried by thirty to forty men.

Evanston claimed one of only three joss houses in the United States. On the Chinese New Year, Chinese came great distances to worship at the Evanston joss house and to watch or march in the parade behind the dragon.

POLITICS

Political activity occupied some of the free time of many Wyoming adults, particularly the men. One argument used for electing territorial delegate and legislators at the same time (finally achieved in 1882) was that it would cut in half the excitement and strife which were part of campaigning and voting. For many people, nevertheless, it seems that regular elections brought cheap entertainment and escape from the workaday world. Meeting leaders from other parts of the territory, reading lively political editorials, and participating in torchlight processions must have helped brighten many a man's life.

Politicians played for keeps, packing primary conventions, stuffing ballot boxes, lying about one another, and buying votes with whiskey and money. While the politicians who avoided such methods had a better chance of success in the 1880's than in the 1870's, many reprehensible practices continued. *Bill Barlow's Budget* (Douglas), for instance, charged in May, 1888, that Lusk and other eastern precincts had voted children, canary birds, and poodle dogs in their futile attempt to win the county seat from Douglas. The *Budget* maintained that in Manville, which ran third, 200 out of 226 votes were fraudulent.

Adding spice were occasional newspaper descriptions of legislative antics. The *Cheyenne Leader* observed that the last night of the session of each legislative assembly was a "corker." Often the newspapers did not have to wait for the last night to get raw material out of which they could fashion lively copy.

CHURCHES

The Methodist, Episcopal, Presbyterian, Baptist, Roman Catholic, and Mormon churches were active in Wyoming before the territory was organized. Congregationalists became active in 1869. A Methodist, Dr. Scott, has been credited with preaching the first sermon in Cheyenne in September, 1867. Much earlier, Wyoming's first Protestant sermon was preached by the Reverend Samuel Parker near present-day Bondurant in 1835, and the first Catholic Mass (with more than just a few in attendance) was celebrated by Father Pierre Jean De Smet at the Green River rendezvous near present Pinedale in 1840. The first regularly stationed clergyman in Wyoming was the Reverend William Vaux, Episcopal army chaplain at Fort Laramie, 1849–1862.

The Union Pacific offered free lots to all congregations along the line, but lack of funds delayed construction of buildings. An Episcopal church was, however, built in Cheyenne in 1868, and Presbyterian and Methodist churches were erected there in 1870. Protestant groups received help from the East. In April, 1869, St. Mark's Episcopal Church in Cheyenne received a 600-pound bell as a gift from St. Mark's in Philadelphia.

Bill Nye found humor in church socials:

The method by which our wives in America are knocking the church debt silly, by working up their husbands' groceries into "angel food" and selling them below actual cost, is deserving of the attention of our national financiers.

. . . This festival is an open market where the ladies trade the groceries of their husbands to other ladies' husbands, and everybody has a "perfectly lovely time." The church clears $2.30, and thirteen ladies are sick all the next day. . . .

The church socials and festivals really made more money than Bill Nye suggested. Catholics in Cheyenne for instance, in October, 1888, held a fair, or bazaar, for seven nights and raised more than $1,400. They charged for suppers and dancing, sold ice cream and lemonade, and sold or raffled all kinds of donated merchandise, ranging from a box of cigars to a cherry bedroom suite.

Greatest problem for early church workers in Wyoming was to gather a quorum. The scarcity of women meant that few persons participated. Governor Campbell's diary included this entry, "No congregation at church," and another, "Mr. Jackson here to preach but no person to listen to him." The *Wyoming Tribune* (Cheyenne) commented in April, 1871: "Our Churches. No one attends once, but what is led to exclaim this may be a God fearing people; but it certainly is not a church going people." The *Tribune* thought the ministers were as much at fault as the people: "Let there be good singing. Let the ministers tell their hearers something new each Sunday. The world today cares little about the color of Nebuchadnezzar's breeches. People long for something of the living present. Let ministers raise voice against today's evils instead of constantly decrying other denominations and sects."

Judge Joseph M. Carey, who wrote a series of editorials for the *Cheyenne Leader* in February, 1873, warned that "the churches must be made more attractive or ministers will preach to empty seats in the future as they have in the past." Again, Carey asked: "What have Christian men and women of Cheyenne done towards aiding one of the poor fallen women of the town?" The Presbyterian minister replied that at least one minister had visited every fallen woman, had given them Christian counsel, and had invited them to church. Christian women, he added, had gone from house to house, pleaded with the fallen women, and prayed with them. More than a year earlier, he said, a society had been formed to reclaim the prostitutes, but insurmountable difficulties had arisen. The society could not afford to start a home for the penitent, and when two or three families offered a home to reformed prostitutes, none came forward to accept the offer.

Within the next year there were Cheyenne sermons on the social evil and on temperance, but in general the ministers preferred to stay away from everyday problems. An exception was the Reverend D. J. Pierce, Baptist exponent of the social gospel in Laramie, who in December,

1880, wrote a letter to the *Sentinel* declaring that "we charge the UP corporation with breaking the laws of God and the laws of nature." There had been a series of accidents on the railroad, with five or six deaths in three months. The principal cause of these accidents, thought Pierce, was the work schedule: "Men are robbed of sleep, of Sunday, of home. . . . Our running men work from 35 to 48 days [shifts], of ten hours each, per month."

The Episcopal church, which had done comparatively little missionary work in the Middle West, was ready to push the work energetically by the time Wyoming Territory was organized. Among its outstanding leaders in early Wyoming were the Reverend George Rafter of Cheyenne and the Reverend John Roberts of the Wind River Reservation, who gained reputations as the "Nestors" or wise men of their communities. In 1887, Ethelbert Talbot arrived to serve as Bishop of the Missionary District of Wyoming and Idaho until 1898. Cheyenne, Laramie, Rawlins, and Boise, Idaho, all invited him to reside with them. He finally accepted the Laramie proposition, which promised construction of a $7,000 residence for him. In his eleven years in the West, Bishop Talbot increased the number of Episcopal churches from seven to thirty-two and the number of clergymen from eight to forty.

While men like Bishop Talbot worked strenuously to church the scattered pioneers, the great majority were not interested. In Laramie in the early 1870's, editor Hayford made the rounds of the churches on Sunday morning and reported that only one person in ten was within and that those present were mostly women. In January, 1881, Hayford could report progress in that there were five "neat Christian Churches. They have their carpets and cushions, bells and organs." Yet not one in ten, he said regretfully, was a churchgoer. "Our pulpits are all supplied with able men; the very best the country can furnish . . . they represent every leading sect, so that everyone can enjoy his or her own preference, and yet people don't go to church."

A separate Roman Catholic Diocese of Cheyenne was established on August 9, 1887. Before that time, Roman Catholic activity in Wyoming had been guided from outside the territory—from Omaha, 1885–1887. By 1889 there were five Roman Catholic priests besides the Bishop in Wyoming. At that time Bishop Maurice W. Burke of Cheyenne found conditions so intolerable that he went to Rome to get the Diocese of Cheyenne attached to a neighboring diocese, but he was turned down. In May, 1891, Bishop Burke sent a circular letter (published in the June 6, 1891, *Leader*) to eastern Catholics asking help: "With no

prospects for the future, no increase in the Catholic population, with
absolutely no support for a bishop, with a large debt on the little church
at Cheyenne, and without any possibility of doing anything whatever
in the interests of religion, I find the situation insupportable. . . . I
earnestly appeal for financial aid."

Mormons antedated territorial organization in southwestern
Wyoming, but were not numerous east of Rock Springs. They built
churches early in Evanston and Rock Springs. A few of them entered
Star Valley in the 1870's, and many more followed in the 1880's; they
also began moving into the Big Horn Basin in the eighties. Polygamists
found that there was less pressure on them to put aside plural wives in
western Wyoming than in Utah. They had a very poor press in Laramie, where their harshest critic was Bill Nye. Yet Heber J. Grant,
president of the Church of Jesus Christ of Latter-day Saints, said in
Cheyenne in May, 1929, that "our people [in Wyoming] have never
experienced the intolerance with which they have been regarded in
some sections of other states."

Although pioneers in small numbers had entered the area east of the
Big Horns in the 1870's, no churches were established there until 1884,
when the Congregationalists organized in Sheridan and Buffalo, with
twelve and ten members, respectively.

After the birth of Douglas in the summer of 1886, the Reverend
Harmon Bross of Chadron, Nebraska, held services and organized a
Congregational church in December, 1886. Roman Catholic and
Methodist services began in 1887 and 1888. Amazingly, Casper, where
buildings were first put up and the first train arrived in June, 1888,
did not have any religious services by an ordained minister until the
Reverend Bross of Chadron preached in a private home on March 3,
1889. The *Casper Weekly Mail* at the time urged the need for a church
building, observing that "while there are but a few of our male adult
population that are ordinarily supposed to have souls (worth speaking
of) to save, there are women and children."

Among the pioneer church leaders in Wyoming was Young Men's
Christian Association organizer Robert Weidensall, who arrived in
Cheyenne in November, 1868. By May, 1870, there were "YMCA
rooms" supplied with papers and periodicals and a few books for free
public use. Later the association opened reading rooms in other towns.
At Rock Springs at the end of the territorial period the organization
claimed almost two hundred members, who had the opportunity to

bathe as well as to read. The Union Pacific assisted the Y.M.C.A. in providing such combination reading room–bath room facilities.

The Census of 1890 attributed 43 church edifices and 11,705 communicants or members—19.28 per cent of the population—to Wyoming. Later, in the publication *U.S. Census of Religious Bodies, 1916*, Wyoming's total membership for 1890 was corrected, making it 12,973, or 21.4 per cent, as compared to 34.5 per cent for the United States. The Wyoming church members were divided: Roman Catholic, 8,453; Methodist Episcopal, 1,322; Protestant Episcopal, 467; Presbyterian Church in the U.S.A., 364; Congregational, 339; Baptists—Northern Convention, 262; Lutherans—Synodical Conference, 48; and all other denominations, 945.

It seems that denominational rivalry was less prominent in Wyoming than in older communities in the East. While many people who had belonged to eastern churches broke these ties when they went west and never joined a church again, others were disposed to affiliate with a new church if their old one were not available.

On the whole, it appears that territorial Wyoming was largely secular. Pioneer cowboys, railroad workers, miners, and soldiers were for the most part not attached to formal religious institutions. Organized religion meant less to them than it did to the farmers and people of the small towns in the Middle West.

EDUCATION

The first school in Wyoming was the one begun by the chaplain at Fort Laramie, the Reverend William Vaux, in the 1850's. The usual date given is 1852, but Mrs. Lodisa Watson, in her M.A. thesis, reports having found a letter written by an army major at Fort Laramie in 1858 complaining that Vaux had not begun instruction until March, 1856, was a most unenthusiastic schoolmaster, and was a negligent chaplain who never visited the sick or concerned himself with the morals of the soldiers. If the major was fair to Vaux, children at Fort Bridger were better served. In 1860 the sutler there, William A. Carter, employed a governess-teacher for his children and welcomed other children to his private school. At any rate, a few children at the military posts were the first pupils receiving formal education in what was to become Wyoming.

The first legislature in December, 1869, supplied the basic law for public education, making the auditor ex officio superintendent of public instruction. He was given five hundred dollars for his educational duties, which included general supervision of all the district schools, recommending uniform textbooks, making reports, and distributing school funds among the counties. Elective county superintendents were to divide the settled parts into school districts, apportion the county school tax and other school funds among the several school districts, examine and certify teachers, visit each school at least twice each term, and generally supervise the schools. In each district a board of directors was to be elected, consisting of a chairman, a clerk, and a treasurer. School-district meetings in May and October were authorized to determine the number of schools and the length of time each would be taught, select the site of each schoolhouse, set the district school tax (subject to the approval of county commissioners), determine what branches of learning should be taught, delegate any of the foregoing powers to the district board, and transact other school business. The district board was specifically empowered to hire and pay teachers. The first legislature provided that where there were fifteen or more colored children in a district, a separate school might be established for them, but no such segregated school was ever started.

The length of school terms varied considerably. The 1873 legislature established the minimum when it required that every child between the ages of six and eighteen attend three months each year. This seems not to have been enforced. Most communities did not have high schools, although high school work was sometimes offered in schools not designated as high schools.

Important in the organization of education was the teachers' institutes, which met annually beginning in 1874. Leaders in these institutes for many years were N. E. Stark and R. E. Fitch, principals, respectively, in Cheyenne and Laramie. The 1877 legislature required all principals of graded schools to attend the institutes, with their traveling expenses to be paid by the territory. The 1882 legislature extended these provisions to cover all public-school teachers. In these meetings, which lasted several days (four to ten days by 1877 law), many common problems were discussed. In a May, 1879, session in Laramie one teacher read a paper condemning emphasis on "the study of dead languages" and urging greater attention to "our own vernacular—on history, literature, science and the modern languages. . . . Instead of teaching so many dry rules let there be more out-door training, more rambles among the beetles and butterflies, rocks and rivulets, forms and flowers of the vegetable world."

Outside speakers often addressed the institutes. Former Governor John W. Hoyt, for instance, told the 1885 meeting at Cheyenne that, in Cheyenne, $25,000 worth of cattle were respected much more than $25,000 worth of brains. The teachers at the institute took time for relaxation, as at Rawlins in September, 1886, when after a long day of papers "the young folks began dancing and all was merry till the wee hours of morn."

One of the better-educated pioneers, who came to Wyoming with considerable training in both law and medicine and who served as the territory's first superintendent of public instruction, was J. H. Hayford, Laramie editor. He wrote in his *Sentinel* on January 10, 1879: "We would have our youth taught something in our schools by which they could make a living." He suggested manual training, watchmaking, telegraphy, and typesetting. Hayford knew the school curriculum well because he had many children. He believed in early acquaintance with work, placing a ten-year-old son in his back shop.

Bill Nye often disagreed with Hayford, but he, too, appreciated the practical in education, as when he wrote: "There are very few households here as yet that can keep their own private poet. . . . The crisp, dry air here is such that hunger is the chief style of yearn in Wyoming, and a good cook can get $125 per month where a bilious poet would be bothered like sin to get a job at $5 per week." Defenders of the traditional curriculum, such as N. E. Stark of Cheyenne, were hard put to defend it.

In 1886, Cheyenne, with two high school teachers, adopted a two-track high school program. Pupils could choose between a four-year college preparatory course and a three-year "business" course. The latter omitted Latin, astronomy, and geology. Such a division had been approved by the territorial institute, and Governor Moonlight concurred when, speaking at the Cheyenne commencement in May, 1887, he urged the importance of obtaining a "practical" education.

The 1877 legislature assigned to the territorial institutes the duty of arranging for county institutes. In the 1880's territorial institutes were dropped as county institutes received greater emphasis.

Dr. T. D. Fromong's study of early Wyoming education shows that by modern standards territorial education was sketchy and minimal. As late as 1893 the average number of days school was in session was 89.21. There were only five high schools in 1895: Buffalo, Cheyenne, Evanston, Rawlins, and Sundance. In 1896 only one pupil in forty-four was enrolled in a high school program.

The University of Wyoming, whose history has been written by Professor W. O. Clough, opened in 1887 at Laramie with a $50,000 building, a faculty of seven, and forty-two students, most of them at the college preparatory level. Indeed, for many years the availability of college preparatory work at the University made it unnecessary for Laramie to establish a separate high school. Poorly supported outside Laramie, it would be many years before the institution could live up to its pretensions as a university. Dean Justus F. Soule recalled: "During the first twenty-five years we never knew whether we should be there or not the next year."

Secretary of the first board of trustees was the versatile editor Hayford, who transferred to the university level his passion for utilitarian education. On May 1, 1886, in his newspaper report of the first board meeting, he set the tone: "While not ignoring the benefits of classical education, the Board recognizes the fact that the world has more use for engineers, mining, civil, gas, electric engineers, for architects, chemists and mechanics, than it has for men who can merely cackle Greek." No doubt from the beginning the trustees were, like most men on the frontier, inclined to emphasize the practical, yet it would be a long time before the little frontier university could turn out many engineers, architects, and chemists. Nevertheless, the inscription on the cornerstone of the first building, Old Main, had significance for Wyoming youth: *Domi habuit unde disceret*, which may be translated "At home he had whence he might learn."

VIOLENCE

Novels, movies, and television shows have exaggerated the amount of violence present in the Rocky Mountain and High Plains West in the nineteenth century. Owen Wister, who crisscrossed the West in fifteen trips in the years 1885–1902 and kept detailed diaries of his experiences, never witnessed a killing, and indeed never saw a man fired upon! One cannot go so far, however, as to assert that there was no more violence then than now, for in proportion to population there was at least ten times as much—long after the turbulent hell-on-wheels era was gone. One who reads the Wyoming newspaper files of 1870 to 1890 finds more shootings, knifings, and general brutality than among the far greater population of the 1960's. Nevertheless, territorial people were, for the most part, civilized. The "rough stuff" usually happened in saloons or houses of ill fame or near them. People who remained sober and avoided these places usually avoided trouble as well.

Exceptional circumstances brought special periods of violence to some communities. In three chapters of her volume *The Cheyenne and Black Hills Stage and Express Routes*, Agnes Wright Spring has chronicled the activities of road agents, horse thieves, and other desperadoes who infested eastern Wyoming in 1877 and 1878 during the Black Hills gold rush. Shotgun messengers, such as Scott Davis and D. Boone May, sheriffs, and soldiers gave the outlaws more than they expected and sent many to death or prison. After it was abandoned by the army in 1882, Fort Fetterman was a wild place for a few years. Thereafter violence bubbled up in one after another of the new towns along the Chicago and North Western and Burlington railroads when, briefly, they were "wide open" and somewhat reminiscent of the Union Pacific hell-on-wheels towns of the 1860's.

Pioneer women, especially in Wyoming, where they had the right to vote and hold office, are sometimes thought to have been accorded honorable treatment universally. They weren't. Sydney Spiegel, in his M.A. thesis study of early Cheyenne, found that "wife beating was a common complaint." Mrs. Esther Morris, of Statuary Hall fame, in South Pass City in 1871 swore out a warrant for assault and battery against her husband, John. Hayford reported in his *Laramie Sentinel* on October 10, 1885: "A worthless whelp named Smith was arrested and jailed this week for assaulting, beating and threatening to murder his equally worthless wife." In August, 1886, in Cheyenne an old woman who had recently come to town with her husband quarreled with him one night and set out to find a policeman so that she might sleep in jail. Three men offered to take her to jail. Instead they took her to the Union Pacific yards, where they undertook to rape her. Her screams brought help.

These unsavory incidents are only a few of many that can be documented. It becomes necessary to question sweeping generalizations by old-timers about pioneer chivalry. The Englishman John J. Fox, for instance, as a young man spent the years 1885–1887 in Wyoming and in his old age recalled: "One thing is certain. No woman of that period in Wyoming, no matter what her age or condition, could have been violently abused or man-handled, as is often shown now-a-days in the screen stories of the Wild West."

In hell-on-wheels days, most of the men carried guns. Indeed, newspaper editors advised them to carry weapons for protection. As long as guns were commonly worn—and they were in the 1870's—false ideas of personal honor, especially when under the influence of alcohol, led to gunplay. The 1875 legislature made it illegal to carry "concealed or openly, any fire arm or other deadly weapon" in village, town, or city. The law was not well enforced. The *Wyoming Tribune* in January, 1886, complained: "The law against this 'gun' carrying ought to be more rigidly enforced. The idea of men perambulating our streets like walking arsenals is the worst kind of reflection upon us as a lawabiding people. The man with his 'pop' is too prone to use it upon every occasion or dispute or difference."

Shooting in self-defense was the standard plea in murder cases, and juries regularly honored such pleas. There were only two legal executions in Wyoming before 1884. A half-breed Indian murderer, John Boyer, was hanged legally at Cheyenne in April, 1871, and a second Indian half-breed, Toussaint Kensler, was hanged at Cheyenne in November, 1874.

In the early 1880's the failure of the courts to punish in homicide cases caused growing resentment, evidenced by editorial complaints. There had been "scores of murders, coldblooded and atrocious," with little in the way of punishment, in the past fifteen years, asserted the *Laramie Times*, quite accurately, in March, 1882. In his *Sentinel* in April, 1882, J. H. Hayford added that "it has actually come to be regarded as less dangerous to kill a man than to steal a horse." Meanwhile, exaction of the death penalty continued to be left to the hands of extralegal groups. In February, 1879, two bodies labeled "Cattle Thieves" were reported found hanging to a tree in the Powder River country. One "Dutch Charlie" Burris was lynched at Carbon in January, 1879, and his pal "Big Nose George" Parrot (or Parrotti) was lynched at Rawlins in March, 1881. Henry Mosier was lynched in Cheyenne in September, 1883.

Most of the people in the territory condoned the lynchings of Dutch Charlie, Big Nose George, and Henry Mosier, since all three were thought to be cold-blooded murderers who might escape punishment unless there was mob action. The Mosier affair evoked widespread discussion. Mosier was accused of murdering a man three miles north of Cheyenne and wounding another in a robbery attempt. He was taken from jail and hanged from a telephone pole at Nineteenth and Eddy [Capitol] streets. Mayor Joseph M. Carey and Territorial Secretary E. S. N. Morgan pleaded with the mob to let the law take its course, but their pleas were rejected. Explained the *Cheyenne Sun*: "There has [*sic*] been so many long winded ceremonious legal farces enacted in the courts of the territory that it seemed to many of our thoughtful citizens

as if the law was being used to protect and not to punish criminals."
Added the *Leader*: "[Mob violence is deplorable.] But unless the laws
and the courts furnish protection to life and punish crime, there is
nothing else left us."

Whether demands for stiffer penalties had much to do with it is hard
to say, but finally, in 1884, there were two legal executions. Leroy
Donovan was executed in Rawlins for the hammer slaying of a sleeping
Rock Springs barber whom he intended to rob, and a cowboy, George
Cook, was hanged in Laramie for murdering his brother-in-law. The
willingness of 1884 courts to convict and apply the death penalty to
someone other than friendless half-breeds marked a significant change
in the administration of justice. Three other murderers were executed
—a man named Booth at Buffalo in March, 1886; Ben Carter at Rawlins
in October, 1888; and George Black at Laramie in February, 1890.
Nevertheless, extralegal executions were not abandoned. The desperado Si Partridge was taken from a stock detective and lynched just
south of Laramie in August, 1885. Gus Kernwood, reputed to be a
horse thief, was lynched on the Stinking Water in December, 1886.
In October, 1888, two hide hunters, N. L. Adams and Charles Putzier,
were lynched near Savery. James Averell and Ella "Cattle Kate"
Watson were lynched on the Sweetwater in July, 1889 (this last case
will be discussed later in Chapter 10). Thus legal executions failed to
keep pace with extralegal ones in the final years of the territory.

COWBOYS AND OTHER MEN AT PLAY

Cowboys were neither better nor worse than other men on the
frontier. There were mean cowboys, given to violence, interspersed
among the many more decent ones. Mont Hawthorne never forgot the
bunch of cowboys who came to Carbon his first Saturday night there
in 1881. They picked on some Finns, "busted the bottoms out of
whiskey bottles by banging them against the bar. They then held on to
the bottlenecks and shoved the broken, jagged edges into the poor
devils' faces, cutting them something terrible. . . . Then they got on
their horses, emptied their guns . . . and galloped off." Two of the six
men legally hanged in the territory were cowboys, George Cook and
Ben Carter.

Owen Wister's Virginian, who waited for the villain to make the
first move for his gun before reaching for his own weapon, seems never
to have had a real-life counterpart in Wyoming Territory. Whether
cowboys or not, men yielded no advantage if they could help it. The

Cheyenne Leader on October 7, 1888, described what it called "the only code duel ever fought in Wyoming." A teen-age cowboy had challenged his foreman on one of the Union Cattle Company's ranges. A cowboy from Virginia made the arrangements. Seconds were chosen. The antagonists took positions fifty yards apart. They agreed to fire once at a count of three by the cook, who was ex officio surgeon. The foreman received a bullet in his right arm, after which the duelists were reconciled. Such honorable combat was certainly exceptional.

In January, 1883, a cowboy named Ed Taylor, otherwise known as Badman Taylor, was shot to death in a Hartville saloon. He was not given a fair chance in a confrontation, but was shot with a rifle through a window. The fact that in the previous month Taylor had shot another cowboy in the thigh may have had something to do with his murder.

In April, 1884, at Cheyenne, two cowboys, Rogers and Sweet, fought with a Seventeenth Street saloonkeeper over credit and a piece of ice. They made no honorable arrangement for settlement of the dispute but, two against one, proceeded to beat the saloonkeeper over the head with a pitcher and an iron statuette.

In September, 1884, several cowboys, smarting under some slight, descended on the "Hog Ranch" near Fort Fetterman, determined to "clean out the concern." Four persons, including a woman, were more or less seriously injured.

In August, 1885, while Charley Williams was standing at the bar of a saloon in Lander, Frank Howard placed a revolver near the back of his head and shot him to death. Formerly gambling partners, they had quarreled.

Cowboy Charley Miley went to Lusk to celebrate in October, 1886, placed his saddle in safekeeping with a prostitute, and proceeded to get drunk. Under the influence he told another prostitute that he was a horse thief. He was soon arrested by Charles V. Trumble, who had been a deputy sheriff but was one no longer. Apparently in an effort to win a reward, Trumble kept Miley in handcuffs for days and otherwise abused him before he had to release him. Then, later, while drinking with Miley in a saloon, Trumble asked Miley at gun point whether he was friend or enemy. Miley replied frankly: "To tell you the truth, Charley, I cannot like you, you have used me so hard." Such candor was a mistake, for it angered Trumble and he shot and killed the unarmed Miley. For this he was sentenced to hang in June, 1887. His lawyers obtained one stay of execution after another. In response to an appeal for a pardon, Governor Moonlight wrote a ten-page letter explaining why he could not pardon the murderer of an "unarmed, harmless and inoffensive man." A new trial was ordered in June, 1889, during which Trumble pleaded guilty to manslaughter. Finally, in February, 1890, Judge Willis Van Devanter sentenced Trumble to six and one-half years in the penitentiary, less three years already spent in county jails.

Ed J. Linn, gambler, amused himself in June, 1887, by trying to shoot off the boot heels of some of his companions as they "balanced on the corner" at a dance at a Fort Fetterman resort known as Dick's Place. Later in the evening he drove past and fired his six-shooter into the dance hall, killing "Old Billy" Parker. Using the defense that another man fired a pistol at the same time, Linn's lawyer was able to limit his punishment to a maximum sentence of four years for manslaughter.

These are random samples of Wyoming's young men at play in the 1880's. When drunk, some of them misbehaved.

No doubt the cowboys contributed their share to frontier violence. Until Buffalo Bill's "Wild West" shows could present them to the world as colorful and daring riders in the 1880's, Theodore Roosevelt could begin to glorify them in his *Ranch Life and the Hunting Trail* in 1888 ("[The cowboys] are as hardy and self-reliant as any man who ever breathed. . . . They are in the main good men; and the disturbance they cause in a town is done from sheer rough light-heartedness."), and Owen Wister could publish *The Virginian* glamorizing them, in 1902, the cowboys were better known for their violent behavior than for their courage and manliness. In recalling his cowboy life of the 1890's, Bruce Siberts wrote: "I had a liking for the girls, but when I went into town with my rough clothes on they wouldn't pay any attention to me. . . . Owen Wister hadn't yet written his book *The Virginian*, so we cowhands did not know we were so strong and glamorous as we were after people read that book."

OUT ON THE RANGE

"Away from settlements the shotgun is the only law," Edward W. Smith of Evanston told the United States Public Lands Commission in 1879. He was not far wrong except that the rifle was used more often than the shotgun. In the country, violence increased in the 1880's as users of the range multiplied. Conflicts over land claims led to many tragedies.

In July, 1883, James Carr shot George Bailey to death at the latter's claim shanty on the Big Laramie River. In November, 1887, Jesse McDowell shot to death two unarmed men, Bird and Madson, on the Middle Fork of the Little Laramie. At Antelope Basin north of Rock Creek in June, 1888, J. L. Batty, unarmed, remonstrated with a rancher named Atkinson, who had been dogging his neighbors' cattle. After hot words, Atkinson ran to get his rifle and shot at the fleeing Batty, shattering Batty's right arm. In May, 1889, Bob Burnett was murdered fifteen miles east of Laramie by George A. Black. Fortunately, however, most disputes on the range did not actually reach the shooting stage.

VIOLENCE IN THE NEWSPAPER OFFICE

Editors sometimes wrote scurrilous attacks on one another and the public. The courts could not be depended upon to give redress, and were rarely appealed to by persons who were libeled. In district court in Cheyenne in June, 1875, W. M. Renton and T. Joe Fisher were acquitted of charges of newspaper libel. Thereafter, editors were involved in fisticuffs and gunplay more often than in libel suits. Yet in more than thirty years at Laramie, J. H. Hayford managed to avoid violence. He used the scalpel rather than the bludgeon except at rare times, such as in June, 1880, when he became so exasperated with editor W. E. Wheeler of the *Evanston Age* that he called him "a drunkard, a pimp, a whoremonger, a dead beat, a man on whom nature or education never fooled away a moment's time."

Bill Nye went into hiding for a few days after writing that at a dance Mr. Sherrod's half-Indian wife had been "painted up like a Shutler wagon." Sherrod came gunning for Nye but cooled off before he found him.

In 1878, E. A. Bradbury, treasurer of Sweetwater County, accosted a Green River printer for things said about Bradbury by the absent editor. In the ensuing argument, the printer shot Bradbury just above the heart. Bradbury recovered, but the printer was sent to the penitentiary for ten years.

In July, 1884, A. S. Mercer of the *Northwestern Live Stock Journal* and his partner, Marney, came to blows. According to the *Laramie Sentinel*, "the wife of Mr. Mercer took a hand and knocked the eternal stuffin out of Marney with a cuspidore. Mr. Marney's condition at last accounts was serious and critical."

In May, 1887, editor Z. T. Brown of the *Rawlins Tribune* was "pitched onto . . . and pounded" by "a cowardly bully named Kelley."

In November, 1888, Dick Keenan, saloonkeeper and chairman of the

Democratic Central Committee in Sweetwater County, "made a brutal and murderous assault" upon N. B. Dresser, editor of the *Rock Springs Independent*.

In September, 1889, former Governor George W. Baxter struck editor E. A. Slack of the *Cheyenne Sun* with a cane and "was knocked down and choked in turn, when friends interfered." Baxter should have chosen a smaller antagonist. Slack was six feet one and weighed 230 pounds in the 1870's and apparently did not lose any weight thereafter. He was known by his editorial contemporaries as "The Cheyenne Avoirdupois," "adipose Archie," and "the obese and oily Col. Slack." [3]

Editors were in a special category. Otherwise the generalization offered above seems to hold valid: territorial people who remained sober and avoided saloons and houses of prostitution normally could expect to enjoy freedom from violence.

AN INSECURE AND TRANSIENT BUT NOT UNHAPPY SOCIETY

Although the pattern was too simple and the change too slow to use the word kaleidoscopic, territorial Wyoming was by no means static. Energetic, optimistic men were busy trying to evaluate and exploit the vast territory's wealth. Disappointments far outnumbered notable successes, with the result that comparatively few people became lifelong settlers. Cheyenne, Laramie, Rawlins, and Evanston looked relatively permanent by 1890, but elsewhere an air of impermanence persisted. Among permanent settlers and transients alike there were the admirable and the despicable. While life for many was "narrow, brutish and short," it was sweet and satisfying to others. No doubt most people had as much fun as their grandchildren do today. Among the happiest were those who planted trees, founded cattle ranches, built churches, and in other ways planned a better life for their descendants.

[3] "Colonel" Edward Archibald Slack (1842–1907) learned the printer's trade in Illinois as a boy. After service in the Nineteenth Illinois Infantry, 1861–1864, he attended "the Chicago University" two years, after which he pursued further collegiate study at Fulton, Illinois. He accompanied his stepfather, John Morris, to South Pass City in 1868, becoming a newspaper editor there, and then at Laramie, 1871–1876. He transferred his editorial activities to Cheyenne in 1876, first editing the *Cheyenne Sun* and later (after he bought it in 1895) the *Leader*. In Laramie, Slack was an Independent and a Democrat, but Republicans financed his move to Cheyenne, where he was a stalwart Republican until his death. Another prominent editor, W. E. Chaplin, who worked for Slack for a few years, recalled: "He was a man of indomitable energy, tremendous will power, and high personal character. . . . As a writer he used the sledge-hammer. . . . When he got thoroughly interested in a subject he seemed to accumulate more and more of it from day to day until his adversaries were literally overwhelmed and driven from the field of action." Slack became the most influential editor in territory and state, though he was not the most gifted editorial writer (that was J. H. Hayford, with John F. Carroll a close second).

CHAPTER 9

Statehood

A FEW PEOPLE IN WYOMING were talking and writing about statehood
as early as 1868. They expected the territory to attain sufficient population to justify statehood within a few years. Ever since the Ordinance
of 1787 had stated that parts of the Northwest Territory might be considered for statehood when a population of sixty thousand had been
reached, that number had been regarded by many people as sufficient
for statehood, and a few states had come into the Union with a smaller
population. For various reasons, which are discussed by John D. Hicks
in his *Constitutions of the Northwest States* (Lincoln, 1923), no state was
admitted between 1876, when Colorado came in, and November, 1889,

236

when four states—North Dakota, South Dakota, Montana, and Washington—were added.

In the discouraging 1870's there was more talk of partitioning Wyoming Territory than of statehood. The economy perked up in the 1880's, permitting Governor Warren to include statehood recommendations in both his 1885 and 1886 reports to the Secretary of the Interior. Thereafter the possibility of statehood was often discussed.

Until neighboring South Dakota and Montana entered the Union in 1889, Wyoming could hardly expect recognition, since both had better claims with their larger population. Dakotans and Montanans understandably worked harder than the Wyoming people for statehood in the 1880's, but their desires were long frustrated because during the years 1883–1889 control of the two houses of Congress was split between Republicans and Democrats. Republicans in Congress were more sympathetic to statehood pleas coming from the Northwest because the territories there were expected to become Republican if they were not already so. When the Republicans won control of both houses of Congress and the presidency in 1888, they prepared to act on their desire for more Republican senators and congressmen. The Democrats in Congress thereupon capitulated and agreed to the admission of North Dakota, South Dakota, Montana, and Washington. They hoped to share in the gratitude of the voters in the new states.

Normally one might expect most of the people in a territory to want statehood, since it would open new opportunities to them. Two senators and one or more representatives would provide better representation in Washington than one delegate in the lower house, and, unlike residents of a territory, people in a state could vote for the President. In a state there would be less dictation from Washington, and carpetbagger appointees in the executive and judicial branches would be replaced by officials elected from resident candidates. It was usually thought also that a state would be more attractive to prospective settlers.

Yet partisan considerations colored the thinking of Wyoming people on the matter of statehood just as it did that of Congress. Republicans led the statehood movement in the late 1880's, with Francis E. Warren and Joseph M. Carey out front. Since they became the first United States senators, it seems plausible that they planned it that way. Certainly Carey's leadership for statehood in 1888 was attributed again and again by Democrats to his ambition to become United States senator.

As a rule, Wyoming Democrats were much less enthusiastic about statehood than the Republicans, but except for a few like Governor Thomas Moonlight and editor John F. Carroll of the *Cheyenne Leader,* they were not actively opposed. The territorial legislature of January–March, 1888, with Democrats in control of the lower house and Republicans the upper house, sent to Washington a petition for statehood.

After Territorial Delegate J. M. Carey presented the petition, a bill for an enabling act was introduced in each house of Congress, to no avail. Tired of waiting, Governor Warren and his associates decided to proceed as if an enabling act had been passed, a tactic not without precedent. Under Governor Warren's guidance, boards of county commissioners in seven of the ten counties adopted resolutions for a constitutional convention. Governor Warren then arranged for an election of delegates, July 8, 1889, to a constitutional convention in September. The election was on a nonpartisan basis, yet party affiliation was not ignored entirely. The Democratic *Laramie Boomerang* complained that workingmen were not taking much interest in the approaching election. They must turn out and vote, urged the *Boomerang*, if they did not want corporations to write the constitution. As it turned out, of the forty-nine men who attended the convention, thirty-two were Republicans and seventeen were Democrats.

On the threshold of statehood, Wyoming appeared to be Republican, since Republicans controlled the constitutional convention and there was a Republican delegate to Congress, although the legislature was split. What had happened to the Democratic majority of earlier days? The Democrats had no leader comparable to Warren and Carey, who stood head and shoulders above all other Wyoming politicians. Republican tariff policies looked good to a majority of Wyoming people. Democratic Governor Moonlight divided the Democrats instead of uniting and leading them.

The Democratic party had also been hurt by a combination of bad luck and poor organization. Unable to agree on a gubernatorial candidate whose name they could press upon President Grover Cleveland in 1885, they had to wait twenty months before Cleveland removed Warren. They were hurt again when, after forty-five days, Cleveland felt compelled to remove his appointee, George W. Baxter, for fencing government land.

Lack of leadership and poor organization cost the Democrats dearly in the fall of 1886. Their convention in Rawlins, just a month before the election, tendered the nomination for delegate to M. E. Post, who declined, whereupon Laramie bank president and stock raiser Henry

G. Balch was nominated. Not until almost two weeks later, long after the convention had disbanded, was it learned that, like Post, Balch would not run; the convention had not obtained his prior consent. He was somewhere in Montana, and not until October 15 was it published that he was not interested. In consequence, Carey was virtually unopposed.

Two years later the Democrats were able to come up with a candidate willing to run, Caleb Perry Organ, Cheyenne hardware merchant who had branch stores in Douglas and Buffalo. He had served one term, January–March, 1888, in the upper house of the legislature. He was not well known, yet he appeared to have qualities which would appeal to many Democrats. Since his arrival in Cheyenne in October, 1867, as a poor mule skinner, he had become general superintendent of Camp Carlin and eventually a prosperous cattleman and merchant. The *Cheyenne Leader* extolled him as a "man of the common people."

"Honest Perry" Organ was a poor public speaker. The *Sundance Farmer* reported that he was making a queer campaign: "He takes a man along with him, who makes the speeches and 'me, Perry Organ,' sets on the platform, looks wise, and intimates to the boys, 'them's my sentiments.'" Carey, on the other hand, could speak at great length, cogently and effectively, though making no attempt at flowery oratory. The *Cheyenne Leader* assigned him to the "dry-as-dust" school of orators: "He revels in statistics and frolics with the dry bones of facts that have long lost their vitalizing principles."

Democratic assertions that Carey was "a kidgloved representative of Washington for cattle barons and dudes" and that "Carey's hands have never been hardened by honest toil" failed to rally workingmen against him. Charges that Carey had called Governor Moonlight "a tramp from Kansas" cost him few, if any, votes. Organ carried only Johnson and Fremont counties and lost to Carey by a vote of 10,451 to 7,557.

Was statehood a significant issue in the Carey-Organ contest? It was an issue, but probably not a crucial one. The platform of the territorial Democratic party in October, 1888, said: "On the question of statehood the Democrats, when the proper time arrives, will be found working enthusiastically in the front of the battle, but we do not believe in indulging in any spread eagle blatherskitism." A few days later, the territorial Republicans stated their position: "We now have the taxable wealth and the population necessary to support a state government and being therefore entitled to admission into the Union we earnestly favor such congressional legislation as will enable us to adopt a constitution and secure the rights of statehood." Thus the Democrats wanted to wait, while the Republicans wanted statehood at once.

John F. Carroll of the *Cheyenne Leader* was a member of the Democratic platform committee, and Edward A. Slack of the *Cheyenne Sun* served on the Republican platform committee. Their editorials corresponded to the platform statements. The *Leader* wanted delay for as much as five years; the *Sun* advocated immediate statehood. The *Leader* argued that statehood at once "would prove little short of genuine calamity. . . . This statehood talk is too highly flavored with [Carey's] senatorial ambitions." The *Leader* contended that Wyoming could not afford statehood, which, it said, would cost at least $95,000 a year more than territorial government. Accordingly, the *Leader* announced that "a vote for Judge Carey is a vote in favor of immediate statehood and consequently ruinous taxation." The Republican *Sun* agreed that "a vote for Judge Carey is a vote for statehood."

After three quarters of a century, when so many circumstances have changed, one might be tempted to think that no one could seriously object to statehood on the grounds that it would cost $95,000 a year. This would be mistaken. Many of Wyoming's citizens were very poor in the late 1880's, and $95,000 looked like a large sum to them.

Perry Organ did not "talk down" statehood directly, nor did he come out for it. His campaign remarks suggest that he was accepting the Democratic platform plank on statehood without comment. Democratic editors in Cheyenne, Rawlins, and Saratoga placed their candidate squarely against immediate statehood, whatever he privately may have thought about it. In Saratoga, George R. Caldwell put it this way: "Organ would rather see Wyoming fostered as a territory than wrecked as a state. Carey would have Wyoming admitted at once to the Union with all the ruinous burden of taxation."

During the 1888 campaign, more noise was made over the statehood issue than any other, yet one senses a hollow ring in the Democratic cries against statehood. Most Wyoming Democrats probably were not really opposed to immediate statehood; rather, their opposition was to a statehood movement led by Carey and Warren, who had been champions of statehood since 1885. With them so strongly for statehood and with the national Republican party for statehood, Wyoming Democrats were less than eager to climb on the bandwagon. They chose halfhearted opposition instead of the available alternative, me-tooism. A week after the Carey victory, the *Cheyenne Leader* plausibly maintained that the statehood question had not influenced one hundred votes either way.

Wyoming Democrats could not get very excited about national Democratic pleas for tariff reform. Nor could they defend very effectively against Republican assaults on Cleveland's land policies, particularly his holding up of land patents, more often for poor men than rich. Carey had the advantage of experience and the better ability to project his personality.

In analyzing the election returns, the *Cheyenne Leader* and *Rawlins Journal* focused attention on a major reason for Carey's victory: Republican control of the labor vote in the mining counties. Carey won Uinta County by 837 votes, Carbon by 769, Sweetwater by 559. Beckwith, Quinn & Company controlled the hiring and firing for the Union Pacific mines. In Uinta County, said the *Leader*, Beckwith, Quinn & Company, at company expense, printed straight Democratic tickets with the single exception of the delegate. The *Leader* and the *Rawlins Journal* added details: hundreds of Finns in Uinta and Sweetwater counties voted as they were told, taking the ticket offered them and presenting it as their ballot. Carbon Precinct in Carbon County cast 909 votes, with an average Republican majority of 400. Even Republican editor J. H. Hayford recognized publicly the influence of Beckwith, Quinn & Company.[1]

No doubt certain reprehensible practices were prevalent in Wyoming and elsewhere in the days before the Australian ballot was adopted in 1890. After the 1882 election the *Cheyenne Sun* had reported frauds by both parties—emigrants being taken from trains to vote; men voting more than once, using assumed names; fifteen-year-old girls voting; and men publicly buying votes at the Seventeenth Street polling place.

Charles A. Guernsey, who was elected to the House in 1884 and to the Senate in 1886, has published a description of some of the unusual features of Wyoming elections as he observed them in Laramie County before the Australian ballot brought changes.[2] After the party conventions, enterprising individuals of both parties printed tickets, selecting candidates from the major tickets. Each person, society, lodge, union, or company printing such a ticket claimed to control a certain

[1] While there can be little doubt that Beckwith, Quinn & Company helped Carey in 1888, the *Leader*'s assertion that the company printed straight Democratic tickets except for Carey is suspect because one Republican was returned to the legislature by Uinta County that year, along with three Democrats.

[2] Charles A. Guernsey, *Wyoming Cowboy Days* (New York: Putnam, 1936), pp. 97–102.

number of votes. A candidate could get on such a ticket by paying the ticket sponsor so much for each vote the sponsor claimed to control, or in some cases on merit alone if the sponsor approved him. Such printed tickets were accepted at the polls. Guernsey recalled that in 1884, he paid the Union Pacific master mechanic for the four hundred votes he claimed to control.

On December 11, 1888, Governor Thomas Moonlight sent Secretary of the Interior William F. Vilas a statement in which he revised radically downward his previous estimates of Wyoming's population. He recalled that Governor Warren had estimated a population of 65,000 in his 1885 report and 75,000 in his 1886 report and that he (Moonlight) had estimated 85,000 in 1887 and 85,000 again in his report of September 19, 1888. Now, less than three months later, Moonlight cut the estimate back to 55,500. He based the revision on an analysis of the November 6 election, in which a full turnout cast only 18,008 votes for delegate. Allowing three persons for each voter and guessing that perhaps 500 legal voters did not vote, he arrived at the figure 55,500. As later events were to prove, this was remarkably accurate. Coming as it did, however, when the Republicans were hot for statehood, Moonlight's supplementary report evoked partisan derision. It smelled like a sour-grapes reaction to the Republican victory.

Even Democrats thought the Governor looked foolish. Formerly his champion, the *Cheyenne Leader* asked on December 22, 1888, whether the Governor might not have employed himself to better advantage in some other way. Placing his low estimate of population before the whole country (it was well publicized) at a time when high estimates were the rule for all other territories could only serve, said the *Leader*, to retard immigration. Editor Carroll related that for many months he had been shaking his head over Moonlight's public policy and general behavior but had withheld criticism out of party loyalty, knowing that his days were limited. The supplementary population report was too much even for Carroll. He wished Wyoming "no better Christmas gift than the assurance of Governor Moonlight's immediate and precipitate removal." The *Rock Springs Miner* and the *Rawlins Journal* seem to have been the only newspapers willing to say a good word for Moonlight's gratuitous supplementary report.

The *New York World* in January, 1889, published the results of interviews with prominent citizens of Wyoming on the subject of statehood. With the exception of editor Carroll, who still maintained that the territory was not yet ready, all others interviewed favored statehood as soon as possible. Soon thereafter even Carroll began to look more favorably upon statehood. The closing of a contract between the Cheyenne City Council and the Union Pacific Railroad in January, 1889, calling for construction of large shops and a general supply depot at Cheyenne in return for city promises of free water and two viaducts to be built by the city, caused Carroll to revise upward his estimate of the territory's economic strength. In March he wrote: "The Leader has never frantically raved for statehood, but it believes the time is now rapidly approaching when the honor must come to Wyoming." Thereafter he did not oppose statehood.

An anonymous attack on Francis E. Warren, the new governor, sent from Cheyenne and published in the *New York Times* in April, 1889, charging him with being a fencer of government land and a tool of the Union Pacific and the cattle barons, was generally condemned in Wyoming. Thousands turned out for Warren's inauguration on a wet, muddy day, April 9. The inaugural address was mainly a plea for statehood. Warren argued that increased expenses would be offset by greater revenues. "Let us have statehood," he urged, promising rapid growth and development once admission to the Union had been accomplished.

THE CONSTITUTIONAL CONVENTION

Governor Warren arranged for a constitutional convention at Cheyenne in September, 1889.[3] Fifty-five delegates had been elected on July 8, all of them men. This might seem rather odd in a territory where much was said about equality of the sexes, yet it is consistent with Wyoming's failure to elect any woman to a territorial legislature.

Of the 55 delegates elected in July, only 49 put in an appearance at the convention, which met in the new capitol building. Brief biographies of 47 members of the convention are available in Mrs. Marie H. Erwin's *Wyoming Historical Blue Book*. Among the 47 were 18 lawyers, 13 veterans of the Union army, and one veteran of the Confederate army (Caleb "Honest Perry" Organ). Only 3 of the 47 had been born in the South, 8 in Ohio, 7 in Pennsylvania, 4 in New York, 4 in Illinois, 6 in New England, and 6 outside the United States—one each in England, Scotland, Wales, Denmark, Germany, and Canada. The origins of the convention members correspond rather closely to the origins of the territory's population as a whole. New York, Pennsylvania, Ohio, and Illinois led the states in supplying Wyoming's 1890

[3] Major source used for the discussion which follows is the *Journal and Debates of the Constitutional Convention of the State of Wyoming* (Cheyenne: *The Daily Sun*, 1893). See the "Sources" section at the end of this volume for a list of other materials used in preparing this chapter.

population. Only 4 per cent of Wyoming's 1890 population had been born in the South; only 94 men were Confederate veterans, as compared with 1,171 Union veterans.

Laramie lawyer Melville C. Brown,[4] who was elected president of the convention, later wrote that the "convention represented all the business interests of the State—bankers, stockgrowers, merchants, farmers, gold miners, coal miners, railroaders and lawyers." The lawyers should have been at the head, not bottom, of the list, for they dominated the convention. They did most of the talking, especially eight of them: Brown from Laramie; A. C. Campbell, E. S. N. Morgan, Charles N. Potter, and John A. Riner of Cheyenne; Clarence D. Clark of Evanston; Charles H. Burritt of Buffalo; and George C. Smith of Rawlins.

Contributing substantially to the debates were these six nonlawyers: George W. Baxter, Cheyenne cattleman and former territorial governor; Henry A. Coffeen, Sheridan merchant; George W. Fox, Laramie merchant; Henry G. Hay, Cheyenne cattleman and banker; John W. Hoyt, president of the University of Wyoming and former governor of the territory; and Hubert E. Teschemacher, Uva and Cheyenne cattleman. All of these fourteen leaders of the convention had been brought up and trained in the States somewhere east of Wyoming. Ten of them had enjoyed formal education beyond high school.[5] There were four

---

[4] Melville C. Brown was born in Maine in 1838, went to California in 1856, and then moved to Boise, Idaho, in 1863. He turned up in Cheyenne and began to practice law in November, 1867. From Cheyenne he moved to Laramie in May, 1868, where he served as that city's first mayor. In 1871–1872, as penitentiary commissioner, he accepted construction bids and then postponed opening them for twenty-four hours. After an investigation, the contract which he had awarded to a friend was canceled (National Archives, Department of the Interior Files, *Wyoming Territory*, *Wyoming Penitentiary 1871–72*, "Charges Concerning Superintendent of Construction"). In 1884 the Wyoming Territorial Supreme Court suspended for a time Brown's license to practice before the court because in talking publicly about the court he had used "vile, opprobrious, and indecent epithets." Republican bellwether Francis E. Warren disliked Brown. He wrote to Joseph M. Carey on March 13, 1889 (Warren Letterbooks, University of Wyoming Library): "Personally, I would rather crawl on my hands and knees in the gutter a block in Cheyenne, than to see even the worst of our three democratic judges replaced by Brown." Nevertheless, Senator Warren in 1900 approved (but possibly to get him out of Wyoming) Brown's appointment by President McKinley to a judgeship in Alaska. In 1905, President Theodore Roosevelt dismissed Brown from the judgeship for having engaged in a water-power venture (cf. Jeannette P. Nichols, *Alaska* [Cleveland: Arthur H. Clark Co., 1924], p. 237 and n. 443). After practicing law for a few years in Seattle, Brown returned to practice once again in Laramie, where he died in 1928.

[5] Clark at the University of Iowa; Potter and Riner at the University of Michigan; Burritt at Middlebury; Brown at the Detroit Law School; Baxter at the University of

Democrats—Campbell, Burritt, Baxter, and Coffeen—and ten Republicans among the fourteen convention leaders.

Some members of the convention contributed little or nothing. A case in point is Stephen W. Downey, highly respected member from Laramie, who would undoubtedly have been a leader in the convention had he attended regularly. It was later said on the one hand that the illness of his father kept him away and on the other that he was miffed over committee assignments.

In the election for president of the convention, after C. D. Clark of Evanston declined to be a candidate, the Republicans divided their votes between two other lawyers, A. B. Conaway of Sweetwater County and Melville C. Brown of Albany County, permitting the Democrats to tip the balance in favor of Brown. Appropriately, Brown presided without partisanship.

Pressure of time was obvious. Tempers were short now and then. On the twenty-fourth day, Cheyenne lawyer A. C. Campbell apologized for having lost his temper eleven days before and asked that his language be expunged from the record. His apology was accepted and the record was changed. Fifty-one years later, Laramie newspaperman W. E. Chaplin, also a member of the convention, recalled the incident in a talk before the Cheyenne Rotary Club. It was, he said, "the only fireworks of a somewhat prosy convention." Campbell had said that he was for woman suffrage but believed it should be submitted to the people separately. Henry A. Coffeen of Sheridan questioned Campbell's motives. White as a sheet, Campbell rose and shouted: "Any man who impugns my motives on the floor of this convention lies, away down in the bottom of his old throat." Possibly Chaplin had a copy of the original record; otherwise his memory of the exact words expunged can hardly be trusted. Chaplin recalled that, fortunately, Coffeen was peace loving, and so a personal encounter was avoided.

Ironically, this most violent personal quarrel of the convention was between two Democrats. On the day after Campbell's apology, an "Address to the People of Wyoming" was adopted, which included the statement that the convention was nonpartisan in character and without division upon party lines. The document said further that sectional

---

Tennessee and West Point; Hoyt at Ohio Wesleyan, Cincinnati Law School, Ohio Medical College and Eclectic Medical Institute; Coffeen at Abingdon College in Illinois; May at Vincennes University and a commercial college; and Teschemacher at Harvard. Campbell, Morgan and Smith had learned their law in offices of other lawyers.

questions were at no time considered, and no outside influences were permitted to affect action. Despite these protestations, a close reading of the journals suggests that the members could not divest themselves entirely of partisanship, that North *versus* South sectionalism was present in mild form, and that lobbyists were on hand. Often overlooked in assessing influences from outside the convention were Governor Warren, Delegate Carey, Willis Van Devanter, and Elwood Mead, who were often consulted and whom convention member W. E. Chaplin in 1934 called "an invisible delegation of extraordinary power."

PROCEDURE

The convention early chose nineteen standing committees of ten, seven, or five members. Five major committees had ten members each, with, insofar as possible, one member from each of the ten counties. The five major committees dealt with the legislative department; the judiciary; boundaries and apportionment; taxation, revenue, and public debt; and railroads and telegraphs.

In convention debate, Cheyenne lawyer John A. Riner once complained that "members of the committees take out this and that from the different state constitutions without taking into consideration for a moment whether they affect the local conditions we have or not." On the other hand, former Governor George W. Baxter justified borrowing by arguing that the ablest men in past ages had formulated the fundamental principles of liberty, justice, and equality in such clear and concise language that "it seems to me, therefore, that so far as nine-tenths of our labor is concerned, we have only to exercise an intelligent and discriminating judgment in our study of the work of the constitution builders who have preceded us." Baxter's philosophy prevailed. How else could the constitution have been produced, in twenty-five working days, except by the scissors-and-paste method? Heavy borrowing from earlier constitutions has been the standard practice in state constitution making.

The Wyoming convention was presented at the outset with a model constitution. It had been drawn up by former Territorial Chief Justice J. W. Fisher and was presented to the convention by E. S. N. Morgan, former territorial secretary, who was a member of the convention. After some debate, the convention decided to distribute the model constitution's parts to the several appropriate committees. What, if any, influence Judge Fisher had on the final product cannot be determined.

The convention apparently had access in the territorial library to the constitutions of all states already in the Union. Five territories not yet admitted had recently held conventions—North Dakota, South Dakota, Montana, Washington, and Idaho. Governor Warren's correspondence shows that he wrote for, and obtained, copies of their constitutions just before the Cheyenne convention. The debates include references to the constitutions of Colorado, Kansas, Illinois, Missouri, Nebraska, Pennsylvania, Texas, and Washington, but the greatest obligation of the Wyoming Constitution's makers appears to have been to the constitutions of North Dakota, Montana, and Idaho.

A section-by-section comparison of the Wyoming Constitution with the constitutions of North Dakota, South Dakota, Montana, and Idaho leads to the conclusion that Wyoming's Article III (Legislative Department) was borrowed for the most part from the Montana Constitution; Wyoming's Article V (Judicial Department) appears to have been borrowed substantially from the constitution of North Dakota; and Wyoming's Article XIX (Miscellaneous), Article XX (Amendments), and Article XXI (Schedule) resemble closely articles in the Idaho Constitution.

Major Issues in the Convention

While the Wyoming Constitution shows heavy obligation to several earlier constitutions, decisions had to be made as to what to borrow and what changes to make in wording. The debates show substantial differences of opinion on several important issues.

Some of the members wanted to make it easy to organize new counties. They did not want to have to travel great distances to reach the county seat. On voice votes, attempts to raise the committee's recommendation of a two-million-dollar valuation for a new county to two and a half or three million dollars were defeated. The go-slow members made it necessary for the old county to be left with a valuation of at least three million dollars. They also provided that a majority of the qualified electors of the area to be separated must approve before the new county could be established.

Another issue over which there was much argument was whether there should be a supreme court separate from the district courts. The territorial arrangement had been to combine the two. The territory had three district judges who now and then sat together as a supreme court. In the first stage of this dispute, all of the lawyers wanted a separate supreme court. "I believe it has been said that the lawyers in this convention have been talking too much," said A. C. Campbell of Cheyenne, but he could not resist talking at length in favor of a separate supreme court. Under the territorial system, he argued, an appeal is taken to a court one-third of whose members is already against you. "What show has the defeated party got?" he asked.

The Harvard-trained cattleman Teschemacher asked if the three supreme-court judges would not have a "soft snap" while the district judges were overworked. Lawyer A. B. Conaway conceded that this might be true at the outset, but pointed out that as a partial offset the committee had planned to give supreme-court judges original jurisdiction in certain matters.

Lawyer George C. Smith of Rawlins asked: "What is the matter of a few thousand dollars compared with the rights of life and liberty?" He conceded, however, that were it not for the vast amount of travel required of the district judges, "one judge could do all the business and not be constantly employed." In committee of the whole, the lawyers won approval for a separate supreme court by a vote of 13 to 8. When the judiciary-department file came up for final reading, however, public opinion had been brought to bear on the convention. Lawyer Charles N. Potter of Cheyenne had changed his mind. His amendment, to eliminate the separate supreme court, lost narrowly, 17 to 21. The debate over what kind of supreme court to have showed clearly that many members of the convention were seriously concerned about the costs of statehood. Economy was the watchword in the convention, although most of the lawyers believed so strongly in a separate supreme court that they would not give it up.

Before the judicial section of the constitution was completed, two other problems took time. How much should the judges be paid? The convention left judges' salaries to the legislature after debating whether the constitution should fix the salary at $2,500 or $3,000. What should the minimum age be? Some thought thirty-five, but the convention agreed on thirty for supreme-court judges and twenty-eight for district judges. A thirty-year-old Lander lawyer, Douglas A. Preston, a Democrat, argued that there weren't three Democratic lawyers in the state who were thirty-five years of age, and Democratic lawyers would soon be needed, he said, for the supreme court.

Lawyer A. C. Campbell of Cheyenne tossed a bombshell into the convention on its fourteenth day when he moved that woman suffrage be offered to the electors as a separate article. No one of any standing in the territory had found fault with woman suffrage since the 1871 legislature, yet a group of Cheyenne people had handed Campbell a petition asking for a separate vote. In proposing a separate vote, Campbell insisted that he personally favored woman suffrage. He said that opponents of woman suffrage had often told him that the people had never been given an opportunity to vote on the proposition and that the legislature had always been afraid to submit the question to popular vote. He believed that the people should have a chance to vote on the matter before it became the fundamental law of the new state. He thought that woman suffrage would be approved by a two-thirds vote.

Campbell's proposal called forth eloquent pleas against a separate vote from Baxter ("I yield to no man in the homage and adoration which I feel and which upon all proper occasions I gladly pay to a pure and lovely woman."), Coffeen ("I am unwilling to stand here and by vote or word or gesture disfranchise one-half the people of our territory, and that the better half. . . . Let us catch inspiration from the glorious features of nature about us, the grand valleys, the lifting mountains, the reverberating hills, the floating clouds so lovely above them."), C. W. Holden ("I say rather than surrender that right, we would rather remain in a territorial condition throughout the endless cycles of time."), M. C. Brown ("I would sooner think . . . of submitting to the people of Wyoming a separate and distinct proposition as to whether a male citizen of the territory shall be entitled to vote."), Hoyt ("No man has ever dared to say in the territory of Wyoming that woman suffrage is a failure. We stand today proud, proud of this great experiment. . . . Why then this extraordinary proposition? . . . I know that one-half of the members of the congress of the United States are in sympathy with this very principle."), and Burritt ("If they will not let us in with this plank in our constitution we will stay out forever.").

Campbell was not completely alone. Louis J. Palmer of Sweetwater County finally rose to support his proposition, stating that there were many voters in his county who were opposed to woman suffrage but who would like to have statehood. They would not vote for the constitution with woman suffrage in it. Conaway, who was also from Sweetwater County, denied that many of his constituents desired a separate vote. On the vote in the committee of the whole, eight votes were cast in support of Campbell's proposition, twenty against.

Long-winded argument preceded adoption of Teschemacher's provision that, unless handicapped by physical disability, one must be able to read the constitution to vote. Teschemacher explained that four earlier constitutions contained similar provisions. Despite spirited opposition, the educational test was included in the constitution, with all residents who had voted before admission being assured that they would not be disfranchised.

Debate raged furiously over the question of apportionment of seats in the Senate. Without very much difficulty the seats in the House of Representatives were distributed according to population, but members of the less populous counties fought for equality in the Senate. They praised the federal plan by which each state of the Union has equal representation in the United States Senate. They argued that in the past the "little" counties had been "preyed upon" by the larger counties.

Potter and Morgan of Laramie County led the attack on the federal plan. Potter rejected the federal analogy, insisting that the relation of a county to a state is not the same as the relation of a state to the United States government. A county, he said, is "simply a medium by which a state conducts its business." Counties have no independence, whereas under the United States Constitution, states have reserved powers. True democracy, he maintained, required that every man count for as much as any other man and that the legislature should represent everyone equally. Morgan argued along the same line: "I ought to have as much right in the . . . enactment of laws for the government as the man who lives in a smaller county."

Preston of Fremont County taunted Potter and Morgan, suggesting that they were afraid that the capital would be moved away from Cheyenne. Baxter of Laramie County (with interests also in Fremont and Johnson counties) rejected the one-senator idea, calling it as extraordinary as it would be to propose that each county should contribute the same amount to the general fund. He asked what justice there could be in permitting a man from the northern part of Wyoming to have five or ten times as much voice as a man in the south. Palmer and Conaway of Sweetwater County, often at odds, were in agreement on this question, both holding that it would be unfair to give Sheridan County, with one-third the valuation and one-half the population of Sweetwater County, equal representation in the Senate with their county.

Had delegates from the five Union Pacific counties united on the issue, it would have been no contest, since they had more than twice as many delegates as the five northern counties. The Union Pacific delegations, however, did not present a united front. President Brown (Albany County) could see no need for two houses if the principle of representation in proportion to population were adopted. He preferred a two-house legislature with the smaller house so constructed that it would be a check on the will of the popular majority in the other house. He considered the federal plan of representation to be "the happiest compromise that ever came to man."

John W. Hoyt, like Brown, supported the idea of one senator per county in the belief that it would best promote the welfare of the state. He thought it desirable to have a differently constituted Senate so that it could serve as a check on the House. Holden of Uinta County likened the House of Representatives to a cup of tea and the Senate to a saucer, explaining that "you have use for the saucer for the purpose of cooling the beverage."

As the showdown vote approached, the presiding officer ordered lobbyists to keep off the floor of the convention. Southern delegations were worried because some of their members had gone home. However, enough southern members who opposed the one-senator idea remained on the nineteenth day to defeat it, 17 to 11, so sixteen senators were provided for the ten counties. On the same day, what was regarded by many as a sop to Sheridan, Johnson, and Converse counties was provided in the form of one additional House seat for each of them; thus the total in the House was increased from thirty to thirty-three. The ten counties received representation as follows: Laramie County, three senators and six representatives; Albany and Carbon counties, two senators and five representatives each; Sweetwater and Uinta counties, two senators and three representatives each; Converse County, one senator and three representatives; Crook, Fremont, Johnson, and Sheridan counties, one senator and two representatives each.

M. C. Brown, president of the convention, led a drive to include in the constitution a tonnage tax on coal. It was generally supposed that coal would be the state's major source of wealth. Nearly two-thirds of current production, Brown estimated, was shipped out of the territory. The consumers would pay such a tax, argued Brown, and he could see no reason why those who benefited from Wyoming coal should not help support the government. Brown stated that coal lands and coal corporations paid only 1.5 per cent of the property tax, even though the coal business was the largest industry in the territory. Coal interests, he said, contributed only $1,250 per year toward the support of the territorial government at a time when it cost the territory more than $3,000 each year to pay a coal inspector and coal engineer. Brown thought that a tax of one and one-half cents on each ton (one cent to the state and one-half cent to the county where mined) would pay half the expenses of the state government and would not be unjust.

Brown's principal antagonist was C. D. Clark of Evanston, who had been an attorney for the Union Pacific and admitted that he was part owner of a coal-mining enterprise at Rock Springs. Clark expressed concern lest the state find itself with a surplus every year: "Do you want to have a provision in our constitution that may heap up more money than we can honestly spend for a state government?" Clark must have been expecting a great increase in production. In the late 1880's, annual production amounted to about two million tons. At that rate, one cent per ton would bring the state only twenty thousand dollars a year, hardly a frightening amount of revenue.

Clark could see no justice in placing on coal a special tax that did not apply to other minerals. "Why," he asked, "single out this infant industry?" He argued that coal would not be raised in price to meet the tax; the burden would fall either upon the mining company or upon the miner. Another coal-mine owner, Henry G. Hay, a Cheyenne banker, also objected to making the "infant coal industry" subject to a direct tax not imposed on the output of other mines.

Coffeen of Sheridan, like Brown, argued that coal lands were not paying their just share. He agreed that, generally speaking, there should be no discrimination, but coal mines were already developed, while other mines were not. Hence the tax should be applied first to coal mines.

Baxter of Cheyenne scoffed at the suggestion that the tax would bring a great surplus to the treasury. He explained that a coal mine was different from an acre of farmland, which, with proper care, would be worth as much in fifty years as it was then, while a mine would become worthless when the coal was exhausted. He thought a production tax justifiable on coal, "as near a proper basis for taxing it as you can reach," but felt that it was best to leave the matter to the legislature.

Brown wanted the tax in the constitution in order to remove it from the influence of lobbyists: "As you have seen in the past men elected to our legislature wearing the brass collars of the great railroad corporation, you will see just such men wear the brass collars of the great monied mining corporations." Brown looked forward to having the coal industry produce $100,000 annually in revenue, almost enough to pay expenses of the state government. He warned that without such a tax, little would be collected from the land before its wealth was exhausted "and you have nothing left but a howling wilderness."

Palmer of Sweetwater County warned that Uinta, Sweetwater, and Carbon counties would not support the constitution if a tonnage tax on coal were included. The controversial production tax on minerals was left to the legislature. Many years later, speaking to a group of Cheyenne pioneers on "Constitution Making," M. C. Brown declared that "the most serious mistake in our Constitution was lack of legislation, failure to fix a tonnage tax upon the output of coal mined in our State being perhaps one of the gravest omissions."

The territorial legislature had already located several institutions. Most of the convention delegates, however, were unwilling to locate them permanently by constitutional provision. Although Evanston had one of the institutions, Clarence D. Clark of that city opposed the permanent location of any public building or institution "in any one place." Coffeen of Sheridan was concerned not to locate the university permanently. Brown of Laramie objected to what he considered an attempt to put "the University on wheels, to be wheeled around anywhere they may please at any time." He would accept location of the institutions for a term of years, but did not want the legislature free to relocate them at any time, as dictated by logrolling. He offered the opinion that "there has been more corruption in legislation, more corrupt trades, more infamous deals instituted in legislative bodies on the location of these public institutions than has ever occurred in the legislature in any other way." Preston of Lander thought it "a good idea to put these buildings on wheels. When we become a state we want to wheel them up into the central part of the state." Riner of Cheyenne suggested that other constitutions generally located institutions for a term of years, after which they might be changed by vote of the people. He doubted that the university would ever be moved, but he felt that it would be wrong to locate any public institution except for a term of years. His views prevailed, and the convention placed in the constitution the provision that institutions should be located permanently by popular vote after ten years.

What little originality there is in Wyoming's constitution is mainly concentrated in Article VIII (Irrigation and Water Rights). This article comprises only five short sections:

SECTION 1. The water of all natural streams, springs, lakes or other collections of still water, within the boundaries of the State, are hereby declared to be the property of the State.

SECTION 2. There shall be constituted a board of control, to be composed of the State engineer and superintendents of the water divisions; which shall, under such regulations as may be prescribed by law, have the supervision of the waters of the State and of their appropriation, distribution and diversion, and of the various officers connected therewith. Its decisions to be subject to review by the Courts of the State.

SECTION 3. Priority of appropriation for beneficial uses shall give the better right. No appropriation shall be denied except when such denial is demanded by the public interests.

SECTION 4. The legislature shall by law divide the State into four (4) water divisions, and provide for the appointment of superintendents thereof.

SECTION 5. There shall be a State engineer who shall be appointed by the governor of the State and confirmed by the senate; he shall hold his office for the term of six (6) years, or until his successor shall have been appointed and shall have qualified. He shall be president of the board of control, and shall have general supervision of the waters of the State and of the officers connected with its distribution. No person shall be appointed to this position who has not such theoretical knowledge and such practical experience and skill as shall fit him for the position.

Wyoming did not originate the idea of recognizing water rights according to priority of appropriation for beneficial use. California and Colorado had pioneered in breaking with the English common law of waters, which gave all who had land along a stream the rights to a "full and undiminished flow." Earlier still, appropriations had been permitted under Mexican sovereignty. Wyoming's major contribution lay in adopting a complete system for state control of water. Wyoming's achievement was such that William E. Smythe wrote in his *Conquest of Arid America*: "It [Wyoming] is recognized as the law-giver of the arid region. It is the State which has contributed most to the working out of the legal institutions on which our great future civilization will rest throughout western America. In this respect its position of leadership is alike unapproached and unchallenged." Smythe's high praise for Wyoming's part in water law needs qualification. Later studies show that Wyoming shares with Colorado the leadership in working out the procedures which have been copied by other western states.[6]

Three men were mainly responsible for drawing up Article VIII— Elwood Mead, territorial engineer, and two convention members, J. A. Johnston, Laramie County farmer, and Charles H. Burritt, Johnson County lawyer. Mead, who had come to Wyoming in 1888 as the first territorial engineer, had learned quickly the deficiencies of existing

[6] Cf. particularly Wells A. Hutchins, *Selected Problems in the Law of Water Rights in the West* (Washington: U.S. Government Printing Office, 1942), pp. 64–109.

water laws. By the time of the constitutional convention he knew what reforms he would like to institute. Johnston was chairman of the committee on irrigation and water rights. Burritt was an extraordinarily effective spokesman for the committee in convention debate. When their report first reached the convention floor, Burritt made a claim, unique in the debates, that the report "in some respects . . . is radical and different from anything that any state or territory in the union now has."

Conaway stated what others must have thought when he said, apropos the claim that all water belongs to the state: "We may be claiming more than we are rightly and legally entitled to." He added: "I suppose it is true . . . that we cannot lose anything by claiming too much." Burritt read from a Mead report to illustrate some of the evils of the territorial irrigation system. The district court, for example, had allowed the Carey Horse Creek Ditch No. 8 to take twenty cubic feet of water per second for 190 acres when one cubic foot was adequate for 50 or 60 acres.

There was much discussion about whether appropriation meant diverting water from a stream, the beginning of work to divert the water, or the application of water to land. In support of Burritt, President Brown argued that the definition of appropriation should be left to the courts. Brown thought the right acquired by appropriation should be qualified or limited in some way. Henry S. Elliott agreed and moved an amendment that after "Priority of appropriation shall give the better right" should be added "but shall not be conclusive in determining the better right." His amendment was lost, 13 to 19. When a further assault was made on the right of appropriation, Burritt pleaded eloquently for its retention. President Brown, who was not convinced, insisted that it was contradictory to say first that the state owns the water and then that priority of appropriation shall give the better right. On the final vote, Brown could get only one supporter, Smith of Carbon County.

On the twenty-fourth day, John W. Hoyt offered a proposition which caused the last significant split in the convention. He moved that "the legislature shall make such provision by law as shall be calculated to secure the best faithful service for all minor places in the state, county and municipal government, regardless of considerations purely political." Hoyt explained that he had no connection with the civil service reform movement but was merely interested in securing the best public service possible. C. D. Clark rose to describe civil service reform as "a delusion and a snare, a lot of political clap trap which does not accomplish the end sought at all." Burritt said "Amen." A. L. Sutherland chimed in that civil service was "one of the greatest frauds that ever was." Even when a pretense was made of finding the "best" man, he noticed that he "is always the man who had the boodle." "I am a mugwump and am proud of it," injected Teschemacher. He alone supported Hoyt in debate, although when it came to a vote, the proposal was defeated only 21 to 11.

THE CONSTITUTION IS APPROVED

On the twenty-fifth day, on a roll-call vote, the constitution was adopted, 37 to 0, and each member present signed the document. That night, the Laramie County delegation was host to the other members of the convention at a banquet at the Cheyenne Club, after which the members dispersed to their homes. Aided by the "Address to the People of Wyoming," which had been prepared by a convention committee, they undertook to win popular approval for the constitution.

At a special election on November 5, 1889, the electorate approved the constitution by a vote of 6,272 to 1,923. It was a disappointingly small turnout, considering that at the general election the year before, 18,008 votes had been cast. Sheridan County voted against the constitution, Johnson County favored it by a majority of only 44 votes, and Fremont County was less than enthusiastic, but the other seven counties supported the document, two to one or better.

Following the ratification, a convention committee presented a memorial to Congress "Praying for the Admission of Wyoming into the Union of States." Delegate Joseph M. Carey then introduced a Wyoming statehood bill in the House of Representatives, and others introduced two omnibus bills including Wyoming.

While they waited for Congress to act on their request for statehood, the people of Wyoming watched their last territorial legislature, which assembled in January, 1890, engage in a slugfest such as occurs occasionally when the state senate is at odds with the governor. The voters in November, 1888, had returned a Republican House (17–6) and a Democratic Council (7–5). The members were handicapped by lack of experience. Territorial legislators rarely sought re-election, finding their service poorly paid and thankless and also finding it hard to spare the time from their occupations. Only four of the legislators who met in January, 1890, had been members before: R. M. Galbraith and Alexander H. Reel in the Council and Thomas B. Adams and Stephen W. Downey in the House.

The new wings on the capitol building were ready for occupancy, so there was no space problem. Governor Warren's 10,000-word message was comprehensive and discreetly cautious in view of the Democratic Council. The *Cheyenne Leader* described the message as "absolutely colorless" and lacking in leadership and said: "When he ventures an inch beyond absolutely safe grounds he makes use of recommendations in the reports of territorial officials . . . or to work of the constitutional convention."

As usual, livestock men were prominent in the 1890 legislature. The *Cheyenne Sun* counted five stock raisers in the Council and nine in the House. W. Turrentine Jackson has counted eight members of the Wyoming Stock Growers Association among the twelve members of the Council (although three of the eight were not active ranchers). The stock interests overcame an effort in the House to do away with the Board of Live Stock Commissioners and were able to push through a $10,000 appropriation in aid of the stock commission's work. House member Thomas B. Adams, secretary of the Wyoming Stock Growers Association, represented the cattlemen effectively.

"The watchword of the legislature should be Retrenchment," said the *Leader*, and it was. The 1886 and 1888 legislatures had spent so much for institutions that the bonded debt was at the limit of $320,000 and the property tax had been pushed up to six mills. Economic conditions were not good, and few people would approve a higher mill levy. The legislature did no more than the absolute minimum for the institutions. To complete the $100,000 penitentiary buildings at Rawlins, $70,000 was required, but nothing was appropriated (the federal penitentiary at Laramie was adequate). Small wonder that Johnson County's request for a college of agriculture, Crook County's request for a normal school, and Sweetwater's request for a hospital were all turned down.

The Democratic majority in the Council treated Governor Warren much as the Republican majority had treated Governor Moonlight two years earlier. The Council refused to approve several of Warren's appointments. It was contended that the incumbent Democratic auditor and treasurer should be reappointed, since it seemed unwise to replace them with inexperienced men for only a few months of service, statehood being expected very soon. To climax their battle with the Governor, the Democrats in the Council balked at a $1,200 contingency-fund item for the Governor and a $600 item for the secretary of the territory. Reconciliation was impossible—the two houses could not get together—and the legislature adjourned without approving the $49,939.20 general-appropriation bill.

One noteworthy piece of legislation came out of the session: the Australian ballot was adopted. There had been so much discussion of voting abuses during the past year, in the constitutional convention and elsewhere, that the secret ballot, which had been gaining favor in the East, was instituted.

Within two weeks after the legislature adjourned, Delegate Joseph M. Carey began his battle for statehood on the floor of the United States House of Representatives. On March 26, 1890, he talked at great length in support of his bill.[7] He declared that Wyoming had ten to twelve million acres of "irrigable land" and was "rich in agricultural possibilities." With respect to minerals, he asserted that Wyoming was "unsurpassed" and was "one of nature's great storehouses." He dwelt at length on grazing development, forest resources, educational leadership, splendid institutions, significant postal statistics, widespread railway construction, the "model" constitution, and the unique place of women.

As expected, there was skepticism about the territory's population. In December, 1888, Governor Moonlight had estimated the population to be only 55,500, and governors' estimates were usually optimistic. In answer to a direct question on the subject, Carey placed the population between 110,000 and 125,000, twice as great as the federal census a few months later would find it to be. He explained the small vote in the election to ratify the constitution by saying that no effort was made to get out the vote and that "the universal exclamation in Wyoming was that day, 'Everybody favors the constitution, and what is the use of voting.'"

The House of Representatives was the major hurdle. Member after member rose to complain that the proceedings leading to the constitutional convention had been irregular, the territory's population was too small, the educational qualification for voting was improper, and woman suffrage should not be permitted. The Democrats who raised most of the objections probably were more distressed at the prospect of

[7] This speech is quoted in full in Marie H. Erwin, *Wyoming Historical Blue Book* (Denver: Bradford-Robinson Printing Co., 1946), pp. 663–703.

another Republican state than they were about woman suffrage, but with Republicans in control of both houses of Congress, it would hardly do to argue publicly against adding a Republican state. So they talked unconvincingly about the evils of woman suffrage.

When Wyoming statehood passed the House on March 26, 1890, by a vote of 139 to 127, victory was virtually assured. News of the House action reached Wyoming the next day and brought a great outburst of cheering in Wyoming towns. Church bells, train whistles, fire bells, cowbells, and trumpets sounded in Cheyenne. All the bunting in town was displayed. A spontaneous parade of men and women marched to Governor Warren's place of business and obtained comments from him. He congratulated the people, especially the ladies. That evening a huge bonfire of packing boxes blazed at the corner of Seventeenth and Ferguson (Carey), after which a crowd filled the opera house to hear speeches. George W. Baxter explained: "It means the dawning of a brighter day, the beginning of an era of unparalleled prosperity. . . . A tide of immigration will set in. Capital will come." Governor Warren assured Wyoming citizens that the United States Senate would act within ten days. Three months later, on June 27, the Senate voted for statehood, 29 to 18, after listening to objections from several Democrats, who gave special attention to the population question and woman suffrage. Again there was an impromptu parade in Cheyenne, with "Clanging Bells, Shrieking Whistles, Incessant Yelling."

President Benjamin Harrison signed the statehood bill on July 10, 1890, thus setting off a third celebration the following day. A drizzle dampened spirits in Cheyenne, but there were the usual bells and whistles, accompanied this time by firecrackers and bombs, "and the yelling was ear splitting and incessant." A 44-gun salute was fired in Laramie, cannon boomed in Rock Springs, Douglas celebrated "louder than ever." A dispatch from Rawlins announced that "Rawlins Town is wild," and another from Buffalo said that "the great north is delighted."

The fourth and official celebration of statehood occurred in Cheyenne on July 23. Committees, with state-wide representation, had begun preparations in March for a formal observance as soon as possible after the President's signature. The formal observance, though attended by upwards of five thousand people, lacked the spontaneity and wild shrieking of the first three celebrations. There was a two-mile parade featuring troops and two bands (Fort Russell and Union Pacific), along with many carriages and floats. On one large float rode forty-two young women representing the older states. It was followed closely by a small carriage in which rode three little girls representing the Goddess of Liberty, the state of Idaho (admitted July 3), and the state of Wyoming. A fat boy in a buggy advertised that he ate ice cream, fruit, and candy at Mrs. Robinson's parlors. A "generous looking cow" represented the dairy where she worked, and a fat steer, properly placarded, represented a livestock commission house.

The parade led to the capitol, in front of which a large throng had gathered for the principal program of the day. Mrs. Theresa A. Jenkins offered the first speech, a review of the struggle for woman suffrage. The *Cheyenne Leader* avowed the next day that her address was the most forceful and eloquent of the day, although it conceded that at one point she was carried away by a "fairest and rarest flight of oratory." Fifty years later, Mrs. Jenkins' daughter recalled for the *Wyoming State Tribune* that her mother had been heard by everyone in the audience, which extended to a point four blocks away, because she had practiced on the open prairie, with her husband riding off in a buggy to greater and greater distances and shouting back, at intervals, "Louder."

After Mrs. Jenkins' address, Mrs. Esther Morris presented to Governor Warren a 44-star silk flag purchased by women of the state. She made no attempt at an address, speaking only two sentences. Then, after a 44-gun salute, Mrs. I. S. Bartlett read an original poem, "The True Republic," the last four lines of which ran as follows:

> *Let the bells ring out more loudly and the deep-toned cannon roar*
> *Giving voice to our thanksgiving, such as never rose before.*
> *For we tread enchanted ground today, we're glorious, proud and great;*
> *Our independence day has come—Wyoming is a State!*

After these stirring sentiments, Melville C. Brown, president of the constitutional convention, presented Mrs. Amalia B. Post, "representative woman of Wyoming," with a copy of the state constitution.

The afternoon program ended with the oration of the day by Clarence D. Clark, Evanston attorney, who had been one of the leaders of the constitutional convention and who later would serve as United States senator. Clark seems to have been a substitute for Joseph M. Carey, who could not be present. That evening there was a fireworks display and a grand ball in the capitol building.

What may be regarded as a fifth celebration of statehood took place three days later when Joseph M. Carey and his family arrived from Washington. Again there was a parade, music, and a speech, followed, said the *Leader*, by a Republican caucus in the Hoffman brothers' saloon. No doubt Republican politicians assembled in some convenient meeting place, for they needed to complete their plans for the state's first election, which was little more than six weeks away.[8]

[8] Missing from the caucus was one of the territory's outstanding Republicans, W. W. Corlett, who had died on July 22, 1890, at the age of forty-eight. Since his arrival in Cheyenne in 1867, he had become the dean of the Wyoming bar, delegate to Congress (1877–1879), and a candidate for a judgeship in 1889. Along with many other Republicans, he could not tolerate his party's presidential candidate in 1884, the corrupt James G. Blaine. He turned Mugwump and made some speeches in support of Democrat Grover Cleveland. Later, in 1889, when President Benjamin Harrison, at the instigation of Joseph M. Carey, was about to appoint Corlett chief justice of the territory, W. W. Peck settled an old score by directing Harrison's attention to Corlett's behavior in 1884. This made Corlett unacceptable to Harrison, who gave the judgeship to Carey's second choice, Willis Van Devanter.

The premature passing of Corlett cost Wyoming the services of an outstanding leader. Upon his death it was said that he had been too honest and independent for the requirements of politics.

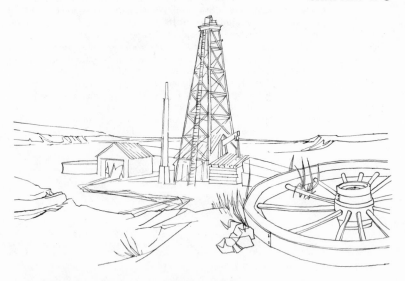

CHAPTER 10

Years of Struggle, 1890–1897

"DON'T EXPECT TOO MUCH," warned the *Cheyenne Leader* on the day after President Harrison signed the Wyoming statehood bill. The future, said the *Leader*, would still depend upon the people, the laws they enacted, their energy and frugality, their skill in attracting immigration and capital, and the intelligence with which capital was used in the development of latent resources. It was a timely warning, for many people appear to have been carried away by notions that statehood would solve most of their problems. This was not to be the case; harsh realities would dispel the aura of optimism.

When the first 1890 census reports became available, they showed that Wyoming had 62,555 people, including 1,850 Indians on reservation.

262

Governor Moonlight had estimated 55,500 in December, 1888, not counting Indians. Delegate Joseph M. Carey, in congressional debate in March, 1890, had estimated between 110,000 and 125,000. When the truth was published in October, 1890, no newspaper twitted Carey about his exaggeration. Statehood had been achieved, and he was the hero of the hour, "the architect of statehood."

There were twelve counties in the young state (Sheridan and Converse had been organized in 1888, and Natrona and Weston early in 1890). While there had been a northward spread of population since 1880, the five Union Pacific counties still claimed almost three-fourths of the total. Leading the cities and towns, Cheyenne had 11,690; Laramie, 6,388; Rock Springs, 3,406; Rawlins, 2,235; Evanston, 1,995. Casper and Sheridan, towns which would later rise to prominence, had only 544 and 281, respectively.

THE ELECTION OF SEPTEMBER 11, 1890

Territorial Governor Francis E. Warren moved quickly to carry out congressional provisions for the establishment of state government. On July 15 he issued a proclamation setting a special election for September 11. State conventions of the Republican and Democratic parties met in Cheyenne on August 11 to nominate candidates for state office and prepare party platforms.

Although the 1890 census showed that Wyoming had only 94 Confederate veterans as compared with 1,171 Union veterans and that only 4 per cent of the people had been born in the Old South, several men from that section were placed on the Democratic ticket, eliciting from the *Laramie Sentinel* the comment, "They utilized all the remnants of the Cleveland, carpet bag, ex-confederate element within reach." The Democratic nominee for governor, George W. Baxter, was a cattleman, born in Tennessee, who had been territorial governor briefly in 1886. The Republican nominee for governor was Francis E. Warren.

During the short campaign (one month), major attention focused on the gubernatorial race. Since Warren was ill and unable to participate until the last ten days, Joseph M. Carey did most of his campaigning for him. He debated Baxter before huge audiences in Evanston, Almy, Green River, Rock Springs, and Rawlins. When Baxter described and condemned Warren's preemption "theft" of the early 1880's, Carey denied knowledge of the incident but said he knew that other people had acquired land without fulfilling the residence requirements. Carey said that Baxter was head of a great cattle trust which was trying to raise the price of beef. Baxter charged that Warren had tried to pack the Rock Springs grand jury at the time of the Rock Springs massacre in 1885. Both Baxter and Carey were effective platform speakers; neither overwhelmed the other, partisan claims to the contrary notwithstanding. Everyone was aware that, should a Republican legisla-

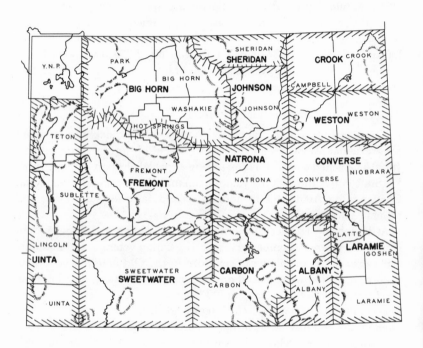

WYOMING, THIRTEEN-COUNTY MAP, 1890

ture be elected, Carey would be the first choice for the United States Senate.

The Democratic press spared neither Warren nor Carey. It charged that Carey had engaged in fraudulent land entries, had taken up thousands of acres under the Desert Land Act through "unprincipled hirelings," and was an enemy of the settler and the laborer. It alleged that of his 80,000 sheep in Laramie County, Warren had returned only

13,210 for assessment (the county commissioners had raised the figure to 22,910). His sheep, it was claimed, were responsible for depredations on small settlers.

Baxter's difficulties over fencing government land were well aired. Everyone learned, if they did not already know, that Cleveland had removed him from the governorship for illegal fencing. Warren defeated Baxter 8,879 to 7,153, and the Republicans won all other state offices by comparable margins, while Clarence D. Clark defeated George T. Beck for the lone seat in the United States House of Representatives, 9,087 to 6,520. Republicans won control of the Senate 13 to 3 and the House 26 to 7.

ME AND F. E.

Democrats in the early 1890's commonly referred to Carey and Warren as "Me and F. E." Carey was forty-five, Warren forty-six in 1890. They had dominated the Republican party for years. Democrats had snapped at them, abused them, and called them representatives of the classes against the masses. Grudgingly, they had to concede, however, that they could not find two men in the Democratic party with the prestige and ability of Me and F. E. In the 1890 campaign the *Laramie Sentinel* noted that the Democratic onslaught was concentrated on "the two men who have done more for Cheyenne and the state than all the men who ever ran for office on democratic tickets in Wyoming, put together." Editor Hayford, who often envied Cheyenne's success, declared that he would rather have Carey and Warren in Laramie than "the B & M railroad, the new U. P. shops and the state capitol, all combined." All three of these items would be in Laramie within two years, he added, if Me and F. E. lived there.

As expected, the legislature, which met November 12, quickly elected Joseph M. Carey first United States senator, but selection of the second senator took more time. When their friends could muster no general support for John W. Hoyt of Albany County, DeForest Richards of Converse County, and Homer Merrell of Carbon County, Governor Francis E. Warren was nominated and was elected on the seventh ballot. He resigned from the office of governor on November 24, 1890, making Secretary of State Amos W. Barber acting governor until 1893.

Warren's decision to give up the governorship two and one-half months after his election in order to accept a seat in the United States Senate brought hoots of derision from Democrats. Some of them had predicted that he would do this and had scouted his campaign statements to the contrary. Not a few Republicans groaned at the turn of events. They wanted a strong governor in the first years of statehood and were not sure that Dr. Barber was adequate to the task. The Douglas surgeon was known as a good mixer with a wide acquaintance among cattlemen and cowboys, but he was inexperienced in politics and government. Some people did not want both senators to come from Cheyenne. Others believed it unconstitutional for the governor to be elected senator, since the constitution said (Article IV, Section 2): "Nor shall he [the governor] be eligible to any other office during the term for which he was elected." [1] Frank Mondell, who was a member of the first legislature, wrote many years later in *My Story* that in Warren's election to the Senate "was sown the seed of future trouble."

Most people in the state nevertheless accepted without complaint the idea of sending Me and F. E. to Washington. The *Newcastle Journal* said: "Both senators are from Cheyenne, but what of it? Governor Warren and Delegate Carey have never for a moment forgotten that they represent the entire state, and they will not now. . . . A strong team!"

In Washington it was decided by lot that Warren should have a two-year, Carey a four-year term. Carey, who had been in Congress as a delegate since 1885, was already well known. He was a large, heavy man with beard and mustache. At six feet, one inch, Warren was taller than Carey and weighed 190. He was described by a Washington reporter as being straight, broad shouldered, with light-brown hair, blue eyes, and a "luxuriant straw colored" mustache hanging well down over his mouth. The droopy mustache, it should be observed, did not set Warren off from his fellows in 1890, when, for example, every member of the Wyoming Legislature except one was similarly adorned.

Carey and Warren moved smoothly into niches as conservative spokesmen for western interests. In January, 1891, however, when they had to choose between conservatism and western interests, they voted

---

[1] No one challenged Warren's eligibility in court, nor did anyone challenge John B. Kendrick's right to run for the United States Senate while still governor in 1916. Finally, however, in 1948 the right of Governor Lester C. Hunt to file for the Senate was challenged in the Wyoming Supreme Court case *State* v. *Crane*. The court held that "provision of the state Constitution that the Governor shall not be eligible to any other office during the term for which he was elected does not prevent the Governor from becoming a member of the United States House of Representatives or the United States Senate, since provisions of the federal Constitution dealing with qualifications of members of the House of Representatives and the Senate are controlling."

against free coinage of silver, which was popular in the West. They had prepared the way for their vote two weeks earlier by obtaining from a small mining convention in Cheyenne a 25–13 vote against a free-coinage-of-silver resolution. The mining-convention vote, said the *Cheyenne Leader*, was "beyond comprehension except that the majority was subservient to Warren and Carey, who needed a home 'endorsement.'" For months thereafter the votes against free silver coinage were discussed in the western press. Previously, both Warren and Carey had shown some interest in helping the development of western mining by aid to silver. Wyoming, it is true, had produced no silver, and would produce none, but there was always hope. Meanwhile, Democrats generally and not a few western Republicans accepted the view that easier money would help the West. In defense of Carey and Warren, the Republican press argued that they were sympathetic with free coinage of American silver but not world silver.

Warren attracted further attention in February, 1891, when he introduced a bill which would have transferred arid lands to the states, with a view to state reclamation of what could be reclaimed and state leasing of the rest. Adjournment came without action on the bill. Republicans and Democrats argued over the origin of the idea of transferring arid lands to the states, both claiming credit, but certainly Republicans Elwood Mead and Francis E. Warren had expressed themselves in favor of the idea as early as 1889.

The First State Legislature

After electing Wyoming's first two United States senators, the legislature settled down to a session which was unusually strenuous because many parts of the constitution required implementation and several hot issues which had been debated in the constitutional convention had been left for legislative decision.

Attention to the constitutional mandate that legislative reapportionment should follow the 1890 census renewed a convention battle in which upstate representatives had fought to limit each county to one senator. Again counties along the Union Pacific with three-fourths of the population were unwilling to give one-fourth of the people control of the Senate. There were enough crosscurrents, however, so that no reapportionment bill was passed, leaving the constitutional convention's distribution of seats in effect for another two years.

The constitutional convention's battle over a production tax on coal was renewed. Such a tax had been omitted from the constitution, but the legislature had been authorized to institute such a tax, which it now failed to do as advocates of the tax had warned would be the case.

After considerable argument, the constitutional convention had left the office of attorney general out of the constitution. The first legislature provided for one, to be appointed by the governor. The legislature created the office of state examiner and established the Board of Charities and Reform, an ex officio board consisting of the treasurer, the auditor, and the superintendent of public instruction.

The legislature also set up a board of land commissioners, an ex officio board consisting of the governor, the secretary of state, and the superintendent of public instruction, to manage and control the extensive land grants made by the federal government to the state, which amounted to more than four million acres. The last territorial legislature had refused to establish a miners' hospital at Rock Springs, but the grant of thirty thousand acres for such a hospital led the first state legislature to provide for one at a site (Rock Springs) to be selected by popular vote in 1892.

The grant of ninety thousand acres for the use and support of an agricultural college raised once again the question whether that college should be separate from the University of Wyoming at Laramie. The first legislature provided that Wyoming College of Agriculture should be located by vote of the people in 1892. Meanwhile, certain federal funds made available for an agricultural experiment station and the agricultural college were by action of the first legislature assigned to the University at Laramie until a separate agricultural college should be established.

The first legislature transacted a vast amount of business. Fortunately, little time was lost in partisan bickering, since the Republicans were in control of all state offices and in command of large majorities in both houses.

THE JOHNSON COUNTY WAR

Attempts of cattlemen to protect their cattle against theft in the 1880's have been discussed in Chapter 7. The big cattlemen were often frustrated. Small settlers were becoming more numerous, and some of them no doubt helped themselves to the beef of the large operators. And when men thought to be rustlers were arrested, juries were apt to turn them loose, either for lack of sufficient evidence or out of sympathy for the accused and his family.

At the very time when big cattlemen thought they were suffering outrageously, many small settlers considered themselves to be the injured parties. Absentee ownership magnified dislike for the big cattle-men. The Maverick Law of 1884 was hated by small settlers at the same time that it failed to satisfy its sponsors. Modification of this despised law in 1886 helped little. Then, in 1888, when control of roundups was given to the Board of Live Stock Commissioners, Governor Moonlight, though a friend of the small settlers, could not avoid appointing leading members of the Wyoming Stock Growers Association to the board. Territorial control of roundups made sense, but small settlers, who had become accustomed to distrusting the association, felt that members of the new board were tools of the association and were not sympathetic with the interests of small settlers. The new board did not solve range problems; in fact, the consensus at the time was that cattle stealing and mavericking increased.

Failing to get justice in the courts, big cattlemen took the law into their own hands. On July 20, 1889, a group of them lynched James Averell and Ella Watson near Independence Rock. A coroner's jury reported that Averell and Miss Watson "came to their deaths by being hanged by the neck at the hands of A. J. Bothwell, Tom Sun, John Durbin, R. M. Galbraith, Bob Connor, E. McLain and an unknown man." The six named men were arrested by Sheriff Frank Hadsell of Carbon County and each was released under five thousand dollars' bond.

Averell had been a painful thorn ever since he had homesteaded on public land used previously by A. J. Bothwell. He had written letters to a Casper newspaper asserting that three men were trying to hog one hundred miles of the meadows along the Sweetwater River. He had asked the Carbon County brand committee five years in a row for approval of a brand without any luck.[2]

Ella Watson, who was known thereafter, if not before, as Cattle Kate, was variously described as a prostitute and Averell's paramour. Some said that she was Averell's wife but kept it secret for homestead filing purposes. It was said also that she accepted stolen cattle from cowboys in return for her favors. Carbon County brand-committee records show that she was refused a brand in December, 1888.

Had only Averell been lynched, little would have been said about it, since his type was expendable. Miss Watson, however, was the only woman ever hanged in Wyoming, legally or illegally, so there was much

[2] The brand committee's record book which shows this is in the Carbon County Museum at Rawlins.

publicity. The *Laramie Boomerang* quoted a cattleman who said that "the lynching of Averell and his woman was the direct outgrowth of the failure of the courts of Wyoming to lend protection to the property of cattlemen." The *Salt Lake Tribune* commented: "The men of Wyoming will not be proud of the fact that a woman—albeit unsexed and totally depraved—has been hanged within their territory. That is about the poorest use that a woman can be put to." *Bill Barlow's Budget* (Douglas) held that "Averell was not a rustler, and while the woman Watson did have stolen stock in her possession it is a fact that she, herself, did not steal, or illegally brand, a single calf. She bought them, as any other prostitute buys."

Owen Wister entered the following comment in his diary on October 12, 1889: "Sat yesterday in smoking car with one of the gentlemen indicted for lynching the man and the woman. He seemed a good solid citizen, and I hope he'll get off. Sheriff Donell [Hadsell] said, 'all the good folks say it was a good job; it's only the wayward classes that complain.'" If so, the wayward classes were numerous, for Miss Watson had many sympathizers. Wister realized his wish. The six cattlemen employed excellent counsel—John W. Lacey, John A. Riner, and J. R. Dixon—and were released after four known witnesses to the crime failed to appear before the grand jury. No one was ever punished for the double lynching. Except for Averell's horse, which was sold at a sheriff's sale, there is no record of what happened to other livestock that he and Miss Watson were said to have had. According to Mari Sandoz, the Averell and Watson homesteads were contested on grounds of desertion by Henry H. Wilson, who after final proof sold them to Bothwell.

In August, 1889, editor J. H. Hayford in Laramie used the term "irrepressible conflict" to describe the war in progress between the "cattle kings" on the one side and "the small ranchmen, who own from half a dozen to half a hundred cattle," on the other. "Each is very much in the other's way," he said.

On October 5, 1889, Hayford took exception to recent editorials by A. S. Mercer in the *Northwestern Live Stock Journal* (Cheyenne) in which Mercer advocated that the few honest men in the territory declare war on thieves and rustlers and go to "hanging them like dogs." Hayford had recently met Mercer at a press convention and described him as follows: "The old gentleman has a very benign and patriarchal look. We should have taken him for a superannuated Methodist preacher. No one would have dreamed that he was the most bloodthirsty monster that ever 'scuttled a ship or cut a throat.'" Hayford disagreed with Mercer's assertion that all editors in the territory except those of Cheyenne were standing in with the thieves.

No doubt there was cattle stealing in Johnson County and no doubt convictions were difficult to come by, but loose statements, often made, that there were hundreds of indictments without convictions are not true. Helena Huntington Smith searched the Johnson County records and found only a few cattle-stealing cases in the years leading up to the Johnson County War: none in 1886; one in 1887 (dismissed); five in 1888 (four dismissed, the other resulting in a petty-larceny conviction and a fine of one hundred dollars); and thirteen in 1889 (all dismissed).[3] Thereafter there were few arrests, as the big cattlemen evidently gave up hoping for convictions in the courts after Judge Saufley's famous 1889 remark that "four [dismissed] men were as guilty men as I have ever tried."

Statehood brought no truce in the "irrepressible conflict." The Board of Live Stock Commissioners, the Wyoming Stock Growers Association (whose members controlled the livestock commission), and the county sheriffs could not quell rustling. At the annual meeting of the association in April, 1891, rustling was no doubt seriously discussed, although the minutes say nothing about it. John Clay, who was president of the organization from 1890 to 1895, recalled in his book *My Life on the Range* (Chicago, 1924) that on July 4, 1891, Frank Wolcott proposed to him "a lynching bee," a plan "so bold and open" that Clay rejected it as "impossible" and asked to be left out of it. According to Clay, he was left out of the project, and first learned of it on the way home from England after it had been carried out. Some did not reject the proposal. The energetic Hiram B. Ijams, new secretary of the association; Vice-President George W. Baxter; executive committee members Frank Wolcott, H. E. Teschemacher, and W. C. Irvine; and others began preparations for action. W. C. Irvine, president of the association from 1896 to 1911, wrote in 1914 that the original plan was to use only hired Texans, but it was decided in an Omaha meeting sometime in 1891 to add some Wyoming men "to show them the way; to point out those we wanted; to give the expedition prestige; and last to prevent mistakes."[4]

[3] Helena Huntington Smith, *The War on Powder River* (N.Y.: McGraw-Hill, 1966).

[4] W. C. Irvine's account is in the University of Wyoming Library and has been included in Lois Van Valkenburgh's 1939 M.A. thesis "The Johnson County War: The Papers of Charles Bingham Penrose in the Library of the University of Wyoming with Introduction and Notes."

While the plan was maturing, a few cattlemen could not wait. Tom Waggoner, reputed to be a rustler, was lynched southwest of Newcastle in June, 1891. An attempt was made on the life of another suspected rustler, Nate Champion, on Powder River in November, 1891. Later that same month, two other small ranchmen, Orley E. "Ranger" Jones and John A. Tisdale, were dry-gulched—shot to death by concealed gunmen—south of Buffalo. Frank Canton, stock detective and former sheriff of Johnson County, was accused of Tisdale's murder, but the case against him was dismissed.

The plan took final shape during the winter of 1891–1892. Johnson County would be invaded by a force of picked men who would surprise designated rustlers and kill them. A Texan, Tom Smith, was sent to his home state to recruit twenty-five men. In *Cow Country Cavalcade*, Maurice Frink, who was employed to write the history of the Wyoming Stock Growers Association, states: "It was not an official function of the Wyoming Stock Growers Association, although leading members of the Association took part in it, the secretary, H. B. Ijams, conducting some of the correspondence with the raising of the invasionary force." Professor Ernest S. Osgood, in *The Day of the Cattleman*, is in doubt: "Whether the Association as a body determined upon the course of action subsequently followed, or whether the matter was decided upon unofficially, cannot be determined, as the records are not available." The association records in the University of Wyoming Library are blank on the subject. For all of 1892 there is only this sentence in Ijams' hand: "No meeting of the Executive Committee held in 1892." Fortunately, however, Dr. Charles B. Penrose and W. C. Irvine later gave their testimony.

It is sometimes said the small settlers in Johnson County who were so hated by the big cattlemen were farmers or sheepmen. On the contrary, they were small cattlemen, many of them former cowboys who had homesteaded and acquired small herds. There was very little cultivation in Johnson County at the time. The 1890 census of agriculture reported that a much larger Johnson County than the present one—extending all the way west to the Big Horn River—had only 3,576 acres under cultivation, mostly in oats. Likewise, there were very few sheep in the county: only 7,300 in 1890 as compared with 100,365 cattle.

The point of view of the small settlers in Johnson County was well presented from time to time by Joe DeBarthe, editor of the *Buffalo Bulletin*. He said on December 24, 1891:

The big cattlemen . . . own thousands upon thousands of acres of rich Wyoming land that they have deliberately stolen from the government; land they hired on to take up, make proof on, and deed over. . . . They . . . gobbled up all the rich creek bottoms they could . . . and the rest of the state was their range. . . . When a man who had been working in one of their outfits had the audacity to take up 160 acres of land for himself the big fellows blackballed him.

DeBarthe regularly argued that rustling was bad but that assassination was much worse.

The Maverick Law of 1884, discussed in Chapter 7, bred deep resentments that persisted into statehood. Changes in the law with respect to the handling of mavericks did not satisfy the small settlers. In 1891 the first state legislature established the Board of Live Stock Commissioners, whose three members were appointed by the governor. The board organized the official roundups after recommendations from the Wyoming Stock Growers Association. The board, made up of big cattlemen, placed inspectors at terminals and furnished the inspectors with a list of "rustler" brands. The receipts for all cattle bearing these brands were forwarded by the brand inspectors to the secretary of the board and held until the shippers could prove ownership of the cattle. Members of the association, not the courts, decided what brands were rustler brands. Alleged rustlers thus could not ship to regular markets. In northeastern Wyoming they found a temporary market in the Burlington construction gangs working between Gillette and Sheridan in 1891–1892, but, naturally, the closing of regular outlets was bitterly resented. The *Cheyenne Leader* of March 22, 1892, declared that the "Board of Live Stock Commissioners does not have legal authority to seize and hold proceeds of cattle sales."

In defiance of the big cattlemen, an unofficial "Northern Wyoming Farmers and Stock Growers Association" at Buffalo gave notice that it would hold an independent roundup beginning May 1, a month before the state roundups. In these circumstances, the "irrepressible conflict" erupted in the form of new violence in April, 1892. The plan of the big cattlemen to punish their tormentors in Johnson County was set in motion.

The twentieth annual meeting of the Wyoming Stock Growers Association met in Cheyenne on Monday morning, April 4, 1892, with "the largest attendance that has been known for years." Eleven individuals and representatives of thirty-six companies responded to roll call. Vice-President George W. Baxter presided in the absence of President John Clay. Secretary Ijams reported that there had been only one meeting of the executive committee during the past year (April 7, 1891). W. E. Guthrie introduced a resolution, which was passed, commending the Board of Live Stock Commissioners for withholding the proceeds of "stolen cattle" until proof of ownership could be made. There is no record of a meeting of the executive committee, which normally met in a closed session after the public sessions of the association were concluded. If the executive committee met, it was in secret.

On Tuesday afternoon, April 5, 1892, a six-car special train left Cheyenne for Casper. As a three-car train, the special had arrived from Denver carrying twenty-five Texas gunmen (sometimes referred to as former United States marshals and deputies). At Cheyenne, three cars loaded with horses, wagons, and supplies were added, and twenty-four "Regulators" boarded the train: ranch owners, ranch managers, detectives, and inspectors. No Wyoming cowboys below the rank of foreman joined the expedition, presumably because they could not be trusted and were not invited. One of the leaders, W. C. Irvine, later wrote: "The men working for the cattle outfits seemed to have an understanding among themselves that they were being paid so much a month for working, not fighting, and it was up to the owner or manager to do his own fighting." Curiously, there were almost as many Texans as Wyoming men.

The commander was Major Frank Wolcott, relieved for a time by Frank Canton and often aided by W. C. Irvine. The three had been prominent in territorial history. Wolcott and Irvine were association members and big cattlemen. Canton was former sheriff of Johnson County, a long-time association detective, and a cold-blooded killer in fact and by universal reputation. Other big cattlemen in the expedition were H. E. Teschemacher, Fred DeBillier, W. J. Clarke, W. E. Guthrie, F. G. S. Hesse, C. A. Campbell, A. B. Clarke, E. W. Whitcomb, and J. N. Tisdale.[5] Pat Flannery, editor of the John Hunton diaries, thought Hunton might have gone were it not for the fact that he was waiting in Cheyenne to be sworn in as United States commissioner on the day of departure. Hunton's partner, A. B. Clarke, did go. For April 5, Hunton noted in his diary: "Expedition started north to round up Rustlers. Sorry I could not go. . . . Fear the results as it is wrong and illegal." Two newspapermen, Ed Towse of the *Cheyenne Sun* and Sam

[5] No relation to John A. Tisdale, who was killed in November, 1891. Also, cattleman C. A. Campbell should not be confused with lawyer A. C. Campbell.

T. Clover of the *Chicago Herald*, went along, as did Dr. Charles B. Penrose, member of a prominent Pennsylvania family who had come west for his health.

Positive conclusions are hard to come by, but the presumption seems justified that Union Pacific officials who furnished the special train knew the intentions of the expedition. It seems also that Acting Governor Amos Barber; Senator Carey; Senator Warren (more doubtful); Cheyenne attorneys Willis Van Devanter and Hugo Donzelman; E. A. Slack, editor of the *Cheyenne Sun*; A. S. Mercer, editor of the *Northwestern Live Stock Journal*; and most members of the Wyoming Stock Growers Association were privy to the plan.

Thomas Tisdale, grandson of John A. Tisdale, who was killed in 1891, and a man who has devoted years of study to the Johnson County War, is probably right in believing that the "Invaders" had different ideas of what to do in Johnson County, although they agreed on a basic plan in advance. Mari Sandoz in her book, *The Cattlemen*, states that the Invaders (variously known as Regulators and White Caps) took along "a Dead List of seventy men," including "Sheriff Red Angus, the new mayor, the commissioners, and other officials and business men down to Nate Champion and some that perhaps were rustlers." She writes further that "their plan was to strike at Buffalo first, where their men waited at strategic points over the town, ready to bring down the city marshal and the sheriff with the first two bullets. . . . Dynamite squads would blow up the courthouse and the store of Foote." [6]

Miss Sandoz' analysis resembles that offered in A. S. Mercer's famous volume, *The Banditti of the Plains*: "The plan of the campaign, it is believed, was to kill Sheriff Angus and his deputies . . . [and] twenty or thirty citizens and then raid the settlements in the county killing or driving out several hundred more." On the other hand, the late J. Elmer Brock, who, although he was too young to be involved in the "Invasion," was a long-time resident of Johnson County, was well acquainted with many of the participants, and as president of the Wyoming Stock Growers Association had access to information, thought the Invaders were on a good-will mission. He told Maurice Frink, who quoted him in *Cow Country Cavalcade*:

[6] These quotes are taken from Mari Sandoz, *The Cattlemen* (New York: Hastings House, 1958), pp. 360–361. Among authors who have written on the Johnson County War, Miss Sandoz in her contempt for the Invaders is surpassed only by A. S. Mercer in *The Banditti of the Plains*.

They planned to go to Buffalo, and take charge of the court house and the weapons of the militia, which were stored there. This was to be done to keep the settlers from getting them. There were also some court records against those who had attacked Champion and Gilbertson in the Hall cabin which the Regulators wanted to destroy. They proposed then to call a mass meeting of citizens of the county. They intended to tell the law-abiding residents that their rights would be recognized and respected. They expected to confess that they opposed the settlers' coming into the country, and had done many things against them for which they were sorry now. They wanted to offer to make amends and obtain the co-operation of the honest settlers in protecting property which everybody knew was being stolen wholesale. They planned, following this meeting, to post a list of the confirmed thieves and those so classified, and give them 24 hours to get out of the country on pain of death.[7]

The Invaders undoubtedly had a list of rustlers, at least some of whom they were ready to kill without twenty-four hours' notice. The written statements of two members of the expedition, Dr. Charles B. Penrose and W. C. Irvine, leave no doubt that the Invaders intended to kill nineteen or twenty men and to drive others out of the country. After the Invasion, the *Chicago Herald* and the *Cheyenne Leader* printed a 35-name list of wanted men supplied by *Herald* reporter Sam Clover. The list of rustlers had been carefully prepared, wrote Irvine later, from nominations made by Wyoming Stock Growers Association members to Secretary Ijams. Ninety per cent of the men on the list were said to be fugitives from other states. The names were submitted to the executive committee of the association for checking.

After sitting up all night, the Invaders arrived at 4 A.M. on April 6 at the stockyards outside Casper, where a few more men joined them and they unloaded their horses and wagons. Hoping that they had not been observed by any early risers among the six hundred citizens of Casper, they quickly rode northward. Six miles north of Casper, they gathered around campfires for breakfast. When the wagon drivers came in and unhitched their horses, the commotion caused some of the riding horses to pull loose from sagebrush to which they had been tied. Five or six hours of precious time were lost as a result. Then it began to snow to delay them further, but they made it to Tisdale's ranch on Willow Creek sixty-five miles north of Casper, where they rested and refreshed for a night and a day.

Up came Mike Shonsey with information that fourteen rustlers had been at the KC Ranch, eighteen miles north of Tisdale's, the night

[7] Maurice Frink, *Cow Country Cavalcade* (Denver: The Old West Publishing Co., 1954), pp. 141–142.

before. Against stout opposition from some members bent on reaching Buffalo without delay, the Invaders decided to investigate the KC. Leaving at 1 A.M., they arrived there before daylight on the ninth. Ed Towse, Dr. Penrose, and H. W. Davis remained at the Tisdale ranch and were to see none of the subsequent action.

The KC Ranch, at the south edge of present Kaycee, was surrounded. An old trapper who had stopped at the ranch for the night was seized and tied up when he came down to the stream for water. A half-hour later, the trapper's young partner appeared for similar treatment. Then Nick Ray, a listed rustler, emerged from the ranch cabin. Ten steps from the door he was shot down by a Texan but managed to crawl back into the cabin, where he died a few hours later. This left only one living man in the cabin, for the rustlers reported by Shonsey were gone; and yet, almost incredibly, the one who remained, Nate Champion, held more than fifty Invaders at bay most of the day. Finally, at four in the afternoon, the Invaders loaded a wagon with pitch pine and hay, pushed it up to the cabin, set fire to it and the cabin, and shot Champion to death before he could run very far.

The Invaders lost much precious time at the KC. During the long day they devoted to the destruction of Ray and Champion, at least two reports of the siege reached Buffalo.

J. Elmer Brock's statement that the Invaders intended to give men on their list twenty-four hours to leave the country cannot be reconciled with events at the KC. Champion and Ray were offered no chance to escape. That the Invaders were bent upon killing some of their enemies without quarter cannot be gainsaid.

The Invaders knew now that time was against them. They hurried on toward Buffalo, fifty miles north, stopping only briefly at a few friendly ranches for fresh horses. At a point seven miles from Buffalo early in the morning of the tenth, they were met by friends from Buffalo who warned that a superior force was alert and ready for them. They then decided to turn back to the TA, a friendly ranch, thirteen miles south of Buffalo, belonging to Dr. William Harris. They fortified the TA as best they could and waited for the Buffalo men to come to them, as the latter did on the morning of April 11, more than two hundred strong, well armed, and led by Sheriff Red Angus.

Red Angus had been a very busy man since he learned, on the ninth, of trouble at the KC. He rode fifty miles to that place with a small posse, only to find that the Invaders had moved on toward Buffalo by a different route from the one he had taken. He then dashed back to

Buffalo to take charge of the defense forces. He and his deputies now laid siege to the TA, much as the Invaders had laid siege to the KC two days before.

Acting Governor Amos Barber in Cheyenne received a telegram from Buffalo on the twelfth describing the state of affairs. The telegraph wires, which the Invaders had cut, had been repaired. Barber decided not to call out the National Guard, although there was a unit at Buffalo. Instead, he wired the President of the United States, stating ambiguously that "an insurrection exists in Johnson County . . . against the government of the . . . state. . . . Open hostilities exist and large bodies of armed men are engaged in battle." He explained that United States troops were located at Fort McKinney (near Buffalo), thirteen miles from the scene, which could be used to suppress the "insurrection." United States Senators Carey and Warren added their appeals. It is often said that they got President Harrison out of bed. At any rate, the President authorized the use of federal troops, and Colonel J. J. Van Horne, with a detachment of cavalry, intervened at the TA on the thirteenth of April. No one had been killed there. The Johnson County people had been just as inept in siegecraft as the Invaders had been at the KC. Colonel Van Horne escorted the Invaders to Fort McKinney, where they were held to protect them from the irate citizens of the county and to answer for the murder of Ray and Champion. Ten days later, forty-three of the Invaders were delivered to Fort Russell to be held for trial.

Meanwhile, the Johnson County War had become the talk of the state, if not the nation. Senator Warren wrote on April 25: "The cattle war is in every newspaper in the east."[8] The *Cheyenne Sun* (Slack) declared that "in Johnson, Natrona, and Converse counties the rustlers are all powerful. . . . Then let us have no namby pamby sentimentalism about the killing of a few stock thieves." The *Rock Springs Review* noted: "Our sympathy, of course, is with the men who dared to do for themselves, that which the law seemed powerless to do for them." Other newspapers were less complimentary toward the big cattlemen. The *Laramie Sentinel* (Hayford) said that "of all the fool things the stock association ever did this takes the cake." The *Lander Clipper* commented: "It is time that the settlers, farmers and small stockmen were beginning to look to their interests by rising en masse and driving these murderous invaders from the fair soil of our beloved young state." And the

[8] This and subsequent quotations from Warren in this chapter are taken from the Francis E. Warren Collection in the University of Wyoming Library.

Lusk Herald said: "They [the Invaders] have proved themselves blood-thirsty murderers and should be given the full extent of the law."

The Invaders, it developed, had not come out of the war unscathed. Two of the Texans, Dudley and Lowther, died of gangrene resulting from wounds described as accidental by W. C. Irvine.

Early in July, the Invaders were taken to Laramie for a change-of-venue hearing. After two weeks in Laramie, their attorneys—M. C. Brown, Willis Van Devanter, W. R. Stoll, and Hugo Donzelman—obtained a ruling that the trial should be held in Cheyenne, where sympathy for the Invaders was strongest. In the meantime, representatives of the Invaders had escorted Jones and Walker—the two trappers who witnessed events at the KC—out of the state and had concealed them in the East so that the prosecution would be unable to use them.

In Cheyenne on August 7, 1892, the Invaders pleaded not guilty to murder before District Judge Richard H. Scott; August 22 was set as the date for trial. When Judge Scott learned that Johnson County was not paying the bills for board and room of the prisoners and the wages of guards, amounting to more than one hundred dollars a day, he ordered all of the prisoners released—the Wyoming men on their own recognizance and the Texans on bonds signed by the Wyoming men. The Texans went back home at once, pausing only to enjoy a farewell party featuring champagne.

On August 21, Judge Scott postponed the trial to January 2, 1893, using as an excuse the pressure of court sessions in Weston and Crook counties. After a further delay, the case was called for trial on January 21. At that time, after more than one thousand veniremen had been examined to select twelve jurors, the discouraged and inept Johnson County prosecutor, Alvin Bennett, moved to proceed no further and all of the defendants were discharged. By now, Johnson County owed $18,000 for costs of the case. When in time it became obvious that the county would not pay the costs, the legislature, in 1899, appropriated $18,000 to settle accounts.

Immediately after the Invasion, ranches belonging to the Invaders in Johnson County were raided and property was destroyed or carried off. Buffalo attorney and mayor Charles H. Burritt, friend of the Invaders, wrote to Senator Warren on May 17, 1892: "Free expression of one's thoughts upon any question growing out of the stock interests is not to be thought of here at the present time." [9] A few days later he wrote to attorney W. R. Stoll in Cheyenne that "One Eyed Tex" had

[9] *Buffalo Bulletin*, August 17, 1961.

recently made the rounds in town wearing a suit of Invader Fred Hesse's clothes.[10] Many men associated with the Invaders feared for their lives. George Wellman, who replaced Laberteaux, one of the Invaders, as foreman of Henry A. Blair's Hoe Ranch, was shot to death. The murderer was never apprehended. Federal troops were brought to central and northern Wyoming that summer to help maintain order.

The major purpose of the Invasion had been to inhibit rustling. Big cattlemen in later years claimed that some of the men on their list left the state after the Invasion and that rustling declined. Some of the hunted men did leave, all right, but it cannot be proved that the Invasion caused their departure.

The Invaders presumably were busy that summer trying to pay the costs of the Invasion, which, according to W. C. Irvine, amounted to more than $105,000. One report stated that one hundred men were to contribute $1,000 each. Just who paid and how much has never been revealed.

People generally thought that Senators Warren and Carey were involved. Warren denied it; Carey said nothing. Warren wrote to Governor Barber on April 19, 1892: "No, you are wrong, I did not know about the decided move that the stockmen were taking against the rustlers until informed by wire through the general press." Warren had not been represented at the Wyoming Stock Growers Association convention on April 4, judging by the official roll call. Carey, on the other hand, was represented at the convention, and his foreman is often said to have had the assignment of cutting the telegraph wires to Johnson County.

Dr. Penrose wrote that the Invaders "doubted Carey's loyalty—and I think with reason. Warren was never doubted." Both, of course, had a hand in the aftermath. Unlike Carey, who destroyed his correspondence, Warren left evidence to show that he gave much time and thought to helping extricate the big cattlemen. He sent at least five telegrams in code to his Cheyenne agent, S. B. Tuttle, and dispatched other letters and telegrams regarding the matter. In a coded telegram to Tuttle dated April 14 he said:

Existing conditions must determine action. Decisive action always popular and will win as colleague and myself informed should say first put stockmen at McKinney out of danger by bringing to railroad if they do so desire. Then consider proclamation pardoning both sides engaged in conflict saying when out-

10 *Ibid.*

bursts occur in which good men engaged there is always a cause real or fancied. If civil authorities fail to protect property from the assaults of evil disposed, good men will protect their property by force. Industries necessary for the prosperity of State being destroyed not by honest but dishonest men. Investigation shows no conflict between settlers and stockmen farmers and cattlemen but between stockmen who want to conduct business and rustlers who defy law. You should warn all persons to desist making roundups except at times and as provided by law. Governor can call into operation all the powers of State civil and military to maintain the laws.

On May 7, Warren wrote to attorneys John W. Lacey and Willis Van Devanter: "We can probably slip along from day to day to cover the necessary time for you to carry out your arrangement for trial. . . . I am now keeping away—as hard as I can—from the President and Secretary of War, because I fear they will urge action." These and other documents show that Warren, and presumably Carey, were completely committed to the cause of the big cattlemen.

On February 7, 1895, the *Buffalo Voice* commented that the Invaders had been offended because Carey had refused to pay his assessment. Commenting on political difficulties for Carey, the *Voice* said: "If Carey had acted like a man and paid his assessment to the fund to carry on the invasion . . . things might have come out differently. . . . He agreed to pay this money and was anxious to see the invasion made a success, but after it proved a failure he refused to pay the money, and now he is getting his reward." Later, E. A. Slack, in his *Cheyenne Sun-Leader*, July 17, 1897, stated that Carey paid five thousand dollars to fulfill his promise, but only after W. R. Stoll had threatened to sue him. There seems to be no way to verify these statements. It may be supposed, however, that the Invasion cost a lot of money, that meeting the cost was not easy, and that men enjoyed discussing rumors about the reckoning.

Hard feelings persisted for years. President John Clay told the Wyoming Stock Growers Association convention in April, 1893: "The policy of the majority of the state is to pull down its principal industry. . . . Technically, legally they [the Invaders] did wrong, but . . . I count every one of them a friend. . . . There will be a day of retribution and the traitors in the camp and in the field will be winnowed like wheat from the chaff."

The Invasion brought both fame and grief to Asa S. Mercer, editor of the *Northwestern Live Stock Journal*, a man of fifty-three in 1892, who had been first president of the University of Washington (Seattle)

before coming to Cheyenne and starting the *Journal* in 1883. As voice
of the big cattlemen, he had urged in 1889 that rustlers be hanged "like
dogs." Then soon after the Invasion he fell out with the big cattlemen,
whether, as the *Cheyenne Sun* said, because he had wanted to send
several squads of four or five killers instead of the one large company,
or for some other reason. In June, 1892, Colonel E. H. Kimball, editor
of the *Douglas Graphic*, violently denouncing the big cattlemen, was
charged with criminal libel by George W. Baxter and was brought to
jail in Cheyenne. Mercer offered to go bail for Kimball (his bond was
rejected), whereupon the big cattlemen took their advertisements out
of the *Journal*. Mercer gave full details in an editorial in the *Journal* of
July 8, 1892, in which he condemned the Invasion and explained that
"we regret the necessity for this action on our part, but our rule thus
far in life has been that if a man slapped our face, we must hit him
behind the ear." Thereafter there was no reconciliation. In August,
1892, C. A. Campbell, an Invader who had just been released on bail,
entered the *Journal* office and struck Mercer so as to break his glasses
and cut him over the eye. In October, 1892, the *Journal* published "A
Confession" of George Dunning, one of the Invaders, stating that he
had been hired in Idaho by H. B. Ijams, secretary of the Wyoming
Stock Growers Association, and that Ijams had promised that the
association would pay each hired man five dollars a day and fifty
dollars for every man killed, had confided that the Invaders planned to
kill about thirty men, had said the Governor and Judge Black were back
of the Invasion, and had given assurances that the expedition would
have the approval of every member of the association before it would
start.

   Beset by creditors, cattlemen, and lawyers, Mercer suffered in 1893.
He gave up trying to publish the *Northwestern Live Stock Journal* in
February, 1893, and began publishing instead the *Wyoming Democrat*.
Then he abandoned the newspaper business entirely in July, 1893, when
he sold his press and other equipment. However, he resumed his attack
on the Invaders in 1894 in his book, *The Banditti of the Plains*, which was
printed in Denver. Mercer's harsh indictment of the big cattlemen
caused them to discourage their friends from buying the book. Mercer
and his son, nevertheless, managed to sell a few hundred copies at one
dollar apiece. Money was scarce in 1894 and selling books in Wyoming,
even controversial ones, was not easy. A few persons have asserted that
the big cattlemen, aided by a court injunction, seized and destroyed
most of Mercer's books. However, it has been impossible to verify these

assertions. The Mercers soon moved from Cheyenne to Hyattville in the Big Horn Basin. In the twentieth century four different publishers issued reprints of *The Banditti of the Plains.* The first (1894) edition became so scarce that a copy sold for eight hundred dollars at auction in 1974 in Austin, Texas.

SUMMING UP

The Johnson County War ranks as the most notorious event in the history of Wyoming. In retrospect, it was an anachronistic vigilante operation, a throwback to the 1850's and 1860's, when vigilantes had often taken the law into their own hands. One can see in it also overtones of rugged individualism and Social Darwinism. More or less successful attempts have been made to justify vigilante activities in frontier communities. The Johnson County Invasion, however, occurred in a later period when there was a state government in which the big cattlemen had great influence. Had the cattlemen been wiser and more patient, they might have been able to solve their problems within the law.

Ironically, at least five of the leaders of the 1889 constitutional convention were involved in the Invasion—W. C. Irvine and H. E. Teschemacher as active participants, George W. Baxter as planner, backer, and apologist, and Charles H. Burritt and M. C. Brown as two attorneys for the defense. Among the convention's fruits was Article XIX, Section 6: "No armed police force, or detective agency, or armed body of men, shall ever be brought into this state, for the suppression of domestic violence except upon the application of the legislature, or executive, when the legislature cannot be convened." Bringing in "an armed body of men" in the form of the twenty-five Texans earned the cattlemen special scorn.

The Invasion illustrates the low value placed on human life in the West in the nineteenth century. Wyoming people were learning only slowly to place human rights above property rights, although each person, of course, valued his own life.

Many judgments have been passed on the Invasion, mostly unsympathetic. Professor Ernest S. Osgood's conclusion is provocative. He notes that it was

as drastic as it was unwise. . . . The mistake of the Wyoming cattle companies . . . in using such methods . . . was in supposing that they were frontiersmen. These large cattle outfits, backed by outside capital, had lost all the characteristics of frontier enterprises; the small ranchmen, and the granger represented what was left of the frontier on the northern ranges.[11]

Maurice Frink's judgment in 1954, in a study paid for and published by the Wyoming Stock Growers Association, also deserves attention. He called the Invasion "indefensible," then added that "it can be understood only when it is placed in perspective against the frontier times in which it occurred."

THE ELECTION OF 1892

Although the Republicans had enjoyed a picnic in 1890, they found the political weather considerably less favorable in 1892. The Johnson County War was used by Democrats to stir up resentment against the Republicans. Democratic papers used the phrase "The Republican Ring Gang of Cattle Barons of Cheyenne." Senator Warren declared that more than half the cost of the Johnson County Invasion had been borne by Democrats. Other Republicans, such as J. H. Hayford, insisted that the Invasion was as much Democratic as Republican and that many big cattlemen were Democrats. Certainly the Invasion was not a Republican project, yet many citizens associated the big cattlemen with the Republican party.

The Democrats held their nominating convention in Rock Springs at the end of July. They read defenders of the Wyoming Stock Growers Association out of the party and nominated Dr. John E. Osborne of Rawlins for the governorship (last two years of Warren's term). Osborne was a handsome man of thirty-four with wavy hair and a mustache. He had prospered in medical practice and the drug business and had then invested in sheep. Partisan critics stated that he was an agnostic, a dude, lacked humor and good fellowship, was stubborn, and "leaves his finger marks on every five cent piece that passes through his hands." H. A. Coffeen, Sheridan merchant, was chosen as the Democratic candidate for Congress.

Convening in Laramie in mid-September, the Republicans nominated Edward A. Ivinson, wealthy Laramie banker, for governor and incumbent Clarence D. Clark of Evanston for Congress.

A third party, the Populists, emerged as a minor force in Wyoming politics in 1891 and 1892. Thomas A. Krueger has traced their history in a typescript M.A. thesis at the University of Wyoming, "Populism in Wyoming" (1960). It is clear that the Populist party never amounted

[11] *The Day of the Cattleman* (Minneapolis: University of Minnesota Press, 1929), p. 248.

to much in Wyoming because there were very few crop farmers and virtually no silver production, because laborers and miners were often intimidated by their employers, and because Populist leaders could rarely agree (thanks, in part, to manipulations by Republicans and Democrats).

In their state nominating convention at Douglas in late September, 1892, the Populists endorsed the national platform, with its planks for free and unlimited silver at the ratio of sixteen to one, a graduated income tax, and government ownership of transportation and communications, and then passed on to place major emphasis on home-made planks: "We demand the repeal of all laws conferring possessory rights on the public domain. 9. We demand the repeal of all laws relating to the Wyoming Stock Association. 10. We denounce . . . the action of the stock commission and invading stock men in introducing an armed force . . . in killing our citizens; in burning our homes." By a vote of 27 to 17, the Populist convention accepted a Democratic proposal for fusion, agreeing to support Democrats Osborne and Coffeen in exchange for Democratic support for Populist presidential candidate James B. Weaver. Bitter debate preceded the decision to fuse, and delegates from Albany, Crook, and Sweetwater counties walked out.

Democrats and Populists could agree enthusiastically on one issue: the Johnson County War. After a few Democrats had been read out of the party for defending the Wyoming Stock Growers Association, the remainder vehemently decried the "Republican Ring Gang," and the Populists joined in the denunciation.

In the main, the Wyoming Populists were defectors from the two old-line parties. Joe DeBarthe, former chairman of the Republican county committee in Johnson County, started a Populist paper in Buffalo, *The Free Lance*. In Crook County, the *Sundance Republican* turned Populist under the name *The Reform*, while Democrat E. H. Kimball in Douglas changed his *Graphic* to a Populist sheet. In Cheyenne, the journalist and historian I. S. Bartlett switched his affiliation from Democrat to Populist, while his wife switched from Republican to Populist.

As usual, however, the Republicans controlled most of the newspapers, although ten were Democratic: *Cheyenne Leader, Lander Mountaineer, Buffalo Voice, Evanston Register, Rock Springs Miner, Rawlins Journal, Laramie Boomerang, Sheridan Enterprise, Lusk Herald,* and *Sundance Apex*. Easily the most influential Democratic newspaper was the *Cheyenne Leader*, edited by John F. Carroll; E. A. Slack's *Cheyenne Sun* held that distinction among the Republicans. Although he was still considered the titular head of the Democratic party, former Governor George W. Baxter, Invasion backer, broke with Carroll over the latter's violent attacks on the big cattlemen. In June, Baxter and Frank A. Kemp brought a suit to force the *Leader* into receivership. Together, Baxter and Kemp owned only sixteen of the two hundred shares of stock in the *Leader*, but they charged that mismanagement and misappropriation of funds endangered their investment. Able Democratic lawyers A. C. Campbell, J. C. Thompson, and Nellis E. Corthell succeeded in delaying trial until after the election, when the case was dismissed.

The Johnson County War was the major issue in the 1892 campaign, and the Democrats and Populists had the more popular side. A secondary issue was Warren's arid-lands bill, which he had pushed unsuccessfully in 1891 and 1892. Democrats asserted that the bill would permit a "land steal" by large corporations. Senator Warren, whose two-year term was about to run out, was subjected to much abuse, being accused of monopolistic practices, land frauds, and hounding small settlers on the fringes of his extensive pastures. Both Ivinson and Osborne were treated by partisan presses as wealthy men with little else to recommend them.

The silver issue entered the campaign quite prominently. Carey and Warren, who had voted against free coinage of silver in 1891, did so again in July, 1892, to the disgust of Democrats and Populists. They were hanged in effigy in Ogden, Utah, as enemies of the West.

In line with the national Populist plank that "our country is on the verge of moral, material, and financial ruin," the Wyoming fusionists exaggerated economic distress, while Republicans tried to make it appear that Wyoming and the nation were more prosperous than they really were.

Adding class warfare to other issues was Populist Henry Breitenstein of Laramie, whose campaign oratory is represented by the following: "Our civilization . . . is the civilization of the wood tick and the honey bee. The wood tick sucks, but it creates nothing. . . . It is the bloated plutocrat of the woods. . . . The people must once again unite to bring about a higher civilization, one that means death to the ticks and fair play to the bees." Another Laramie Populist, Shakespeare E. Sealy, was dismissed by editor Hayford as one who worked "his jaw more than his hands." His character and reputation were so malodorous, said Hayford, that "it would make a horse leave his oats if Sealy came between him and the wind."

The remarkably bitter campaign ended with a fusionist victory, or at least a Democratic victory. Carrying all counties except Laramie, John E. Osborne was elected governor with 9,290 votes to 7,509 for Edward A. Ivinson, and Henry A. Coffeen was elected to Congress with 8,855 votes to 8,394 for Clarence D. Clark. Republican presidential electors, however, were chosen by margins of about 750, suggesting that Democrats (particularly in Laramie County) did not adhere to their bargain as faithfully as the Populists did. President Harrison's victory in Wyoming was based on the fact that northern Republicans supported him, although they voted against Ivinson and Clark.

In the election, also, Lander was chosen as site for the location of the agricultural college. This decision would never be implemented by any future legislature, however, the effect being to leave the college at the university in Laramie.

The legislature chosen in 1892 was divided. The Republicans—thanks in part to holdover members—controlled the Senate by a margin of eleven to five. In the House there were sixteen Democrats, twelve Republicans, and five Populists. Thus the Democratic governor was confronted by a hostile Senate, while the five Populists held the balance of power in both the House and the joint sessions which would try to elect a United States senator.

Although he finally made good his claim to the governor's chair, John E. Osborne had a comic-opera time of it. Newspaper reports of returns from all counties gave him a substantial margin, yet week after week no official confirmation was forthcoming from Cheyenne. Osborne became more and more impatient. He thought that the Republicans were purposely holding up his official notification until they could settle a few contests in their favor and so gain control of the legislature.

Tired of waiting, Osborne went to Cheyenne, where, on December 2, he arranged for a notary public to take his oath of office. He then took possession of the governor's office and issued a proclamation stating that he had "duly and legally qualified as governor." Acting Governor Barber justified the delay by saying that the election returns of Converse and Fremont counties had not been received. Finally, on December 8, the canvassing board met and declared Osborne elected, after which, on January 2, Osborne took his oath of office a second time.[12]

In the meantime, the press fed more fuel to partisan fires. Republican reports said that Osborne had acted childishly, that he had climbed in

[12] The Wyoming Supreme Court later called Osborne's assumption of authority on December 2 "premature and invalid."

through the window of the governor's office after crawling along an outside ledge. Cheyenne editor John Charles Thompson, Jr., later reported that not Osborne but a boy entered the office by way of ledge and window and opened the door from the inside. All accounts agree that Osborne spent the night of December 2 in the office, afraid that if he left he would be locked out. Newspaper accounts during the next few days told of a wrestling match between Osborne and Barber's secretary, R. H. Repath, for possession of the office key, the Republican press declaring Repath the winner, the Democratic press, Osborne.

THE SECOND STATE LEGISLATURE

In his message to the 1893 legislature, Governor Osborne declared that the state had not advanced in prosperity or increased in population during the past year. He had an explanation ready: the "lawless invasion . . . with its accompanying crimes" and the bad publicity given by Republican leaders, who had thought it "necessary to wantonly slander our State to excuse the crimes of the invaders."[13]

Much of the time of the 1893 legislature was devoted to fruitless attempts to choose a United States senator. Thirty ballots were taken at intervals during the session. "The joint sessions were the principal attraction of the capitoi city and were attended by all of the politically-minded and fashionably disposed portion of the population," recalled Frank Mondell, who was president of the Senate. There were twenty-three Republicans, twenty-one Democrats, and five Populists in the two houses, making twenty-five votes necessary for election. Had the Democrats and Populists been able to combine as in the past campaign, they could have elected a senator. On one ballot, Democrat John Charles Thompson, Sr., received twenty-four votes. Later it was often alleged that Democrat Nat Baker, Converse County representative, who would not vote for Thompson, had been bribed. Francis E. Warren, whose two-year term was ending, was the leading Republican candidate, although he never received more than thirteen votes.

Senator James "Uncle Jimmie" Kime, Fremont County Democrat from Miner's Delight, became very ill for several days as the result, it was thought, of a poisoned cocktail. Senator Leopold Kabis, Cheyenne Democrat, was accused of complicity in the poisoning. A joint committee recommended the unseating of Kabis, but the legislature chose only to censure him.

---

[13] A convenient gathering of Osborne statements can be found in C. P. Hill, *Public Papers, Messages and Proclamations of Hon. John E. Osborne, Governor of Wyoming, 1893–4, Together with Some Public Addresses and Correspondence of Interest* (Cheyenne, 1894).

Occupied as it was with intrigues and joint sessions, the legislature found little time for lawmaking. Only thirty-three laws were adopted, besides six resolutions and memorials. Frank Mondell, in his autobiography, recalled that "we managed at odd times to consider and pass the necessary appropriation bills and essential legislation." Not so well satisfied, editor J. H. Hayford said: "Never has our young state been so degraded and disgraced." No action was taken on Osborne's recommendations for more stringent laws to protect game and birds, revision of the election laws, abolition of the Board of Live Stock Commissioners, and organized efforts to encourage immigration. An apportionment bill was passed, however, providing for eighteen senators and thirty-seven representatives. Laramie County was assigned three senators; Albany, Carbon, Sweetwater, and Uinta were given two each; and the other seven counties received one each.

When the legislature did not abolish the Board of Live Stock Commissioners, Osborne vetoed the $12,000 appropriation for the board, making it necessary for the Wyoming Stock Growers Association to supply funds for board operation during the next two years. Osborne also vetoed a $4,500 item to cover the salary and expenses of the state veterinarian and a $600 item to reimburse H. B. Ijams, secretary of the Board of Live Stock Commissioners, for money paid out for clerical help.

Appropriately in the circumstances, the legislature did find time to approve a memorial to Congress in favor of popular election of United States senators. After the legislature had adjourned without naming a senator, Governor Osborne appointed A. C. Beckwith of Evanston to fill the vacancy. Although he was generally known as a Democrat, Beckwith's appointment received more approval from Republicans than Democrats. The latter complained that the wealthy banker, merchant, and stockman was too closely associated with the Union Pacific and had taken no part in the last campaign.

Francis E. Warren, it seems, narrowly missed appointment. Osborne had planned to go to Washington for the March 4 inauguration of President Cleveland, but changed his mind. Had he gone, Secretary of State Amos Barber would have been acting governor, and he intended to appoint Warren, on the theory that Wyoming's vacancy did not occur until March 3, the end of Warren's two-year term. The Republican United States Senate might have seated Warren. Warren wrote to Willis Van Devanter: "Had Barber appointed as well as Osborne, the Barber appointee, in my judgment would have had the best of it." And he wrote to Barber on March 3, 1893: "I thank you sincerely for your kindness and confidence expressed in me. I shall have been very glad of the appointment had Mr. Osborne absented himself as proposed because it would have been a particularly useful and profitable document to have had here—my appointment dated March 4th as against Beckwith's dated February 23rd." [14]

After waiting more than five months without being seated, Beckwith on August 7 sent his resignation to the United States Senate "owing to a combination of circumstances." Osborne deferred naming a replacement until he could see what happened to a Montana appointment. The Montana man was refused a seat, the Senate explanation being that "to secure representation in Congress for states where legislatures failed to elect last winter, it is necessary to reconvene such bodies and consummate such an election." Governor Osborne chose not to call a special session, having no assurance that such a session would do any better than the regular session. And so Wyoming had only one United States senator, Joseph M. Carey, from 1893 to 1895.

THE REPUBLICANS DISCARD CAREY

The Republican party in Wyoming, strong in 1890, weak and on the defensive in 1892, was vigorous once again in 1894. At the nominating convention in Casper on August 1, William A. Richards, a rancher from Red Bank in the Big Horn Basin who had been surveyor general of Wyoming, 1889–1893, was nominated for governor; Charles W. Burdick of Saratoga, secretary of state; William O. Owen of Laramie, auditor; Henry G. Hay of Cheyenne, treasurer; Estelle Reel, Cheyenne, superintendent of public instruction; and Frank W. Mondell of Newcastle, representative in Congress. The Republican state platform indorsed the McKinley high-tariff bill, advocated liberal pensions for Civil War veterans, and urged free coinage of gold and silver at the ratio of sixteen to one. The decision to support free coinage of silver represented surrender to the western easy-money philosophy. Wyoming produced no silver, but many of its people sympathized with other western states that did and thought that free coinage of silver would increase the amount of money in circulation and help to overcome hard times.

United States Senators Carey and Warren had been berated by many western editors for voting against silver. Carey had stuck to his guns, while Warren's public utterances thereafter showed him hedging, and willing to follow the wishes of a majority of Wyoming people on

[14] Warren Letterbooks, University of Wyoming Library.

the subject. The pro-Carey *Wyoming Tribune* suggested that the free-silver plank in the Republican platform was inserted merely to catch votes.

Failing to arrange fusion in 1894, Democrats and Populists advanced full slates of candidates for state offices, and each entered a candidate for Congress. Democrats were handicapped because their party was split nationally. Wyoming Democrats did not like Cleveland's defense of the gold standard, nor did some of them approve the free-wool schedule of the Wilson-Gorman Tariff of August, 1894.

Republicans campaigned hard everywhere. Congressional candidate Frank W. Mondell recalled in *My Story*:

As we drove into the little village of Afton in the rich mountain-rimmed Star Valley, we were met by a pleasant capable appearing man who bade us welcome as Mayor and Republican committeeman. After these salutations he said smilingly that he thought we ought to know he was a polygamist, in case that might affect our attitude. [Polygamy had been outlawed by Congress in 1887.] We assured our friend we were not disposed to question the propriety of his family affairs and would be glad to accept his hospitality. Thereupon our party partook of a fine supper in the modest home of very pleasant and comely wife No. Three, and thereafter, leaving Miss Reel with her, the remainder of our party was comfortably housed in the larger homes of Wives One and Two.

This peculiar situation perhaps requires some explanation. When the federal authorities began action against the polygamists in Utah, the fathers of such households naturally sought means to escape prosecution without abandoning their families, and there came a transplanting of families into the adjacent states. . . . Wisely the Wyoming authorities ignored these family relations and welcomed these capable, orderly, and industrious settlers. . . .[15]

The Republicans won a smashing victory. William A. Richards received 10,149 votes for governor to 6,965 for William H. Holliday (Democrat) and 2,176 for Lewis C. Tidball (Populist). Other Republican candidates scored comparable victories. The legislature became overwhelmingly Republican, with eighteen Republicans to four Democrats in the Senate and thirty-four Republicans to two Democrats and one Democrat-Populist in the House.

Senator Joseph M. Carey was now discarded by the party which had sent him to Washington with such enthusiasm in 1890. Two United States senators were chosen by the 1895 legislature, Francis E. Warren and Clarence D. Clark. In the public balloting, not a single vote was

[15] Frank W. Mondell, *My Story*, in *Wyoming State Tribune* (Cheyenne), September 6, 1935. Mondell's autobiography, referred to several times in this chapter, ran serially in the *Tribune* from August 1, 1935, to February 4, 1936.

cast for Carey, all Republican votes going to Warren on the first ballot for the six-year term and to Clark on the first ballot for the four-year term. Newspapers reported that even in the Republican caucus there had been no votes for Carey, although M. C. Brown of Laramie had received eight votes against Clark.

There can be no doubt that Carey desired re-election. How, then, can this amazing reversal be explained? Carey's adherence to the gold-standard policy of the national Republican party was an important factor, since Warren was ready to support the state-party plank and Carey was not. Carey later said that his gold-standard views caused his rejection. Another factor was the desire of Republicans outside Cheyenne to limit Cheyenne to one senator. Frank W. Mondell, who as candidate for Congress was in the thick of the 1894 campaign, recalled in his autobiography that "the people of the state would not stand for two senators from the capital city." Warren, after his failure to win re-election in 1893, had improved his time, mended his fences, and was prepared to nudge Carey aside when one of the two strong men had to go. In a long letter to M. C. Barrow dated December 12, 1894, Warren explained his refusal to stand aside for Carey. For instance, he wrote: "Tenth, I know of no reason on 'God's footstool' why I should always play second fiddle in the Carey-Warren or Warren-Carey combination. Now I am not *against Carey*, but I am *for Warren*. . . . Please be assured however, that it is the other side who are bluffing and not me. . . . If either J. M. C. or F. E. W. go to the Senate in 1895 it will be F. E. W." [16]

The two most influential Republican editors in the state, Slack and Hayford, chose to back Warren. To help his last-ditch cause, Carey in December, 1894, bought control of the *Wyoming Tribune*. In commenting on the ensuing battle between the *Tribune* and the *Cheyenne Sun*, Hayford declared in his *Laramie Sentinel*: "We believe it is the almost universal opinion that there should be but one senator elected from Cheyenne, and that one should be F. E. Warren. We hoped, however, there would be no mud slinging and that the matter would be settled without acrimony and bitterness." There was bitterness, however, and the Carey-Warren feud would endure until 1918.

Warren became the head of the Republican party in Wyoming in

[16] Warren Letterbooks, University of Wyoming Library. This letter and others show that Warren and Carey had been drifting apart for several years for a variety of reasons.

1895 and would remain so until his death in 1929. Willis Van Devanter, Cheyenne attorney, was credited with helping to engineer the Warren-Clark elections. He and Hayford and Slack and many others who took Warren's side in 1895 were subsequently rewarded with appropriate political appointments.

THE 1896 ELECTION

In 1896 the Populists, who were obviously weaker than they had been in 1894, offered to fuse with the Democrats if the latter would support the Populist candidate for Congress, William Brown of Big Horn, and Populist presidential electors in return for Populist support for four state judgeships. The Populists weren't offering much, since they apparently had no candidates for the judgeships. The Democrats declined the offer, after which the jerry-built Populist organization fell apart, as Democrats tried to take the Populist candidates off the ballot and Republicans schemed to keep them there. Democrats and Republicans alike realized that most of the Populists, if they had no candidates of their own party, would vote Democratic.

Warren's letterbooks for the campaign period reveal that he obtained railroad passes and $250 in expense money for J. W. Paterson, chairman of the Populist state committee, so that Paterson could rally Populists to stand by William Brown and the Populist electors. Warren also supplied passes for Brown, and was able to keep Brown and two Populist electors on the ballot (a third Populist elector accepted a place on the Democratic ticket vacated by a Democrat). Meanwhile, the battle was joined between fusionist and antifusionist Populists, and it was apparent that the Populist vote would be split between Democrats and Populists.

On September 14, 1896, in an appeal for money addressed to national Republican boss Matthew Quay, Warren explained that railroad workers were deserting the party: "The receivers and managers of the [Union Pacific] road are as anxious for McKinley as we can desire, but unfortunately, cannot control their men as railway managers usually do, because the road is in the hands of receivers." [17] Warren also told Quay that he was somewhat more hopeful of getting coal miners' votes: "Coal miners here—always easily stampeded—were almost uniformly for Bryan upon his nomination, but are being gathered for McKinley in large blocks, and if we have oil enough to properly

[17] *Ibid.*

take care of their machinery the last weeks of the campaign, with
enough in the meantime to keep the bearings smooth, we will have
them."

Principal issue in the 1896 campaign was silver. Osborne and Bryan,
and Populist William Brown as well, urged free coinage of silver.
Mondell and McKinley equivocated, trying not to stray too far in the
free-silver direction from the Republican party's national plank: "We
are opposed to the free coinage of silver except by international agreement with the leading commercial nations of the world, which we
pledge ourselves to promote, and until such agreement can be obtained
the existing gold standard must be preserved."

Osborne defeated Mondell for the seat in Congress, 10,310 to 10,044.
The three Democratic presidential electors defeated the Republican
electors by an average margin of 255. Populist William Brown received
648 votes; the two Populist electors received 486 and 427 votes. The
judgeship contests were won by two Democrats, a Republican, and an
Independent. The Republicans retained control of the two houses of
the legislature, 14 to 5 and 23 to 15. Included among the fifteen non-
Republicans in the House were three fusionists and one Populist.

In addition to subsidizing Populist candidates, the Republicans had
voted one hundred Finnish miners at Hanna and Carbon who could
not read English. They had printed in the Finnish language an
excerpt from the Wyoming Constitution for use by the miners in case
they were challenged to read the constitution at the polls. The defeated
Democratic candidate for treasurer of Carbon County in November,
1897, won a Wyoming Supreme Court decision which held that the
constitution's provision requiring voters to be able to read the constitution meant that they should be able to read it in English.

Organizing the Finns and subsidizing the Populists brought the
Republicans close to victory, but only close. And yet Francis E. Warren
was not far wrong when he boasted in a letter to B. B. Brooks dated
November 11, 1896, that in comparison with surrounding states the
Wyoming Republicans had in the Bryan-McKinley contest "scored the
greatest success in the United States."[18] Bryan defeated McKinley six
to one in Colorado, five to one in Utah, four to one in Idaho, and four
to one in Montana.[19] All of these states, to be sure, were much more
excited about the silver issue than was non-silver-producing Wyo-

[18] *Ibid.*
[19] The ratios are derived from figures given in E. E. Robinson, *The Presidential Vote,
1896–1932* (Stanford: Stanford University Press, 1934).

ming.[20] While Bryan's lead in South Dakota was razor thin and Nebraska gave him only a 12,000-vote lead, the west end of Nebraska and the southwest corner of South Dakota preferred Bryan two or more to one.

It was really Uinta County that made the difference in Wyoming, voting Democratic almost two to one. After analyzing the returns, Warren first blamed the Mormons, but later conceded that Uinta County Mormons were no more Democratic that year than the county's non-Mormons and actually gave the Republicans a much better vote than did their neighbors in Utah and Idaho.

HARD TIMES

Economic depression prevailed in the United States during the 1890's. The Panic of 1893 was followed by substantial depression until 1898. Throughout the country appeared the familiar manifestations of depression: falling farm prices, reduced wages, widespread unemployment, strikes, business stagnation. The Union Pacific Railroad—so important to Wyoming—went bankrupt in October, 1893.

The Warren Livestock Company went into receivership in August, 1894, with debts in excess of $200,000. The company, the largest of its kind in Wyoming, had about 90,000 sheep, 2,500 cattle, 2,000 horses, and 2,500 Angora goats in 1889. In March, 1892, Warren wrote to his father that he had between 80,000 and 120,000 sheep. Warren controlled more than 250,000 acres of land, of which only about 25,000 acres was patented. He had bought 125,000 acres of land from the Union Pacific in 1884, but had sold most of this land in the following year. Warren's letterbooks in the University of Wyoming Library show Warren remarking on hard times regularly in the years between 1888 and 1897. The Warren Mercantile Company, which was also the largest of its kind in Wyoming, avoided bankruptcy, but was under great financial strain for several years.

Wyoming's increase in population from 62,555 in 1890 to 92,531 in 1900 was disappointingly slow to residents of the new state whose optimism had soared when statehood was achieved in 1890. They had been told again and again that their sixty-two million acres were rich in undeveloped resources. As in the 1870's, they suffered disillusionment and frustration.

[20] Another factor helping the Republicans in Wyoming in 1896 was the unpopularity of the Democratic free-wool schedule. The wool industry, which was important in the state, needed tariff protection, which had been taken away under Cleveland in 1894. Hides, too, lost their protection in 1894, to the annoyance of cattlemen.

One index of economic growth is found in property valuations. Wyoming's property valuation for tax purposes changed as follows from 1890 to 1898:

Year	Valuation
1890	$30,665,197.00
1891	32,536,400.00
1892	32,357,500.00
1893	32,356,801.96
1894	29,198,041.20
1895	29,838,938.79
1896	30,028,694.65
1897	30,300,462.31
1898	30,789,291.74

The important cattle industry suffered shrinkage which was partially offset by an expansion in sheep, although there was a difference of opinion as to how well the wool industry was doing. Governor Osborne maintained that he and others in the industry were making a satisfactory profit. Free use of government land may have made this possible. And yet Wyoming wool brought little more than half as much in 1894 as it had in the years 1890–1893, and, as noticed above, the Warren Livestock Company went broke.

Since the state depended for its revenue almost entirely upon the property tax, usually levied at between six and seven mills, expansion of public services was virtually impossible. "There is . . . urgent demand for a reduction of expenses in all departments of the public service," Governor Richards told the legislature in 1895. The total expenditures for all purposes by the state, nevertheless, did increase slowly from $168,000 in 1890 to almost $250,000 in 1897. The state contributed $15,000 a year to maintain the university during the first two years of statehood, then cut back to $5,000 or less thereafter.

There were fifteen banks in Wyoming at the time of its admission—eleven national and four state and private. Two of these and two new ones, which were opened soon afterward, failed within the next few years. The Cheyenne National Bank closed in November, 1891; the First National Bank of Cheyenne and T. A. Kent's Bank of Cheyenne closed in July, 1893; and the First National Bank of Sundance closed in October, 1893. Meanwhile, deposits and loans were shrinking. State funds amounting to $44,147.31 were lost in the Kent bank failure.

There were few industries at the beginning of the decade, and some of them closed. The most industrialized city, Laramie, lost some of its plants. Its flour mill and its cigar factory closed in 1891. Its rolling mill operated fitfully after peak employment of 180 men in 1890. Its glass-works had closed in 1889 and could not be reopened. Said the *Cheyenne Leader* in February, 1891: "Negotiations for establishment of manufac-turing plants here always fall to pieces. . . . There is too much irre-sponsible twaddle at public meetings held to consider new enterprises. Wind and gush never accomplish anything. We have had too much spread eagleism already."

In 1897 the McKinley Administration adopted the high Dingley Tariff, which was heralded as a big help to infant industries. Scoffed the *Laramie Boomerang* in October, 1898: "The Dingley bill has started one new industry in Wyoming. They have started a broom factory in the Laramie pen. It is a peculiar republican enterprise and we must give them credit. Great is the Dingley bill! Great is McKinley prosperity!"

A few attempts had been made by communities in the 1880's to sub-sidize small industries, such as the Laramie glassworks, but Wyoming communities generally felt too poor to do this in the 1890's. Cried editor Hayford in March, 1892:

But our citizens will not bankrupt themselves, individually and collectively, and give everything they have made by years of struggle . . . and bankrupt our city and county with debt to put up for mythical schemes of impecunious adven-turers who come here and tell us "Cheyenne will give a hundred thousand dollars! What will you give?" We ain't bidding against Cheyenne wind or any-body else's wind.

General Jacob S. Coxey, a Populist of Massillon, Ohio, in 1894 called for a march on Washington in support of a public-works program he was promoting. Many members of "Coxey's Army," also known as "Commonwealers" and "Coxeyites," commandeered trains in the West and passed through Wyoming in April and May, 1894, on their way to Washington. Some Wyoming towns gave them provisions rather than have them overrun the communities in search of food. In May, 1894, United States Marshal Joseph P. Rankin and many deputies recap-tured a train from Coxeyites in Green River and arrested fifteen leaders. Four companies of troops from Fort Russell answered an appeal from Rankin and took charge of the Commonwealers, escorting most of them to Idaho. The fifteen leaders were sentenced to four- and five-month jail sentences in Cheyenne by United States Judge John A. Riner. Other Coxeyites were jailed in Evanston.

At its company town near Chicago in 1894 the Pullman Company laid off one-third of its employees and cut the wages of the rest, whereupon the remaining employees struck. Railroad workers in Wyoming and elsewhere struck in sympathy. President Cleveland ordered the United States Army to break the strike, under the pretext of protecting the mails, and the strike soon ended. More than eight hundred Union Pacific employees in Wyoming lost their jobs for participating in the short sympathy strike. They were discharged on federal-court order, the railway company being in the hands of the federal court while in receivership. In Rawlins a rigorous boycott was instituted against the soldiers and United States marshals. No one would sell them anything. Five Rawlins men were arrested, including the city marshal, a court clerk, and a newspaper editor.

Wyoming labor, already sore beset, suffered another blow in March, 1895, when a coal-mine explosion at Red Canyon, seven miles from Evanston, killed sixty-one men. They were mainly Scots, nearly all of them heads of families and some of them leading citizens of Evanston.

Dreams of new railroad construction were forgotten. After completion of the Burlington across northeastern Wyoming in 1894, no new projects could be launched during the decade. From Alliance, Nebraska, the Burlington reached Newcastle in November, 1890, Gillette in August, 1891, and Sheridan in November, 1892. Edward Gillette, chief of the line's surveying party, said in his memoirs: "A line had been located into Buffalo and contract ordered to be let to construct the road, when on account of the Rustler or Cattlemen's war, construction was postponed and not resumed." Sheridan was the terminus until construction was renewed in 1894 and the line passed on into Montana.

Despite Joseph M. Carey's glowing report to Congress in 1890 about vast mineral wealth, only coal was produced in significant quantities in the 1890's. Output rose from 1,870,366 tons in 1890 to 2,744,960 tons in 1897. The Union Pacific's wholly owned subsidiary, the Union Pacific Coal Company, organized in 1890 to take the place of the Union Pacific Coal Department, produced most of the state's coal from its mines at Rock Springs, Hanna, Almy (closed in 1900), and Carbon (closed in 1902). There were smaller, non–Union Pacific mines at Glenrock, Inez, Newcastle, and Sheridan. New mines opened at Diamondville and Kemmerer, the latter town being named after M. S. Kemmerer, a Pennsylvania investor.

In August, 1893, a prospector named J. C. Carter turned up in Casper with the news that he had found the legendary Lost Cabin mine in the Big Horn Mountains. For more than thirty years there had been tales about this rich mine, whose original owners, it was said, had been killed by Indians, except for two who had disappeared after reporting the tragedy at Fort Fetterman. Several Casper citizens accompanied Carter to his discovery, which proved to be, not a mine, but only a rude structure erected by Indians as a hunting "blind."

During the nineties, Casper prospectors devoted most of their attention to Casper Mountain, whence came frequent reports of rich finds of gold, silver, copper, galena, and asbestos. Much perspiration was poured over the mountain without any important return. Minerals there were, of many kinds, but they were all low grade.

Soda lakes in the Laramie Plains and the Sweetwater country had attracted attention in the territorial period. Chicago men in 1892 organized the Syndicate Improvement Company, capitalized at three million dollars, to develop some of the Sweetwater properties. Machinery was installed, and many men were employed briefly at the new city of Johnstown. Within two years, however, the project collapsed, with explanations that costs exceeded the market value of the product.

As in the previous decade, promoters from time to time released stories about promising new developments at various gold mines in the Medicine Bow Mountains, all of which proved negligible—on Brush Creek in 1890, at Gold Hill in 1890 and 1891, at Centennial in 1892, on Douglas Creek in 1893, and so on. Gold was also reported near the Encampment River beginning in 1896. The elusive Lost Cabin gold mine was once again falsely reported found in the Big Horns southeast of Cloud Peak in 1897. Mining exchanges were organized in Laramie and Rawlins in 1896 to advertise opportunities. The Laramie Mining and Stock Exchange published folders giving facts about twenty-five mining camps tributary to Laramie.

Even Wyoming editors who were usually tolerant of extravagant claims expressed skepticism about a Rawlins letter published in the *Chicago Herald* in November, 1897, with respect to a new discovery of gold at Grand Encampment. The letter described a rich find in Purgatory Gulch, near the Encampment River, and said: "People here and all around are mad. Everybody is rushing to Grand Encampment. . . . The excitement is higher than anything within the memory of the oldest miner, not excepting the days of '49." In December a Union Pacific immigration agent described at Cheyenne the gold madness in the East resulting from the rich finds at Grand Encampment: "Every paper throughout the country is talking Grand Encampment." He expected a stampede, he said. He considered that besides the gold at

Grand Encampment, the copper district there was "without question the richest copper proposition known on the globe." Such exaggeration was offset by one reality in the form of small iron-ore shipments from Hartville to Denver and Pueblo which began in November, 1897.

State geologist Wilbur C. Knight reported six thousand barrels of oil produced in 1897. Building Wyoming's oil production to six thousand barrels had been a slow process in the sixty years since the eastern public had first learned from Washington Irving's *The Adventures of Captain Bonneville U.S.A.*, published in 1837, of the presence of a "great tar spring" near South Pass. Mountain men at the Green River rendezvous of 1832 had told Bonneville of the spring, which he found, with great difficulty, on the Little Popo Agie southeast of present-day Lander. Thereafter, many surface indications of oil were observed by Oregon Trail travelers and territorial pioneers. Small quantities were collected from pits dug near Evanston and along the Belle Fourche River in the 1870's, and in 1883, Wyoming's first flowing well was brought in southeast of Lander, near Bonneville's "great tar spring," in what was to become known as the Dallas Field. In that same year, the first claim notices in the Salt Creek area were filed by Stephen W. Downey of Laramie. The former Delegate to Congress did not follow up his claims with affidavits of assessment work and permitted them to be taken over by others. Downey deserves to be called a man of vision in several respects, but in mineral development he was shortsighted and guessed wrong. He poured much money into abortive gold-mining schemes, while the Salt Creek claims which he permitted to lapse lay close to the center of a 22,000-acre area north of Casper which has produced 400,000,000 barrels of crude oil.

Dr. Samuel Aughey, territorial geologist, in his annual report of January 1, 1886, described the Salt Creek oil basin in favorable terms, which required no special brilliance because the presence of a broad anticlinal dome is obvious on the surface. Cy Iba, an old California gold prospector, filed his first placer claim at Salt Creek in 1887, after which he and other members of his family filed claim after claim and did much assessment work.

The man in the street's opinion of Wyoming's oil prospects at the time is well represented by the following editorial comment which appeared in the *Casper Mail* in January, 1889: "There are springs in various localities that flow all the way from one gallon to ten barrels per day. It is by these springs that the oil belt of Wyoming is traced for more than two hundred miles."

In 1889, Phillip Martin Shannon, successful Pennsylvania oilman, filed claims on a large area just north of Salt Creek and extending into the north edge of Salt Creek. Shannon and his associates drilled a 1,000-foot well in what came to be known as the Shannon Field. The venture produced five or ten barrels a day, enough to justify drilling three more wells in the vicinity. Since there was no market in Wyoming, the crude was put up in barrels, hauled by freight wagon to Casper, and shipped east on the Chicago and North Western. To obtain more capital, Shannon and his associates organized a Wyoming corporation, the Pennsylvania Oil and Gas Company. They built a refinery in Casper in 1894–1895, capable of producing one hundred barrels of lubricating oil per day. At every opportunity, Casper people proudly escorted visitors through the little refinery.

Meanwhile, in 1893 the University of Wyoming had published a remarkably clear and accurate geological report on the Salt Creek Field written by Professor Wilbur C. Knight with the collaboration of Professor E. E. Slosson. This favorable report, which told where the oil was, brought no rush of drilling crews in the 1890's, a commentary on transportation and marketing problems of that era.

In the state geologist's report of oil production worth $54,000 for 1897 lay the greatest hope for Wyoming's twentieth-century mineral production. At the time, however, it was as an acorn to an oak, and worth very little to the contemporary economy.

RECLAMATION

Many ranchers in the 1890's were enjoying cheap irrigation of hay meadows along small streams, yet the large rivers carried most of the state's water unused into other states. Corporate organization and large capital expenditures would be required before there could be significant expansion of reclamation. Great promises were made in the nineties, but accomplishments were woefully small. Joseph M. Carey assured the United States House of Representatives in March, 1890, that Wyoming had "ten to twelve million acres that may be irrigated," naming as his authorities John Wesley Powell and Elwood Mead. In the previous year, Francis E. Warren had declared in his governor's report to the Secretary of the Interior: "It is estimated that between 12,000,000 and 15,000,000 acres can be successfully cultivated." Despite such glowing assurances from persons in whom they had confidence, the residents of Wyoming in the troubled decade of the 1890's began to learn that it would take "blood, sweat and tears," plus money, to make the desert blossom.

While they waited for dreams to come true, Wyoming people followed with great interest the activities of one Frank Melbourne, an Irishman who had come to the United States by way of Australia and New Zealand. He first attracted attention as a rainmaker at Canton, Ohio. In August, 1891, he transferred his activities to Wyoming. After failing to deliver more than a sprinkle in Casper, he moved to Cheyenne, where he agreed to produce one-half inch of rain within three days for $150. He set up shop in the loft of a stable, permitting no one to watch his operations. Smoke issued from a hole in the roof of the loft. Before the expiration of the 72-hour period, two thundershowers delivered a half-inch of rain. Melbourne collected the $150, was lionized in Cheyenne, and enjoyed much favorable publicity all over the country. Locally, some people scoffed, others were skeptical and required further proof, while still others became firm believers. After a few days of delay to placate ranchers who wanted to complete their haying, Melbourne was offered $100 if he would produce another half-inch of rain. This time he failed. He soon left the city to carry on other rain-making experiments in Utah, Idaho, Kansas, and Texas. In June, 1892, he was back in Cheyenne under another contract. Again he worked secretly, this time from a more elevated perch in the dome of the capitol building. He soon claimed credit for rains at Rawlins and other distant places, but the Cheyenne committee insisted on precipitation closer to Cheyenne, which he could not produce. He left Cheyenne without his pay, regarded by most of the citizens as a fraud.

A more reliable aid to the Wyoming farmer and rancher than Frank Melbourne was Elwood Mead. In the 1890's this outstanding state engineer brought order out of the chaotic water-rights situation. Under Article VIII of the Wyoming Constitution and subsequent legislation, Mead surveyed ditches, gauged streams, adjudicated water rights, and established a reliable centralized record of approved water appropriations. In trying to increase the amount of water applied to the land, however, Mead and other state officials were disappointed more often than not. Governor William A. Richards, himself an experienced canal builder of the Big Horn Basin, told the 1895 legislature of "this vast wealth of land and water lying idle, side by side, awaiting only the magic touch of labor and capital, intelligently combined, to be coined into wealth." Enthusiastic though he was, Mead conceded in late 1896 that not more than 33 per cent had been added to the total acreage of irrigated land since 1890. He blamed the slow progress on hard times. Ever the optimist, he added that the amount of Wyoming land under irrigation could be increased tenfold. In his biennial report submitted to the 1897 legislature, he declared that the limit of irrigation through small, short ditches was near at hand, while "our rivers are untouched."

Calculated to help enlarge the sphere of reclamation was the famous Carey Act, which was adopted by Congress and received President Cleveland's approval in August, 1894. Named after its author, Wyoming's Senator Joseph M. Carey, the law was designed to supply federal and state aid to irrigation projects. It provided for donation by the federal government of up to one million acres of arid lands to each state having such lands on condition that the state cause the lands to be reclaimed and settled by actual settlers on small tracts.

The Carey Act stirred the imagination and soon induced considerable promotional activity. Yet Democratic politicians in Wyoming fought both the Carey Act and Senator Francis E. Warren's earlier attempts to get something like it in 1891 and 1892. They doubted that the state, without financial outlays beyond its means, could make the scheme succeed, and they suspected that most of the benefits, if any, would go to corporations rather than the actual settlers. Henry A. Coffeen, United States representative from Wyoming, for instance, charged in congressional debate in August, 1894, that land syndicates, big cattlemen, and "non-irrigating representatives" were behind the bill for their own aggrandizement. The Carey Act, it should be noted, did leave out certain sensible provisions, which Democrats had found objectionable in Warren's bills, that would have allowed the state to lease for grazing purposes lands of the federal grant not taken up by irrigators.

Wyoming was the first state to accept the federal government's offer under the Carey Act. In a ten-page law of the 1895 legislature, the Board of Land Commissioners and the state engineer were given detailed assignments. They were to study the feasibility of proposals for irrigation works advanced by individuals or companies and to make contracts when projects appeared sound. The state would charge the settler fifty cents per acre for the land, and the private construction company would charge him twenty dollars or more per acre for perpetual water rights. By January, 1897, eight projects had been approved, of which only two in the Big Horn Basin were pushed with any vigor.

The Big Horn Basin Development Company, headed by S. L. Wiley, received state approval in June, 1895, to take water from the Greybull

River. The Shoshone Land and Irrigation Company, with William F. (Buffalo Bill) Cody as president and George T. Beck as construction superintendent, received state approval in September, 1895, to divert water from the South Fork of the Stinking Water (renamed Shoshone in 1901). Both companies suffered bitter disappointments in subsequent years.

A third irrigation project, which would become a Carey Act project in time, was that of the Wyoming Development Company. Organized in 1883 by Joseph M. Carey, William C. Irvine, Horace G. Plunkett, John W. Hoyt, Morton E. Post, Francis E. Warren, and Andrew Gilchrist (Thomas Sturgis joined them in 1884), the company founded the Wheatland Colony, taking water from the Laramie River to irrigate more than fifty thousand acres. After a painfully slow start, the Wheatland community prospered after 1900, but the company did not, its losses to 1951 amounting to $1,622,687.48.

Meanwhile, a few hundred Mormon families had settled on the north side of the Greybull River beginning in 1893. They completed a ditch and harvested a crop in 1895 without Carey Act land and established small towns at Burlington and Otto. As more people entered the Big Horn Basin, a campaign was launched for the organization of a separate Big Horn County, with boundaries coinciding with those of the Big Horn Basin; this was achieved in 1897. In the meantime, the most spectacular county-seat fight in Wyoming history raged in 1896, with Otto and a younger town, Basin City, the principal contenders. Basin City (later Basin) won the battle, partly, it seems, because at the last moment Cody entered the contest, probably at the instigation of Basin City editors and politicians. Cody could scarcely hope to win, but it managed to attract a number of Burlington votes which would otherwise have gone to Otto.

Big Horn was the only new county established in the 1890's, and it was organized in disregard of the two-million-dollar minimum valuation specified in the constitution. Optimists who had talked in the constitutional convention about rapidly multiplying counties were sobered by the conditions of the nineties.

Hungering for others to join them on their sixty-two million acres, Wyoming people of the nineties were nevertheless somewhat particular. They did not like the Chinese, a few hundred of whom remained at Rock Springs under the protection of federal troops. The 1895 legislature petitioned Congress to restrict immigration to the United States.

The legislature's objection to immigrants seems to have been based less on resentment against the foreign-born already in Wyoming than on acceptance of the arguments of the national Immigration Restriction League formed in 1894. The foreign-born were blamed for assorted ills of the country, including the depression. Almost one-fourth of Wyoming's people in 1890 were foreign born. Of the 14,913 foreign-born in the state, 3,147 had come from England, 2,037 from Germany, 1,900 from Ireland, 1,380 from Scotland, 1,357 from Sweden, 1,314 from Canada, 794 from Russia, 680 from Denmark, 533 from Wales, 474 from China, 345 from Norway, 259 from Italy, 232 from Austria, and 127 from France.

Indians, who had never been appreciated in Wyoming, received special attention in 1895 and 1896. Under the Fort Bridger Treaty of 1868, the Bannocks, who lived mostly in Idaho, had been assured the right to hunt on the unoccupied lands of the United States "so long as game may be found thereon, and so long as peace subsists between the Indians and whites on the borders of the hunting districts." Accordingly, they hunted in western Wyoming, particularly in Jackson Hole, without paying any attention to Wyoming game laws. Governor William A. Richards told the 1895 legislature that "there is no exaggeration in the statement that more large game is killed by Indians for the hide alone than is killed by our citizens for food purposes." Then in October, 1895, Sheriff John Ward of Uinta County arrested a Bannock named Race Horse for unlawfully killing seven elk the previous July. Race Horse's attorneys obtained his release on a writ of habeas corpus, after which the United States Circuit Court in Cheyenne held that Wyoming's game laws could not be enforced against the Indians. People in northern Uinta County were furious. In time they had their way, however, because Willis Van Devanter, representing Sheriff Ward, carried an appeal to the United States Supreme Court, where he won his case. The high court held that the hunting privilege conferred by the 1868 treaty was repealed by Wyoming's act of admission, which gave Wyoming all the powers of other states and reserved no privileges to Indians.[21]

Two hundred Negroes, mostly from Harrison County, Ohio, were brought to Dana (near Hanna) to work in the coal mines in January,

---

[21] Later, in October, 1903, some Sioux Indians ventured into eastern Wyoming to hunt antelope. Weston County Sheriff Bill Miller and a posse tried to arrest them on Lightning Creek north of Douglas. A battle ensued in which the sheriff, a deputy, and four Indians were slain.

1890. Most of them did not stay long. Newspaper references to them and to the few other Negroes who were in the state in the 1890's suggest that there were divided opinions with respect to their acceptance by whites.

While many Wyoming people viewed Chinese, Indians, Negroes, and European immigrants with disapproval, a few rather pathetic efforts were being made to attract farmers from the Middle West. The legislators talked about reviving the territorial immigration bureau but could not bring themselves to appropriate any money for it. Instead, several county immigration societies were organized. They accomplished little. A small German-Russian colony from Chicago arrived in the Big Horn Basin in May, 1896, piloted by the old scout Frank Grouard, to establish the new village of Irma with eight log houses.

The most impressive promotional literature dealing with Wyoming in the nineties was a pamphlet, *Wyoming*, put out in new editions from time to time by the Union Pacific Railroad. It summarized the agricultural, stock-raising, and mineral resources of the state.

Not much land was filed on or patented from 1890 to 1897. In those eight years there were 4,441 homestead filings and 1,385 desert-land filings in Wyoming. In the same period there were 1,547 homestead patents and 667 desert-land patents. The great era of public-land entries in Wyoming would be in the twentieth century, with the peak years 1920 and 1921.

After eight years of experience in Wyoming, Elwood Mead, in his 1897 biennial report, blamed the land laws for Wyoming's slow development. He urged that the federal government cede grazing lands to the states. He advocated that the state then give each settler and irrigator of 160 acres the right to lease 2,560 acres of contiguous grazing land at one cent per acre. Such a program, he said, would solve the state's "most important" agricultural problems. Setting up a large number of such farming-grazing units would, he felt, "prevent the destruction of the native grasses, now taking place, reduce taxes, provide ample revenue for county and state government, increase the profits of farmers, put an end to range conflicts." Nothing came of Mead's proposal, and the range conflicts of which he took cognizance became worse. They will be discussed in the next chapter.

RELAXATION IN THE DEPRESSED NINETIES

Most forms of territorial fun continued with little change in the 1890's. The old stand-bys of the frontier, the saloon, gambling hall, and

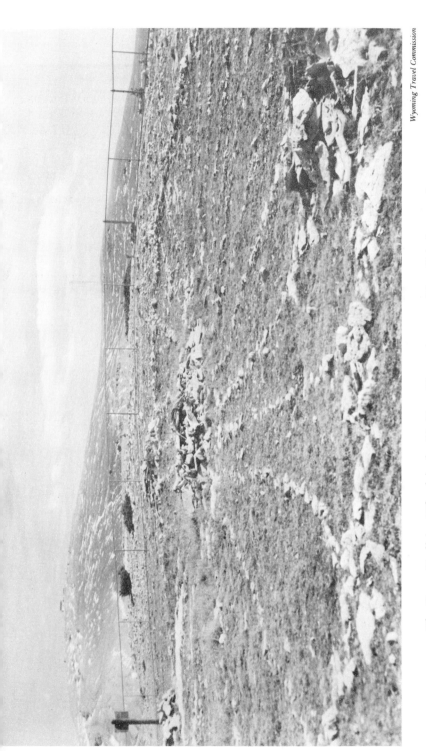

The Great Medicine Wheel, in the Big Horn Mountains east of Lovell, is the most famous of Wyoming's Indian relics. It is thought to have been constructed for ceremonial purposes.

Independence Rock, located on the north bank of the Sweetwater River southwest of Casper, was a famous landmark on the Oregon Trail. Inscriptions on the rock date back to the 1830's.

Painting by W. H. Jackson, courtesy University of Wyoming Library

Fort Laramie in 1842

Painting by W. H. Jackson, courtesy University of Wyoming Library

Fort Bridger as it looked 1843–1847

Old Bedlam at the Fort Laramie National Historic Site

Hostile Sioux chiefs (l. to r.) Sitting Bull, Swift Bear, Spotted Tail, and Red Cloud and their interpreters

Esther Morris statue

Esther Morris, 1870

William H. Bright

James H. Hayford

Bill Nye

Thomas Moonlight

John W. Hoyt

S. W. Downey

Medicine Bow, about 1885

Perils of early railroading near Laramie

Salt Creek area Shannon Well no. 1, 1889

Oil refinery at Casper, 1895

Cheyenne Club, 1880's

Grub time at a cattle roundup camp, 1898

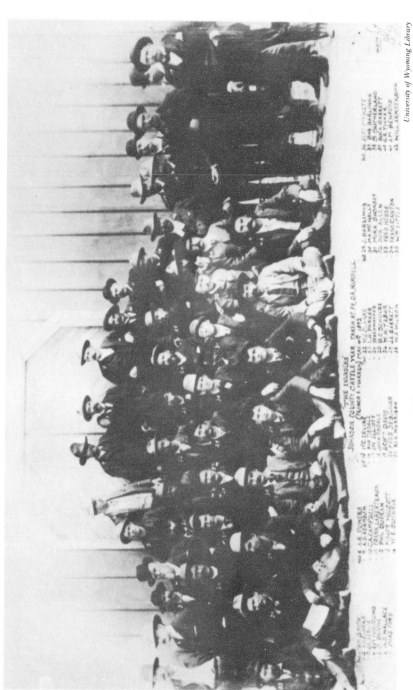

The Invaders, 1892

Sheridan Inn, built in 1893 and recently restored

Green River Brewery, about 1900

Joseph M. Carey

Francis E. Warren

Frank W. Mondell

John E. Osborne

Bishop Ethelbert Talbot

E. A. Slack

Clarence D. Clark

John B. Kendrick

Grand Encampment copper smelter, about 1903

The herder, his dogs, and his flock

Stimson Collection, University of Wyoming Library

Breaking prairie near Cheyenne about 1910

U.S. Bureau of Reclamation

Irrigating beans near Powell

Lower Falls of the Yellowstone

Photo by H. R. Crandall

The Teton Range and Jackson Lake

William B. Ross

Nellie Tayloe Ross

Leslie A. Miller   Joseph C. O'Mahoney   Tracy McCraken
(about 1934)

Nels H. Smith

Robert D. Carey

University of Wyoming Library

Wyoming National Guardsmen at Fort Lewis, Washington, 1942

Tom Parker photograph, Casper Tribune-Herald

Heart Mountain Japanese Relocation Center, 1943

Branding time

Big and husky bulls, the kind range men like, on Frank Wadsworth ranch near L
Tree

Wyoming Travel Commission

Frontier Days rodeo is rough on man and beast

Photograph by Bill Peery, Rocky Mountain News

Wind River Canyon

World's largest hot spring, Hot Springs State Park, Thermopolis

Marina at Alcova Reservoir near Casper

The annual cutter races in Jackson Hole

Wyoming Game and Fish Department

ild game abounds on the prairies and in the mountain valleys of Wyoming. Above, elk,
d below, antelope.

Lester C. Hunt

William (Scotty) Jack

Frank A. Barrett

William H. Harrison

Velma Linford

Minnie A. Mitchell

Keith Thomson

Thyra Thomson

Joseph J. Hickey

Jack R. Gage

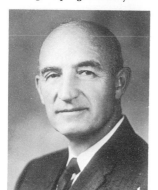

Milward L. Simpson

Clifford P. Hansen

Stanley K. Hathaway

Gale W. McGee

Malcolm Wallop

Teno Roncalio

Science Center and Classroom Building, University of Wyoming

Jim Bridger Power Plant

Sprinkling for dust control in strip mine north of Sheridan

Ed Herschler

James B. Griffith

State Capitol

Wyoming Game and Fish Department

Edwin J. Witzenburger

Robert G. Schrader

The Buffalo Bill Historical Center, located in Cody, houses the Buffalo Bill Museum, the Whitney Gallery of Western Art, and the Plains Indian Museum.

Robert Russin's Prometheus statue in front of the Natrona County Library, Casper

Robert Russin's statue of Lincoln, located between Laramie and Cheyenne

Devils Tower, the nation's first national monument, created in 1906

Medicine Bow peak

house of prostitution, remained popular resorts although they were losing a little ground as the preponderance of single men declined. The Reverend Daniel L. Rader, Cheyenne Methodist minister, told a temperance meeting in Laramie in March, 1891, that in his extensive travels over the state he had seen more women drunk than men. He had seen seven drunk women and six drunk men. Rader's statement brought him so much criticism that he offered to resign his pulpit, but his bishop refused to accept his resignation.

Profanity was prevalent in male circles. Dr. Charles B. Penrose wrote to Owen Wister in May, 1892: "Of course, during the past two months 'son of a bitch' has been a favorite expression in this country. Wyoming is in the son of a bitch stage of her civilization and could not get along without it any more than she could without a lariat and a branding iron."

The penitentiary at Laramie was crowded with the wayward. The Board of Charities and Reform reported in 1897 that among the 174 convicts there were 26 cowboys but only one sheepherder.

Since the passage of a law by the territorial legislature in 1888, saloons were supposed to be closed on Sundays, but the law was not generally enforced. Gambling was under attack, but its opponents could not get a law passed to make it illegal. The practice of collecting monthly fines from prostitutes continued.

Outdoor life included fishing, camping, hunting, tennis, and cycling. Indoors there were card parties (high five and whist). At a ladies' card club banquet in Laramie in November, 1895, sixteen ladies played high five and dined on fried oysters, wafers, celery, turkey, mushroom patties, potato salad, cranberry jelly, olives, almonds, ice cream, cake, and coffee. Some of the churches considered it sinful to play cards, and doubly so to play cards for prizes.

Holidays were observed in the traditional ways. One of Casper's most memorable Fourths of July was the one of 1893, when tremendous excitement centered around a horse race between Doc Middleton, owned by Charlie Richards, Bates Park rancher, and Sorrel John, owned by Jim Dahlman of Chadron, Nebraska. Large sums were wagered. The local horse won, as he did in a second race two weeks later.

Small circuses, with their bunko men and thieves, visited the larger railroad towns in summer, as in the 1880's. Newcastle got its first circus in 1892. Boisterous young spirits found release in Halloween vandalism and in charivaris. Roller skating was less favored than in the 1880's, and firemen's tournaments began to lose their former prominence.

The building of ostentatious mansions ended in the depression-ridden nineties. In 1891, on a hill in Evanston, Dr. William A. Hocker built a mansard-roof frame house with ten large rooms. Some of the natives called the place "Hocker's Hotel," though the doctor's large family needed the space. Mayor Frank Mondell in 1892 built a tall frame house with several chimneys, locating it on a hill overlooking Newcastle. In the same year, banker Edward A. Ivinson erected an outsize Romanesque dwelling in Laramie.

Emerging as spectator sports were football and the rodeo. After watching football games in February, 1894, between the Laramie Athletic Club and Fort Russell and between Laramie and Cheyenne high schools, editor J. H. Hayford observed: "We are not familiar enough with the game to give any technical or detailed report of it. It looks to a man up a tree like a rough and tumble Donnybrook fair fight minus the shallalas. Several of the participants were more or less hurt and carried off the field. . . . It is a very rough game as now played."

Roping and riding contests in the West have been traced as far back as 1847. Several occurred in Texas in 1883, yet Clifford P. Wester-meier, in *Man, Beast, Dust: The Story of Rodeo* (1947), gives Lander, Wyoming, credit for having held the first commercial rodeo, in 1893. The Labor Day program at Laramie in 1895 closed with an exhibition of "broncho bucking." In November of the same year, cowboys staged an "exhibition of wild horse riding" at the Laramie stockyards; the public was admitted free. The cowboys offered a reward of twenty-five dollars to anyone who could produce a horse they could not ride. In November, 1896, the Laramie Plains cowboys put on another such show, attended by one thousand people.

There was a "Wild West" exhibition at the Cheyenne fairgrounds on a Sunday afternoon in May, 1897. The *Wyoming Tribune* reported: "A small crowd attended owing to a general dislike of such sport and rainy weather." The editor evidently frowned on the new sport because it was so rough: "The exhibition had hardly commenced when several riders were thrown violently to the ground. Some escaped with bruised limbs, faces, etc., while others were quite badly stove up." After one contestant had been carried off to the county hospital, the exhibition was stopped. Unlike the editor, others fancied the new form of entertainment. In the following September, Cheyenne's first Frontier Day celebration was held, with Warren Richardson as chairman of the first committee. Well supported by the Union Pacific Railroad and Fort

Russell personnel and enthusiastically advertised by editor E. A. Slack in the *Sun-Leader*, Frontier Day was a success from the first.

Dancing lost none of its popularity in the depressed nineties. Johnson County pioneer Charles S. Washbaugh recalled in 1959 the country dances of his youth.[22] He attended his first dance, wearing his first pair of long pants, at the age of eight. The men wore Levi's, the women long dresses. People came in buckboards, spring wagons, lumber wagons, or on horseback. Married couples brought their children, who began dancing at the age of twelve or so, while younger children slept in a room set aside for them. Washbaugh remembered only violin music at his first dances. There were square dances, waltzes, two-steps, and schottisches. Favorite tunes were *Turkey in the Straw, Arkansas Traveler, Zip Coon,* and *Buffalo Girls.* Washbaugh recalled that pranksters sometimes switched the front and back wheels on the buggies belonging to young swains, causing the rigs to tip toward the back instead of slightly forward. At other times, gates were wired shut, to the vast annoyance of the first guests to leave.

In the 1963 volume *Tales of the Seeds-Ke-Dee,* sponsored by the Sublette County Artists' Guild, Wilda Springman has described sundown-to-sunup dancing in the hall above D. B. Budd's store in Big Piney in the 1890's, with waltzes, quadrilles, polkas, schottisches, and Virginia reels. Oyster suppers preceded the Christmas and New Year's dances, while a box supper was featured at the Valentine's Day dance. The biggest dance of the year in Big Piney was the masquerade affair on St. Patrick's Day.

At a private party in Laramie in 1895 more than forty guests danced until 3 A.M. to the music of a Cheyenne mandolin orchestra. The carpets were covered with canvas. Dances included waltzes, lanciers, newports, schottisches, polkas, yorks, tuckers, and, after midnight refreshments, the german.

Cowboys, who had been sniffed at in the territorial period, were gaining social acceptance in the cities during the nineties. On November 18, 1895, cowboys sponsored a public dance, attended by "several hundred people," at Männerchor Hall in Laramie. The ceiling was decorated with saddles, bridles, ropes, spurs, and "large hats." The program chairman had found appropriate names for the twenty-four dances, such as "start on circle," "cutting out the beef steers," "catch that maverick," "catch your top horse," "cowboys in town," and "cut out your string and go home."

[22] *Buffalo Bulletin,* July 2, 1959.

CHAPTER 11

Into the Twentieth Century

AFTER SEVERAL DREARY, depressed years in the 1890's, the Spanish-American War kindled prosperity and revived frontier exuberance. J. H. Hayford had suggested in 1894 that a foreign war was needed to lift the country out of depression. A few years later, two New York editors, Joseph Pulitzer and William Randolph Hearst, with aid from politicians, whipped up enthusiasm for war with Spain. Remote as Wyoming was, its men fell over one another in eagerness to participate when war came in April, 1898.

There was no draft. Instead, states were assigned quotas of volunteers. To satisfy the original quota request for 231 infantrymen for two years, most of Wyoming's National Guard regiment was mustered into service. The four strongest companies of the seven in the regiment were chosen: C of Buffalo, G of Sheridan, F of Douglas, and H of Evanston. Then part of Company A of Laramie was added to Company F, making 338 men in the battalion.

Commanded by Colonel F. M. Foote of Evanston, the guardsmen assembled at Fort Russell, moved to San Francisco in May, embarked June 27, left ship in the Philippines on August 6, and fought in the Battle of Manila on August 13, the day after the armistice which officially ended the war. News of the armistice did not reach the Philippines until August 16. It was asserted later, not without challenge, that the first United States flag raised in Manila was that of the Wyoming battalion.

A second Wyoming volunteer unit, the Alger Light Artillery, consisting of 125 Cheyenne men, also went to the Philippines, arriving there December 7, 1898. Both units remained in the Philippines, obliged to fight native insurgents, whom they thought they had come to free. Somewhat disillusioned, they returned to great home-coming demonstrations in Wyoming in August, 1899.

Still a third unit left Wyoming during the war, the Second United States Volunteer Cavalry, commonly known as Torrey's Rough Riders. Colonel Jay L. Torrey was a Big Horn Basin rancher with previous experience in the Missouri National Guard. He was in the forefront of the Rough Rider movement, but lacked the impetuosity and political influence of Theodore Roosevelt, whose Rough Riders won all the glory. Torrey recruited 842 cavalrymen, of whom 591 were from Wyoming, and trained them at Fort Russell. Not anticipating how short the war would be (115 days), Torrey spent weeks searching the region for horses that could meet his high standards, when the only hope for glory lay in getting to Florida quickly, with or without horses. More than eighty thousand horses were assessed in Wyoming that year, but Torrey found it hard to buy a few hundred good horses at prices he wanted to pay.

Finally, on June 22, the Rough Riders entrained for Camp Cuba Libre, Jacksonville, Florida, only to be met by misfortune in Mississippi. At Tupelo on June 26 the second section of the troop train ran into the first section and five Wyoming troopers died. Among the fourteen injured was Colonel Torrey, whose feet were badly bruised. Further delays followed before the regiment settled down in camp at

Jacksonville for the duration. The Florida heat and failure to reach Cuba seared the morale of Torrey's Rough Riders before they were mustered out of service in October, 1898.

Wyoming's casualties in the Spanish-American War totaled sixteen: the five Rough Riders who died at Tupelo, ten infantrymen of the National Guard battalion, and one artilleryman. Apparently no one died in battle. The total United States casualties in the war included only 289 killed or mortally wounded in battle, plus about thirteen times that many who died of disease. Rather surprisingly, not one Wyoming man served in the navy during the Spanish-American War.

The 1899 legislature appropriated $1,500 toward the erection of a monument on the capitol grounds in memory of the Wyoming war dead. The same legislature passed a resolution congratulating President McKinley "for the masterly and praiseworthy administration of the affairs of the National Government during the eventful and critical year just past."

During the war, Wyoming women engaged in several home-front projects. Mrs. Harry B. Henderson of Cheyenne was credited with originating the idea of supplying each soldier with a pocket case containing pins, needles, buttons, and thread. Women in Cheyenne, Laramie, Saratoga, Rawlins, Rock Springs, Green River, and Evanston prepared many such cases. Meanwhile, Clara Barton, founder of the American Red Cross, had urged the preparation of flannel abdominal protectors for soldiers going to tropical countries. These accessories were said to be an excellent precaution against fevers, dysentery, and other diseases. Wyoming women went to work, making the garments double thickness of good-quality all-wool flannel. Unaccustomed to wearing heavy wool underwear in hot weather, Wyoming men failed to appreciate the protectors.

Next to Colonel Torrey, Captain John D. O'Brien, a guardsman from Douglas, received the most publicity. Described as a family man and a veteran of four wars, the Captain became involved with a fair young mestizo woman in Manila. He loved her and left her, reported Manila newspapers as they made much of his alleged desertion. Wyoming friends defended him, insisting that he was a gallant soldier in spite of his advanced years.

Retiring Governor William A. Richards estimated the state's manpower contribution to the war at four and one-half times "our proper quota." The 1,054 volunteers certainly did constitute a large contingent for a sparsely populated state of fewer than 90,000 people. Still enthusiastic about it all, the 1901 legislature appropriated $750 for the purchase of bronze medals for the volunteers who had served with honor in the Philippines.

The optimism which characterized frontiersmen and which had been muted in the depression of the mid-nineties revived vigorously in 1898, in part because of the successful war, which everyone seemed to think had had such a high moral purpose. The Wyoming Legislature resolved "that our people are most reverently thankful that our own government is the very forefront of the world's guardians of Liberty, Peace and Progress." Hopes long deferred could now be realized. C. G. Coutant set the tone in the opening paragraphs of his *History of Wyoming* (Laramie, 1899):

[Wyoming] with beauty as rare and scenery as grand as can be found in the known world; with a wealth of mineral resources which will equal, if not surpass, all other geographical divisions of the United States. . . . The vast storehouses filled with coal, oil, iron, copper, gold, silver and countless other minerals, await capital and enterprise. . . . The inexhaustible quantity of water for irrigation. . . . Wyoming is, so to speak, the backbone as well as the heart of the continent. . . . Where else on this or any other continent has nature bestowed so many rich blessings to be utilized by mankind?

Then, after touching on the glorious achievements of the pioneers, he asked:

But what of the future? Will the brave blood of the pioneer when assisted by the pure air of these high altitudes result in a race of men and women bordering on physical as well as intellectual giants? All we can answer is that the foundation has been laid for such a result. Time alone will answer such a question. . . .

And Casper pioneer B. B. Brooks told the Natrona County Pioneer Association in November, 1902:

Look about you, and see what has been accomplished in fourteen years. Then tell me, oh, ye prophets, what will it be like, when the first half of this new century is history? What sort of people will then inhabit this oasis in the Great American Desert? I will tell you. Women so surpassing fair that all the world pays homage. Men of vigorous strength, with an unheard of power for effective action, capable of solving the deepest riddles of the ages. Giants, physically, intellectually and morally. Made so by their natural environment. Made so by an omnipotent, omniscient, omnipresent force. . . . Made so by the spirit of these rugged mountains, by the voiceless influence of these matchless plains, by the intoxicating ozone of this high, dry, perfect atmosphere. . . .[1]

[1] A. J. Mokler, *History of Natrona County, Wyoming, 1888–1922* (Chicago: R. R. Donnelly & Sons, 1923), pp. 60–61.

For ten years governors' messages were consistently optimistic. B. B. Brooks, elected governor in 1904, proclaimed in 1905 that "the present wholesome prosperity stands without parallel in our history."

Joining the work force were thousands of immigrants from southern Europe and Japan. Many were coal miners. Before 1900, Wyoming's foreign-born had come mainly from the British Isles, Scandinavia, Germany, and China. Census takers in 1910 found the birthplaces of Wyoming's foreign-born to be as follows: Austria, 3,966; England, 2,985; Germany, 2,638; Sweden, 2,497; Italy, 1,961; Greece, 1,915; Scotland, 1,812; Japan, 1,575; Finland, 1,380; Ireland, 1,359; Denmark, 884; Russia, 763; Norway, 623; Hungary, 437; China, 204. The large total for Austria included people who would be listed after World War I as having come from Austria, Italy, Yugoslavia, and Czechoslovakia.

In October, 1907, a financial panic visited the nation and the world. It was followed by a depression accompanied by considerable unemployment. State newspapers in November quoted Senator Warren: "I am not a prophet, or the son of a prophet . . .; nevertheless, I will in this case prophesy that the financial flurry will soon be over." Within a year the depression was gone, making it one that was much less painful than those following the panics of 1873 and 1893. The economic setback in 1907 and 1908 was less severe in Wyoming than in the industrial East. Not one Wyoming bank failed. The Union Pacific reduced hours for shopmen, laid off some operating workers, and in January and February, 1908, furloughed 750 miners in Hanna and Rock Springs. As usual in depressions, there was heavy migration of tramps, via the Union Pacific, from east to west and then from west to east. Drought hurt the farmers and ranchers in 1909 and 1910 and there were other indications of economic weakness, but on the whole the state passed through the first decade of the twentieth century quite prosperously.

POLITICS

The Republican party benefited from the enthusiasm for the Spanish-American War and from returning prosperity. The tremendous national popularity of the McKinley Administration resulted in an unprecedented Republican surge in Wyoming which in 1898 carried the Warren political machine to complete control of the legislature, state executive positions, and seats in the United States Senate and House of Representatives. The Wyoming Senate consisted of thirteen Republicans and six Democrats, while the House was Republican by a margin of thirty-five to three. DeForest Richards, Douglas banker, became governor; Fenimore Chatterton, secretary of state; LeRoy Grant, auditor; George E. Abbott, treasurer; Thomas T. Tynan, superintendent of public instruction.

The 1898 campaign was enlivened by the oratory of Constantine P. Arnold, father of Thurman Arnold, who was to gain fame forty years later. The *Laramie Boomerang* described Arnold, the Democratic candidate for Congress, as "irridescent in oratory and invincible in argument." He spoke regularly, for an hour and a half at a time, mainly on the need for free and unlimited coinage of silver. He agreed with the Republicans on the need for tariffs on wool and hides "to protect our Wyoming ranchmen." Arnold's opponent, Frank W. Mondell, pointed to better beef, mutton, and wool prices and increased coal output. He declined to debate Arnold, yet won the election by a vote of 10,762 to 8,466. Free coinage of silver had lost some of its appeal.

Democrats were scarce indeed in the legislatures during the next decade. They had only nine of the fifty-seven seats in the two houses in 1899 and could do no better until 1909.

In his autobiography, Frank W. Mondell described the campaign dances of the period: "I enjoyed these campaign dances, though one had to be careful not to confine his attention to the younger and better dancers." Alfred J. Mokler, Casper editor, helped Mondell and other Republican candidates campaign in Bates Hole in 1898. He recalled traveling with the candidates in a Concord coach drawn by six horses. They took along some two-gallon jugs. Mokler explained: "During the campaign in those days there were always a great many 'doubtful voters,' and it sometimes required several quarts of liquor and an unlimited number of cigars to convince them. . . . [The candidates] had to make the contributions or be termed as pikers, and a piker in those days could not get very far in any game." Speeches in the Freeland schoolhouse were followed by food at 11:30 P.M. and dancing until morning to music from a fiddle and a mouth harp. Square dances were relieved by a few polkas, schottisches, and waltzes.

DeForest Richards and Fenimore Chatterton campaigned together in the fall of 1898. They traveled fifteen hundred miles by buckboard, going through South Pass to Lander, through the Big Horn Basin, and across the Big Horn Mountains. In his memoirs, Chatterton recalled concluding all of forty-five rallies with dancing. "This was quite a task. . . . Fortunately, some of the ladies did not dance, so I could sit out those dances in animated conversation." At Buffalo, where the people still blamed the Republicans for the Johnson County Invasion, only one person, the Republican county chairman, appeared at the rally.

Rollin Lynde Hartt, in the February, 1900, issue of *Atlantic Monthly*, asserted that the Mormons held the balance of political power in Wyoming. Examination of voting patterns in the years 1898–1908 provides no support for the statement. The Republican victories were overwhelming in these years, and the Mormon counties regularly gave Republican candidates about the same majorities as other counties did. Had all the Mormons voted Democratic, the Republicans still would have won most contests.

A POTENT OLD GUARD TRIO

Dominating the political scene in Wyoming at the turn of the century were three mustachioed Republicans who made up the congressional delegation: Francis E. Warren, Clarence Don Clark, and Frank W. Mondell. Warren and Clark had been elected to the Senate by the 1895 legislature. Warren was to remain in the Senate until his death in 1929, Clark until 1917. Mondell was elected to Congress in 1894, was defeated in 1896, and then in 1898 began a series of twelve consecutive victories in congressional races. These men were able, energetic, and conservative and presented a united front on major issues for many years. Rarely has any state been able to keep its congressional delegation intact for such a long time.

Warren was the undisputed leader. He was the junior senator because in 1895 he took the long term, leaving the short term for Clark. Since Clark was considered to be completing the term which began in 1893 and was sworn in first, he was senior to Warren. This mattered in Washington, but not in Wyoming, where it was customary to speak of the Republican political machine as the "Warren Machine."

After long and close acquaintance with Warren, Cheyenne publisher W. C. Deming listed the Senator's outstanding quality as business acumen. Starting with nothing, Warren had become the richest man in the state, worth millions—five, according to the *World Almanac* in 1909. He had recovered from his 1894 bankruptcy without default. Second, said Deming, Warren was the best political organizer he had ever known. And third, his "crowning characteristic" was loyalty, "as he stuck to his friends through thick and thin, and through good and evil report." Deming said further that Warren "declined to acknowledge that a man, even of opposite politics, was his enemy." This should not be taken to mean that Warren did favors for political enemies—unless he could gain something thereby. Fenimore Chatterton, who had led four other Republican rebels against Warren in the 1893 legislature and had helped keep him out of the Senate for the next two years, wrote in his memoirs that "because I had been the leader for the defeat of the 'machine,' for many years thereafter many stones were placed in my pathway."

In 1905 and 1906, Warren was accused of carrying two men on the Claims Committee payroll while they were residing in Cheyenne and doing private work for him; carrying his son Fred on the government payroll as a folder in the Senate folding room while Fred was attending Harvard; improperly leasing his buildings in Cheyenne to the government; using his influence as chairman of the Military Affairs Committee to secure a contract for his electric-light company to furnish electricity to Fort Russell; and violating the law against enclosing the public domain. Despite denials, at least some of the charges appear to have been true, although it does not follow that Warren was guilty of behavior remarkably different from that of many of his contemporaries given similar opportunities. Wrote Senator Robert LaFollette about Warren a few years later: "He is the boss of Wyoming, with a powerfully entrenched political machine of the 'pork barrel' and 'patronage' type. He is one of the high moguls of the Old Guard." And the *Cheyenne Leader* (Democratic) concluded that "as a man, both in his private life and in his public acts he is not one whom conscientious parents can consistently commend as a pattern for their sons."

As chairman of the Senate Military Affairs Committee, Warren favored a large standing army, with as many men as possible stationed in Wyoming. Thus Fort D. A. Russell at Cheyenne became a full regimental post, Fort Mackenzie at Sheridan was well supported, and troops were kept at Fort Washakie until 1909.

Warren was elected president of the American Protective Tariff League in 1897 and president of the National Wool Growers Association in 1901. Thus other senators had no doubts about how he stood on the wool tariff and protective tariffs in general. Some senators resented that Warren himself was the greatest single beneficiary of his successful efforts to maintain a high tariff on wool.

In earlier years, Warren had run cattle as well as sheep, and he kept his friends among the cattlemen. No one could say that he worked harder in Washington for the sheepmen than he did for the cattlemen. As far back as 1891 he had advocated leasing the public domain. After

1900, when most of the cattlemen came to favor leasing, Warren found himself arrayed with them against the wool growers, whose national president he was! Warren's own sheep business was so organized that leasing would be beneficial to him, while most wool growers, especially the small transients, would suffer under leasing. Yet a good case can be made for the view that leasing was the statesman-like solution, best for the general welfare.

As a member of the Senate Committee on Public Buildings and Grounds, 1902–1912, Warren obtained more than one million dollars in appropriations for public buildings and sites in Wyoming: buildings in Cheyenne, Laramie, Casper, Douglas, Sheridan, Evanston, Lander, Rawlins, and Rock Springs; sites in Basin, Cody, Green River, and Buffalo.

After he had overcome his early skepticism about Theodore Roosevelt, Warren was a frequent guest at the White House. In 1903 he proposed a 56-mile horseback ride for the President from Laramie to Cheyenne. The ride took place on May 30. Since he loved to excel as an outdoorsman, the President was pleased to have Warren, who now weighed more than two hundred pounds, fail to ride the full fifty-six miles. During his Wyoming visit, the President, according to Chatterton, jumped his horse over some of Warren's illegal fences without knowing that they were illegal, and was a guest at one of Warren's ranches.

Clarence Don Clark, handsome and eloquent Evanston lawyer, worked well with Warren. Coming from the western end of the state, he was acceptable to many who earlier had objected to having two senators from Cheyenne. He generally supported Warren in public-domain, reclamation and tariff legislation, differing with him only on leasing of the public domain. Since he had been a Union Pacific attorney and was brother of D. O. Clark, vice-president of the Union Pacific Coal Company, he was sometimes called a tool of the Union Pacific. He guarded the ramparts against coal imports as assiduously as Warren blocked wool imports. As chairman of the Senate Judiciary Committee and with help from Warren, Clark was able to get their intimate friend the ultraconservative Willis Van Devanter appointed to the United States Supreme Court in 1910. Van Devanter previously had been Assistant Attorney General of the United States (1897–1903) and federal circuit judge (1903–1910).

Clark lacked the Warren color, introduced few bills, and rarely had anything to say on the floor of the Senate, yet he was a topnotch errand boy for his constituents. By 1911 he ranked sixth in Senate seniority and could get things done.

The third member of the puissant Old Guard trio, Frank W. Mondell, had first come to Wyoming in 1887 as an employee of the Kilpatrick brothers, who were involved in the construction of the Burlington Railroad and the development of coal mines in northeastern Wyoming. After serving as Newcastle's first mayor, Mondell became the youngest member of the state senate in 1890 and then moved on to Congress. Aggressive and outspoken, he was a harsh critic of the Forest Service. He scored the inclusion of land without trees in the national forests and objected to federal control of game. Like Warren and Clark, he was a high protectionist and was especially interested in Wyoming products, such as coal, wool, hides, and sugar. In land legislation, he fought vigorously for retention of the Homestead Act, the Desert Land Act, and the commutation clause. He had tried dry farming for a few years near Newcastle and was identified more with the small settlers than was Warren. Although married to the daughter of Dr. William Harris, on whose TA Ranch the Johnson County Invaders were besieged, he seems to have thought that the cattlemen would eventually give way before the farmers. On occasion, like Clark, he supported the settlers and wool growers against Warren's long-established position in favor of leasing the public domain to stockmen.

Mondell was more uncompromising than Warren on public-domain issues. Warren and Roosevelt worked together on these, each influencing the other. In general, however, there was little perceptible difference among Warren, Clark, and Mondell with respect to their ultraconservative inclinations. All three were more at home with the principles of McKinley and Taft than with those of Roosevelt, although they were more protectionist than Taft, who wanted cheap raw materials for manufacturers. They chose to stand shoulder to shoulder with Taft against Roosevelt in 1912.

JOSEPH M. CAREY REVIVES THE DEMOCRATS

After experiencing many lean years, the Democrats began to feel stirrings of hope once again as 1910 approached. Mondell attributed the long supremacy of the Republican party to good organization, capable leadership, and honest and able administration of state affairs. On the whole, his explanation is valid, yet demands for change in Wyoming became louder in the later years of Governor B. B. Brooks, coinciding with national criticism of the Taft Administration. Progressive reform talk was on many lips.

Except for a brief recession in 1907–1908 following the financial panic of October, 1907, good times continued in the nation. But not everyone was happy. Many people began to feel that they were not getting their share of the progress and prosperity they had heard so much about from standpat Republican politicians. In 1907 they lost confidence in the nation's business and financial leaders, who only recently had asserted that financial panics could not happen in twentieth-century America. Muckraking magazines and books stirred up further discontent with the *status quo*. In Wyoming there were special complaints against the entrenched Republicans. Some of their much advertised state-sponsored reclamation projects had come a cropper, and dry farmers attracted by state promotion had failed.

Not all Republicans loved the Warren Machine. Rejected office seekers grumbled. Most useful to the Democrats proved to be Joseph M. Carey, lifelong Republican and a conspicuously able man. His leadership talents had been unable to find any expression in the Republican party after he was shoved aside in 1895 when seeking re-election to the United States Senate. Thereafter the existence of a Warren-Carey feud became known to all. Carey nevertheless announced in May, 1910, that he was a Republican candidate for governor. In a letter to the people, he explained that he believed, "as a great majority of the Republican party do," that candidates should be chosen by the voters. Carey had many friends in the Republican party, and was a sure winner if he could only get the nomination from the party convention. He found during the summer, however, that the machine would not accept him unless he would submit to party discipline. Recognizing that nomination by the machine was impossible unless he knuckled under, on September 10, five days before the Republican convention, Carey announced his candidacy as an independent Republican. At the same time, he criticized Republican management of state and nation and identified himself with the "insurgents," the Progressive Republicans who had become disenchanted with Taft and his standpat supporters. Predictably, the Republican convention, meeting in Rawlins on September 15, passed over Carey and nominated W. E. Mullen, a Sheridan lawyer, who was the state's attorney general.

In their convention at Sheridan the Democrats looked back over the many lean years and concluded that although their party strength was growing, they had no probable winner to advance for the governorship. So they conferred with Carey, who was in Sheridan ready to negotiate. Carey agreed to accept the Democratic nomination after a mutually satisfactory platform had been worked out. The Johnson County delegation walked out, and the delegates who remained were not wildly enthusiastic over their choice. The platform as approved by the convention included endorsement of a direct-primary law; the initiative and referendum and recall; the Australian headless ballot; the eight-hour day for women and children under eighteen in industry; good roads throughout the state; conservation of natural resources, with the state rather than the national government in charge; enactment of a law to eliminate the influence of lobbyists; and termination of the leasing system in the state penitentiary.

During the campaign, Democrats began calling Carey the "Grand Old Man" as they reviewed his past services for the information of newcomers: his work as delegate to Congress, as "father of statehood," as author of the Carey Act. Carey's known sympathy for protective tariffs was made palatable to free-trade Democrats by editorial explanations that the tariff was not an issue in the gubernatorial race.

In campaign speeches Carey expressed disdain for machine politics and bosses. He vehemently condemned the state contract under which Otto Gramm of Laramie received fifty-seven cents per day for feeding the state-penitentiary prisoners and received all the proceeds from the penitentiary's broom factory. He urged outdoor employment of prisoners, with the proceeds going to the state.

Occasionally during the campaign, Carey was called a tax dodger. Such charges were usually blunted by evidence that Warren and Governor Brooks enjoyed even lower property-tax assessments.

In the election on November 8, Carey overwhelmed Mullen by a vote of 21,086 to 15,235. Socialist W. W. Paterson polled 1,605. Carey carried with him to victory Democratic candidates Frank L. Houx (secretary of state) and Rose A. Bird (superintendent of public instruction). Houx's plurality was only 37, Miss Bird's 1,343. Frank W. Mondell, who was so sick that he could not campaign, retained his seat in Congress, defeating the Democratic contender, William B. Ross, 20,312 to 14,659. The returns constituted a great personal triumph for Carey. For the Democrats, the triumph was less exciting, although they had won state offices for the first time since 1892. In the legislature, the Republicans won control of both houses, 19 to 8 and 29 to 27.

THE ADMINISTRATION OF JOSEPH M. CAREY, 1911–1915

Joseph M. Carey proved to be one of the most outstanding governors in all of Wyoming history. He understood Wyoming problems, knew what he wanted to do about them, and was persuasive enough to sell some of his ideas to the legislature. Carey had been known as a conservative ever since he first came to Wyoming in 1869, so few people expected his temporary association with the Democrats or his identification as a Progressive Republican to bring much of a leftward deviation. At the outset Carey had to tread carefully, since the Democrats, under whose auspices he had been elected, were in a minority in both houses. However, he had a few "insurgent" friends among the majority Republicans, and regular Republicans found some of his recommendations palatable.

Governor Carey's opening message to the 1911 legislature is a remarkably comprehensive document, full of recommendations on many subjects. By way of introduction, Carey told the legislature that he was not striving to build up a party machine but only to build up the state. He asked bipartisan support in developing the resources of the state and improving the state's institutions.

In keeping with the platform on which he had campaigned, Carey asked for the Australian headless ballot, which had been adopted by the 1890–1891 legislature but had been substantially modified in 1897. He obtained certain changes, but could not get party labels removed from column heads.

Carey asked for a direct-primary law such as was in effect in many other states: "Under the present system but few of the voters of a party have anything to do with the nominations. They are fixed often by one man, at best by a very few men of the party, in advance of the assembling of the convention." The legislature followed his recommendation and adopted the direct primary.

The Governor urged adoption of a corrupt-practices act which would compel publication of election expenses and would limit campaign expenditures. He obtained a law limiting expenses by or on behalf of any candidate, including United States senators, to 20 per cent of one year's salary for the office, except for travel and a few other minor items.

Carey recommended adoption, by constitutional amendment, of the initiative, referendum, and recall devices, which were popular among Progressives, especially in the West, at that time. The legislature submitted to the people an initiative-and-referendum amendment, which the voters in the 1912 general election favored 20,579 to 3,446, but since the total vote in the election was 42,296 and the amendment had to have a majority of the electors, it failed of passage by a narrow margin. The legislature did not act on the Governor's recommendation of the recall, under which elected officials could be unseated by popular vote before the end of their terms.

Governor Carey recommended enabling legislation permitting cities to adopt the commission plan of government, which, he said, had been very successful wherever tried. This plan was made permissive for cities with more than seven thousand residents.

Carey pointed out that since another decennial census had been taken, reapportionment was imperative. The legislature, using population as the basis in both houses, distributed twenty-seven Senate seats and fifty-seven House seats among the fourteen counties.

There had been considerable talk about the need for new counties. Carey stated that new counties should be established if population and taxable wealth justified their creation, keeping in mind that the old counties must not be impoverished. Seven new counties were added by the 1911 legislature: Campbell, Goshen, Hot Springs, Lincoln, Niobrara, Platte, and Washakie. The new counties brought the total to twenty-one, leaving the last two of the state's twenty-three, Sublette and Teton, to be added in 1921.

Unlike his predecessors, DeForest Richards and B. B. Brooks, Carey said nothing about how prosperous the state was. Drought in 1909 and 1910 made rural people feel pretty poor. Paradoxically, they were willing to undertake new commitments by increasing the number of counties by 50 per cent, but otherwise, with Carey's hearty approval, they clamped a tight lid on taxes. Property taxes supplied most of the revenue for the state, as well as for counties and school districts. The total taxes levied for all purposes, state, county, and schools, for the year 1900 had been only $853,563.33, or $11.35 per capita, said Carey. In 1910 the total had increased to $2,090,318.03, or $15.55 per capita.

Carey advocated registration of lobbyists at the capitol, but no action was taken on this proposal. He called for a law to prevent members of the legislature from competing for contract awards made possible by laws and appropriations they had helped to pass: "I very much regret that it has been a practice, fortunately not in many cases." The legislature passed no such law.

Carey had long been a booster for agricultural development. To help the farmers help themselves, he proposed a corporation law enabling them to organize cooperatives for marketing and other purposes. No legislation of this type resulted.

The Governor believed in promoting immigration, yet conceded that the department of immigration created in 1907 had failed. He called for greater effort, to be based in part on help from private corporations and individuals. The legislature complied by setting up a five-man board which would choose a commissioner of immigration and would solicit money and publicity materials from railroads and other corporations and individuals. The state appropriated forty thousand dollars toward the cost of the stepped-up program.

The Wyoming Central Irrigation Company had done virtually nothing during the four years it had been responsible for reclamation on the Riverton project. Carey now suggested the passage of a law authorizing the issue of state bonds not to exceed two million dollars, the proceeds from which were to go into an "Irrigation Trust Fund" for use by the state in developing the Riverton project. The legislature, however, chose not to take such an active part in reclamation.

Major issues in the campaign had been conditions at the state penitentiary at Rawlins and the contract with Otto Gramm and his associates under which he fed the prisoners and worked them for private profit. The contract system had been in existence throughout the statehood period. Carey's proposals for prison reform were instituted by the legislature. An act was adopted setting up the office of warden and establishing a state commission on prison labor. Another act provided for the establishment of the Wyoming Industrial Institute, for young prisoners, which by vote of the people in 1912 was located in Worland.

The 1909 legislature had established a state general hospital at Casper in addition to the state's general hospitals already in existence at Rock Springs and Sheridan. Carey proposed that some way be found to rid the state of the "incubus" of state-supported general hospitals. With irony he suggested that either the state should get rid of the general hospitals or it "should proceed as rapidly as possible to give every county in the State . . . a hospital, and establish an independent hospital government for their control." Incubus or not, the three general hospitals retained their state support.

The insane, said Carey, "are more deserving of sympathy than any other class." To improve conditions at the state hospital for the insane at Evanston, he urged the employment of a full-time director. The legislature failed to act on this proposal.

Governor Carey asked the 1911 legislature for a remarkably long list of reforms. He did not get them all by any means, and yet at the end of the session, some of the state's editors correctly observed that the eleventh legislature had passed more reform laws than any previous legislature in the state's history.

The legislature's failure to give Carey everything he wanted was matched by the Governor's vetoes of 15 of 110 bills. He vetoed a bill appropriating $20,000 for a nurses' home at Sheridan. He vetoed a bill appropriating $25,000 to reimburse Big Horn County for the cost of prosecuting some cattlemen who were found guilty of murdering three sheepmen near Tensleep in 1909. Big Horn County was wealthy, he said, and the act would establish a precedent which "would plague the state at every session of the legislature." He also vetoed a $60,000 wolf bounty bill with the explanation that frauds had been committed, the state had been imposed upon, and state bounties had not reduced materially the number of predators. All told, he lopped off $270,000 from various appropriations bills.

THE ELECTION OF 1912

Reminiscent of 1892 was the campaign of 1912. It was quite as bitter. Also it included a significant third party—this time the Progressive in place of the Populist. There were really five parties in the field in 1912: Democratic, Republican, Progressive, Socialist, and Prohibition. The last two, however, were insignificant.

"Senator Warren . . . comes up for reelection soon. . . . Why doesn't Wyoming send Governor Carey to the Senate? He is a good insurgent." Thus wrote Mark Sullivan in *Collier's Weekly*, November 11, 1911. Carey, although he was quite ready to help oust his old foe, had never been an avowed candidate for the Senate since his defeat in 1895, did not express any interests in the position in 1912, and knew very well that Warren's regular Republicans controlled the state machine. Carey, however, did assume leadership of the insurgents in Wyoming. In January, 1912, a widely disseminated letter announced the intentions of an executive committee consisting of Robert D. Carey (the Governor's son), Fred H. Blume of Sheridan, and Boise C. Hart of Basin to form Progressive associations in each county. A state meeting, it was explained, would be held at a later date to perfect a permanent organization.

In February, at Theodore Roosevelt's instigation, Governor Carey
and six other governors wrote to the former President urging him to
run against incumbent William Howard Taft. When the national
Republican convention nominated Taft in June, the Roosevelt Republicans bolted to organize a Progressive party. In preparation for the
August national convention of the Progressive party, Carey called his
long-planned state meeting in late July. Only about twenty men
gathered in the offices of J. M. Carey & Brother for the state convention. Reported as present at the Bull Moose meeting were, besides the
Governor, the Governor's two sons, Robert D. and Charles, Sheridan
Downey of Laramie, C. Watt Brandon of Kemmerer, Roy Schenck,
state immigration commissioner, and several other state officeholders.
Obviously, the Warren Machine was still intact. Roosevelt's appeal in
Wyoming would have to be to the rank-and-file voters, since the
politicians were not deserting their familiar standards.

The Taft regulars—Warren, Clark, and Mondell—used their imposing seniority to move through Congress their bills for six new
federal buildings in the state. "Raids upon the treasury," cried Democratic editors.

"The campaign was not a pleasant one for regular Republicans anywhere," recalled Frank Mondell in *My Story.* "It was certainly not a
happy one in Wyoming where our organization, strenuously and faithfully supporting Taft, was tremendously embarrassed by the candidacy
of Roosevelt." Beyond question, Roosevelt's popular appeal in Wyoming put the Warren Machine to a real test.

Muckraking magazines dusted off the arguments they had used
against Warren in 1906. "Old residents . . . will give no attention to this
burned powder—stuff that had no effect six years ago and which will
have no effect now," asserted the *Laramie Republican.*

In the August primary the Republicans expressed their preference
for Warren, the Democrats for John B. Kendrick. The Progressives
advanced no senatorial candidate. Republicans were pleased to see
Warren poll 12,092 votes in the primary to 7,216 for Kendrick,
although, of course, everything depended on which party could win
control of the legislature. To improve his chances, Kendrick, in
January, 1912, had acquired control of the *Sheridan Enterprise* and the
Cheyenne Leader. He was also supported in the campaign by the *Rawlins
Journal,* the *Laramie Boomerang,* and the *Encampment Herald.*

In September, Republican newspapers published Warren's replies to
a series of questions posed by C. P. Connolly in the *Collier's Weekly* of

August 31, 1912. According to Leslie A. Miller's memoirs, Miller and Governor Carey helped Connolly to gather material for his article.

To Warren's influence as chairman of the Senate Military Affairs Committee had been attributed the jumping of his son-in-law, Captain John J. Pershing, to brigadier general over the heads of 862 officers who outranked him. Now, in September, 1912, Warren declared that he did not know Captain Pershing existed at the time of the extraordinary promotion. Only a lapse in memory can account for this statement, since Pershing had married the Senator's daughter, Helen, on January 26, 1905, some twenty months before he made his famous leap to the rank of brigadier general on September 20, 1906.

To the oft-repeated charges that he had perjured himself to obtain title to a pre-emption claim, Warren quoted an 1889 statement by Special Agent E. N. Bonfils that he probably had resided on the land for the minimum period required. To a question about his having relatives on the Senate payroll, Warren answered that this was not illegal and that he believed in hiring the best people he could get. To the charges concerning illegal fencing, he referred to a General Land Office letter stating that reports showed that in August, 1907, the month in which the final investigation had been completed, he had no unlawful enclosure.

The Senator answered allegations that he had benefited through the leasing of state lands, selected by state officials with his needs in mind, by claiming that the Warren Livestock Company had a smaller percentage of state lands leased in proportion to the number of acres owned than almost any other company renting lands from the state. This is plausible, since the state's published list of leases in effect in 1910 shows the Warren Livestock Company, Francis E. Warren, and Fred Warren together holding only 2,533 acres of state leases in Laramie County (much less than in earlier days).

Warren did not deny charges that he had drawn a double salary as governor and United States senator but, rather, evaded the question by saying that "I never presented a bill or request for payment" as governor.

Since no Progressive candidate was advanced for the Senate, John B. Kendrick, the Democratic candidate, was the beneficiary of all anti-Warren activity by Carey and his Progressive organization. Kendrick was shelled rather lightly by Republican editors. Since his public record was small (state senator once, in 1911), there wasn't much ammunition at hand. Someone found evidence that in 1908, Kendrick, to get Montana timber, had given his residence as Montana. He explained that from 1899 to 1909 he had resided most of the year in Montana "and yet during all this time I continued to claim my political residence in . . . Wyoming." Charges were also advanced that Kendrick had government land under fence and that he had used employees and dummies to homestead land for him. It may be supposed that he was like other big cattlemen of his day with respect to these practices. He answered the fencing charges by stating that he acquired some illegal fences when he took over the Converse Cattle Company's property but removed them after a warning from a special agent. He parried attacks upon the national Democratic low-tariff position by saying that he would not vote for any law injurious to Wyoming interests.

The general-election results in 1912 were about as expected. The state's electoral votes went to Democratic presidential candidate Woodrow Wilson, whose Wyoming electors received more than 15,000 votes, while Taft's electors received 14,000 and Roosevelt's, 9,000. As had been predicted from the beginning, the Republican split assured victory for Woodrow Wilson. Taft did better in Wyoming than he did nationally, where he ran third.

In Wyoming, however, the Republican split did not bring other Democratic victories. Frank Mondell was returned to Congress by a large plurality. The Republicans won control of both houses of the legislature, although their control of the House of Representatives hung in the balance for a time, and Kendrick was thought to have a chance to unseat Warren.

THE LEGISLATURE OF 1913

The leading Republican political reporter in Wyoming in 1913 was John Charles Thompson, Jr., who wrote for William C. Deming's *Wyoming State Tribune* in Cheyenne. Twenty-six years after the event, Thompson, in his "Old Wyoming" column in the *Wyoming State Tribune*, described the 1913 legislative session as "the most disorderly" in Wyoming history. There were, he recalled, "conspiracies, counter-conspiracies, contests, cross, double-cross, and super-double-cross, shouting, tumult, riot, criminal charges. For more than a fortnight the state was agog."

The Republican margin in the Senate was substantial, 16 to 11. The Republicans also appeared to have a 30–27 lead in the House. In a number of counties there had been "Independent" candidates for both houses of the legislature, but they won few votes, so only Republican and Democratic candidates were elected. Then, to the consternation of the Republicans, the Democrats, with assistance from Governor Carey, "seduced," as Thompson put it, two of the Republicans of the House, changing the 30–27 Republican control of the House to a 29–28 Democratic margin. Martin Luther Pratt, representative from Park County, apparently agreed to accept Democratic discipline in return for election to the speakership. Pratt was a partner in "Pratt Brothers Big Store" in Powell in private life. In public life he was a neophyte, a freshman in the House who would have had no conceivable claim to the speakership were it not for his balance-of-power position and over-weening ambition. Like Pratt, E. H. Manson, a weighman at the Superior mines in Sweetwater County, was elected as a Republican but stood ready to vote with the Democrats. Both Pratt and Manson pro-fessed in Cheyenne to be Progressives, although there can be no doubt that they had run as regular Republicans. Republican papers insisted that they had been persuaded by the Careys to turn their coats after the election.

With the help of Pratt and Manson, the Democrats organized the House and instituted contests against three Republican representatives from Lincoln County. Democrats claimed that executives of the Dia-mond Coal and Coke Company had herded to the polls as Republican voters many foreign-born employees who were not citizens, did not fulfill the residence requirements, and could not read the constitution in English.

What did the Democrats and the Careys have in mind? Some observers suspected that there was a plan for the House majority to refuse to ballot for United States senator, in which case there would be a repetition of the situation in 1893, when the state had only one senator for two years. Other observers thought there was a plot to elect Democrat John B. Kendrick or a dark-horse Progressive. Robert D. Carey was mentioned, and Martin Luther Pratt seems to have aspired to the position as well.

Learning that the Democrats were in control of the House, Senator Warren hurried home from Washington to take command of his troops. Whatever plans the Democrats and Progressives may have entertained went up in smoke when, after ten days, Speaker Pratt reneged on his promises to the Democrats. Whether, as Democrats later insisted, he had accepted a large Republican bribe in a Denver hotel room is beyond proof, but he certainly deserted his new-found Democratic friends and took himself and his speakership into the Republican fold.

In his memoirs, T. Blake Kennedy explains that "it took a long time to convince Pratt that the Democrats were using him for their own purposes since should they be able to secure a majority in the body by throwing out a number of Republicans he would undoubtedly be unseated and go with them." When challenged, Pratt seized the Democratic speaker pro tem and hurled him from the rostrum, whereupon a battle royal erupted. The globular Union Pacific lobbyist Charlie Irwin rolled down to the governor's office to urge that the National Guard be called out. The riot was soon quelled, however, without summons of the Guard.

Manson did not follow Pratt back into the Republican camp. Ten days after he had aligned himself with the Democrats, Manson was visited by a sheriff from West Virginia who wanted to take him back there to answer for a ten-year-old forgery charge. Governor Carey, however, refused to extradite Manson, whose real name, the West Virginia sheriff insisted, was F. E. Roberts. Carey declined to honor the requisition on several counts, among them being this one: "I will not recognize a requisition that I know was obtained to influence the election of a United States senator."

No matter what might happen to Manson, Pratt's return to the Republican fold assured Republican control of the House, 29 to 28, seating of the three Republicans from Lincoln County, and Warren's re-election.

PROGRESSIVE AT BAY

Governor Joseph M. Carey in his message to the 1913 legislature called for fewer reforms than he had asked of the 1911 legislature. Even so, his 1913 message was far from the usual routine review of state government. In keeping with his posture as a Progressive, Carey asked that the minimum age for boys working in mines be raised from fourteen to sixteen and requested a presidential-preference primary law, the Australian headless ballot, another initiative-and-referendum amendment, the recall, and elimination of certain delays in the courts. The legislature, less tractable than in 1911, did nothing about any of these proposals.

Governor Carey espoused a "Blue Sky Law," such as Kansas had adopted in 1911, to minimize fraudulent promotion schemes. He thought no state had been more cursed than Wyoming by companies selling worthless stocks. Capital shunned the state in consequence of many past frauds, he said. No Blue Sky Law was passed, although Democratic and Republican editors alike had been asking for one.

"The state is on the eve of a great growth," Carey promised. "There never has been a time when Wyoming was so well or so favorably known as the present," he continued. He was proud of the work of the Board of Immigration, for which he urged further support. The Republican legislators were less than enthusiastic about the immigration office. They frowned on Commissioner Roy W. Schenck's Progressive political activity. Some critics asserted that the promotion work was mainly for Governor Carey's Wheatland project. Others said too much was being spent in the East, when the Middle West was a more promising field for promotion. Leslie A. Miller (later governor) worked for Schenck for a while and relates in his memoirs how he discovered that Schenck had rigged the drawing for a free Wyoming irrigated farm so that the woman in charge of the state's Pittsburgh exhibit could win it. Perhaps it was just as well that the legislature appropriated nothing for immigration promotion in that session.

Carey renewed his plea for efforts to exchange poor state lands for better lands still held by the federal government. "In many instances the state has selected as worthless lands as are found within its boundaries, apparently to secure the paltry income of from one and a half to five cents an acre rental per annum, and to suit the convenience of someone." The legislature in this instance went beyond the Governor's proposal and asked for the cession of all vacant and unappropriated lands to the state.

Taxation remained a matter of profound concern to Carey. He asked, as he had in 1911, for a nonpolitical tax commission authorized to study taxation and revenue and endowed with powers "advisory, directory and if necessary, compulsory." He did not get it.

To help enforce laws against gambling, prize fighting, and illegal sale of intoxicants, Carey asked for authority to remove county officers who failed to perform their duties. The legislature passed a law—amending and re-enacting an old law—which authorized Carey to remove delinquent county commissioners after they had been found guilty by a district judge with whom written charges had been filed. This was not what the Governor wanted and needed for compelling local law enforcement.

Ruefully, Carey remarked that if the last legislature could have anticipated the winter of 1911–1912, which was so destructive to the sheep industry, several of the seven new counties might not have been organized. He saw no need for any more counties, and none was added, though several were proposed.

Governor Carey recommended passage of a workmen's-compensation act such as those in operation in Wisconsin and Massachusetts. The old system, under which the employees had to seek compensation through damage suits, was costly and unsatisfactory, said Carey. He reported that only 29 per cent of the damages for injuries reached the employee or his beneficiary. In this case the legislature was persuaded, and submitted a constitutional amendment authorizing workmen's-compensation acts, which the electors approved in 1914.

The Governor asked for and obtained a favorable vote on the proposed amendment to the United States Constitution providing for popular election of United States senators. As his final reform proposal, Carey recommended that some better way be found to amend the Wyoming Constitution. The legislature, however, was satisfied to let the difficult old method stand.

Thus Governor Carey's 1913 message stood second only to his 1911 message in its far-reaching proposals for reform. The legislature left much undone, more indeed than in 1911. For one thing, too much time had been lost in the hubbub over House organization and the Senate election. For another thing, Carey was not on as good terms with the lawmakers in 1913 as he had been two years earlier. He was a Progressive at bay.

Harsh words were exchanged over a joint legislative resolution to send a committee to investigate the state hospital at Rock Springs and other state institutions. Carey vetoed the resolution, stating that he would sign no measure the purpose of which was to reflect upon him or to dwarf his powers. The committee chairman was a Democrat, Edward S. Murray, a Rock Springs doctor who had criticized the management of the hospital. Without actually naming the Senator, Carey left no doubt in anyone's mind as to whom he was talking about when he said in his veto message that a doctor had been detected stealing supplies and destroying state equipment.

The Republicans, it seems, had been using the Rock Springs hospital business as an entering wedge for an investigation of the penitentiary. Carey had been criticized during the campaign for mismanagement of the penitentiary, suggestions being made that conditions had deteriorated since termination of the old contract system. Giving the critics aid and comfort, the prisoners had mutinied in mid-October,

1912, and burned the broom factory, and twenty-seven of them had escaped. One Rawlins citizen was shot to death by an escaping prisoner. Carey suggested that the mutiny had been politically inspired, an assertion which seems as implausible as the contrary one: that reorganization of the penitentiary had caused the riot. At any rate, Carey was dead set against having the hospital and the penitentiary investigated by a committee headed by a known enemy. The *Rock Springs Miner*, a Republican newspaper which had previously opposed Carey, stated that conditions at the Rock Springs hospital had never been better and that the Governor was right on principle—a person bringing charges should not sit as a judge. It was late in the session, and the joint committee did not go to Rawlins and Rock Springs to investigate the state institutions.

After the legislature adjourned, Governor Carey trimmed the appropriations bill by $378,272.31, a vast sum for those days, which represented 21.5 per cent of the total appropriations. His major cuts were $95,000 from the $135,000 set aside for the Wyoming Industrial Institute at Worland, $67,500 for an addition to the state capitol, $57,600 for county agricultural agents, $50,000 for California expositions, and $20,000 for a wing to the Casper hospital.

The Governor had vetoed several measures during the session, and added to the list of vetoes after adjournment until there were sixteen, one more than in 1911. Most important of his vetoes was one killing Shoshone County, which would have been formed from the northeastern part of Fremont County. Shoshoni would have become the county seat, with Riverton and Lander remaining in Fremont County. The new county would have had as its principal tax base forty-seven miles of the Burlington Railroad. In his veto message, Governor Carey read affidavits purporting to show that state leaders of the Republican party had threatened to divide Fremont County if it sent a Democratic delegation to the legislature—which it did. A similar attempt to divide Fremont County had failed in 1911, at which time the name Waconda was suggested for the proposed new county. In 1913 the bill, introduced by Representative Robert Grieve of Natrona County, passed both houses by a party-line vote, with the Republicans for it and the Democrats against it.

Not one of Carey's vetoes was overridden. Said the *Laramie Republican*, quite correctly: "For veto messages Governor Carey easily leads all Wyoming governors." The *Casper Tribune*, after the Governor had concluded his vetoing and pruning, said: "Governor Joe is not as popular as he was two years ago, but . . . he is a scrapper, and although he has been pounded into the ground a dozen times, he always comes up and throws a handful of mud at the fellows who landed on him."

Most severe critic of the 1913 legislature was the *Cheyenne Leader*, whose president was John D. Clark and whose principal owner was John B. Kendrick. "Wyoming has never seen such an imbecile legislature," said the *Leader* after adjournment. "They waged a bitter and senseless warfare against the governor of the state because he has opposed their idol, Francis E. Warren."

Looking back over the administration of J. M. Carey, one sees a frugal, well-informed, capable Progressive who was often unhorsed by the fractious majority Republicans. Nationally in this era, Progressives worked for political, humanitarian, and economic reforms. In comparison with other Progressive leaders, Carey was primarily interested in reforms designed to purify the political system, secondarily in humanitarian reforms, and scarcely at all in reforms calculated to circumscribe big business. Carey's accomplishments were noteworthy. When one considers the political circumstances, one must credit him with no mean achievement.

THE ENCAMPMENT BUBBLE

In Wyoming mining history the turn-of-the-century copper excitement in the Encampment area is comparable to the South Pass gold excitement of thirty years earlier. Mining claims had been located in the Sierra Madre Mountains as early as 1868, and reports of copper discoveries appeared from time to time thereafter. In 1881, George Doane and associates found copper carbonates near Battle Lake and began the development of the Doane-Rambler mine. In 1897, Ed Haggarty located the Rudefeha mine, which he named by adding the first two letters of his own name to the first two letters of each of the names of the three men who had grubstaked him—J. M. Rumsey, Robert Deal, and George Ferris. The Rudefeha had rich copper ore in sufficient quantity to interest a remarkable promoter, Willis George Emerson, who with partner Bernard McCaffrey bought the town-site of Encampment and began selling town lots and mining stock. Emerson brought a gifted newspaperman, Grant Jones, to the area to turn out news releases for national distribution.

The Rudefeha mine, which was becoming known as the Ferris-Haggarty, produced ore promising enough to warrant construction of a copper smelter at Encampment by the Boston and Wyoming Smelter,

Power and Light Company in 1902. An aerial tramway sixteen miles long began carrying the ore from the mine to the smelter in June, 1903. The tramway was regarded as one of the wonders of the West, and indeed it was a remarkable engineering achievement. Three hundred and four towers supported the cables which conveyed the ore in buckets of seven hundred pounds' capacity.

In August, 1902, the North American Copper Company acquired the Ferris-Haggarty mine and the partially constructed smelter and tramway for one million dollars, after which Emerson and Jones undertook to market twenty million dollars' worth of stock in the company and its subsidiaries. The Penn-Wyoming Company took over the North American Copper Company in January, 1905, and proceeded to enlarge the smelter and to build a railroad between Encampment and the main line of the Union Pacific at Walcott.

A series of disasters soon began for the Penn-Wyoming Company. On March 28, 1906, the concentrating mill at the Encampment reduction works was destroyed by fire. In the following year, fire destroyed part of the smelter. Then in 1907 and 1908, the price of copper dropped from twenty cents a pound to thirteen cents, causing the mine and smelter to shut down for good. The Penn-Wyoming Company managed to unload its holdings to the United Smelters Railway and Copper Company in 1909. The latter soon slipped into bankruptcy, followed by litigation which involved the Penn-Wyoming Company as well.

During the years 1899–1908, twenty-three million pounds of copper were produced in Wyoming, and the state ranked among the leading copper producers. The Encampment District, however, proved to be no Anaconda, no Bingham Canyon, for its rich ores were soon exhausted. The Wyoming economy was damaged somewhat by the pricking of the Encampment bubble. Where there had been as many as fifteen hundred men in the Sierra Madre Mountains and close to that many at Encampment, there remained only a few hundred after 1908.

Wyoming people, lacking money to invest, lost little in the Encampment failure. Said the *Cheyenne Leader* in commenting on foreclosure proceedings in federal district court in Cheyenne in 1913: "The facts are that the Penn-Wyoming project was picked up by crooks who exploited the property three different times to draw large sums of money for the sale of stocks from eastern people and even from Europe." On one occasion after the collapse, incredulous stockholders chartered a special train and traveled to Encampment to survey their decaying property. Ultimately, after various receivership sales turned up no prospective operators, junk men were permitted to move in.

Grant Jones and Willis George Emerson, who had performed yeomen's service in blowing up the Encampment bubble, were not on hand to suffer from the collapse. Jones died of heart disease on June 19, 1903. Emerson, who had been a central figure in the incorporation of the North American Copper Company, moved to California in 1904 after being frozen out by eastern financiers.

Before leaving Wyoming, Emerson caused a small flurry of excitement in late 1903 when he announced that he was organizing a syndicate to build a new capital near the center of the state. The 1901 legislature had authorized a vote of the people in November, 1904, to decide on the permanent location of the state's institutions. Emerson's syndicate, it was said, would build a model capital, without cost to the people, at a point midway between Casper, Rawlins, and Lander. The capital was to be named Emerson or, some said, Muskrat. Before the election, Emerson left the state, and his proposed new city was not in the running. Cheyenne received 11,781 votes, Lander 8,667, and Casper 3,610. At the same time, by popular vote, the university was permanently located at Laramie, the penitentiary at Rawlins, and the insane asylum at Evanston.

COAL AND OIL

While copper passed through its boom-and-bust cycle, coal became more and more important in the state's economy. Production more than doubled between 1898 and 1910, rising from 3,260,000 tons to more than 7,000,000 tons. Although most of the production continued to be along the Union Pacific, several coal camps were opened north of Sheridan: Carney and Monarch in 1904, Kooi in 1907, and Acme and Model in 1911. Dietz, the oldest of the Sheridan County coal camps, dated from 1893. Cambria and Gebo were important northern producers in 1910. All told, in 1910 there were 42 producing coal mines with 8,106 employees.

Two disasters marred the otherwise flourishing coal business. On June 30, 1903, an explosion in Union Pacific Coal Company's Mine Number One at Hanna killed 171 miners. Said the *Denver Times*: "Martyrs not to our civilization, but to our ignorance, thoughtlessness and greed!" The *Times* thought that there had been inadequate safety measures. Almost 150 women were widowed, and 600 children lost their fathers. A second disaster, involving two explosions, occurred in the same mine on March 28, 1908, killing 58 men and leaving 33 widows and 103 fatherless children.

Since Inspector David M. Elias of the southern district had been killed in the second of the 1908 explosions, Governor B. B. Brooks ordered Noah Young, inspector of the northern district, to make an investigation. Four months later, Young reported that the first of the 1908 explosions was directly due to the desire of the Union Pacific Coal Company to open up too soon an entry in which a fire was burning and that coal companies had been very lax in obeying laws regulating coal mines. The Wyoming press quoted figures released by T. P. Fahey, district organizer of the United Mine Workers of America, for compensation paid by the Union Pacific Coal Company in the 1908 disasters: eight hundred dollars to each surviving widow; fifty dollars additional for each child under fifteen.

The oil industry was marking time at the turn of the century, awaiting demand for Wyoming products. Prospectors and speculators, looking ahead, filed claims and battled over them. The Placer Mining Law, which applied at the time, required that trenches be dug, shafts sunk, and oil seeps developed for assessment purposes.

In 1900 and 1901 nearly one million acres of federal land in Natrona County was withdrawn from agricultural entry as possible oil land. Pioneer farmers and ranchers had not yet filed on the land because better land for their purposes was available elsewhere. Most of the withdrawn land was restored to agricultural entry in 1903 after more than two-thirds of the taxpayers of the county had petitioned for such restoration.

Many exciting races occurred among rival claim jumpers on New Year's Eve in 1901 and 1902 in the Popo Agie, Uinta, and Salt Creek fields. It had become known that many filings would lapse for failure to do assessment work. The only way for the former owners to retain their claims was to relocate. Horsemen rode all night to drive stakes and to file their claims in the county clerk's office. Fist fights and gunfire enlivened the contests, as stakes were often pulled. An Evanston report was carried in the *Laramie Boomerang*:

Up to midnight last night a person could well imagine themselves in the heart of a hostile country. Fires marking the corners of claims were lighted by thousands, and these, together with the hundreds of locators camped near them, reminded one of a bivouac in war. Colonel Ketchum, at the head of twelve

cowboys, well armed and mounted carried the Aspen country by storm. . . .
From the present outlook it seems that the larger concerns will gobble up nearly
all the valuable land. . . .

For a sum variously reported as $360,000 and $600,000, the refinery
and other properties of the Pennsylvania Oil and Gas Company,
pioneer in the Salt Creek Field, were taken over in 1903 by the "Wyoming Syndicate," which consisted of two Parisians and three Londoners,
who soon indulged in an orgy of stock manipulations in Brussels. The
syndicate promised to build railroads from Casper to Lander and Salt
Creek and to erect a refinery, for which Casper, Lander, and Orin
Junction competed, but neither the railroads nor the refinery materialized. Instead, the old refinery was razed as a fire hazard at the demand
of the disgusted Casper town council.

Placer locations continued apace in Salt Creek and multiplied after
a Dutch company in October, 1908, brought in Salt Creek's first gusher
at a depth of 1,050 feet. Notable newcomer was William M. Fitzhugh,
California engineer, who in 1909 began jumping claims right and left.
He and others who aspired to monopoly were hamstrung by President
Taft's executive order of September, 1909, withdrawing all of the Salt
Creek area from location under the mining laws. The government
thereafter would recognize all well-established rights, but lawyers found
profitable employment for many years, since the area was full of vague
and overlapping claims and claim jumpers were hiring armed men to
prevent assessment or development work by earlier claimants.

Bankruptcy overtook the Wyoming Syndicate by 1910, and its assets
were acquired by a Delaware corporation, the Franco-American
Wyoming Oil Company. In the next two years this company laid a six-
inch pipeline from Salt Creek to Casper and built a small refinery at
the west end of town. More important, also in 1910, Verner Z. Reed
of Colorado Springs, Colorado, and his associates invested Colorado
gold-mining profits in Natrona County. They organized the Midwest
Oil Company, bought a lease on 560 acres of the rare patented land in
Salt Creek, acquired other interests, and laid a six-inch pipeline to a
new refinery which they built at the west end of Casper. They persuaded the Chicago and North Western Railroad to convert its locomotives to oil burners in return for the opportunity to haul gasoline and
kerosene eastward. Marketing arrangements were worked out with the
Standard Oil Company of Indiana. The Midwest Oil Company prospered, took over Franco-American, and changed its own name to
Midwest Refining Company. Standard of Indiana built a cracking

plant in Casper in 1913, buying residue oil from Midwest. The arrival of this major oil company was auspicious for the future of Salt Creek.

United States District Judge John A. Riner ruled in June, 1913, that President Taft's 1909 withdrawal order was void, but in 1915 the United States Supreme Court, in an epochal decision, reversed Riner and upheld the withdrawal order, thus providing a foundation for the government's subsequent policy of retaining oil lands and allowing production under lease.

Until 1915 the Wyoming oil story is largely the story of Salt Creek, and involves the laying of foundations on which a great superstructure would be erected in later years.

RAILROADS

In keeping with the prevailing optimism at the turn of the century, there soon came a great burst of railroad construction. All had been quiet on this front since the completion of the Burlington line across northeastern Wyoming in 1894. In 1900 and 1901 the Union Pacific revamped its main line, making extensive improvements and introducing much double track. The famous old Dale Creek Bridge was abandoned as the line was moved four miles southward. In his autobiography, Governor Leslie A. Miller recalled that between seventeen and eighteen hundred men were employed on Sherman Hill. Virtually all of them were brought in from outside the state, and they left in 1901. According to Miller, the workers were counted twice in the federal census of 1900, once for Cheyenne and again for Laramie. Their temporary presence helps to account for the fact that a comparison of 1900 and 1910 census figures shows Cheyenne losing population and Laramie standing still for the decade.

In western Wyoming in 1901 the Union Pacific pierced Aspen Hill with a 5,900-foot tunnel, which shortened the route ten miles and eliminated several steep grades.

The Chicago, Burlington & Quincy, commonly known as the Burlington, built a short line from Alliance, Nebraska, to Guernsey early in 1900. In April, 1900, the Great Northern and Northern Pacific railroads jointly bought 97 per cent of the Burlington's common stock. In subsequent years, the new owners linked the Burlington lines in Wyoming with their own extensive trackage in the Northwest and added several hundred miles of track in Wyoming. Mormon farmers, who had recently colonized in the Big Horn Basin, prepared the grade for a new line from Toluca, Montana, to Cody in 1901. From Frannie on this line tracks were laid southward in 1906 via Greybull, Basin, and Worland, reaching Kirby in September, 1907.

In December, 1908, the Burlington acquired the Colorado and Southern, whose line in southeastern Wyoming, originally the Cheyenne and Northern, tied in with a line from Denver to Texas and the Gulf of Mexico. Thereafter the Burlington joined its Big Horn Basin line with its lines in southeastern Wyoming. The long connecting link passed through Wind River Canyon and reached Casper in October, 1913, and Orin Junction in October, 1914. The Chicago and North Western, which had terminated at Casper in 1888, built on to Shoshoni, Riverton, and Lander in 1906.

Completing the railroad construction of this period were two short lines in southeastern Wyoming. The Laramie, Hahn's Peak and Pacific was incorporated in Laramie in 1901, with plans for a line from the Union Pacific at Laramie west to Gold Hill in Carbon County and thence southwest to Baggs. The line crept slowly across the Laramie Plains, arriving at Centennial in April, 1907. After pausing there for a while in consequence of the financial panic of that year, the owners abandoned plans to go to Gold Hill and instead built southwest to Colorado's North Park. By 1912 the line had crossed the southern flank of the Medicine Bow Mountains by way of Albany, Fox Park, and Northgate and had terminated at Coalmont, just beyond Walden, Colorado. The line did not prosper and was taken over by the federal court in Cheyenne in 1912 and sold in 1914.

In 1905 the Saratoga and Encampment Railway was incorporated to facilitate development of the Grand Encampment mining country. The line stretched forty-five miles from Walcott on the Union Pacific to Encampment, reaching Saratoga in August, 1907, and Encampment just one year later. By the time the railroad was completed, the Encampment boom had collapsed, so the new line passed into receivership along with the Penn-Wyoming Company.

Beginning at this time was much publicity about the Denver, Laramie and Northwestern. Hoping to build from Denver to Seattle via South Pass, Jackson Hole, and Boise, the line never got out of Colorado. The company was forced to give up coal properties fraudulently acquired near Elk Mountain.

In the years 1900–1914 the state's railway mileage almost doubled, reaching nineteen hundred miles. There would be more paper roads, and even some further construction, but not much. A new era, that of autos and trucks, had begun.

In the early years of the twentieth century, railroads were under attack from many state legislatures on several counts. It appears that Wyoming railroads, protected by effective lobbies, did not suffer much from such attacks. Governor Brooks told the legislature in 1905 that railroad-property valuations had remained practically unchanged for a number of years. Two years later he said that "it is generally believed among our people that railroads do not pay their just proportion of taxes." Citing the figures, he reported that all surrounding states, except possibly South Dakota, placed much higher valuations on comparable railroad property.

Although attempts to increase railroad taxes were bipartisan, the Democrats generally were more critical of the railroads than were the Republicans. The state Democratic platform in 1906 included this plank: "We demand the enactment of a law making it a criminal offence, punishable by imprisonment, to give, offer or accept a free pass or ticket over any transportation line within the state to any state, county or municipal official or members of the judiciary or legislature." The *Cheyenne Leader* (Democratic) said editorially on January 30, 1908: "The Union Pacific has ruled Wyoming ever since it was organized as a territory. It controlled and used the republican machine and has owned every legislature with one possible exception in forty years." The *Leader* was angrier than usual in this instance because of layoffs in Cheyenne following the October, 1907, financial panic.

Upward adjustments were made in railroad assessments as an attempt was made by the tenth legislature (1909) to assess all property at full value. Higher assessments and additions to the state's railway mileage in 1910 pushed the valuation of railroad property up to $48,469,000, about one-fourth of the state's total property valuation.

Part of the animosity toward Wyoming railroads resulted from the appalling number of deaths and injuries to trainmen and from the difficulty of getting any compensation in such cases. These were grievances of long standing. Working on the railroad, particularly the busy Union Pacific, was almost as dangerous as working in a coal mine. There was some improvement after 1901, yet several men were killed every year. Normally, the responsibility was hotly disputed. A Wyoming railroader of this period, Ernest M. Richardson, has written quite plausibly that "fiction writers . . . seem to have completely missed the potentially dramatic possibilities inherent in early day railroading, a vocation infinitely more hazardous than bustin' broncs, or branding mavericks."

The 1913 legislature at last gave the railroad employee some protection that he had previously lacked. A law was adopted which stated that the railroad corporation should be liable for injury or death of employees at work due to the negligence of the corporation or its agents or to defects or insufficiencies in equipment. Contributory negligence should not bar recovery, but should diminish the damages in proportion to the amount of negligence by the employee. Contracts or rules restricting liability were declared void.

Democratic attempts to obtain a railway commission with regulatory powers failed in the 1911 and 1913 legislatures. Governor Carey had not asked for such a commission, although every state except four was reported to have one.

RELAXATION

At the turn of the century, saloons, gambling halls, and houses of prostitution were still well patronized. A. J. Mokler reported that Casper became a "Sunday school town" in 1898 when lewd women were ordered to keep off the streets and out of the saloons. The lewd women, however, were not asked to leave town. And, unlike some Wyoming towns which required Sunday closing, Casper kept its saloons open on Sundays until 1911.

In 1901 the legislature, after discussions on the subject in many previous sessions, finally prohibited gambling. The law, which went into effect in 1902, was reported in 1905 to be enforced in only five of the thirteen counties. Sheridan, for example, began licensing gambling places in July, 1904, in utter disregard of the statute. Mokler noted in his *History of Natrona County, Wyoming* that the gambling tables were moved into the back rooms, where crooked gamblers replaced the honest ones.

Society women were still playing high five and whist in their clubs. They added euchre to their repertoire in 1901.

A steam "merry-go-round outfit" under canvas made the rounds of Wyoming towns, charging a nickel a ride on the wooden horses, goats, elk, and sheep and dispensing free music from the steam calliope. Ringling Brothers Circus came to Cheyenne in August, 1901, with special trains totaling sixty-five cars. The circus parade was described as the longest in the history of Cheyenne. Half the seats were taken down after the first performance, and the show lost money, said the manager, but he added that the circus had needed a rest stop.

Cheyenne's Frontier Days, which originated in 1897, attracted many people from the immediate vicinity. They came at special rates on Union Pacific excursion trains. The two-day show in September, 1898, included a half-mile gymkhana race in which the contestants rode one-quarter of a mile, dismounted, turned their coats inside out, remounted, rode one-eighth, dismounted, lighted their cigars and put up their umbrellas, mounted, and rode in with umbrellas up and cigars lighted. Other features were re-enactments of the first election in Wyoming, a lynching, a pioneer wedding, an Indian attack on an emigrant train, and two stagecoach holdups.

Novelties introduced on the Wyoming scene in the period were golf in 1900 and basketball in 1902, with both men and women playing. Grace Raymond Hebard carded a sixty-nine for six holes of golf at Laramie in 1900 and went on to win the state championship for women.

Buffalo Bill brought his Congress of Rough Riders to Cheyenne in 1897. He became identified with the state through investments in Sheridan and the Big Horn Basin. He was a founder of Cody, which was named after him. His unsuccessful attempts to obtain a divorce in Cheyenne and Sheridan courts in 1905, so that he might marry an English actress, caused him to lose some of his admirers. "With what a dull, sickening thud . . . do our gods go glimmering," wrote Bill Barlow in Douglas.[2]

For lack of transportation, picnicking and camping in the mountains continued to be unavailable to most Wyoming residents except on rare occasions. Aven Nelson, botanist at the university, wrote in 1899 that three-fourths of the people lived in railroad towns and that two-thirds of these towns lay on open, comparatively barren plains. He lamented that "girls and boys are nearing maturity in some localities in the state to whom any tree would be of interest and to whom a glimpse of a fruit tree in blossom would be as a glimpse into Paradise."

In the northwest corner of the state, Yellowstone National Park,

[2] Merris C. Barrow (1857–1910), better known as Bill Barlow, published a weekly newspaper, *Bill Barlow's Budget*, in Douglas from 1886 to 1910. In Wyoming his reputation as a rural philosopher was excelled only by that of Bill Nye. During the years 1904–1910 he published a little monthly magazine, *Sagebrush Philosophy*, which he advertised as "Pure Stuph" and as "pungent but always palatable." His jokes, proverbs, and rambling tales no longer amuse. Unhappily, the same judgment must be passed on George R. Caldwell, another humorist, known in his day as the "Lurid Liar of Lander," who was active in several Wyoming towns from 1886 to 1906.

founded in 1872, was beginning to attract attention.[3] Park officials began sprinkling the roads in 1901 and reported a total of 18,769 visitors for that year. The visitors arrived mainly by train, and were hauled around the park in stagecoaches.

Slowly entering upon the recreational-travel scene was the automobile. The first successful car had been made in the East by the Duryea brothers in 1893. Wyoming's first horseless carriage was one which ran on gasoline and was built by Elmer Lovejoy in his Laramie machine shop in 1897–1898. It weighed 940 pounds and had iron buggy tires, which were later replaced by pneumatic tires. Apparently it was Lovejoy who also brought the first automobile to the state from the outside, a Locomobile steamer in 1898.

The early automobiles offered sport for spectators as well as for owners. Thousands of Wyoming people remembered all their lives the "New York to Paris" automobile race, which passed through the state from east to west in March, 1908. The American, French, German, and Italian crews who drove the racing cars enjoyed great ovations in every town.[4] Finding roads impassable in western Wyoming, the American car took to the Union Pacific track.

Casper got its first automobile in 1908 at a time when Douglas already claimed fifteen. In August of that year an auto parade was a feature of state-fair week at Douglas, and a few hundred miles to the northwest some people from Chicago negotiated Togwotee Pass in their Oldsmobile, which was hailed as the first automobile in Jackson Hole.

On occasion cowboys threatened to shoot road hogs who were speeding on country roads, frightening horses and endangering lives. Auto owners in 1909 were further threatened by a bill introduced in the legislature which would have required them to stop their machines on public roads in the presence of frightened horses and to give their names and addresses to anyone on demand. The bill failed of passage. By 1913, however, the automobile age had advanced to the point at which the

[3] Good books on Yellowstone include Richard A. Bartlett, *Nature's Yellowstone* (Albuquerque: University of New Mexico Press, 1974); Merrill D. Beall, *The Story of Man in Yellowstone* (Yellowstone Park: Yellowstone Library and Museum Assn., 1960); and Aubrey L. Haines, *Yellowstone National Park* (Washington, D.C.: U.S. Govt. Printing Office, 1974).

[4] Another race, an endurance horse race sponsored by the *Denver Post*, attracted considerable attention two months later. Beginning in Evanston, Wyoming, on May 30, 1908, the racers took seven days along the route, which led through Green River, Rock Springs, Rawlins, Laramie, Cheyenne, and on to Denver. See Dean F. Krakel, "Dode Wykert and the Great Horse Race," *Colorado Magazine*, XXX, 3 (July 1953), 186–193.

legislature thought it appropriate to provide for "the registration, identification, and regulation of automobiles." Motor-vehicle operators were required to stop on signal until restive animals had passed.

Members of "Good Roads Clubs" in many towns devoted free time to volunteer work on the roads, removing rocks, filling ruts, and repairing bridges. They regularly carried sacks of gravel on their running boards, prepared to stop and dump the gravel into the first mudhole. Ranchers who at first had cursed them soon bought automobiles for themselves, after which they were more sympathetic with the problems of auto owners.

New hotels began to sprout like mushrooms after rain, all because of good times and automobiles. The Plains in Cheyenne and the Virginian in Medicine Bow opened in 1911. Erected by United States Senator Francis E. Warren and Cheyenne bank president Thomas A. Cosgriff, the Plains soon became very profitable under its lessee, Harry Hynds. The Connor Hotel opened in Laramie in 1912 and the LaBonte in Douglas in 1914. Soon three hotels were built in Casper, and other new hotels appeared in almost every town and city in the state.

CHAPTER 12

Huggermugger on the Range, 1898–1914

SENATOR FRANCIS E. WARREN declared in an August, 1897, interview that "stockmen in Wyoming are feeling unusually jubilant. . . . [The] range has never been better. . . . Prices are good . . . cattlemen and sheepmen are equally happy." The Dingley Tariff, adopted in July, 1897, had placed substantial import duties on raw wool and hides, both of which had been on the free list since 1894. The sheep industry was already advancing and would now move rapidly forward, while the cattle industry would begin a vigorous comeback after being more or less depressed since 1886. Agricultural prices in general would increase

346

nearly 50 per cent between 1900 and 1910. Thus the important farm-and-ranch segment of the Wyoming economy was destined to enjoy a dozen years far more favorable than the decade just past. There would be, nevertheless, a full measure of frustration and huggermugger.

Go North, Young Man

At last the northern part of the state would begin to fill up. Even before the hostile Indians were cleared out in 1876 and 1877, the north had been regarded by many as the best part of the territory. Northern delegates to the constitutional convention had promised that their section would soon overtake the southern counties in population. The five Union Pacific counties increased in population by only 22 per cent from 1900 to 1910, while the nine counties north of the Union Pacific increased by 137 per cent. The five Union Pacific counties grew from 63,532 people to 77,540, the northern counties from 28,630 to 67,906. The population of the state as a whole increased from 92,531 in 1900 to 145,965 in 1910.

Tens of thousands of settlers occupied the country both east and west of the Big Horn Mountains. Enjoying its boom decade, Sheridan County more than tripled in population, from 5,122 to 16,324, as coal miners, farmers, and townspeople flocked in. The town of Sheridan became a city, burgeoning from 1,559 to 8,408; with a huge flour mill built in 1903 and a brewery added in 1907, it was prepared to supply two staples prized by frontiersmen.

Agriculture formerly had been organized on a small scale as an adjunct to the livestock industry. It supplied hay and a small amount of feed, mainly oats. Then in the early years of the twentieth century all-out efforts were made to convert much more of the state to farming as possibilities were tested in many places. The number of farm and ranch units increased from 6,095 in 1900 to 10,987 in 1910. Of the 10,987 units in 1910, almost one-half (or 5,219) were under 175 acres in size. The number of persons occupied in general and crop agriculture increased from 8,299 in 1900 to 15,631 in 1910. The expansion in farming occurred in two forms, one with and one without irrigation.

Reclamation

The University of Wyoming Agriculture College and Agricultural Experiment Station report of 1895 had promised that irrigation "will some day reclaim fully ten million acres of our fertile valley lands." Appropriation of Wyoming waters by individuals continued wherever possible. State and federal aid were summoned in situations where the work was beyond the capacity of individuals.

By the Carey Act of August 18, 1894, provision was made for the donation to each desert-land state of not more than 1,000,000 acres of such land as the state might cause to be irrigated, occupied, and cultivated by actual settlers. Eight years after the passage of the Carey Act, Wyoming, which led the states in taking advantage of that law, had filed application for 457,500 acres of land but had been able to carry through to final patent only 11,321 acres. Thus the Carey Act had fallen short of expectations. One million acres of desert land, though offered free to the state, did not represent much capital. Construction companies, which were expected to contract with the state to do the work, shied away from many projects and usually lost money on those they undertook—that is, investors, if not the promoters, lost money. Their costs mounted far above estimates. When companies did succeed in delivering water, farmers often could not afford to pay the prices required to meet the costs.

Dissatisfied with the slow progress under the Carey Act, irrigation promoters again turned to the federal government. State engineer Fred Bond said in his biennial report in 1900: "It is agreed that only the General Government can undertake the work [of impounding flood waters with reservoirs] and carry it to a successful issue. The amount involved . . . is too great for private enterprise." Senator Francis E. Warren and Congressman Frank W. Mondell worked for passage of the Newlands Act (or Reclamation Act) of 1902, named after Congressman Francis G. Newlands of Nevada, which authorized the federal government to undertake reclamation projects with money obtained from the disposal of public lands.

As a result of the Carey Act of 1894 and the Reclamation Act of 1902, reclamation became a three-ring circus. Before 1894 the whole show had been concentrated in one ring, where unalloyed private enterprise prevailed. The original ring would always be the largest in terms of acreage involved, though not in terms of money spent. The addition of a state ring in 1894 did not end activity in the first ring, nor did the introduction of a federal ring in 1902 terminate performances in the first two rings. There ensued a pell-mell scramble for leftover water rights. "Every spring and rivulet is now as eagerly sought for as if it were in fact the last available supply of water in the state," reported the state engineer in 1902.

VENTURES UNDER THE CAREY ACT

S. L. Wiley's Big Horn Basin Development Company, which had undertaken the diversion of Greybull River water to the Germania Bench in the state's first Carey Act project, approved in 1895, completed that project in 1902. Some six hundred persons, mainly Germans, were brought from Illinois and Iowa to occupy land around the town of Germania (renamed Emblem in World War I).

Meanwhile, in 1900 the state launched another promising Carey Act project in the Big Horn Basin. Officials of the Church of Jesus Christ of Latter-day Saints were sufficiently impressed by the success of Mormon pioneers on the Greybull River in the 1890's to support organization of a sizable colonization company. A. O. Woodruff, member of the Council of the Twelve Apostles, led a large migration from Utah and Idaho to the north side of the Shoshone River in the spring of 1900. The colonists were organized as the Big Horn Colonization Company. Wyoming officials offered assistance under the Carey Act. In the summer of 1900, construction of the Sidon Canal began, and townsites were laid out at Byron, Cowley, and Lovell. In subsequent years, other Carey Act segregations were made on the south side of the Shoshone River and on both sides of the Big Horn River.

Flushed with the success of his Germania Bench venture, S. L. Wiley in 1902 obtained Carey Act contracts to irrigate the Oregon Basin with water from the South Fork of the Shoshone. More than 200,000 acres were segregated. Prospective settlers were promised water early in 1908 at the rate of forty dollars per acre. Consequent to a national publicity campaign, homeseekers converged on Cody in preparation for the grand opening announced for May 12, 1908. Publicity releases announced special excursions from Chicago, St. Louis, Omaha, Kansas City, and Denver and promised that 245,000 acres of land could be drawn for in a lottery to be held at Wiley, a new town twelve miles from Cody.

There had been a slight oversight: there was no water, and Oregon Basin, with five or six inches of precipitation a year, was just plain desert without it. Early in May the state engineer, who was on the scene, wired Governor Brooks that the opening would have to be postponed because water would not be available. Thirty miles of canal had been dug, but the system was incomplete. The state land board, in emergency session, decided to permit the opening as scheduled on the twelfth, subject to the proviso that all moneys paid by settlers would be held in escrow until the company could make good its promises, and Brooks wired the state engineer: "It is too late to call it off now." When they learned of these developments, the humbugged land seekers, except for seventeen who made filings, returned to their homes with harsh words for Wyoming. Soon thereafter Wiley's company, having spent almost half a million dollars, went into receivership. The state tried to find some other company to proceed with the Oregon Basin project, which it was never able to do. It appears that Wiley and the state land board had erred in thinking that the project was feasible. Commented the *Sheridan Enterprise*: "This gives another black eye to Wyoming's reputation. It was already known as the field of the grafter and swindler."

Many small projects were undertaken during the decade, some with Carey Act aid, others without. The state engineer reported in 1904 that "never before in the state's history were so many irrigation enterprises launched, nor were there ever so many miles of new ditches constructed in the same period of time in the state." He promised: "Within the next ten years Wyoming is to be one of the most important agricultural states in the West." Outstanding among the private enterprises was the Wyoming Development Company's "Wheatland Reservoir" of 120,000 acre-feet established thirty-five miles north of Laramie on the Big Laramie River in 1901–1902. This was made possible by an 1883 direct-flow appropriation and an 1898 reservoir right. Subsequently the company enlarged its Wheatland project to include a total of sixty thousand acres in crops by the addition of Carey Act lands and two new canals.

With normal summer flow generally appropriated, the irrigators planned more and more reservoirs to impound flood waters. Because of spring runoff from mountain snowbanks, it is not unusual for Wyoming streams to carry ten times as much water in May and June as in August. Fish that frolic in bank-high streams in June scarcely find enough water in the stream bed to cover their dorsal fins in August. Elwood Mead observed: "Farmers have learned that dependence on a canal which is empty half of the season is worse than waiting for rain in a humid climate." In 1905 and 1906 the state engineer issued 343 reservoir permits, compared to only 575 issued in all of the fourteen years preceding. Likewise, more lands were included under permits granted by the state engineer in 1905 and 1906 than were under irrigation as the result of all past efforts. The pace quickened thereafter until by the end of 1910 filings had been made on virtually all projects which appeared to be at all feasible.

THE RIVERTON PROJECT

Fremont County witnessed the first installment in a long series of reclamation difficulties. By an act of Congress of March 3, 1905, slightly less than one and one-half million acres of the Wind River Reservation was opened to settlement and entry under the Homestead Act. In response to far-flung publicity, some 10,559 persons registered as applicants for the land, of whom 7,240 were given the right to draw for sixteen hundred homesteads. Dates in August, 1906, were announced for drawings at Lander and for the official opening of the area to filings.

In preparation for the lottery, a flood of land-hungry people poured into Fremont County, most of them coming by train to Shoshoni, the new town at the railhead of the Chicago and North Western, which was building west from Casper. Shoshoni in the summer of 1906 was a canvas town, somewhat reminiscent of Union Pacific hell-on-wheels communities of an earlier generation. The law-abiding element embarked on an antigambling crusade which caused three gamblers to shoot to death Warner Moody, town attorney, and his friend George D. Anderson. A special train in late July brought a militia company from Douglas to maintain order.

Since water was essential for a livelihood on the ceded lands, the state engineer had begun to worry about their reclamation in 1905. He could not interest the federal government, so he turned to private enterprise. Preliminary surveys, delayed by the Commissioner of Indian Affairs, who was reluctant to permit trespassing before the official opening, led to the conclusion that 265,000 acres of the cession could be irrigated. Just before the opening, the state gave the Wyoming Central Irrigation Company, whose president was Joy Morton of Chicago and whose general manager was Secretary of State Fenimore Chatterton of Wyoming, a contract to build a canal system in the ceded area. There were to be two large canals, thirty-five and forty miles long, from the Wind River. The company agreed to sell perpetual water rights at twenty to thirty-eight dollars an acre, the price varying with the terms of payment.

The company laid out a townsite at Riverton. A few hundred squatters descended from Lander and Shoshoni on August 15, 1906, only to be driven out by a troop of cavalry until orderly disposal of lots could be worked out a few days later. During the first winter, many of the citizens of Riverton lived in "boarded-up tents, set on platforms," and hauled their water from the river in barrels.

As the company began planning its canal system, actual occupation of the farmland proceeded much more slowly than expected. In the first two weeks after the opening, filings were made by only 388 persons, who were joined by close to 200 more entrymen before winter set in. Since these pioneers now had their free government land without having promised to take water from the Wyoming Central Irrigation Company, they postponed making commitments. The matter inevitably got into politics. Said the state Democratic party platform in the fall of 1906: "We condemn the Republican party's policy in the opening of the Shoshone reservation whereby every settler is confronted with a private corporation exorbitant water tax." Added the *Carbon County Journal* (Rawlins): "Hundreds of prospective settlers—eastern farmers—have been driven from the state by the rotten contract given to the Wyoming Central Irrigation Company by the state officials." Thinking that they could irrigate their lands more cheaply themselves, in 1907 the homesteaders formed the Settlers' Cooperative Irrigation Company and asked state permission to irrigate thirty thousand acres of the land. They were turned down by the state and by the district court after an appeal.

Failing to get enough signatures on water contracts, the Wyoming Central Irrigation Company postponed major construction from year to year. Disenchanted with the Wyoming Central, the state engineer made several futile trips east to find a more venturesome company. No one would touch the project unless provisions of the Carey Act could be applied. In March, 1910, the state made preliminary moves toward applying the Carey Act, with the intention of permitting the Wyoming Central to continue under a new name, the Fremont Irrigation Company. A few months later, however, after company engineers had reported that much of the land was not suited to irrigation, all rights of the Wyoming Central Irrigation Company were cancelled. After the ceded lands had been placed under the Carey Act, the state engineer declared: "The project is so good from a physical standpoint that there is no excuse for delay." Time would prove him wrong. The state's new contract with the E. R. Tallmadge and D. C. Buntin Company led only to further delays and frustrations.

The Republican state administration was on the defensive in the 1910 political campaign, as Democrats alleged that there had been political graft and unconscionable profiteering by the Wyoming Central Irrigation Company. In 1911, Governor J. M. Carey recommended that the state assume direct responsibility, construct irrigation works, and sell the water at a reasonable price. The legislature was not prepared, however, to take over the Riverton project, and private capital refused to do it under the Carey Act. Eventually, in 1920, the United States Bureau of Reclamation was persuaded to add the scheme to its growing list of Wyoming projects. By spending more than twenty-six million dollars, the bureau was able to irrigate 52,945 acres, which was much less than the 265,000 acres the state engineer had thought irrigable in 1906. Apparently the Wyoming Central Irrigation Company was lucky to get out of the Riverton project when it did, for this item became a perennial object lesson in the formidable difficulties inherent in large-scale reclamation projects in the West.

THE LARAMIE PLAINS

The Laramie Plains interested irrigation promoters from earliest times, water rights there going back to 1867. The pioneers watered meadows along the Big and Little Laramie rivers and other streams by means of small, inexpensive ditches. In 1878–1879 the Pioneer Canal Company began a more ambitious project, diverting water from the Big Laramie, near Woods Landing, to irrigate lands several miles from the river and all the way to Laramie. In 1884 the Wyoming Central Land and Improvement Company was organized to buy up and develop a few hundred thousand acres of Union Pacific land. This company took over the Pioneer Canal Company, reorganized it, and enlarged the canal. In the previous year (1883), however, Joseph M. Carey's Wyoming Development Company had begun an appropriation of Big Laramie water below the Laramie Plains. Eventually, adjudication would establish that the Pioneer Canal Company's 1884 appropriation, a large one, had to take second place behind Carey's 1883 right. In short, Carey's priority made possible the development of the Wheatland community and stymied the Pioneer Canal Company and its successor, the Wyoming Central Land and Improvement Company.

From time to time there was talk of using the Big Hollow as a reservoir. No doubt this huge depression, twenty miles long and several miles wide, caused by wind erosion, would hold a lot of water. With most of the Laramie Plains water already appropriated, however, no one could ever find a river to direct into the great natural reservoir.

And had they been able to fill the Big Hollow, getting the water out again would have been a challenging problem.

Freewheeling promoters representing the E. R. Tallmadge and D. C. Buntin Company of Chicago appeared in Laramie in 1908 carrying substantial bank rolls with which they acquired assorted water rights and land. The company even announced plans, which were never carried out, to erect a dam in Cummins Canyon on the Big Laramie south of Woods Landing. The company also promoted settlement on a Carey Act project near Bosler, dependent on water brought from James Lake. In October, 1908, the company opened 14,500 acres to settlement, offering the land in tracts of 160 acres or less at fifty cents an acre, the usual Carey Act price in Wyoming, and perpetual water rights at $350 an acre, payable one-fourth down and the balance in ten annual payments. A lottery at Bosler determined the order of selection. The down payment was high and the timing was bad, the opening coming too soon after the fiascoes at Riverton and Wiley. Although not many settlers came to buy, Tallmadge and Buntin persisted, aided by enthusiastic assistance from Laramie newspapers. The company brought many prospects from the Middle West to look at the development in 1909. Kansas excursionists came singing this song:

> The excursion train came round the bend,
> Goodbye, my lover, goodbye,
> All loaded down with Kansas men,
> Goodbye, my lover, goodbye,
> We're going west to buy some land,
> Goodbye, my lover, goodbye,
> They say they have water and don't need rain,
> They'll make all rich who ride this train,
> We'll all buy land and settle down,
> Goodbye, my lover, goodbye.

Some of the Kansans who stopped in Laramie before going on to Bosler were discouraged by local skeptics, who in turn were berated by a local editor for being "knockers." The *Lander Mountaineer*, aware of the 7,000-foot altitude at Bosler, suggested planting figs, dates, and peanuts on the new project.

Federal census takers in April, 1910, could find only 264 persons in the Bosler region, and some of them soon left because of that year's drought, which dried up the sources of water. Tallmadge and Buntin had money and imagination but could not master Wyoming problems. They put other irons into the fire, but none got hot. They started to colonize on the Heart Ranch southwest of Laramie, but accomplished less there than they had at Bosler. They agreed to be colonizing agents for a large tract of land to be irrigated from Lake Hattie and also entered into futile negotiations with the state to take over the stalled Riverton project. Their colonization efforts for the Lake Hattie development came to naught. Pennsylvania promoters, who spent two million dollars on this project before their money ran out, planned to take supplementary water from Douglas Creek.

On the Laramie Plains, as elsewhere, Wyoming people were learning that (1) water was more limited than had been assumed, (2) moving water long distances from stream beds took large sums of money, and (3) recurring drought would sear the soul of both investor and farmer.

There was great attrition among Carey Act projects. Struthers Burt wrote in his *Diary of a Dude Wrangler* (1925): "On the surface this is an excellent act and was intended as such, but its actual workings have been weird and devious." Between 1894 and September, 1910, the state engineer had issued Carey Act permits for the reclamation of about 2,000,000 acres under fifty-seven different systems but had seen only 92,000 acres actually patented. In another thirty years the patented acreage under the act would increase only to 202,000. Obviously, the Carey Act did not work very well.

An incidental irritation bothered some people. Segregated Carey Act lands were used as cattle ranges for long periods of time while awaiting reclamation work that never came. Sometimes it was charged that the promoters merely wanted free grazing land, which they had never intended to irrigate. How much promoters under the Carey Act prospered at the expense of company stockholders has not been studied. Cody's Caroline Lockhart, in her novel *The Lady Doc* (1912), included crooked reclamation promoters in her cast of characters. Many years later she wrote to me: "I drew as accurate a picture of Cody as I could and keep out of jail."

Likewise, the original, strictly private ring of the reclamation show had its problems. T. S. Parsons, University of Wyoming agronomist, reported in January, 1913, that the early settlers, through excessive flooding of meadows, had killed out many of the finer grasses, leaving only the coarser, rushlike grasses that made poor feed.

RECLAMATION BY THE FEDERAL GOVERNMENT

Soon after the passage of the Newlands Act in 1902, Reclamation Service engineers began various feasibility surveys giving special attention to the Shoshone and North Platte rivers. Wyoming's first federal project, the Shoshone (later to be renamed Buffalo Bill), in 1904 took over the stalled work started in 1899 by Buffalo Bill and Nate Salsbury. They had run out of money in this Carey Act enterprise and were ready to relinquish their water rights, which the state then issued to the federal government. Said state engineer Clarence T. Johnson in his 1904 report: "The great government enterprise on the Shoshone is probably the most important yet issued with the possible exception of that for the Oregon Basin project. Both of these projects will utilize the water from the Shoshone River and each will lead to the reclamation of 200,000 acres of arid land."

The company to which the Reclamation Service first awarded the Shoshone Dam contract in 1905 soon abandoned it, making it necessary to turn the work over to another company in 1906. In the meantime, the contractor to whom the Corbett Tunnel phase of the project was assigned moved so slowly that the Reclamation Service itself took over that work in 1906. By 1910, crops could be grown on fifteen thousand acres of the Shoshone project in the vicinity of Ralston, Powell, and Garland. The Shoshone Reservoir (Buffalo Bill Dam) was completed in 1910, after which the Reclamation Service obtained a permit to irrigate ninety thousand acres under the Garland Canal and enlarged the Garland Canal system. While this was being done, it was learned that the nature of the soil required the installation of a drainage system as well as the irrigation works.

Although the Shoshone project has not lived up to early expectations, it may well be regarded as the most successful federal reclamation project in Wyoming. By 1975 it had cost $25,820,713 and was furnishing water to about 94,000 acres. It also provided power from the 5,600-kilowatt Shoshone power plant and the 5,000-kilowatt Heart Mountain power plant and offered recreation on the reservoir.

The state's second federal project, the North Platte, under permit of February, 1905, called for construction of Pathfinder Dam in a canyon of the North Platte River forty miles southwest of Casper and for a North Platte River diversion dam at Whalen, a few miles above old Fort Laramie. From Whalen the Interstate Canal was to carry water to thirty thousand acres in Wyoming and eighty thousand acres in Nebraska. Water was turned into the first forty-five miles of the Interstate Canal in May, 1906, and Pathfinder Dam was completed in 1911. Progressive disillusionment with the Pathfinder project can be seen in this 1912 report of state engineer A. J. Parshall:

Reclamation by the Federal Government had not yet been tried out, and nearly everyone expected to see the country in the vicinity of the Reclamation

Service projects develop wonderfully. The applications which were filed [for the Pathfinder project] indicated that it was the intention of the Reclamation Service to irrigate nearly 700,000 acres of land, the bulk of which was in the State of Wyoming. . . . Reclamation Service now [1912] reports only 129,270 acres of which 107,521 acres are in Nebraska, and 21,749 acres are in Wyoming. Of this 21,749 acres, 17,874 acres are lands of the North Platte Canal and Colonization Company which operates the Whalen Falls Canal, and a large part of these lands are being reclaimed under the Carey Act. This leaves less than 4,000 acres to be reclaimed in this State as a result of the construction of the Interstate Canal; a very small area to reclaim after submerging 22,000 acres with the Pathfinder Reservoir. A large part of the land so submerged was improved and irrigated land. . . .

The federal government began its third reclamation project in Wyoming when it built a temporary rock-filled crib dam at Moran at the Snake River outlet of Jackson Lake in 1906–1907. After the log dam failed in 1910, the Bureau of Reclamation erected a concrete dam in 1910–1911. This was reinforced and enlarged in 1916 in order to raise the water level of Jackson Lake seventeen feet. Jackson Lake Reservoir stores water almost entirely for Idaho's huge Minidoka project and has done virtually nothing for Wyoming, except to enlarge Jackson Lake.

STATE-FEDERAL FRICTION

An unfortunate aspect of the three-ring circus of private, state, and federal reclamation activity in the early years of the twentieth century was the friction between agencies. Many of the pioneers who at the outset had been enthusiastic about the Carey Act and the Newlands Act later became resentful over some of the concomitants of federal aid. Governor B. B. Brooks declared in his message to the 1909 legislature: "Unfortunately the present policy . . . seems to be to accomplish all reforms through federal agencies . . . whose meddlesome activity frequently acts as a hindrance to our development, and hence irritates our people." State engineer Clarence T. Johnson grumbled in 1910: "The Carey Act is but of little value. . . . The Interior Department with its endless rules and regulations and its army of employees must have its own way."

There were frequent complaints about long delays in securing federal approval of segregations. Wyoming Commissioner of Public Lands S. G. Hopkins, in his 1912 report, conceded that the Carey Act had fallen into disrepute because of abuses in early projects—incompetent engineers, deceptive literature, lax administration by the state. In consequence, he said, the federal government became very exacting, making it difficult to get approval for legitimate projects.

Operation of the Newlands Act was accompanied by little friction as long as people expected great benefits. When results turned out to be relatively small, recriminations multiplied. Scornfully, state engineer Parshall wrote in his 1914 report:

As an illustration of the "paralyzing hand of bureaucratic sloth" the records of the State Engineer's office will show that the sturdy settlers, without capital or credit further than the God-given capital of brawn and energy, have reclaimed more acres of arid land than the millions of capital and army of employees in the service of the Government, in the same length of time, and more than that, each settler contributes his share, in the way of taxes, toward the support of our institutions. (The public lands of the Federal Government are exempt from taxation.)

Moreover, conflicts arose between federal and state laws. State engineer Parshall accused the Reclamation Service of ignoring state laws, riding roughshod over the rights of individuals, and looting the state of its water supply for the benefit of other states. Said he in his 1914 report: "The present attitude of the Reclamation Service must change radically before any real good can be accomplished in this state by it."

THE STATE AND THE IRRIGATORS

By 1910 the state employed almost fourscore men to supervise the distribution of waters: a state engineer, two assistant state engineers, three deputy state engineers, four division superintendents, and sixty-six part-time water commissioners. In dry years, it was impossible to keep the irrigators happy, for many could not be allowed the water they needed. Theft of water was common, and the state engineer often deplored overuse of water. Reported Frank Bond, for example, in 1900: "Burlington Flats soil has become so saturated with water that the traveler is not safe from bogging down both in the high road and upon the fields. The resulting injury to the land by bringing large quantities of alkali to the surface is apparent." State engineer A. J. Parshall noted no improvement in 1914:

Wyoming farmers are not scientific irrigators. It is the prevailing custom to use two or three times the amount of water specified by law. This unlawful and wasteful use of water is a disgrace to our state. An alarming percentage of our irrigated land, which has no natural drainage, is becoming marshy, swampy and covered with alkali sloughs. . . .

State engineers and experts at the Wyoming College of Agriculture had their hands full trying to improve irrigation practices. University of Wyoming Experiment Station bulletins published information on proper irrigation methods, but their advice was often ignored.

In 1911 the state assessed 456,737 acres of cultivated irrigated lands and 351,764 acres of uncultivated irrigated lands. Laramie County led with 100,919 acres of cultivated irrigated lands. Big Horn County followed with 76,650 acres, Sheridan with 44,617, Johnson with 28,672 and Fremont with 21,524.

No other decade has seen so much promotion of irrigation, so much actually accomplished, and yet such a large gap between promise and performance. The decade's momentum carried over for two more years, the assessed acreage of cultivated irrigated land reaching a peak of 531,130 and of uncultivated irrigated land 511,308 in 1913, after which there was a falling off in both categories. During the next ten years, reclamation development was virtually at a standstill.

Meanwhile, many of the irrigation farmers were in trouble. They had been misled by promoters, lacked the capital necessary for success, and could not pay their debts. Elwood Mead, back from seven years in Australia, told an irrigation conference in Denver in April, 1914, that the United States government should follow the example of the Australian government and give more aid to settlers on irrigated lands. Said Mead: "Often there is much hardship. . . . Many a poor settler's wife has aged ten years in ten months." He concluded that "the marvel is not that many fail, but that any endure." This was a wiser Mead than the enthusiast of the early 1890's.

DRY FARMING

Farming without irrigation was not tried much in Wyoming in the nineteenth century. Many people evidently thought that Bill Nye was not too far wrong about Wyoming agriculture when he wrote at Laramie under date of June 10, 1880:

It has snowed a good deal during the week, and it is discouraging to the planters of cotton and tobacco very much. . . . Unless the yield this fall of moss agates and prickly pears should be unusually large, the agricultural export will be far below preceding years, and there may be actual suffering. I do not wish to discourage those who might wish to come to this place but the soil is quite coarse, and the agriculturist, before he can even begin with any prospect of success, must run his farm through a stamp-mill in order to make it sufficiently mellow. This, as the reader will see, involves a large expense at the very outset. Hauling the farm to a custom mill would delay the farmer two or three hundred years in getting his crops in, thus giving the agriculturist who had a pulverized farm in Nebraska . . . a great advantage. . . . We have, it is true, a large area of farming lands now lying on the dump, but they must first be crushed and then treated for alkali, in which our Wyoming farms are very rich. Then, again, the climate is erratic, eccentric and peculiar . . . [and] the early frosts make close connections with the late spring blizzards, so that there is only time for a hurried lunch between. . . .

The first annual report of the University of Wyoming Experiment Station in 1891 gave substantial support to the Nye views. Dice McLaren, M.S., station agriculturist, wrote: "Though many parts of Wyoming have yielded occasional good crops without irrigation, the northeastern part of the State alone has sufficient rainfall for fair results. The ditch of water is as necessary as the acre of soil. All crops must be irrigated."

Yet the temptation to try farming proved irresistible, especially along the eastern edge of the state, where precipitation approached and occasionally exceeded sixteen inches. According to I. S. Bartlett's *History of Wyoming*, a few Swedes from Iowa began successful dry farming in the Salem community forty miles northeast of Cheyenne in the late 1870's. Other pioneers dry-farmed in Crook County and at Manville in Niobrara County in the days of Governor Moonlight. Frank W. Mondell, later a congressman, dry-farmed successfully five miles northwest of Newcastle from 1889 to 1893. Generally, however, dry farmers delayed their invasion of Wyoming until the twentieth century, when a few thousand entered the eastern counties to occupy selected lands all the way from Colorado to Montana. Their activity in Wyoming was not to be compared with that in Colorado, Kansas, Nebraska, North Dakota, and Montana. Considering Wyoming's small population, however, the dry-farming excitement was an important phase of the state's history.

The philosophy of Wyoming dry-farming promoters can be seen in a statement by state engineer Frank Bond in his biennial report of 1902: "It is impossible to consider the vast expanse of territory and especially the little which it produces without speculating on the possibility of increasing its value and usefulness." Wyoming's next state engineer, Clarence T. Johnson, suggested in 1904 that the "Campbell System," named after Hardy W. Campbell, a dry-farming exponent whose ideas had been tried extensively in Nebraska, Kansas, and Colorado, "should lead to the utilization of large areas in Wyoming. . . . Either the State or the Government should lead in the investigation and these experiments should be carried on on a large scale."

The preliminary promotion by state engineers soon enlisted the talents of others. Publisher W. C. Deming began preaching the gospel of dry farming in his *Wyoming State Tribune*. A Cheyenne committee was chosen, consisting of A. D. Kelley, H. B. Henderson, Sr., Clarence B. Richardson, Clarence T. Johnson, and Deming. They solicited funds with which they brought an Oregon expert, Dr. V. T. Cooke, to give advice in 1905 and 1906. Experiments were soon under way in several parts of the state, with support from the Cheyenne Board of Trade, the College of Agriculture, the United States Department of Agriculture, and the Union Pacific, Burlington, and Colorado and Southern railroads.

After the legislature in 1907 appropriated $5,000 for dry-farming experiments, the state employed Dr. Cooke as "Director of Dry Farming Experiments," in which capacity he traveled all over the state giving advice and assistance. Governor B. B. Brooks told the 1909 legislature: "Experiments so far have been very encouraging. . . . Unquestionably, a considerable portion of our remaining public land has some value for agricultural purposes."

Bulletin No. 80, "Dry Farming in Wyoming" (March 1909), summarized the experiences and methods of pioneer dry farmers in the state as collected through a questionnaire. Those who responded had been moderately successful for periods extending to twenty-five years. Most of them cropped the land every year, yet said they thought seeding alternate years was better. The bulletin stated that Wyoming had 14,250,000 acres (almost one-fourth of the state) with a rainfall of over fifteen inches and declared flatly that "it is safe to say that the plow land of this area can be profitably farmed on natural precipitation, by thorough practice of dry farming methods." The bulletin said further that the state had 29,500,000 acres (almost one-half of the state) with an annual precipitation of between twelve and one-half and fifteen inches and avowed that "practically all of the plow land of this area will grow profitable crops by dry farming in a majority of seasons. It is a safe prediction that very much of this land subject to homesteading under the 320-acre law will eventually come under the plow." For the other quarter of the state, where precipitation was below ten inches, the bulletin recommended further testing before judgment could be passed on dry-farming possibilities. Professor James DeLoss Towar, director of the University of Wyoming Experiment Station and author of the bulletin, had been trained in the Michigan College of Agriculture, where he had earned a Master of Science degree, and had become acquainted with dry farming in Australia before coming to the University of Wyoming.

A talented Laramie Plains promoter, Colonel E. J. Bell, gained much free publicity for Wyoming agriculture, both irrigated and dry, with his offers to wager ten thousand dollars that he could raise more oats on a section of ground in Albany County than could be raised on any other section in the world. He had won blue ribbons for his irrigated oats at national expositions in St. Louis and Portland, Oregon. Waving a certified check for ten thousand dollars, he challenged any and all at the International Dry Farming Congress at Billings, Montana, in 1909. For one reason or another, the ebullient Colonel could find no taker.

Congressman Frank W. Mondell aided the dry-farming cause by introducing and getting passed in Congress a 320-acre homestead law in February, 1909, which doubled the amount of free land available to homesteaders, except in northwestern Nebraska, where the Kinkaid Act of 1904 had already allowed 640-acre homesteads. Appropriately, Mondell was elected president of the International Dry Farming Congress in 1909.

The enlarged-homestead act brought more dry farmers to Wyoming. The Christian church headquarters at Dayton, Ohio, even founded a dry-farming community at Jireh, five miles west of Manville, and opened a junior college. Unhappily, in 1910 and 1911 came drought, causing widespread crop failures, which were reflected in reduced dry-farming acreages: 621,447 acres were assessed as dry-farming lands in 1911, but only 412,772 acres were so assessed in 1912. The 1910 disaster in Crook County can be seen in the assessment figures: 461,329 acres in 1911, only 43,371 in 1912, and even smaller acreages in 1913 and 1914. For the state as a whole, good crops in 1912 and 1913 pushed the dry-farming assessed area to 818,191 acres in 1914. Indeed, the Board of Immigration claimed agricultural production to be worth more than thirty-five million dollars in 1912, as compared to thirty million dollars for livestock.

In 1912, Congress lowered the homestead residence requirement from five years to three and permitted the homesteader to absent himself from the property for five months each year. These concessions gave renewed emphasis to dry farming.

Taking Crook County's place at the head of the dry-farming parade was Laramie County, with 101,713 acres assessed in 1912, 396,846 in 1913, and 591,612 in 1914. The Laramie County expansion lay mainly southeast of Cheyenne in what was known as the Golden Prairie District, where wheat, oats, barley, rye, flax, corn, and potatoes were grown.

Sweetwater County appeared on the assessment rolls with 166,424 acres of dry-farming land in 1912, then reported no such land in 1913 and 1914. Behind Laramie County with its 591,612 acres in 1914 came Hot Springs with 73,839, Crook with 33,266, Weston with 23,463, Sheridan with 18,000, and Niobrara with 17,342.

Helping to boost dry farming—and everything else in the state—in 1911 and 1912 was the Board of Immigration, created by the 1911 legislature and supplied with forty thousand dollars. The board's biennial report for 1911–1912 shows impressive activity, unimpressive results. Commissioner Roy W. Schenck said he had in eighteen months mailed out 301,000 "pieces of literature" and 42,000 letters. A standard paragraph in his letters stated: "There is absolutely no question as to the fertility of the soil in Wyoming. It is rich, and will produce enormous yields as compared with farms of the Middle West." Schenck reported that he had a list of 175 names of persons whom he and the immigration board had influenced to move to Wyoming. That the list was no longer than it was, Schenck appeared to attribute to the state's very bad reputation. His report said:

Regardless of the cause, the fact is apparent to this office, that Wyoming has anything but an enviable reputation among prospective homeseekers, immigrants, or investors. This undesirable impression apparently has been growing greater instead of less.

Hundreds and even thousands of letters and personal interviews have convinced us that investors of capital are reluctant to examine a proposition when informed that it is located in Wyoming. Homeseekers or farmers are ready to consider locating in any other state in the Union, or even in Canada, before giving Wyoming a thought as even a possibility. These are facts that we do not like to hear but they are true nevertheless. What is the matter?

There is only one answer. The people of Wyoming have not properly attended to their own advertising. They have allowed outsiders to gain their only knowledge of the State through reading lurid tales of the barrenness of our deserts, the outlawry of our citizens and the general undesirability of everything pertaining to the State. In other instances fake mining, irrigation, and oil propositions have been launched, and thousands have gained their estimate of Wyoming by being swindled. Misleading information has been spread broadcast for the past twenty or thirty years. . . .

Schenck argued that were he permitted to tell the truth long enough, excellent results would follow. He was full of schemes, such as placing an immigration agent at the docks in New York City and having the state prepare well-improved farms for sale on easy terms, but the 1913 legislature cut him and his board off without a penny.

Although most of Wyoming's dry farmers came equipped with farming experience gained in Nebraska, South Dakota, Colorado, Kansas, or Iowa, conditions were different and adjustments had to be made. The University of Wyoming Experiment Station staff members were learning along with the farmers. Some of them, like Professors J. D. Towar and Aven Nelson, for a time became dry-farming enthusiasts. Dr. Nelson, in a paper read before the Young Men's Literary Club of Cheyenne in March, 1911, said that for thirty years the country's press had printed and reprinted Bill Nye's "funny but fatal fallacies." Now "farming as such is to be the backbone of our prosperity. . . . There might as well be two millions of people. . . . When our agricultural possibilities are finally appreciated people will flock in eager for the unparalleled opportunities that are opening."

University President Charles O. Merica became infected by the Towar-Nelson enthusiasm. He wrote an article entitled "New Wyoming" for the November, 1911, issue of the *Wyoming Farm Bulletin,* a monthly publication of the agricultural college and experiment station. He proclaimed that "from now on there must be a hundred spears of grass where before there was one. One hundred cattle must fatten where before one raced with the cowboy of story and song." He decried the presence in the state of the "carping, the critical, the fault finding, and the men who are the 'dogs-in-the-mangers.'" In that same month, the *Saturday Evening Post* carried a depressing article entitled "The Autobiography of a Wyoming Homesteader," describing in detail the woes of a homesteader at Garrett. Said the *Laramie Boomerang*: "There should be some way of preventing such men as the 'homesteader' from breaking into print."

The 1913 legislature required agriculture to be taught in the public schools of the state. In that same year, the cornerstone was laid for a $100,000 College of Agriculture building at the university, and A. E. Bowman was placed in charge of the University of Wyoming Experiment Station's dry-farming work. Trained at Utah State Agricultural College, Bowman brought knowledge of Mormon experience. Fremont County got the state's first county agricultural agent in 1913, followed soon by Sheridan County.

As personnel at the experiment station learned more about Wyoming's capabilities, they provided better guidance. In the August, 1913, issue of the *Wyoming Farm Bulletin*, for example, the editor stated that "the farmer who comes to Wyoming cannot expect to always tread a path of roses. . . . Some land has been taken up which might better go back to cattle and sheep ranges until such time as we are in greater need of land than we will be for some time to come." The last sentence looks strange indeed when placed alongside statements appearing in the same publication only a few years earlier.

CATTLE AND SHEEP

Frederick Jackson Turner said in 1893:

Stand at Cumberland Gap and watch the procession of civilization, marching single file—the buffalo following the trail to the salt springs, the Indian, the fur-trader and hunter, the cattle-raiser, the pioneer farmer—and the frontier has passed by. Stand at South Pass in the Rockies a century later and see the same procession with wider intervals between.

Turner adhered to the conventional wisdom in regarding Wyoming cattlemen as merely the advance guard of the farmers. Many people in the East thought it inevitable that farmers would supersede the stockmen in Wyoming. Quite a few people in Wyoming thought so, too.

The inroads of farmers were certainly annoying to many ranchers. While the total acreage appropriated by the farmers, wet and dry, was less than 3 per cent of the state's total by 1910 and may appear trivial, the farmers distressed the livestock men more than the acreages and percentages suggest. For one thing, the farmers often took over winter grazing grounds and watering places, which upset traditional patterns. For another, some of the farmers placed a few cattle or sheep on the open range in competition with the stockmen. And still again, as had been the case since the 1870's, the big cattlemen suspected the settlers of rustling and mavericking.

In 1905 the Board of Live Stock Commissioners dropped the long-standing practice of arranging official cattle roundups. There had been so much fencing (some of it by the cattlemen themselves) that cattle could no longer stray great distances. The veteran cattleman John Clay, in *My Life on the Range* (1924), recalled that the great Swan Land and Cattle Company disposed of its cattle in 1910. "The settlers," he said, "were too much for them." And he said also that "you can fight armies or disease or trespass, but the settler never. He advances slowly, surely, silently . . . pushing everything before him." And yet Wyoming cattlemen were found to have deeper roots than most people gave them credit for. Mainly because of the state's aridity, the farmers did not overwhelm the cattlemen as they were expected to do in the years 1898–1914. The most severe challenge for the cattlemen came, not from farmers, but from sheepmen.

Although land filings were stepped up, the total acreage filed on for all purposes in the seventeen-year period under scrutiny amounted to less than 8,400,000 acres and the total acreage patented less than 2,500,000 acres. Cattlemen and sheepmen, as well as farmers, were involved in these land entries. Five-sixths of the land in the state was still publicly owned in 1914, and most of the privately owned land was grazing land. Large ranches, for the most part, were not being broken up into small farms in these years.

CATTLEMEN AND SHEEPMEN RAMPANT

In Washington at the turn of the century the stockmen were well served by United States Senator Francis E. Warren, with occasional assistance from Senator Clarence D. Clark and Representative Frank W. Mondell. Edward N. Wentworth, in *America's Sheep Trails*, credits Warren with being "the author, or principal instigator, of legislation protective to the sheep growing industry for over a quarter of a century." Warren did not neglect the cattlemen, for he fought to retain high tariffs on hides as well as on wool. His achievements for the wool industry, it is true, were especially noteworthy. Senator J. P. Dolliver of Iowa in June, 1909, twitted Warren about being the largest single beneficiary of his successful efforts for the wool industry, calling him "the greatest shepherd since Abraham." Such slurs troubled Warren very little. He seems to have lost no sleep over conflict-of-interest problems. Useful also to Wyoming stockmen in this period was William A. Richards, former governor, who served as Assistant Commissioner of the General Land Office from 1899 to 1903 and as Commissioner from 1903 to 1907.

Floored by the winter of 1886–1887, Wyoming cattlemen had recovered slowly. The Johnson County War and the long depression of the 1890's prolonged the convalescence. By 1898, however, the cattlemen were on their feet and ready to mix it up with the onrushing sheepmen.

The bulletin "Wyoming Agricultural Statistics," published jointly in 1925 by the United States Department of Agriculture, Bureau of

Agriculture and Economics, and the Wyoming Department of Agriculture, offers the following estimates for cattle and sheep numbers in the period under discussion:

ESTIMATED NUMBER OF WYOMING LIVESTOCK, JANUARY 1, FOR THE YEARS 1898–1914

Year	Cattle	Sheep
1898	706,000	1,940,021
1899	713,000	2,328,025
1900	767,000	2,840,190
1901	769,000	5,449,074
1902	792,000	5,885,074
1903	816,000	5,826,150
1904	823,000	4,602,658
1905	832,000	3,267,887
1906	776,000	4,575,042
1907	887,000	4,986,796
1908	861,000	5,885,000
1909	896,000	6,091,000
1910	767,000	5,397,000
1911	658,000	5,019,000
1912	593,000	4,600,000
1913	552,000	4,072,000
1914	583,000	3,827,000

These figures are probably low, but they are the best available. The bulletin placed the "farm value" of the cattle higher than that of the sheep for all of these years except 1908 and 1910.

The secretary of the Board of Sheep Commissioners in October, 1899, reported that even though the ranges were already crowded, "hundreds of parties are going into the sheep business and those already in are buying more." Sheep thus overcrowded the public lands in the years 1899–1901. In the hands of capable herders, sheep could adjust more readily to the diverse grazing conditions than could cattle. They could make better use of the browse type of forage. They could thrive in the Red Desert in winter or on the high mountain slopes in summer.

Many of the flockmasters of the period were leading citizens of the state, men such as B. B. Brooks; Thomas A. Cooper; John and Thomas Cosgriff; W. W. Daley; J. A. Delfelder; Frank A. Hadsell; John W. Hay; W. T. Hogg; Frank, Bert, and Joe King; Tim Kinney; John Mahoney; W. P. Noble; J. D. Noblitt; J. B. Okie; P. J. Quealy; Pat Sullivan; George Taylor; L. E. Vivion; Francis E. Warren; Dr. J. M. Wilson; and J. D. Woodruff. Socially, the flockmasters were on a par with the cattlemen. One of them, J. B. Okie, in 1898 built a palace, said to have cost $100,000, for his ranch home at Lost Cabin. The state's position in the nation's wool industry in the period is indicated by the selection of Senator Warren as president of the National Wool Growers Association, 1901–1907, and Dr. J. M. Wilson of Douglas as vice-president in 1906.

Owners of the great herds of cattle and flocks of sheep were confronted by several formidable challenges, not all of their own making. The weather at times was awesome. The winter of 1898–1899 was a bad one. The growing practice of winter feeding held down the losses, yet the United States Department of Agriculture estimated Wyoming cattle losses from exposure and disease in the year ending April 1, 1899, at 46,599 and sheep losses at 236,683. The cattle losses that year were the greatest since 1886–1887 and the sheep losses the greatest for any year up to that time.

PREDATORY ANIMALS

Wolves and coyotes preyed on herds and flocks. The state, through a system of bounties, waged all-out war on the predators. "Every civilized country has recognized the necessity of state aid in the extermination of predatory wild animals," said Governor DeForest Richards to the legislature in 1901. In the decade beginning in 1895, state outlays in bounties ranged from $5,613.50 in 1897 to $25,177 in 1904. Normally in these years the state spent more for killing wolves and coyotes than it did for supporting the state university (not counting federal aid to the university). Some counties added their own bounties. Wyoming paid more generous bounties than surrounding states, with the result that, despite threats of penalties for false affidavits, the state seems to have been paying for imported pelts.

Edward N. Wentworth has written that "bounty payments in the West never eradicated predators and normally failed even to restrict them after the first few years." Yet Governor DeForest Richards in 1903 and Governor B. B. Brooks in 1905 thought some progress was being made against the predators. The 1905 legislature, however, appealed to the United States Congress for help.

While they waited for federal aid, the stockmen regularly obtained bounty laws from the legislature. Governor Carey vetoed one in 1911 and another in 1913. Before the end of the 1913 session, however, he relented and approved another bounty bill which included certain safeguards that he had required. Eventually, federal hunters, trappers, and poisoners appeared in the state in response to various appeals for aid. Still later, the beneficiaries assumed more of the burden by organizing predatory-animal districts and approving mill-levy assessments on sheep.

Poisonous plants, such as woody aster, larkspur, and loco, took their toll. Wyoming Experiment Station Preliminary Bulletin No. 88 (April 1911), blamed woody-aster plants for sheep losses running into millions of dollars a year. A station specialist estimated that woody aster caused twice as many sheep losses as coyotes did. Later studies have established that sheep will eat woody aster only when starved to it.

That sheep were starved into eating poisonous plants is a commentary on overgrazing, which was widespread on the public grazing lands and which was accepted as inevitable by informed observers of the period. It was a constant problem. B. C. Buffum and W. H. Fairfield of the University of Wyoming Experiment Station wrote in the 1900 report of the station: "The natural ranges have greatly deteriorated through overstocking, which has prevented the best grasses from reseeding themselves for so long a time that they have run out." They reported that many ranchers had bought sacaline and Australian saltbush with which to improve their ranges. They advised that sacaline had proved "absolutely valueless" and that the Australian saltbush was a tropical plant which would not flourish in the Wyoming climate.

RANGE CONFLICTS

State engineer Elwood Mead had reported in 1897 that range conflicts were threatening the peace and prosperity of many communities. As the sheep multiplied at the turn of the century and were trailed onto public lands used previously only by cattlemen, the conflict became so violent that it must be rated as a major theme of the state's history.

Cattlemen claimed that they had been in Wyoming first, which was true, generally speaking, although there had been a few pioneer sheepmen in the early years of the territory. The newcomers replied that no legal rights had been established by prior use and that the free public grazing lands were open to one and all. The pattern of conflict was complicated by the fact that many cattlemen switched to sheep when they appeared to be more profitable, and sometimes vice versa.

George Rollins, in his 1951 University of Utah doctoral dissertation, "The Struggle of the Cattlemen, Sheepmen and Settler for Control of Lands in Wyoming, 1867–1910," noted that range wars in Wyoming usually followed a set pattern: first, warnings by cattlemen to sheepmen to keep sheep out of a certain area; second, announcement of a dead line which sheep must not cross; third, confrontations, often ending in destruction of flocks and assaults on the herders. Sheepmen stubbornly persisted. The controversy was exacerbated by religious prejudice against Mormon sheepmen, by charges that Utah sheepmen were introducing scab-infected sheep, and by further charges (often true) that transient sheep escaped Wyoming taxation.

Sheepherders and sheep for a time were sitting ducks for the bellicose cattlemen, since a herder normally was alone with his band of two thousand or so sheep. Bullets might or might not be used. Hundreds of incidents were reported in the newspapers, and presumably others were not reported. For instance in May, 1897, cattlemen of Jackson Hole appointed a committee of safety and published a notice that "no sheep will be allowed to pass through Jackson's Hole . . . under any circumstances." Let one other example suffice. In July, 1902, about fifteen herds of sheep belonging to Rock Springs parties crossed a dead line in the New Fork country of the Green River Valley and were attacked by 150 masked men. At least two thousand sheep were destroyed, one herder was killed, and the other herders were driven out of the country and their herds scattered.

And so it went year after year, with the sheepmen advancing on many fronts and the cattlemen offering vigorous resistance. Arrests and convictions were rare, because it was almost impossible to identify the masked men, who were together only briefly before dispersing. The sheepmen, however, were getting more numerous and more influential every year. Even as the cattlemen had organized in the 1870's to combat thieves, so the sheepmen now organized to combat the masked men, although this was not the only reason for forming a state association. They also needed to unite to fight sheep scab and to improve their lobbying in Cheyenne and Washington.

Representatives of ten county associations at a meeting in Cheyenne on March 27, 1902, failed to form a state association. Finally, however, in Cheyenne, April 10–13, 1905, the wool growers were able to organize the Wyoming Wool Growers Association. Dr. J. M. Wilson was elected first president, John Hay vice-president, and George S. Walker secretary and treasurer. A board of trustees of thirteen members, one from each county, was provided for, with the president and vice-president ex officio members of the board.

The Wyoming Wool Growers Association flourished, as might be expected from the events of the decade. Starting out with 40 charter members, the association picked up new members fast. At its second meeting eight months later in Casper, 271 members answered to the roll call. By January, 1909, the association had 541 members (646, the highest ever, a year later) and claimed to be the largest organization of its kind in the country. County associations were active in ten counties —all except Laramie, Fremont, and Crook. Secretary George S. Walker's report to the governor in December, 1908, showed that Wyoming led all states in wool production, both in the grease and scoured. It is not unreasonable to rate wool as the state's leading industry in the years 1908–1910.

Nevertheless, attacks on sheep and their herders continued. The executive committee of the Wool Growers Association, meeting in April, 1907, at Cheyenne, offered a reward of one thousand dollars for the conviction of any sheep-camp raiders and decided to raise a fund of fifty thousand dollars to be used for several purposes. The order in which the purposes were listed in newspaper reports may not have been entirely fortuitous: the fund was to be used "in combating sheep camp raiders, combinations against wool growers, Pinchot's forest reserve policy and President Roosevelt's land leasing policy."

The climactic events in the long range war between cattlemen and sheepmen occurred in 1909. In April, fifteen or more masked men attacked a sheep camp on Spring Creek, a branch of the Nowood, near Tensleep in the Big Horn Basin. They killed in cold blood two wealthy wool growers, Joe Allemand and Joe Emge, and one of their herders, Joe Lazier. Big Horn County Prosecuting Attorney Percy Metz and Sheriff Felix Alston began a thorough investigation. The county wool growers association and the state association each offered rewards of one thousand dollars for the capture of the murderers. Other money was contributed, and the National Wool Growers Association announced that it was ready to support the prosecution with twenty thousand dollars. While a grand jury was considering evidence, one of the witnesses committed suicide, leaving three letters implicating prominent cattlemen of the area. Seven men were arrested in May: George Sabin, M. A. Alexander, Thomas Dixon, Herbert Brink, Charles Faris, Albert F. Keys, and Ed F. Eaton. While they were awaiting trial, Keys and Faris turned state's evidence. The other five under arrest then pleaded guilty and received penitentiary sentences varying from three years to life. For the wool growers, the combination of organization, money, energetic prosecution by county officials, and

luck had finally paid off. Detectives employed by the Wyoming Wool
Growers Association were a deterrent to raids thereafter, and cattlemen
quit murdering sheepmen and herders.

An observer of the events of 1909 might with some reason have ventured the opinion that cattlemen were on the run and that sheepmen
would soon dominate the ranges of the state. This was not to be the
case. Overgrazing, drought, dry farmers, a destructive winter (1911–
1912), and loss of the tariff on wool in 1913 withheld the fruits of victory
from the flockmasters. Although the cattlemen suffered several anxious
years, they could not be dislodged. In Wyoming's cattle-sheep conflict,
1897–1909, fifteen men and a boy, and perhaps ten thousand sheep,
were killed.[1] Men working on the range, however, were really in less
danger than those who worked in the coal mines or on the Union Pacific
Railroad.

Tom Horn

Mingling with the many amateur regulators who tried to control the
Wyoming range at the turn of the century was a professional killer:
Tom Horn. Before coming to Wyoming, Horn had worked in New
Mexico and Arizona territories as Indian scout and stock detective and
for a time in Colorado as Pinkerton detective. It is sometimes asserted
that he was in Wyoming as early as 1892 and had a hand in the Johnson
County Invasion. Probably, however, he did not come to Wyoming
before 1894.

Horn's first employment in Wyoming seems to have been in some

---

[1] Professor Harold E. Briggs, in his generally excellent book *Frontiers of the Northwest*
(New York: Appleton-Century, 1940), has made the cattlemen-sheepmen conflict,
bad as it was, appear much worse. He writes: "The mountain gorges and plains of
Wyoming contain the bones of many a sheep herder who was murdered at night as
he slept in his isolated wagon or tent and the evidence hidden as the camp was burned
or the body thrown into some deep valley or chasm." He adds: "One reliable writer
states that in the years from 1893 three scores of men were killed and five times that
number were wounded in the conflict that extended pretty well over the state."
Briggs identifies the "reliable writer" as Clara M. Love, whose article "History of the
Cattle Industry in the Southwest" appeared in the *Southwestern Historical Quarterly* in
two parts (XIX, 4 [April 1916] and XX, 1 [July 1916]). On p. 13, Vol. XX, of the
Quarterly we read: "From 1893 to 1903 a score of men were killed and five times that
number wounded in this series of petty wars, which extended pretty well over the
grazing states." Briggs erred remarkably in reading "a score" as "three scores" and
"the grazing states" as "the state." Miss Love's statement in its original form is
plausible enough, but, like all historians, she nodded occasionally, judging by her
inclusion of this whopper: "On one occasion 800,000 sheep were driven from Utah
and Wyoming into Colorado. The cattle men there took the herders and held them
until every sheep was killed, after which they warned the herders not to return."

capacity with the Swan Land and Cattle Company and then as a stock detective for the Wyoming Stock Growers Association. J. M. Carey, chairman of the association's secret committee in charge of the detective work, is said to have dismissed Horn as soon as he learned that he was more interested in liquidating men than in getting evidence for use in court. After Horn's dismissal by the association, some of the big cattlemen hired him to assassinate their enemies at five hundred dollars per head. John C. Coble and Ora Haley have often been identified as Horn's employers by hearsay, though not by any valid proof.

The 1895 murders of two small ranchers living on Horse Creek in the Laramie Mountains are usually credited to Horn. William Lewis was shot in the back three times in August, and Lewis' neighbor Fred Powell was shot from ambush the following month. Both had been suspected of stealing cattle. Horn was questioned about these deaths, but neither he nor anyone else was arrested. Two murders in Brown's Park, Colorado, in 1900 were also attributed to Horn by hearsay evidence. Then in July, 1901, Willie Nickell, a thirteen-year-old boy, was shot to death from ambush in the Iron Mountain section of the Laramie Mountains. Willie's father, Kels P. Nickell, carried two bad marks on his escutcheon: in a fight in 1890 he had slashed John C. Coble with a knife, and later he had introduced sheep into the cattle country around Iron Mountain. Apparently, the son was mistaken for the father. The son was large for his age, was wearing his father's hat and coat, was riding his father's horse, and was killed in the poor light of early dawn. A week after Willie was dry-gulched, the father, Kels Nickell, was shot in arm and hip from ambush. A few days after that, some of his sheep were clubbed.

Six months later, under the influence of liquor, Horn boasted to Deputy United States Marshal Joe LeFors that he had killed Willie Nickell. Unknown to Horn, two witnesses, Deputy United States Marshal Les E. Snow and court stenographer Charles J. Ohnhaus, were listening through a crack in the door; Ohnhaus made a stenographic record of the LeFors-Horn conversation. On the strength of this unsigned "confession," Horn was found guilty and was hanged in the Laramie County jail in November, 1903. The best legal talent in the state (John W. Lacey, Timothy F. Burke, R. N. Matson, T. Blake Kennedy, Nellis E. Corthell) could not save him. Looking back on the affair a half-century later, Federal Judge T. Blake Kennedy confided in his memoirs that, while he did not like to lose the case, "probably it was good riddance."

There was much excitement in southeastern Wyoming at the time of the Horn trial, imprisonment, and execution. Many people thought his employers could not afford to let him hang, lest in his last moments he name them. In his memoirs, Fenimore Chatterton, who was acting governor during Horn's last months, recalled that he received many letters threatening his life if he did not commute the sentence, that prominent politicians and cattlemen pleaded with him for commutation, and that one "emissary of the cattlemen" said: "Governor, there is a hundred thousand dollar fund ready to defeat any political ambition you have, if you do not commute the sentence." Horn escaped once, but was recaptured. He never named his employers, although it was common knowledge that John C. Coble was the "pay-off man," as Chatterton called him.

PUBLIC LANDS

The public lands, which comprised more than five-sixths of Wyoming's area at the turn of the century, were constantly involved in controversy. It is often said that eastern congressmen have never understood western needs and have saddled the West with improper land laws. There is an element of truth in this, because most of the land laws have been better suited to a humid area than to a semiarid region like Wyoming. The root of the problem lay in the fact that it was virtually impossible for a stockman, within the law, to get possession of enough land for his needs. It took much scheming, scrambling, and perjury to assemble the acreage needed for a sound ranch operation.

In trying to acquire control of the land they needed, Wyoming ranchers behaved much as did ranchers in neighboring states. The United States attorney for Wyoming, Timothy F. Burke, was reported by an Interior Department special agent in 1906 to have justified his failure to prosecute for land frauds by saying that "inasmuch as three-fourths of the public domain had been proved up by perjury, to let them have it; that the paying of taxes was enough punishment for the deed, and what the State needed was the land on the tax rolls to reduce taxes."

It won't do to blame eastern congressmen for all the inadequacies of the land laws. It should not be overlooked that westerners normally could not reach a consensus about their needs. They often disagreed violently about the terms of land laws and their administration. Had the advice from the West been less confused, some of the difficulties might have been avoided.

It is regrettable that Wyoming cattlemen, as discussed in Chapter 7, scorned the 1879 proposal that they buy large blocks of land at five cents an acre or pay one-half cent per acre for long-term leases. Had the pioneer cattlemen supported the proposition and had Congress approved it, there would have been much less grief later for all concerned. In time, the leasing idea attracted advocates among Interior Department officials and cattlemen, large and small. Leasing had an advantage over outright ownership, since ownership entailed taxation.

Governor William A. Richards told the 1897 legislature that about four-fifths of the state had no value except for pasturage. He suggested that if the state could control the grazing lands and lease them to farmers and stockmen at a low rental, it would reduce overgrazing, lower taxes, and end the range conflict. A few months later the Wyoming delegation in Congress unsuccessfully asked for a five-million-acre federal donation of grazing lands to the state. The proposal was looked upon by many in Washington and Wyoming as a land grab by monopolistic cattlemen who would control leasing of the land by the state. It was recalled that Senator Warren had proposed the cession of arid lands to the states in 1891 and 1892, with provision for leasing land not occupied by small settlers. "Warren's land steal" had been the cry at that time, and the new proposal in 1897 was likewise viewed with suspicion.

Wyoming Democratic editors in 1897 and 1898 denounced Republican methods of leasing state lands, pointing in particular to the lease of twenty-two thousand acres to J. M. Carey & Brother in Natrona County. Republican editor E. A. Slack joined the Democrats in calling this a "Carey land grab scheme." Obviously, many people in the state refused to recognize the fact that the cattle business required large units for efficient operation.

By 1899 an increasing number of big cattlemen were coming to recognize that their best chance to survive the sheep invasion lay in leasing federal grazing lands. A well-known Cheyenne stock raiser, J. W. Hammond, said in August, 1899: "We, the cattlemen of Wyoming, thought at first we could not afford to have the arid lands; now we realize that we cannot afford to do without them." The National Live Stock Association's convention at Fort Worth in January, 1900, adopted a resolution "that such of the public lands of the United States as are adapted for grazing should be subject to lease by stockmen . . . at reasonable rental." In retrospect, a program of leasing the public lands, either under federal or state control, deserved wider support than it had in 1900. The cutthroat competition between cattlemen and sheepmen on the one hand and between sheepmen and sheepmen on the other (the latter was almost as vicious as the former) could lead only to overgrazing, sheep slaughter, and homicide.

Senator Warren recognized the merit of a leasing program, but the warring groups at home withheld general support. Old suspicions of the cattle barons would not down. Many sheepmen and some small cattlemen thought that their interests would suffer under leasing. They feared that the big cattlemen and a few privileged sheep kings would be the principal beneficiaries of leasing, whether it was by the federal government or the state.

Governors of western states, meeting in Salt Lake City in April, 1900, passed a resolution in opposition to federal leasing; they preferred cession to the states and state administration of the public lands. An outspoken advocate of cession was Governor DeForest Richards of Wyoming.

A federal public-lands commission which made a study of public-land policies in 1904–1905 consisted of William A. Richards of Wyoming as chairman, F. H. Newell, and Gifford Pinchot. As in 1879–1880, members of the commission traveled extensively in the West, took voluminous testimony, and tabulated responses to a circular letter. Of the 1,400 stockmen replying, 1,090 wanted some form of government control. Among the 218 Wyoming graziers who responded to the circular were 76 who raised cattle and horses, 50 cattlemen, 33 sheepmen, and 18 who ran both cattle and sheep. They favored federal control of grazing lands 175 to 23. In its first report, March 7, 1904, the commission made some revealing comments about the magnitude and complexity of the problems:

Often in any one State the conditions are so diverse that the man who argues for certain points is usually found to base his argument upon conditions which exist in his locality. If not limited by geographical environment the view point is almost always that of a special industry, such as sheep or cattle raising, irrigation, etc., and the arguments are based upon a knowledge of conditions which affect that industry. . . . The information obtained . . . discloses a prevailing opinion that the present land laws do not fit the conditions of the remaining public lands. Most of these laws and the departmental practices which have grown up under them were framed to suit the lands of the humid region. . . . In spite . . . of the recognition that the land laws might be improved, there is a general fear of change and a wide demand that the present laws be allowed to stand. This is due to dread of the introduction of unfamiliar requirements and to the fear that new enactments may recognize physical conditions even less than the present ones, and may be even less suited to the needs of the country. By the use of practices sanctioned by custom, the people have heretofore been able to get along fairly well; any change in their minds is associated with more difficult requirements, and they dread innovations which may hinder rather than help home making.

CONSERVATION

Another circumstance besides the bloody competition between cattlemen and sheepmen that pushed Wyoming graziers toward leasing was the national conservation movement, which gained momentum in the 1890's and crested in the administration of Theodore Roosevelt. Usually, conservation activities were frowned upon in Wyoming, and their leader, Gifford Pinchot, head of the Forest Service under Roosevelt, was often abused.[2]

In the 1890's, Presidents Harrison and Cleveland began a policy of setting aside forest reserves under authority of an act of Congress of March 3, 1891. Among the forest reserves established were the Yellowstone in 1891, the Big Horn and Uinta in 1897, the Medicine Bow in 1902, the Sierra Madre in 1906, and the Bear Lodge in 1907. At first, little attempt was made to regulate use of the new reserves. In 1902, however, Wyoming artist-rancher A. A. Anderson initiated a plan for converting the Yellowstone Forest Reserve and other land into the first real national forest of any size. An area of 9,500 square miles on all four sides of Yellowstone National Park was assigned to Anderson, who was named Special Forest Superintendent. He divided the reserve into four divisions—the Shoshone, Wind River, Absaroka, and Teton—each with its supervisor and rangers. He and his men began to limit the use of the forests, despite the bitter hostility of sheepmen. Most of the state's editors assailed Anderson. The *Meeteetse News* said: "Mr. Anderson can by a single stroke of his diamond-bedecked hand put out of existence that noble animal that clothes his unclean body." Anderson sued the

---

[2] Earlier, the Wyoming pioneers in the late 1870's and mid-1880's had been exasperated by restrictions placed on sawmill operators. Cheap native lumber, fence posts, and cordwood were important to the pioneers in country and town. Grumbled editor J. H. Hayford in May, 1879: "Nobody dares to bring a load of wood into town for sale now." And again in July, 1886, Hayford wrote: "The proper thing to do would be to take these 'stumpage collectors' and duck them in a horse pond for the first offense and hang them up to dry for a second." By 1878 law the pioneers were permitted to go out and cut enough for individual needs, but most of them were not in a position to do so. Thus they were embittered by conservation controls and stumpage fees imposed on sawmill operators. Then, in the 1890's, companies cutting ties on the public domain were in hot water.

News and extracted an apology. Gradually, with the hearty cooperation of Gifford Pinchot and Theodore Roosevelt, grazing excesses were eliminated in Anderson's bailiwick.

Restrictions on freedom to use the forests and the 1906 introduction of fees for grazing brought loud complaints from graziers, lumbermen, and miners until Congress, in 1907, barred forest extensions in Wyoming and five other western states without the consent of Congress. By that time, virtually all timbered areas in Wyoming outside Yellowstone National Park and some patches without timber had been placed in national forests—the area amounting to 8,998,723 acres on June 30, 1908. Limited in the number of permits they could get for grazing in the national forests and barred entirely from Yellowstone National Park, cattlemen and sheepmen competed more keenly than ever for the unreserved public domain.

CONSERVATION OF COAL AND OTHER MINERAL LANDS

The Theodore Roosevelt Administration gave attention to land frauds of all kinds, and did not spare the coal-mining companies in Wyoming. Since 1873, coal lands could be bought at not less than twenty dollars an acre if within fifteen miles of a completed railroad and not less than ten dollars an acre if more than fifteen miles from a railroad. However, only 160 acres could be bought by an individual and only 640 acres by an association or corporation. The Union Pacific Railroad had received much coal land in its land grant, but in order to round out its coal properties, it wanted to acquire some of the even-numbered sections retained by the government. Unable to buy lands in the quantities desired, the Union Pacific Coal Company used dummies, vagrants, and respectable citizens, much as the cattlemen had used their cowboys. The land was fraudulently acquired by assorted individuals for agricultural purposes and then transferred to the coal company. In other cases, individuals bought 160 acres of coal land, as they were entitled to do, and then transferred title.

In October, 1906, President Roosevelt directed the Department of Justice to institute legal proceedings against the Union Pacific Railroad to obtain restoration of extensive coal lands to public domain. This was eventually accomplished. Similar proceedings led to the recovery of other coal lands fraudulently acquired by the Wyoming Coal Company in Sheridan County, the Wyoming Coal & Coke Company in the Cumberland-Kemmerer district of western Wyoming, and the Owl Creek Coal Company at Gebo. In the last case, and perhaps others, the company emerged from its bout with the government possessed of a lease and an agreement to pay royalties.

While condemning fraudulent acquisition of coal lands through agricultural entries and fraudulent assignments, President Roosevelt in 1907 recognized the problem when he told Congress that "the present limitations have been absurd . . . and often render it necessary that there should be either fraud or else abandonment of the work of getting out the coal." Yet Congress persisted in retaining the limitations of 160 acres per individual and 640 acres per company.

Government land agents testified before the Interstate Commerce Commission at Salt Lake City in November, 1906, that they had been compelled to see Senator Francis E. Warren regarding official business of the General Land Office. Warren could not avoid suspicion whenever land frauds were aired in this period because he was considered mainly responsible for the appointment of Wyoming's William A. Richards as Commissioner of the General Land Office and the appointment of Wyoming's Willis Van Devanter as Assistant Attorney General for the Interior Department, in which position he was "the legal conscience of the land department" during the years 1897–1903.

Like Warren, Senator C. D. Clark and Representative Frank W. Mondell were much interested in furthering the Wyoming economy, which included, prominently, the Union Pacific Railroad and its subsidiary coal companies. Clark and Mondell probably understood coal problems even better than Warren did. Clark had worked for the Union Pacific Coal Department in territorial days. His older brother, Dyer O. Clark, was vice-president and general manager of the Union Pacific Coal Company from 1904 to 1911 and had worked for the Union Pacific in various capacities since 1868. Mondell knew the coal business first-hand, having developed coal properties at Cambria in the late 1880's.

To stop the acquisition of coal lands through agricultural entries, President Roosevelt, by executive order in 1906 and 1907, ordered 66,938,000 acres of land withdrawn from agricultural entry until it could be determined whether the land was underlain with merchantable coal. There were further withdrawals in the next few years. Some 17,000,000 acres of Wyoming land were tied up in this way for a few years, to the disgust of Representative Mondell, who protested violently against "locking up" the coal lands and blocking agricultural entries. Mondell asserted that the western coal industry was being paralyzed, coal-land prices were too high, monopoly was being fostered, and consumers would have to pay more for their coal. By November 1, 1910, Wyoming public lands totaling 4,213,508 acres had been classified as coal lands. A few million more acres were added in the next few years. On July 1, 1913, the government had 7,180,509 acres of coal lands listed in Wyoming at an average price of $53.20 per acre. In the meantime, much of the land temporarily withdrawn had been classified as noncoal and reopened to agricultural entry.

In his 1907 report, Commissioner of the General Land Office Richard A. Ballinger had recommended that surface rights and coal rights be separated, so that farmers and ranchers could file on the land under the agricultural laws while the government could retain the mineral rights for future leasing. Representative Mondell introduced a bill providing for this separation, and it became law March 3, 1909. In his memoirs, Mondell stated that he took greater pride in this law than in any other law for which he was responsible. Certainly it did represent a significant forward step.

As of November 1, 1910, the Interior Department, in other phases of its conservation program, had in Wyoming 1,267,494 acres of phosphate-land withdrawals outstanding, 243,334 acres of oil-land withdrawals, and 84,655 acres of power-site withdrawals.

ENCLOSING PUBLIC LAND

Fencing government land had become common practice in the 1880's. The first Cleveland administration applied considerable pressure and succeeded temporarily in discouraging the practice. For a decade thereafter, little attention was paid to the fencers and they enclosed much land illegally. In the last days of Cleveland's second term, in February, 1897, a special agent of the Interior Department notified ranchers in the vicinity of Lusk to remove unlawful fences. Pressure, however, eased under McKinley.

Two months after President Roosevelt took office, Addison A. Spaugh, on November 21, 1901, was charged in federal district court in Cheyenne with illegally enclosing 225,000 acres near Manville. Settlers had complained, and he had been indicted by a grand jury. Spaugh was convicted by the trial jury. Judge John A. Riner postponed sentence until January 2, 1902, implying that leniency could be expected if the fences were removed in the meantime. After Spaugh had taken down the fences, Riner gave him a token sentence of one day in jail and a fifty-dollar fine.

Federal officials at the time threatened an all-out prosecution of "land grabbers" and caused so much concern that the Wyoming Stock Growers Association, in convention the following April, passed a resolution petitioning President Roosevelt to stay further proceedings until the leasing of public lands could be worked out. The resolution stated that the 1885 law against fences on public lands had never been generally enforced and that sweeping government action would cause financial panic, since bankers would lend money only on fenced cattle and would call in loans, "ruining countless homemakers." Nevertheless in the year ending June 30, 1902, proceedings had been instituted against twenty-three Wyoming outfits which special agents said had 950,000 acres unlawfully fenced. Then on February 1, 1903, William A. Richards, former governor of Wyoming, moved up from Assistant Commissioner to Commissioner of the General Land Office. With Richards in that position in Washington and with Timothy F. Burke, another friend of the stockmen, as United States attorney in Cheyenne, pressure on the Wyoming fencers let up appreciably, although stockmen in other states, such as Nebraska, were not so fortunate.

Senator Francis E. Warren, to whom Richards and Burke and the people in the Cheyenne Land Office all owed their jobs, should have been as free as anyone from danger of investigation, yet enemies of the Senator kept talking about his fences. In the 1905 legislature, Democratic State Senator S. A. D. Keister of Fremont County presented a resolution asking for an investigation of charges against Warren. Instead of acting on the Keister resolution, the legislature, which was overwhelmingly Republican, adopted a memorial repudiating the "malicious resolutions" and expressing "entire confidence in the wisdom, patriotism, integrity and fidelity of our Senator Warren." Late that same year, however, Secretary of the Interior E. A. Hitchcock detailed Inspector E. B. Linnen and Special Agent W. C. Hintz to investigate complaints against Warren. Their findings were summed up in the "Linnen Report," which was submitted to Hitchcock on September 7, 1906.[3] The report stated that the Warren Livestock Company had 46,330 acres of government land unlawfully enclosed in Laramie County and 1,120 acres in Weld County, Colorado, and that the enclosures had been maintained for twenty years or more. The report said further that William A. Richards, Commissioner of the General Land Office, must have known about the unlawful fencing when he was governor of Wyoming and that prosecution could not be expected from United States Attorney Timothy F. Burke. The report

[3] The Linnen Report is included in *House Report 1335*, 62 Cong., 3 Sess.

included assorted affidavits, such as one by a Mrs. D. Mantey stating that "persons who have filed within the Warren Live Stock Company's pastures have been persecuted . . . and have been run off the land; their fences have been cut . . . and they have been compelled to sell out or move out." The Warren Livestock Company had been notified in October, 1905, to remove the unlawful fences but had done nothing about it.

Ordinarily, such a report would have led to court action, but that was not to be the case in this instance. Secretary Hitchcock may have been thinking of Warren when he wrote in his annual report on November 30, 1906, that in his efforts to protect the public domain, "I have not considered either the station or the power of the guilty . . . [and] the higher the offender the greater the crime against society and law, because of the force and influence of the higher example." Although he was able to send United States Senator John H. Mitchell of Oregon to jail for land frauds, he could not even initiate an action against Warren. When he got wind of the Linnen Report, Warren wrote his good friend Theodore Roosevelt denying the charges and asking that Hitchcock be stopped from issuing news stories about the matter. President Roosevelt complied with Warren's request. He referred the Linnen Report to the Justice Department, where it was discredited on various grounds, one of them being that one of the fences involved probably was not Warren's, although it served the purpose of enclosing government land for Warren.

The Justice Department decided that no good case had been made against Warren. At the time Roosevelt reported this to Secretary Hitchcock, January 26, 1907, he told him that Timothy Burke's reappointment had become impossible "because he evidently has not been in hearty, zealous sympathy with the enforcement of the laws against the parties guilty of illegal inclosure of public lands." For reasons not published, William A. Richards resigned as Commissioner of the General Land Office, effective March 4, 1907. Timothy Burke was reappointed after eloquent pleas in his behalf by Warren, Clark, and Mondell.

As a rule, President Roosevelt was not inclined to be lenient with unlawful fencers. Although he wanted no embarrassment for his friend Senator Warren, the President had now become fully aware of the situation in Wyoming. The Linnen Report, which dealt mainly with Warren, mentioned incidentally that thirty-four or thirty-five others, such as Governor B. B. Brooks, John Arbuckle, Colin & Hunter, R. S.

Van Tassell, Ora Haley, and Dr. John Carey (J. M.'s brother) had about half a million acres of government land unlawfully under fence. In January, 1907, all special agents and local land officials were notified that the 1885 law would be enforced. All unlawful fences must be removed before April 1, 1907. President Roosevelt and his successor, President Taft, meant business; lawsuits were instituted, and the fences came down at last. A dozen or more Wyoming men (Warren was not one of them) were given token one-day jail sentences, very lenient treatment indeed, considering that the 1885 law authorized punishment up to a fine of one thousand dollars and a year in jail.

As long as Republicans controlled both houses of Congress, as they did from 1895 to 1911, it was not to be expected that Senator Warren would be investigated in Congress for his alleged fencing activities. In 1911, however, the Democrats finally got control of the House, though not of the Senate. So much public fuss had been made about Warren's fences that the House Democrats could not resist looking into the matter. They timed their probe so that their findings could be released to the press during the 1912 campaign. Then, in 1913, their final report was published as House Report No. 1135.

The House committee charged with investigating Warren's activities was the Committee on Expenditures in the Interior Department. The committee printed Linnen's 1906 report in full. The four Democrats on the committee concluded that at the time of the Linnen Report, the Warren Livestock Company was maintaining unlawful enclosures. The two Republicans on the committee, Frank W. Mondell and Charles H. Burke, filed a minority report, in which they said that there was no claim of any unlawful enclosure within the past six years, that the case had not been proved in 1906, and that the investigation was started in 1912 to embarrass Warren just before the 1912 election.

Deprived of their unlawful fences, cattlemen and a few big sheepmen like Warren looked on leasing with more favor than they had before. In a stormy session in April, 1907, the Wyoming Stock Growers Association passed resolutions in favor of leasing of the federal range at fees varying from one-half cent to one and one-half cents per acre. Governor Brooks tried his best to block the resolutions. At the National Live Stock Association convention in Denver in January, 1908, a letter from Gifford Pinchot was read declaring that whatever men of the West wanted in regard to government control and leasing would be done. The convention voted $386\frac{1}{2}$ to $39\frac{1}{2}$ for a leasing policy. The Wyoming Stock Growers Association in convention in April, 1908, approved "some plan to put the . . . unoccupied public domain under control of the department of agriculture for grazing purposes, under some form of individual lease, or community permit, dependent upon the demands of the stockgrowers of given sections." They suggested grazing fees of one-half to one and one-half cents per acre or a fair per-head charge.

Meanwhile, the sheepmen continued to be overwhelmingly against leasing. The Wyoming Wool Growers Association in January, 1907, resolved that the passage of a leasing law "will result in the grossest abuses . . . and . . . will retard the development of the state and . . . will result in interminable litigation, dispute and expense." Congressman Frank Mondell declared in December, 1907, that "a large majority of western people believe that any kind of a federal leasing system would seriously endanger the settlement and development of the west." In January, 1908, Wyoming wool growers reiterated their opposition to leasing. They endorsed the work of Senator Clarence D. Clark and Congressman Frank Mondell in opposition to Pinchot's policies. They condemned the *Wyoming State Tribune* and the *Laramie Republican* for supporting Pinchot, explaining that their editors (W. C. Deming and William E. Chaplin) held positions in the Cheyenne Land Office. Senator Warren, the state's leading wool grower and president of the National Wool Growers Association, was not mentioned, for the good reason that he had approved Roosevelt's leasing policy. In January, 1908, the National Wool Growers Association retired Warren from the presidency. News reports from the Helena convention said that Warren had lost all of his former supporters except the Wyoming delegation, "and even in that there are dissenters." George S. Walker, secretary of the association, gathered fifty thousand names on a petition which viewed with alarm the leasing of the public domain and other Pinchot policies. More than four hundred Cheyenne names were included on the petition, which was forwarded to Congressman Mondell in February, 1908.

In his message to the 1909 legislature, Governor B. B. Brooks praised the Homestead Act and condemned leasing, charging that it would retard settlement. Thereafter, the leasing question continued to be discussed hotly for several years. A good many leasing bills were introduced in Congress, only to die in committee. The dry farmers who flocked to the state in years 1909–1913 followed Mondell's lead in opposing leasing. The 1913 legislature approved a memorial asking Congress not to enact into law a bill providing for the leasing of public lands. Governor Carey vetoed the memorial, however, with the statement that he believed that the interests of the people of Wyoming would best be served if the remaining public lands were leased. In 1913, Congressman Frank Mondell proposed a 1,280-acre grazing-homestead law. Three years later, in 1916, grazing homesteads were made available, but they were limited to 640 acres and the federal government retained the mineral rights.

Wild game animals and men who pursued them contributed to the huggermugger on the range. Although game laws had been on the books since 1869, not until 1899 was a state game warden provided for, and for some years he and his deputies were inadequate for the task at hand. "Tusk hunters," who killed bull elk for their tusks, which they sold as Elks Lodge emblems, so enraged Jackson Hole citizens in 1905–1906 that they organized vigilantes. In 1907 the legislature assisted by making the killing of big game for tusks, antlers, or heads a felony. As the threat of the tuskers declined, the elk, given a few mild winters, multiplied too fast for the available range. The spread of ranching and fencing in Jackson Hole and the upper Green River Valley, coupled with a hard winter in 1909–1910, brought a legislative decision to introduce large-scale winter-feeding programs. State and federal game preserves and refuges and game-management programs were soon inaugurated.[4]

In retrospect, there was more going on, and more chaos, on the Wyoming range in the years 1898–1914 than in all other years of Wyoming history taken together. Out of it all, a pattern could be seen emerging. Cattle, sheep, and big game rather than irrigators and dry farmers would occupy most of the range for the foreseeable future. Conservation of timber, minerals, and big game in the national interest became permanent policy in Washington, and permanent also became state-federal friction over programs designed to implement conservation policy.

---

[4] See James P. Blaisdell, "A History of the Conservation Effort in Wyoming and the Wyoming Game and Fish Commission to 1950" (Unpublished M.A. thesis, University of Wyoming, 1964), for a full account of game and fish problems and solutions.

CHAPTER 13

The First World War

WHEN AUSTRIA DECLARED WAR on Serbia on July 28, 1914, the *Laramie Republican* editor (W. E. Chaplin) observed that "if a general war is brought on in Europe the waste will be tremendous. It will take years of 'trimming' American tourists to get the money back." Two weeks later, after the great powers Germany, Russia, France, and Great Britain had joined the war, Chaplin recognized that "it will probably prove to be the greatest war known in history."

Wyoming seemed a long way from the battle front in the first months of the war. With Germany generally regarded as the aggressor and with only 2,500 German-born in the state, the Allies received sympathy from the beginning. In the fall of 1914 there was a state-wide drive to

386

raise money with which to purchase flour for destitute Belgians, whose country had been overrun by the Germans. The Wyoming Federation of Women's Clubs organized the state for participation in a Red Cross tag day on which about $2,500 was raised for the war-relief fund. No one in Wyoming in 1914, 1915, and 1916 appeared anxious to take an active part in the war, and the great majority supposed that the United States could remain aloof while enjoying rising prosperity.

THE ELECTION OF 1914

In the early months of 1914, leading Republican editors, such as W. C. Deming of the *Wyoming State Tribune*, W. E. Chaplin of the *Laramie Republican*, and A. J. Mokler of the *Casper Tribune*, promoted reconciliation between Progressives and regular Republicans. The peacemakers did not go so far as to propose a place for J. M. Carey on the Republican ticket, but they were much interested in making sure that the nine thousand who had preferred Roosevelt to Taft in 1912 would support regular Republican candidates in 1914. On the whole, they succeeded.

Four parties—Republican, Democratic, Progressive, and Socialist— entered candidates for state offices, although the last two won few votes. The Progressives advanced candidates for four of the state's elective offices, but not for the governorship. They chose to support the Democratic candidate for governor, John B. Kendrick, a Sheridan County rancher who had distinguished himself as a state senator in 1911 and 1913. Principal opposition for Kendrick came from the Warren Machine man, Hilliard S. Ridgely, a lawyer whom Buffalo Bill had brought from Nebraska in 1903 to be his personal representative in Cody. Ridgely had later moved to Basin and then to Cheyenne.

Kendrick defeated Ridgely 22,387 to 19,174, winning his home county by a margin of more than two thousand votes and in general carrying the north, while Ridgely won all of the Union Pacific counties. Kendrick was especially attractive to the stockmen because he was one of them. In the north, people made much of the opinion that it was time for that section to have a governor, while they called Ridgely a tool of the Union Pacific. The Republicans were criticized for voting frauds they were alleged to have perpetrated in Lincoln County in 1912. On the whole, however, there was little bitterness, in sharp contrast to the campaigns of 1910 and 1912.

Frank L. Houx, incumbent Democratic secretary of state, was returned to that office by a mere 120-vote margin. Otherwise the

Republicans were victorious. They re-elected their perennial congressman, Frank W. Mondell, won three of the five state elective positions,
and continued their traditional control of the legislature, winning the
Senate 18–9 and the House 42–15.

During the 1914 campaign, Republican editors remarked that Kendrick spoke in a slow, halting manner and that he was willing to spend
generous amounts of his considerable personal fortune in order to win.
They conceded that he never abused his opponent or indulged in per-
sonalities, yet complained that he placed the newspapers he controlled
under no such restraints. But they accepted Kendrick's victory with
equanimity, approving of his long residence in the state, his business
success, and his reputation for courage. The Democrats, of course,
couldn't say too much for their hero. They had finally found a leader
whom they could call their own, one worthy of high office and able to
win. Four years earlier, after many years of frustration, they had looked
over the field, had seen no one who could inspire confidence, and had,
with some reluctance, embraced the outcast Republican, Carey. Kendrick was a "Woodrow Wilson type man . . . quiet, unassuming,
sincere," said James L. Kilgallen, editor of the *Laramie Boomerang*, which
was owned by Democrats at the time.

The new governor was just the type of Democrat who could get
along with a Republican legislature, since there was nothing in his
political philosophy to distinguish him from a regular Republican.
Only the accident of Texas birth, it seems, can account for his being a
Democrat. He was a tall, rugged man with a square jaw, a plain "man
of the people" whose formal education had ended in the seventh grade.
As a cattleman and as past president of the Wyoming Stock Growers Association, he had many Republican friends in and out of the
legislature.

As the 1915 legislative session approached, there was no editorial
attempt to stir up trouble between Democratic governor and Republican legislature. To the credit of both Democrats and Republicans,
partisanship, which had been so rampant two years before, was subdued
in 1915. The *Wyoming State Tribune* (W. C. Deming and John Charles
Thompson) even undertook to reconcile J. M. Carey and the regular
Republicans.

Governor Kendrick's message to the 1915 legislature was concise and
matter of fact—less than half as long as either of J. M. Carey's messages. There was nothing to suggest that the speaker knew he was
talking to an audience predominantly of a different political party. He
congratulated the legislators and the people upon the satisfactory

condition of the state's affairs and its institutions, noting, however, that Wyoming "is the one state capable of supporting a large population, that is without that population." He said that the rate of taxation "is already more or less excessive" and that "it is universally admitted that the expense of county government . . . is at present unwarranted." He warned against working a hardship on or incurring the hostility of any industry.

Rarely has a Republican governor, let alone a Democratic one, worked more harmoniously with a Republican legislature than Kendrick did in 1915. Most of what the Governor asked for, he got: workmen's-compensation act, public-utilities commission, constitutional amendment permitting farm-loan legislation, extension of women's rights, an elaborate game and fish law, authority for the Board of Equalization to equalize assessments, two new experimental farms, provision for removal of unfaithful county officers, amendment of the direct-primary law, and capitol-building extension (through a special levy).[1]

The Workmen's Compensation Act, which covered extra-hazardous occupations, except for railroads engaged in interstate commerce, was properly hailed as very important, although its schedule of payments was not very generous. For instance, a single man suffering total disability would receive a lump-sum payment of one thousand dollars. The legislature appropriated thirty thousand dollars to start the industrial-accident fund. Employers in extra-hazardous occupations were required to pay into the fund a sum equal to 2 per cent of the wages they paid. In the next legislature, it was possible to discontinue state appropriations and to reduce the percentage paid by employers because withdrawals from the fund had been small.

The livestock industry and farming were not covered by the Workmen's Compensation Act.[2] Editor Chaplin of the *Laramie Republican* grumbled in October, 1919, that the range business was much more hazardous than printing, which was included. Chaplin went on to

---

[1] Thus the third phase of capitol construction was authorized. In her *Wyoming Historical Blue Book* (Denver: Bradford-Robinson Printing Co., 1946), pp. 1365–1369, Marie H. Erwin gives a detailed history of the capitol. David W. Gibbs of Toledo, Ohio, was architect for the first unit, built of Rawlins and Fort Collins stone in 1887–1888. He also drew the plans for the second unit, consisting of the first east and west wings, added in 1888–1890. William B. Dubois of Cheyenne was architect for the second set of east and west wings, which were added in 1915–1917.

[2] Dr. Edmund L. Escolas, in an article entitled "Wyoming's Workmen's Compensation System, 1915–1960," *Wyoming Trade Winds*, IV, 10 (December 1961), 8, writes: "Coverage of occupations to Wyoming's Workmen's Compensation Act represented a political compromise of dominant economic groups. In a frontier economy dominated

explain that the rural representatives who controlled the 1915 legislature had stated frankly that they would kill any bill including the farm and stock business.

Governor Kendrick signed 161 bills, modified the general-appropriations bill only slightly, and vetoed eight bills. Only one of his vetoes attracted much attention—the bill would have legalized twenty-round boxing matches.

Governor Kendrick's only notable setback at the hands of the legislature came on the last night of the session when he failed to get a $24,000 item inserted in the general-appropriations bill to pay the expenses of the state immigration commission for the ensuing two years. The legislature gave him everything, said the *Snake River Sentinel*, "but the power to appoint some worthless officeseeker to the position of commissioner of an immigration bureau."

Remarkably, in his message to the 1915 legislature Governor Kendrick said not one word about the war, which was then in its seventh month. And no act passed by the legislature was war connected, unless one can so construe an appropriation of $2,100 for the purchase of uniforms for public-school cadet organizations.

On June 3, 1916, Congress passed the National Defense Act, authorizing expansion of the National Guard. War Department orders followed on June 19, 1916, for the mobilization of two battalions of the Wyoming National Guard for service in patrolling the Mexican border. After training at Fort Warren, the Guardsmen departed for the Mexican border on September 28, 1916.

As the war entered its third year in the fall of 1916, no one in Wyoming appeared to take seriously the possibility of United States involvement. Germany was observing its May, 1916, pledge not to sink merchant vessels without warning. Neither Woodrow Wilson nor Charles Evans Hughes, the major candidates in the 1916 presidential election, showed any inclination to take the United States into war.

THE ELECTION OF 1916

When Theodore Roosevelt and the national committee of the Progressive party chose to support Republican candidate Charles E. Hughes in 1916, the weak Progressive party became inactive in

---

by extensive agriculture, cattle and sheep raising with coal mining predominant along the line of the Union Pacific Railroad, Wyoming's Legislature satisfied both of these interests . . . by exempting agriculture while adopting the proposals of the coal operators."

Wyoming. With no avowed Progressive candidates in the state campaign, Republican leaders expected to do better than they had done in 1912. Wyoming people, however, liked the Democratic slogan, "He

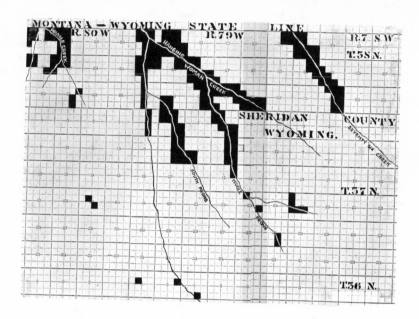

GOVERNOR KENDRICK'S TEN-THOUSAND-ACRE LAND PURCHASE

kept us out of war," and handed Woodrow Wilson a plurality of 6,500. But Wilson was not able to carry with him to victory John D. Clark, Cheyenne lawyer, who lost the race for Congress to the veteran Frank W. Mondell by 537 votes.

In the state's first popular election of a United States senator, Governor John B. Kendrick defeated incumbent Clarence D. Clark by more than three thousand votes. Kendrick was charged with having violated the Wyoming Corrupt Practices Act in the campaign. He had filed a statement listing his 1912 Senate campaign expenditures at about nine thousand dollars, when the Corrupt Practices Act limited him to three thousand dollars (20 per cent of the Senate salary). This was done "unwittingly," explained Kendrick. The Governor was also criticized for not resigning the governorship until after his election as senator. The state constitution was often quoted: "Nor shall he be eligible to any other office during the term for which he was elected." This argument against Kendrick "fell rather flat," recalled Frank Mondell in his memoirs, in view of the precedent set by Francis E. Warren in 1890.

Keeping alive the Warren-Carey feud, Joseph M. Carey chose to campaign for Kendrick, as he had done in 1912 and 1914. Republican newspapers pictured Kendrick as an "enormously wealthy" man as opposed to the "poor, honest public servant" Clark. Kendrick's land acquisitions were scrutinized. He had bought 9,666 acres of state lands in November, 1915, while governor and president of the state land board, apparently in ignorance of the state law which said that state lands "shall not be sold to any member of the board." Just before the election, Republican papers published reproductions of a large, carefully prepared map showing how the 9,666 acres had been selected, often in forty-acre parcels, to control the waters of Waddle Creek, Hanging Woman Creek, and Seventy Six Creek in northern Sheridan County. Democrats replied that Warren, too, had bought state lands. Republicans countered that Warren had not been a member of the state land board at the time of his purchase and that "Warren's purchase did not run down a lot of streams in such a way as to gobble up ten times the amount of land his state leases and purchase covered."

The cattleman governor was too colorful and popular for the Warren Machine to defeat, at least in a year when President Wilson had such a large following in the state. That the Democratic tide was running stronger than usual was shown in the returns for the legislature. The Democrats picked up seats in both houses, but still had to accept Republican majorities, 16–11 in the Senate and 32–25 in the House.

Cheyenne attorney T. Blake Kennedy, who in 1921 was rewarded with a federal judgeship for long and faithful service to the Republican party, later commented (in his memoirs)[3] on the 1916 campaign as follows:

I had a great deal to do not only in that campaign but in former campaigns in arranging the itinerary of the different speakers. . . . When handed an itinerary completely arranged as to detail Mondell would say when he arrived from Washington, "Well, that may be all right but I thought that a different plan for me would be better;" pulling a completely new itinerary out of his pocket

[3] In typescript in the University of Wyoming Library.

and no matter what we could say or do he would insist on following his own plan regardless of our advice in regard to where he would be able to do the most good. Senator Clark would whine and almost cry like a baby when shown his itinerary which might include some outlying districts rather difficult of approach and say, "Blake, I can't do that. That's too much of a trip for me. I'm an old man;" but eventually he would accept his schedule and fulfill it nobly. Senator Warren when approached and handed his schedule would never look at it but say, "When do we start and what is my first stop?" This analysis rather indicates the individual character of the three men.

THE 1917 LEGISLATURE

Governor Kendrick, who would go to the United States Senate on March 4, 1917, chose to continue as governor through the state legislative session before permitting Secretary of State Frank L. Houx to become acting governor. Once again, as in 1915, his relations with the Republican legislature must arouse the envy of other governors who have had to deal with legislatures in which their own party was in the minority. As before, appointments received unanimous approval. Among four vetoes, the only one of particular note was a bill raising salaries of state elective officers.

As in 1915, the Governor's message was short, cautious, and unexciting. The assembly was told that not much legislation was needed, since "our state has kept abreast of the times." Like Carey before him, Kendrick indulged in no blarney about remarkable prosperity and progress. He stressed the "extreme importance of economizing." He recommended adoption of a budget system such as "has recently been introduced in several of the states."

It was time, after the 1915 state census, to reapportion seats in the legislature. Kendrick suggested reduction in the size of the legislature, which he said could be accomplished by allowing one senator to each county and either one or two representatives, depending on population. No other Wyoming governor has gone so far in favoring county equality.

Kendrick, who had said nothing about prohibition in 1915, now favored it. The drys had sent many petitions to the 1915 legislature, and a few prohibition bills had been introduced without success. By 1917 the national trend toward prohibition had become stronger. When he asked that the people be given a chance to vote on the question, Kendrick said: "Wyoming stands in a vast dry area, as the one state which permits the sale of intoxicants with little or no restriction."

As in 1915, Kendrick ignored the war. Except for a statement that legislation was required to qualify the Wyoming National Guard for federal recognition and aid under the June, 1916, National Defense Act, there was nothing in the message even remotely connected with the war.

Kendrick was able to get most, though by no means all, of the things he asked for. He did not get a budget system, a Blue Sky Law, immigration promotion, taxation of mortgages and securities, and his reapportionment scheme. Population was given more consideration than land in the reapportionment, which assigned four counties two senators apiece and one to each of the others, and varied the number of representatives from one to six.

The legislature petitioned Congress for a grant of two million acres of land, which was to be sold and the proceeds used for loans to qualified settlers on irrigable lands. The petition recognized the impasse reached in the state's reclamation work by stating that hundreds of thousands of acres under completed irrigation systems were unoccupied. A revolving fund was deemed essential for "the new settler in the arduous costly task of transforming raw, sagebrush land into an irrigated farm."

WAR

The First World War, which had seemed so remote for two and one-half years, suddenly threatened to involve the United States when on January 31, 1917, the German government announced termination of its *Sussex* pledge. German submarines henceforth would sink all vessels on sight in a specified zone around the British Isles and in the Mediterranean. When United States claims of neutral rights were rejected, President Wilson broke off diplomatic relations, still hoping, however, to avoid war.

In these critical days, Wyoming was quite clearly less isolationist than the Middle West. Pacifists were scarce in Wyoming, apart from the fourteen hundred unobtrusive citizens who had voted Socialist in 1916. Some two thousand German-Americans were probably hoping for continued neutrality, yet they said little publicly. Actions of the legislature give us some idea of how most of the people felt. The legislature unanimously approved a resolution in favor of conscription before Congress acted on it, and also unanimously passed a resolution commending President Wilson for severing diplomatic relations with Germany. Thus war clouds brought no strife to a peaceful legislative session, which was brought to a close after a statement by minority leader W. H. Holliday testifying to "the absolute harmony which has prevailed during the session."

The United States teetered on the brink of war as German submarines sank five American ships in the month of March. Although expecting war, Wyoming people were much less excited than people in the East, apparently because distance from the seacoast offered insulation and security. On March 26, 1917, a second battalion of the Wyoming National Guard was ordered into federal service, along with other National Guardsmen in the nation.

Responding to a presidential request, Congress, on April 6, 1917, declared war on the Central Powers. Patriotism, hitherto quite subdued, erupted all over the state as there were mass meetings, flag displays, and resolutions in support of the President. Newspapers carried a large front-page picture of Uncle Sam pointing a compelling finger at the reader and saying: "You! Enlist today. Your Country Needs You!" Many young men did enlist. Sheridan, for example, was reported to have set a record with forty-nine navy enlistments in a few days.

In late April the *Chicago Tribune* polled congressmen and senators on their views with respect to conscription, soon after President Wilson requested it. Warren was for it, Kendrick was noncommittal, and Mondell was opposed. All three, however, voted for the Selective Service Act of May 18, 1917.

The nation surprised the enemy with the dispatch with which it supplied fighting men, food, raw materials, equipment, and munitions. Except for the last two categories, Wyoming contributed its share and more.

Approximately 12,000 Wyoming men entered military service— about 6 per cent of the population. This was somewhat above the national average, which was to be expected since the state had more men than women. Washakie County, with more than 10 per cent of its population in uniform, claimed to lead the nation, and similar claims were made for Natrona County. Of 8,279 Wyoming draftees who were examined, 78.85 per cent were accepted for active service. Only Oklahoma and Arkansas had higher percentages. The state was credited with having 3,948 volunteers in service in addition to the draftees.

After training at Fremont, California, Wyoming National Guardsmen went to France in December, 1917, as part of the Forty-first, or Sunset, Division. Most of the Wyoming soldiers who enlisted or were drafted received their training at Camp Lewis, Washington, and joined the Ninety-first Division, which was used as a replacement pool after it landed in France in July, 1918.

Two regiments of cavalry were stationed at Fort D. A. Russell (Cheyenne) for a time during the war. In anticipation of the departure of the cavalry, the War Department in June, 1918, proposed the establishment of home-guard companies to handle any trouble which might arise in the absence of troops. Under Major George M. Sliney of Thermopolis, seven home-guard companies were organized at Basin, Casper, Laramie, Newcastle, Sheridan, Thermopolis, and Wheatland.

The names of 468 Wyoming servicemen who died during the war appear on the bronze memorial tablet in the rotunda of the state capitol. The home-service department of the Red Cross compiled a list of 881 other Wyoming men who were wounded. The total number of American lives lost in the war was 125,500 out of a total of 4,800,000 men in service.

CENTRALIZED CONTROL

Virtually everything was directed from Washington during the nineteen months between America's declaration of war, April 6, 1917, and the Armistice, November 11, 1918. Congress gave the President extensive powers, which he delegated to many agencies, such as the War Industrial Board, the War Food Administration, the War Trade Board, and the Railroad Administration. The Council of National Defense, made up of six cabinet members and an advisory board of seven civilians, supervised the assorted boards. The Council of National Defense directed state councils, which in turn directed county councils. The Wyoming Council of National Defense was headed first by Dr. Henry G. Knight, dean of the College of Agriculture at the University of Wyoming, and later by Maurice Groshon of Cheyenne.

AGRICULTURE AND LIVESTOCK

Called upon to do so because allies of the United States could not produce what they needed, Wyoming farmers and ranchers stepped up their production to the limit. They enjoyed a few years of unprecedented prosperity, receiving magnificent prices for record yields. Wheat prices rose from 72¢ a bushel in 1913 to $1.98 in 1918, and production increased from 2,250,000 bushels to 6,600,000. In the same period, corn prices and production doubled. Oats and hay prices doubled, although production remained about the same. Cattle were estimated to number 552,000 and to be worth $21,721,000 on January 1, 1913. Numbers and values increased gradually until on January 1, 1919, there were 1,172,000 head valued at $73,824,000. In the same period, sheep numbers declined from 4,072,000 to 3,300,000.

The United States Employment Service, the United States Department of Agriculture, and the Wyoming Council of National Defense helped round up agricultural labor. Convicts from Rawlins helped with the Goshen County potato harvest in 1917. At a Cheyenne meeting of the Wyoming Council of National Defense in February, 1918, the labor shortage was said to be the state's most difficult problem. Saloons and poolrooms, it was reported, harbored many idle men who spurned the jobs offered them. Later that year, editor Watt Brandon of the *Cokeville Register* declared that demands of sheepshearers were "little less than the acts of highwaymen." Businessmen volunteers in Sheridan, Lander, Pine Bluffs, and other towns helped the farmers.

INDUSTRIAL DEVELOPMENT

Oil production doubled between 1916 and 1918, rising from about six million barrels to twelve and one-half million. Acting Governor Houx valued the gasoline marketed in 1917 at $37,500,000 and other oil products at $11,250,000. He listed 23 proven fields, 475 producing wells, and 5 refineries—2 at Casper, 2 at Greybull, and one at Cowley. The major producing fields were Salt Creek, Grass Creek, Elk Basin, and Big Muddy. Governor Houx proudly declared: "A minor industry of the state in 1912, the oil business in 1917 has become second in importance of Wyoming's industrial activities, ranking below agriculture only and representing a gross business only four per cent less than that of agriculture."

Coal production mounted rapidly to 8,800,000 tons in 1917 and to more than 9,000,000 tons in 1918. Major mines in production were at Rock Springs, Reliance, Superior, Hanna, Cumberland, Kemmerer, Gebo, Hudson, Cambria, and Sheridan. At Sunrise the Colorado Fuel and Iron Company extracted 600,000 tons of iron ore in 1917 and more than 1,000,000 tons in 1918 for its steel plant at Pueblo.

There was heavy traffic on Wyoming railroads, particularly on the Union Pacific. In December, 1917, the Union Pacific's general manager, William Jeffers, in an attempt to increase the efficiency of some of his workers, persuaded Governor Houx to appeal to mayors to close saloons at nine in the evening. Some, but not all, city governments complied. Ten days later the federal government took over the nation's railroads with assurances of fair compensation to the owners.

Sugar shortages, real or anticipated, led to the building of sugar factories at Sheridan in 1914, Lovell in 1916, and Worland in 1917. Half a dozen small flour, grain, and feed mills began production.

The state labor commissioner reported that labor conditions in 1917 and 1918 were "very satisfactory and encouraging," with jobs plentiful and wages rising. In 1918, coal miners were earning $4.98, refinery workers $4 to $5.50, painters $6, carpenters $7, and locomotive engineers $8.50 for an eight-hour day. Female stenographers were earning $10 to $35 per week, laundry workers $7 to $20. Wages scales generally would rise 35 per cent more in the next two years. In 1918 the commissioner estimated that there were fourteen thousand organized workers in the state, which he considered to be "very gratifying as compared with a few years ago, when organized labor was almost unheard of in Wyoming."

Home-Front Activities

"Four-Minute" speakers addressed public gatherings, recommending economy in the use of wheat, meat, and sugar. "Wheatless Mondays" and "Meatless Tuesdays" were proclaimed. "Hoover menus," so called because Herbert Hoover headed the War Food Administration, listed rye bread, no meat, and honey in place of sugar. Meatless days were soon discarded, but later a national request was made for a general reduction in the quantities of food prepared each day. On the whole, it seems probable that the customary diet of Wyoming citizens changed very little during the war.

Citizens gathered to give hearty send-offs to draftees, offering street demonstrations, band concerts, fireworks, suppers, dances, and farewell gifts. Governor Houx wrote to mayors in late September, 1917: "Complaints are coming to me from a great many different parts of the state that during the time of the departure of the last detachment of drafted men, many of them departed in an intoxicated condition." The mayors generally complied thereafter with the Governor's request that saloons be closed for a few hours before detachments left town. In October, 1917, the state adjutant general ordered all draftees and their luggage to be searched for liquor before they boarded the trains, although the state still remained wet.

Women were registered to facilitate using them as replacements for men in an emergency and to obtain pledges from them regarding food conservation. They entered the labor force in increasing numbers in 1918, some of them even doing heavy work in railroad shops. Housewives devoted much time to knitting and preparing bandages and other materials for hospitals under Red Cross supervision. Knitting needles clicked merrily in May, 1917, after the captains of the battleship *Wyoming* and the monitor *Cheyenne* asked for knitted vests, jackets, scarfs, and wristlets. Women did most of the work in collecting twenty thousand books for servicemen.

At the University of Wyoming, enrollment dwindled as men in the Reserve Officers Training Corps program left for training camps. President Aven Nelson, a devout Methodist, endeavored to stimulate patriotism and Christianity. He told the graduating class in June, 1918: "It is not presumption to think of our nation as the hand-maid of liberty, God's own instrument with which to scourge brutal might from the throne." On October 1, 1918, six weeks before the end of the war, a 174-man unit of the Student Army Training Corps was installed on the campus under the command of Captain Beverly C. Daly.

GENERAL PROSPERITY

"Never in the history of Wyoming has the entire people been more prosperous than now," said the *Laramie Republican* in September, 1917, adding six months later that "from every section of the state the same story comes. Wyoming is prospering as never before in its history." The state commissioner of labor and statistics reported November 1, 1918: "The two years which have elapsed since this office was established are without parallel in the history of the state." There can be no doubt that most people in the state prospered during the war. Inevitably, however, inflation favored some economic groups more than others as the cost of living in the United States increased 74.4 per cent between 1913 and 1918.

Government bonds were sold in five great drives, four during the war and one in the following spring. Like every other state in the Union, Wyoming oversubscribed all bond sales quotas. It stood thirteenth among the states in percentage of oversubscription, purchasing $23,621,700 worth of bonds in the four wartime drives. The bond interest rates were attractive, rising from 3.5 per cent in the first loan to 4.75 per cent in the fifth.

Three Laramie men, Captain Thurman Arnold, First Lieutenant Samuel H. Knight, and Ralph E. McWhinnie (a university student who served as business manager of the group), promoted the sale of Victory bonds by exhibiting a small tank in many communities, transporting the tank from town to town on a railway flatcar. Purchasers of bonds were rewarded with rides in or on the tank. The vehicle climbed over brick piles, entered and climbed out of excavations, and attracted large crowds wherever it went.

Between bond purchases, Wyoming citizens contributed an esti-mated $1,357,225 to the Red Cross, Y.M.C.A., Salvation Army, United War Work, and sundry forms of relief.

CONFORMITY AND INTOLERANCE

Because German-Americans, who often sympathized with the Cen-tral Powers, and Socialists, who were pacifist, were numerous in some parts of the country and because there was thought to be too much apathy and indifference, Congress early in the war created the Com-mittee on Public Information. This committee and other agencies sought to establish universal patriotism as they whipped up hatred of Germany. The propaganda was so persuasive that many excesses occurred.

Significant anti-Americanism seems to have been absent in Wyoming. Although none of the country's fifteen hundred arrests for espionage and sedition occurred in the state, many people apparently thought there were spies in Wyoming. Witness this statement by Casper editor A. J. Mokler: "The Standard and Midwest refineries had many extra guards at their plants, guards were stationed at the Pathfinder dam, railroad bridges were guarded and every precaution was taken against German spies, there being every reason to believe that quite a number were located in and around Casper."

Following a November 16, 1917, presidential proclamation, German aliens were registered by the police. Although aliens gave no serious trouble in the state, feeling ran high in some communities and several individuals who probably should have been ignored were abused. Citizens forced a Basin man to kiss the flag because he had criticized President Wilson. In Thermopolis, "disloyal" persons were required to kiss the flag; in Lander, others were forced to take positions on their knees. Newspaper reports of the incidents did not explain the nature of the disloyalty. In perhaps the most egregious manifestation of patriot-ism run wild, a Union Pacific employee of Russian ancestry in Cheyenne was stripped and painted yellow because he refused to buy a Victory bond.

Basin, Thermopolis, Lander, and Douglas had "vigilance com-mittees," Powell a "Patriot League." At the suggestion of the Council of National Defense, "100 Per Cent American Clubs" were formed in Cheyenne and Laramie to keep an eye on aliens, ferret out sedition, and promote patriotism.

At Greybull and a few other places, German books were burned. At

Garland the school board expelled three high school pupils for burning some of the German textbooks, whereupon six other pupils seized the German teacher in a fruitless attempt to make him burn the remaining German textbooks. According to state librarian Agnes Wright's 1916–1918 biennial report, her staff had "cooperated with the Government by removing from our shelves German propaganda, books explaining the making of explosives and books on neutrality." The town of Germania was renamed Emblem, and French replaced German in the curricula of many high schools. The *Laramie Republican* boasted in June, 1918, that "Wyoming is 100 per cent clean so far as publication of foreign language papers is concerned. There is not a paper published in a foreign language issued in this state."

The only reported manifestation of pacifism in the state was at Powell, where the school board asked a pacifist teacher to resign.

THE ELECTION OF 1918

Wyoming politicians found time for politics almost as usual in 1918. In the United States Congress, the Republicans, after six years of Democratic domination, won control of both houses, while in Wyoming, for the first time since 1908, the Republicans captured all of the major elective offices and both houses of the legislature.

Senator Warren, who was approaching seventy-five, almost retired. He had suffered a great tragedy when his only daughter, Helen (Mrs. John J. Pershing), and her three daughters lost their lives on August 27, 1915, in a fire at the Presidio in San Francisco. A few days before the United States declaration of war in April, 1917, the Senator wrote to state Republican chairman Patrick Sullivan that he intended not to run again, whereupon Congressman Frank Mondell and Rock Springs banker John W. Hay announced their candidacy for Warren's place on the Republican ballot.

Republican editors, however, early in 1918 began suggesting that Warren's experience, efficiency, and ability were indispensable. In May, 1918, after Mondell and Hay had been campaigning for months, Warren announced that he had changed his mind and would run again, whereupon Mondell and Hay dropped out of the Senate race, Mondell returning to his familiar place as a candidate for the House of Representatives. In opposition to Warren, the Democrats advanced John E. Osborne, who had been governor (1893–1895), congressman (1897–1899), and First Assistant United States Secretary of State (1913–1915).

Warren was advertised as more than a sheepman; it was said that he was engaged in large-scale dry farming. Much was made of his devoted support of Wilson's war measures and his seniority, since only two men were senior to him in the Senate.

The Democrats called Warren a reactionary and directed attention to President Wilson's request for the election of only Democratic senators and representatives. The threadbare fencing and land-fraud charges, which had been used against Warren again and again, had proved of little value in past elections and were left in the closet in 1918. And certainly, now that General John J. Pershing was commander-in-chief of the American Expeditionary Forces, no one brought out the old accusation that Warren had been responsible for his son-in-law's rapid promotion to general's rank in 1906.

Republicans recalled Dr. Osborne's "clownlike antics" in 1892 and derided him as a carpetbagger for having lived recently in Denver. They traced his fortune to the Rawlins drugstore where, it was said, he had in pioneer days sold "firewater" without a prescription and done his own prescribing. Osborne was popular, but failed by six thousand votes to overtake Warren.

Mondell had no difficulty in besting a comparative unknown, Hayden M. White, by more than eleven thousand votes. To no avail, Democrats decried Mondell's war record. Before United States entry, he had dragged his feet on preparedness. He had said in 1913 that European governments would not fight for fear of bankruptcy. After the outbreak of war in Europe, he had declared that there was less chance of American involvement than before. He had opposed expenditures for battleships and a larger army. He had opposed conscription until the final vote. Despite this type of campaign, which was calculated to be effective in an atmosphere of patriotic hysteria, Mondell led his ticket.

At long last the quarter-century feud between Joseph M. Carey and Francis E. Warren was blunted. The bitter enmity between these two outstanding Republicans, which often had hurt the party through the years, subsided when the Warren Machine decided to support Carey's son, Robert D., for governor. The two Careys brought the remnants of Progressivism into the Republican party. Young Carey's assets were widely advertised: native son, president of the Wyoming Stock Growers Association, experience on state commissions, devotion to a protective tariff, and "the advantage of bringing together the Progressives and Republicans in Wyoming."

Republicans derided Carey's opponent, Acting Governor Frank L. Houx, sneering that Kendrick had not trusted him in 1917. After his election to the United States Senate, Kendrick had remained in office until after the 1917 legislative session rather than permit Secretary of State Houx to govern. Late in the campaign, full-page advertisements appeared in which it was alleged that Houx had accepted a bribe from a favored state oil-land lessee. Republicans also published pictures of what was said to be the log-cabin saloon Houx once operated in Cody, a nasty trick because he had recently become a fervid promoter of prohibition.

Scrambling desperately for issues, the Democrats used newspaper advertisements headed "Hun Kultur at Careyhurst." The ads declared that a German alien, Fred J. Wiedeke, had been employed by J. M. Carey & Brother since March 1, 1914. Wiedeke was described as "the unregenerate offspring of Hunland" and the "subject of the Beast of Berlin." It was alleged that he was in a position "to insidiously and constantly influence Robert D. Carey." Joseph M. Carey replied that Wiedeke was entirely loyal, had declared his intention to become a United States citizen, had tried to enter service, and had engaged in home-front war work. Robert D. Carey was elected by five thousand votes.

Rounding out their general victory, the Republicans installed Ishmael J. Jefferis as auditor, A. D. Hoskins as treasurer, and Mrs. Katherine A. Morton as superintendent of public instruction. And they bagged the Senate, 17 to 10, and the House of Representatives, 43 to 11. Reflecting on the great Republican victory, the *Wyoming State Tribune* editorialized about Wyoming politics on November 8, 1918:

A campaign . . . is a good deal like a battle—no matter how careful you may be some noncombatants may be hit. It cannot be entirely helped. . . . But absolute immunity and safety cannot be found either in politics or on the battle front. . . . If any noncombatants were struck it was rather more incidental than intentional. If any one in the enemy camp was unnecessarily bombarded or if any bad shells were used, that too was the result of error and not malice. . . .

CLIMAX OF THE WAR, AND PEACE

American troops were thrown into the European holocaust in ever growing numbers in the summer and fall of 1918. Half a million Americans won an important victory at Saint-Mihiel in September, 1918. Americans made substantial contributions in the Meuse-Argonne offensive, which began September 26 and continued into November. After Bulgaria, Turkey, and Austria surrendered, Germany finally gave up the hopeless struggle against mounting odds and signed an armistice on November 11, 1918. Cried the *Wyoming State Tribune*: "This is the greatest day in the history of Christendom since that Easter morn on Calvary when Christ rose." All over the state, residents congregated in town and city business districts for mutual congratulations. Bells, sirens, whistles, and auto horns greeted the breath-taking news. In Cheyenne, thousands marched in a parade, listened to addresses by the governor and the mayor, and watched the Kaiser burning in effigy. A band played *There'll Be a Hot Time in the Old Town Tonight*. After participating in one celebration or another, the citizens settled down to thinking about what adjustments were needed and when the servicemen would return.

Newspaper editors discussed Wilson's proposed League of Nations, generally (except for Deming in Cheyenne) opposing United States membership in the League without substantial reservations. President Wilson "hurled defiance at League enemies" in an address at the Princess Theater in Cheyenne on September 24, 1919. Senator Kendrick usually supported Wilson's efforts to put the United States into the League of Nations without Senator Lodge's reservations. In March, 1920, however, Kendrick broke with Wilson and voted with Warren and the majority for the League with reservations. The vote, 49 to 35, was short of the necessary two-thirds required for treaty ratification.

SPANISH INFLUENZA

A deadly epidemic of Spanish influenza assailed the nation late in the war. It struck Wyoming in October, 1918, and continued into January. In the nation and in Wyoming there were many more deaths from flu than from all war-connected causes. In Wyoming there were 780 fatal cases, 169 of which were attributed to flu and 611 to flu and pneumonia combined.

Public meetings were banned; schools and churches were closed. In the belief that smoke might carry the disease, leaf burning was prohibited. In Cheyenne, stores that did not close were limited to five customers at one time for each twenty-five feet of store front. When show houses and churches reopened in January, people occupied only alternate seats.

THE 1919 LEGISLATURE

His contemporary, the historian Mrs. Cyrus Beard, wrote: "In his messages Governor Robert D. Carey exemplifies the man of large affairs, practical minded and generous, with a sympathetic attitude towards efforts labeled 'progressive' and which have to do with social and economic betterment." Robert D. Carey was accustomed to wealth. He had been graduated from the Hill School and Yale University. "Keep the appropriations as low as possible," he told the 1919 legislature, "but remember that money spent for a useful purpose is never wasted." And again, he remarked: "We are spending large sums of money to protect our live stock from disease, but I fear we have been overlooking the welfare of our people." To be sure, times were still good in 1919. Nothing had happened yet to prick the bubble of inflation; property valuations and state revenues were on the increase; thanks mainly to oil, land sales, leases, and royalties were bringing more revenue into the state treasury than property taxes.

Governor Carey said more in behalf of labor than any previous Wyoming governor had said. The war, he felt, had demonstrated the "vital importance of labor to the welfare of the nation. . . . The labor organizations, particularly in Wyoming, have demonstrated their loyalty and patriotism."

The Republicans had large majorities in both houses of the legislature. They were generally sympathetic with Carey, and the minority Democrats could find little cause for complaint. The remarkable good feeling noticed in the 1915 and 1917 legislatures characterized the 1919 session as well. The Governor's appointments received unanimous approval. Although he trimmed out twenty appropriations items, they totaled only $63,150. His only two vetoes, apart from the appropriations items, were of slight importance. A Democratic spokesman at the end of the session acknowledged that "political differences have been buried during this session and never permitted to interfere in the least in our deliberations." Even another attempt to split Fremont County received scanty support.

Carey got most of the things he asked for. Among his more striking achievements were an executive budget system, Blue Sky Law, changes regarding the labor commissioner, increased salaries for many officers, significant state-highway legislation, a state board of immigration, prohibition effective July 1, improvements at various state institutions, and increased workmen's compensation.[4] "Splendid Record of Accomplishment," judged the *Wyoming State Tribune.*

OIL AND THE AUTOMOBILE

Oil and the automobile brought great changes to Wyoming beginning in the second decade of the twentieth century. After 1910 the demand for Wyoming oil increased from year to year and received a further boost from the First World War. Casper was transformed from a wool town to an oil city, with pretensions to being the oil capital of the Rockies.

Speculative fever raged in Casper in 1916 and 1917 after exciting discoveries on the Muddy east of Casper. A. J. Mokler recalled: "Men in all walks of life neglected their business and their professions to buy and sell oil stocks." Most of the trading was done in the lobby of the Midwest Hotel, which later became the Henning, and customers overflowed into the street on many evenings. Each new discovery was followed by the organization of scores of new companies which issued millions of shares of stock, mostly worthless. Leslie A. Miller, who had recently served four years as chief clerk in the state land office, testified before the United States House of Representatives Committee on Public Lands on February 15, 1918, that Wyoming had a "whole herd" of promoters. He said: "For the greater part they do very little drilling. Once in a while to protect themselves from the Post Office Department they do a little drilling, but their chief aim is to sell stock."

Discovery of the Second Wall Creek Sand on August 26, 1917, at a depth of 2,200 feet enhanced the value of the Salt Creek Field several times over and attracted new companies. In 1918, Salt Creek's production rose to 5,500,000 barrels, almost half the state's total. Other fields were opened during the war years: Grass Creek and Elk Basin in the Big Horn Basin, Big Muddy at Glenrock, and Lance Creek northwest of Lusk.

The United States Supreme Court's 1915 decision in the case of *United States* v. *Midwest Oil Company,* upholding the right of the President of the United States to withdraw and protect public lands without approval of Congress, was greeted with indignant denunciations. Wyoming's Senator C. D. Clark asserted that the decision had put "a stop to the largest and greatest industry" of Wyoming. Oilmen soon

[4] Governor Carey summoned a special session of the legislature, the state's first, in January, 1920, to ratify the woman-suffrage amendment to the United States Constitution.

reached a consensus that they must persuade Congress to pass a leasing act for oil lands like those already in effect for coal and phosphate lands. Western senators and congressmen, with help from oil lobbyists, finally pushed through the Oil and Gas Leasing Act of February 25, 1920. Thereafter, most of Wyoming's oil production would be from federally owned land by private companies paying one-eighth royalty.

Oil-industry growth was, of course, dependent upon the "gasoline buggy," which evolved rapidly from a novel luxury to a necessity. The state legislature in 1911 asked the federal government for a grant of one million acres of public lands to be used for the building and maintenance of good roads—without result. The same legislature arranged for the Board of Charities and Reform to supervise road construction by convicts. The state engineer, who hitherto had been mainly concerned with reclamation, was assigned the additional duty of providing highway plans and specifications. In the next few years the counties did most of what little highway work was done, though they were restrained by Governor Carey's 1913 veto of a legislative measure authorizing county bond issues for roads.

The voluntary Wyoming Highways Association was formed in 1912 for the purpose of promoting through routes. The national Lincoln Memorial Highway Association in 1913 endorsed the southern-Wyoming Overland Trail, along the Union Pacific, as the state's link in the transcontinental Lincoln Highway. Much of this famous highway's route between Rawlins and Rock Springs at first utilized an abandoned Union Pacific grade. In the north the Black and Yellow Trail came in 1914 from Minneapolis to the Black Hills and on to Newcastle, Gillette, Buffalo, Tensleep, Worland, Cody, and Yellowstone Park. Left off the Black and Yellow Trail, Sheridan helped promote the Custer Battlefield Highway from the Black Hills to Glacier National Park via Sheridan. Other through routes followed: Yellowstone Highway, National Park to Park Highway, Grant Highway, and Rocky Mountain Highway. Inevitable jealousies developed.

Yellowstone Park was officially opened to autos in 1915 after a period of controversy in which it was argued that the park roads were too narrow for both autos and teams.

The legislature took a significant step forward in 1917 when it established a state highway department under a state highway commission and authorized the acceptance of federal aid on a matching basis. To get federal aid in needed quantity, the state had to raise matching funds through a bond issue of $2,800,000, approved overwhelmingly by popular vote in April, 1919, and through a second bond issue of $1,800,000, approved in 1921. These two bond issues exhausted the state's constitutional bonding capacity. Fortunately, the Oil and Gas Leasing Act of 1920 soon began to pour royalty money into the state's matching fund, and a gasoline tax was of further help.

By 1918 the state had 15,900 registered automobiles, ten times as many as five years earlier, and substantial increases occurred each year thereafter.

Every town had to provide a municipal campground. During the summer of 1920, some forty thousand people camped at the north edge of Cheyenne, three thousand from thirty-two states being there during Frontier Days that year. Truly, oil and the automobile were bringing revolutionary changes to Wyoming.

PROHIBITION

Temperance was a plant of slow growth in the man's world of Wyoming until the First World War. Governor Joseph M. Carey told a Cheyenne meeting of the Anti-Saloon League in 1914 that he had frequently attended banquets where, among fifty or one hundred men, he was the only one who did not drink. He shocked the league by stating his belief that temperance could never be brought about through law but only through education. That same year, the state convention of the Wyoming Federation of Labor opposed prohibition by unanimous vote. Statewide prohibition was impossible, said the *Laramie Republican*, until the "tremendous public sentiment against a prohibition law" had been changed through education.

In 1915 the Woman's Christian Temperance Union and the Anti-Saloon League, with help from the churches, presented the legislature with petitions bearing ten thousand signatures and asking for submission of the question to a vote of the people. Although no action was taken in that session, wets were thrown on the defensive thereafter as one state after another bordering Wyoming adopted prohibition. Colorado did so in 1914, Idaho in 1915, Nebraska, South Dakota, and Montana in 1916, and Utah in 1917. Temperance leaders in other parts of the country could not understand why Wyoming, which had enjoyed the benefit of woman suffrage for so long, should be so obstinate on the question. The pressure increased. In January, 1917, Joseph M. Carey reversed his 1914 position and recommended prohibition. Governor John B. Kendrick likewise thought it was time for action. Upon his recommendation, the legislature decided to give the people an opportunity in November, 1918, to vote on a prohibition amendment to the state constitution.

With the nation at war, the Wyoming Council of National Defense in January, 1918, asked for a presidential order closing the saloons, arguing that the liquor business had reduced labor efficiency by at least 40 per cent. True or not, such allegations made the wets look unpatriotic, if not downright traitorous.

Temperance leaders said in 1918 that, as the one wet spot in the Rocky Mountain region, Wyoming had become the dumping ground for shady characters and the supply depot for surrounding dry states. Crime, they said, abounded in the border towns of Evanston and Cheyenne. The W.C.T.U. and the Anti-Saloon League campaigned with vigor in the fall of 1918 and were thrilled by a tremendous victory at the polls. By a vote of better than three to one, the state adopted the prohibition amendment submitted by the 1917 legislature. In recognition of the overwhelming dry sentiment, the 1919 legislature followed Governor Robert D. Carey's recommendation and provided for statutory prohibition on July 1, 1919, six months before the state's constitutional amendment would become effective.

So Wyoming went dry on July 1, 1919, *de jure* but not *de facto*. The night before was described as one of the wildest in Cheyenne's history as hundreds of Nebraska and Colorado visitors joined local citizens in a final fling. Said the *Wyoming State Tribune* next day: "The melancholy days have come. . . . Cheyenne awoke this morning with a headache, a yearning thirst, a fuzzy taste in its mouth, and not a chance for the morning eye-opener." Not everyone, however, was deprived of "the morning eye-opener," because many who could afford it had, with official approval, stocked their cellars. Newspapers had reported in March that "those who choose to violate the law to the extent of keeping a supply on hand for their own use will not be molested by the officers of the law." The state prohibition commissioner affirmed this policy in July, 1919; and in December, 1920, the Wyoming Supreme Court held that liquor acquired prior to July 1, 1919, for use in private homes was not contraband. The next legislature, however, in 1921, changed the law in order to make such liquor contraband. Meanwhile, hijackers sometimes invaded well-stocked cellars. In February, 1920, State Senator Patrick Sullivan of Casper suffered the loss of five barrels of eight-year-old whiskey valued at five thousand dollars. In April, 1920, hijackers made off with a large quantity of Old Taylor whiskey stored in a warehouse by two prominent Cheyenne attorneys.

Many men who had no caches of bonded stuff soon prepared substitutes. Just three weeks after prohibition began, forty-two men and women were arrested in a raid on a disorderly house in West Cheyenne. A newspaper report stated that "a tray full of glasses containing a drink that has not yet been identified, led police officers to believe that a still is in existence somewhere in the city and that it is producing a weird drink." The later history of Wyoming's part in the "Noble Experiment" will be discussed in the next chapter.

CHAPTER 14

Depression Years, 1920–1939

THE TITLE OF THIS CHAPTER may surprise some readers who have accepted the standard American-history textbook interpretation of the 1920's as a decade of prosperity after a short depression in 1920–1921. Although textbooks offer a picture of over-all prosperity in the nation, they usually concede that agriculture and coal mining did not share in that prosperity. Agriculture and coal mining were important in Wyoming, as was oil, another industry that suffered a severe setback in Wyoming in the twenties.

Because of deflation and the 1919 drought, the livestock business suffered extraordinary distress. Where there had been 1,172,000 cattle

411

in 1919 worth $73,800,000, there were only 795,000 in 1925 worth $23,000,000.

The wool industry fared no better. With the facts fresh in mind, the prominent Laramie Plains wool grower Frank S. King wrote in 1922:

The summer of 1919 was one long to be remembered; drought was universal throughout Wyoming and in the fall at least one-third of the livestock had to be shipped out of the State. The remaining herds compelled the purchasing of hay and grain at prices that were appalling. Winter started from a month to six weeks earlier than the average and in October snow covered the State. Long cold months followed, ending with an April storm that has been unequalled since the March storm of 1878. This resulted in the loss of about one-third of the stock of the state and in many cases the cost of carrying through the winter was more than the sheep were worth in the spring. On top of this calamity came the depression in prices and sheep and wool were among the first to feel its effects. In a week wool fell from 80 to 25 cents and sheep from $18.00 to $10.00 and then later to $6.00. The price of lambs fell from $8.00 to $12.00 down to $3.00. Of credit there was none and the stockmen were up against a stone wall.[1]

The farmers, too, were in trouble. Although crop production meant less than livestock to the state, many people were dependent upon crop production, and there was half a crop or less in the drought year of 1919. Yields were better thereafter for several years, but prices were consistently discouraging. Cattle prices, on the other hand, were good for a few years, 1926–1928, so as to strengthen that industry against impending troubles.

The Union Pacific laid off one-third of its men during the four months beginning in December, 1920. A year and a half later, Wyoming railroad shopmen participated in widespread shopcrafts' strikes against reduction in wages, and National Guardsmen were mobilized when striking shopmen in Sheridan attacked a nonunion worker.

National coal strikes affected the state in 1919 and 1922. Aliens in the Wyoming coal camps were under suspicion during the national postwar "Red scare," but Wyoming miners, who were well organized by the United Mine Workers, were more cautious and conservative than miners in some other states. No one in Wyoming was arrested as a dangerous alien. In 1928 the Wyoming miners accepted a $1.20 cut in their daily wage (to $6.72) without a strike. Meanwhile, employment in the state's mines gradually declined from 7,511 in 1923 to 4,675

[1] Quoted in R. H. Burns, A. S. Gillespie, and W. G. Richardson, *Wyoming's Pioneer Ranches* (Laramie: Top-of-the-World Press, 1955), p. 554.

in 1931. The Wyoming trend corresponded to the national trend in coal mining.

Some addition (Spanish-American) to Wyoming labor occurred in the beet fields, as sugar-beet culture expanded. On the other hand, with declining petroleum production after 1924, there was a corresponding reduction of employment in oil fields and refineries.

With three of the state's major economic supports—agriculture, coal mining, and petroleum—showing substantial weakness, the 1920's must be regarded as years of depression for Wyoming, despite the apparent prosperity of the middle and upper classes in the nation's big cities. Everything considered, it is rather remarkable that the state's population increased from 194,402 in 1920 to 225,565 in 1930.

BANK FAILURES

Wyoming had 153 banks in January, 1920, and 32 others were opened in the decade which followed. However, 101 banks closed, most of them of necessity. In short, most of the banks of the state closed their doors in what has been called for the nation a prosperous decade! The failures were due mainly to inability to collect on real-estate and live-stock loans. Many depositors lost their savings, and a few bankers committed suicide. Wyoming's bank closings were spread out over the decade as follows:

YEAR	NUMBER OF BANKS CLOSING	
	State Banks	*National Banks*
1920	4	0
1921	9	0
1922	8	1
1923	8	3
1924	23	12
1925	9	1
1926	4	0
1927	4	7
1928	0	5
1929	2	1
	71	30

Source: Unpublished data obtained from Norris E. Hartwell, State Bank Examiner, 1963.

Wyoming had entered statehood in 1890 with only fifteen banks. Only a few new ones appeared in the depressed 1890's, but thereafter they multiplied, with ten or more being founded in each of the years 1906, 1907, 1912, 1916, 1917, and 1919. Then in the 1920's so many were eliminated that only eighty-three of the hardiest remained on June 30, 1930, with deposits of $56,000,000 and total resources of $71,341,000. The Great Depression of the 1930's trimmed out twenty-seven more, seven of them in 1932 and seven more in 1933.

CLIMAX OF HOMESTEADING

The extraordinary prosperity enjoyed by farmers and ranchers in 1917 and 1918 persuaded many rural people to enlarge their holdings by exhausting whatever unused rights they had under the various land laws. Some large stockmen, who were favorably situated with respect to free federal range, had opposed the 640-acre grazing-homestead act of 1916, but when it was adopted, they filed on what free land they could get, if for no other reason than to keep others from getting it. For example, the Cheyenne Land Office reported that during the first two weeks of January, 1917, there were 1,250 filings in that office, nearly all of them by Wyoming residents "for the purpose of squaring up ranches." Then in the spring, townspeople and newcomers joined in the homesteading spree, some for speculation, others with serious intentions to make permanent homes. The greatest boom years, however, proved to be 1919, 1920, and 1921, despite the devastating drought of 1919, which should have given pause to even the most land hungry and speculation prone.

LAND ENTRIES IN WYOMING UNDER THE HOMESTEAD ACTS DURING THE FISCAL YEARS 1915–1935 (For each year, first row gives original entries, second row gives final entries.)

Year	Number of Homestead Entries	Acres
1915	3,030	679,677
	1,652	331,617
1916	5,380	1,305,017
	1,652 (same as for 1915)	353,109
1917	5,332	1,404,912
	1,888	419,425
1918	4,411	1,140,749
	2,235	491,687
1919	7,083	2,226,249
	1,907	432,265
1920	11,327	3,899,451
	3,857	966,048
1921	10,051	3,719,778
	4,993	1,426,649
1922	4,869	1,682,865
	5,656	1,702,619
1923	2,914	1,014,401
	4,635	1,468,004

Year	Number of Homestead Entries	Acres
1924	1,788	643,657
	3,687	1,201,583
1925	1,497	573,947
	3,068	1,025,583
1926	1,192	487,389
	2,214	734,078
1927	1,582	695,391
	1,417	461,572
1928	1,686	763,296
	1,323	451,691
1929	2,112	1,021,766
	1,084	356,420
1930	2,180	1,096,300
	811	287,161
1931	2,175	1,098,655
	723	268,815
1932	1,903	989,834
	809	328,172
1933	1,302	677,253
	367	138,175
1934	1,529	794,275
	756	338,107
1935	769	346,389
	944	381,865

Source: Reports of Secretary of Interior, except for 1933. Data for 1933 from G.L.O. Statistics Report. A 1962 Bureau of Land Management publication, *Homesteads*, gives final homestead entries, by years, 1868–1961, but does not list original entries. The publication's figures for Wyoming differ slightly from those above, which have been taken from annual reports of the Secretary of the Interior.

Thus almost ten million acres of land were patented under the homestead laws in the decade of the twenties, and another one and one-half million acres passed to patent in the 1930's before vacant, unreserved, and unappropriated lands were withdrawn by executive order on November 26, 1934, after the passage of the Taylor Grazing Act of June 28, 1934. Private ownership of land in the state was doubled during the twenties, rising to approximately 40 per cent. No other decade compares with that of the twenties in the matter of turning Wyoming land from public to private ownership.

Assisting in the promotion of Wyoming settlement in 1919 and 1920 was the Board of Immigration. Governor Robert D. Carey in 1919 persuaded the legislature to revive work of the board, which had been inactive since 1912 for lack of appropriations. Commissioner of Immigration Charles S. Hill reported in 1920 that his office had distributed 54,000 pieces of literature, with most attention given to Nebraska,

Kansas, Iowa, the Dakotas, Montana, Utah, Idaho, Colorado, Oklahoma, Texas, Missouri, Illinois, and Indiana, "where experience has taught that it is reasonable to expect the greatest result." Hill conceded that it was difficult to estimate the real value of his work, yet he declared that the immigration board was responsible for bringing hundreds of war veterans to the state. The board helped to publicize homestead openings on the Shoshone and North Platte reclamation projects. Veterans received preference and could, for time served, deduct up to two years of the three years of residence required on the homesteads.

Despite the spectacular acquisition of land under the homestead laws, the number of farm and ranch units increased only from 15,748 in 1919 to 16,011 in 1929, and the rural farm and ranch population increased only from 67,076 to 72,905. People who were already on the land in 1919 sooner or later came into possession of most of the newly homesteaded land. They enlarged their units from an average size of 749.9 acres in 1919 to 1,469 acres in 1929. Moreover, they were not plowing up much of the newly acquired land. Cropland harvested increased only from 1,153,624 acres in 1919 to 2,007,751 in 1929. The acreage harvested in 1929 represented only 3 per cent of the state's area, illustrating once again the persistent dominance of livestock and grazing in the state's agriculture. Wyoming in 1930 had 824,000 cattle and 3,426,000 sheep. And most of the crops grown were used as livestock feed, with alfalfa the leading crop.

Thousands of homesteaders gave up in the 1920's and either abandoned their lands before patent or sold them after patent to more successful neighbors. The veteran stockman and banker John Clay was quoted by the *Wyoming State Tribune* on January 1, 1922: "The retreat of the dry farmer and 640-acre homesteader has begun. . . . A few of the thrifty will stay, and will acquire some cheap land as it is foreclosed or sold for taxes." An examination of the table of entries and patents from 1915 to 1935 shows approximately 72,700 homestead entries in Wyoming and only 45,300 patents during that 21-year period.

Some of the homesteaders of the twenties were war veterans attracted by the $2,000 property-tax exemption granted to them by the 1921 legislature. Whatever their primary motive may have been, the Wyoming homesteaders who were not just enlarging their holdings found it difficult to make a living because this period of farm depression reached almost everywhere and because little of Wyoming's land can be farmed successfully without irrigation and even less can be ranched successfully in 640-acre units.

Evidence for the deflation and depression which plagued Wyoming in the 1920's can be found in property valuations. Although the land area in private ownership doubled, the total valuation of taxable property changed little, varying between $400,000,000 and $460,000,000, the lowest valuation coming in 1922, the highest in 1925. More land was added to the tax rolls in the 1930's, yet total property valuations dropped below $400,000,000.

Rapid as the transfer of land to private ownership was, more than 60 per cent of the state still remained in public ownership in 1927, causing the legislature of that year to petition Congress for a 2,560-acre homestead law. Said the petition: "Millions of acres of public lands remain vacant, unoccupied and unused in the state." Major John Wesley Powell had made the same proposal in 1878. No such law was passed, and half of Wyoming would still be owned by the federal government in the 1960's.

Besides stepped-up homesteading and the general depression, several developments in Wyoming agriculture are worth passing notice. Head lettuce was tried as a cash crop on the Laramie Plains in the years 1922–1926. The experiment proved a failure because of marketing problems and early frosts at the 7,200-foot altitude. Turkeys, which were introduced in large numbers in eastern counties, likewise proved a failure. Sugar-beet production was pushed vigorously, with better luck, in the irrigated oases of Goshen, Platte, Sheridan, and Fremont counties and in the Big Horn Basin. Corn, mostly dry-farmed, became popular in the eastern tier of counties, and barley found much greater favor than previously. Yet oats and wheat remained the favorite grains, with winter wheat more popular than spring wheat after 1924.

After deflation began in 1920, Wyoming farmers and ranchers sought help from the legislature. Their mortgage debt, according to the federal census, was already more than $15,000,000 in 1919 (27.5 per cent of the value of their property), and their average interest rate was 7.7 per cent. The 1921 legislature set up a state farm-loan board, made possible by a constitutional amendment adopted in 1916, and authorized 6 per cent loans on farmlands, limiting each borrower to $5,000. The legislature authorized the board to lend up to $1,000,000 from the common-school permanent fund. The 1923 legislature cut the interest rate to 5 per cent and raised the limit for each borrower to $15,000. The ceiling on total loans was raised gradually to $8,000,000. On September 30, 1930, the loans outstanding amounted to $6,672,553 (2,549 individual loans). By the spring of 1935, the state held 250 farms and ranches as the result of foreclosures. Prosperous years beginning in World War II made it possible for the farmers to pay off their loans. By July 1, 1963, Treasurer Everett T. Copenhaver could report that the Wyoming Farm Loan Department "has never lost one dollar."

Wyoming was fortunate in that it got into the farm-loan business late and conservatively. In contrast, South Dakota launched its rural-credits program in 1917, lent vast sums obtained through bond issues, and eventually lost $57,000,000. Montana, Idaho, and Utah also lost heavily on farm loans. Federal loans also were made available to farmers and ranchers.

Wyoming farmers were not prosperous in the 1920's, yet they suffered less than their more numerous counterparts in Montana. Half the farmers of Montana lost their farms in twenty thousand mortgage foreclosures in the years 1921–1925. The Montana catastrophe was due in good part to terrible drought in 1918, 1919, and 1920, which mercifully spared Wyoming, except in 1919.

An unusually wet year brought bumper crops in 1927, bringing renewed interest in dry farming. Then came dry years in 1930, 1931, 1933, 1934, and 1936. In 1936 a federal agency, the Resettlement Administration, undertook to resettle 134 stranded, drought-stricken Wyoming families on what was regarded as better land near Sheridan and Lingle. Hundreds of other rural families in the state needed help, but only those in the most desperate straits were resettled. Assisted families were furnished dairy cows, beef cattle or sheep, horses, chickens, and pigs in return for promises of repayment in thirty years.

An erosion-control demonstration area was established by the federal Soil Conservation Service in Goshen Hole (in Goshen and Platte counties), where wind erosion had damaged much of the land. The Soil Conservation Service introduced strip-cropping and retired some of the land from cultivation. Another erosion-control area was established on the Wind River Reservation.

RECLAMATION

Only a few thousand acres were reclaimed in Wyoming in the 1920's, although, as always, there was much discussion of the subject. For a number of years the federal government's emphasis was on salvaging and improving old projects rather than making new starts.

In December, 1924, John B. Kendrick introduced in the United States Senate a bill which, according to the *Wyoming State Tribune* (Cheyenne), would "prevent alike the colonization of one unfit to farm, one fit to farm on land unfit to farm, and one unfit to farm on land unfit to farm." Kendrick's bill, which was not adopted, called for more careful classification of newly opened lands and accurate appraisal of the value of each unit. It would have required applicants to have at least one year's experience on a farm, plus farm equipment valued at fifteen hundred dollars, and would have permitted amortization in forty years.

Elwood Mead, who had become United States Commissioner of Reclamation in 1924, supported Kendrick's bill, pointing to what he called great human waste on Wyoming's Garland, Frannie, and North Platte projects. Unable to get federal-government action, Mead told a reclamation conference in Cheyenne in June, 1925, that the state should take charge of settlement and farm development, adding that "whoever does it will have a difficult task. . . . We should either assume this burden or quit building canals." Neither the federal nor state government was ready to move. Secretary of the Interior Hubert Work, after an inspection trip which included Wyoming, declared in Washington in July, 1925, that "there is no need of more reclamation projects until the present ones are put on a sound basis: One third of the projects are insolvent and one fourth of them should never have been built." Meanwhile, between 1921 and 1924, Congress had passed four relief measures, all providing for postponements in payments by the water users on federal projects.

A new enthusiast for reclamation appeared on the Wyoming horizon with the election of Charles E. Winter as a Republican congressman in 1922, replacing Frank W. Mondell when the latter ran unsuccessfully against John B. Kendrick for the United States Senate. Winter joined Mead and Kendrick in their efforts to obtain aided and directed land settlement.

Beginning in the 1920's, there were protracted negotiations over division of Colorado River water. State engineer and later governor Frank C. Emerson was mainly responsible for guarding Wyoming's rights in its Colorado River tributaries, the Green and the Little Snake. Representatives of the seven states involved—California, Arizona, Nevada, New Mexico, Colorado, Utah, and Wyoming—drew up a compact at Santa Fe in November, 1922. The upper-basin states— Wyoming, Colorado, Utah, and New Mexico—agreed to deliver at Lees Ferry 75,000,000 acre-feet of water in each ten-year period, or 7,500,000 acre-feet in each year—approximately half the flow of the river. Nevertheless, very complex negotiations followed over a period of many years. Arizona and California could not agree on lower-basin problems, while upper-basin states were worried about the future of their rights vis-à-vis the lower-basin states and one another. Although the compact was ratified by the Wyoming Legislature in 1923, only herculean efforts by Frank Emerson maintained the state's loyalty to the compact in the 1925 and 1929 sessions of the legislature. Since allocation of waters among the four upper-basin states was not included in the 1922 compact, it was feared that Wyoming's water rights were not adequately protected. Governor Emerson assured skeptics in 1929 that Wyoming would get its share "when the time was right."

The formidable Riverton project, which had flooded the Wyoming Central Irrigation Company and state officials with several acre-feet of frustration, was finally taken over by the United States Bureau of Reclamation in 1920. During the next decade, a first installment of four million dollars was devoted to the project, and further funds were expended for the construction of Bull Lake Dam in 1936–1938.

Wyoming and Colorado fought occasionally over problems concerned with the division of Laramie River waters. The United States Supreme Court decreed in 1922 what amounts Colorado might divert and for what purposes, but controversy continued.

Idaho and Wyoming bickered over division of Snake River waters. The mountain barrier to the east and south has prevented extensive use of Snake River water in Wyoming, yet Wyoming people have never become completely reconciled to the use of Jackson Lake as a reservoir for the Minidoka project in Idaho.

From time to time, Idaho and Montana proposed converting Yellowstone Lake into a reclamation reservoir for the benefit of one or the other. The Department of the Interior and the National Park Service have had little sympathy for such proposals, nor has Wyoming, since the irrigation would not be in Wyoming. The Wyoming Planning Board in 1937 investigated the feasibility of diverting water from the Snake River to the Green River watershed. Such a diversion would have to be based either on an encroachment upon Idaho's rights or on use of Yellowstone Lake for Wyoming purposes, and there has been little hope of getting support outside Wyoming for either.

The Kendrick project (known as Casper-Alcova until 1937) attracted more attention than any other reclamation project for eighteen years, beginning in 1927, when Governor Emerson and Congressman Winter launched a drive for the new start in central Wyoming. It was argued that Natrona County had made vast contributions to the reclamation fund in the form of oil royalties and that with the anticipated exhaustion of the Salt Creek Field, Casper's economy desperately needed such help as the project might give.

In his memoirs, Leslie A. Miller recalls that Senator John B. Kendrick was so delighted at having carried Natrona County by two votes against home-town candidate Winter in 1928 that he went to Casper and asked how he might best show his appreciation. The Chamber of Commerce gave top priority to the Casper-Alcova project, which the Senator then doggedly pursued for the next five years. He could get no encouragement from President Hoover, and the Bureau of Reclamation and Commissioner Elwood Mead worried about feasibility. The more obstacles were interposed, the more enthusiastic Kendrick became. "The future of one-fourth of Wyoming depends on the early development of the . . . project," he said in Sheridan in August, 1932.

Victory for Roosevelt and the Democratic party in 1932 gave Kendrick new hope. He and W. F. Wilkerson of Casper called on Roosevelt at Albany, New York, soon after his election and obtained his tentative promise of support. As hopes for the project rose, an ugly three-state war broke out because Colorado and Nebraska looked upon it as a threat to their use of North Platte waters. For a time, Colorado blocked Wyoming at every turn; there was much talk of a Wyoming boycott of Colorado merchants in retaliation. Kendrick wrote to Wilkerson in January, 1933, expressing the hope that "our people in every town in Wyoming will do whatever they can in the way of trade relations to see that the so-called sister state has reason to regret her unneighborly attitude." Governor Leslie A. Miller frowned on the spreading boycott, explaining that it might prejudice final determination of the issue. Finally, in July, 1933, Kendrick was able to get the President's approval. Kendrick argued that Wyoming contributed most of the water in the North Platte, the federal government had taken thirty million dollars in oil and gas royalties from Natrona County, and Casper was a badly depressed community. Commented the *Denver Post*: "Senator Kendrick has a way of getting things done. Wyoming sends big men to represent her in Congress. We send professional politicians who seem to have no influence." Kendrick scorned questions of feasibility:

This word 'feasible' . . . has been the most deadly word ever written into the English language. I have been compelled to marvel at the comfort derived by members, in discussing this matter both on and off the floor of congress, in the use of this word as an alibi for their action in despoiling my state for the benefit and advantage of their own states. . . .

Prolonged negotiations ensued, intrastate and interstate, in search of adequate water rights for the new project. State engineer Edwin W. Burritt issued a 1904 water right, with the reservation that the permit should not affect the rights of appropriators taking water from above Pathfinder Dam under permits issued since 1904. Burritt, with Governor Miller remaining discreetly silent, justified his grant of a 1904 water right by explaining that the Reclamation Service had filed its original plan for North Platte River development in 1904 and was finally getting around to the Casper-Alcova unit of the original plan. Wyoming irrigators in Goshen, Platte, and Converse counties were furious because the South Side Canal, built in 1915, would have to yield to the recently issued 1904 right. The Wyoming Water Users Association filed suit in Wyoming District Court against the extraordinary water right, and the state of Nebraska soon filed an action against Wyoming in the United States Supreme Court to prevent threatened damage to Nebraska irrigators who held senior water rights.

Secretary of the Interior Harold L. Ickes announced in October, 1934, that further expenditures on the project had been stopped until the water-rights dispute could be settled. Finally, in February, 1935, President Roosevelt approved the project, with a 1934 rather than a 1904 water right, after the Bureau of Reclamation had agreed to proceed with plans to leave out the north section of the project, thus trimming the number of acres to be irrigated from sixty-six thousand to thirty-five thousand. The Bureau of Reclamation had recognized that it could not win the suit brought by the Wyoming Water Users Association.

The state of Nebraska continued its assault upon the project. In this instance, the best method of solving interstate water disputes, through compact, could not be arranged. In September, 1935, Nebraska's attorney general filed a motion in the United States Supreme Court asking appointment of a Special Master to take testimony and make recommendations in the dispute. Colorado was drawn into the suit, as was the United States. The suit dragged on for ten years and cost Wyoming more than $135,000. In 1945 the Supreme Court handed down its decree, which protected vested rights to the extent possible in an overappropriated river. Both Colorado and Wyoming necessarily were limited in the water they could divert or store.[2] Priority of appropriation was the guiding principle. Said Justice Douglas, who delivered the majority opinion:

[2] For the text of the decree, see Earl Lloyd and Paul A. Rechard, *Documents on the Use and Control of Wyoming's Interstate Streams* (Cheyenne: State of Wyoming, 1957).

Apportionment calls for the exercise of an informed judgment on a consideration of many factors . . . physical and climatic conditions, the consumptive use of water in the several sections of the river, the character and rate of return flows, the extent of established uses, the availability of storage water, the practical effect of wasteful uses on downstream areas, the damage to upstream areas as compared to the benefits to downstream areas if a limitation is imposed on the former—these are all relevant factors. They are merely an illustrative not an exhaustive catalogue. . . .

While the lawyers argued, the first unit of the Kendrick project was completed in 1940, although operation was delayed for several years for lack of water. Unhappily, the Kendrick project would never come up to early expectations. By 1961 there were only 23,957 irrigable acres, of which 20,790 were watered. The valuation of all crops raised that year, one-half in acreage and value being alfalfa, was about one million dollars, scarcely enough to justify Senator Kendrick's assertion that the future of one-fourth of Wyoming depended on the project.

BURGEONING TOURISM

In the 1920's almost every town, urged on by national promotions, set up a municipal campground of some kind as autos multiplied. Wyoming, for example, had 24,000 autos in 1920 and 62,000 in 1930. Cheyenne's free campground in 1922 offered police protection, electric lights, hot and cold water, a community house, toilet facilities, shower baths, wood, scavenger service, laundry tubs, a bathing beach, boating facilities, and a community store. The following year, an area with the best facilities available was set aside for tourists able and willing to pay fifty cents a night. This gave rise in Cheyenne and other communities to complaints that to charge money was contrary to the spirit of the Old West.

Hitchhikers soon lined the highways. Came also the automobile graveyards. "Almost day by day the accumulation of unsightly hulks upon the city's edges grows visibly and its offensiveness becomes the greater," said Cheyenne editor John Charles Thompson in 1926. A year later he complained about obnoxious advertisements daubed on ledges and boulders along the Lincoln Highway.

"Cottage camps" sprang up to cater to tourists who did not want to carry their own tents and other camping equipment. Communities permitted facilities at their free campgrounds to run down as they looked with greater favor on persons able and willing to spend some money. Meanwhile, dude ranches multiplied, especially around Sheridan, Cody, Dubois, and Jackson. The Eaton brothers are commonly credited with starting the first real dude ranch at Wolf, Wyoming, west of Sheridan in 1904.

By 1937, tourists had begun traveling with trailers—"cottage trailers," they were called—and communities began providing trailer parks with special facilities.

There was much discussion of the value of tourism. On the basis of returns from a questionnaire, the state highway department estimated that tourists spent between six and seven million dollars in the state during the summer of 1926. Yellowstone National Park was recognized as the great tourist attraction, drawing 260,000 visitors in 1929 and more than 300,000 in 1935.

Every community tried to come up with some gimmick that would hold tourists overnight. Each thought that it had special recreational opportunities and scenery, but the average tourist dashed on to Yellowstone Park or hurried across the state on the Lincoln Highway (Highway 30) with scarcely a pause. Cheyenne's Frontier Days held many tourists for a few days, but other cities and towns could conjure up no comparable attraction. Their rodeos had to depend mainly on natives.

"Loud Shirts And Four-Gallon Hats For Business Men," said a Cheyenne newspaper headline in July, 1922, over a story about the Frontier Days committee's efforts to "create an atmosphere for the visitors." Said a committee member: "We want them to know that they are out west." Such pleas were made regularly in many towns thereafter. In 1939, George Houser, head of the Wyoming Department of Commerce and Industry, tried to get all the natives to wear "western garb," urging them to "give our guests what they expect." No doubt the persistent promotion made big hats and bright shirts more common than they had been among the pioneers.

Lack of revenue held down expenditures for good roads. After the First World War the state received from the federal government surplus road-building equipment and materials valued at $1,500,000. After 1921, when the state's bonding capacity was exhausted, there was a constant struggle to obtain funds needed for matching federal financial aid. Oil royalties after 1920 and a gasoline tax after 1923 became the major sources of matching funds.

Despite revenue problems, mile after mile of highway was surfaced, first with gravel, later with oil. The state highway department in 1924 began to experiment with treating gravel roads with black oil, which was abundant and cheap. By 1929 the state had eighty-seven miles of oiled roads in Albany, Carbon, Goshen, and Natrona counties. Meanwhile, the federal Bureau of Public Roads had oiled the main-loop roads in Yellowstone Park in 1927. By 1939, all main roads in the state had been oiled.

In 1934, deaths in auto accidents surpassed one hundred for the first time.

The auto age changed the lives of Americans remarkably in the 1920's and 1930's. In particular, it made them much more mobile. No longer were there quiet, remote communities in Wyoming where strangers were novelties. No longer were most Wyoming citizens confined to small areas. They spent their weekdays in their flatland towns along the railroad, as before, but many of them now dashed off to distant mountains on summer week ends. The state's scenic attractions also made it possible for tourism to grow so that it could inject a little dynamism into an otherwise static economy.

THE AIR AGE

Close on the heels of the auto age followed the air age. An airplane visited Wyoming as early as 1911, when Colorado daredevil George W. Thompson flew a Denver-built plane at Gillette's Fourth of July celebration. Six weeks later, Riverton people, celebrating the fifth anniversary of their city, were privileged to witness the state's second airplane flight when one W. A. Adams shipped a plane to town, assembled it, and flew away. Planes, however, remained novelties in the state until after the First World War. Then, with the inauguration of New York to San Francisco airmail service in September, 1920, Cheyenne and Rock Springs, particularly the former, had visions of greatness, for they were two of the fourteen stops on the transcontinental route. Converted army De Havilland biplanes with open cockpits were used for several years, capable of flying one hundred miles per hour and attaining an altitude of ten thousand feet. At first the planes did not fly at night, the mail being transferred from plane to train at night and from train to plane in the morning. In February, 1921, when night flying began on an experimental basis, beacons were provided in the form of large bonfires placed every fifty miles between Chicago and Cheyenne.

Cheyenne's municipal airfield in the later 1920's became one of the best equipped in the nation, and it was thought that the city might remain a major air terminal. For several reasons, however, Cheyenne lost its air-age leadership as Denver and many other large cities forged to the front.

CESSION OR LEASING OF THE PUBLIC LANDS?

In 1926, Congressman Charles E. Winter launched a campaign to transfer the public lands in the eleven western "public land" states to those states. Thus he dug up an old demand that earlier Wyoming politicians had discarded as hopeless many years before. No one before, however, had ever been such a dedicated champion of cession as Winter became.

Perry W. Jenkins, president of the state senate, joined Winter's campaign. He steered through the 1927 legislature a memorial to Congress for the "return" to the states of "all vacant and unappropriated lands, together with all resources, including water power, power sites, forests and minerals, now held in trust by the Federal Government within the borders of any of the said states."

Winter spoke repeatedly on the subject, in Congress and elsewhere. A lawyer, he used involved legal arguments in an attempt to establish that the states had absolute rights to the lands within their borders and that the federal government was merely a temporary trustee. Using a less sophisticated argument, he told the Wyoming Wool Growers Association in July, 1927: "The four sons of Uncle Sam, North, East, South and West, were entitled to their equal inheritance. North, East and South duly received theirs. Now when the West comes of age and asks for its equal share, North, East and South step up and say, 'Now we'll divide the last quarter among the four of us for the benefit of all the people.'"

In 1928, Winter, who was in his third term in Congress, tried to unseat Democratic United States Senator John B. Kendrick, while Perry W. Jenkins aspired to Winter's vacated seat in Congress. The two Republicans made public-land cession their principal campaign plank. Early in the year, Jenkins set out to visit the governors of the other ten public-land states in an effort to win their support. He soon had support from the governors of Utah and Arizona, as well as from Governor Emerson of Wyoming, but other governors were less enthusiastic. Likewise, Winter in the summer of 1928 could not organize the united front he had hoped for from the senators and congressmen of the public-land states.

Senator Kendrick rejected the proposal of cession in 1928. Similar bills, he said, had been introduced over a period of many years and had always been referred to committee and allowed to die. Whatever the merits of the respective arguments may have been, Kendrick trounced

Winter by six thousand votes. Vincent Carter, who won the Republican nomination in a contest with Perry W. Jenkins, was elected to Congress, defeating W. S. Kimball by three thousand votes.

In the summer of 1929, the Hoover Administration came out tentatively for cession to the states of the surface rights only on 190,000,000 acres of public-domain grazing land for the benefit of the public schools. In the proposed cession were 17,035,537 acres in Wyoming— 27 per cent of the state's area.

Cession of the grazing rights only was not what Winter, Emerson, Jenkins, and their Wyoming cohorts wanted. Governor Emerson soon issued a formal statement recognizing Hoover's proposal as "in the right direction" but requiring the addition of mineral rights to be satisfactory. Fenimore Chatterton, former acting governor, took the position that it would be unwise to acquire merely the surface rights. A Worland attorney, C. F. Robertson, who spoke often on the subject, expressed the opinion that the states would lose money trying to administer only the surface rights.

Although the Wyoming Legislature, by unanimous vote, had proposed cession of surface and mineral rights in 1927, it soon appeared that the people were not in complete agreement. Conservationists preferred federal control. Even Frank W. Mondell, who had often done battle with conservationists in years gone by, preferred now to leave ownership of minerals to the federal government. Reclamation interests suspected that when federal royalties ended, the reclamation fund would dry up. Dude ranchers also took a jaundiced view of cession.

President Hoover, with the approval of the 1929 Western Governors' Conference, appointed a 22-man Committee on Conservation and Administration of the Public Domain under the chairmanship of James R. Garfield, who had been Secretary of the Interior under President Theodore Roosevelt. Among the members of the committee were Perry W. Jenkins of Big Piney, Wyoming, and Elwood Mead, Commissioner of Reclamation. On January 16, 1931, after hearings and conferences, the committee, as expected, recommended cession of the grazing lands to states which would accept them. With respect to minerals, the committee offered a compromise which was unacceptable to vocal elements in Wyoming. The federal government would retain rights to minerals known to exist and specifically named at the time of the grant and would retain control of its defense areas, parks, forests, monuments, reclamation and reservoir sites, and migratory-bird refuges.

The committee's report gave rise to another spate of discussion. Wyoming wool growers in their convention that year passed a resolution asking for cession of all remaining public lands without reservation. Mart T. Christensen, editor of the *Snake River Sentinel* and registrar in the Cheyenne Land Office, wrote that homesteaders and cattlemen were opposed to cession because they were afraid of what might happen to their individual rights and privileges.

Just as there were differences in Wyoming, so were there from state to state. Some of the public-land states in which the federal government held no valuable minerals saw nothing to be gained for them by awarding rich oil lands to Wyoming—they stood to lose reclamation projects which could be paid for by Wyoming contributions to the reclamation fund if the federal government retained the mineral rights.

THE LEASING QUESTION IS REVIVED

The old question of federal leasing of grazing lands, which had split Wyoming and the West wide open in the years 1906–1913, came up again. The proposal that the federal government withdraw all public land not already withdrawn from entry and adopt a general leasing program became a burning issue, especially after it became apparent that there was no enthusiasm for the Hoover committee's recommendations.

The Hoover committee's proposals were embodied in a bill introduced by Senator Gerald P. Nye (North Dakota) and Congressman John M. Evans (Montana). The bill would grant to the states all unreserved, unappropriated, nonmineral land. The state could sell the land at a minimum of three dollars per acre and lease lands not sold, the proceeds to be held in trust for schools and educational institutions. The President would be authorized to create a national range of its public domain in states not accepting cession. Charles E. Winter called the bill better than nothing and with prescience warned that unless the West got behind the bill, the grazing lands would be leased under federal regulations with permits and fees.

In 1932, Winter published in Casper a 349-page volume, *Four Hundred Million Acres: The Public Lands and Resources*, in which he traced the history of the public lands and presented arguments for cession of both surface and subsurface rights to the states. He suggested that after cession the state could establish a homestead law or sell the land, lease at low rates until sale, and lease mineral rights at royalties low enough to encourage development.

While Winter favored acceptance of the Nye-Evans bill as better than nothing, he urged a continuing battle for eventual transfer of all the remaining lands and their resources, excluding the national parks. He conceded that complete transfer "will not be obtained unless the representatives of the West united in a determined campaign to convince Congress."

The united western effort desired by Winter was not forthcoming. The Nye-Evans bill was dropped because in extensive hearings many objections were raised to it from both West and East. Wyoming witnesses who participated in the hearings included Senator Kendrick, Thomas Cooper, president of the Wyoming Wool Growers Association, and Perry W. Jenkins. Kendrick suggested that subsurface rights be included in the cession. Cooper testified that three dollars per acre was too much to ask for the land. Jenkins urged the inclusion of mineral rights: "We cannot tolerate the existence of a dual government over the same piece of land."

In February, 1933, Senator Kendrick introduced a compromise bill which would cede surface and mineral rights to the states with the proviso that 52.5 per cent of the revenue from mineral acreage would go to the federal government. The federal government would continue its reclamation work, apportioning expenditures among the states on the basis of what they paid into the fund. This would have been favorable to Wyoming, major contributor to the reclamation fund, but the bill had little appeal to other states and was rejected. After Senator Kendrick's death, his successor, Joseph C. O'Mahoney, introduced a similar bill which also got nowhere.

Winter had warned that rejection of the Nye-Evans bill would be followed by federal leasing of the grazing lands. This came to pass with the adoption of the Taylor Grazing Act of June 28, 1934. Winter's replacement in Congress, Vincent Carter, objected strenuously: "This bill will give the Secretary [of the Interior] practically dictatorship over our livestock industry of the West and can be compared to the dictatorship of Russia." The Wyoming Stock Growers Association resolved against it. The association president, Dugald R. Whitaker, called the bill "a most iniquitous measure . . . another example of the bureaucrats in Washington trying to extend their power and their control more and more." After going on record against the Taylor bill, the association adopted a resolution asking summer grazing for twenty-five thousand head of cattle in Yellowstone Park. This alarmed conservationists, even though it was only an emergency request based on drought distress and did not anticipate permanent use of the park for grazing.

The Taylor Grazing Act and the complementary Executive Order

6910 of November, 1934, are important milestones in western history. The executive order virtually ended homesteading, except on reclamation projects, and meant that the federal government would hold on to the bulk of its remaining land, classifying and conserving it. The Taylor Act authorized the Secretary of the Interior to establish great grazing districts on the 173,000,000 acres of withdrawn land (approximately 16,000,000 acres in Wyoming). Five districts were set up in Wyoming on which upwards of 150,000 cattle, 14,000 horses, and 1,500,000 sheep were permitted to graze on a fee basis. By 1939 some 1,500 licenses and permits had been issued in the state, with stockmen being given a voice in the management of the lands through service on advisory boards. Although it took several years, stockmen finally began to give grudging credit to the Taylor Act. Reported Maurice Frink in *Cow Country Cavalcade*: "Many of the ranchers eventually agreed that the Taylor Act, while far from perfect, was one of the best land laws the West has ever had." In particular, the graziers found that they had much more to say about the management of Taylor Act lands than about lands controlled by the Forest Service.

President Hoover and Assistant Secretary of the Interior Joseph M. Dixon had talked of overgrazing in 1929. Secretary of the Interior Ickes noted in his diary in June, 1933: "The public range is being overgrazed to an alarming extent." In pushing his bill, Congressman Taylor of Colorado revived this justification for closer federal supervision under leasing when he said: "There is hardly a spear of grass left in Wyoming." The title to his bill read: "A bill to stop injury to the public grazing lands by preventing overgrazing and soil deterioration." Wyoming graziers resented the overgrazing talk. They conceded that there wasn't much grass, but attributed the scarcity to drought, and they insisted that the range would come back after the resumption of normal rain. Reports of surveys made in 1897 and 1926 by Dr. Aven Nelson, University of Wyoming botanist, were produced to show that the Wyoming range had not deteriorated between these years.[3]

Because of the great influence of the cattle and sheep interests in Wyoming and because there was more federally owned oil in Wyoming than in any other state, public-land issues received more attention in Wyoming than elsewhere in the 1920's and 1930's. Yet many Wyoming

[3] James C. Malin, no foe of conservation, in *The Grassland of North America* (Lawrence: James C. Malin, 1956), pp. 131–141, has filed a protest against "misinformation and misuse of information" by government officials and private individuals "in an excess of zeal to sell conservation policies to the public." As Malin points out, there were dust storms and erosion in the West long before cattlemen and farmers arrived.

people in towns and cities paid little attention to the extensive discussions of public-land problems. The *Wyoming State Tribune*, for example, in April, 1934, complained about public apathy with respect to the Taylor bill as it moved toward adoption. Moreover, on final passage, Senator O'Mahoney voted for the bill. That fall, he defeated Vincent Carter, who had been an outstanding critic of the bill, by thirteen thousand votes. As in earlier years, there was no consensus regarding public-land policies. For the most part, each person looked to his own interest, and many people could not see clearly where their own best interests lay.

THE PETROLEUM INDUSTRY FALTERS AND BECOMES CONTROVERSIAL

Everyone was optimistic about the future of Wyoming's oil industry at the end of the First World War. Everyone knew that the state had great oil reserves and that the multiplying automobiles would have to have gasoline.

The Oil and Gas Leasing Act of 1920 appeared to solve certain problems that had been plaguing the industry for years. Federal lands would now be thrown open to oil companies on a lease basis, and the state stood to benefit from both the production and the royalties. The government's royalty would be divided: 10 per cent to the general treasury, 52.5 per cent to the United States Reclamation Fund, and 37.5 per cent to the state where the oil was produced. Wyoming's congressional delegation and Governor Robert D. Carey fought for a state share of 45 per cent but had to settle for 37.5. The state would use its portion for roads and schools. After a few changes, the Wyoming distribution would be established as follows: 50 per cent for public schools, 41 per cent for highways and roads, and 9 per cent for capital improvements at the University of Wyoming. The state would also share in the royalty money which accrued to the United States Reclamation Fund. Wyoming's 37.5 per cent amounted to $748,445 in 1921, $1,743,875 in 1922, $2,424,481 in 1923, and $4,223,298 in 1924. Thereafter the royalty income declined, along with production, and remained below the 1924 figure until after World War II, when it rose to new highs.

Meanwhile, since 1913, the state and its counties had been collecting property tax on all crude oil produced. Other revenues came from leases on state lands. Particularly profitable was a school section in the Salt Creek Field which brought many millions to the state.

Expanding oil production cushioned the state's economic difficulties

in the early 1920's. The Midwest Refining Company and Standard of
Indiana built refineries at Laramie in 1920–1921, using crude from the
Rock Creek Field, and Standard enlarged its Casper refinery until it
was recognized for a few years as the largest in the world. Standard of
Indiana took over Midwest operations at Casper, Laramie, and Grey-
bull in 1921 and became the dominant oil company in the state.

Oil production rose from 1,600,000 barrels in 1912 to almost
13,000,000 barrels in 1918 and on up to 44,000,000 in 1923. In 1922
the state geologist had asserted that, thanks to oil, the mining industry
was more important than either livestock or agriculture in the state's
economy. After 1923, however, production declined gradually, to a
low point of only 11,500,000 barrels in 1933, before beginning to climb
once again. For many years other states had marketing advantages, and
in particular Wyoming's heavy black crude was not in demand.

Since many people expected more benefits from the oil industry than
it delivered, politicians and editors harried the industry from several
directions. Indeed, war against the oil interests was a salient theme of
the state's history in the twenties and thirties.

Beginning in 1921, there was much controversy over the low prices
paid by the Standard Oil Company for Wyoming crude. Independent
oilmen organized the Independent Oil Association and talked about the
need for an independent refinery or a pipeline to Chicago to boost
Wyoming crude prices. Then came much dispute over the Teapot
Dome affair, a complex one which had far-reaching repercussions and
was given national headlines for years. Thirty miles north of Casper
and just south of the Salt Creek Field lies the Teapot Dome formation.
For years it had been a navy petroleum reserve. Early in 1922,
Leslie A. Miller and other independent oilmen complained to
Senator Kendrick of rumors that Teapot Dome was being leased
privately without competitive bidding. Senator Kendrick asked
questions in the Senate, and on April 16, 1922, the Senate adopted his
resolution calling upon Secretary of the Navy Edwin Denby and
Secretary of the Interior Albert B. Fall to advise the Senate whether
negotiations were in progress for the leasing of the 9,481-acre Teapot
Dome Reserve without competitive bidding. Kendrick's resolution
elicited the admission that a contract had been signed by the government and Harry F. Sinclair's Mammoth Oil Company for development
of Teapot Dome.

In Wyoming the Republican press, as well as the Democratic,
objected to the lease. It was argued that the lease would allow oil to be

piped out which should be refined in the state. The rights of other bidders were also stressed. Governor Robert D. Carey and former Governor B. B. Brooks maintained that in view of the national surplus of petroleum, the reserve should be left untapped. Some Wyoming people, such as Laramie editor W. E. Chaplin, argued that the contract was favorable to Wyoming because it would broaden the market for Wyoming oil and increase the price of the state's crude. They argued further that Salt Creek development was draining oil from Teapot Dome, making it necessary for offset drilling to protect the government's interest. Majority opinion has held, however, that Teapot Dome cannot be drained from Salt Creek.

As American-history textbooks relate, investigations and prosecutions led eventually to the resignations of Denby and Fall, cancellation of the Teapot Dome lease and the Elk Hills Reserve lease in California, and prison terms for Secretary of the Interior Albert B. Fall and oilman Harry F. Sinclair. Wyoming's Federal District Judge T. Blake Kennedy upheld the Teapot Dome lease, but he was overruled by the Circuit Court of Appeals and the United States Supreme Court.

While the Teapot Dome scandal was being ventilated, there developed a drive for a state severance tax on oil. It was commonly thought that Wyoming's oil would soon be gone and therefore a special tax should be imposed on this "exhaustible resource" during its short life to compensate the state for painful adjustments. Even state geologist G. B. Morgan said in 1922: "The oil will be largely exhausted in the U.S. inside of 20 years and that is also probably true of the oil fields of Wyoming." Absentee ownership aroused opinions such as those expressed by Fred Hoffman in a letter to the *Wyoming State Tribune* dated January 6, 1923:

Too many look upon Wyoming as an excellent milch cow to be milked dry; and have not even the decency to leave the skim milk, nay, they even refuse to furnish a wisp of hay for her sustenance. . . . From now on, we shall see that this cow, Wyoming, gets a square deal. Don't forget that . . . we'll be here when the cow is dry, and these foreign milkers leave and search for another cow. . . .

Legislators from both political parties proposed bills for a severance tax in 1923. Since the Republicans were in control, the bill introduced by John A. Stevenson, Republican rancher from Albany County and chairman of the Oil and Gas Affairs Committee, was given the right of way. His bill would assess a 1 per cent tax on the gross value of crude oil and similar taxes on other mineral products. Dozens of lobbyists gathered, and the battle was furiously fought. "Kill the oil industry in the state of Wyoming and half the population would be thrown out of work overnight," cried the *Casper Tribune-Herald.* Governor William B. Ross importuned a joint session to defy the oil lobby. The House killed the Stevenson bill 29 to 20. One factor in its defeat was the suspicion, well propagated, that it was unconstitutional. Also, it was argued that the property tax collected on oil since 1913 was enough of a burden on the industry. Unwilling to drop the subject, the 1923 legislature voted to submit a constitutional amendment to the people, including the provision that in addition to the production tax already authorized in the constitution, "there shall be levied a severance license tax based on the actual value of the gross product." As the 1924 election approached, Governor Ross spoke repeatedly in favor of the amendment. The amendment failed because, while 39,109 voted for it and only 27,795 against it, many persons at the polls did not vote on the amendment, and therefore the 39,109 yes votes did not constitute a majority of the 84,822 electors. Though often renewed later, the drive for a severance tax would never again come so close to victory.

In April, 1923, the state land board renewed its lucrative lease of Section 36 in the Salt Creek Field to the Midwest Oil Company, which was now a producing subsidiary of Standard of Indiana. The company had been paying one-third royalty. The new lease, to go into effect October 1, 1924, called for 65 per cent. Again there was argument, some saying that it should have been 65 per cent all along, while oilmen replied that in the 1923 renewal the company had been whipsawed by competing bidders and had agreed to pay too much. Further controversy stemmed from the fact that not until May, 1923, did the Board of Land Commissioners decide to employ someone to check on and verify the oil royalties from the Salt Creek Field. Ever since 1917 there had been complaints that it was not good business to let the lessees alone decide how much royalty they owed.

In a dramatic illustration of what oil could do for the state, the Producers and Refiners Corporation in 1922–1923 built a refinery and model town for fifteen hundred persons six miles east of Rawlins. Crude oil was piped from the Lost Soldier and Salt Creek fields. The "Wonder Town of Wyoming," as it came to be known, with its striking Spanish architecture, was named Parco from the initials of the company. Later, when the Sinclair Oil Company acquired the property in a receivership sale in 1934, the name of the town was changed to Sinclair.

The price of gasoline has been a constant annoyance to Wyoming people, who cannot understand why they should pay more than people

living in states without oil fields and refineries. Leslie A. Miller, an
independent oil dealer, told the Young Men's Literary Club in August,
1923, that Standard of Indiana dominated the oil industry in Wyoming
and other states and through the "Tulsa plus" system charged Wyoming people excessive gasoline prices. The "Tulsa plus" system meant
that the region's base price was set for Tulsa, Oklahoma, and then
consumers in Cheyenne, for example, would have to pay the base price
plus the freight from Tulsa. What had been a recurring irritation
became, in 1927, a constant and nonpartisan itch that persisted until
World War II and beyond. Two Republican editors, Watt Brandon in
the *Sheridan Journal* and John Charles Thompson in the *Wyoming State
Tribune* (Cheyenne), began complaining in the spring of that year.
Other editors soon joined them.

The 1929 legislature asked Governor Emerson to direct an inquiry
into the retail prices charged for gasoline. The committee reported to
the 1931 legislature that the nominally higher costs of refining did not
justify the higher prices on gasoline in Wyoming as compared to other
states, whereupon Senator George B. McClellan of Washakie County
proposed legislation to institute state refining and retailing, but he got
nowhere. In 1932, Thomas A. Nicholas, Gillette city attorney, took the
lead in organizing a nonprofit corporation called the "United Gas
Users," which began state-wide agitation for lower gasoline prices and
state refining.

Lower prices were discussed in the political campaign of 1932.
Advertisements bore the slogan "A vote for Miller is a vote for lower
gasoline prices in Wyoming." Soon after his inauguration, Governor
Leslie A. Miller called a conference of oil-company representatives and
listened to familiar arguments about the greater costs of doing business
in Wyoming.

Assorted bills were introduced in the 1933 legislature, despite
Attorney General James A. Greenwood's opinion that the state had no
jurisdiction to fix retail prices on gasoline. Later that year, the depres-
sion-spawned National Recovery Administration approved gasoline
prices which Governor Miller called unfairly high for Wyoming. His
administration filed a lawsuit against the Continental Oil Company in
September, 1933, charging discrimination against the state and certain
parts of the state and asking for cancellation of the company's permit to
do business. In July, 1935, the case was decided against the state in
district court at Cheyenne.

In December, 1938, a committee on the preservation of state
resources reported that although gasoline prices were relatively high,

nothing could be done about it without risking the closing of refineries. Republican Governor Nels H. Smith nevertheless told the 1939 legislature that gasoline prices in the state were too high and that there should be legislation to compel price reductions. Three days later, gasoline prices in Cheyenne rose two cents a gallon. Assorted gasoline-price bills introduced in the Republican-controlled legislature were all defeated. Attorney General Ewing T. Kerr declared in August, 1939, that a gasoline trust existed in the state and sent a telegram to Roosevelt's trust buster Thurman W. Arnold asking help in breaking the trust. Arnold arranged for the Federal Bureau of Investigation to help probe Kerr's contention that in Wyoming "the major oil companies have not only set the price but have contacted independent dealers with a view to getting them to raise their prices on all occasions when the major companies advance their retail prices." Arnold also promised to proceed nationally on the issue of the basing-point system.

Kerr summoned representatives of four major oil companies to appear and answer accusations on September 12, 1939. The company representatives denied charges of price fixing and conspiracy. Kerr told the companies that they were also charged with violating the state's unfair-competition laws. Standard Oil Company attorney G. R. Hagens of Casper warned Kerr that enforcement of these acts would force "the companies to the wall. If that is the case, the companies may as well get ready to pack and leave Wyoming." Such threats had served to silence critics on previous occasions.

In his message to the 1941 legislature, Governor Nels Smith reported that his administration had been successful in reducing gasoline prices in the state an average of approximately three cents a gallon in the past two years. Nevertheless, there was further talk of state refining, and Democratic Senator Roy Montgomery of Gillette introduced an unacceptable bill to place full control of prices and the licensing of gasoline dealers in the hands of the Public Service Commission. World War II soon put an end to talk of state control of gasoline prices. Whether the efforts to reduce gasoline prices brought any changes in pricing that would not have come had there been no agitation is a moot question.

CONSERVATION OF OIL AND GAS

From time to time conservation issues agitated the oil and gas industry and the legislature. In 1921, "anti-carbon black" legislation disturbed what was an otherwise harmonious session of the legislature.

The 1919 legislature had prohibited carbon-black manufacturing plants within ten miles of an industrial plant or an incorporated city or town. The issue arose because the American Carbon Company's carbon-black plant at Cowley was burning millions of cubic feet of natural gas per day from the Byron Field. It was explained that carbon-black was made by a process similar to holding a metal sheet over a candle, the "black" being all that was taken from the gas. Meanwhile, the Western Sugar Company, the Lovell Brick and Tile Company, and the town of Lovell were also using natural gas from the Byron Field, and they feared that the carbon-black plant would soon exhaust the supply. After the American Carbon Company's allegation that the 1919 law was unconstitutional had been denied by the United States Supreme Court, lobbyists for the carbon-black industry persuaded the 1921 legislature to repeal the 1919 law. Governor Carey, however, vetoed the repeal measure after adjournment and advised carbon-black manufacturers to move outside the ten-mile limit. Another desperate attempt by the carbon-black lobby to repeal restrictions failed in the 1923 legislature.

Secretary of the Interior Ray Lyman Wilbur in March, 1929, announced suspension of further permits for oil exploration on the public domain. Only fifty-six leases had resulted from thirty-four thousand permits issued since the Oil and Gas Leasing Act of 1920. Secretary Wilbur said that too many individuals and companies appeared to be obtaining permits for speculative purposes instead of development. The announced purpose of the suspension was to clean up the misuse of outstanding permits and to clear the way for "constructive conservation." Wilbur also spoke of the waste of natural gas, loss of gas pressures, consequent losses in total oil yield, and wasteful diversion of oil from gasoline to fuel.

A thousand citizens attended a meeting in Casper in April, 1929, at which Governor Frank Emerson and B. B. Brooks, president of the Rocky Mountain Oil and Gas Association, alleged that there was no legitimate reason for locking up public-land oil reserves. President Hoover, after listening to protests from western senators, including Warren and Kendrick, invited the governors of western oil states to send representatives to a June, 1929, Colorado Springs conference to consider the possibility of creating an interstate compact for oil conservation.

During the next few years, national overproduction of oil and the Great Depression drove the price of Salt Creek crude down to nineteen cents a barrel in 1931. In July, Acting Governor A. M. Clark appealed to President Hoover, asking him to halt the sale of crude from government lands in Wyoming because the low prices meant minuscule royalty payments and consequent difficulties for school financing and highway construction. Acting Secretary of the Interior Joseph M. Dixon replied to Clark that in the Oil and Gas Leasing Act of 1920, Congress did not authorize federal price fixing for crude oil. He suggested that oil-producing states must take the initiative in solving the oil crisis through proration of production and markets.

After much talk, six states—Texas, Oklahoma, Kansas, New Mexico, Illinois, and Colorado—in 1935 entered into the Interstate Compact for Conservation of Oil and Natural Gas, approved by Congress. The expressed purpose of the compact, which from time to time was joined by other states, was "to conserve oil and gas by the prevention of physical waste thereof from any cause." Wyoming chose not to join the compact in 1935, preferring to wait twenty years. The long delay was due to fear that Wyoming oilmen would be asked to restrict production and might lose their independence of action. In 1941, when only Wyoming and California among the major oil states remained outside the compact, Governor Nels Smith asked the legislature to authorize the state to join the compact. He insisted that nothing in the voluntary compact could restrict Wyoming's production. Smith was afraid that unless all the oil states could provide a united front, there would be federal controls and federally imposed production quotas. The Governor's proposal was defeated in the Senate, and Wyoming remained outside the compact until 1955.

Another oil-industry issue flared up in the 1930's over pipelines. R. W. Fenwick, editor of the *Casper Times*, was credited with beginning a fight to block construction of a pipeline from Lance Creek, the booming field of the period, to Denver. The Casper Trades and Labor Assembly in August, 1938, asked for a special session of the legislature to halt construction of the line. Casper refinery workers also proposed a severance tax on oil taken out of the state for processing elsewhere. No special session was called, and the Continental Oil Company built its line to Denver. The following year, protests flowed to Cheyenne regarding a proposed pipeline from Fort Laramie to Salt Lake City. Wyoming labor organizations insisted that the line would throw hundreds of railroad workers and other men out of work. The county commissioners of Uinta, Lincoln, and Sweetwater counties asked for a special session to halt construction. Oil-company and pipeline officials replied that they thought they were doing Wyoming a favor by building the line. Said one: "If Wyoming prevents the building of the line, many of the fields will have to be closed down. . . . What good is our crude if we can't sell it?" Former Governor B. B. Brooks, head of the Rocky Mountain Oil and Gas Association, urged Governor Smith to let the line be built, and it was built.

A Lost Cause: Prohibition

An observer might easily have made the mistake of concluding that prohibition would be easy to enforce in Wyoming, since the state voted for it better than three to one at the November, 1918, election. After prohibition went into effect on July 1, 1919, events soon showed that the state's notorious aridity did not extend to alley, cellar, and parlor. Hundreds of raids turned up liquor and stills in all sorts of places, some in cities, some in rural areas far from settlements. In 1961, Jim Griffith, Sr., Lusk publisher, looked back to the 1920's and recalled that "times were tough then and many a small rancher who was otherwise a law-abiding citizen, in order to make ends meet, had embarked in the business of making moonshine. . . . And most of them made a pretty good brand of drinking liquor."

After one year the *Wyoming State Tribune* reported that there were fewer drunks and fewer arrests than before prohibition, yet anyone who wanted a drink could find it: "First there is old stuff that has been kept but costs a small fortune, then there is the home-made brew, and then comes perfume, hair tonic, flavoring extracts and patent medicines. . . . These produce some peculiar results and make some men wild."

Federal, state, and local officers converged on violators. In December, 1921, federal officers announced that in Sweetwater County they had completed the biggest and most successful raid of its kind west of the Mississippi River. They arrested 62 persons in Rock Springs, Green River, and Superior and confiscated 1,400 boxes of raisins, 3,000 gallons of "dago red" wine, and 1,000 gallons of other intoxicants. Those arrested who pleaded guilty in federal court in Cheyenne were fined $200 each, Judge T. Blake Kennedy's usual penalty for possession. Penalties were usually not heavy enough to discourage offenders from repeating their offenses, and much evidence was suppressed in court on grounds that the search and seizure provision of the United States Constitution had been violated. In 1922, federal agents made 208 arrests for illegal manufacture and 598 for illegal sale. Many other persons were arrested by the state law enforcement department, county sheriffs, and city police.

So many arrests could not be accomplished without occasional gun-play. Bootleggers and officers alike were killed. Three trigger-happy state agents near Laramie in September, 1919, riddled a passing automobile and killed an innocent young rancher, Frank Jennings, whom they mistook for a bootlegger. All three of the agents received long penitentiary sentences. In June, 1923, county officers lay in the sage-brush near a moonshine cache four miles north of Cody. When two unarmed Greybull men approached, the agents fired, killing one and shattering the leg of the other. Quite beside herself, Caroline Lockhart wrote in her *Cody Enterprise*: "It looks to the people of this locality as if human life was getting pretty cheap when any person with a nickel star pinned on him can go out and shoot and kill in the name of the law and order without a warrant, for an offense which, at most, is only a misdemeanor." She said that one of the gunmen was the courthouse janitor. The county attorney sued Miss Lockhart for libel, but failed to collect anything.

Excessive zeal was less common than laxity among the local officials. The state superintendent of the Anti-Saloon League complained in 1920: "Folks have grown indifferent—too many have laughed over violations. . . . Too many towns and counties have failed to do their duty." Governor Robert D. Carey told the legislature in 1921 that "in some counties open saloons are being permitted." Governor William B. Ross told the 1923 legislature: "The violation of this law is grave enough in itself, but in addition it is breeding contempt for all laws." He asked for, and got, authority to remove any county officer who failed to discharge his full duty. Before his death, which came less than two years later, Governor Ross brought about the resignations of a county sheriff and a county attorney.

The 1920's have been called the "Roaring Twenties," the "Lawless Decade," and the "Era of Wonderful Nonsense." All three designations are appropriate in view of some of the transactions in Wyoming. Let two examples suffice. In his memoirs, Federal District Judge T. Blake Kennedy related that the state prohibition commissioner once came to him and borrowed two quarts of gin for a party, promising to return a like quantity within a few days. Concluded the Judge: "If he could replace it, it seemed to me that he was getting liquor from an illegal source. The fact was that I never enjoyed the fulfillment of his promise as I was out two bottles of gin." Again, Mike Perko refused to pay full price for three tons of grapes he had bought from the Rock Springs Commercial Company. The Wyoming Supreme Court in September,

1927, required Perko to pay, despite his declaration that the grapes were "musty, damp, green and did not make wine but vinegar."

Enthusiasm for prohibition, so evident in 1918, waned in the twenties. Senators Warren and Kendrick reported in April, 1926, that their heavy mail showed that Wyoming opinion was evenly divided, yet in 1927 the state Senate cast only four votes in favor of a proposed memorial to Congress stating that prohibition was a failure and asking for a referendum.

Heavier penalties were tried as a deterrent in the late 1920's. Governor William B. Ross had recommended imprisonment for first offenders in 1923. Imprisonment did become more common thereafter, but as the penalties stiffened, convictions became more difficult. The 1927 legislature passed, and Governor Frank Emerson approved, a measure making possession of a still subject to a three-year penitentiary sentence. The vote was close. In the House debate, Representative Milward L. Simpson, then of Big Horn County, was reported to have said: "My county is sopping wet and the saloons run wide open." Juries, he said, would not convict if conviction meant a jail term. The federal Jones-Stalker Act of 1929 (called the "Five and Ten Law") authorized penalties up to five years in the penitentiary and fines up to ten thousand dollars for illegal possession of liquor. The first two men to be sentenced under the new law in Wyoming, however, were fined only five hundred dollars each, although one of them was also sent to the county jail for thirty days. During 1929, some 425 persons were arrested in Wyoming by federal agents on charges of violating federal prohibition laws, as compared with 393 in 1928 and 806 in 1922.

Repeal was a major national issue in the presidential campaign of 1928. The three chapters of the Woman's Christian Temperance Union in Cheyenne chose as their slogan: "We are going to dry clean Al Smith with a Hoover." Mrs. Nellie Tayloe Ross, who had been governor from 1925 to 1927, said at a Cheyenne rally just before the 1928 election that although she was a prohibitionist, she supported Al Smith because violations of the law were so numerous and flagrant. The state gave Hoover a majority of almost two to one, which should not be taken to mean that the state was vehemently dry in 1928, since other issues besides prohibition were involved.

Two magazine polls in 1930 obtained contradictory results. The *Pathfinder* found the state dry, the *Literary Digest*, wet. Judging by the *Literary Digest* poll, Wyoming and Montana were the wettest states in the region, and both were wetter than the nation as a whole.

The drys clearly were on the run after 1929. Prohibition agents were regarded with more suspicion than ever after William C. Irving, state law-enforcement commissioner from November, 1927, to December, 1928, was sentenced to serve eighteen months in federal prison following conviction in February, 1930, on charges of conspiracy to violate national prohibition laws. There were four other convictions in the same conspiracy, two from Thermopolis and two from Kemmerer. While he was head of the state's law-enforcement department, Irving collected thousands of dollars in "protection money." For example, speak-easies at Rawlins paid him fifty dollars each, and operators of a large still at Thermopolis paid him one dollar per gallon.

City officials in Thermopolis and Rock Springs in May, 1930, were charged with conspiracy to violate the national prohibition law. It appears that they used a system of fines as a form of licensing. Some of the Thermopolis officials who pleaded guilty were fined $250 each by Judge T. Blake Kennedy. There was no element of personal gain, said the Judge; they were collecting revenue "with a view of benefiting the municipality." Other Thermopolis citizens—ranging from red-light district ladies to club owners—pleaded not guilty and were acquitted by the jury. City officials and others indicted in the Rock Springs "conspiracy" were likewise found not guilty by the jury.

The mayor and chief of police and thirty-four other citizens of Casper were indicted and tried on conspiracy charges in 1933. Deputy United States Attorney Ewing T. Kerr asserted that "something more than the prohibition law is involved. The issue of men in public office who betrayed every trust the citizens of Casper imposed in them is involved in this case." The jury found the accused not guilty of accepting protection money.

Meanwhile, public sentiment swung rapidly in the direction of repeal. Mrs. Dora McGrath of Thermopolis, the state's first woman senator, declared in January, 1931, that "I do not think the prohibition law can be enforced. . . . I wish we were back where we started from." The legislature gave the voters a chance to express their opinions for or against repeal at the November, 1932, election. In the referendum, 52,957 (71.5 per cent) voted for repeal and 21,015 favored retention of the prohibition law. Thereafter the only question was how soon the details of state and national repeal could be worked out. By December, 1933, three-fourths of the states, including Wyoming, had ratified the Twenty-first Amendment, and the Noble Experiment was at an end, except in a few states and localities which chose to remain dry.

The end of prohibition was celebrated with excitement reminiscent of the last pre-prohibition hours. In Wyoming, 3.2 beer became legal at midnight, May 19, 1933. Cheyenne, Laramie, and Evanston streets were jammed "to greet the return of a prodigal." Since the return of beer was delayed in Utah, cars from that state filled the streets of Evanston, where the town siren sounded at midnight as the sale of beer began. The 3.2 beer proved disappointing to many people, so they settled down to waiting for the legalization of stronger stuff, which came to Wyoming in April, 1935. The legislature chose to establish a state liquor commission which would engage in liquor wholesaling. The Republican minority opposed such "socialism," but the Democratic majority felt that the new source of revenue was needed.

THE GREAT DEPRESSION

. Accustomed as they were to frugal living, the people of Wyoming suffered less from the Great Depression of the 1930's than did the nation. Yet further belt tightening was required, and the agony was considerable. The state's taxable valuation, which had changed little in the twenties, shrank from $448,000,000 in 1929 to $300,000,000 in 1935. Assessed oil production dwindled to ten million barrels valued at only six million dollars in 1934. Motor-vehicle registration dropped 15 per cent between 1931 and 1933. The Bureau of the Census reported the state's retail business down 46 per cent between 1929 and 1933, motors and apparel showing the sharpest declines. Fewer tourists entered the state, and those who came spent less money than in former times.

President Herbert Hoover's 1932 position that "it is not the function of the government to relieve individuals of their responsibilities to their neighbors, or to relieve private institutions of their responsibilities to the public" was accepted in Wyoming longer than elsewhere in the country. Wyoming was the only state that rejected the Reconstruction Finance Corporation's 1932–1933 offer of loans to states for emergency-relief purposes on the condition that the loans would have to be repaid out of future federal-aid road appropriations. Editors and political leaders took pride in the state's posture of self-reliance. In December, 1933, however, Governor Leslie A. Miller told a special session of the legislature that self-help had failed. Surveys had revealed thousands of cases of undernourished children and many cases of inadequate clothing. A total of $95,443 had been accepted, he reported, in outright grants from the federal government for relief purposes. The state could qualify for one dollar in federal grants for every three dollars expended by state and local agencies. Since almost all of the county poor and pauper funds were overdrawn, the Governor asked for and got a state appropriation of $75,000 for distribution to the counties for food, clothing, fuel, and shelter. At the close of 1933, one Wyoming person in five was receiving some form of relief and the unemployed numbered twenty thousand.

In 1935, after the worst phase of the emergency had passed, the federal government decided to return the burden of direct relief to the states but continued the administration of work relief. That same year, the state established the Department of Public Welfare and assigned to it the general administration of public relief and the supervision of county departments which issued aid to dependent children, the blind, the aged, and others in need.

Wyoming relief rolls remained long throughout the 1930's. Governor Miller explained to the 1937 legislature why they did not shrink quickly with improving conditions:

At the outset of the depression there were many people ordinarily unemployed who were being taken care of by relatives and friends. After a while many of these relatives and friends became sorely beset and were forced to turn such responsibilities over to relief agencies. When the employables found the going rough, they first resorted to the use of their savings and investments, but when the depression drew out to such a length of time, these resources dwindled away and finally many of this class had to move in with relatives and friends and ultimately turned in large numbers, along with the unemployables, to the relief rolls.

Now, most of the unemployables who formerly were cared for without resort to public funds are still on the relief rolls and will be indefinitely because it will be a long time before their former sources of support will be rehabilitated to the extent they can be taken back. Moreover, it has been accepted that these people properly are public charges and it is doubtful if it will again be regarded as disgraceful to be carried on public charity as it once was. Then there is the problem of men being displaced by machinery— we have examples in Wyoming of road machinery, single units of which will do the work of dozens of teams and men as roads were built only a few years ago. . . .

Drought compounded the state's distress in 1933, 1934, and 1936. The federal government purchased starving cattle and sheep, slaughtering on the range some of them that were unfit for human consumption. The government transported other animals to more favored areas and supplied loans to ranchers and farmers at a time when the state farmloan fund was virtually exhausted.

The Agricultural Adjustment Administration paid many farmers for reducing wheat and sugar-beet acreages in 1935. When that agency was declared unconstitutional in 1936, a soil-conservation program was substituted. In late 1936, the Resettlement Administration purchased 300,000 acres of land in Goshen, Platte, Converse, Campbell, and Weston counties at a cost of nine million dollars. Conservation practices were introduced in 1937 to begin restoration of the purchased land.

The Wyoming Stock Growers Association, which had been weak in the 1920's, became powerful once again in the 1930's and 1940's. The Association membership increased from 262 in 1930 to 2,102 in 1945. In the 1930's ranchers and farmers suffered as much as urban folks, although they had one advantage—they almost always had something to eat. The well-known self-reliance of the stockmen eroded as they accepted government subsidies. Oda Mason, president of the WSGA in 1945–1946, recalled that stockmen accepted subsidies "because everyone else was doing it." The federal government spent $141,185,431 in Wyoming in the period 1933–1939, which was more per capita than all other states except Nevada and Montana received. The stockmen got their share.

Most popular New Deal innovation was the Civilian Conservation Corps, which had nineteen camps in Wyoming in 1934. The boys in the corps thinned forest trees, eliminated rodents, prepared public campgrounds, built trails and bridges, and removed dead trees from the shore line of Jackson Lake. Each boy earned thirty dollars a month, of which twenty-five dollars was sent home to his family. For most of the boys, the opportunity to spend a year or two in a Wyoming C.C.C. camp was a memorable privilege.

The federal Public Works Administration put up many buildings: post offices at Powell, Wheatland, Lusk, and Riverton, a liberal-arts building and a student union at the University of Wyoming, the Wyoming Supreme Court building at Cheyenne, and thirty-three school buildings. Highway construction boomed as federal aid made possible a network of oiled roads. Reclamation projects—out of favor in the 1920's—gained new support as job-giving public works. Federal expenditures on the Kendrick, Riverton, and Shoshone projects helped the state. The Rural Electrification Administration increased the number of electrified farms and ranches from 527 in 1935 to 3,300 in 1939.

Unemployed transients abounded all through the decade. Federal aid for transients was instituted in October, 1933, with the Salvation Army doing most of the work. Beginning in August, 1935, indigent transients were required to work for their room and board at five camps located at Cheyenne, Laramie, Green River, Casper, and the 0-7 Ranch near Casper.

The National Youth Administration offered jobs to needy students at the University of Wyoming, where projects offered opportunities to work up to thirty hours a month at thirty cents an hour.

Many people in the big cities looked to Communism as a possible solution for the nation's economic ills. Just as the "Red hunt" following the First World War turned up few dangerous aliens in Wyoming, so also were there few Communists in the state during the Great Depression. Communist party candidates for governor, congressman, and secretary of state in 1934 received between 150 and 170 votes, some of them probably being cast as protest votes by non-Communists. The Communist Party of Wyoming held a convention in Cheyenne in July, 1936. The party, which seems to have been active mainly in Cheyenne, could muster only 91 Wyoming votes for its presidential candidate that fall.

The churches, traditional refuge in times of trouble, may have meant more than they usually did to their old members in the depths of the depression, but they did not attract many new members. Only 30 per cent of the state's population were church members in 1936, as compared to 45.45 per cent for the nation.[4]

As was true for the nation, Wyoming's birth rate in the 1930's was down and its suicide rate was up. Those old enough to remember it will never forget the Great Depression, which shook the country and the state as a great war might do and left an indelible impression on all who lived through it.

[4] The percentages are based on 1930 populations. Figuring the percentage in each case on the population of the previous decennial census, Wyoming had 25.9 per cent church members in 1906; 27.1 per cent in 1916; 32 per cent in 1926; and 30 per cent in 1936. The actual count of members in 1936 was as follows: all denominations, 67,770; Roman Catholic, 17,695; Latter-day Saints, 16,497; Protestant Episcopal, 6,284; Methodist Episcopal, 6,147; Presbyterian Church in the U.S.A., 4,549; Northern Baptist, 4,017; Congregational and Christian, 2,496; Lutheran Synod of Missouri, Ohio and Other States, 2,157; all other bodies, 7,928. The state's percentages of Methodists, Presbyterians, Northern Baptists, Congregationalists and Christians, and Lutherans were close to the national percentages for those denominations. Wyoming's percentage of Roman Catholics (7.8) was less than half the national percentage for that faith (16.2). On the other hand, the state's percentage of Latter-day Saints (7.3) was much greater than the national percentage for the Latter-day Saints (0.05). Wyoming had very few adherents to several faiths which ranked very high nationally: Jewish, Negro Baptist, Southern Baptist, and Methodist Episcopal South. No religious census has been taken in the United States since 1936.

CHAPTER 15

Politics and Government, 1920–1940

THE TERM "GRAND OLD MAN" has been applied to three Wyoming
political leaders. One of them, Joseph M. Carey, died February 5,
1924, at the age of seventy-nine. His contributions to territory and state
have been mentioned often in earlier chapters. In brief, he served as
United States attorney for Wyoming (1869–1871), associate justice of
the Wyoming Territorial Supreme Court (1871–1876), territorial
delegate to Congress (1885–1890), United States senator (1890–1895),
and governor (1911–1915). He was "father" of the Wheatland Colony
and owner of the famous CY cattle brand. Federal District Judge T.
Blake Kennedy wrote in his memoirs that Carey was "possessed of a
peculiarly vindictive disposition and temperament oft-time akin to a

447

school girl." Said Kennedy: "He took to heart any opposition to himself and punished those who had opposed him in an exceedingly icy manner." Nevertheless, Kennedy called Carey "perhaps the most astute and effective stump speaker that Wyoming has produced." The Judge considered Carey a man of "preeminent ability . . . a big man in big things."[1]

The second Grand Old Man, Francis E. Warren, died November 24, 1929, at the age of eighty-five. His contributions have figured prominently in earlier chapters. He was territorial governor, 1885–1886 and 1889–1890, and first state governor briefly in 1890 before going to the United States Senate. He served in the Senate thirty-seven years and four days, which was the longest period of Senate service on record until Carl Hayden surpassed it in 1964. Just before his death Warren was making plans to run again in 1930. As chairman of the Senate Appropriations Committee from 1921–1929, he did just about all a senator could to further the interests of his constituents. The *Denver News* in June, 1929, called him the "West's great patronage dispenser." Head of the Republican party in Wyoming for many years, he was so well regarded by a majority of his constituents that he scarcely needed to campaign. Six months before he died, the *New York Times* said of him that "few Americans have led such useful lives. . . . He . . . works incessantly, always knows his subject, never says anything unless he has to and then something completely to the point tending to expedite the matter he has in hand."

The third Grand Old Man, John B. Kendrick, died November 3, 1933, at the age of seventy-six. Unlike Carey and Warren, he was a Democrat. He was governor from 1915 to 1917. Elected to the United States Senate in 1916, he was re-elected in 1922 and 1928. In all of his four major election contests he was confronted by above-average opposition. He entered the Senate by ousting the four-term veteran Clarence D. Clark in 1916, kept his seat in 1922 against the formidable challenge of Frank W. Mondell, who left the position of majority floor leader in the United States House of Representatives to run against him, and then in 1928 defeated three-term Congressman Charles E. Winter. No matter whether it was a Democratic or Republican year, Kendrick was invincible in popular elections. In 1928, for instance, when Republican Herbert Hoover carried the state by a plurality of 23,449, Kendrick trounced Winter, no pushover, by almost

[1] Judge T. Blake Kennedy's memoirs (in typescript) are in the University of Wyoming Library.

6,000 votes. Kendrick was not an ardent partisan, stating in the 1928 campaign, for example, that he had always tried to avoid partisan politics, desiring only to serve as a representative businessman. Charges which might have defeated many a politician had no apparent effect when directed against Kendrick. While governor, he violated the state's corrupt-practices act and the law forbidding a state board member to buy state land. While senator, he often missed roll-call votes. He was not an orator. He did not pretend to be a statesman. He was merely an accomplished vote getter, recognized in 1928 by Jim Griffith, Sr., Lusk editor and Republican pundit, to be "the craftiest politician the state has ever produced."

To what did Kendrick owe his phenomenal success? Though blessed with only seven years of formal schooling, he possessed an uncommon drive to succeed. As a cowboy of twenty-one he left his native Texas in 1879 and rode with a trail herd to northern Wyoming, where in the next few years he studied by lantern light while other cowboys caroused. He married the boss's daughter, built a great estate, and then late in life turned to politics. In the United States Senate he concentrated on furthering Wyoming's economic interests, with particular attention to cattle, sheep, sugar beets, and reclamation.

In 1922 a young county chairman, Pat Flannery, was distressed when at the time scheduled for a meeting in the schoolhouse at LaGrange, the speaker, Kendrick, had disappeared. Flannery finally found the Senator perched on a manure pile talking over old times with several veteran cowhands. As Flannery and Kendrick made their way to the schoolhouse, Kendrick patiently explained that he had garnered more votes on the manure pile than he could win in the schoolhouse, for the cowhands would campaign vigorously for him. Significantly, Kendrick looked and lived up to the western ideal: rugged, masculine, direct, frank, and unassuming—the Virginian in the flesh.

All three of the Grand Old Men were large, strong men and rugged individualists. All three were livestock men, although Kendrick was the only one who actually lived in the country for any length of time. All three were basically conservative in economic philosophy, although Carey was for some time a Bull Moose Progressive and Kendrick was a lifelong Democrat. Kendrick was one of three Democratic senators who voted for the high-protection Fordney-McCumber Tariff Act of 1922. His high-tariff record was just as good as Warren's, and these two men saw eye to eye on almost everything. They often lunched together, and they cooperated closely in furthering the interests of their constituents.

They did not run against each other after the bitter contest, won by Warren, in the 1913 legislature. Thereafter, when one stood for election, the other offered only token opposition.

Patrick J. Sullivan, Casper sheepman, a Republican, was appointed to the United States Senate in 1929 to fill out Warren's term. Sullivan chose not to run in 1930, when Republican Robert D. Carey, former governor, defeated Casper attorney Harry H. Schwartz. Six years later the same two contestants squared off, with the Democrat Schwartz emerging as the victor. Neither Carey nor Schwartz could attain distinction in their single Senate terms.

Joseph C. O'Mahoney, Cheyenne newspaperman, who studied law at Georgetown University while serving as Senator Kendrick's secretary (1917–1922) and then practiced law in Cheyenne, was appointed to fill out Kendrick's Senate term in 1933 and was elected to a six-year term in 1934. For a few years O'Mahoney appeared to be a loyal New Dealer, ready to support President Roosevelt on everything. Then in 1937 he distinguished himself by becoming one of the leaders in opposition to Roosevelt's Supreme Court reform plan. This annoyed the President briefly, but on the other hand, it endeared O'Mahoney to his constituents. Quite clearly, O'Mahoney took his position with respect to the Supreme Court matter on principle. It was his good fortune that the great majority of Wyoming voters felt the same way about it. Rarely has a first-term senator made so much political hay by a single action.

Further favorable publicity accrued to O'Mahoney from his work as chairman of the Temporary National Economic Committee, which set out in 1939 to investigate the facts of American business organization, with special attention to concentrations of power. The committee collected thirty-seven volumes of testimony and published forty-three monographs. O'Mahoney was generally credited with fairness and objectivity in his handling of the investigation.

Another Wyomingite, Assistant Attorney General Thurman Arnold, led a crusade against trusts. As the New Deal's chief prosecutor in anti-trust cases, 1938–1943, Arnold brought more than two hundred suits for restraint of trade or other monopolistic practices. He made cigarette manufacturers halt price collaboration, established restrictions on block booking of motion pictures, opened the Associated Press news service to all newspapers willing to pay the assessments, and obtained many indictments against building and construction industries. Both Arnold and O'Mahoney were famous when World War II ended the fact gathering and trust busting.

The dapper Irish orator from Boston, Joe O'Mahoney, snowed under native son Milward L. Simpson in November, 1940, winning re-election to the Senate by more than nineteen thousand votes. In his campaign, Simpson tried to revive the anti-Communist hysteria of the early 1920's. With some encouragement from the Republican party's national-campaign planners, he asserted that the New Deal had packed "key" positions of the federal government with Communists and fifth columnists. He reported that the Dies Committee had "shown that there are more than 700 people in the employ of the government who are out-and-out Communists" and had established that there were "at least 300,000 dangerous fifth columnists in America." Only twenty-five thousand Communists had overthrown the Russian government, he warned. Most of the Wyoming voters were not frightened. They preferred to accept O'Mahoney's opinion that the fifth-column talk was "the purest kind of bunk." Nor did they accept Simpson's statement that O'Mahoney "is a firm believer in the New Deal and therefore in national socialism."

MEN IN THE HOUSE OF REPRESENTATIVES

Wyoming's lone place in the House of Representatives has often proved to be a slippery steppingstone for would-be United States Senators. After thirteen terms in the House, Frank W. Mondell slipped in 1922 when he tried to leap to the Senate in competition with Kendrick. Charles E. Winter, Casper novelist, poet (state song), lawyer, and judge, occupied for six years the place vacated by Mondell. Then he, too, tried the leap to the Senate and slipped. He could never regain his winning stride, although he tried again for the Senate and for the House. Vincent Carter, another Casper attorney, who had been state auditor, won the House seat vacated by Winter and, like Winter, served three terms before he slipped in trying for the Senate against O'Mahoney in 1934. Paul R. Greever, Cody lawyer, in 1935 moved into the congressional seat given up by Carter and served two terms. Greever was the first Democrat to win the state's seat in the House since John E. Osborne left it in 1899.

GOVERNORS

In an International News Service interview in February, 1928, Senator Francis E. Warren advised young men not to enter politics "if they feel self confident enough to do anything else." Said he: "It ought to be the last hope of any young man starting out in life, unless he has the unselfish motive of serving his country without reward. All governments are ungrateful." Had Warren been governor of Wyoming in the 1920's or 1930's, he might have been even more emphatic in rejecting politics, for no governor appeared able to satisfy the people for long.

In 1920 the Republicans had given the Democrats a memorable drubbing. For President, Warren G. Harding received twice as many Wyoming votes as James M. Cox. For the House of Representatives, Frank W. Mondell submerged his opponent, Wade H. Fowler, 34,689 to 14,952. The Democrats elected only one candidate to the legislature, Thurman W. Arnold of Laramie in the lower house. The Democrats, it is true, had three holdover senators.

Governor Robert D. Carey, who had been elected as a Republican to a four-year term in 1918, found that much of the optimism of 1919 and 1920 had vanished when the legislature met in January, 1921. Livestock and agricultural prices had plummeted, the debt burden was oppressive, and banks were beginning to fail—three since the November election. Carey called for fiscal retrenchment, yet he did not batten down all the hatches, for he had inherited a penchant for reform from his father. The legislature gave him a state department of law enforcement after he had cited glaring examples of lax enforcement by county attorneys. He also obtained a strengthened board of health after his assertion that the state was far behind many other states. He repeated his 1919 charge that more was spent to protect livestock than people. Other pieces of legislation that can be traced to his specific requests are elimination of the state's branch hospitals at Casper and Sheridan; creation of a state farm-loan board to lend public-school funds on first mortgages on farm lands (overwhelmingly approved by popular vote in 1916); curbs on real-estate agents; and provision for annual meetings of assessors and members of the several boards of county commissioners with the state board of equalization in Cheyenne.

Many World War I veterans did not think the bronze medals which all had received from the 1919 legislature were adequate recognition for their sacrifices. Carey was sympathetic with the idea of a veterans' bonus, but thought it should be a federal-government responsibility. Nevertheless, he approved what amounted to a state bonus for all United States veterans in the form of exemption of property from taxation. Exempted was "the property of all honorably discharged veterans of the Civil War, the Spanish-American War and the World War and their widows during their widowhood, and all nurses who served during the World War to the amount of Two Thousand ($2,000) Dollars in assessed valuation."

The legislature was reapportioned, much as in 1917, with four counties (Laramie, Natrona, Sheridan, and Sweetwater) receiving two senators, the others only one, and all getting from one to six members in the House of Representatives. Counties 22 and 23, Sublette and Teton, were added, the first new counties since 1911—and the state's last.

The 1921 legislature gave more attention to the problem of prostitution than ever before. Three laws were passed, one threatening the keeper of a house of ill fame with jail and fine, with each day of continuation to constitute a separate offense; a second declaring to be a nuisance any building used for prostitution, gambling, or liquor violations and providing for the abatement thereof; and a third providing for repression of prostitution and confinement in jail or reformatory for various violations.

Governors' wives sometimes influence legislation. Federal Judge T. Blake Kennedy, for example, attributed to Governor Robert D. Carey's wife, Julia, passage of the legislative act providing for state purchase of the Saratoga Hot Springs Reserve (420 acres) for fifty thousand dollars. The bill had been sidetracked, and then Julia became interested. She wagered six pairs of gloves with Kennedy that she could get the bill out of the wastebasket and passed by the Senate. Kennedy's recollections (in his memoirs) were:

She got the bill removed from an indefinite postponement, restored to the calender and passed. . . . The Governor . . . knew nothing about this episode but when the Bill came to him he immediately sent for me and asked how it had occurred. . . . I then told him of the incident and ventured the assertion that he was "sitting on a hot-spot" and if he didn't approve the Bill he would be more ridiculous in the eyes of the public than if he would meet the criticism of too much expense. He evidently saw the situation as I had explained it to him and approved the Act.

Except for the wrangle over carbon-black legislation, discussed above, there was no public bickering in 1921 among the Republicans, who were in complete control. Among Governor Carey's proposals which did not lead to legislation were these: appointment, instead of election, of assessors; an income tax; a department of agriculture; a tribunal for arbitration of industrial disputes; an eight-hour day for women; and replacement of the Board of Live Stock Commissioners, the Board of Sheep Commissioners, and the state veterinarian by one livestock board.

The cost of state government had been rising more or less steadily. Expenditures from the general fund, 1908–1924, were as follows:

Two years ending September 30, 1910 .   .   . $ 762,455.65
Two years ending September 30, 1912 .   .   .   879,674.42
Two years ending September 30, 1914 .   .   . 1,112,250.10
Two years ending September 30, 1916 .   .   . 1,213,071.97
Two years ending September 30, 1918 .   .   . 1,716,431.39
Two years ending September 30, 1920 .   .   . 1,830,569.66
Two years ending September 30, 1922 .   .   . 2,717,220.59
Two years ending September 30, 1924 .   .   . 2,397,637.16

When one considers the growth in population and wealth, the trend of
state expenditures seems to have been not at all out of line. The deflation of the early 1920's, however, temporarily ended the upward trend
of government expenditures.

Governor Carey vetoed $280,000 in appropriation bills in 1921, but
he did not economize enough to satisfy many hard-pressed taxpayers,
and so he was rejected by his own party in the August, 1922, primary.
Cheyenne and Rock Springs banker and sheepman John W. Hay, who
challenged Carey, was considered to be the Union Pacific and coal-
mining candidate. He presented what amounted to a one-plank platform: economy. He promised that he would reduce the cost of state
government by one-third. When asked where there was waste and
inefficiency in Governor Carey's administration and what bureaus and
commissions he would abolish, Hay declined to be specific. He received
substantial support from the press. Typically, the *Lusk Herald* said: "It
is not that Mr. Carey has been a poor governor but that Mr. Hay will
be a better one. . . . The fact that many people like Governor Carey
personally does not make them forget that taxes are beyond the
ordinary man's ability to pay." Carey's friends countered that the per
capita tax for state purposes was only eight dollars; thus little could be
saved for the average taxpayer, even by drastic elimination of state
services.

The primary battle became fierce before Hay won out by a mere 443
votes. Hay netted two more votes in a recount demanded by Carey in
Sweetwater County, where Hay had a 5–1 lead. Carey campaigned for
his party that fall, but the primary contest left scars that permitted
Democratic candidate William B. Ross, Cheyenne lawyer, to defeat
Hay by 723 votes. Many of Carey's Republican friends apparently
voted for Ross, and so did some dry Republicans who thought both
Carey and Hay too wet for their taste.

Playing a minor role in the 1922 election was the Nonpartisan
League, which could transfer to Wyoming only a small part of the

influence that it had enjoyed for several years in North Dakota. The league advocated state hail insurance; state ownership of elevators, flour mills, and packing plants; rural-credit banks at cost; and tax exemption for farm improvements. After league organizers had held meetings in several Wyoming counties, the Thermopolis Chamber of Commerce took the lead in calling a state-wide conference of people opposed to the league. Out of the conference emerged the Wyoming American Association, which was designed to start a backfire of education against the league's socialistic ideas. In March, 1922, the *Wyoming State Tribune* announced that Henry M. Lux, league manager for Wyoming, had moved to Nebraska and that the league was dead. Although it was not dead, the league did not thrive. In July, 1922, league representatives joined with other farm and labor groups to form a Conference for Progressive Political Action, which was part of a national Progressive movement. The conference, in session at Douglas, voted to fuse with the Democrats, whose leaders, Leslie A. Miller, Thurman W. Arnold, and Joseph C. O'Mahoney, were in Douglas for the amalgamation discussion. After the August primary, the Conference for Progressive Political Action threw its support behind the entire Democratic ticket.

Ku Klux Klan activity, which was extensive in other parts of the country in the 1920's, amounted to little in Wyoming. In late September, 1922, the letters KKK were painted on front doors, front steps, and sidewalks at ten or twelve Cheyenne homes. Otherwise there was little evidence of the Klan's presence.

In view of the depression, retrenchment became the watchword for both gubernatorial candidates. Ross, however, emphasized economy somewhat less than Hay did and, unlike Hay, pledged to shift some of the tax burden to the railroads and other corporations.

John B. Kendrick, who was re-elected to the United States Senate by more than 9,000 votes, did not need the support of the Conference for Progressive Political Action. The conference could, however, lay some claim to tipping the scales for William B. Ross, whose margin of victory was only 723 votes. Republicans won the other state offices and the seat in Congress and maintained control of the legislature, 20 to 5 in the Senate and 37 to 23 in the House.

Governor Ross urged "strictest economy" upon the legislature and "retrenchment in every possible way." He fared very well in his dealings with the Republican legislature, generally getting what he asked for. Notably, the legislature adopted an improved child-labor law, hiked inheritance-tax rates sharply, passed a one-cent gasoline tax instead of the two-cent tax requested, and declined to adopt any kind of interim severance tax, although it did submit a severance-tax amendment to the people.

The Senate confirmed the recess appointment of state engineer

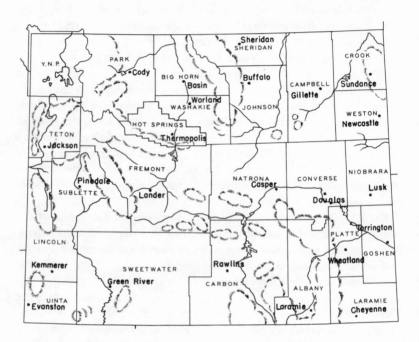

WYOMING, COUNTIES AND COUNTY SEATS SINCE 1923

Frank C. Emerson for a six-year term, made by Governor Carey after the adjournment of the 1921 legislature. Carey's appointment had been delayed intentionally in order to make Emerson eligible for a salary increase authorized by the 1921 legislature. After the 1923 legislature adjourned, Governor Ross had Emerson ejected from his office by the county sheriff after Emerson had refused to tender his resignation as requested. In district court, however, Emerson established his right to the office, subject only to removal for cause.

As the 1924 popular vote on the severance-tax amendment approached, Governor Ross campaigned for approval. He became ill after speaking on the subject in Laramie on September 23. Two days later, he was operated on for acute appendicitis, and on October 2, 1924, at the age of fifty-one, he died of complications following the operation.

Governor William B. Ross had earned the respect of Republicans and Democrats alike. He was modest, yet courageous. He was a natural orator. He is remembered particularly for his energetic enforcement of the prohibition laws and for his unsuccessful crusade to obtain a severance tax on oil.

THE FIRST WOMAN GOVERNOR

The death of Governor William B. Ross occurred just a month and two days before the general election of November 4, 1924, and necessitated the election of someone to fill out the last two years of his four-year term. Special party conventions met in Cheyenne on October 14. The Republicans nominated Eugene J. Sullivan, a Casper attorney, who had been mayor of Basin and speaker of the Wyoming House of Representatives. He had interests in irrigation farming in Big Horn County and in an independent oil company. The Democrats nominated the late Governor's widow, Mrs. Nellie Tayloe Ross, who had not been active in politics. She had taught kindergarten briefly in Omaha before her marriage in 1902, after which she had been busy bringing up three sons. A fourth son had died in infancy.

Sullivan campaigned vigorously for three weeks, while Mrs. Ross announced: "I shall not make a campaign. My candidacy is in the hands of my friends. I shall not leave the house." A few small advertisements quoted her as saying that she would "be governed by the underlying principles by which he and I, side by side, have sought to conduct our lives during our 22 years together." Mrs. Ross defeated Sullivan by more than eight thousand votes, polling more votes than Francis E. Warren, who won his seventh term in the United States Senate. The *State Tribune-Leader* (Cheyenne) correctly appraised the situation: "Chivalry and sympathy were the factors of chief consideration."

There was Ku Klux Klan activity in Laramie County during the 1924 campaign, as in 1922, but there is no reason to suppose that the Klan affected the outcome of any major political race.[2]

[2] In an interview in her home in Washington, D.C., in December, 1964, Mrs. Ross told me that she thought the Klan had no significant influence in Wyoming in 1924. Jerry A. O'Callaghan, however, who worked on Senator Joseph C. O'Mahoney's

The national Conference for Progressive Political Action was back on the Wyoming scene. In a stormy session in Wheatland in June, 1924, Cheyenne labor delegates failed in an attempt to commit the conference to support of the Democratic party. The labor delegates insisted that a third party would throw the election to the Republicans. The Wyoming conference, like the Ku Klux Klan, affected the outcome of no major race, but the national conference's candidate for the presidency, Robert M. LaFollette, ran much stronger in Wyoming than he did in the nation. Calvin Coolidge, Republican, received 41,858 votes; LaFollette, Progressive, 25,174; and John W. Davis, Democrat, only 12,868.

Few Wyoming governors have received more favorable notice outside the state than Nellie Tayloe Ross. Although she was elected on the same day as Mrs. Miriam A. "Ma" Ferguson of Texas, she was acclaimed the first woman governor because she assumed office twenty days before Mrs. Ferguson.

Like her husband, Mrs. Ross had to deal with a legislature that was predominantly Republican (16 to 11 in the Senate, 45 to 17 in the House), and, also like her husband, she was the only Democrat among the five state elective officials. Predictably, she did not dominate the many state boards on which she sat with the four Republicans, and, predictably, too, she did not control the Republican legislature. In her brief opening message to the legislature, she dealt only with the subjects that she considered to be of "greatest immediate importance." She explained at the outset that she had been aided in preparing her message by extensive notes assembled by her husband for the message that he had planned to deliver. With pride she reported that during her husband's administration, the valuation of railroads for tax purposes had been increased by eleven million dollars and that the total state taxes had been reduced. She urged the legislature to continue shifting the tax burden from small property holders to large ones. Recalling a coal-mine disaster at Kemmerer in which one hundred persons had died on August 14, 1923, she asked for improved safety regulations. She called for increased state investment in farm loans to aid depressed agriculture. She repeated her husband's complaint that Wyoming had

---

staff for a few years, recalls that O'Mahoney attributed his defeat by Robert R. Rose in the August, 1924, senatorial primary to Klan activity, particularly in the Big Horn Basin. No doubt the Klan was much stronger in Colorado. See David M. Chalmers, *Hooded Americanism* (New York: Doubleday, 1965), and W. P. Randel, *The Ku Klux Klan: A Century of Infamy* (Philadelphia: Chilton, 1965).

not kept pace with progressive states in restricting work hours for women, and she recommended ratification of the Child Labor Amendment, which had been submitted to the states by the United States Congress.

Republican drys who thought their own candidate too wet had helped elect Mrs. Ross's husband in 1922. Appropriately, Mrs. Ross announced that she stood "unequivocally for . . . thorough enforcement" and proposed the enactment of a statute that would make it as great a crime to buy liquor as to sell it.

Contemplating the awesome fact that 35 of the state's 120 banks had failed in the past year, Mrs. Ross asked for a "sound banking law" and "some form of a guaranty provision."

The legislature adopted new coal-mine safety regulations, passed a new banking code, and enlarged the farm-loan fund, but such actions were coincidental rather than indicative of Republican willingness to follow Democratic leadership. Also, a child-labor law barring employment of children under sixteen in hazardous occupations was adopted— a law which would stand virtually unchanged until 1963. Otherwise, the legislation enacted by the 1925 legislature showed little similarity to the Governor's message.

Although she was elected "on trust," as she herself once put it, Mrs. Ross proved to be a good governor who gave the state a respectable, dignified, and economical administration. Intelligent, tactful, and gracious, she soon became a competent administrator and an effective public speaker. Appropriately, in 1926 her party nominated her for a four-year term, while the Republicans advanced Frank C. Emerson, state engineer, whose ouster both she and her husband had tried to accomplish without success.

Considerations of sympathy, charity, and chivalry were no longer important by 1926. Moreover, many Republican women who had crossed party lines to vote for a woman in 1924 voted for Emerson in 1926. Mrs. Theresa A. Jenkins, venerable champion of woman suffrage who had delivered an oration at the statehood celebration in 1890, asked in an open letter during the 1926 campaign: "What has Mrs. Ross done to particularly deserve the votes of women? Has she ever, since coming to Wyoming taken any interest in Woman's Suffrage?" A prominent Casper Republican, Mrs. H. C. Chappell, declared in a public address: "I am not against a woman for governor, but I am against a woman who is not fitted for the office and who was elected through appeals and prejudices that have no place in politics." Mrs.

Ross's critics charged that she had not given other women a chance to demonstrate their capacity for public office, that she had appointed 174 men and only 5 women, and that she had named not a single woman to an office formerly held by a man.

The Republicans alleged that Mrs. Ross was merely a figurehead and that four men were really running her administration: Cheyenne lawyer Joseph C. O'Mahoney, state examiner Byron S. Huie, Attorney General David J. Howell, and Interstate Streams Commissioner S. G. Hopkins.[3] Democratic advertisements defended the Governor with statements that she had reduced the expenses of state government in all departments, had equalized the tax burden by increasing the share paid by corporations, and had upheld the state's water rights.

Frank Emerson was presented as a businessman and engineer who would bring development to the state. A typical advertisement asserted: "Wyoming has retrogressed while neighboring states progressed. What's wrong with Wyoming? Wyoming needs leadership. Frank Emerson can meet its need." Another Republican advertisement, placed in a box on the front page of the *Wyoming State Tribune*, said: "In 20 words Wyoming needs Vision, Experience, Leadership, Information, Comprehension, Knowledge of Men, Ability to read men's motives, in the office of governor."

Among that year's Democratic candidates, Mrs. Ross easily ran the best race, but she lost by 1,365 votes. She lost, not because she was a woman, but because she was a Democrat in a Republican state and because she could not avoid being blamed for the state's economic aches and pains. She never again sought public office in Wyoming. Her work for the Democratic national committee subsequently brought her appointment as director of the United States Mint, in which capacity she served from 1933 to 1953. Living in retirement in Washington, D.C., she said in 1964: "I am very grateful for all that the wonderful people of Wyoming have done for me." Mrs. Ross died at the age of 101 on December 19, 1977.

THE ADMINISTRATION OF FRANK C. EMERSON

"Wyoming is now in a position to make rapid strides forward in every way," proclaimed Percy C. Spencer, chairman of the Republican Central Committee, after the 1926 election. He referred to the fact that his party was now in complete control of all branches of state govern-

[3] In an interview in her home in Washington, D.C., in December, 1964, Mrs. Ross told me that she had relied mainly on advice from O'Mahoney and Howell.

ment. Time established, however, that the campaign talk about Emerson's ability to get Wyoming moving was just talk. Throughout his administration, valuation of property in the state was below what it had been under Mrs. Ross. Nothing happened on the industrial front, either, except for the construction of a cement plant at Laramie in 1928–1929.

Perry W. Jenkins, Republican president of the state senate, told its members in 1927 that "natural resources are seized by special interests and conveyed into richer and stronger neighboring states [and] . . . our state is drained of its life blood and our development is long deferred." He mentioned specifically iron ore, oil, timber, phosphates, water, and water power. Whether Jenkins properly identified the cause of the state's slow growth or not, the export of raw materials continued.

Governor Emerson gave most of his time to reclamation matters. He was an able reclamation engineer who had the misfortune to become governor when expansion of Wyoming reclamation was blocked by the federal "no new starts" policy and the questionable feasibility of remaining Wyoming projects. His major achievements in his special domain of reclamation consisted of (1) getting Wyoming into the Colorado River Compact; (2) holding her there, against much home-state opposition, so that water would be available when Green River development began in the 1960's; and (3) maintaining Wyoming's rights to North Platte River waters against the claims of Nebraska and Colorado.

Emerson lived up to his reputation as a businessman. He dealt quite effectively with legislators, most of whom were of his own party, and was elected for a second term in 1930, defeating Democrat Leslie A. Miller 38,058 to 37,188.

Second only to his interest in reclamation was Governor Emerson's concern about highways. He wanted especially a secondary system to serve people not on the primary system of highways. Burgeoning highway needs exhausted funds available from federal oil royalties, the gasoline tax (increased to three cents a gallon and then to four cents), the sale of automobile licenses, and bond issues. The university enrollment grew, necessitating increases in expenditures there. Likewise, the doubling, since 1920, of the number of persons cared for in the state's twelve institutions made increased appropriations unavoidable. Yet Emerson tried hard to hold the line on appropriations, constantly emphasizing the need for efficiency and economy.

It was politically impossible (and not seriously considered) to raise property-tax assessments or the state mill levy. Emerson talked regularly about the need for assessment of intangible property, without getting significant action. In desperation he proposed in 1931 a state income tax, but the legislature refused to submit the constitutional amendment thought necessary.

Emerson, who insisted on handling farm loans on a business-like basis, had no hesitation about foreclosing. Not wishing to run the risk of suffering the heavy losses incurred in other states of the region, he would not recommend a state loan fund larger than eight million dollars. Private lenders had withdrawn from the farm-loan field, so in 1931 he and the legislature petitioned the Federal Farm Loan Board and the Federal Land Bank of Omaha for greater activity in Wyoming.

Governor Emerson fell ill of influenza during the 1931 legislative session and died of pneumonia on February 18 at the age of forty-eight.

GOVERNORS A. M. CLARK AND LESLIE A. MILLER

Secretary of State Alonzo M. Clark, a Republican, became acting governor February 18, 1931, and served until January 2, 1933. Clark had taught school in Glenrock, Lusk, and Gillette, had homesteaded while teaching at Gillette, and had even tried his hand at ranching before becoming county clerk of Campbell County. He was elected secretary of state in 1926. Since the legislature was only a few days away from adjournment when Clark became acting governor, he contributed little to the 1931 session except for a few appointments and five vetoes. The most important veto was one of an act to legalize pari-mutuel wagering on horse races.

As the depression worsened, taxpayers groaned even more audibly than they had in the 1920's. J. Elmer Brock, president of the Wyoming Stock Growers Association, in behalf of various groups, called a meeting at Casper in March, 1932, to organize the Wyoming Tax League, forerunner of the Wyoming Taxpayers Association. Such a league, he said, should not "submit or recommend any new form of raising public revenues until the per capita expense of government shall have been reduced 50 per cent below the 1931 cost." Most of the state's counties were represented in the league's organizational meeting, at which Sheridan coal operator Ed R. Lee was elected president. Leslie A. Miller represented Laramie County at the meeting. The league began at once to look for ways to reduce the cost of state and local government, looking forward to influencing the next legislature.

The Republicans in convention in May, 1932, passed over A. M. Clark and endorsed Harry R. Weston, state treasurer from Jackson, for the governorship (for the two years remaining in Emerson's term). In their convention, the Democrats were confronted by two candidates, Leslie A. Miller, Cheyenne businessman, and Thomas D. O'Neil, Big Piney rancher, and chose to endorse neither.

Both parties adopted platform statements favoring sharp reductions in costs of state and local governments and urging the elimination of all nonessential state activities. Miller defeated O'Neil in the Democratic primary, after which both Miller and Weston campaigned on economy planks, with Miller winning by a margin of 3,438 votes. For the first time in the state's history, the Democrats also won complete control of one house in the legislature, the lower one, 42–20, while the Republicans retained control of the Senate, 15–12. Illustrating the hairpin turns which they can take, the state's voters, who had given Herbert Hoover a plurality of more than 23,000 in 1928, now rejected him in favor of Franklin D. Roosevelt by almost 15,000 votes.

Unlike any of his predecessors, Governor Miller had served in both houses of the legislature. Long business experience qualified him as well. To the legislature he reported a general-fund overdraft of more than half a million dollars. He promised to take a salary cut and said he would not move into the governor's mansion, thus saving the cost of heat, light, redecorating, and refurnishing. He recommended reduction in state travel allowance, elimination of two of the nine judicial districts, halving the university's extension service, elimination of the law-enforcement department, curtailment of highway construction, and many other economies. In general, he got what he asked for. Finally, after several governors had recommended it, the Board of Live Stock Commissioners, the Board of Sheep Commissioners, and the state veterinarian's office were consolidated into a livestock and sanitary board. And, also after many attempts, female labor was limited to eight hours in any one day and to forty-eight hours in any one week.

It was time, after the 1930 census returns, to reapportion the legislative seats. As usual, there were those who wanted just one senator for each county. However, the established pattern was followed: counties received from one to six seats in the House; four counties were allowed two senators (Laramie, Natrona, Sheridan, and Sweetwater), the others just one. There would be no change thereafter until 1963.

In a special message to the 1933 legislature, Governor Miller presented a proposal, originating in the Wyoming Tax League, for a study by experts of budget and tax reforms, consolidations of counties and school districts, and other possible changes. The legislature authorized the study, the results of which were to be presented at a special session later in the year. The Governor recommended deep cuts in appropriations and complimented the legislators when they cut deeper than he had thought possible. State expenditures were reduced by about 30 per cent.

A bipartisan legislative committee employed the firm of Griffenhagen and Associates of Chicago, paying the company $8,750, to study Wyoming problems. As planned, a special session of the legislature met December 4–23, 1933, to consider the Griffenhagen report and other depression-induced business. The firm suggested more centralized state control and consolidation of the 399 school districts; a state police force to absorb the duties of sheriffs, livestock inspectors, water commissioners, the state highway patrol, and other law-enforcement personnel; reduction of the number of counties from twenty-three to twelve or even six; a one-house legislature of nine to twelve members elected from the state at large by proportional representation; election of the governor by the legislature from among its members, or by the electorate directly, to serve as presiding officer of the legislature and as official head of the state government but not as an administrative officer; a state administrator chosen by the legislature as general manager of the state government, to be appointed without term and to appoint heads of all administrative departments; and other far-reaching reforms. The proposals were too drastic, and were rejected *in toto*, amid groans that in trying to find ways of saving money, many thousands of dollars had been wasted. The special session was not pointless, however, since it adopted sixty-one acts, plus eight resolutions and memorials. The legislature had to act on several fronts if it wished to take advantage of opportunities offered by the New Deal. The special session approved the Temporary Federal Deposit Insurance Fund, the Home Owners Loan Corporation, the State Industrial Recovery Act, the State Relief Act, and a $300,000 federal loan for a university liberal-arts building. Except for a three-cents-per-gallon beer tax, solution of the revenue problem was postponed: bills for a sales tax, an income tax, and a six-mill levy for schools were all defeated. Appropriations of the two sessions of the 1933 legislature totaled $3,550,863, as compared with $4,458,656 for 1931–1933 and $4,264,962 for the 1929–1931 biennium.[4]

The Democratic party's star has never ascended higher in the Wyoming heavens than it did in 1934. At the November elections that year, Democratic candidates won all five elective state offices: governor, Leslie A. Miller; secretary of state, Lester C. Hunt; auditor, William "Scotty" Jack; treasurer, J. Kirk Baldwin; superintendent of public

---

[4] These figures for appropriations include legislative, state auditor, statutory, and continuing tax levies, and are taken from governors' budget reports.

instruction, Jack R. Gage. Governor Miller won over Alonzo M. Clark by the biggest margin in the state's history up to that time. Best vote getter of all was Jack Gage, whose principal political stock in trade was a steady stream of jokes, mainly directed at himself. Joseph C. O'Mahoney was sent back to the United States Senate by a 13,000-vote margin over Vincent R. Carter, and Paul R. Greever won the seat in Congress over former Congressman Charles E. Winter by almost 16,000 votes. For the first time in history, the Democrats won control of both houses of the legislature, 14 to 13 and 38 to 18.

In his opening message to the 1935 legislature, Governor Miller explained that inasmuch as assessed valuation of property would be only about $300,000,000, the constitutional maximum of four mills would limit property-tax revenue to not more than $1,200,000 per year, or $2,400,000 for the biennium. The Governor made it clear that expenditures must be cut and new sources of revenue found.

Major pieces of legislation to emerge from the session were an act adopting a 2 per cent sales tax on retail purchases and an act providing for state wholesaling of liquor through the Wyoming Liquor Commission. The two measures, particularly the first, would go a long way toward solving, for many years to come, the revenue problem, which had been critical since 1921. The sales tax was chosen in preference to an income tax, which was also considered. Governor Miller made a personal plea for the sales tax before the House of Representatives, where labor opposition was strong.

In 1936, the year in which he carried all states but Maine and Vermont, Franklin D. Roosevelt carried all counties in Wyoming except Johnson and Crook. Roosevelt was so popular that, although there was shrill criticism of the New Deal in Wyoming, as elsewhere, the Democrats, for the second time, won control of both houses of the legislature, 16 to 11 and 38 to 18. For the seat in Congress, Paul R. Greever, Cody lawyer, bested Frank A. Barrett of Lusk, another lawyer, by fifteen thousand votes, while Casper lawyer Harry H. Schwartz, who had lost to Robert D. Carey in 1930, turned the tables and won a seat in the United States Senate.

THE 1937 LEGISLATURE

The economy showed signs of improvement during the 1937 legislative session. In general, however, the spirit in Cheyenne was one of caution rather than exuberance. Total appropriations were slightly below those of the previous biennium after Governor Miller had slashed a third of a million dollars from the total approved by the legislature. Miller approved almost the exact amount he had recommended in his budget message. There was only one item which later lent itself to charges of extravagance: $12,000 to rehabilitate and refurnish the governor's residence. The mansion, erected and furnished at a cost of $33,000 in 1902–1903, had stood unoccupied from 1931 to 1933 and had then been rented to the Federal Relief Administration from 1933 to 1936 before Miller decided that he would like to use it.

The desire of certain elements to legalize gambling, outlawed in 1901 but never vigorously suppressed, was discussed by the Governor in his 1937 message. Recalling that he had vetoed such a bill in 1935, he said: "No act of mine since I have been in office brought to my desk such a flood of commendation." Advocates of legalized gambling argued, first, that it might as well be recognized that gambling was widespread and could not be suppressed and, second, that municipalities needed the revenue which legalized gambling could provide. Miller conceded that enforcement was lax in many counties and then proceeded to list many familiar arguments against gambling and its legalization. A parimutuel bill was introduced, but it failed to pass after the legislators received a flood of post cards from women who wanted no gambling.

The Governor unsuccessfully tried to revamp the revenue pattern. He recommended to the legislature a sales-tax increase from 2 per cent to 3 per cent, exemption of foodstuffs from the sales tax, a use tax on articles shipped into the state, and submission to a vote of the people in 1938 a constitutional amendment authorizing the legislature to provide for a graduated income tax. In short, Miller believed in modest use of all three taxes—property, sales, and income. A 2 per cent use tax was adopted, the sales tax remaining at 2 per cent, with food included, but modified so that the first penny would be collected at twenty-five cents instead of thirteen. No income-tax amendment was submitted to the electorate.

One last action of the 1937 legislature is worth remembering. It gave the state game and fish department something many sportsmen had long desired: considerable independence from the legislature. Provision for a bipartisan six-man commission, first set up in 1925, was continued.

Leslie A. Miller Is Rejected

A more energetic, well-informed, economy-minded governor than Leslie A. Miller is hard to imagine. He was frank, straightforward, outspoken, courageous, and stubborn. In August, 1937, the *Wyoming State Tribune* (Cheyenne) said of him: "His judgment is not infallible, but if it's his considered judgment he stands by it. He does not maintain a closed mind, may be convinced by reason, facts and circumstances, but he is about as difficult to drive as a Brahma bull." He served the people of Wyoming conscientiously, 1933–1939, during one of the most difficult periods of the state's often difficult history. Why, then, should the voters, who in 1934 enthusiastically approved the first two years of his service, turn him down, with even more enthusiasm, in 1938? He had won in 1934 by the largest gubernatorial margin in the state's history up to that time. In 1938 he was defeated by an even larger margin, 18,787 votes. He won only two counties, Albany and Uinta, and these by only a few votes.

Two factors contributed to Miller's defeat. First, Wyoming governors normally find it hard to get re-elected, and Miller was trying for an unprecedented third term, a doubly risky undertaking. Second, the Democratic leadership was at loggerheads. Many Democrats believed that Miller had promised to step aside for Paul Greever in 1938 if Greever would support him in 1934. Miller was thus hurt by "betrayal" charges. Greever ran instead for re-election to Congress and was defeated by dude rancher Frank O. Horton of Saddlestring. Finally, the five Democrats elected to state offices in 1934 could not get along. There were several crosscurrents such as are often induced when a party has been in power for a few years.

Used more or less effectively against Miller in 1938 were his failure to win the long fight for lower gasoline prices, the unpopularity of the sales tax (especially as it applied to food), the attempt to get a 1904 water right for the Kendrick project, and expenditures for refurbishing the executive mansion ("tribute to vanity . . . [and] grandiose ideas of regal splendor at the taxpayers' expense"). Growing disenchantment with the New Deal affected Miller unfavorably, although he was a conservative who had misgivings about many New Deal measures.

Nels H. Smith came along at the right time. Better-known Republicans were not eager to enter the ring against a man with Miller's credentials. Smith, who was virtually unknown in politics, was the 54-year-old operator of an 18,000-acre cattle and wheat ranch in Weston County. Six feet four and handsome, he attracted all kinds of voters who found something to complain about in the course of events during the past six years.

GOVERNOR NELS H. SMITH, 1939–1943

The rare spectacle of Democrats controlling the legislature, as they did in 1935 and 1937, ended at the polls in 1938. Republicans won both the Senate, 16 to 11, and the House, 37 to 19. Moreover, the

Republicans won control of the state boards by electing, along with Governor Smith, Mart T. Christensen as treasurer and Esther L. Anderson as superintendent of public instruction. Two Democrats were re-elected: Lester C. Hunt, secretary of state, and William "Scotty" Jack, auditor. "Wyoming, fundamentally a Republican state, has returned to the normality of sound Republican government," said the *Wyoming State Tribune*.

Governor Smith delivered to the 1939 legislature one of the shortest opening addresses on record—less than three thousand words. He said that a majority of the people "are seeking a rest from new and troublesome regulations of their business and social lives." In particular, he wanted no more taxes. "I am in favor of hewing governmental taxes to the bone," he had said in his campaign. Past legislative sessions had been concerned with more stringent highway rules. To the delight of truckers, Smith said: "I feel highway laws should be as free from unnecessary restrictions as possible." Arousing groans among teachers, he said that "most of our school districts are in good shape . . . therefore they can doubtlessly get along with a slight decrease." He wanted utility rates and the price of gasoline reduced. He wanted to be given control of the state game and fish commission, which had been set up in 1925 as a bipartisan six-man board. He asked to be made ex officio member of the board, arguing that "the Chief Executive should be in position to demand prompt correction of administrative abuses." Otherwise he was content to let the legislators initiate legislation.

Smith soon became the butt of jokes about his use of English. "You done good," he told the university student body. More serious were criticisms of what appeared to be his inclination to use his office to balance an accumulation of personal accounts. Before the legislature met, nine or ten game and fish employees, mainly deputy game wardens, were dismissed in response to an ultimatum from the Governor.

Smith won legislative approval for reorganization of the Wyoming Game and Fish Commission, to which he gave top priority. He failed in a second-priority enterprise to remove the sales tax from foodstuffs. The Wyoming Farm Bureau Federation opposed the sales-tax proposal, believing that such a change would tend to increase the weight of property taxes. Explaining that he did not wish to increase the burdens of the school districts, Smith vetoed a measure which would have provided that the state's teachers pay 1 per cent of their salaries into a retirement fund and the school districts contribute a like amount.

At the end of the session, he trimmed a quarter of a million dollars from the appropriations, but found it impossible to bring them down to 1935 and 1937 totals.[5]

No state senator, Democrat or Republican, voted against confirmation of Governor Smith's appointments in 1939. His most significant appointments, it appeared later, were those of three Republicans, Milward L. Simpson, Frank A. Barrett, and Peter Sill, to the university board of trustees. The first two were well known, but not so the third. Sill was a Laramie baker whose nomination was a puzzle until it dawned on observers that he was chosen to facilitate the ouster of President Arthur G. Crane of the University of Wyoming.

Nothing caused Governor Smith more grief or gave him worse publicity than his inept handling of university affairs. Dr. Crane, who had fostered a reputation as "Crane, the Builder," had been president of the university since 1922. He was an excellent public speaker and a forceful, hard-working administrator who, according to Professor W. O. Clough's history of the university, "no doubt . . . had become somewhat impatient of advice or suggestion, and hypersensitive to criticism." He had made many friends and not a few enemies. A few of the latter had sufficient influence with Governor Smith, who had no personal ax to grind, to persuade him that Crane should be fired. In August, 1939, Smith asked Attorney General Ewing Kerr for an opinion with regard to the duty and authority of the university board of trustees in appointments and dismissals. Kerr replied that appointments and dismissals were "of sufficient importance that the Board of Trustees should be consulted on the action to be taken." Under pressure, the board announced in March, 1940, that President Crane had been offered a one-year renewal of contract at a salary of $6,000. He had been receiving $8,000 since 1933, when the legislature had passed an act (without the signature of Governor Miller) cutting his salary from $12,000. The trustees explained in March, 1940, that they were creating a new office, that of comptroller, which would relieve Dr. Crane of some of his duties. Crane was given two weeks in which to accept or reject the new contract, and he chose, just before the deadline, to accept.

In the meantime, Governor Smith wrote to Fay E. Smith, secretary of the board of trustees, asking him to request that President Crane

[5] Including legislative, state auditor, statutory, and continuing tax levies, the total biennial appropriations in the later 1930's were as follows: 1935–1937, $3,467,611.43; 1937–1939, $3,791,174.18; 1939–1941, $4,213,010.71.

hold up delivery of the contracts of two deans and nine other prominent members of the faculty and staff: Dean Carl Arnold of the law school; Dean Ralph D. Goodrich of the college of engineering; Fred Ambrose; F. Elton Davis; George Gerling; Arthur Himbert; Fred Hultz; R. L. "Red" Markley; A. W. McCollough; H. T. Person; and John W. Scott. Explained the Governor: "The facts are that a number of instructors at the university, drawing in the neighborhood of $4,000 a year, actually spend but one hour a week in classroom instruction, and in many instances some teach as little as two or three hours a week. . . . These are, in fact, pensions." When the salaries and schedules of the eleven men were published a few days later, it was obvious that the Governor had been misinformed. Trying another tack, he offered other objections. Nevertheless, the contracts in dispute were soon signed, and the board of trustees published a statement that "Governor Smith is entirely satisfied."

By this time, people who had not really become acquainted with Smith during his five-minute campaign speeches were getting to know him better. It became clear that he was a simple, unsophisticated, uncomplicated man who desired, as he said, to run the state as he ran his ranch. Unhappily, he could not know state problems as intimately as he knew ranch problems. He had to take advice from others, and could not tell good from bad. Once he took a position, he usually clung to it. Republicans as well as Democrats began calling him stubborn as they noticed that the normal give and take of politics was alien to his nature.

When Dr. Crane chose to accept the rather insulting salary cut in 1940, he was merely postponing his separation from the university. In March, 1941, the board of trustees announced the termination of his contract, effective June 30, 1941. While some of the board members had become disenchanted with President Crane, there seems to be little doubt that, if left alone, they would have permitted him to stay on until he reached retirement age in 1943. Governor Smith's cat's-paw participation in Crane's ouster, as much as anything else, assured his defeat when he sought re-election in 1942.

SECTIONALISM

Like other states, Wyoming has had battles over the location of the capital, county-seat fights, bitter rivalries between cities, and chronic sectionalism.

After several years of competition with South Pass City and Rock

Springs, Green River became county seat of Sweetwater County in 1875. South Pass City soon ceased to be a serious rival, but Rock Springs people have sometimes shown resentment because they, who have the larger city, do not have the county seat. Douglas, Lusk, and Glenrock contested for the county seat of Converse County, as did Dayton, Big Horn, and Sheridan for the county seat of Sheridan County. Casper won its battle with Bessemer in 1890. Basin bested Otto and became county seat of Big Horn County in 1896.

Major intercity rivalries in modern times have involved Sheridan and Buffalo, Riverton and Lander, Casper and Cheyenne, Rock Springs and Green River, and Cody and Powell. For years Sheridan coveted the Buffalo Land Office. And Buffalo resented the closing of its Fort McKinney and the establishment of Sheridan's Fort Mackenzie. Later it would be highway location that set the two communities at each other's throats. The pioneer city of Lander and the newcomer Riverton (born 1906) have found many divisive issues. Likewise, the pioneer city of Cheyenne has been challenged often by the younger city of Casper, which, though born in 1888, did not amount to much until World War I. Casper tried to get the capital moved from Cheyenne to Casper in the 1923 legislature, arguing the advantage of central location. Understandably, hard times sharpened the competition. In 1931, Cheyenne won a Veterans Bureau hospital desired by Casper, Thermopolis, and Sheridan. Thereafter, Casper and Cheyenne were often at odds.

Cheyenne and Laramie had been cutthroat rivals in pioneer days. Laramie's editor Hayford wrote in 1883 that "both towns have now pretty well outgrown this boyishness." The observation was a trifle premature, yet certainly in modern times a spirit of friendly cooperation has characterized Cheyenne-Laramie relations. Rarely does anyone go as far as Laramie's famous lawyer N. E. Corthell, who in 1936 painted out the bucking horse on his license plate with the complaint that the horse and rider were being used only to advertise Cheyenne's Frontier Days.

North *versus* south rivalry has often emerged, as in the constitutional convention of 1889. Among the issues have been legislative representation, capital location, and location of institutions. For a long time the more populous south was dominant. In 1935 there was much talk of the desirability of a new state, Absaroka, to be formed from the northern third of Wyoming, the southern part of Montana, and the western part of South Dakota. All three sections had often felt isolated and neglected.

Sheridan people led the discussion and hoped that Sheridan would be capital of the projected state. "It can't be done," said Governor Miller, and he was of course right because prior approval of all three states and Congress would have been required.

In some instances the north *versus* south rivalry has been mainly a Casper *versus* Cheyenne battle. Casper wanted the state liquor warehouse, which was placed in Cheyenne by the state liquor commission in 1935. When Casper failed to get the warehouse, a group of Casper businessmen organized the Better Wyoming League for the ostensible purpose of selecting representative men for state and federal offices and to see that when elected they would serve the state as a whole. Communities in central and northern Wyoming were asked to cooperate. Governor Miller scored the league in a speech at Casper in July, 1935, charging that it was organized "to punish Cheyenne for that city's alleged greediness in public affairs, functions and legislation." Miller felt that only harm could come from inflaming sectional feelings. Editor Deming of the *Wyoming State Tribune* (Cheyenne) thought that Casper had done "mighty well" in getting the state headquarters for the Civilian Conservation Corps, the Home Owners Loan Corporation, and the National Recovery Administration, the district office for the United States Reclamation Service, and the regional office for the Works Progress Administration.

While Casper, which was hard hit by shrinkage of the oil business, received sympathy and encouragement from many communities, there was nothing approaching unanimity in the north. Said the *Lovell Chronicle* in August, 1935: "[We do not believe] that the liquor warehouse was located in Cheyenne because of selfish community reasons, but because that is where it belongs." L. L. Newton of the *Wyoming State Journal* (Lander) likewise would not cooperate. He argued that there were sound reasons for keeping all departments of state government in Cheyenne. After listening to Governor Miller's attack on the Better Wyoming League, the editor of the *Lusk Free Lance* correctly concluded that the league "is one of those things designed to live but a short time." He did not expect sectional rivalries to disappear, however, nor would they.

CHAPTER 16

The Second World War

WORLD WAR II, as it summoned almost everyone to make special contributions, brought greater changes to Wyoming than had all the events of the previous twenty years.[1] Hitler's invasion of Poland on September 1, 1939, touched off the war, which quickly spread around the world. The United States became more and more involved until the Japanese attack on Pearl Harbor on December 7, 1941, caused Congress to declare war on Japan and its Axis allies. The surprise

---

[1] This chapter is a condensation of my book *Wyoming's War Years, 1941–1945* (printed by Stanford University Press for the University of Wyoming in 1954), a thoroughly documented volume which may be found in many libraries, although it is now out of print.

473

attack on Pearl Harbor united Americans, who had been divided the day before, some wanting war, others not. When he heard the shocking news, Governor Nels H. Smith wired President Roosevelt: "The people of Wyoming and the officials of our state assure you of our unanimous and vigorous support in the prosecution of this war." Men of all ages flocked to army, navy, and marine recruiting stations. They had to strike back at what the *Wyoming State Tribune* called "the yellow scum of the Pacific—the Japanese tools of the beasts of Berlin."

Wyoming men numbering 5,560 were already in uniform when war was declared: 1,879 in the Regular Army; 1,439 draftees in army training; 1,288 mobilized National Guardsmen; 804 in the navy; 224 in the Marine Corps; and 26 in the Coast Guard. War increased the flow of men and women to training camps until, on June 30, 1945, Wyoming was credited with 23,611 men and 515 women in service. All told, allowing for those who had been discharged, close to 30,000 men and women of the state entered service before the war ended. In the Spanish-American War, and to a lesser extent in World War I, Wyoming had surpassed most other states in percentages of participants. In World War II, however, equality of sacrifice was the watchword, and the Selective Service System made virtually the same demands on all states.

Wyoming had 22.2 officers per 100 enlisted men in the army, compared with 11.4 officers per 100 enlisted men for the United States as a whole. Wyoming thus had relatively more brass in the army than any other state, mainly, it seems, because of the large number of reserve officers trained in prewar years in the R.O.T.C. program at the University of Wyoming.

The state's only concentration in a single unit was in the 115th Cavalry Regiment, the designation of the state's National Guard after it was mobilized in February, 1941. This unit was stationed for training at Fort Lewis, Washington, until war was declared, when it was given coast-defense duties. Before war's end, Wyoming Guardsmen had been scattered, for it became official policy not to permit large concentrations of men from one community or state in single units.

Up to January 1, 1943, Wyoming's ratio of enlistments to population was sixth in the nation. Thereafter, enlistment ratios became less significant because a new regulation required men of draft age to be inducted through Selective Service. Patriotism, love of adventure, and frontier aggressiveness are not the whole story of the early eagerness to enlist. Wyoming lacked the attractive defense jobs that tempted young men in many other states to stay at home.

The War Dead

An honor list of 1,095 Wyoming war dead was prepared after the war. In their memory, the 1945 legislature adopted a joint resolution:

Whereas they have offered not only their endeavor and sacrifice but even life itself on the altar of our country bringing glory and credit to the State of Wyoming, and the nation . . . Now, therefore, be it resolved . . . that the sacrifices, hardships and contributions of the men and women of the State of Wyoming as members of the armed forces by this memorial be engraved on the hearts of the people of this state. . . .

Selective Service

Almost 60 per cent of Wyoming's servicemen were delivered for induction by the state's Selective Service organization, headed by Colonel R. L. Esmay, who had been state adjutant general for many years. Esmay's efficient administration gave Wyoming the reputation of "no trouble state" in national headquarters. Deferment problems in agriculture and coal mining were most troublesome, for employers in these necessary activities found it very difficult to maintain work forces.

Several hundred older men in the state gave much time without compensation to Selective Service work. Of 126 presidential appointments made for Selective Service positions in Wyoming on or before November 16, 1940, 89, or 70.6 per cent, were still serving on August 31, 1945. This percentage was surpassed by only one other state, Rhode Island, with 70.7.

The Office of War Information reported in February, 1943, that Wyoming had the lowest percentage of Selective Service registrants deferred for mental, moral, or physical reasons. Only 5.15 per cent of Wyoming's registrants were deferred for these causes and classified 4-F, as compared with 8.38 per cent for the nation. "It Must Be the Climate," trumpeted the *Wyoming Eagle* (Cheyenne). By the end of the war, however, Wyoming had slipped to fifth place among the states, with 8.9 per cent 4-F's, as compared with 14.8 for the United States. Idaho, Nebraska, Wisconsin, and South Dakota had lower percentages than Wyoming.

Another way of measuring the fitness of Selective Service registrants was through rejection rates for the men forwarded to induction stations. Up to August 1, 1945, 25 per cent of the Wyoming men aged eighteen to thirty-seven who had been physically examined for induction or enlistment had been rejected. The United States rejection rate was 30.2. Five states—New Jersey, Utah, Kansas, Nevada, and Iowa—

had lower rejection percentages than Wyoming. Although both yard-
sticks, one based on 4-F percentages and the other on rejection percentages, are subject to some qualifications, the conclusion is warranted
that Wyoming's young men rated very well in physical fitness.

Entering military service was the greatest thing a man could do.
Rich and poor, well known and obscure, the model boy and the
juvenile delinquent—all were treated as heroes when they volunteered
or answered the draft board's summons. There were farewell parties
by the thousands. Casper's Aloha Committee, which was unexcelled for
its send-offs, permitted no recruit to leave town without special honors
and without a standard package containing two candy bars, a package
of cigarettes, and a deck of playing cards. The Casper recruit carried
with him also an American Legion booklet of helpful advice, five post
cards from the American Legion Auxiliary, and a memo book from the
American War Mothers.

In a few communities, recruits celebrated their departure by getting
drunk. When Lander editor L. L. Newton deplored such an incident,
a woman wrote him in defense of the right of the men to "pitch one
before leaving for the war." She continued: "Would you destroy a
custom as old as God, war, life, and death? . . . for heavens sake let's
not have any more such drivel. The only available home town paper is
not supposed to be a comic strip . . . please let our service boys get
drunk in peace." A major project for the service centers consisted of
rounding up and chaperoning girls ("hostesses") who danced with and
otherwise entertained the boys.

GI Joe was fed frequently while in the States. He was fed at his farewell party; he was fed at all hours at the U.S.O.; he was fed at can-
teens while traveling. The Red Cross canteen at the Burlington station
in Sheridan fed 126,500 persons in thirty-four months.

It was standard practice for communities to enroll the names of
service personnel on honor-roll boards erected in public places. When
decorations were given, newspapers proclaimed the news. The Congressional Medal of Honor was awarded (posthumously) to only one
Wyoming man, a native of Oklahoma, who had entered service in
Cheyenne—Technical Sergeant Charles F. Carey, Jr.

MILITARY INSTALLATIONS

Wyoming political and business leaders scrambled to obtain military
installations for the state. They won three awards: expansion of Fort
Francis E. Warren at Cheyenne, a new army air base at Casper, and a
prisoner-of-war camp at Douglas.

Old Fort Warren was filled almost to capacity by a garrison of 3,500 officers and men in October, 1940, when it was announced that there would be new construction of 261 buildings for a Quartermaster Replacement Center. Most of the construction was completed by April, 1941, when the name was changed to Quartermaster Replacement Training Center. The mission of the center—to train more than 122,000 quartermaster specialists—was completed by July 1, 1943, when deactivation was ordered. When activity was at its peak in 1942 and early 1943, more than 20,000 men were regularly stationed at Fort Warren.

Deactivation of the Quartermaster Replacement Training Center did not mean complete abandonment of Fort Warren facilities. Many thousands of men of various classifications, such as Negro Quartermaster troops, railroad battalions of the Transportation Corps, and prisoners of war occupied the fort until after the end of the war. Finally, on June 2, 1945, Fort Warren was made a redeployment center for Quartermaster and Transportation Corps troops. All told, the economic and social impact of wartime Fort Warren on Cheyenne and the state was tremendous.

The state's second wartime military installation in size and importance was the army air base eight miles west of Casper. Built in the summer of 1942, it was activated September 1, 1942, changed its name from Army Air Base to Army Air Field, Casper, Wyoming, in February, 1944, and was deactivated March 7, 1945. Designed to accommodate between three and four thousand men, the base was much smaller than Fort Warren; yet it meant much to the oil city, which had languished in economic doldrums for almost twenty years.

Major mission of the Casper base was to give the final phase of four-engine bomber training. Mile-square target areas were fenced off west of the base for bombing practice by crews flying B-24 Liberator heavy bombers. Casper was in more desperate economic straits than Cheyenne at the beginning of the war, and appreciated the benefits correspondingly more. Apparently, too, the Air Force men were more glamorous than the Quartermasters. The official "History of the Army Air Base, Casper, Wyoming," [2] which was not written to be read by Casper citizens, includes a statement that "true western hospitality was experienced almost invariably by the Army men."

[2] The official "History of the Army Air Base, Casper, Wyoming," in 1953 was in the custody of the United States Air Force University, Research Studies Institute, Maxwell Air Force Base, Alabama. Some of the information in the "History" was abstracted, declassified, and forwarded to me by my former student Dr. Victor Cohen for use in preparing my *Wyoming's War Years, 1941–1945.*

History of Wyoming

The state's third military installation, the prisoner-of-war camp, one mile west of Douglas, had a normal complement of 500 enlisted men, 50 officers, and 2,500 prisoners of war. The camp was constructed in 1943 at a cost of two million dollars and included 180 buildings, mainly army-style barracks, surrounded by a wire stockade. At a "grand opening" in June, 1943, attended by sight-seers from seventeen counties, the visitors were particularly amazed by the 150-bed hospital, described in the press as "equipped to the nth degree with the finest equipment available." The first prisoners, 412 Italian enlisted men, arrived in August, 1943. German prisoners came later.

Management of the prisoners was governed strictly by the International Convention of July 27, 1929. No internal disturbances occurred at Douglas, since the prisoners, particularly the Italians, were glad that the war was over for them. Many of the prisoners were taken to side camps, near which they were put to work in agriculture and lumbering. After the 1945 harvest, the prisoners were quickly repatriated. Considering the state's population, it appears that Wyoming managed to obtain a little more than its share of wartime military bases. Cheyenne, Casper, and Douglas—and the whole state as well—benefited from the three installations assigned to the state.

HEART MOUNTAIN RELOCATION CENTER

A Japanese relocation center in Park County brought benefits to Wyoming that were not fully appreciated at the time. Because it was thought at the beginning of the war that the security of the Pacific Coast required transfer of Japanese to inland places, 110,442 persons were evacuated from western Washington and Oregon, California, and southern Arizona. Against the wishes of many citizens of Wyoming, one of ten relocation centers was established at Heart Mountain, halfway between Cody and Powell.

The Heart Mountain center looked like a temporary army camp except for the barbed-wire fence and guard towers surrounding it. There were 465 barracks (tar-paper "hutments"), each 20 by 100 feet, and various auxiliary buildings to accommodate 11,000 persons of all ages. The barracks were divided into family-size apartments. There were community mess halls, baths, and toilet facilities.

The army transferred the evacuees to the camp, where they came under the control of the War Relocation Authority, an independent civilian government agency. Military Police aided in camp control. The evacuees at Heart Mountain at the outset were two-thirds

American-born and therefore United States citizens. In 1943 the evacuees were screened according to loyalty, those who expressed a desire to go to Japan (about 8 per cent) being sent to a segregation center at Tule Lake, California. In the meantime, the War Relocation Authority had begun issuing temporary leaves for voluntary work, mainly in agriculture, and indefinite leaves for permanent resettlement of loyal Japanese. Despite the official policy to terminate the camps, they continued to flourish until after V-J Day. The Heart Mountain center, which had a population of 10,872 in October, 1942, still had 8,663 in February, 1945.

For many of the Japanese, their stay in Wyoming was tragic. As noted, two-thirds of them were United States citizens who had done nothing to suggest that they were disloyal to the United States, yet they were herded eastward and imprisoned on a bleak desert. For the most part, Wyoming people displayed little of their famous western hospitality in dealing with the Japanese. "A Jap is a Jap," agreed many Wyomingites as they failed to distinguish between loyal United States citizens and warlike enemies across the Pacific. Although there were many fair-minded citizens in the state, they tended to remain silent while alarmists and racists were noisily vocal.

Some people in the vicinity of the relocation center were afraid that the Japanese might break out and attack them. Gradually, such fears dissolved. Governor Nels Smith and many other persons, however, were afraid that the Japanese would settle in the state after the war. One of the best friends the Japanese had in Wyoming was editor L. L. Newton of the *Wyoming State Journal* (Lander). When he learned that the evacuees were coming, he wrote: "Let us demonstrate to them what real Democracy is, that it is the application of the same Christian principles of living and dealing with others which have made America what it is today." A more typical reaction was that of the *Wyoming Eagle* (Cheyenne), which asked: "Has Mr. Newton Gone Berserk?"

Heart Mountain became a political football in February, 1943, when Republican United States Senator E. V. Robertson announced that the administration was "pampering" the residents of Heart Mountain. Robertson helped the *Denver Post* obtain data for use in a series of sensational articles which charged pampering, high living, and hoarding of scarce food. After it became apparent that the articles were grossly exaggerated, Governor Lester C. Hunt wrote that "[Jack] Carberry was sent to the Center to write a political story." The Governor explained that "food stuffs cannot be brought into a city to feed 13,500 people in a wheel barrow and it would not be good business to bring it in every day." After a visit to the center, he concluded that the "living standard was, to my way of thinking, rather disgraceful."

Wyoming people gradually mellowed toward the Heart Mountain Japanese, partly because of the remarkable achievements of Japanese units in the United States Army. Heart Mountain contributed more than 900 men to the army, of whom 20 were killed in action. Although Wyoming people became more considerate of the Japanese in their midst, they wanted them to leave after the war. Governor Hunt received petitions and letters on the subject and wrote to War Relocation Authority Director Dillon Myer: "We do not want a single one of these evacuees to remain in Wyoming." Alarm lest many Japanese would stay in the state proved groundless; the state's Japanese population declined from 643 in 1940 to 450 in 1950. A law adopted by the 1943 legislature contributed to the exodus by barring the evacuees from voting and owning property in the state.

A substantial part of the $5,000,000 spent for Heart Mountain construction entered the state's trade channels, and after the center was in operation, Jerry Housel, project attorney in 1943, estimated that the state received financial benefits of more than $500,000 a year from the camp. The Japanese subjugated eighteen hundred acres of virgin benchland; waterproofed a section of irrigation canal; produced pork, poultry, and eggs; raised more than six million pounds of crops; and supplied much seasonal labor in agriculture outside the camp. Although the Japanese guests were hated, feared, and despised, they really deserved sympathy and gratitude.

CIVILIAN DEFENSE

Civilian defense in the Second World War covered many activities, which may be divided into "protective" services and "home and health" services.

Under authority of Congress, the Wyoming Legislature in February, 1941, provided for a state defense council of eighteen members. Adjutant General R. L. Esmay became executive vice-chairman of the council. Colonel Goelet Gallatin of Big Horn served as chairman of the council until July, 1943, when Edwin J. Zoble of Casper took charge. First task of the council was to set up a state guard which could take over civil protection functions in the absence of the National Guard. The state guard consisted of 488 enlisted men and 52 officers, divided into a headquarters troop in Cheyenne and four cavalry squadrons (two troops in each) with headquarters in Sheridan, Casper, Rock Springs, and Torrington. Arrayed in special uniforms, the guardsmen drilled once a week without pay. Except for some duty fighting forest fires, they were never called out for any emergency. At war's end the state guard included 271 enlisted men and 70 officers; more than 200 had left to enter the armed forces.

Before Pearl Harbor, Wyoming's state and county defense councils had already been organized with guidance from the national Office of Civilian Defense, which served as a planning and coordinating body, without local authority. The state defense council met in emergency session in Cheyenne on December 12–13, 1941, in the wake of the Pearl Harbor attack and launched a ten-point program: registration of civilians willing to volunteer for civilian defense; registration of all private pilots and private airplanes for a civilian air patrol; complete housing inventory to determine what facilities would be available in case of widespread coastal evacuations; formation of an air-raid warning system; organization of a health and nutritional program; organization of a medical service for the state guard; training and organization of amateur radio operators; formation of fire districts to protect forests and ranges; establishment of training classes in blacksmithing and farm-machinery repair work; and participation of local defense councils in war drives. Volunteer defense workers were registered and assigned in subsequent months: 332 staff, 2,914 air-raid wardens, 610 auxiliary firemen, 640 auxiliary police, 586 decontamination, 187 demolition and clearance, 342 drivers, 475 emergency food and housing, 782 emergency medical, 808 fire watchers, 559 messengers, 197 nurse's aides, 292 rescue squads, 195 road repair, and 285 utility repair.

Everyone in authority, from President Roosevelt on down, advised "Keep Calm" in late 1941 and early 1942, yet full-page spreads in all newspapers, telling what to do in case of air raids, made some people go look for shelters. They investigated caves and mine shafts. Most people in Wyoming, however, avoided panic, and the state's civil-defense preparations fell far short of those in coastal areas of the country. Besides, far more Wyoming people registered for defense work than actually followed through with training courses. Yet by 1944, some 9,117 persons had received first-aid training certificates.

The American Legion throughout the country took over the training of air-raid wardens. The Wyoming membership summoned a group of 125 persons to a four-day civilian-protection school in Casper in July, 1942, involving lectures on protection against gases, the use and care of gas masks, and types and composition of incendiaries. The 125 then returned to their communities to instruct the local wardens. At the same time, Governor Smith, at the demand of the federal government, set up an air-raid warning communication system, which included many control centers with elaborate panel boards.

Two state-wide blackout tests were held, one in December, 1942, and the other in May, 1943. While it was officially reported that the tests were quite successful, many people did not turn their lights off as required, or turned them back on before the all-clear signal. For a month after Pearl Harbor, some people expected air raids, but by the time blackout tests were ordered, few except the air-raid wardens took the defense measures very seriously, for enemy action seemed far away from Wyoming. Interest in civilian defense gradually waned. The pervasive organization which, by February, 1943, had enrolled 19,352 of the state's citizens was by late 1944 regarded as superfluous. President Truman in May, 1945, ordered the Office of Civilian Defense disbanded.

Late in the war, a few air-raid wardens got something to do as a result of a Japanese paper-balloon scare. Quite a number of paper balloons carrying small bombs came to earth at widely scattered points in the United States and Canada. They caused a few small fires, and several persons who tampered with unexploded bombs were killed. A few balloons descended in Wyoming without causing any damage or injury. After the war, Japanese sources revealed that some nine thousand bomb-laden balloons had been launched, with the hope that prevailing westerly winds would carry them into America. Set to explode forty or fifty hours after launching, the bombs were supposed to start forest fires and frighten civilians. Evidently, many of the bombs dropped in the Pacific.

CIVILIAN DEFENSE: HOME, HEALTH, AND WAR SERVICES

As the war progressed, the Office of Civilian Defense, under its general instructions to promote all war programs, gave less attention to strictly defense activities than it did to nondefense "home, health, and war" services, which involved everyone. The O.C.D. received much assistance from the Red Cross. Three thousand Wyoming women took the Red Cross 24-hour home-nursing course, which was designed to relieve the pressure on hospitals, doctors, and regular nurses. Complementing the home-nursing work was the more exacting nurse's-aide program. By July, 1944, almost 400 Wyoming women who had completed the 80-hour nurse's-aide training course were working in hospitals without pay. Another Red Cross enterprise enlisted 63 Wyoming women as Gray Ladies, who participated in a program of ward visiting, recreation, and entertainment in military hospitals, particularly in Cheyenne. Red Cross "production work" occupied more time than any other phase of the home and health services. Wyoming women produced vast quantities of surgical dressings, kitbags, scrapbooks, and garments.

Knitting was a slightly less important activity in World War II than it had been in World War I, since the services were better prepared to equip their men with the clothing they needed. Yet Wyoming women knitted and sewed more than fifty thousand garments for Red Cross distribution, besides completing more than twenty thousand kitbags according to army and navy specifications. The kits, designed for servicemen going overseas, included soap, playing cards, cigarettes, shoe-polishing cloths, pencils, writing paper, envelopes, chewing gum, shoelaces, a waterproof matchbox, razor blades, a pocket-size novel, and a "housewife" equipped with buttons, needles, and thread. The contents of the bags were purchased through the Red Cross at wholesale prices.

The O.C.D. home and health services enlisted the aid of youth. In many communities, Junior Red Cross workers made scrapbooks, writing portfolios, memo pads, napkins, menu covers, Christmas cards, and other items for hospitals and military camps.

While home and health services were primarily in distaff domain, men joined in planting Victory Gardens. Every civilian-defense council in the state promoted Victory Gardens, with the result that the state's garden production doubled.

SALVAGE

A major home-front operation was the recovery of thousands of tons of scrap metals, paper, rubber, clothing, kitchen fats, silk, and nylon. Most of the scrap-metal collecting took place in the fall of 1942 and the fall of 1943. The state's biggest single salvage operation scrapped thirty thousand tons of rails from the North Western line west of Casper. Consolidation of parallel lines of the North Western and the Burlington made possible the elimination in 1943 of eighty-seven miles of North Western track.

After the Japanese conquest of Singapore and the Netherlands East Indies had cut off natural-rubber supplies, a great national drive in

1942 brought together huge piles of old tires and other rubber articles. Old silk and nylon hosiery was gathered for making parachutes and gunpowder bags. Kitchen fats were salvaged for the manufacture of explosives, paint, soap, and food. The women of Wyoming led the nation in the salvage of fats in January, 1943, on a per capita basis.

An astonishing variety of items was called for at one time or another: fur for the manufacture of Merchant Marine vests, duck feathers for bedding, old keys, athletic equipment, games, canes, radios, hair clippers, phonograph records, small arms, hunting knives, and jewelry. Natives of the South Pacific were said to be willing to work harder for old jewelry than for money.

FINANCIAL MOBILIZATION

With rare prescience, the Wyoming Legislature had memorialized Congress in 1939 to abolish the Sixteenth (Income Tax) Amendment to the United States Constitution. Within the next five years, individual income-tax returns in the state rose fortyfold. Treasury Department figures show the following payments by individuals and corporations in Wyoming:

Year	Individual Income Tax Returns	Corporation Income Tax Returns
1939	$ 613,000	$ 516,000
1940	1,567,000	711,000
1941	5,664,000	1,899,000
1942	14,318,000	3,671,000
1943	23,743,000	3,321,000
1944	26,006,000	3,166,000
1945	25,603,000	3,200,000

Between May 1, 1941, and December 31, 1945, the United States government spent $350,000,000,000, collected $147,000,000,000 (net) in taxes and other revenues, and borrowed $225,000,000,000. As was true elsewhere, bond sales in Wyoming exceeded income-tax collections. There were seven federal war-loan drives and a victory drive, in each of which the state exceeded its quota.

Distribution of war bonds in World War II was one of the greatest selling jobs in history, considering the amount of high-pressure salesmanship, the number of people participating, and the results. Newspapers and the movie industry contributed enormously to the selling effort in Wyoming, with assistance from radio stations and clubs.

The people of the state contributed generously to many war-connected causes. The National War Fund, for which money was collected in 1943, 1944, and 1945, used the Community Chest idea of consolidating many causes in one giant drive for funds. People welcomed such consolidation, since in three previous years they had been overwhelmed by appeals.

PROSPERITY

Wyoming could and did carry its share of the financial burden of the war because its principal industries—agriculture, livestock, transportation, oil, and coal—flourished and because the federal government spent more than $130,000,000 for war-supply contracts and war facilities in the state. With a few exceptions, the war did not bring new industries to Wyoming, and tourism suffered somewhat, yet income payments and bank deposits warrant the conclusion that the state was much better off financially at the end of the war than at the beginning.

Income payments in the state (total income payments to individuals) rose, at an almost constant rate, from $141,000,000 in 1939 to $287,000,000 in 1945. Since the consumers' price index rose less than 30 per cent from 1939 to 1945, the state enjoyed good times, as it had in the Spanish-American War and the First World War. Testifying to the prosperity of the war years, Wyoming bank deposits increased from $63,900,000 on June 30, 1939, to $210,900,000 on December 31, 1945. Nevertheless, the state's per capita income increased more slowly than that of the nation, rising from $567 in 1939 to $1,153 in 1945, while the national per capita income rose from $539 to $1,177. Wyoming was very weak in the first of four dynamic components which accounted for wartime expansion in national income: increased wages and salaries in war manufacturing industries, agricultural income, federal civilian payrolls, and pay for the armed forces.

RATIONING AND PRICE CONTROLS

Wartime scarcity of essential goods brought rationing and price controls by the Office of Price Administration (O.P.A.), which was set up by Congress in January, 1942. The first phase of the controls program felt in Wyoming was the rationing of tires and tubes. Automobiles, trucks, tractors, trailers, typewriters, and bicycles were soon added to the list of commodities which could not be bought without a certificate from the local rationing board. Sugar was rationed beginning in May, 1942, although the rations were large enough so that very few people were inconvenienced. Coffee was rationed for nine months beginning in November, 1942. Gasoline rationing, which had been imposed in the East in May, 1942, came to Wyoming in December of that year. The basic ration in Wyoming was four gallons per week until October, 1943, when it was cut to three gallons. It was cut further to two gallons in March, 1944, then raised to three gallons in June, 1945. Shoes were rationed beginning in February, 1943. The long-expected rationing of food (other than sugar and coffee) began in March, 1943.

For the most part, Wyoming citizens accepted food rationing in good spirit. While most consumers thought meat rationing was necessary, producers groused about it, knowing that they could get better prices in a free market. Wyoming was comparatively free from black-market operations in meat, even though authorities in the state did little beyond issuing an occasional warning to petty chiselers on farm and ranch. No serious attempt was made to enforce the slaughtering rules, although it was well known that some Wyoming people were supplementing their rationed supplies illegally. Under meat-rationing rules, livestock raisers could slaughter for their own household use without a federal license, but not for sale or gift unless they collected ration stamps and made monthly reports to the Office of Price Administration.

In general, enforcement of O.P.A. rules was no more popular in Wyoming than in other parts of the country. The public acknowledged the need for price controls, but was apathetic about enforcement. Customers sympathized with retailers, who let them know regularly that regulations and red tape were almost unbearable. Not many people passed up opportunities to get steaks or gasoline in violation of the rules. Publisher Tracy McCraken wrote in his *Wyoming Eagle* in April, 1945:

We're a funny lot, we Americans. . . . Mrs. Jones—Mr. Jones is no better— says she is as patriotic as anyone. . . . But, says Mrs. Jones, when everyone else is getting a little stuff here and there without points, why should my family hold back? And says the restaurant owner and other retailers of rationed items, we wouldn't be doing it at our place except that we know our competitors are doing it and you can't expect us to let them take all our business away from us, can you? Besides what difference does it make? If we don't take the black market meat offered us, someone else will. . . .

Although occasional violators of O.P.A. rules were legion, controls worked pretty well most of the time, and there was much less inflation than in World War I. The O.P.A. program avoided the runaway prices and the speculative hoarding that almost certainly would have come had there been no controls. The Bureau of Labor Statistics price index for moderate-income families in large cities rose from 99.4 in 1939 to 128.4 in 1945 (1935–1939 = 100). Wyoming prices were not tabulated and converted into an index, but there is little evidence to suggest that the Wyoming situation departed far from the national one. In its price-administration history, the state differed from the national norms mainly in two particulars: the absence of large-scale black-market activities and the absence of any enthusiasm among O.P.A. officials to crack down on violators.

AGRICULTURE

"The greatest industry in the State of Wyoming is agriculture and its kindred activity, the raising of livestock," Governor Lester C. Hunt told the twenty-eighth legislature in 1945. Oil and the tourist business would catch up fast after the war, but they were still far behind agriculture in wartime. War made the farmer's work seem much more important than it had been in the 1920's and 1930's, when surpluses and low prices were the rule. Suddenly, slogans appeared, such as "All-out production for war" and "Food will win the war and write the peace."

Wyoming's most spectacular production increase was in cattle. There were 827,000 cattle valued at $37,523,000 in 1941 and 1,043,000 cattle valued at $68,734,000 in 1945. Sheep declined in numbers from 3,778,000 in 1940 to 3,040,000 in 1945.

Cash receipts from the marketing of Wyoming crops rose from $8,259,000 in 1939 to $21,539,000 in 1945 as production increased in winter wheat, oats, barley, beans, and potatoes. Significantly, the increase in production was achieved with fewer farm workers. Crops were harvested with the help of high-school students, volunteers from towns, prisoners of war, Japanese internees, and seasonal workers brought in from Arkansas, New Mexico, and Arizona. There were adequate machines and spare parts. The United States Census of Agriculture reported 10,157 tractors on Wyoming farms and ranches in 1945 as compared with only 6,534 in 1940. Motor trucks increased from 6,341 to 8,638 in the same period. Fortunately, precipitation for the state was well above normal except in 1943, when it was 89 per cent.

Farm prices rose faster than wages, climbing 131 per cent between the summer of 1939 and the summer of 1945, while hourly earnings of labor increased only 61 per cent. The difference was offset in part by the fact that farm prices, except for livestock, were well below parity when war came and also by the fact that hourly earnings of labor are not the whole story of labor rewards, since labor in wartime enjoyed fewer layoffs, longer workweeks, and overtime pay.

Restraints on fat-cattle prices irritated cattlemen, who, as a result, had to take less for their feeder cattle. Returns from a questionnaire distributed by the Wyoming Stock Growers Association in the summer of 1944 showed that all cattlemen thought costs were advancing faster than prices. Production costs doubled during the war, while receipts did not quite double. The Bureau of Agricultural Economics, United States Department of Agriculture, reported that annual cash receipts from marketing Wyoming livestock and livestock products advanced from $39,036,000 in 1939 to $76,386,000 in 1945. Beef-cattle prices were already above parity in 1939. President George A. Cross of the Wyoming Stock Growers Association reported in 1945 that the association was "on the soundest financial basis of recent years."

On the other hand, there was genuine distress among sheepmen. Many wool growers could not meet competition from foreign wool, despite a tariff of thirty-four cents a pound. With price ceilings on lamb, mutton, and wool, the sheepmen could not keep up with wartime costs of labor and feed. Some sheepmen switched to cattle or quit the business. Those who stayed with sheep were brave indeed because the huge stockpiles of domestic and foreign wool, which had been built up as strategic reserves, threatened to demoralize the domestic market for years to come.

Like the wool growers, Wyoming milk producers got caught in the squeeze between price ceilings and increasing costs. O.P.A. Director Henry D. Watenpaugh reported to Senator Joseph C. O'Mahoney in January, 1944, that other agricultural prices had increased by more than 88 per cent over the 1939 level, while milk prices had increased not more than 12 to 20 per cent, exclusive of subsidy payments.

Although sheepmen and dairymen failed to catch the prosperity train, others rode at least part way on it. Cash receipts from Wyoming farm and ranch marketings, including government payments, were as follows:

Year	Livestock	Crops	Government Payments	Total Cash Receipts
1939	$39,036,000	$ 8,259,000	$3,805,000	$51,100,000
1940	41,723,000	9,058,000	3,684,000	54,465,000
1941	50,030,000	12,136,000	3,539,000	65,705,000
1942	62,952,000	16,597,000	3,597,000	83,146,000
1943	71,826,000	19,460,000	3,448,000	94,734,000
1944	74,444,000	19,654,000	2,960,000	97,058,000
1945	76,386,000	21,539,000	4,529,000	102,454,000

Wyoming's agricultural income did not advance as much during the war years as did national agricultural income. The state's total cash receipts increased 100 per cent, while the nation's cash receipts rose 156 per cent. Yet Wyoming farmers and ranchers came out of the war much better off financially than they went in. In particular, they avoided the excesses of World War I, moved conservatively, consolidated their holdings, and paid off their debts.

THE UNION PACIFIC RAILROAD

Wyoming's greatest single industrial enterprise, the Union Pacific Railroad, performed brilliantly, carrying a tremendous volume of freight and passengers efficiently. Net operating revenues rose from $168,164,258 in 1940 to $506,590,966 in 1944. Since operating expenses and taxes also rose rapidly, net income advanced somewhat less spectacularly: $19,445,880 in 1940; $28,857,420 in 1941; $62,083,985 in 1942; $45,293,259 in 1943; $41,070,894 in 1944; and $33,031,580 in 1945.

Wyoming's other railroads enjoyed increased traffic and revenue and made their contributions to the war effort, but, not being so strategically located, their activities were dwarfed by those of the Union Pacific.

INDUSTRY

The national industrial expansion which came with the war scarcely touched Wyoming. The final report (1941) of the Temporary National Economic Committee (Senator O'Mahoney, chairman) recommended decentralization of industry. Nonetheless, most of the new facilities were located in areas already heavily industrialized. The Bureau of Labor Statistics reported that only Wyoming and New Mexico showed an increase of less than five hundred wage earners and salaried employees in manufacturing employment between April, 1940, and June, 1943. The number of wage and salary workers in manufacturing in Wyoming rose from 4,500 in 1940 to 5,400 in 1945. At war's end, Wyoming had the smallest "war" manufacturing-industries payroll of all states. The usual explanations were offered for the state's failure to attract war industry: high freight rates, lack of water, lack of power, lack of labor, and lack of capital. The last item, however, was less significant than usual, since the government was supplying most of the capital.

Most of the early talk about getting defense subcontracts for the state came to nothing. The Rowley Brothers Electric Motor Company of Casper did some armature winding and motor-repair work, and the Ideal Laboratory Tool and Supply Company in Cheyenne obtained contracts for making test apparatus and tools. The Linde Air Products and Prest-O-Lite companies in Casper also won subcontracts. The state's most successful subcontractor, however, was the Wyott Manufacturing Company of Cheyenne, which was able to convert from making cream dispensers, coffee-urn faucets, and display cases to special valves for use by the navy. The Wyott Company won four awards for high achievement in production, entitling it to display the Army-Navy "E" flag with four stars.

Aviation activities at Cheyenne expanded rapidly. Most important was the United Air Lines Modification Center, which installed new guns and instruments and otherwise modified thousands of B-17 Flying Fortresses and smaller numbers of other bombers. Two huge hangars were built for the work in 1942, and additional improvements were made in 1943. For a time, the modification center employed sixteen hundred people, half of them women, on three shifts. The center earned two Army-Navy "E" flags.

Most of the state's manufacturing workers in 1940 had been employed in thirty oil refineries (most of them small). In response to many entreaties, Petroleum Coordinator Harold L. Ickes finally authorized government support for two 100-octane refining plants, one an eight-million-dollar expansion of the Frontier refinery in Cheyenne and the other a ten-million-dollar expansion of the Sinclair refinery at Sinclair. Both plants began operating in 1944.

MINERAL PRODUCTION

Wyoming oil, coal, and iron ore played vital roles in World War II. Crude-oil production rose steadily from 21,537,000 barrels in 1939 to 35,359,000 barrels in 1945. Coal production rose from 5,373,000 tons in 1939 to 9,847,000 in 1945. Iron-ore production at the Sunrise mine rose from 658,000 tons in 1939 to 1,104,000 tons in 1941, then declined to 912,000 in 1943 and to 679,000 in 1945.

A very important oil discovery occurred in 1943 in the deep Tensleep Sand of Elk Basin. The field had been discovered in 1915, but the deeper wells gave it new life. Other, less important discoveries were made in deeper zones of the Oregon Basin and Little Buffalo Basin fields and in the new Gebo and Steamboat Butte fields. Wildcatting flourished. The state's proved reserves increased from 306,000,000 barrels in 1939 to 600,000,000 in 1945. With good reason, state mineral supervisor Pierre LaFleiche proclaimed in a Denver address that "up in Wyoming our latchstring is out to the oil man." The tax structure, he explained, "is as equitable, or more equitable, than that of any other major oil producing state in America."

Wyoming's wartime coal production flowed from one hundred mines in fifteen counties. Most of it was used to fuel Union Pacific steam locomotives.

RESEARCH FACILITIES

Three government research plants were established in Laramie. The Bureau of Mines Petroleum and Oil-Shale Experiment Station was given new housing (at a cost of $574,000) in a handsome structure of native stone. A $4,500,000 alumina pilot plant was erected to experiment with the extraction of alumina from anorthosite. A small Bureau of Mines sponge-iron plant operated temporarily.

LABOR

As in other states, workers enjoyed full employment and good pay in Wyoming during the war. There was much overtime at time and a half, and unions signed up more members than ever before. Workers could shop around for jobs until the government, in 1943, restricted the shifting of workers in essential industry. In the year 1944, only 242 persons in the state filed claims for unemployment compensation, of whom 38 collected benefits totaling $3,055. Women stepped into all kinds of jobs, driving trucks and taxis, serving as filling-station attendants, working in agriculture and in all war manufacturing plants. They were especially prominent at the United Air Lines Modification Center in Cheyenne, the Wyott Manufacturing Company plant, the Union Pacific Railroad, Fort Warren, and Casper Army Air Field. The 1943 legislature amended the Female Labor Law in order to permit employment of females in excess of eight hours per day and more than forty-eight hours per week when an emergency has been declared by the President of the United States.

There was only one notable work stoppage—part of a nation-wide strike in the coal industry, it idled 3,890 Wyoming workers for 43,800 man-days in June, 1943. Although work stoppages were at a minimum, not all was moonlight and roses between employers and employees. Senator E. V. Robertson suggested that workers should be put in uniform and ordered to produce. At a time when many persons all over the country were charging United Mine Workers leader John L. Lewis with treason, the Wyoming Stock Growers Association in convention in June, 1943, passed a resolution describing Lewis as "a traitor who should swing from a cottonwood tree." Wyoming's conservative press had many nasty things to say about coal miners and their leaders. The state's only important labor paper, the *Wyoming Labor Journal*, which became the *Wyoming-Utah Labor Journal* in January, 1945, lashed back repeatedly at labor critics. Labor was "being made the goat by the millionaire press and politicians," said the *Labor Journal* in December, 1941. In later issues there was much attention to high profits. Prices affecting labor, it was asserted, were rising much faster than prices affecting the wealthy. On Labor Day, 1943, the *Labor Journal* lamented that the workingman "finds that he is not much freer than Uncle Tom on Simon Legree's plantation." After consistently crying havoc during the war, the *Labor Journal* experienced a remarkable change of heart. In November, 1945, in an editorial headed "The Honeymoon is Over," the editor declared that the Wyoming worker had been lucky, along with the rest of organized labor.

SUMMARY OF INDUSTRIAL AND BUSINESS DEVELOPMENTS

The United States Bureau of the Census reported Wyoming's participation in major war-supply contracts and war-facilities projects from June, 1940, to June, 1945, as follows:

County	Combat Equipment	Other	Industrial	Military
	MAJOR WAR-SUPPLY CONTRACTS		MAJOR WAR-FACILITIES PROJECTS	
Albany	...	$ 2,067,000	$ 4,670,000	$ 509,000
Big Horn	...	1,927,000	...	...
Carbon	...	11,967,000	6,750,000	...
Converse	...	250,000	...	1,588,000
Hot Springs	...	310,000	...	...
Laramie	$12,670,000	43,377,000	13,197,000	9,924,000
Lincoln	...	204,000	...	...
Natrona	50,000	3,482,000	...	11,410,000
Park	...	4,326,000	918,000	...
Sheridan	50,000	1,147,000	...	...
Sweetwater	...	362,000	...	...
WYOMING	$12,770,000	$68,419,000	$25,535,000	$23,431,000

An over-all view shows that the state's industry and business in war-time had strong spots and weak spots. Transportation and mineral development were strong, while manufacturing development was negligible, except for refinery expansion. Small business fared pretty well, enjoying a nervous, harassed prosperity. Government money was very helpful. All in all, the state emerged from the war in better economic condition than ever before.

POPULATION CHANGES

Unprecedented population fluctuations occurred during the war, and many communities found their population swinging first one way and then another. Servicemen departed. Thousands of the state's workers were attracted to war jobs in other states. Later, other thousands of workers had to be brought in to work in the coal mines, on the railroads, and on special construction jobs. Women and children followed their menfolk to out-of-state training camps and defense jobs. Other women and children arrived to be with men who were stationed at Fort Warren and Casper Army Air Field.

For the first time in history, Wyoming suffered an over-all drop in population. Thirteen counties lost between 20 and 30 per cent of their civilian population between the 1940 census and October, 1943, when registration for War Ration Book Four gave an accurate count. On the other hand, four counties had gained civilian population by October, 1943. Park, thanks to the Japanese internees, had gained 83.5 per cent, Laramie 35.8 per cent, Sweetwater 3.2 per cent, and Carbon 3.1 per cent. When the flow back and forth subsided, it was found that Wyoming had lost by the exchange. The United States Bureau of the Census estimated that the state suffered a net loss of 7,000 civilians from 1940 to 1950. In the decade, Wyoming gained 40,000 in population because of a 41,000 excess of births over deaths and a 6,000 gain at Fort Warren. In short, many people who left Wyoming during the war, never came back. The state's most spectacular population change was part of a national exodus from farm and ranch. The state's rural farm and ranch population declined from 72,674 in 1940 to 53,424 in 1945, and most of the people who left the rural areas never returned.

LIFE ON THE HOME FRONT

Servicemen sometimes thought that the 4-F's and those too old or too young to fight enjoyed a soft life back home. Some did, and some got rich, but for the most part those who stayed home worked harder than usual, gave up some of their usual comforts, and suffered from unwonted tensions. Inflation, though restrained, caused suffering to fixed-income groups. For example, Governor Lester C. Hunt told the legislature in 1945 that the income of the state's old-age pensioners, dependent blind, and dependent children had not kept pace with the rising cost of living.

Production for civilian use was stopped in automobiles, mechanical refrigerators, washing machines, radios, typewriters, and many other items. A Casper store advertised in July, 1942: "Ladies! Take Warning! Girdles are going to war. Our last shipment has arrived. Anticipate your needs."

Despite shortages, the wartime standard of living was well above that of the 1930's, and fat bank accounts promised fun for most people as soon as industry could begin to catch up with consumer requirements.

Only a small minority thought that there should be no gaiety on the home front. The official government view was that a limited amount of play would contribute to maximum work output. Wyoming in wartime enjoyed fewer fairs, rodeos, race meets, and circuses. The Cheyenne Frontier Days committee, recalling that the show had not been called off in World War I, decided to go ahead. Broncs turned up with such names as "Wake Island," "Midway," "Flying Fortress," and "Slap-a-Jap."

The most popular form of relaxation was the movies. Lack of gasoline restricted pleasure driving and left more time for motion pictures, which could be reached on foot. Cheyenne publisher Tracy McCraken, in his *Wyoming Eagle* column, wrote a "Letter to a Soldier" in May, 1943:

Well, sir, we can't say things are normal, for they're far from that. The busy places in Cheyenne are the USO, the ration board offices, the churches and the movies. At the USO they dance, at the ration offices they cuss, like they've never cussed before, at the churches they pray as they have never prayed before, and to the movies they flock as they've never flocked before. . . .

A popular form of relaxation, following the fortunes of the athletic teams at the University of Wyoming, was interrupted in 1943 when the university abandoned football, basketball, baseball, and track after most of the previous year's athletes had joined the armed forces. Sports fans, however, had a pleasant memory to sustain them. In the spring of 1943, the University of Wyoming basketball team had won recognition as the best collegiate team in the nation, first winning the National Collegiate Athletic Association tournament and then defeating the winner of the National Invitation Tournament.

Golf and winter sports languished. While residents bought fishing licenses at the prewar rate, there was a sharp drop in sales of tourist and nonresident licenses. Although the fish harvest declined, the game harvest increased. Meat rationing made hunting more attractive than ever. The annual game kill, which had never reached 10,000 in the years 1935–1939, exceeded 33,000 in 1943. Wyoming Game and Fish Commission officials would have preferred a smaller kill, but stockmen demanded an increase, and the United States Fish and Wild Life Service insisted that the elk migrating to the federal elk refuge be reduced to save feed, prevent starvation, and supply meat.

Courtship persisted, and was often accelerated in wartime. Cheyenne girls captured husbands at Fort Warren; Casper girls, at the air base; Laramie girls, among military trainees at the university. Wyoming servicemen found brides in cities adjacent to southern training camps or in distant lands.

GOVERNMENT AND POLITICS

Wyoming's wartime government was conducted quite efficiently and economically, though not without political bickering and sniping. In 1941, three Republicans and two Democrats held office: Nels H. Smith, governor (R.); Lester C. Hunt, secretary of state (D.); Mart T. Christensen, treasurer (R.); William "Scotty" Jack, auditor (D.); Esther Anderson, superintendent of public instruction (R.).

Besides the usual interparty strife, there was trouble within the dominant Republican party. Governor Smith could not persuade his livestock and sanitary board to oust its paid executive officer, Dr. H. D. Port, whom Smith disliked (although Port was a Republican), so he set out to change the board. When the terms of two highly respected Republican board members, Fred E. Warren and D. P. Espy, expired, the Governor dared not submit substitutes to the Republican Senate. Instead, he waited until the Senate had adjourned and then named two ad interim replacements, only to have the Wyoming Supreme Court confound him by ruling that Warren and Espy should continue on the board, since their successors had not been approved by the Senate.

Secretary of State Lester C. Hunt ran against and defeated Smith when the latter sought re-election in 1942. The 1942 campaign was both hard fought and personal, and the spiteful spirit of the campaign spilled over into the 1943 legislature, where Governor Hunt was confronted by hostile majorities in both houses, 39–17 and 17–10. At session's end, Hunt wrote: "The Legislature that just adjourned was the most political minded Legislature [with] which I have ever had any contact." He added later: "I am thoroughly convinced that had I not had the support of a loyal Senate minority . . . practically every prerogative the Governor has would have been taken from me." The ten Democrats in the Senate were just enough to keep the 17 Republicans from overriding the Governor's vetoes.

Important legislation included adoption of a retirement system for teachers and authorization of a bipartisan interim committee to study state fiscal practices.

Hunt had to bargain for approval of his appointments, and he later recalled: "Of thirty-two recommendations I made in my message . . . only two were adopted, and anything they knew I was interested in never saw the light of day."

In keeping with his campaign pledge to eliminate all nonessential spending, Hunt cut more than half a million dollars from the general-appropriations bill. He was genuinely zealous for economy and at the same time in doubt about the next biennium's revenue.

Partisanship boiled over in October, 1944, when Governor Hunt appointed William "Scotty" Jack secretary of state after Mart T. Christensen died on October 12, and named Carl Robinson auditor to fill the position vacated by Jack. Thus Hunt gained three-to-two control of state boards and reversed the ratio established at the 1942 election. The Republican state committee demanded a special election for the position of secretary of state. The Wyoming Supreme Court, however, upheld the Governor's contention that it was his right to fill the vacancy by appointment, since it had occurred less than a month before the next general election.

In November, 1944, the Republicans won control of the House of Representatives, 36 to 20, and of the Senate, 21 to 6, which permitted them to punish the Governor for an accumulation of grievances. As in 1943, they paid little attention to his recommendations. Then, by refusing to confirm ten of the Governor's key appointments, the Senate extended the terms of incumbents.

When it was not chastising the Governor, the 1945 legislature gave thought to the servicemen who would soon be coming home and passed ten acts for their benefit. Most important was one giving all honorably discharged veterans who had entered service from Wyoming and returned to the state exemption from property taxation to the amount of two thousand dollars in assessed valuation. The act represented an extension of an act adopted in 1921 for the benefit of World War I veterans.

As before, Governor Hunt was very cautious in fiscal affairs. He repeated his 1943 warning about the difficulty in estimating future revenue. Yet despite energetic efforts to hold the line, general-fund appropriations, as approved, climbed to $8,547,282.61, which was more than $1,000,000 above the 1943 figure.

THE CONGRESSIONAL DELEGATION

Wyoming's three-man congressional delegation during World War II included Senator Joseph C. O'Mahoney, who served from beginning to end; Senator H. H. Schwartz and Representative John J. McIntyre, who served until 1943; and Senator E. V. Robertson and Representative Frank A. Barrett, who served from 1943 until after the war.

O'Mahoney, who had been in the Senate since January 1, 1934, held a prominent place in the national government by virtue of his leadership qualities and seniority in the majority party. Outside Wyoming he was recognized as one of the best men in the Senate. *Time* magazine so identified him, and Robert S. Allen and William V. Shannon, in their volume *The Truman Merry-Go-Round*, sized him up as follows:

O'Mahoney is an excellent senator, except for an occasional bit of special pleading on behalf of Wyoming cattlemen or the cement and steel industries' price-fixing basing-point bill. . . . [It] will be a sad day for the country, for Wyoming, and for the Senate when the trim, dapper, perky figure of Joe O'Mahoney disappears through the swinging doors of the upper chamber for the last time.

Senator O'Mahoney's wartime record included vigorous support of large appropriations for Fort Warren. He introduced the Synthetic Fuels Act of 1944, calling for studies to broaden the utilization of Wyoming's vast coal deposits. He was responsible for the establishment of the alumina plant at Laramie. He presented to Congress in 1944 the over-all plan for the development of the Missouri River Basin. He labored indefatigably in behalf of Wyoming's small business, agriculture, livestock, and mineral industries.

The other wartime senators, Harry H. Schwartz and E. V. Robertson, were one-termers who worked conscientiously without gaining special distinction. Schwartz supported the administration too consistently to please many of his conservative constituents. Apparently expecting that his experience and support of the administration were sufficient credentials, Schwartz campaigned for only two weeks in 1942. He discovered that the ultraconservative Robertson was more to the taste of Wyoming voters at the time. Robertson had gained stature by scorning a government subsidy check tendered him for his ranching operations. After election, he achieved a reputation for isolationism. At the national Republican convention in June, 1944, he offered a foreign-affairs plank which included the statements: "We oppose an international police force. We oppose an international New Deal with the U.S. playing the role of Santa Claus." The convention adopted a more internationalistic plank offered by Michigan's Senator Arthur H. Vandenburg.

Congressman John J. McIntyre, like Senator Schwartz, found the antiadministration tide running too strong in 1942. Frank A. Barrett, who in his first attempt for a House seat in 1936 had been snowed under by Paul Greever, found the political climate more favorable in 1942 as he defeated McIntyre by one thousand votes. Barrett soon acquired a reputation for folksiness, alertness to the needs of his constituents, and attention to details.

STATES' RIGHTS

Resentments, going back to territorial days, against federal-government interference reached flood tide in wartime. The expansion of federal power in the 1930's had been accepted as a necessary evil in view of the Great Depression, but with the advent of wartime prosperity the state's leaders in industry, business, agriculture, and politics craved less government. At the state inaugural ceremony in January, 1943, both the outgoing Republican Governor Smith and the incoming Governor Hunt warned of the dangers of federal bureaucracy. Not to be outdone, Senator O'Mahoney often decried the multiplication of executive orders which transferred authority from elected representatives to anonymous experts. He told the National Association of Manufacturers in December, 1943, that the "greatest evil of our time is centralization of power." Although the state's political leaders attacked centralization, they sometimes conceded that the trend was inevitable in wartime and retreated to the position that it must be reversed when peace returned.

There was much criticism of bureaucratic bungling, red tape, and silly government orders. Such criticism was not limited to Wyoming, for people everywhere were irritated by new burdens, often unhappy with the course of events, and regularly in need of a scapegoat. The Democratic *Wyoming Eagle* noted that the "favorite indoor sport" was saying nasty things about bureaucrats. Businessmen found question-naires especially hateful, while cattlemen found price controls and rationing of meat equally distasteful. Speaking for the cattlemen, Senator O'Mahoney argued that ceilings on livestock were "inconsistent with the Administration's program for maximum food production."

Scattered shots along the states' rights front multiplied and merged into a steady drumfire when, by executive order, President Roosevelt established Jackson Hole National Monument on March 16, 1943. Never before had federal-government actions stirred up such a storm of disapproval in the state.

The President's executive order was a milestone in a long dispute. It set aside 221,610 acres of land adjoining Grand Teton National Park on the east. It included 49,117 acres of private land, of which 32,117 acres had been purchased over a period of years by John D. Rockefeller, Jr., with the intention of conveying it to the government. The extension of federal control in Jackson Hole had been tried on previous occasions. Wyoming Senator Robert D. Carey in 1934, for instance, had introduced a bill to extend the boundaries of Grand Teton National Park by including the Rockefeller lands. His bill did not pass, and realization that states' rights champions in Congress would not permit passage of park-extension legislation prompted Roosevelt to take the executive-order short cut.

Arrayed in opposition to the executive order stood Governor Hunt, Senator O'Mahoney, Senator Robertson, Congressman Barrett, Milward L. Simpson, J. Elmer Brock, Charles A. Myers, Clifford Hansen, Felix Buchenroth, the Wyoming Stock Growers Association, the Dude Ranchers Association, the Wyoming Taxpayers Association, and practically all of the state's newspapers except the *Labor Journal*. Residents of Teton County cried that the monument would take one-third of the county's taxable property off the tax rolls and would threaten grazing rights, hunting and fishing privileges, and control of the famous elk herd. Jackson banker Felix Buchenroth warned that this was merely the opening wedge of a movement designed to add much of northwestern Wyoming to Yellowstone Park.

Congressman Frank Barrett introduced a bill to abolish the monument. He and Senator Robertson later introduced bills to make it impossible for the President to create a national monument without the approval of the legislature in the state affected. Governor Hunt enlisted the aid of the governors of California, Nevada, Arizona, Colorado, and Utah, who joined him in signing a resolution condemning the monument. Hunt told the governors that he would use his police power to remove any federal official who assumed authority in the monument area.

In May, 1943, President Roosevelt explained that concern for national benefits had prompted him to establish the monument, that all private interests would be protected, and that the monument would attract money to Teton County when tourist travel resumed. The following month, Charles A. Myers, Wyoming Stock Growers Association president, told the annual convention of the association: "The cloven hoof of our most ruthless bureaucrat [Ickes] was never more plainly in evidence than in the proclamation. . . . This is the 'Boston Tea Party,' and we will never rest until we are in fact, as well as in name, Sovereign States. Not only will we retake the Monument, but the Taylor Grazing Lands with the mineral rights that should pass to our state with them." By unanimous vote the convention pledged to support Governor Hunt "in his efforts to retain State Sovereignty."

Secretary of the Interior Harold Ickes, testifying before a hearing of the House Committee on Public Lands, attributed the antimonument campaign to a few "self-seeking individuals." Horace M. Albright, former Director of National Parks, likewise told the committee that opposition consisted of a "small group of Wyoming people fighting for their special stake." He asserted that all but a few citizens of Wyoming always had been in favor of public use of the land in question. Milward Simpson, attorney for the Citizens Committee of Jackson Hole, countered with a challenge that a plebiscite be taken to determine the attitude of Wyoming people.

For a time it appeared that no resident of the state would openly support the monument. Then former Governor Leslie A. Miller stepped forward for the defense, and he was given halfhearted support by the *Labor Journal* and the Izaak Walton League. The *Casper Tribune-Herald*, while holding that the monument creation was wrong because it was accomplished "by subterfuge" and by "an abuse of executive authority," conceded that there was a good reason for park extension or monument creation in the need to protect the area in front of the incomparable Teton Mountains: "Purchases of land by the Rockefeller interests afforded this protection at a time when it appeared that the highway bordering the park and commanding a magnificent view of the Tetons would be converted into a long lane of unsightly structures that would mar the primitive beauty of the area."

Leslie A. Miller published a four-column statement on the "Other Side" of the controversy in the *Casper Tribune-Herald* in July, 1943. He traced the history of Jackson Hole, voiced gratitude to Rockefeller, and predicted that if opposition to the monument were successful, the day would come "when Wyoming will hang her head in shame." The executive director of the national Izaak Walton League joined Miller, declaring that

the many dramatic stories about dispossessing the ranchers, ruining the cattle business, and taking upwards of 200,000 acres off the tax rolls, amount to nothing but hysterical or malicious bunk. The League . . . believes the area embraced within the monument has outstanding scenic, biologic and recreational values and that the consummation of the Jackson Hole plan, to make a national recreational area for the enjoyment of all the people of the U.S., represents the highest and best use of the area; and furthermore, that some unified federal management is essential to prevent private exploitation from ruining its public values.[3]

After further fireworks, both houses of Congress passed in December, 1944, the Barrett bill to abolish the monument. The bill, however, was pocket-vetoed by President Roosevelt. For several years thereafter, amendments to Interior Department appropriation bills prevented the expenditure of funds on administration of the monument. Finally, in 1950, a compromise bill sponsored by Senators Joseph C. O'Mahoney and Lester C. Hunt was passed by Congress and approved by President Truman. The measure abolished the monument but added most of the disputed area to Grand Teton National Park. It provided for reimbursement of Teton County for the loss of tax revenues on a declining scale, rights of way for livestock, preservation of existing leases and permits, and cooperation between state and nation in the management of the elk herd. After summarizing the Jackson Hole monument controversy, John Gunther, in *Inside U.S.A.*, concluded:

This story has a moral. . . . It is that even the best-principled and most austere of public servants are at the mercy of their constituents on a *local* issue if it burns deep enough. No Wyoming official could dare whisper a word for Jackson Hole, no matter what he might think privately, because it would mean political suicide. Yet it is not the people of Wyoming as a whole who are against the monument, but only a splinter fraction.[4]

[3] *Casper Tribune-Herald*, July 31, 1943.
[4] John Gunther, *Inside U.S.A.* (New York: Harper, 1947), pp. 233–234.

EDUCATION

Wyoming's educational system endured assorted pressures. The state war board of the United States Department of Agriculture recommended in February, 1942, that the entire state go on a six-day school week so that youth could be released a month earlier than usual in the spring for work. Special arrangements were made to release high-school youth as needed, but not all schools adopted the six-day week.

Superintendent of Public Instruction Esther Anderson urged retention of the fundamentals, "even if the frills had to be discarded for the time being." Many curriculum adjustments were made. Thirty-two high schools adopted courses in preflight aeronautics, and nearly all high schools expanded their physical-education, science, mathematics, and vocational-education programs. More high schools than ever before offered world history, American history, international relations, government, and world geography.

Public-school enrollment declined in Wyoming, as in the nation. High-school youth took jobs, while the number of elementary pupils was down because fewer babies had been born during the Great Depression. The state's total public-school enrollment declined from 56,220 in 1939–1940 to 49,248 in 1943–1944. Maintaining a staff of competent teachers was very difficult, particularly since school boards seemed unable to raise salaries enough to meet competition. Biennial reports of the state superintendent indicate that from 1941 to 1945, the pay of Wyoming public-school teachers increased between 20 and 30 per cent, while the state's per capita income increased 78 per cent. Married women, whose services had been shunned in the 1930's, took over between one-third and one-half of the teaching jobs in the state.

The 1943 legislature authorized the state board of education to accept federal aid to education provided that no matching or other contribution of funds by the state were required. This act would cause much partisan strife later.

The University of Wyoming, the state's only institution of higher education, faced major uncertainties because most of its students were young men subject to the draft. Attempts were made to procure special training programs. Most important of several assigned were the Army Specialized Training and Reclassification School and the Army Specialized Training Program. The S.T.A.R. School, which was preliminary to the A.S.T. Program, brought 5,000 army men in uniform, six or seven hundred at a time, for brief periods in which they were given tests, refresher work, and reassignments. The A.S.T. Program, known as the A.S.T.P., trained mainly engineers. The fall of 1943 marked the high tide of the university's A.S.T. Program, when there were 525 men in the basic engineering course, 290 in advanced engineering, and 125 in the foreign area-language group. The A.S.T. Program terminated in the spring of 1944. Since the ground forces were critically short of enlisted men, many disgusted A.S.T.P. men were sent into the infantry as privates, without reference to the specialized training they had received. Much of the gap left by the departure of the A.S.T.P. men remained unfilled until after the war.

Against the wishes of the university board of trustees and President J. L. Morrill, a junior-college system was approved in 1945. The issue was hard fought in the legislature, where finally a bill was passed, in the form of an enabling act, authorizing any school district with an accredited four-year high-school program to vote a special levy up to two mills for junior-college work. Casper promptly launched its college, to be followed in later years by Sheridan, Powell, Torrington, Rock Springs, Riverton, and Cheyenne, in that order.

In the last two years of the war, education leaders planned for the anticipated flood of returning veterans, many of whom would want to go to college. When President Morrill moved on to the University of Minnesota, the responsibility for supervising the postwar building program and the education of returning GI's devolved upon George Duke Humphrey, who took office as the university's new president in August, 1945.

POSTWAR PLANNING

War had scarcely begun before idealists began thinking about the problems of peacemaking. Typically, the Reverend E. K. Feaver talked in Laramie in December, 1941, on the subject "Will We Be Wise Enough to Win the Peace?" Most Wyoming planners were mainly concerned about the prospects for postwar jobs. The first editorial in the *Rawlins Republican Bulletin* after Pearl Harbor asked: "How are we going to find jobs when this emergency is over?" Many people remembered the distressed deflationary period that followed World War I, and everyone knew that prosperity had been very elusive in Wyoming for twenty years.

Governor Hunt could not make up his mind whether the war would be followed by boom or bust. Once he asserted that the nation's stored-up demand "will create jobs in our factories and on the farms as never before." At other times he remembered the woes of the early 1920's.

He told the 1943 legislature, for instance, that "when the boys come home from the war and the great defense industries begin to close, the country will be face to face with a condition as serious as was the depression and almost as serious as the war itself." Senator O'Mahoney was named chairman of a Senate subcommittee to study postwar economic policy. "America," he said, "is determined that our returning soldiers must not face the 'apple economy' that greeted them after the last war."

Representatives of western states, meeting in Salt Lake City in April, 1943, voted to create a postwar planning council to stimulate future industrial expansion and protect water rights. Governor Hunt named William "Scotty" Jack to represent Wyoming at a Denver meeting in September, 1943, at which a thirteen-point program was approved, including one point which called for "the immediate preparation of plans and specifications of an adequate and needed public works program by each of the states to absorb the slack between industry's effort and the needs of retraining service men and war workers."

On December 27, 1943, Governor Hunt named thirty-two persons to the Wyoming Postwar Planning Committee. He told the committee's first session, held in Cheyenne in February, 1944, that there were 160 national organizations working on postwar plans. He added: "I was taken to task a few evenings ago by Mrs. Hunt when we returned from a social gathering, for of the some forty people assembled, I seemed to be the only one who did not have a postwar plan." The group elected an executive committee, with Earle Burwell of Casper as chairman, Dr. H. G. Fisk of Laramie as vice-chairman, and G. O. Houser of Cheyenne as secretary-treasurer.

Throughout its life, the committee emphasized local planning. Sheridan and Casper had developed postwar plans before the state committee met, and other communities began planning when prodded. Secretary Houser reported in September, 1944, that "most every town in the state has given thought to postwar planning and many have plans well along." The committee published an eight-page brochure to encourage community planning; on the cover appeared the statement: "When Johnny Comes Marching Home and Hangs His Gun On The Wall . . . Are We Going To Have a Job for Him Under Our System of Free Enterprise? It is Your Problem!" The brochure announced that the state's returning servicemen would require twenty-four thousand jobs. In search of these, the committee explored various areas of the economy, always returning, however, to four major hopes:

private enterprise, highway construction, reclamation, and public buildings.

Both Governor Hunt and Secretary Houser declared that the greatest expansion of Wyoming's economy would come through reclamation. Hunt told the state planning committee in February, 1944, that the United States Reclamation Service had told him that when full development of reclamation had taken place in the state, an additional 1,600,000 acres of land would have been brought into production, 10,500 new farms and homes would have been created, and the state's population would have been increased 157,000. The future of the state, said the Governor, depended on the expansion of agriculture. Upon request of the Governor, the state's institutions submitted proposals for capital outlays totaling about $5,000,000; of this amount, the university asked for more than $3,700,000.

Governor Hunt suddenly deactivated the Wyoming Postwar Planning Committee in January, 1945, explaining that the army and navy felt that postwar planning led to complacency, which interfered with the war effort. Federal agencies, however, stepped up their planning as more veterans returned home. The Selective Service System, the United States Employment Service, and the Veterans Administration facilitated smooth readjustment to civilian life.

Wyoming, with its insignificant war industry, suffered little reconversion unemployment. Some older workers, women, and youth withdrew from the labor market. Staggered discharges facilitated assimilation of GI's. In October, 1947, Governor Hunt reported that "Wyoming has been particularly fortunate in finding jobs for the returning veterans. The employment rate is high. Employers have been especially cooperative in returning veterans to their old jobs." Thus it became evident that there had been much unnecessary worry about postwar jobs and that the nightmarish aftermath of the First World War would not be repeated.

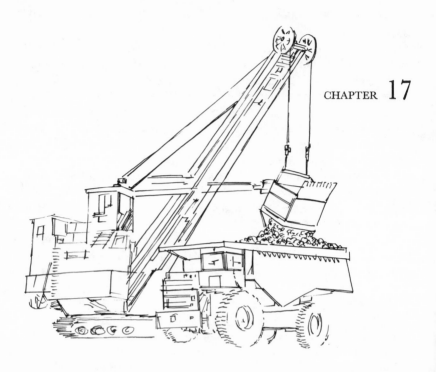

CHAPTER 17

The Postwar Economy

FOR MORE THAN THIRTY YEARS after World War II most Americans enjoyed prosperity such as they had never known before. Wyoming people shared in the rising productivity and the abundance of consumer goods.

Although this was the general picture, there were ups and downs, and not nearly enough growth to satisfy many chambers of commerce. Half a dozen national recessions slowed economic growth at intervals, and Wyoming in the 1960's had its own special slump which bottomed out in the winter of 1966–1967.

Accustomed to more bad years than good and remembering the deep recession that had followed World War I, many citizens expected

506

stormy economic weather after 1945. Instead, accumulated savings, pent-up demand for consumer goods, and vast federal expenditures associated with the Marshall Plan and the cold war military buildup fueled inflation and contributed to full employment.

The Korean War (1950–1953) and our progressive involvement in the Vietnam conflict during the next twenty years brought further increases in the Gross National Product, and prosperity for those who could keep ahead of inflation. The Korean War called many World War II veterans back into service, along with quite a few raw recruits, and snuffed out 70 Wyoming lives. Yet for the many citizens who were not directly involved, the sacrifices were small in comparison with those which had been demanded by World War II. The Vietnam War, from which the United States finally extricated itself in 1975 after a ceasefire in 1973, taxed Wyoming more severely, taking 129 lives and causing much social and economic stress. Nonetheless, most people enjoyed a rising standard of living in the 1960's and 1970's, although many of them did so only because housewives took jobs to supplement the family income.

It is noteworthy in Wyoming's economy, 1945–1973, that (1) the state continued to be what it had always been, primarily a producer of raw materials to be exported for processing and consumption elsewhere; (2) the state's population increased more slowly than that of the nation; and (3) regular infusions of federal money were essential to keep the economy viable.

From 1910 to 1950 the state had kept approximately abreast of the nation's growth in population. In the 1950's, however, Wyoming's increase was only 13.6 per cent, compared to 18.5 per cent for the United States. Wyoming's population increased from 290,529 in 1950 to 330,066 in 1960 because of the excess of 83,999 births over 24,752 deaths. There was a net outmigration of 19,710 during the decade. Editor Lewis Bates of the *Wyoming State Tribune* (Cheyenne) in 1960 looked on the bright side: "Wyoming . . . is wonderful! Its industrial and business development over the last few years . . . has been nothing short of sensational. It has been highly diversified resource tapping. . . . The advance is terrific and constant."

Thereafter stagnation really set in, bringing an actual loss of population, 1960–1966, before a moderate rebound in the next four years made possible a gain of 2,350 (less than one per cent) for the decade, and a 1970 population of 332,416. If we define stagnation as failure to progress or develop, the term applies here, except for the minerals area.

Many of the oil and gas producers and exporters were profiting hand-somely, and they were doing it with less manpower than before. Their pipelines, once installed, required few maintenance men. And a sub-stantial part of their income flowed to nonresident owners.

In the years 1960–1966 the net outmigration must have exceeded 50,000, although most of the emigrants were balanced by the excess of births over deaths. The situation would have been worse had there not been great federal government expenditures at and around Warren Air Force Base, Cheyenne, in the years 1959–1965, when the base became a major intercontinental missile center. First twenty-four Atlas and then two hundred Minuteman installations were distributed over a large area in southeastern Wyoming, western Nebraska, and north-eastern Colorado. The dismantling of obsolete Atlas missiles began in 1964.

Many Wyoming citizens were disturbed in the years 1945–1970 by the state's slow growth and the persistent outmigration of young people. Concerned citizens visualized strengthening the economy by adding manufacturing payrolls. As always, the state's economy was handi-capped by lack of diversification. Employment in manufacturing, which had always been small, declined to 6,500 in 1964, the lowest among the fifty states. Most of the 6,500 were employed in petroleum refining (1,800), food and kindred products (1,200), and lumber (700).

While the search for the elusive manufacturing plants had been con-ducted intermittently since earliest times, the postwar years brought renewed activity. To be sure, many residents preferred to have Wyoming remain an uncluttered, uncrowded commonwealth without factories, but usually they were outnumbered by boosters.

The legislature created the Natural Resources Research Institute at the University of Wyoming in 1943, the Natural Resource Board in 1951, the Division of Business and Economic Research in the College of Commerce and Industry at the university in 1955, and the Department of Planning and Economic Development in 1969 (replacing the Natural Resource Board). The Pacific Power and Light Company in 1961 published a brochure in which a California economics consultant tried to attract industrialists with this glowing account of opportunities:

Wyoming has virtually every requisite—except population—to become one of the greatest industrial states in the union. . . . It is endowed with an abundance of diversified natural resources, possesses one of the greatest reserves of energy in the United States, has an intelligent citizenry, benefits from a conservative state government, enjoys healthy climate and is rich in scenic beauty. . . . Wyoming is the ideal state in which new industry may profitably be located. . . .

Labor-management conditions are ideal. . . . The University of Wyoming ranks among the top 10% of American universities. . . . Wyoming governors and state officials have followed a policy of maintaining "good business climate." The state legislature has always been conservative. . . . No income taxes or burdensome corporate taxes are levied. . . . Wyoming tax laws are among the most favorable to business and industry in the nation. . . . Wyoming is the last "frontier state" in the nation.

The author of this tract optimistically estimated that Wyoming would have a population of 450,000 by 1970.

Some of the problems confronting promoters were analyzed in O. D. Turner's *Resources of Wyoming and Their Relations to Industrial Development* (University of Wyoming, 1959). Turner asked manufacturers already present in the state to list factors which they thought would limit future growth and expansion of industry. They listed in order of importance: lack of markets, lack of skilled labor, increased competition, high labor costs, lack of financial assistance, lack of raw materials, miscellaneous, lack of adequate water supply, unfavorable climate, unfavorable tax structure, and high cost of fuel and power. Earlier in the century such negative information would have been suppressed. Turner suggested that "climate will probably become an even more important industrial location factor in the future" because "managements are tending more and more to choose locations in climates which appeal to workers and executives."

The Natural Resource Board in September, 1963, reported that twenty-five Chicago-area firms had been asked if they had ever considered Wyoming as a site for a branch plant, and all had replied that the state's weather was too severe. No doubt, the state's reputation for long, cold winters deterred economic growth, notwithstanding the readiness of many natives to boast about their fine year-round climate.

In his 1962 campaign for the governorship, Clifford Hansen emphasized the need for a more diversified and more stable economy. Later, as governor, he spoke often on the same subject, usually adding a warning against accepting government help which might lead to loss of individual freedom.

The adoption of a right-to-work law by the 1963 legislature failed to bring the new factories promised by proponents. Instead it may have caused some union labor to leave the state. One argument for such a law had been that new factories would be attracted to states where union wages did not have to be paid. It seems to have worked out that way in some southern states but not in Wyoming.

The Natural Resource Board, headed by Glen Sorenson, president of the Kemmerer Coal Company, promoted industrialization with more enthusiasm in the 1960's than had been evident in the 1950's when cattleman J. Elmer Brock and woolgrower J. Byron Wilson headed the board.

Governor Stan Hathaway (1967–1975) vigorously promoted growth in the late 1960's, yet was generally unable to overcome the well-known obstacles. The feeble revival noticed in the economy was primarily in mining, oil and gas, tourism, and utility plant expansion at Glenrock and Kemmerer. Three small manufacturing plants were added—bicarbonate of soda in Sweetwater County and electronics plants at Riverton and Casper. Light, clean, "quality growth" plants were especially desired, but they were sought in other states as well and usually avoided Wyoming.

In 1968 Governor and Mrs. Hathaway and a score or more "Wyoming ambassadors" visited New York City, Los Angeles, and other cities on a promotion tour, entertained investment bankers at wild-game dinners, and came home without have persuaded anyone except a reporter to venture to the "Lonesome Land." The reporter wrote a story which was published on the front page of the *Wall Street Journal* under the headline "The Lonesome Land," and the subheading "Wyoming Is Emptier and Its Economy Lags as People Move Away but Many Love the Solitude and Bristle at Campaign to Attract New Industry." A rancher told the reporter that more industry would bring "a lot of undesirable people." A barber told him: "There are all the ———— ———— people here now that I care about." Such anti-growth sentiment was offset by boosters who complained about those who are suspicious of outsiders and "think small." As fate would have it, not manufacturing but the production of minerals would dominate the 1970's in Wyoming.

Measured by the yardstick of cash receipts, the minerals industry had become number one in the 1950's and steadily increased its lead. Beginning in 1960, oil and gas brought in as much money each year as agriculture-livestock and tourism taken together, while trona, uranium, iron ore, coal, and bentonite brought in additional millions.

PETROLEUM AND NATURAL GAS

In the 1970's Wyoming was more dependent on petroleum than any other state with the possible exceptions of Alaska, Louisiana, and Texas. Wyoming had become a major oil producer after World War II when exploding demand and new pipelines solved marketing problems. The fourfold increase in production between 1945 and 1960 leveled off thereafter near 140 million barrels per year. No major field had been discovered since 1918, but many new small fields and at least one medium-sized one (Hilight in Campbell County) made possible an all-time high of 156 million barrels in 1970. Production declined thereafter to 120 million barrels in 1976.

In 1976 two counties, Park and Campbell, produced 45 per cent of the state's oil output, and eight counties (Park, Campbell, Sweetwater, Converse, Hot Springs, Natrona, Big Horn, and Fremont) produced 86 per cent. In the same year Sweetwater, Fremont, and Sublette counties produced 60 per cent of the state's natural gas output, and eight counties (Sweetwater, Fremont, Sublette, Campbell, Converse, Lincoln, Carbon, and Park) produced 88 per cent. In 1977 oil and gas contributed 39.5 per cent of the property tax collected in the state, while other minerals contributed 9.5 per cent. The 1977 tax was based on the 1976 production data.[1]

The mineral severance tax revenues for fiscal year 1977 totaled $45,576,641.48. In 1977 the state also received about $59,000,000 as its half of the mineral royalties collected by the federal government on production from its mineral properties in the state.

Fourteen refineries, the largest of which were those in Sinclair, Cheyenne, Casper (three), Newcastle, and Cody, processed about one-half of the crude oil. The other half flowed in pipelines to refineries in Denver, Salt Lake City, Wood River, Illinois, and elsewhere.

For many years Wyoming had watched its proved oil reserves increase. After the mid-fifties, however, heavy withdrawals reduced the reserves from 1.6 billion barrels to about 850 million in 1977. Although the proved reserves amounted to only six or seven years' supply at the 1977 rate of production, new discoveries and secondary recovery measures were expected to postpone exhaustion. Professor Don L. Stinson, head of the Mineral Engineering Department, University of Wyoming, in 1977 estimated that Wyoming would be producing 60 million barrels of oil in the year 2020 with twice as many production workers as were required in 1977.

Reserves of natural gas were 3.7 trillion cubic feet in 1977, an eleven-

---

[1] The average assessed valuation of 1976 production was $7.51 per barrel of crude oil and 51¢ per thousand cubic feet of natural gas. The prices and valuations varied widely, depending upon whether the oil and gas came from old wells, stripper wells, or new wells. Stripper wells were wells nearing exhaustion.

year supply at the 1977 rate of withdrawal. However, extensive drilling, particularly in the Overthrust Belt in southwestern Wyoming, at depths below 10,000 feet, located substantial amounts of new gas in 1976 and 1977. A fourfold rise in the price of natural gas made the deep drilling feasible. The deepest well in the Rocky Mountain states to date was one costing ten million dollars that reached 23,081 feet in Park County in July, 1977. More than 100 drilling rigs were active in 1976 and 1977, the count rising to 129 in September, 1977, when new gas would bring more than $1.50 per 1,000 cubic feet and new oil about $15 per barrel. About two-thirds of the state's gas flowed by pipeline to other states, as did most of the gasoline refined in the state.

As natural gas reserves dwindled in the 1960's and early 1970's, the flaring of gas from oil wells provoked criticism. Before that time, oil men had often looked upon gas as a nuisance. Hundreds of billions of cubic feet had been flared in the 1920's. There was little demand for Wyoming gas at the time and what could be sold was valued at from three to seven cents per thousand cubic feet. Rather than cap the wells that flowed both oil and gas, the oil was produced for sale and the gas was wasted. Usually it was burned at the well to reduce the danger that accumulations in low places would explode.

Flaring continued into the 1970's, especially in the new Hilight Field in Campbell County. Governor Stan Hathaway, chairman of the Oil and Gas Conservation Commission, defended the decision to allow some flaring by explaining that the commission "tried to fulfill its responsibility to conservation and at the same time not let the momentum of development die." Critics thought natural gas was becoming too valuable for the Governor to be so solicitous about the "momentum of development" and the producers' desire for quick cash. Yet Wyomingites in general were still growth-hungry enough to condone flaring until producers themselves recognized that they might be losing future profits.

OTHER MINERALS

Trona, uranium, and coal aided oil and gas in establishing the over-all dominance of minerals in the state's economy, and a dozen other minerals made smaller contributions. Already in 1977 the number of workers employed in oil and gas extraction (12,100) was exceeded by the number in other phases of Wyoming mining (12,300).

Fifty million years ago beds of trona (sodium sesquicarbonate) were deposited in southwestern Wyoming when all the water evaporated from salty lakes. A U.S. Geological Survey scientist discovered the trona in oil well drill cores in 1939. Drill tests began in 1944, and mining and refining in 1952. The Westvaco Chemical Corporation, whose president was William B. Thom, a native of Buffalo, Wyoming, pioneered in this development. Westvaco later became a subsidiary of the Food Machinery Corporation. Two other giant chemical companies, Stauffer and Allied, entered the field in the early 1960's and the Texasgulf Corporation began production in 1976. Together the four companies mined about 8.8 million tons of trona in 1976 and refined it into 5.6 million tons of soda ash (sodium carbonate), an off-white, powdery substance which has many industrial uses. Bulk rail cars carried most of the soda ash to factories east of the Mississippi River. About half of the soda ash was used in the manufacture of glass, and 20 per cent in phosphates, silicates, and soaps. Some of the soda ash was turned into baking soda and packaged in Sweetwater County.

All four of the trona mine-mill complexes were located in the northwest quarter of Sweetwater County, fifteen to twenty-five miles northwest of the thriving city of Green River. More than half of the workers commuted from Green River and about 25 per cent from Rock Springs.

The mining was done with costly machines in tunnels 800 to 1,600 feet below ground level. Twenty-four beds of trona had been identified, some of them 12 feet thick. Beds not yet mined lay all the way from 400 to 3,500 feet below ground level. In 1977 more than 3,700 workers in the Wyoming trona industry received annual pay averaging $17,500.

Sweetwater County supplied most of the nation's soda ash and had 67 billion tons of reserves, the greatest in the world. There was competition from three synthetic plants in New York, Michigan, and Texas and from a plant in California which produced natural soda ash from brine. However, the Wyoming trona industry, with its vast reserves and favorable market situation, seemed to be a desirable addition to the state's economy until evidence of environmental damage appeared. A University of Wyoming scientist reported in 1977 that sodium salt, a by-product of soda ash fallout around the mills, destroyed the big sage plants and caused three of the four species of grass native to the area to die out. Also, as much of Sweetwater County's soil was being denuded for various developments, clouds of dust made life miserable for many of the residents.

While trona enjoyed fairly steady and predictable progress for a quarter of a century, uranium in contrast experienced remarkable uncertainty and drama. The Atomic Energy Commission (AEC), established by Congress in 1946, began looking for domestic sources of uranium as it stockpiled A-bombs and planned other uses for nuclear energy. After it became known that Russia was working on nuclear weapons, the AEC in 1948 guaranteed a market for all domestic ore of not less than 0.10 per cent uranium oxide (yellowcake) discovered and developed in the next ten years. Bonuses were added in some circumstances.

Small uranium deposits had been found near Lusk in 1918, and it was thought that a thorough search would turn up richer deposits. The AEC issued information circulars and distributed maps suggesting likely locations as determined by AEC reconnaissance planes. Hundreds of people bought Geiger counters and joined in the search. They found enough to justify filing many claims. Paying quantities were found in 1949 in the Black Hills of Crook County, where they were soon exploited by the Homestake Mining Company.

In 1951 Dr. J. David Love of the U.S. Geological Survey directed attention to the possibilities of the remote, sparsely settled Pumpkin Buttes country in southwestern Campbell County. Prospectors soon located small deposits there. Then in 1953 Neil McNeice and Lowell Morfeld of Riverton made the famous Lucky Mc strike in Gas Hills in eastern Fremont County. In the next few years prospectors ransacked the state and filed thousands of claims, some in every county. The most productive mines developed in the 1950's and 1960's were in eastern Fremont County (Gas Hills and Crooks Gap) and in northeastern Carbon County (Shirley Basin).

During the prospecting craze of the mid-1950's it seemed like old times as once again there was huggermugger on the range. Confusion reigned because of the complex pattern of rights to land and minerals. While early land laws gave surface and subsurface rights in one grant, the homestead acts of 1909 and 1916 gave only surface rights, retaining the mineral rights for the federal government. Later, leaseholders under the Taylor Grazing Act of 1934 received only the use of the surface. Also, state-owned lands were scattered through every county, usually with the surface rights leased and the mineral rights retained by the state. Most ranches consisted of a hodgepodge of private and public land with assorted rights.

After Dr. Love's discovery at Pumpkin Buttes, the Interior Department in March, 1952, before much exploration had occurred there, withdrew from public entry 65,343 acres of public land in that locality.

Later, after a survey, it was announced that the government's rights in the Pumpkin Buttes area would be thrown open to public entry on May 3, 1955. Since the Pumpkin Buttes were now famous, a great rush of prospectors was anticipated. This distressed the ranchers, who were not accustomed to visits from strangers except during antelope season. Ranchers held surface and mineral rights to about 30 per cent of the Pumpkin Buttes uranium country and surface rights to about 60 per cent. They wanted no hordes of prospectors. When some of the ranchers threatened to use force to prevent trespass on their ranges, Governor Milward Simpson instructed the National Guard to close the area in case of violence. Alarmed by the possibilities, the Interior Department postponed the opening date from May 3 to November 17, 1955.

The delay gave ranchers time to organize the Pumpkin Buttes Mining District, covering 46,400 acres. They announced that prospectors must have "mining entry" cards issued for a fee by mining-district representatives and must file claims through the mining district rather than the county clerk. They stipulated that each claimant must promise to pay the holder of surface rights a royalty on production.

About four hundred prospectors entered the area on opening day, outnumbering the permanent residents. There had been no comparable invasion of the area since Colonel Sawyers and his wagon-road construction party had passed the Buttes in 1865. There was no violence. Some prospectors registered claims with the mining district, others with the county clerk. Eight or ten small but profitable mines resulted, the ore being shipped first to Edgemont, South Dakota, and later to Gas Hills for milling. Ultimately the Wyoming Supreme Court ruled that the Pumpkin Buttes Mining District was illegal.

Lawyers enjoyed a field day because there were many legal tangles. Disputes arose between persons holding separate surface and subsurface rights, and between conflicting oil and mining laws. Claim jumpers were as abundant as they had been in the early years of oil exploration. Production occurred mainly on claims with clear titles. The multiple-use statute passed by Congress in August, 1954, cleared up one area of dispute by stipulating that oil exploration should be governed by the Oil and Gas Leasing Act of 1920 and uranium exploration by the General Mining Laws.

Most of the prospectors suffered disappointment. Even with a clear title to their claims, development costs were beyond their means. Thousands of claims lay undeveloped. Unless the claim was very rich, no one was eager to buy it. Gradually the better claims were consolidated until a small number of companies emerged as important producers. Among the pioneer entrepreneurs who helped round up the necessary capital were W. H. H. Cranmer of the Lucky Mc complex, Bob Adams of Western Nuclear, and Cotter Ferguson of American Nuclear.

The AEC first bought ore at temporary buying stations until areas could support private mills authorized by the AEC. Then contracts were negotiated with the mill owners at guaranteed prices. Still worried about future needs, and underestimating the quantity of ore being located, the AEC in 1956 extended the promise of guaranteed prices through 1966. In 1957, however, the commission decided that ore was being mined too fast. Alarmed at the prospect of large government stockpiles, subject to deterioration, plans were announced to cut back production and terminate authorization of new mills.

Wyoming had lagged behind other states in mill construction. Uranium miners and their friends were afraid that the state's growing reserves would be cut off from markets, as had been the case in the pioneer phase of the oil and gas industry. Given a choice between unnecessary federal spending and contraction of the economy, they chose the lesser of two evils. Governor Milward Simpson in August, 1957, declared that the state must have more mills (only one had been completed and one other was under construction). In December, 1957, U.S. Senator Frank Barrett asked for more mills, arguing that the government's promise to buy ore must be honored. While Governor Simpson led a delegation to Washington to plead for more mills, state newspapers deplored the government's unfairness. Relenting, the AEC authorized five more mills in the next few years, making a total of seven, three at Gas Hills, two in Shirley Basin, and one each at Crooks Gap and Riverton. Wyoming was able to take second place behind New Mexico in production as well as in reserves. In the 1960's more than half of the state's production was in Fremont County, and Riverton claimed to be the uranium capital.

AEC authorization for the additional five mills, and their subsequent construction, did not mean rapid expansion, because concern about overproduction lingered. President Lyndon Johnson announced a 25 per cent cutback in the production of enriched uranium in 1964, and the AEC adopted a "stretch-out" policy. Mill operators were persuaded to reduce annual production in return for guaranteed prices to 1970 instead of 1966, as promised earlier. Despite the "stretch-out," the market was such that production increased, although slowly, every year for a decade after 1966, except for a setback in 1969. Exploration continued because it was thought that the market was bound to improve in time.

The pace of exploration quickened in the 1970's as many nuclear power plants were built (none in Wyoming) and a number of giant utility corporations signed contracts for long-term deliveries of yellowcake. Several utilities joined in the search. President Jimmy Carter's opposition in 1977 to breeder-reactor technology, which would produce electricity while at the same time generating additional fuel, meant greater demand for yellowcake, and more activity in Wyoming.

Summarizing recent developments, a headline in the *Riverton Ranger's* annual mining and industrial development edition, June 16, 1977, proclaimed that the "Lid Pops Off Uranium." "The price rose," wrote Roy Peck in an editorial, "and a slumbering segment of Wyoming mining, uranium, sprang back to life." The price of yellowcake had soared from eight or ten dollars in the 1950's and 1960's to more than fifty dollars a pound in 1977.

The five operating mills could not keep up with demand. An old mill in Shirley Basin, idle since 1974, was reopened. Four new mills were under construction, one in the Red Desert in northeastern Sweetwater County and the other three in the Powder River Basin.

The major Powder River Basin ore bodies that made the new mills feasible lay in the Pumpkin Buttes area of Campbell County and in northwestern Converse County. Millions of cubic yards of overburden were removed, in some cases to depths of 500 feet. The fifty-dollar price tag on yellowcake made such depths feasible, and also warranted the mining of lower-grade ore. Whereas all the early production had been by strip mining, some of the mining in 1977 was underground at a 900-foot level or in situ by acid-leaching methods.

Before 1977 the Powder River Basin uranium in Campbell, Converse, and Natrona counties had not been comparable to that of the Gas Hills (Fremont County) and Shirley Basin (Carbon County), but in 1977 the Powder River Basin was credited with having half of the state's reserves. With extensive core drilling, additional reserves assured Wyoming of ranking either first or second among uranium-producing states for many years to come.

Coal

Rarely does an industry that has suffered a serious setback make so spectacular a comeback as coal did in Wyoming beginning in the

1960's. Coal had been of some importance every year for eighty years, from the creation of the Territory in 1868 until after World War II. In 1949 six million tons were mined, but in the 1950's the railroads retired their coal-fired steam locomotives in favor of diesel oil-burning units, and other coal users also turned to gas or oil. Major underground mines at Rock Springs and Hanna shut down as the state's output slipped below two million tons a year. Rock Springs business languished; Hanna's population dropped from 1,200 to 600.

Then, after ten years of virtual hibernation, the industry showed signs of life again. Coal-burning electric utilities at Glenrock and Kemmerer expanded, drawing on strip mines close to their plants for fuel. By 1970, unit trains were delivering low-sulphur coal from strip mines near Rock Springs, Hanna, and Sheridan to power plants in Iowa, Illinois, and Wisconsin. Before the Arab oil embargo of October, 1973, added new impetus, many one-hundred-car unit trains, each carrying 10,000 tons of coal, were making regular runs to seventeen states. Wyoming's output approach 20 million tons in 1974 and exceeded 23 million tons in 1975 and 30 million in 1976. The production of the Amax Belle Ayr strip mine near Gillette approached 15 million tons in 1977, with about three hundred men on the job. It was but a beginning. Firm, long-term orders gave reasonable assurance that the state's production would reach 100 million tons in 1980 and 200 million tons in 1985. No more than 440 million tons had been mined in a century, 1870–1970. Probably more than that would be mined in just a two-year period in the late 1980's.

Coal underlay more than 40 per cent of the state. Seven of the state's twenty-three counties were significant producers in 1977. Ranked according to output, they were Campbell, Carbon, Lincoln, Sweetwater, Converse, Sheridan, and Hot Springs, with Campbell and Converse having most of the known economic reserves. Wyoming had reserves of 900 billion tons, of which 24 billion lay in strippable beds 10 to 200 feet thick without much overburden. Only Montana and North Dakota had greater reserves.

Three per cent of the Wyoming coal is bituminous, 96 per cent subbituminous, and 1 per cent lignite. Although Wyoming coal is generally below eastern coal in heat content and leaves more ash, it contains less sulphur and is able to meet federal sulphur-emission standards in electric power generation.

Certainly much Wyoming coal would be used in the 1980's for fueling electric utility plants. Already in 1977 there was a 1,500-

megawatt plant in Sweetwater County, another 1,500-megawatt plant at Glenrock, a 750-megawatt plant in Lincoln County, and a 330-megawatt experimental air-cooled plant at Gillette. The Sweetwater County plant (Jim Bridger) was scheduled to have a 500-megawatt addition completed in 1979. A new 1,500-megawatt plant, begun in 1976 in Platte County, was scheduled for completion in 1983. Two other large plants were being considered for construction in Carbon and Sheridan counties.

Probably some coal would be used in gasification or liquefaction plants. Two small experimental plants in Carbon and Campbell counties were testing the possibilities of coal gasification in 1977. The one at Hanna produced 170 BTU gas, which is about one-sixth of the heating value of natural gas. The Energy Research and Development Administration (ERDA) turned down the application of WYOCO ALGAS for a proposed coal gasification plant in Johnson County, which would have used Texaco's coal and water. Other proposals from Illinois and Indiana were given government contracts by ERDA, apparently because they asked less subsidy from the government.

Natural gas had generally taken the place of coal for heating homes and public buildings in the 1930's. In the 1970's Wyoming citizens expected to have to convert back to coal, beginning in the 1980's, if not before.

Almost everyone expected that most of the Wyoming coal to be mined in the 1980's would be transported, as in the 1970's, by rail to utility plants in the Midwest. To expedite export by rail, construction began in 1977 on a 126-mile rail line from Gillette to Douglas, where it would connect with existing lines. There was, however, a well-financed plan to lay a 1,000-mile coal slurry pipeline from Campbell County to Arkansas, capable of carrying 25 million tons of coal a year. The slurry would be a mixture of half pulverized coal and half water. The idea was not new, having worked already in Ohio and Arizona. Energy Transportation Systems, Inc. (ETSI) won approval from the 1974 legislature and the state engineer to sink wells 3,000 feet deep and pump water for the slurry from the Madison limestone formation. The legislature had been led to believe that the Madison formation water would be brackish. After adjournment, test wells established that the water would be potable, which caused many people to protest. It was argued that water was too precious in Wyoming to lose 15,000 or 20,000 acre feet every year. It would be too expensive to pump the water back uphill to Wyoming. Railway unions and management opposed the pipeline on the basis of competition. The Nebraska and Kansas legislatures refused to grant the right of eminent domain necessary before the pipeline could cross railway rights of way in the two states.

A coal pipeline bill was then introduced by Bob Eckhardt, Texas Democrat, in the U.S. House of Representatives. The bill would empower the Secretary of the Interior to grant certificates of public convenience and necessity to coal slurry pipeline companies to exercise the power of eminent domain. Teno Roncalio (D., Wyoming) chaired a subcommittee hearing in Cheyenne on the bill, in June, 1977. Governor Ed Herschler led the opposition, arguing that 15,000 acre feet of water was too much to lose for a state already having difficulty in supplying its industrial and agricultural needs. State Senator Bob Johnson (D., Sweetwater County) objected to congressional action in the matter as an invasion of states' rights. State Senator Eddie Moore (R.) of Converse County favored the pipeline because it would give the railroads competition.

Former governor Stan Hathaway, who was unable to attend the hearing, submitted a statement enthusiastically supporting the bill. He had recommended legislative approval of the ETSI plan in 1974. He argued that the pipeline would do less harm to the environment than railway transport; would cause less inconvenience than trains; that the railroads would have more hauling to do than they could do efficiently; that 15,000 acre feet had been reliably estimated to be only 10 per cent of the annual recharge of the Madison formation; and that pumping the water from depths below 2,500 feet could cost more than two hundred dollars per acre foot, which would be prohibitive for agricultural users. Other coal slurry lines had been suggested, including one from northeastern Wyoming to the Pacific Northwest. The whole slurry business appeared to hinge on whether Congress would adopt the coal pipeline bill. If ETSI won its battle, much of the credit would have to go to Frank Odasz, tireless promoter, who spoke everywhere on the subject, and to Stan Hathaway, an influential convert to the cause. Congress was expected to act on the slurry bill in 1978.

Wyoming's stereotype as lonesome cow country began to disintegrate as knowledge about the state's uranium and coal spread and developers and workers poured into the state. With lots of oil, gas, uranium, and coal to occupy the newcomers, it was perhaps fortunate that another energy source fizzled. Wyoming's oil shale had been heralded since the first years of Wyoming Territory as the foundation for a great future oil-producing industry. Southwestern Wyoming and the adjacent corners of Utah and Colorado had great reserves. During World War II a U.S. Bureau of Mines oil-shale experiment station was established in Laramie. For thirty years its engineers and chemists studied oil shale and expressed confidence that oil from shale would fill the void when the oil wells ran dry. However, when the federal government invited corporations to offer bids for rights to develop shale in government tracts in the three oil-shale states, bids were offered for only the Utah and Colorado tracts, and the successful bidders soon appeared to be sorry that their multi-million-dollar bids had been accepted. No doubt the oil is there in vast quantity; no doubt it can be extracted. The tristate shale province had thirteen times as much oil in its shale as the world had in proved reserves in its oil fields. But serious technological and environmental problems must first be solved before there can be large-scale production of oil from shale. To help in the problem solving, the federal Energy Research and Development Administration (ERDA), which had been established in January, 1975, gave the old petroleum and oil-shale experiment station at Laramie a new name, LERC, for Laramie Energy Research Center, and gave it responsibility for the government's in situ mineral-processing effort in the areas of coal, tar sands, and oil shale.

Other minerals besides the energy-producing ones played supporting roles in the state's rapidly expanding economy. Trona, which has already been discussed above, had the major supporting role in the 1970's. Next in importance was iron ore. The Sunrise mine in Platte County continued to supply ore for the Colorado Fuel and Iron Company's steel mill in Pueblo, Colorado, as it had done since the turn of the century. Two or three hundred miners produced about half a million tons of hematite ore each year. An upgrading plant began pelletizing the mine's large reserves of low-grade ores in the late 1960's. Meanwhile the U.S. Steel Corporation in 1961–1962 had built a sixty-million-dollar mine and mill complex in historic South Pass to develop a taconite (low-grade iron ore) deposit. Production soon amounted to four million tons a year. An upgrading plant converted the ore into pellets, which were shipped to the corporation's steel mill at Provo, Utah. The company built a seventy-nine mile railroad to connect the South Pass mill with the Union Pacific Railroad near Rock Springs. Thus Wyoming ore fed Colorado and Utah steel mills employing thousands of men while Wyoming's hopes of steel mills at home were deferred until mention of the subject in the exciting 1970's brought no more than a shrug of the shoulders from the average booster and a shake of the head and a smile from the typical environmentalist.

Other minerals which were of relatively minor significance in Wyoming in the 1970's, except locally, were bentonite, sulphur, gypsum, titanium, vermiculite, copper, limestone, anorthosite clay, and jade. Experiments with anorthosite clay to produce aluminum had been carried out at Laramie in World War II, leading to occasional rumors in later years that the anorthosite near Laramie was about to be developed.

Even without shale oil, steel mills, and an aluminum plant, Wyoming's minerals industry was robust enough in the late 1970's to make some of the natives yearn for the uncrowded days of the 1960's. Some of them thought relevant the story of the eight-hundred-pound gorilla. "Where does he sleep?" "Anywhere he wants!" If all the people in the state who had substantial direct or indirect interests in the minerals industry got together to further a common purpose, it would indeed be a formidable assembly. Oil, gas, coal, and uranium interests often dovetailed. Oil companies, whose oil reserves doubled or tripled in value as a result of the OPEC cartel, used some of their windfall profits to add to their already substantial investments in uranium and coal. Among the major oil company investors in Wyoming coal were Exxon, Kerr McGee, Sun, Texaco, Shell, Continental, Standard of California, Mobil, and Atlantic Richfield. Very active in the uranium sphere were Getty, Kerr McGee, Exxon, Mobil, and Union. Electric utilities, particularly Pacific Power and Light, owned much of the coal. The Burlington Northern and Union Pacific railroads, thanks to land grants of the nineteenth century, were among the ten greatest coal owners in the United States. U.P.'s coal was mainly in Wyoming, BN's in Montana and North Dakota (originally granted to one of BN's ancestors, the Northern Pacific). Coal-owning railroads were two-way beneficiaries, reaping income from both hauling and sales.

Minerals service and supply companies multiplied; many of them joined the Wyoming Mining Association, which in June, 1977, listed 63 mining companies as members and 150 service and supply company members. The association was reported to have 600 individual memberships as well. Casper's leadership position in the state's minerals industry is indicated by the addresses listed by the Mining Association's service and supply company members: Casper, 53; Denver and its suburbs, 25; Billings, 12; Riverton, 7; Cheyenne, 6; Rock Springs, 5; and fewer members from each of many cities all over the United States.

Casper's central location, its proximity to most of the mineral deposits, and the availability of water in the North Platte River destined it to be the state's mining supply headquarters, trade and distributing center, convention center, and metropolis. It was no longer just the Oil City or the Energy Center. The Mining Association's board of directors, nonetheless, voted in 1977 to move its headquarters from Casper to Cheyenne, to be closer to state government.

A remarkable industrial development in modern Wyoming was the evolution of the Union Pacific Railroad into a holding company with extensive interests in real estate and natural resources development. The railroad's 1864 land grant furnished the land and natural resources: oil, natural gas, coal, trona, uranium. Much of the development was handled through joint ventures; for example, with Standard of Indiana in oil and gas, Stauffer Chemical in trona, Mono Power Company in uranium, and Arch Minerals in coal. An integrated oil company, Champlin, was purchased for $240 million. Union Pacific earnings doubled between 1971 and 1976, with much greater expansion in the energy area lying ahead.

AGRICULTURE AND LIVESTOCK

Governor Lester C. Hunt said in 1945, without contradiction, that "the greatest industry in the State of Wyoming is agriculture and its kindred activity, livestock." In the 1950's, however, the agriculture-livestock industry slipped back into the number two position, and in some years thereafter it lagged behind both minerals and tourism. Among ranchers and farmers, lamentation, hand wringing, and discouragement were more noticeable than optimism. One or two years of high prices and pride were commonly followed by several of marginal profits and chagrin. Participants in a lenders' seminar in Jackson in 1977 suggested the need for a debt moratorium, low-interest loans, and a floor under the price of beef to avert disaster for many operators.

Of the state's 62 million acres, the amount of land devoted to livestock (more than 35 million acres) and to crops (less than 2 million acres) changed little. The number of people living on farms and ranches fell from 72,674 in 1940 to about 35,000. Farm and ranch employment, which had exceeded 25,000 in 1940, was only 20,120 in July, 1977. The number of farm and ranch units declined from 15,018 in 1940 to 7,900 in 1977, as the average size of all units more than doubled from 1,866 acres to more than 4,500.

The 1969 U.S. Census of Agriculture reported that Wyoming had 435 ranches that averaged 26,673 acres in size. Of these, 268 averaged 40,023 acres. Three thousand smaller ranches averaged little more than 5,000 acres. Farms ranged in size from irrigated patches of 40 acres to wheat farms of several thousand acres. Wealthy individuals and corporations, more of the former than the latter, were buying up hundreds of ranches with an eye to recreation, subdivision, mining, water rights, or tax write-offs. Some of the new owners joined the Wyoming Stock Growers Association; its 2,600 members in 1976 included 140 out-of-state residents.

The state's total cash receipts from the farm and ranch sector, which had doubled from about $50 million in 1940 to $100 million in 1945, did not grow as fast thereafter, particularly when inflation is considered. In the 1950's and early 1960's the totals averaged about $147 million, ranging between $193 million in 1951 and $115 million in 1955. In the fifteen years between 1950 and 1965, roughly 60 per cent of the total came from cattle, 20 per cent from sheep, and 20 per cent from crops (the traditional three leaders, hay, sugar beets, and wheat, and others such as oats, barley, corn, beans, and potatoes). The most important crop, hay (mostly wild but also alfalfa) was consumed by livestock on the ranch and so played a minor role in direct cash transactions. Among the ranchers, 1,500 were public lands permittees who had additional problems in the form of federal regulations.

Continuing inflation pushed the total cash receipts above the $300 million level in 1972, and above $400 million thereafter. The gross farm and ranch income in 1974 came 47 per cent from cattle and calves, only 7 per cent from sheep and wool, and 46 per cent from crops, other livestock, and government payments.[2]

The press gave much attention to the problems of agriculture and left the impression that the ups were never adequate and the downs threatened disaster. Senator Cliff Hansen, Jackson Hole rancher and former president of the Stock Growers, wrote President Gerald Ford in October, 1976, that livestock producers were "in deep, deep trouble." He recommended that the President order increased purchases of beef by federal agencies and that steps be taken to reduce imports. "Eat more Lamb: 10,000 coyotes can't be wrong" and "Eat

[2] University of Wyoming Agricultural Experiment Station, *Research Journal 104* (March 1976), p. 2. The exceptionally high world price of sugar contributed to the high percentage attributed to crops because in 1974 Wyoming beets brought more than ever before or since.

More Beef" bumper stickers were popular in Wyoming at the very time when the *Wall Street Journal* reported that half the people in the country were limiting meat purchases to hamburger because they could not afford other meat products, and a special Senate committee headed by George McGovern was advising people to eat less meat for health reasons.

Senator Hansen pursued the matter of beef imports further in 1977. He reported that Wyoming's net farm income had dropped from $123.7 million in 1973 to $61.7 million in 1974 and to $14.2 million in 1975. "Losses suffered by livestock producers," he said, "have accounted for almost all of this shocking decline." On the other hand, Kim Krueger, president of the WSGA, urged the cattlemen in annual convention in June, 1977, to make no effort to change the 1964 meat import quota law because eastern congressmen might decide to increase instead of reduce imports. President Krueger had suggested in the April, 1977, issue of *Cow Country* that the livestock problem was "one which could be easily alleviated if the federal bureaucracy and the American consumer would rescind some of the pressure that they exert on the farmer and rancher, and allow him to receive a small profit for his labor and investment." In the same issue of *Cow Country* the WSGA executive manager, Dean T. Prosser, Jr., blamed the cattlemen themselves: "We absolutely must not allow ourselves to again overproduce our markets in response to high prices . . . the real culprit is the guy that looks back into the mirror while preparing for your daily shave." Prosser expanded his remarks at the annual convention in June, 1977. He cited the example of the milk producers, who were solving their oversupply problems through marketing associations. Unless agricultural people modified their rugged individualism, he said, and organized effectively, agricultural production in the U.S. would continue its slide into hands of men subsidized by income from other sources.

One self-help attempt failed in 1977 because cattlemen nationally would not give it enough support. A check-off system to fund beef promotion received only 57.6 per cent support when 66.7 per cent was required. Wyoming cattlemen voted 80 per cent for the program.

That bankruptcies were rare can be explained by the availability of outside income, such as oil and gas leases and royalties, and the rising land values, which made larger loans possible despite low cash flow. Sympathetic legislatures answered rural entreaties by granting one tax exemption after another. The Bureau of Land Management (BLM) postponed scheduled fee increases on its grazing lands, which were lower than comparable private rentals. The national director of the BLM, however, warned that stockmen must get over the idea that the leased land belonged to them. In 1977 it was apparent that many stockmen, as in the past, were unhappy with federal supervision of lands they leased from the BLM and Forest Service. Despite adversity the WSGA survived. It was announced at the June, 1977, convention that the membership was growing and the association was "as strong and as sound as it has ever been."

Cattle numbers in postwar years varied from 1.0 to 1.7 million. Herefords predominated. Perhaps 10 per cent of the cattle were black angus, and there was a growing number of crossbreds. In Wyoming, as well as in the nation as a whole, there had been high cattle prices and herd increases in the early years of each decade until the inevitable price breaks came. In Wyoming, cattle numbers peaked at 1.7 million in 1973–1974, after which they declined with falling prices (and drought in 1977).

Sheep, which had been almost as important as cattle in the years 1900–1940, slipped badly during and after World War II, in Wyoming and nationally. A stopgap federal program instituted in 1955 saved the industry temporarily by providing payments to make up the difference between the market price of wool and an established incentive price. In 1972, for example, payments in excess of $100,000 went to each of six Wyoming outfits, while about one hundred woolgrowers received government payments of between $20,000 and $100,000. The *Casper Star-Tribune* listed the names and amounts received by many rugged individualists who were not happy about being identified as recipients of government subsidies. A congressman who called these payments "nothing more than welfare for the wealthy" did not understand the difficulties confronting woolgrowers. Synthetics, imported wool, predators, labor problems, and weak consumer demand for mutton and lamb drove the number of sheep in the state down to only one million in 1977. Of some 339 Wyoming woolgrowers who quit the business in the years 1968–1974, about 72 per cent shifted to cattle; some of them regretted the change, as woolen clothing became popular once again and the market for wool improved.

Seventy-seven of the 339 dropouts from the wool industry responded to an Agricultural Extension Service questionnaire and listed predation losses as the most important factor for quitting, shortage of good hired labor as second in importance, and poor lamb prices as third. Although there should be no doubt that predators were a serious threat, many persons outside the industry were skeptical about the extent of predator losses. Critics in the early 1970's doubted that predators killed 162,000 lambs in 1971 and 150,000 in 1972, as reported.[3] An assistant secretary of the Interior Department told Senator Gale McGee, chairman of a subcommittee studying the predator-control program, that losses claimed by stockmen were consistently in error and sometimes much inflated. Some critics suggested that inflated figures made unwarranted income tax deductions possible. A study group from the University of Michigan, after spending three months in the Routt National Forest of Colorado, concluded that most of the sheep and lamb losses attributed to coyotes there had not been killed at all but had simply wandered away from their herders.

A federal ban, first on the use of poisons on federal lands, and later on the use of poisons altogether, dismayed woolgrowers, who insisted that they would be driven out of business if they could not use poisons to control coyotes. They objected strenuously to the federal government's plan to phase out federal predator controls.

Eagles were included among the predators by the woolgrowers, who claimed that they killed 5,300 Wyoming lambs in 1971 and 6,100 in 1972. Woolgrowers generally took no action against eagles because they were protected by federal law, especially the scarcer bald eagle, the national bird. In 1971, however, investigations turned up evidence indicating that hundreds of golden and bald eagles had been slain illegally by poisoning and gunfire. U.S. Attorney Richard Thomas charged before U.S. District Judge Ewing T. Kerr in Cheyenne that the wealthy seventy-nine-year-old rancher Herman Werner was a key figure in the deaths of seven hundred eagles. According to the prosecutor, Werner wanted the eagles killed, and two helicopter pilots from Buffalo and Casper flew "sportsmen" over the range while they enjoyed the rare sport of shooting contraband eagles on the wing. Eight gunners were each fined one hundred dollars and one of the pilots was fined five hundred dollars. Defendant Herman Werner, who had pleaded innocent, died in 1973 as the result of an auto accident before he could be brought to trial. Some of his close friends insisted that it would have been out of character for him to harm eagles. At the time (1973) the Wyoming Game and Fish Department estimated that there were 9,000 golden and 700 bald eagles in the state. The state joined the

---

[3] The 1972 report of 150,000 lamb losses was based on estimates submitted by about 350 ranchers and farmers who owned about 40 per cent of the state's lambs.

federal government in protecting eagles in 1973 when the legislature made it a second-degree misdemeanor to take one.

RECLAMATION AND WATER DEVELOPMENT

Irrigation promoters, who had suffered one disappointment after another in the 1920's and 1930's, met further reverses thereafter. Governor Lester C. Hunt's crystal ball had been clouded in 1944 when he told the state planning committee that after World War II full development of reclamation would create 10,500 new farms and increase the state's population by 157,000. Instead, the number of farms and ranches declined, although the U.S. Bureau of Reclamation spent $373,000,000 on multiple-purpose projects in the state in the years 1945–1976. Major projects and federal expenditures on them in these years were: Yellowtail, $92,547,589; Flaming Gorge, $71,786,008; Glendo, $46,102,676; Boysen, $33,840,143; Seedskadee, $25,060,000; Kortes, $14,745,126; Lyman, $12,066,814; Eden, $11,113,327; Owl Creek, $6,839,215; Riverton Reauthorization, $5,137,000; Hanover-Bluff, $5,130,527; Keyhole, $4,721,870; and Transmission Lines, $44,587,000. It should be noted, however, that the two most expensive projects, Yellowtail and Flaming Gorge, benefited other states more than Wyoming.

Wyoming's first federal project, the Shoshone, authorized in 1904, may not have come up to expectations but its cost-benefit ratio has been outstanding. As of June 30, 1975, it had cost $25,820,713 and was furnishing water to 93,682 acres. It also provided power from two small hydroelectric plants and offered recreation on the Buffalo Bill Reservoir. Some of the later projects, which could develop little agriculture, had to be justified by other benefits. In 1963 a Bureau of Reclamation study group reported that most of Wyoming's reclamation projects were handicapped by poor soil and high altitudes. In 1964, farmers on the ill-starred Third Division of the Riverton project were given a chance to sell their unproductive holdings to the government.

While many persons in other parts of the country criticized federal expenditures for reclamation in the West, only a few in Wyoming objected, Leslie A. Miller, former governor, being one of the exceptions. The usual assumption was that even if only a few thousand acres were reclaimed, other benefits such as employment, flood control, electric power, and, most of all, recreation, justified the projects.

Wyoming had a better claim to federal reclamation expenditures than other states in one respect. The major source of reclamation funds was federal income from the Oil and Gas Leasing Act of 1920. From 1920 through June 30, 1975, the reclamation fund received $1,355,034,329 under the 1920 act. Of this total, public lands in Wyoming yielded $544,839,166. No other state contributed nearly that much. Wyoming was the only state whose contributions in the form of royalty and lease payments exceeded Reclamation Service expenditures ($450,000,000). Thus, in one sense, Wyoming was in the unique position of having paid in full for its reclamation projects.

The 1945 settlement of the ten-year-old North Platte River suit (discussed in Chapter 14) and a series of interstate compacts dividing the waters of the Colorado, Snake, Yellowstone, Belle Fourche, and Bear rivers stabilized reclamation affairs. The Colorado River Compact of 1922 had divided the Colorado River waters between upper and lower states; subsequently in 1948 the upper states divided the waters assigned to them as follows: 51.75 per cent to Colorado, 23 per cent to Utah, 14 per cent to Wyoming, and 11.25 per cent to New Mexico. The Upper Colorado River Compact opened the way for federal funding of the Flaming Gorge, Seedskadee, and Lyman projects on the Green River. Several problems, however, held up funding of the Savery–Pot Hook project on the Little Snake River and the Polecat Bench project on the Shoshone River.

The federal government's reluctance to fund any more projects in Wyoming led to consideration of state funding. Wyoming had title to water in the Big Horn and Green rivers which it had never put to use. Downstream states had enjoyed the free use of this water. Wyoming's full use of its entitlement would entail expensive facilities for diversion and storage.

The legislature in 1975 authorized the Interdepartmental Water Conference to enter the water-development field. The heads of eleven state agencies concerned with water began advising the director of water planning with respect to policy. The legislature in 1977 levied a 1.5 per cent excise tax on coal production, the proceeds from which were to be deposited in the water-development account until the account reached a balance of one hundred million dollars. Even with such an account to draw upon, the state water developers would be unable to satisfy many applicants because little surplus water was available in such a dry state. Most of the Green River and Big Horn

River flow was preempted. All of the North Platte flow was preempted, most of it by Nebraska. All of the Snake River flow was preempted, 96 per cent by Idaho. No diversion would be permitted from the Yellowstone River in Yellowstone National Park.

The state's limited water was threatened on several fronts in 1977. The U.S. Corps of Engineers claimed jurisdiction over all streams with a normal flow of five cubic feet or more per second. Legislation was pending, however, to limit the Corps' jurisdiction to rivers that had been used or could probably be used for navigation. Indians on the Wind River Reservation were also claiming more water rights than had been conceded to them. A third threat stemmed from the national Water Resources Council's proposal for an extension of the federal government's control of western waters, against which 23 western U.S. senators protested. The senators were able to get a ninety-day extension on implementation of the policy for hearings. The Interdepartmental Water Conference offered no major development proposals in 1976 and 1977, and Frank Trelease, director of the water planning program for the state engineer's office, lamented in July, 1977, that "water rights have the state buffaloed on new projects."

During most of its history Wyoming recognized preferred water use for domestic, municipal, and transportation purposes. In 1955, however, the legislature extended preferred-use status to steam power-generating plants, and in 1957 to an iron-ore upgrading plant in South Pass. Industrial users were not empowered to condemn existing water rights, but they were authorized to buy existing irrigation rights and to claim unappropriated rights. Industry found that it was easier to buy water rights from agriculturists than to develop new sources. Some ranchers and farmers could not resist the premium prices offered for their water, with the result that crops, livestock, and wildlife were all threatened.

Sprinkler irrigation based on well water spread over Laramie, Platte, and Goshen counties, until evidence that ground-water levels were dropping alarmingly in eastern Laramie County caused the state engineer to declare a moratorium on well drilling for irrigation or industrial purposes in some areas until effects on water tables could be studied. Waiting and watching the depletion of water reserves were many municipalities, which, if growth continued, would certainly have to have more water. In short, all phases of agriculture—cattle, sheep, and crops—were in jeopardy in the late 1970's.

TOURISM AND RECREATION

Given the nature of Americans and Wyoming, it was inevitable that tourism would flourish. The state has enjoyed a steady increase in popularity as a summer playground ever since early visitors in the middle of the nineteenth century found time to leave the Oregon Trail. Away from the trail they found mountains, woods, and lakes, spectacular scenery, and good hunting and fishing. In territorial days sportsmen came seeking trophy heads. Guides and outfitters encouraged them to return again and again. Excursion trains began bringing non-hunting tourists to the north and west entrances of Yellowstone Park in the 1880's. In the park horse-drawn stage coaches were replaced by automobiles and buses in the 1920's. Some of the early campgrounds and dude ranches, with refinements added, have survived, but the primitive "cottage camps" of the 1930's, with rare exceptions, have been displaced by motels and great motor hotels.

Trailers, trailer parks, and motor homes that appeared in the 1930's have become more elaborate. The number of four-wheel-drive recreational vehicles, trail bikes, snowmobiles, and backpackers multiplied after World War II.

Tourism expanded as fast as the oil and gas industry. Out-of-state tourists spent an estimated $40 million in the state in 1948, $107 million in 1963, $180 million in 1971, $313 million in 1974, and $345 million in 1975.[4]

Frank Norris, Jr., director of the Travel Commission, 1963–1977, developed one of the best travel-promotion organizations in the United States. He and the commission won many national awards before his untimely death at age fifty-one in June, 1977. One of his understudies, Randy Wagner, took charge in Norris's place.

A perennial problem in the 1960's and 1970's was the preoccupation of tourists with getting to the state's two great national parks, Yellowstone and Grand Teton, as quickly as possible. About three million people a year visited each of these parks, close to 10 per cent more appearing in Grand Teton than in Yellowstone. Most of them toured both parks on the same trip, since they lie side by side in the state's northwest corner. The crowds taxed the park facilities from mid-June until early September.

[4] Estimates by the State Travel Commission, based on sales tax receipts and questionnaires.

Dr. James Pikl, economics professor at the University of Wyoming, declared that he would rather have seven thousand permanent residents than seven million tourists who spent only ten dollars each outside the national parks. Chambers of commerce sought ways to slow down the rush to and from the parks. Cheyenne's Frontier Days celebration held tourists for a few days during the last ten days of July, but no other community had comparable success. The State Fair at Douglas, Central Wyoming Fair at Casper, Cody's Stampede and Buffalo Bill Historical Center, Laramie's Jubilee Days, All-American Indian Days, at Sheridan, re-enactment of the Green River rendezvous at Pinedale, Fort Laramie, Fort Bridger, and Devils Tower did well to hold the tourists for one day. Most of the other celebrations and events, including seventy small rodeos, drew more natives than tourists.

The bucking horse logo was a great favorite in Cowboy State advertising. Chambers of commerce asked the natives to "dress western" each summer. "Let's give people what they expect and have fun doing it" was a typical plea. When the Utah native Bernard DeVoto, who spent his adult life in the East, complained that western people who donned cowboy boots and hats were "coerced advertisers," he missed the point that, at least in Wyoming, most townspeople who dressed up as cowboys and cowgirls did so because they enjoyed doing so.

Fort Laramie promised to become a major tourist attraction as the National Park Service pushed its program of restoring old buildings at that famous national historic site. The Wyoming Recreation Commission was active all over the state, with restorations at old South Pass City, Fort Bridger State Park, and Fort Fetterman State Park, and with the upgrading of the eight other state parks for which it was responsible. After Independence Rock was acquired in 1977, plans were made for establishing an eleventh state park there. The Recreation Commission cooperated with other agencies in locating and marking historic trails, including "mountain man" trails. By 1977 the commission had enrolled more than one hundred historic sites on the National Register of Historic Places, and had a backlog of several hundred sites for future recommendation. The 1,100 members of the Wyoming State Historical Society, through their promotion of museums and pageants, summer treks, and publications, made substantial contributions to tourism.

No outrageous tourist trap comes to mind, although erroneous information is sometimes peddled. Visitors are sometimes told that a grave at Fort Washakie is the burial place of Sacajawea of the Lewis and Clark expedition, when most scholars agree that Sacajawea's grave is in South Dakota.[5] Again, they are told that Esther Morris, first woman justice of the peace, was the prime mover in causing Wyoming to adopt woman suffrage, which she probably was not.

Efforts to keep roads in Yellowstone Park open through the winter were not very successful, although over-snow vehicles did make it possible for more than twenty thousand persons to visit the Old Faithful area each winter. The promotion of winter sports brought disappointing results because the dozen or so ski areas were too remote from great population centers, could not get jet plane service, and all too often lacked enough snow for good skiing. Jackson Hole offered the state's most sumptuous skiing facilities.

The economic importance of game and fish increased. As the Game and Fish Commission's planning coordinator, Douglas M. Crowe, pointed out, hunting and fishing "is a way of life. In earlier days it was a matter of survival; in more recent years it has become a much-sought-after form of recreation." Game and fish did double duty, serving the recreational needs of both tourists and sportsmen. In his University of Wyoming M.A. thesis (1957), Tom Bell reported that expenditures for hunting and fishing in 1955 ($23,350,000) amounted to more than the cash value of all agricultural crops produced in the state. A 1976 Game and Fish Department study found that 196,000 big game hunters had spent $38,500,000 and 239,000 fishermen had spent $39,300,000 in the state. Bird hunters and small game hunters had spent an additional $4,500,000, making the total impact of hunting and fishing $82,300,000. One hunter had the temerity to suggest that it would be best to exclude sheep from the Red Desert and give antelope (pronghorns) full possession.

Except for two national parks, the Medicine Bow, Big Horn, Wind River, and Absaroka mountains, with their dude ranches, hunting, and fishing, served more effectively than anything else to detain tourists, although reclamation reservoirs occupied growing numbers of fishermen and water-sports enthusiasts. The national forests, which generally coincided with the mountain ranges, contributed much more to tourism than to lumbering, a small industry because the conifers take a century to mature in the high, dry climate.

September, October, and November were the big hunting months. The Game and Fish Commission, and the guides and outfitters, worked

[5] For the best presentation of the evidence, see Irving W. Anderson's article "Probing the Riddle of the Bird Woman," in the Autumn 1973 issue of *Montana: The Magazine of Western History.*

534 History of Wyoming

overtime then to keep all interests happy. The game and fish represented natural resources to be harvested and to be conserved at their optimum numbers. If they became too numerous, they would starve. Habitat must be provided and protected. Ranchers and farmers must not be expected to feed wildlife at the expense of their own livestock without adequate compensation. Multiple use and balance must be established on publicly owned grazing lands.

The simultaneous increase in residents and nonresidents in the 1970's boded ill for hunting and fishing. Resident as well as nonresident hunters must draw for all big game animal licenses except for antelope. Joe White, chief of the fish division, noted in 1977 that most of the complaints he got were about fishermen, not fishing. "The problem," he said, "appears to be that the tolerance limit of one human in Wyoming for his fellow species is remarkably low." Whereas in 1974 the complaints had been almost entirely about Coloradans, a few years later people in Sublette County objected to Sweetwater County people fishing in Soda Lake, and Carbon County people resented the pressure of Natrona County folks fishing the Upper Platte "and so on ad infinitum." Symptoms of problems in the hunting sphere included a Casper hunter's complaint that he had applied for a moose hunting permit for thirty-seven years without success, and a report that the annual pheasant harvest had dropped in twenty years from 120,000 to 30,000. The latter was explained by a steady decline in habitat; as irrigated land became more valuable, farmers cleaned out weedy and brushy areas, leaving much less cover for birds. Tension between hunters and ranchers increased partly because of greater hunting pressure, and partly because many ranchers felt generally put upon by contemporary society. More ranchers than ever before collected trespass fees in 1977.

In spite of evidence indicating that hunting and fishing were deteriorating, the state could still boast of having more antelope, mule deer, elk, and moose than any other state. The estimated populations of game in 1977 were 280,000 mule deer; 168,000 antelope; 63,000 elk; 51,000 white-tailed deer; 7,500 moose; 3,100 bighorn sheep; 2,100 black bears; and 70 Rocky Mountain goats. Between 25 and 30 per cent of the game animals were harvested annually.[6] Fifty-five to 65 per

[6] The estimated 1976 harvest was as follows: 64,644 mule deer; 58,480 antelope; 14,705 elk; 11,298 white-tailed deer; 1,678 moose; 293 black bears; 125 bighorn sheep; and 4 Rocky Mountain goats.

cent of the Game and Fish Department's income in the 1970's came from nonresidents. Nonresident hunters were required to employ licensed guides.

COLONIALISM

In the eighteenth and nineteenth centuries, European states used colonies to supply raw materials and absorb surplus manufactures. More recently, many people thought of western America, and Wyoming in particular, as a colonial area in which the natives worked for absentee owners to supply the industrial East with raw materials. Drawing upon his experience in Wyoming, Thurman Arnold, for example, testified before Senator O'Mahoney's Public Lands Committee in 1941 that industrially the West was only a colony whose interests were subordinated to those of the East.

For a long time the West suffered from high transportation costs and the basing-point price system. Modifications came in the 1940's. In May, 1945, the Interstate Commerce Commission ordered a uniform system of freight classification for the whole country and a 10 per cent reduction in class rates in the West and South. The U.S. Supreme Court upheld the order, and it went into effect in May, 1947. This provided some relief for Wyoming consumers. Moreover, the basing-point price system was outlawed by the U.S. Supreme Court in April, 1948. Nonetheless, relatively high gasoline prices persisted, even with the "Tulsa plus" price system outlawed. High costs and sharply reduced sales in winter were the usual explanations given.

After 1948 there was less talk of western colonialism. Leonard J. Arrington, Utah State University economic historian, reported in 1963 that the Mountain West was less colonialistic than formerly. His data showed, however, that Wyoming was the most colonialistic western state, with the largest percentage of people employed in "export" industries.

Typical license fees in 1976 for nonresidents were: for bighorn sheep, $150; elk and fishing, $125; moose, $125; deer, $50; antelope, $50; and black bear, $30. Fees paid by residents, who were issued many more licenses, were as follows: for bighorn sheep, $30; moose, $25; elk and black bear, $15; deer and black bear, $10; antelope (pronghorn), $10; black bear, $5. Nonresident fishing licenses cost $25, resident licenses $5. Five-day licenses cost less.

The number of fishing licenses was not limited, although the number of hunting licenses was. In 1976 hunters drew for 65,000 antelope licenses, 50,000 elk licenses, and 50,000 deer licenses.

536 History of Wyoming

HELPFUL UNCLE

After World War II, Wyoming exported raw and semiprocessed materials, such as crude oil, natural gas, coal, soda ash, yellowcake, iron ore, cattle, sheep, wool, and wheat. It also exported mountain scenery and recreation. It imported manufactured goods, transportation, communications, insurance, meat, milk, fruits, and vegetables. Paying for the imports posed a problem. Economist Robert Garnsey of the University of Colorado explained in *America's New Frontier* (1950) that the Rocky Mountain region was able to pay for its imports only because the federal government sent more money into the region than it took out.

In the next twenty years the Library of Congress Legislative Reference Service reported repeatedly that Wyoming was receiving more money from the federal government than it was paying in federal taxes. The imbalance reached an extreme point in fiscal 1968, after several years of severe weakness in the Wyoming economy.[7] Neal R. Pierce in his *The Mountain States of America* (1972) observed that "the prime irony of Western politics is that this totally dependent region is the same one which produces so many rugged, independent frontiersmen who are ready to denounce the federal government for its every transgression."

A *National Journal* survey found that in 1975 Wyoming was still receiving more back than it was sending to Washington. The *National Journal* reported (June 26, 1976) that in fiscal 1975 the federal government spent $1.21 in Wyoming for every dollar of federal taxation collected.

There appeared to be three good reasons, however, why the balance could be expected to swing the other way: (1) New England and the Middle Atlantic states, suffering from economic setbacks and high unemployment, wanted more federal aid for themselves and less for the West, and they had many representatives in Congress; (2) Wyoming, enjoying a great boost from minerals production, was in a position to export its tax burdens through severance taxes if it would, and should be able to get along with less federal aid; and (3) there were a few signs

[7] Taking 100 as the index number for the U.S. average, Wyoming's index for its exchange with the federal government was 116 in 1952, 118 in 1958, and 128 in the three-year period 1959–1961. The Library of Congress reported that in fiscal 1968 Wyoming taxpayers had paid the federal government $107 million and had received $210 million in return, broken down as follows: federal aid $100 million; federal wages and salaries, civilian, $42 million, military, $25 million; old-age, survivors', disability, and health payments, $32 million; veterans' benefits, $17 million. Also the federal government awarded $15 million in primary military construction.

that Wyoming people were losing what had appeared to be an insatiable thirst for federal aid. Governor Herschler in June, 1977, issued a directive requiring state agencies to obtain his written approval before accepting federal funds. Federal grants, he explained, too often entailed the addition of state employees and unanticipated financial obligations.

That the turning point might have come already was suggested by a *National Journal* follow-up study published July 2, 1977. It revealed that in fiscal 1976 the federal government took $1,533 in taxes from each person in Wyoming and spent only $1,530 in Wyoming. Perhaps after more than a century, Wyoming had come of age and would no longer be so dependent on the federal government and the states of the Northeast and Midwest.[8]

LABOR

The *Casper Star-Tribune*'s opinion that Wyoming in 1977 was "a paradise for labor" evoked most dissent from union organizers. Wyoming was one of twenty right-to-work states, having become one by act of the legislature in 1963. Union workers, if they constituted a majority in a plant or mine, could become the bargaining agent for the work unit, but non-union workers did not have to pay union dues. Union members insisted that non-union workers enjoyed all the benefits won by the bargaining efforts of unions, past or present, and should be compelled to pay part of the union's expenditures.

Union membership, which had exceeded 20,000 during World War II, had slipped to 13,100 in 1963 in a nonagricultural work force of about 125,000. In 1976 union membership totaled about 25,000 in a nonagricultural work force of about 155,000. State Department of Labor surveys indicated unmistakably that most of the blue-collar workers would rather not pay union dues as long as they could get equal treatment without doing so. Younger workers who did not know the history of the labor movement felt no obligation or loyalty to unions. Only 35.8 per cent of 13,452 construction workers belonged to unions in 1976, and unionization varied remarkably among the state's industries.[9]

[8] Critics question the validity of some aspects of the *National Journal*'s analysis, but eastern politicians were making the most of it in 1977, and almost certainly they would try harder than before to get their full share of federal appropriations.

[9] Of construction craft workers in 1976, the percentages of union members ranged as follows: iron workers, 74.4; bricklayers, 69.9; electricians, 63.2; sheetmetal workers, 54.8; teamsters, 33; plumbers, 29.7; carpenters, 24.6; painters, 24.4; laborers, 17;

Wyoming employers appeared able to counter union organizing efforts quite effectively by paying union wages (or not much below them), while providing good working conditions, grievance procedures, and seniority systems. They met walkouts with delaying maneuvers which wore out the pickets, and sometimes they made life unpleasant for union organizers without violating the letter of the law. Wages were higher than might be inferred from the state's minimum hourly wage, $1.60 in 1977. Average hourly earnings in 1976 were $8.07 in oil refining, $7.65 in coal mining, $7.48 in contract construction, $6.57 in transportation and public utilities, $6.15 in oil and gas extraction, and $3.43 in retail trade.

The *Casper Star-Tribune* said in September, 1976, that right-to-work was a dead issue. The National Right to Work Committee (with headquarters in Fairfax, Virginia) must have had some doubts on the subject, because it ran many full-page advertisements in Wyoming newspapers during the 1976 political campaign, advocating "the principle of individual freedom." They published a map showing the twenty states that had right-to-work laws—eleven in the South plus the tier of four states just east of Wyoming, plus Iowa, Utah, Arizona, Nevada, and Wyoming. Another series of the committee's ads purported to show that the areas of substantial unemployment were all in the thirty states that did not have right-to-work laws.

Wyoming's unemployment averaged 4.1 per cent in 1976, compared to 7.7 for the nation, and dropped to 3.5 per cent in 1977, as the national percentage slipped to 7.0. With the national rate so high, finding workers was usually not much of a problem except for low-pay service jobs. Job seekers from other states who could not find work in Wyoming normally moved on because strict eligibility rules were enforced for unemployment compensation, and welfare payments were below national averages.

To enjoy Wyoming's "paradise," workers had to adjust to a few mundane circumstances—extremes of weather, high living costs, and the need to travel great distances for services and recreation. Gas-

cement masons, and plasterers, 14.5; and drywallers, 0.0. About 93 per cent of 1,140 strip coal miners were union members in 1975. About 75 per cent of 2,328 workers in trona mining and milling were union members (United Steel Workers) in 1977, but only 3.9 per cent of 3,403 workers in crude petroleum and natural gas production were unionized. Slightly more than half of 1,921 workers in the uranium industry were unionized.

guzzling pickup trucks were the preferred means of transportation. Many thousands lived in trailers that had to be tied down lest they blow away. Enforcers of the Clean Air Act found it impossible to do much about the blowing dust around most of the many places where the land surface was disturbed.

Occasionally the newcomers were not welcomed by natives who looked upon them as troublesome intruders who caused environmental impact problems. One of Wyoming's most eloquent gadflies, Mike Leon, columnist for the *Sheridan Press*, suggested that impact was falling "most brutally" upon the newcomers who should be receiving more sympathy and understanding than they had been accorded so far.

RESTRAINTS ON RUNAWAY GROWTH

Wyoming's century-long slow growth had been the consequence of great obstacles. The obstacles did not go away; they continued to restrain growth by making it difficult and expensive.

Lack of water was a major obstacle. It made very difficult, if not impossible, some kinds of industrial expansion, particularly in coal gasification, coal liquefaction, and electric utilities. It posed serious problems even for mining and urban growth.

The complex land-ownership pattern also restrained growth. The federal government owned the mineral rights under 72 per cent of the land and owned 48 per cent of the surface. The state owned about 5 per cent of the land. County and state governments were gradually imposing stricter zoning regulations, though not without stiff opposition.

Capital-formation problems killed some enterprises. A coal gasification or liquefaction plant might cost two billion dollars. The oil industry, which provided much of the capital for coal and uranium mining, wanted the federal government to put up the risk capital for gasification and liquefaction projects.

Industrial developers encountered a fourth obstacle in environmentalists, whose demands for impact studies delayed projects and sometimes made them more expensive if not impossible. But environmental protection laws came too late to prevent a legacy of many great, ugly uranium pits, which may never be filled up, and some mill tailings piles that continue to emit radioactivity. Aroused to environmental problems, the state legislature for several years became more demanding in this regard each time it met: it passed an Air Quality

Act and Outdoor Advertising Act in 1967; Open Cut Mining Reclamation Act and Land Use Act in 1969; Plant Siting Act in 1971; Environmental Quality Act and Surface Mining Act in 1973; and Land Use Planning Act in 1975. The 1977 session of the legislature paused for breath, as members resisted further restrictions on industry except for small increases in severance taxation on uranium and trona, and a larger increase in the coal severance tax. In 1977 bills were rejected that would have protected stream channels, established a river protection system, begun an energy export policy, authorized the Environmental Quality Council to declare a moratorium on the receipt of mine permit applications, and required more lead time before major industrial facilities could get permits. Another rejected bill would have deleted an existing provision "that no zoning regulation shall prevent any use or occupancy reasonably necessary in the extraction or protection of mineral resources."

At the time of the Arab oil embargo in October, 1973, Wyoming expected an influx of major industrial plants. Four years later, among the many projected plants, only one had been started (ground was broken in 1976 for a 1,500-megawatt utility plant in Platte County). The lack of water had proved to be the greatest obstacle of all, blocking many projects entirely and causing much grief for the promoters of the Platte County project. The state's water problem was starkly exposed in August, 1977, when Granger, a town of 300 in southwestern Wyoming, lost its water supply as the Ham's Fork River dried up. The mayor of Granger went to Washington, hat in hand, seeking $1.5 million with which to lay a fifteen-mile pipeline to the Green River. The pipeline by itself would not be enough; water rights would have to be obtained from someone.

Considering that only one large new industrial plant had been started, the state's unprecedented population growth from 332,401 in 1970 to perhaps 400,000 in 1977 was surprising. Part of the increase came from the expansion in the mining, processing, and transportation of trona, uranium, and coal. Part of it came from construction of additions to pre-1973 utility plants, feverish minerals exploration and leasing activities, impact studies, housing construction, real estate developments, and assorted speculative enterprises.

Thanks to the restraints, the lack of water in particular, Wyoming's unprecedented growth of the 1970's did not get completely out of hand. Yet for a state that had known so little growth in the past it was truly spectacular. The U.S. Commerce Department reported in

November, 1977, that between the last quarter of 1973 and the second quarter of 1977 the overall income of Wyoming's wage earners had increased 54 per cent. Among the fifty states, only Alaska's percentage of income growth exceeded Wyoming's. Overall income in the mining industry had increased 174 per cent. Some of the growth was temporary and would certainly come to a halt.

Most Wyomingites wanted to keep ranching and farming, wildlife, open space, uncrowded countryside, and tourism. They might have a chance to save all or most of these if the population climbed no higher than 500,000 by 1985.

CHAPTER 18

Postwar Politics and Government

POLITICS IN WYOMING is a game played seriously by a few hundred people, most of them men. In even-numbered years they maximize their efforts and activate temporarily a few thousand recruits.

Civil servants are watched closely. In the 1960's one man lost his state job for padding his expense account. In the early 1970's two other state employees went to the penitentiary for somewhat larger embezzlements. Then in 1977 citizens were puzzled by a controversy that after six months caused tremendous excitement and suspense. In May, 1977, differences between Attorney General Frank Mendicino and Neil F. Compton, director of the state's criminal investigation division, led to charges, countercharges, and Compton's dismissal by Governor

542

Ed Herschler. Compton, a holdover from Hathaway's administration, at first accused Mendicino merely of postponing or blocking investigations into alleged misuse of funds in state institutions. Then the allegations expanded from week to week until they involved serious charges against mayor Paul Wataha of Rock Springs, state Democratic chairman Don Anselmi, and Governor Ed Herschler. Reports in metropolitan newspapers and in the nationally televised program "60 Minutes" heightened excitement. A state grand jury began studying the matter on November 21.

Politicians pondered the potential impact of the investigation on the election of 1978, to which they looked forward with more interest than usual. Eligible voters in Wyoming go to the polls very faithfully (more than 82 per cent in 1976). The Republicans generally win the elections and the spoils. Beginning in 1938 they won back most, but not all, of the losses suffered earlier in the 1930's. In 1976, 45 per cent of the registered voters were Republicans; 40 per cent, Democrats; and 15 per cent, Independents.[1]

Republicans controlled state government with rare interruptions, so they had continuity of leadership with which to supervise the perpetuation of their power. The Democrats controlled (30–26) the state House of Representatives in 1959 and held one-half of the seats in the state Senate in the 1975 and 1976 sessions. They also had members of their party in the governor's chair during thirteen of the thirty-two years from 1946 to 1978, and had 3–2 control of state boards two of the thirty-two years. The Democrats fared best in elections to the U.S. Senate, winning six and losing six contests. The only Democrat in the U.S. House of Representatives in postwar years was Teno Roncalio, who won the state's only place in that body five times.

Both major parties in the state were somewhat more conservative than their national organizations. Wyoming electors voted for the winners in postwar presidential elections, except in 1960, when they voted for Richard Nixon instead of John F. Kennedy, and in 1976, whey they voted for Gerald Ford instead of Jimmy Carter. In 1976 Wyoming's delegates had supported Ronald Reagan in the national GOP convention. The voters' positive distaste for Hubert Humphrey in 1968, George McGovern in 1972, and Jimmy Carter in 1976 precluded the possibility of any coattail ride for other Democratic candidates.

[1] Statewide registration was not mandated before 1968. In the primary elections of 1946 through 1964, Republican voters averaged 6,000 more than Democratic, compared to 14,000 more in the primary elections of 1912–1932.

Laramie County lost its bellwether distinction in 1976 when for the
first time ever it voted for the losing presidential candidate. Third-
party candidates played no significant role in postwar elections, although George Wallace received 11,105 votes (8.7 per cent) as an
Independent candidate for the presidency in 1968, not enough to
affect appreciably the Nixon-Humphrey contest.

Although Republican strength was obvious, there were occasional
surprises because a candidate's personality and leadership qualities
counted for as much as his party affiliation and his stand on issues. It
was, however, virtually impossible for a Republican to carry Sweetwater County and almost as difficult for a Democrat to win in several
northern counties. Wyoming's voters abhorred extremism, especially
of the left, and it was customary for candidates to exaggerate the lean-
ings of their opponents. The Wyoming electorate included very few if
any Communists and Nazis, and only a few hundred members of the
John Birch Society.[2]

Republicans were dominant in the northern counties and in small
towns and rural areas; Democrats did best in the cities along the Union
Pacific Railroad. The Farm Bureau Federation, Stock Growers,
Medical Society, Taxpayers Association, Mining Association, and
employer organizations generally, as well as most newspapers, supported the Republicans, while Democratic success depended on turning
out the labor vote. The oil industry preferred Republican candidates but
prudently supported major candidates of both parties so long as they
endorsed industry demands, which the candidates—prudent as well—
did with regularity.

Except in local elections along the Union Pacific, labor in Wyoming
has never been a potent political force. The right-to-work law, adopted
by the legislature in 1963, weakened labor still more. Republicans
who had worried about what the influx of people in the 1970's might
do to their dominance were relieved to learn that the newcomers were
quite conservative and in the main not strongly committed to either
party.

Republican candidates for state and national office usually campaigned for decentralization of federal authority, reduced federal
expenditures (except for national defense and reclamation), and states'
rights. Democrats were more inclined to favor foreign aid, federal aid
to education, civil rights legislation, rights of women and minorities, and

[2] A law adopted by the legislature in 1955 imposed severe penalties on Communists
who did not register. No one has ever registered or been arrested for failure to register.

expenditures for social services. The Republicans usually raised and spent more money in their campaigns and organized more effectively.

THE YEARS OF LESTER C. HUNT AND ARTHUR G. CRANE

In 1946 Democrats won the two top offices (U.S. senator and governor) but lost everything else. Senator Joseph C. O'Mahoney and Governor Lester C. Hunt were re-elected, while Republicans won the other four state offices. The GOP won control of the legislature, 19–8 in the Senate and 44–12 in the House. Hunt, who prevailed over Earl Wright, Farson rancher and state treasurer, had rare energy, a well-deserved reputation for economy, and relentless ambition. His advertisements were not far-fetched when they boasted that "he had placed the State in its soundest financial condition in its history . . . yet Wyoming's per capita tax is the lowest of the eleven western states."

The first postwar legislature met in January 1947. Governor Hunt, recalling the aftermath of World War I, warned that deflation lay ahead. The state must, he said, "look into the future and prepare for the trip down the other side of this inflationary peak." The Senate majority floor leader, R. L. Greene (R.), also expected deflation and a drop in state revenues. Time would prove that Hunt and Greene were wrong, but their go-slow recommendations won general consent. Construction proposals were tabled. Past inflation forced general-fund appropriations above $18 million, compared to $8.5 million two years earlier. A constitutional amendment permitting a six-mill state levy for public school support was submitted to the people and adopted in 1948. Labor successfully sidetracked a right-to-work bill. Another controversial bill, which would have moved the university's College of Agriculture to Sheridan, was defeated by arguments that the state could not afford two four-year schools.

World War II veterans flocked to the University in such numbers that a special session of the legislature had to be called June 28–30, 1948. The legislature appropriated two million dollars for the university and other institutions and departments, and also passed a hospital federal-aid enabling act.

Governor Hunt moved on to Washington as U.S. senator at the midpoint of his second term (in 1948), turning the governor's chair over to the secretary of state, Arthur Griswold Crane, former president of the University of Wyoming. While at the university, Crane had loved the designation "Crane, the Builder," and his emphasis on buildings had not changed. He strongly urged the legislature to approve money requests for construction of permanent improvements. He presented a budget prepared by Hunt, who by this time had realized that the die was cast for inflation instead of deflation. While Crane had been a dominating university president, he kept his hands off the legislature, explaining: "I hold that it is not the responsibility of the governor to initiate legislation or to endeavor by influencing the legislature to enact any particular program."

The great blizzard of 1949, ending about the time the legislature convened, left the livestock industry in distress. Governor Crane wired President Truman for aid. Following other appeals from governors of the region, federal agencies joined in opening roads and moving feed to starving animals. The legislature appropriated $700,000 for emergency relief, which helped to hold cattle losses down to about 4 per cent.

A well-supported severance tax bill threatened the oil industry. The specter of such a tax had haunted oilmen ever since 1923, when the legislature submitted a constitutional amendment which almost won approval. There were two schools of thought, one favoring a tax on all crude-oil production, the other preferring to tax only exported crude. The latter school produced the 1949 bill. It would have placed half of the revenue in a "replacement for depletion of natural resources" fund, permitting expenditure of only the interest earned. The bill was sponsored in the House by Frank C. Mockler (R.) of Fremont County, E. L. Chamberlain (R.) of Goshen, and John Sullivan (D.) of Albany. E. J. Zoble (R.), senator from Natrona County, argued that the proposal was discriminatory, unconstitutional, and in need of further study. Lewis E. Bates, editor of the *Wyoming State Tribune* (Cheyenne), called a severance tax inevitable, and warned that Wyoming children would grow up to find nothing left but pipelines and holes in the ground. R. F. McPherson, editor of Tracy McCraken's other Cheyenne paper, the *Wyoming Eagle*, replied that the tax would be passed on to the consumer, and moreover was unnecessary. After an amendment had cut the 4 per cent in half, the bill passed the House 31–24, with Democrats voting for it 17–9 and Republicans opposing it 15–14. The Senate killed the bill 16–10.

Appropriations corresponded closely to executive recommendations and exceeded $21,000,000. A year later Governor Crane called a special session (February 14–23, 1950), primarily to appropriate money to fight off an anticipated grasshopper invasion. After appropriating $750,000 for grasshopper control, the legislature established the

Wyoming Home and Hospital for the Aged at Thermopolis and authorized a new cell block for the penitentiary at Rawlins.

FRANK BARRETT AND "DOC" ROGERS

The strongest gubernatorial candidate in sight for the Democrats in 1950 was William "Scotty" Jack. After ten years as auditor and two as secretary of state, Jack had declined to run for office in 1946, preferring to give full time to private business. Hopes that he might be drafted in 1950 were dashed when he accepted a position as executive vice-president in charge of public relations for the Rocky Mountain Oil and Gas Association. He had been bought off, cried critics, but Jack insisted that he had never intended to run for office in 1950. With Jack unavailable, the Democrats nominated John J. McIntyre as their gubernatorial candidate. A Casper lawyer, McIntyre had served one term in Congress (1941–1943). He had lost two congressional races to Frank Barrett, in 1942 and 1946. McIntyre's opponent in 1950 was once again Frank Barrett, who left the House of Representatives after four terms.

Barrett was the idol of the cattlemen and woolgrowers. As chairman of the House Subcommittee on Public Lands he had presided over hearings in Grand Junction, Colorado, and Rawlins, Wyoming, with such marked sympathy for livestock men that the *Denver Post* had described the hearings as "Frank Barrett's Wild West Show." Critics complained that the hearings were rigged, with little time allowed for Forest Service spokesmen and conservationists.

Severance taxation became the major issue in the 1950 campaign. McIntyre wanted a tax on crude oil taken out of the state for refining. That a severance tax proposal should come out of the Oil City (McIntyre's home) surprised some observers. The prominent cattleman J. Elmer Brock spoke against the tax, asserting that consumers would pay it and that, once applied to oil, it would soon be applied to cattle, sheep, and grain. The fact that some ranchers enjoyed income from oil leases and royalties may have made them more sympathetic to the oil industry than they had been in the 1920's. Two Republican members of the Public Service Commission said that a severance tax would be unsound, illegal, and a disastrous precedent. Frank Barrett, who opposed McIntyre's specific plan, said that he favored an investigation of severance taxation by a legislative interim committee. The Republicans had a field day, taking all statewide contests and winning control of the legislature 17–10 and 39–17. Barrett's majority over McIntyre was 12,000.

Unlike his predecessor, Governor Barrett held a tight rein on the legislature, and with the substantial majorities in both houses there was little audible dissent. Few legislators were out of sympathy with Barrett's emphasis on economy. Appropriations totaled $22,869,952.14, not much more than one million above the preceding biennium's total. Only once did Barrett disregard economy. He pushed through a bill increasing the number of university trustees from nine to twelve. The Democratic minority opposed the idea, and for once had most of the state's newspapers on its side.

Governor Barrett resigned in 1952 to run for the U.S. Senate, leaving C. J. "Doc" Rogers, secretary of state, to become acting governor. The Eisenhower landslide left few Democrats to oppose Rogers in the 1953 legislature. Republicans controlled the two houses, 45–11 and 21–6. Like Crane four years earlier, "Doc" Rogers showed no inclination to lead the legislators. The chief executive, he said, "should refrain from needless interference with the legislature at all times." He did announce his opposition to any increase in taxation and legalization of gambling. As might have been expected from a filling station operator, which he had been in private life, Rogers vetoed a bill providing for Wyoming participation in the Interstate Oil Compact. He explained that membership in the compact might "impose undue restrictions on citizens and interests which we may have cause to regret." Although economic indicators were favorable, appropriations from the general fund were held to $24,400,088.66, which was not much more than the totals of 1949 and 1951.

MILWARD SIMPSON AT THE HELM

When Milward Simpson, Cody attorney, native son (third-generation), and long-time president of the University of Wyoming board of trustees, was at his magnanimous best, he could be very charming indeed, and this was the case in 1954 when he ran for governor against the formidable Scotty Jack, who had not lost any of his seven past political contests. Simpson called Jack his "splendid opposition" and explained that he could not speak disparagingly of Democrats because his father and mother were Democrats. He declared that Wyoming and the nation were sick and tired of abusiveness in politics. He ignored the

Communists, whom he had campaigned against in 1940, and whose alien ideology Wyoming politicians had regularly opposed ever since. Simpson seemed to know most of the people in the state by their first names when the campaign began, and all of them by election day.

A wealthy man of generous instincts, Simpson was suspected by some people of wanting to spend too much of the state's revenues. On the other hand, Scotty Jack, a canny Scot who had herded sheep in Niobrara County as a young man, spent much of his time explaining how he could save money for the state. He compared the current cost of government to the much lower cost in 1946. He promised to cut the governor's contingency fund from $100,000 to $5,000. The severance tax was no issue, because Jack would not turn against his recent employers and Simpson had substantial oil interests.

The Simpson-Jack content was one of the cleaner ones in Wyoming history. Simpson won by only 1,112 votes, and in keeping with the amicable spirit of the campaign, he later appointed Jack to a membership on the Public Service Commission and Board of Equalization.

Once again there was a take-charge governor. The state had never had a greater promoter in the statehouse. Said the *Wyoming State Tribune* of Simpson: "His enthusiasm and zeal for all things Wyoming knows no bounds." Though hardly a wastrel, he was readier to spend money than most governors had been. The legislature, which was controlled by Republicans, appropriated $31,929,626.84 for the two years beginning July 1, 1955—about $7.5 million more than the 1953 general fund appropriation.

To balance the budget, the legislature abolished the $500 property tax homestead exemption and limited to $800 the benefit that could be derived from the $2,000 veterans' property tax exemption. Veterans' organizations fought the curtailment, although veterans owning property still enjoyed the best state bonus in the United States.

By a vote of 28–20 the House killed an interim committee's "ton mile" truck bill. Two other truck tax bills got through the legislature, only to be vetoed by the governor on various grounds. Cody trucker Richard R. Jones, Republican senator, led the opposition. John A. Reed, Kemmerer banker and president of Wyoming Highway Information, asserted that the Wyoming Trucking Association "has shown that it is the only group in the United States able to dictate its own taxes." Reed complained that "during the past year the truckers employed virtually every lawyer in the legislature from the central and upstate areas."

The legislators were not desperate enough for revenue to give serious consideration to a 2 per cent severance tax bill, defeating it in the House 37–10. However, after twenty years of abstention, the oil industry permitted the legislature to approve the state's joining the Interstate Oil Compact for Conservation of Oil and Gas. Consent came only after oil men had been reassured by inclusion of a statement that "this Act shall never be construed to permit or authorize the Governor, or any court to make, enter or enforce any order, rule, regulation or judgment requiring restriction of production of any pool or of any well to an amount less than the well or pool can produce."

The 1955 session ended in a spate of excitement over Governor Simpson's final-week request for enabling legislation that would permit a state commission to purchase and operate the concessions held by the Yellowstone Park Company in Yellowstone National Park. The Governor's enthusiasm and eloquence sufficed to win over the legislature, despite objections that partisan politics could not be avoided in the distribution of park jobs, the state should not go into such "socialistic" activity, and the National Park Service would not approve. Sharp criticism of the proposal flared up in Montana and Idaho, but Simpson carried much of Wyoming with him. The prospect of many new jobs and the hope that accommodations in the park could be improved influenced opinion. In the following year negotiations terminated when no agreement could be reached on a price for the concessions.

Governor Simpson incurred the wrath of his birthplace, Jackson, when he closed down gambling there in 1955. Wyoming's 1901 statute prohibiting gambling had not been enforced conscientiously in some communities. Attorney General Harry Harnsberger had cracked down on violators in Jackson during Governor Barrett's administration, but enforcement soon lapsed. Enterprising newsmen presented so much evidence in the summer of 1955 that Simpson intervened. He obtained the resignation of the Teton County sheriff and the forty-five-day suspensions of four liquor licenses. Officially, at least, gambling stopped amid laments that Jackson's tourist industry was doomed.

Privileged to have another Republican legislature, Governor Simpson fairly bubbled over with enthusiasm when he delivered his 1957 state-of-the-state message: "There never was, and there never will be a better state, or a better system of government." His 12,500-word message was one of the longest and one of the more eloquent in state history. He got most of what he asked for—the creation of a Department of Revenue, authorization of voting machines and a personnel director, a Division of Mental Health, an increase in school funding, higher state salaries, an underground water code, and a civil rights bill.[3]

The Ways and Means Committee cut more than $1.5 million from Simpson's appropriations requests, leaving $32,208,315.55 to be drawn from the general fund. This was less than $300,000 above the previous biennium's appropriation. Three Republican senators—Richard Jones, Albert Harding, and R. L. Greene—led an abortive attempt to cut the budget 10 per cent across the board. Revenues were bolstered by higher cigarette and highway-user taxes. Casper's attempt to locate the State Highway Department's new building in the Oil City instead of Cheyenne barely failed.

High gasoline prices—irksome to many people ever since the 1920's—led Senators Frank C. Mockler (R.) and Rudolph Anselmi (D.) to introduce a bill authorizing an investigation. The bill cleared the Senate but was defeated in the House 25–16, with the Natrona County delegation leading the opposition. The House quickly killed a 2.5 per cent severance tax measure.

THE 1958 ELECTION

Wyoming, along with the rest of the nation, moved sharply toward the Democrats in 1958. The Democrats won 3–2 control of state boards as Rawlins attorney Joseph J. Hickey (D.) defeated incumbent Governor Simpson by 2,582 votes, while Sheridan postmaster and former state superintendent Jack Gage was elected secretary of state, and Velma Linford, incumbent state superintendent of public instruction, was re-elected. The two parties divided control of the legislature, the Democrats taking the House 30–26, and the Republicans the Senate 16–11.

Joe Hickey's victory was a surprise. Astute observers rated Simpson one of the best governors in Wyoming history—personable, energetic, forthright, and courageous. A highway-location squabble hurt him more than anything else. Sheridan wanted Interstate Highway 90 to come to Sheridan from the east along old Highway 14 and not along a new, more southerly route favored by the highway department which

---

[3] The civil rights bill, which had been drawn up by Teno Roncalio, stated: "No person of good deportment shall be denied the right of life, liberty, pursuit of happiness, or the necessities of life because of race, color, creed, or national origin." Simpson, who approved the bill, in 1964 would be one of six U.S. senators who voted against the federal civil rights bill which became law.

would touch Buffalo before turning north to Sheridan and Billings. The latter route, said Carl Rott, publisher of the *Sheridan Press*, would mean economic "destruction" for Sheridan, Clearmont, Dayton, Ranchester, Greybull, Lovell, and Powell. The highway commission approved highway department recommendations, and Governor Simpson refused to intervene. Sheridan was afraid that tourists, once they reached Buffalo, would leave the Interstate highway there and travel on Highway 16 across the Big Horns to Worland on their way to Yellowstone Park, instead of leaving the Interstate Highway at Sheridan to cross the mountains on Highway 14.

Sheridan County, which had given Simpson a majority of 741 in 1954, opposed him by a majority of 1,708 in 1958. In Sheridan, Powell, and Lovell, Simpson lost more than enough votes to account for his defeat. He gained very few votes in Buffalo and Worland, cities which would benefit from the highway location. A few vicious murders made Simpson's opposition to capital punishment unpopular, and his crackdown on gambling cost him a swing of 496 votes in Teton County from 1954. In addition, some veterans resented the eight-hundred-dollar limit placed on their bonus.

JOE HICKEY AND JACK GAGE

After his surprising defeat of Milward Simpson, Joe Hickey, true to his campaign promises, stressed economy. He pared 1959 budget requests by more than $5 million, recommending appropriations of only $30 million. By session's end the total had grown to $33,447,599.16. Revenue in sight would permit no greater expenditures, and there was little disposition to add new taxes. A 2 per cent severance tax got nowhere. Governor Hickey could not deliver on a campaign promise to restore the five-hundred-dollar homestead exemption because the revenue could not be spared.

The legislature modified a 1943 law which had forbidden the State Board of Education to accept federal aid that required matching or other contribution of funds by the state. The modification permitted acceptance of funds if the Board of Education certified that the federal budget was in balance and that the need could not be met with state and local resources.

Governor Hickey and legislators of both parties became much excited about states' rights with regard to choice of color used in painting stripes on federal-aid highways. It was a common belief in Wyoming that yellow lines were invaluable in a snowstorm. However, the federal highway administrator notified the Governor that the state would have to abide by federal standards and use white paint.

Governor Hickey obtained a commission to study and recommend reorganization of state government. As it turned out, however, the legislature provided only five thousand dollars for the project, and efforts to obtain private foundation support failed. Hickey had talked of eliminating most of the power of existing boards and commissions, limiting each department to one function, separating accounting and auditing, establishing direct lines of authority to the governor, and giving the legislature control of game and fish commission funds.

The 1959 session was more than ordinarily frustrating. Appropriately, more steam than usual was released the last night, especially in the House. Visitors, not House members, however, were guilty of moving a mounted buffalo from the capitol rotunda to the front lawn. To entertain the weary legislators at midnight, House employees sang "The Yellow Stripe Blues" to the tune of "The Yellow Rose of Texas."

REPUBLICANS BOUNCE BACK

The political balance swung to the right in 1960. People were leaving the state faster than they were coming in. Democrats tried to capitalize on economic discontent as they talked of the need for new industries to counteract outmigration. The *Wyoming State Tribune* accused Democratic candidates of making a career of "gloomshouting . . . weeping and wailing, and the wringing of hands." In the presidential phase of the 1960 election, Democratic leaders at the Los Angeles convention did not climb on the Kennedy bandwagon until his nomination was assured, with the notable exception of Teno Roncalio, state chairman. Kennedy's identification as a big-city liberal and the suspicion that he wanted to eliminate the oil-depletion allowance handicapped him in Wyoming. Although Tracy McCraken wrote a front-page editorial decrying attacks on Kennedy for his religion, Catholicism had been no handicap for other Wyoming politicians such as Vincent Carter, Joe O'Mahoney, Frank Barrett, and Joe Hickey, and probably did not cost Kennedy many votes in Wyoming in 1960; yet Richard Nixon carried the state by 14,000 votes.

Keith Thomson (R.), after three terms in the U.S. House of Representatives, was elected to the U.S. Senate, something that other congressmen have found very difficult to do in Wyoming. Thomson, a lawyer with a splendid World War II combat record, had defeated Rawlins railroad conductor and mayor Sam Tully in 1954; Jerry O'Callaghan, historian and journalist, in 1956; and Ray Whitaker, Casper attorney, in 1958. In 1960 it was Whitaker again who challenged him, this time for the Senate seat left vacant when O'Mahoney decided to retire. Just a month and a day after his election to the Senate, Thomson died of a heart attack. He was only forty-one. Governor Joe Hickey then resigned, effective January 2, 1961, and Secretary of State Jack Gage, as acting governor, appointed Hickey to fill the Senate vacancy.

This left Gage to preside over the state government for the next two years. Both houses of the legislature were back in Republican hands after the 1959 aberration of having one house controlled by the Democrats. Gage, who was sometimes known as "the Will Rogers of the Rockies," in his message to the legislature offered a mixed bag, now reading from a sober, formal text, now ad-libbing humorously. Some Republicans complained that they could not tell when he was serious and when he wasn't. He criticized socialism, the merit system, and federal aid. He warned that there must be no more tax increases, except possibly for aid to municipalities. Politicians of both parties agreed that Gage was more conservative on economic matters than either Simpson or Hickey. Gage submitted the budget prepared by Hickey, without having had time to study it. Despite a general inclination to hold the line, continuing inflation and built-in increases forced general-fund appropriations upward to $38,545,926.16, which was more than $5 million above those of the previous biennium.

Proposals for a severance tax and a sales tax increase were killed in the House. The session's most furious battles raged around three issues: reapportionment, trading stamps, and federal aid to education. All reapportionment bills were rejected. So were all trading stamp bills pushed by housewives who wanted to remove a ban on them. The 1959 enabling act under which the state could accept matching funds for public schools was repealed, making Wyoming the only state unable to accept such aid. Between bouts over these issues, the legislature recodified election laws, strengthened civil rights, adopted a model business corporation code, provided for a new school for the deaf in Casper, and authorized the sale of the Saratoga Hot Springs State Reserve.

Governor Hickey had attached great importance to the study which he had instigated to reorganize state government. On December 15, 1960, two weeks before he resigned and accepted appointment to the

U.S. Senate, he had sent a ponderous report to legislators recommending centralized accounting and data processing, and reorganization. Recommendations included an adequately staffed Department of Administration reporting directly to the governor. The report had been prepared by two public administration professors from the University of Southern California and Dr. Floyd Harmston, director of economic research, University of Wyoming, and partly by a Remington Rand UNIVAC five-man survey team. Since Jack Gage preferred the status quo, Hickey's reorganization plans were quietly interred.

After two years as acting governor, Jack Gage in 1962 filed for a four-year term. He disposed of a worthy rival, Scotty Jack, in the primary; then he was trounced in the general election by a newcomer to politics, Clifford P. Hansen. Cliff Hansen, who was fifty, was a third-generation Jackson Hole cattleman who had been president of the Wyoming Stock Growers Association and president of the University of Wyoming board of trustees. In his campaign, Hansen matched Gage's enthusiasm for states' rights, appealed to city people by recognizing the need for financial relief for municipalities, and reassured the oil industry by declaring his opposition to severance taxation. His unaffected manner, modesty, willingness to learn, and engaging personality caught the fancy of Democrats as well as Republicans. His public utterances assayed less than the customary amount of campaign claptrap. He won by a majority of 10,672.

Gage blamed his defeat on "liberalism among Democrats." He said that "the people of Wyoming are conservative people." His record suggests that ideologically he belonged in the Republican party. As he left the governorship, Gage commented wryly that the post "is well covered with tinsel. The tinsel falls off it much more rapidly than off anything I know." One unpleasant aspect of the job that he may have had in mind was the hostile legislature. Of the ten Democratic governors and acting governors in Wyoming since statehood, only one, Leslie Miller, had been privileged to have a legislature controlled by his own party.

The Republicans also won the other four state elective offices. Swept out of office was Velma Linford, probably the most intelligent, forceful, and energetic state superintendent of public instruction in the state's history up to that time. She lost by 737 votes to Cecil M. Shaw, a former professional basketball player who had come from Oklahoma three years earlier, and had changed his party registration from Democrat to Republican only a short time before he filed for office. In her two terms, 1955–1963, Linford had fought enthusiastically and against great odds for acceptance of federal aid to education, equalization of educational opportunity, higher teacher standards, and consolidation of school districts. A native of Star Valley who had taught school for many years in Laramie before being elected state superintendent, she received an appointment in the federal government in February, 1963, and held various administrative posts in Washington thereafter. She loved Wyoming, but four defeats convinced her that she was too liberal and outspoken to expect political preferment there. She lost her first race for state superintendent in 1946, a primary battle for the U.S. Senate in 1960, her state superintendent's job in 1962, and a contest for the U.S. House of Representatives in 1968.

As Linford left state government in 1963, another outstanding woman, Thyra Thomson (R.), entered, having been elected first female secretary of state. Her career will be discussed below. She was the widow of Keith Thomson, who had died of a heart attack in 1960, just after his election to the U.S. Senate.

Another able female public servant, Minnie Mitchell (R.), was elected state auditor in 1962. She was in the middle of a long political career, 1952–1971, in which she served one and one-half terms as treasurer after being appointed to fill her deceased husband's place as treasurer in 1952, and three terms as auditor. Unlike Velma Linford, Thyra Thomson and Minnie Mitchell were Republicans and were somewhat less aggressive and outspoken.

Governor Hansen, who took office in January 1963, delivered a message to the 37th legislature that pleased the Republicans, who had control of the House, 37–19, and of the Senate, 16–11, and gave no offense to the Democrats. He repeated his campaign pledge to serve out his full four-year term, mindful that three of the four immediate past governors elected to four-year terms had caused annoyance by moving on to the U.S. Senate at midterm. He praised balanced budgets and the free-enterprise system, suggested relief for municipalities, directed attention to the need for reapportionment, and urged fair and equitable treatment for industry. Unlike most of his predecessors, he offered no advance warning against new taxes, preferring to wait until he "could get the whole picture." His budget recommendations were respected, and led eventually to general fund appropriations of $41,591,158.46, which was $3 million above the 1961 total.

Cliff Hansen did not dominate the 37th legislature. As a newcomer to state office he was feeling his way and left leadership pretty much to senior Republican legislators. Wyoming became the twentieth state to adopt a right-to-work law ("an act to provide that employment shall not be conditional upon membership or non-membership in, nor upon the payment or non-payment of money to, a labor organization"). Chief sponsor of the law was a state-wide organization backed by the Wyoming Farm Bureau Federation, Associated General Contractors, Trucking Association, Automobile Dealers, Stock Growers Association, Wool Growers Association, Retail Merchants Association, Mining Association, Wyoming Division of the Rocky Mountain Oil and Gas Association, and others. Spokesmen for labor objected vehemently. Governor Hansen asked the National Guard to stand by (in the capitol basement) during the final debate and vote before crowded galleries in the House. The bill carried 15–11 in the Senate and 33–23 in the House, with substantially a party-line vote—only three Democrats voted for the bill and six Republicans against it. Governor Hansen took no stand until after passage, when he said as he signed the act, "I sincerely believe that this is in the best interest of all the people of Wyoming . . . the measure is designed to restore full freedom of choice to the working men and women of Wyoming."

Blocked were determined drives to repeal a 1959 law limiting the use of trading stamps, to place in Casper a game and fish commission headquarters building planned for Cheyenne, and to legalize parimutuel betting on horse racing and rodeo events.

Ever since 1869 a favorite pastime of Wyoming legislators has been to send resolutions to Congress. The 1963 resolutions placed the legislature on record:

1) Opposing any future increase in the social security tax rate.
2) Asking Congress to call a convention for the purpose of proposing an amendment to the U.S. Constitution permitting legislatures of two-thirds of the states to propose constitutional amendments, which would become effective when approved by legislatures of three-fourths of the states.
3) Asking Congress to call a convention for the purpose of proposing an amendment to the U.S. Constitution establishing a "Court of the Union" consisting of the chief justices of the fifty states. The new "super court" would be empowered to review and reverse decisions of the U.S. Supreme Court relating to the rights reserved to the states or to the people by the Constitution.
4) Opposing the creation or extension of wilderness areas within the state and suggesting that "areas adjacent to centers of population be

purchased and returned to wilderness state, believing that such a
program would make wilderness areas available to more people of
the country than the creation of such areas in the West."
5) Asking Congress to call a convention for the purpose of proposing an
amendment to the U.S. Constitution providing that the federal
government may not, through legislative or judicial action, restrict
or limit any state in the apportionment of representation in its
legislature.

Since the John Birch Society, which claimed a few members in Cody
and Casper, favored several of these resolutions, some Democrats wondered whether that ultraconservative organization had taken over the
legislature, but no legislator was an avowed Bircher. Apparently, the
1963 resolutions represented just another outburst of hostility toward
the federal government. Although long-standing public-lands controversies had lost some of their old fire after settlement of the Jackson
Hole Monument dispute, federal activities in other areas caused new
flare-ups and warranted the conclusion that throughout its history,
Wyoming had suffered more tension in its federal relations than any
other state outside the South.

The 1963 legislature finally did what no other legislature had been
able to do since 1933—reapportion the seats in the legislature as required by the state constitution after every decennial census. The
House membership was increased from 56 to 61 and the Senate membership decreased from 27 to 25. In particular, two counties, Sheridan
and Sweetwater, each lost one of its two senators. Thus all counties were
left with one senator, except Laramie and Natrona, which retained
two. Democrats were not pleased with the Senate reapportionment and
challenged its constitutionality in federal court. Eventually, after much
deliberation and a special session of the legislature in July, 1964, which
failed to solve the problem, three federal judges in October, 1965,
ordered the number of senators increased from 25 to 30 and apportioned
them on the basis of "one man, one vote," in accordance with the U.S.
Supreme Court decision in *Baker* vs. *Carr* (1962).

THE DEMOCRATS REGROUP

In 1964, better than ever before, the Democrats organized at the
grass roots, and managed to raise and spend almost as much money as
the Republicans. The "reactionary record," as they called it, of the
1963 legislature gave Democrats more to talk about than they had had

in many years. In particular, the right-to-work and apportionment issues stirred up union labor and city voters.

In the Republican state convention in May, 1964, conservative Arizona senator Barry Goldwater won all of the Wyoming votes, and the Wyoming delegates yielded to no one in their enthusiasm for Goldwater in the San Francisco convention where he won his party's presidential nomination. Wyoming Democrats had no difficulty in agreeing to support Lyndon Johnson, who had advanced from vice-president to president when John F. Kennedy was assassinated in October, 1963.

Early in the campaign, neutral observers labeled Wyoming "Goldwater country," and perhaps it was for a few months, but not in November. When the votes were counted, the Democrats had won their greatest victory since 1936. President Johnson carried the state by 18,720 votes. The Democrats also won control of the state House of Representatives, 34–27, and reduced Republican control of the Senate to 13–12. All five of the state's elective officials, however, remained Republicans, having been elected in 1962 for four-year terms.

After two years in office, Cliff Hansen was prepared to assume stronger executive leadership than before. Sensing that the 38th legislature was less conservative than the 37th, Hansen in January, 1965, delivered the most progressive gubernatorial message in the state's history since Joseph M. Carey emptied his cornucopia of reform proposals in 1911. Carey's reform ideas had been of the low-cost variety. Governor Hansen seemed less concerned with cost than need, in keeping with the philosophy expressed in his message: "Positive action to strengthen state government is the constructive way to oppose centralization. States' rights are without force unless they are coupled with state responsibility. We propose to accept every responsibility that we can successfully discharge at the state level."

Hansen recommended initiative and referendum procedures, repeal of the ban on federal aid to education, an enabling act to allow urban-renewal projects, an act to raise the minimum wage from seventy-five cents to one dollar, higher workmen's compensation payments, reapportionment of the state Senate to conform with rulings of federal courts, more generous support for the University of Wyoming and other institutions, greater use of the regional cooperation programs of the Western Interstate Commission for Higher Education, stricter qualifications for establishment of community colleges, greater free-port privileges, a fair employment practices act, elimination of the requirement that a natural parent appear at adoption hearings, repeal of laws prohibiting interracial marriages, higher retirement pay for state employees, more generous state and local support for public schools, uniform school district legislation and other changes in the school system, and a long-range tax structure study.

Among the recommendations that fell by the wayside were the initiative and referendum, reapportionment, stricter qualifications for the establishment of community colleges, and the tax study. Democrats tried to repeal the right-to-work law. They had no difficulty in the House, and for a time it appeared that they might succeed in the Senate after it became known that one Republican had been won over. The repeal bill, however, was brought up in the Senate on a day when one Democrat was absent, with the result that it lost by one vote.

In getting most of what he asked for, the moderate Republican governor did remarkably well, considering that many of the Republicans in the legislature were more conservative than he was, and that some of the Democratic legislators appeared eager to embarrass him. Ultimately the general fund appropriations totaled $52,213,210.83. To supply additional revenue needed, the legislature increased the sales tax from 2 to 2.5 per cent and extended the tax base to include lodging. Municipalities and counties were authorized to levy an additional 0.5 per cent by local option.

THE HATHAWAY YEARS

A young lawyer from Torrington, Stanley K. Hathaway, had the privilege and distinction of presiding over the state's affairs (1967–1975) during the period of its greatest economic growth up to that time. Hathaway had been state chairman of the Young Republicans, the Goldwater for President Committee, and the Republican party. He defeated Ernest Wilkerson, Casper lawyer, by 10,375 votes in the gubernatorial race in 1966.

Wilkerson's slogan was "Wyoming's Wealth for Wyoming's People." Like John J. McIntyre in 1950, Wilkerson campaigned mainly on the severance tax issue and found the oil industry too potent a foe. Wilkerson also stressed the need to invest state funds at higher rates of interest, an idea Ed Witzenburger would develop in the 1970's.

Stan Hathaway's political base in the statehouse was wider than Cliff Hansen's had been. The Republican party in 1966 rebounded from its setback of 1964, giving Hathaway 18–12 and 34–27 majorities in the two houses of the legislature. The reapportionment imposed by three federal judges resulted in the election of more freshmen than usual, yet in each house there remained quite a few veteran Republicans ready to assist Hathaway, who like Cliff Hansen had never served in the legislature. In particular, Dick Jones, Earl Christensen, Pete Madsen, and Howard Flitner in the Senate, and Ward Myers, Cliff Davis, and W. F. Craft in the House were old hands. Dick Jones, who had been chairman of the Ways and Means Committee since 1961, was president of the Senate in 1967, then chaired Ways and Means again until 1971, and then chaired the Appropriations Committee (the new name for Ways and Means) in 1971 and 1973.

Hathaway also had three experienced officers to work with on state boards—Thyra Thomson, secretary of state; Minnie Mitchell, treasurer; and Everett Copenhaver, auditor—and a capable newcomer, Harry Roberts, as superintendent of public instruction. All were Republicans, and so were most of the people in the state bureaucracy.

Thus the state was in the hands of a cautious, conservative crew. They maintained, as had Cliff Hansen, that the federal government had become too powerful and that it would be stopped only by making the state economy and government strong. Hathaway began his eight-year regime just as the ailing Wyoming economy began to recover, thanks to oil discoveries and the rising external demand for Wyoming trona, coal, uranium, oil, gas, and electric power.

Throughout his eight years in office, Hathaway had two main preoccupations, economic growth and government reorganization. He stressed both in his opening address to the legislature. Earlier governors had pushed for both, but never as purposefully and enthusiastically. In the economic sphere, Hathaway promised that the state government would "dedicate itself to creating a congenial environment for business growth." He urged larger appropriations for the Natural Resource Board and the Travel Commission, the "state's two principal promotional agencies, insofar as attracting business and tourists to Wyoming are concerned." He added that a private, nonprofit industrial development corporation would soon be formed. He recommended and obtained legislation enabling the corporation to accept federal Small Business Administration loans which would be passed on as venture capital to entrepreneurs. After the session Hathaway wrote personal letters inviting sixty executives of major corporations to a meeting at Little America in Cheyenne, where he got them to buy stock in the Wyoming Industrial Development Corporation. The corporation has been active ever since in promoting growth.

In the sphere of reorganization, Hathaway recommended that the Recreation Commission be created to combine the Land and Water Conservation Commission with the State Parks Department and Historical Sites agency, and that the Board of Equalization and Public Service Commission be separated. Both changes were made.

Although Governor Hathaway later received low marks from environmentalists, he included in his 1967 message the declaration "I can conceive of no greater legacy this Legislature could pass on to succeeding generations than the enactment of legislation designed to protect the quality of Wyoming's environment." Moreover, he promised that a bill relating to air pollution would be introduced, and one soon was, by Thomas Stroock (R.) of Casper. The Wyoming Air Quality Act created an Air Resources Council with responsibility "to protect the purity of the air resources . . . and to prevent, control and abate air pollution." Of significance also was the Governor's recommendation that water laws be modified "so as to recognize recreation as a beneficial use."

With full support from Hathaway, the legislature, in order to expedite economic expansion, momentarily forgot that private property is sacred and the Union Pacific untouchable, and gave chemical companies which were mining trona in Sweetwater County eminent domain rights against the Union Pacific. This allowed them to dig tunnels through U.P. "checkerboard" section corners in order to connect their own leased sections so they did not have to sink a shaft in every section they owned.

Efforts by the Democrats to repeal right-to-work legislation and to impose a 3 per cent severance tax on oil and gas were easily turned back. Republican attempts to subdistrict so as to have one-member legislative districts were thwarted by Democratic filibusters in both houses. Democrats detected gerrymandering in the bill.

To promote tourism, Hathaway signed a local-option parimutuel wagering bill like one Jack Gage had vetoed. Although budget requests were cut severely, the general fund appropriations bill reached a new high, $64,437,058,12. For revenue the state sales tax was raised from 2.5 to 3 per cent and its coverage was extended to include services.

After adjournment, Hathaway said that the greatest achievement of the session was the submission of a constitutional amendment providing for initiative and referendum. This had been talked about off and on since 1910 and had been turned down most recently in the 1965 legislature. Giving the electorate such rights had been considered progressive in 1910, but in later years political scientists lost their enthusiasm for them, contending that the measures tended to be used too much or too little, depending on how many petitioners were required. In Wyoming requirements that petitions be signed by 15 per cent of the number of voters in the previous general election, and that petitioners be included from two-thirds of the counties proved to be too burdensome. In the nine years immediately following approval by the voters in 1968, only one initiative was attempted and it failed to get the necessary number of signers.

The state's conservative electorate liked the record of the 39th legislature (1967) and the evidences of economic recovery. After the 1968 election the Republicans controlled the House of Representatives 45–16, and the Senate 18–12. With such majorities and with Republicans covering other elements of state government like a blanket, the GOP dominated legislation in 1969 and during the next six years.

In 1969 the pressure for a severance tax became so great that one per cent had to be conceded. State government had to have more revenue, and the alternatives, higher sales tax or an income tax, were even more dangerous politically. Some observers suggested that Ernest Wilkerson's advocacy of severance taxation in 1966 had educated the public and made severance taxation possible. Neal R. Peirce in his book *The Mountain States of America* (1972) called the one per cent severance tax "a true watershed, a stinging rebuke for one of the most powerful lobbies every organized in any American state." A rudimentary open-cut mining reclamation act and a land-use act indicated concern for the environment.

Hathaway asked for and got a Department of Economic Planning and Development (DEPAD). Its four divisions dealt with four areas of development: water, industrial, mineral, and planning. The water development division would lend money for small water projects— sprinkler irrigation, reservoirs, and canal systems. The industrial division prepared community profiles of thirty-five communities, to be made available to industrial prospects. Also a planning coordinator and a Department of Health and Social Services were provided to centralize authority and eliminate duplication. Advising Hathaway was an eleven-man bipartisan, blue-ribbon committee he had appointed in December, 1967, to recommend ways in which state government could be improved. General fund appropriations in 1969 totaled $81,575,819.71.

Governor Hathaway believed in law and order. He used the phrase in his state-of-the-state message in 1967. In May, 1970, two days after four students were killed at Kent State University by National Guardsmen, one hundred or a few more students at the University of Wyoming, some of them university prepsters, demonstrated. Protesting against the U.S. invasion of Cambodia, as the Kent State students had been doing, the Wyoming students raised a peace flag above the United States flag on the flagpole on Prexy's Pasture at the center of the campus. When he learned of this "unpatriotic" act, Hathaway ordered all available highway patrolmen in southern Wyoming, and the city and campus police in Laramie to remove the peace flag from the flagpole. Well armed, they marched to Prexy's Pasture and found the students unarmed and packed six deep around the flagpole. The National Guard stood by in the armory, a mile away, under orders from the Governor. Colonel Theron F. Stimson of the Laramie National Guard telephoned the Governor, urged him to "cool it," and prevailed. After an all-night vigil, the students, patrolmen, and police drifted away, permitting Colonel Stimson to remove the offensive peace flag without further incident.

The electorate later in 1970 gave Hathaway a strong vote of confidence for his enthusiasm for growth, his conservative fiscal policy, and his avoidance of violence at the University of Wyoming. They reelected him. John J. Rooney, Cheyenne attorney, gave him only weak opposition, losing by more than 30,000 votes. Again the Republicans won the other four elective state offices, Thyra Thomson winning her third term as secretary of state with a majority of more than 35,000. Everett Copenhaver was elected auditor, Jim Griffith, treasurer, and Robert G. Schrader, superintendent of public instruction, all with about 17,000-vote majorities. The 41st legislature (1971) was Republican (19–11 and 40–20), with one Independent.

The Republican team approved a Legislative Service Office (LSO), a Department of Administration and Fiscal Control (DAFC), a revised criminal code, a new state office building, and the submission of six constitutional amendments, one of which would establish annual sessions of the legislature, and another, a new system (called the Missouri system) for selecting district and supreme court judges. The LSO and the annual sessions of the legislature may be traced in part to a national study published in 1970 which rated Wyoming's legislature forty-ninth among fifty. The Wyoming legislature was marked down mainly because it had no service office and met only every other year, and for only forty days. General fund appropriations totaled $99,013,399.15.

As usual, there were objections to Republican reapportionment after the decennial census. A three-judge panel, however, in June, 1971, held constitutional the legislature's reapportionment act, which increased the number of representatives from 61 to 62 and left the number of senators at 30. Albany, Campbell, and Natrona counties each gained a representative; Sheridan and Washakie each lost one. Later the 41st Legislature also met in special session, July 8–9, 1971, to ratify the 26th Amendment (eighteen-year-old vote) to the U.S. Constitution.

After another favorable election in 1972, the Republicans controlled the Senate in 1973, 17–13, and the House, 44–18. Hathaway's fourth legislature (the 42nd) met in 1973 for forty days as in the past, and twenty days in 1974 for budget purposes. The regular 1973 session was noteworthy for creating a Department of Environmental Quality, with authority to regulate air and water quality and mined-land reclamation; authorizing a land-use commission; ratifying the federal Equal Rights Amendment; raising the govenor's salary from $25,000 to $37,500 (not effective until after the 1974 election); authorizing construction of a new $800,000 governor's mansion to replace the old one, built in 1904; creating a nine-member higher education council to study and make recommendations concerning the university and seven community colleges; adopting a Surface Mining Act, tougher than the one of 1969; and submitting a constitutional amendment which would make a state income tax virtually impossible. The amendment, approved by the electorate in 1974, stated that "no tax shall be imposed upon income without allowing full credit against such tax liability for all sales, use, and ad valorem taxes paid in the taxable year by the same taxpayer to any taxing authority in Wyoming." General fund appropriations by the regular 1973 legislative session totaled $154,172,463.92.

The twenty-day budget session of 1974 increased the minerals severance tax from 1 to 3 per cent, approved a coal slurry pipeline from Campbell County to Arkansas, increased state aid to public schools substantially, adopted a new election code, amended earlier water quality provisions, and supplemented appropriations of the 1973 session, which had budgeted for two years. Not many bills were introduced because the 1972 constitutional amendment providing for annual sessions stipulated that nonbudget bills in the short sessions required a two-thirds vote for introduction.

In 1973 and 1974 one product of Hathaway's reorganization program, the Department of Administration and Fiscal Control (DAFC), drew much criticism. Many said it was merely another layer of bureaucracy.

State employees and Cheyenne businessmen did most of the complaining. It had been designed in 1971 to consolidate various housekeeping activities of the executive department. It included divisions of budget, purchasing and property control, personnel, centralized accounting and computer services, central services, statistics and research, and (added later) motor vehicle management. In particular, central purchasing and central mailing drew fire from department heads who thought the old, decentralized system was more convenient and efficient. DAFC director Leo Galeotos conceded that the staff and budget had grown rapidly, but so had state government in general.

After Hathaway announced in December, 1973, that he would not seek a third term, three Democrats and five Republicans, one of whom withdrew before the primary, lined up to compete for the vacancy. Most of them found fault with DAFC when that subject came up in the campaign. On the sideline, Hathaway defended what was recognized as the major item in his reorganization program. He said he was proud of the fiscal control and central purchasing achieved by DAFC. Former purchasing policies had been ridiculous, he added. Thus Hathaway ended his eight years in state government as he had begun, staunchly supporting government reorganization. Dedicated to growth, he had taken the reins when the state for several years had been losing population. Almost at once a turnaround occurred; when he departed, the population had grown by perhaps 50,000, and the economy hummed as never before.

While some critics did not like DAFC, and others thought growth had been overemphasized at the expense of the environment, most people gave Hathaway high marks for his over-all performance. The first governor to serve more than six years, he left the statehouse a tremendously popular man. Taking his place was Ed Herschler, Democratic lawyer-rancher from Kemmerer, a World War II Marine sergeant with a Purple Heart and Silver Star. Herschler had defeated State Senator Dick Jones of Cody by more than 15,000 votes. Jones was too conservative for many members of his own party, and had made quite a few enemies during his twelve years as chairman of the Ways and Means and Appropriations committees.

President Gerald Ford nominated Stan Hathaway for the post of Secretary of the Interior April 4, 1975. Many of the state's leaders in both political parties, including Governor Ed Herschler and Senator Gale McGee, endorsed the nomination. Senators McGee and Hansen worked very hard to win Senate confirmation against spirited opposition from environmentalists who testified in the hearings that Hathaway had been too much preoccupied with industrial growth and could not be trusted to give sufficient thought to the environment. Spearheading the Senate attack were Floyd K. Haskell of Colorado, James Abourezk of South Dakota, Richard Stone of Florida, and John Glenn of Ohio. Bart Koehler of the Wyoming Outdoor Council appeared prominently among the critics. Confirmation came by a vote of 60–36 after extended hearings.

Secretary Hathaway soon learned that he would not be allowed to pick his own undersecretary and that many key positions in the Interior Department were occupied by environmentalists who would make it very difficult for him to achieve his energy development goals. After a few frustrating weeks in Washington's bake-oven summer heat, Secretary Hathaway was hospitalized for what was reported to be exhaustion, depression, and a mild case of diabetes. From his hospital bed he sent his resignation to President Ford; he had been secretary of the interior from June 12 to July 25, 1975. Hathaway soon returned to Cheyenne, where he received a hero's welcome before opening a law office specializing in energy development matters.

GOVERNOR ED HERSCHLER

After twelve years of Republican rule, divided control of state government returned. The Democratic Governor Ed Herschler had to share the responsibilities of major state boards with four Republicans: Thyra Thomson, secretary of state; Ed Witzenburger, treasurer; Jim Griffith, auditor; and Robert Schrader, superintendent of public instruction. In the legislature the Senate was divided 15–15, and the House of Representatives had 32 Republicans, 29 Democrats, and 1 Independent.

Herschler had campaigned on a "quality of life" platform, the main planks of which were a strong plant-siting bill, a strengthened Department of Environmental Quality, more assistance to impacted communities (boom towns), effective taxation of energy industries, stronger human services programs, state development of water resources, repeal of the right-to-work law, increased support for education at all levels, a community-oriented medical school, and an increase in the severance tax on trona, coal, oil, and natural gas from 3 to 6 per cent.

Among the more important bills enacted were ones providing for land-use planning, plant siting, water resources development, pay raises for state employees, and a 1 per cent increase in the severance tax on oil and gas, bringing it up to 4 per cent. The Land Use Planning Act required that local governments hold hearings and prepare and adopt land-use plans before December 21, 1977. The amount of state sales tax going to local governments was increased from one-sixth to one-third. Small sales tax rebates were authorized for needy senior citizens and handicapped persons. Funds were provided for planning and preliminary development of a medical school at the University of Wyoming and a residency program at Casper. Appropriations from the general fund in 1975 totaled $224,485,548.00. At the end of the session, veteran senator Pete Madsen (R.) of Sheridan observed that it was the most liberal legislature that he could remember in his eighteen years. "There is less representation from agriculture and more of the urban philosophy," he explained.

The hubbub over DAFC decreased after Leo Galeotos resigned and Governor Herschler appointed Kirk Coulter, Gillette contractor, to replace him as director. Coulter said that he had no further expansion in mind. However, the Jacobs study, which led to a reclassification of state employees, sparked a new flare-up of criticism for DAFC in 1976, while old complaints about the car pool, mail service, duplicating services, and purchasing persisted. DAFC had 380 employees and received almost $35 million for its operations in the 1975–1977 biennium.

The legislature met for twenty days in 1976 and developed a general fund budget bill for the 1976–1978 biennium. This involved taking over about one-half of the 1975–1977 budget and adding money for the 1977–1978 fiscal year. During the 1976 session, football fans lobbied unsuccessfully for additions to the University of Wyoming stadium and a plastic dome to cover it. The legislature refused to give Governor Herschler the additional severance taxes he needed to carry out his programs. It pared his budget requests for travel, technical assistance for land-use planning, and the Department of Environmental Quality. Also it limited executive prerogatives by adding footnotes to the appropriations bill, and started a drive to require the governor to submit all rules and regulations to the legislature's management council for review. Disgusted with the treatment he had received, Herschler in his final remarks to the two houses said that "some legislators seemed to forget they were here to serve the people of Wyoming and not the special interests which were so well represented in the lobbies."

In the November, 1976, elections the Republicans picked up three

Senate seats while leaving the distribution of House seats unchanged. Consequently Governor Herschler found himself in 1977 in the typical plight of Democratic governors in Wyoming, with both houses of the legislature controlled by Republicans, 18–12 in the Senate and 32–29–1 in the House. All the committees were controlled by Republicans and the two majority floor leaders were from the oil industry. Herschler maintained a low profile, working behind the scenes, and relying on friendships in both parties dating from his ten years in the legislature.

Governor Herschler gave top priority to a measure designed to fund a $250 million account for capital facilities construction. Realizing that there was no way to get Senate approval for any increase in the severance tax on oil and gas, he based his facilities bill on a 1.5 per cent increase in the severance tax on coal, trona, and uranium. It was a hard fight but he won. The first facilities authorized, to be paid for by a bond issue made possible by the fund, included a new penitentiary at Rawlins to replace the old one, several remodeling projects in Cheyenne, purchase of a warehouse in Cheyenne, several remodeling projects at the university, and some new construction there.

An additional 2 per cent severance tax on uranium and trona, and 3 per cent on coal, left total severance taxation on major minerals at the end of the session as follows: 10.1 per cent on coal, 5.5 per cent on uranium and trona, and 4.0 per cent on oil and gas.

An act of Congress in 1976 had increased the state's share of mineral royalties collected by the federal government from 37.5 to 50 per cent, making it necessary for the legislature to decide on a formula for distributing the 12.5 per cent increase, which amounted to about $12 million per year, at the 1976 rate of production. After considerable wrangling, 30 per cent was assigned to cities and towns, 30 per cent to the State Farm Loan Board for distribution to impacted communities; 24 per cent to a new highway fund for six years and thereafter to a special account to be administered by the legislature; and 16 per cent to school construction.

Governor Herschler obtained authority to reorganize the Health and Social Services Department. The legislature gave needy senior citizens larger tax rebates and sweetened the retirement benefits for state employees not yet retired. Because the State of Nebraska would no longer house Wyoming's female prisoners, the legislature authorized remodeling Sheridan Hall at the State Hospital in Evanston for use as a temporary women's prison.

The Wyoming Outdoor Council rated the session a poor one in

comparison with the one of 1975 in environmental and social legislation, although it praised improvements in the Plant Siting Act. A
scenic easements bill, amendments to county planning statutes, and a
coal export bill were lost, and the Land Use Planning Act narrowly
missed repeal. Only a strong effort by the Governor saved the eleven
new positions requested by the Department of Environmental Quality
(DEQ). The DEQ declared that all of the eleven positions were needed
because the federal government would be monitoring the state's enforcement of strip mining reclamation. Secretary of the Interior Thomas
Kleppe had agreed in December, 1976, to permit Wyoming to enforce
its mined-land-reclamation law on federal as well as state and private
land as long as Wyoming law was stricter than federal law.

Falling by the wayside were bills providing for legislative income
disclosure, prohibition of smoking in public places, a uniform probate
code, no-fault insurance, consumer protection, public employees' and
teachers' negotiations, and regulation and control of natural gas. The
Governor wanted a sunset law, which died on general file in the Senate
after passage in the House.

FEDERAL RELATIONS AND REGIONALISM

In the American federal system, power is divided between the central
government and state governments. Certain powers are delegated by
the U.S. Constitution to the central government, others are reserved
to the states, and some are shared. The U.S. Supreme Court is the
arbiter when the locus of power is in dispute. If a Supreme Court decision is objectionable to enough people, they may try to amend the
Constitution. Since this is difficult, Wyoming has lost most of its
arguments with the federal government.

Federal expenditures in Wyoming have always been of great importance. Some of these expenditures require the supervision of the
governor. This has been a heavy burden, in recent years, to a very busy
man. Governor Herschler said in 1976 that he needed to be three
persons—state executive officer, federal administrator, and participant
in a multitude of ceremonies. The federal dollars also made necessary
large appropriations for subordinate administrative personnel, causing
the state budget to expand alarmingly. However, as explained in
Chapter 17, Wyoming's spectacular economic growth in the 1970's
could very well reverse the balance of payments between state and

federal governments and reduce the federal presence in the state, relatively if not absolutely.

Another factor that could modify federal relations is the trend toward regional organization, a development which has been encouraged from Washington. If Rocky Mountain or western states, or a coalition of southern states with conservative states in the West, could agree, they might influence legislative and executive decisions in Washington. Such prospects were not very bright in the 1970's. The Federation of Rocky Mountain States, organized in 1966, disbanded in 1977. A majority of western governors wanted to sever connections with the national Council of State Governors and form a western policy office to coordinate planning on energy, natural resources, human services, and water. However, the governors of California, Idaho, Nevada, Oregon, and Washington turned down the idea in September, 1977.

THE CONGRESSIONAL DELEGATION

Most of Wyoming's U.S. senators since World War II were one-termers. Only three—Joseph C. O'Mahoney, Gale W. McGee, and Clifford P. Hansen—served longer than six years. O'Mahoney served twenty-five, McGee eighteen, and Hansen twelve.

O'Mahoney, who had been appointed to fill a vacancy in 1933, was elected in 1934 and re-elected in 1940 and 1946. His advertisements in the 1946 campaign stressed his work in promoting agriculture, oil development, individual rights, full employment, and the rights of labor. John Gunther in his book *Inside U.S.A.* wrote that "O'Mahoney, by any count, is one of the two or three ablest men in Washington, and by all odds the first figure of the state." The *Denver Post* called him "a powerful and relentless opponent of too much centralization of government at Washington." His Republican opponent in 1946, Harry B. Henderson, Cheyenne attorney, concentrated on attacking him for being a "New Dealer." O'Mahoney won by 10,000 votes.

Six years later O'Mahoney had become too much of a statesman for many voters who wanted their senators to think of state problems rather than national. It was said that he had become "too big for Wyoming." He had not come home often enough. His opponent in 1952 was Frank A. Barrett, Lusk lawyer, who had spent four terms in the U.S. House of Representatives, and was at the midpoint of a four-year term as governor. With reference to the Korean War, Republican advertisements promised "Barrett can restore peace with prosperity," and added that "Barrett will drive the Communists from government service, . . . eliminate waste and extravagance . . . will devote all of his time to Wyoming."

Frustration over the stalemate in Korea hurt O'Mahoney. The Wisconsin demagogue Senator Joseph McCarthy campaigned for Barrett, who introduced him with the statement "I have come to love and respect Joe McCarthy." [4] The soft-on-Communism charge, which was often used against Democrats in the 1940's and 1950's, was not applied directly to O'Mahoney because his attitude with respect to security risks in government had become very conservative in the 1950's. Although *Time* magazine called O'Mahoney one of the best men in the Senate, he went down to defeat by a margin of 4,255 votes. Dwight D. Eisenhower's coattails may have helped Barrett, since Eisenhowever vanquished Adlai Stevenson in Wyoming by no less than 33,113 votes.

O'Mahoney got an opportunity to return to the Senate two years later when his colleague in the Senate, Lester C. Hunt, committed suicide. After serving six years as governor, Hunt had been elected to the Senate in 1948, defeating the incumbent, right-wing Republican E. V. Robertson. Hunt had described himself as "a liberal and a progressive but not a radical." He gave strong support in the Senate to public housing, an enlarged health program, and federal aid to education. On June 19, 1954, overwhelmed by personal and political problems, he carried a rifle under his coat to his Senate office and shot himself to death. [5]

Democrats drafted O'Mahoney, who had been practicing law in Washington since his defeat in 1952, to represent the party in the 1954 election. He won by 3,438 votes over Congressman William Henry Harrison. During the campaign O'Mahoney was labeled a foreign agent because as a Washington attorney he had accepted a retainer from the U.S. Sugar Council, which was composed of U.S. citizens with investments in Cuba. Speaking in Cheyenne, U.S. Senator Richard Nixon said that the Democrats were "ignorant and blind" to the Com-

---

[4] Barrett remained loyal to McCarthy to the end, being one of the minority when the U.S. Senate in December, 1954, voted 67–22 to condemn McCarthy for repeatedly abusing an elections subcommittee, calling the Senate censure committee an "unwitting handmaiden" of the Communist party and charging McCarthy with engaging in conduct "unbecoming a member of the United States Senate."

[5] Acting Governor "Doc" Rogers appointed E. D. "Ted" Crippa (R.), Rock Springs automobile dealer, to fill out the remaining months of Hunt's term.

munist inroads made on American government. O'Mahoney's victory gave the Democrats control of the Senate by a majority of one. O'Mahoney chose not to run again in 1960, having reached the age of seventy-five.

SENATOR GALE W. McGEE (1959–1977)

Gale McGee (D.) was the most gifted public speaker and debater the state had ever had, its greatest expert on foreign relations, and the man who had channeled more federal appropriations to Wyoming than anyone else had ever done. Yet, after eighteen years in the Senate, and still in his prime at age sixty-one, he was defeated by Malcolm Wallop, forty-three-year-old Sheridan County cattleman and meat packer, by a margin of 14,252 votes. Ninety per cent of the "experts" had expected a McGee victory. What happened?

In retrospect McGee had done very well to hold his coalition of Democrats, Republicans, and Independents together for eighteen years in such a conservative Republican state. Probably there was no way in which he could have won in 1976 unless the Republicans had opposed him with a weaker adversary than Wallop.

Like O'Mahoney in 1952, McGee in 1976 had become "too big for Wyoming." He had aspired to statesmanship, had published a book on American foreign policy, and was in great demand as a speaker in university audiences outside of Wyoming. On the day after the election, Carl Bechtold, editor of the *Green River Star*, reflected that until the recent revolutionary changes in Wyoming "we didn't have as many giant problems as other states. We could afford to donate one Senator for national and foreign affairs. . . . Yesterday's vote showed that Wyoming citizens turned down 'clout' of experience and seniority for a hope of having another Senator dedicated only to Wyoming."

Yet Wyoming is part of the United States, and American foreign policy is important. Had every voter in Wyoming read McGee's book, *Responsibilities of World Power*, before the election, McGee might have won. Yet defeat did not mean that his superior talents would be wasted. With Wallop taking over the errand-boy chores for Wyoming's special interests at home, McGee could concentrate on what he knew best. In January, 1977, President Jimmy Carter named him ambassador to the Organization of American States, and he was confirmed without opposition.

McGee, who was a protégé of O'Mahoney, forgot in his 1976 campaign that O'Mahoney had dissociated himself as much as possible from the federal government, and had regularly deplored the centralization of power in Washington. McGee tried to defend the federal government but could not do so convincingly in Wyoming, where people had long been dependent on the federal government but had developed a love-hate relationship with it. The wave of anti-government sentiment was overwhelming in 1976.

McGee was blamed for inflation, federal deficits, not being tough enough in Panama Canal treaty negotiations, high postal rates, poor postal service, burdensome safety and health regulations, favoring national health insurance, promoting postcard voter registration, not appropriating enough for national defense, and not returning to Wyoming more often. Full-page advertisements in many newspapers, paid for by the National Taxpayers Union, described him as "the bureaucrat's best friend." He had "consistently taken the lead in advocating higher pay, greater benefits, more generous retirement for government employees." The National Taxpayers Union added: "We don't know anything about McGee's opponent. But he could hardly be worse than McGee." Other full-page ads, paid for by the National Right-to-Work Committee, attacked efforts by labor and McGee to repeal the state's right-to-work law and remove federal restrictions on labor union organizers.

McGee might have done better than he did, had he more thoroughly researched voter opinions about issues and about himself before planning his campaign. He chose to take the high road, stand on his own record, and ignore Wallop. An aggressive attack on his opponent might have closed the vote spread somewhat. Wallop had covered the state in his unsuccessful primary bid for the governorship in 1974 and did so again in 1976. In order to double his coverage, his wife, Judy, campaigned separately. Gale and Loraine McGee had not canvassed many of the byways since 1970, felt obligated to spend precious time in Washington while the Senate was in session in 1976, and by campaigning together were unable to come close to the number of personal contacts the Wallops made. Many young voters and people who had come to Wyoming since 1970 had no opportunity to meet the McGees.

The veteran Senator placed great emphasis on his experience and seniority, on what he had done for Wyoming, and what he could do in the future because of his "clout." This fell flat because many voters accepted editor Jim Flinchum's assessment in the *Wyoming State Tribune* (Cheyenne): "The public is beginning to understand that the more boodle a congressman or senator brings back to his state or district from Washington in the long run means just more government spending and more money out of his constituents' own pockets."

Wyoming's prosperous citizens, which included not a few non-union blue-collar workers, were enjoying the benefits of full employment and thought that McGee's seniority, combined with his readiness to approve appropriations for social programs in less favored parts of the country, threatened their status. They thought that Gerald Ford would win the presidency and would need Wallop to sustain his vetoes. To their surprise, Carter won, although he lost Wyoming by more than twice as many votes as McGee did. Thus Ford's coattails were of some help to Wallop.

McGee had always supported the Equal Rights Amendment. Wallop had voted against its ratification in the Wyoming Senate in 1973. Differences here did not affect the U.S. Senate race because relatively few Wyoming voters were deeply concerned about that issue in 1976.

The tradition that it was to the state's advantage to have one Democratic and one Republican senator was generally discounted in 1976. The fact that McGee and Hansen had worked together very effectively in advancing Wyoming's special interests won very few votes for McGee.

Environmentalists tended to favor Wallop because he had campaigned as a "quality of life" candidate in his unsuccessful 1974 gubernatorial contest. They paid little attention to the water and air pollution caused by Wallop's meat-packing plant at Ranchester. They gave McGee little credit for his pioneer work in the environmental movement in the 1960's—his opposition to clear cutting, support of the Wilderness Act of 1964, support of the nuclear test ban treaty, and early support of federal strip-mining legislation. They considered McGee to be too favorable to the oil industry. He was a supporter of that industry, as Wallop would be.

Although McGee was a sportsman who loved to hunt and fish, he had voted in 1968 in favor of an amendment which would have given states power to require registration of hand guns. He did this because he thought, mistakenly, that this was the only way to avoid federal registration of guns. Many gun owners never forgave him for his vote in 1968, although the National Rifle Association in 1976 gave him a "defender of individual rights" award for his support of N.R.A. policies since 1968.

Neither candidate lacked funds. Wallop set a new record for Wyoming Senate elections, spending $326,688.69, almost four dollars for each vote he received, not counting other expenditures by the National Taxpayers Union, National Right-to-Work Committee, and other conservative organizations and individuals. McGee spent $169,521.36.[6]

A few thousand Democrats who had deserted McGee in 1970 because he supported President Nixon's Vietnam policy were still estranged in 1976. Meanwhile, Republican state chairman Tom Stroock, Casper oil man, did a remarkable job in unifying his party, considering that it had been hurt by Watergate and had some obvious divisions. He persuaded the divided leaders to conceal their differences and concentrate on the task of downing the Democrats. He papered over a wide gap between the Ronald Reagan and Gerald Ford factions, and induced Stan Hathaway's friends to forgive Wallop for withholding his support of Hathaway's Interior appointment until the Senate hearings, at a time when many Democrats as well as most Republicans were demanding confirmation long before the hearings.

Stroock assured his state central committee in April, 1976, that "there isn't an item of philosophy that Malcolm isn't a staunch, conservative Republican rancher on." With clairvoyance he promised, "You're going to be surprised at the votes he's going to pull out of the woodwork all over the state." Later, after checking Wallop's votes, columnist Lee Catterall reported May 5, 1977: "Wyoming's Republicans who worried about sending a maverick environmentalist to the senate can rest easy. . . . Wallop is voting like the conservative Republican he is." And in late October, 1977, United Press International reported that "Wyoming has the most conservative one-two punch in the U.S. Senate." The conservative Committee for the Survival of a Free Congress, on the basis of 249 Senate votes taken from January to August, 1977, had rated Hansen 91 and Wallop 82. No other state had such a conservative pair of senators.

SENATOR CLIFF HANSEN (1967–1979)

Clifford P. Hansen, called Cliff by his host of friends in Wyoming, had been the only cattleman in the Senate. With the arrival of another

[6] Data taken from January 31, 1977, year-end reports filed in the Wyoming Secretary of State's Office by the McGee for Senate Committee and the Wallop Senate Drive. Receipts exceeded expenditures for both candidates, Wallop's by $3,566, McGee's by $18,017. McGee also had 1975 receipts which brought his excess of receipts over expenditures for two years to $120,464. It should be noted, too, that Wallop received more help from his state central committee. The Republican committee spent $226,017.98, the Democratic committee, $50,232.77.

cattleman (Wallop), Hansen decided to retire. He surprised the Wyoming Stock Growers in their June, 1977, convention by announcing that he would not seek a third term in 1978. Few observers doubted that his re-election was almost a certainty.

After a term as governor, 1963–1967, Hansen had gone to the Senate in place of Milward Simpson, who had chosen to retire. Hansen defeated Congressman Teno Roncalio by a 4,407-vote margin in 1966, and won a second term by more than 60,000 (101,314–40,753) votes in 1972, trouncing Mike Vinich of Hudson. No doubt Cliff had the right mind-set for the majority of Wyoming voters in 1972. He had entertained some liberal thoughts while governor but outgrew them in the U.S. Senate.

Hansen and McGee worked both sides of the aisle to keep federal funds flowing to Wyoming. With Teno Roncalio's cooperation in the House they upped the state's share of federal mineral royalties from 37.5 to 50 per cent, which meant twelve million dollars more per year at the 1976 rate of production. They also won Senate confirmation of Interior Secretary appointee Stan Hathaway.

On the other hand, Hansen and McGee often canceled each other's votes on national issues, especially so-called "people" legislation. For example, on the basis of their votes in 1974, the National Council of Senior Citizens rated McGee 82, Hansen, 0; the Friends Committee for National Legislation rated McGee 60, Hansen, 0; the Women's Lobby, Inc., rated McGee 60, Hansen, 0; the Consumers Federation of America rated McGee 50, Hansen, 5; and the League of Women Voters rated McGee 75, Hansen, 20.

Conservative, business-oriented organizations reversed the ratings. For example, on the basis of their votes in 1974, the U.S. Chamber of Commerce rated Hansen 95, McGee, 16; the American Farm Bureau Federation rated Hansen 100, McGee, 20; the Americans for Constitutional Action rated Hansen 98, McGee, 18; and the American Conservative Union rated Hansen 91, McGee 11.

The American Security Council rated Hansen 100 and McGee 86. Both were willing to spend money for military hardware, Hansen especially. In political terms Hansen was farther right of center than McGee was left of center. Indeed, some liberals who had supported McGee enthusiastically in 1958 deserted him later for getting right-of-center ratings from the Americans for Democratic Action.

Cliff Hansen appeared to work harder than ever in the fall of 1977, advancing the interests of his constituents. He received major credit for strengthening surface owners' rights in strip-mining areas. It was evident that his eleven years of experience had given him the knowledge and seniority needed to get things done in the Senate.

Cliff Hansen was sixty-four when he announced his intention to retire. As Roy Peck wrote in the *Riverton Ranger*, he had "given enough of himself to public service." Others had long wondered why anyone who owned a ranch in Jackson Hole would exile himself and his wife to Washington, D.C. for twelve long years.

THE REPRESENTATIVES

Except for Frank W. Mondell, who spent twenty-six years in the U.S. House of Representatives (1895–1897 and 1899–1923), Wyoming politicians have not stayed in the House long enough to receive much national recognition. They get lost among the other 434 members. They no sooner arrive on Capitol Hill than they begin planning to become senators. They do not like having to campaign every two years, nor do they like the fact that they must work harder than senators to garner campaign contributions.

In the four decades after World War II, William Henry Harrison (R.) and Teno Roncalio (D.) each served ten years (five terms). Harrison, a Sheridan lawyer, occupied the office during two four-year stints and one isolated term. His first stint (1951–1955) terminated when he chose to run for the Senate against O'Mahoney. His second stint (1961–1965) ended when Teno Roncalio first ran for office and took the House seat from him. His third stint (1967–1969) began when he defeated twenty-six-year-old Al Christian of Rock Springs and ended when John Wold, Casper geologist, ousted him in the 1968 Republican primary. Against Wold, Harrison who was seventy-two, stressed his seniority and experience, but to no avail.

The other five-term Representative, Teno Roncalio, served during the years 1965–1967 and 1971–1979. His first term ended when he tried to enter the Senate and could not quite make it against Cliff Hansen. Four years later he upset incumbent John Wold. He had little trouble getting re-elected in 1972, 1974, and 1976.

Teno Roncalio, who was almost universally known simply as Teno, was the son of a Rock Springs coal miner. After undergraduate study and a term as student-body president at the University of Wyoming, he earned a Silver Star as a combat infantry officer in World War II.

He then studied law at the University of Wyoming, passed the bar at age thirty-one, and quickly accumulated a competence amounting to "more than $500,000" in law and banking in Cheyenne.

In Congress, Teno was a dove with respect to the Vietnam War. Otherwise, his political philosophy was similar to that of Senator McGee. Eleven liberal organizations in 1975 gave Teno an average rating of 78, compared to 61 for McGee. Eight conservative organizations liked neither very well, their average rating being 32 for Teno and 24 for McGee. Teno was a tireless, dynamic campaigner, who won the affection of voters of all ages.

In 1976 well-known Republicans thought so little of their own chances against Teno that they stepped aside for an unknown candidate, Larry Hart. He was a naval officer, aged thirty, whom few voters had ever heard of outside of Powell, where he had attended high school before accepting an appointment to Annapolis. He was released in June, 1976, from naval duty at Northwestern University, where he had been teaching in the ROTC program.

One of Hart's typical advertisements proclaimed,

YOU GOTTA HAVE HART!

1. To reduce the role of federal government in our economy and private lives.
2. To maintain a strong national defense, trimming out waste.
3. To reduce government spending in order to ease the burden of inflation.
4. To restore credibility of Congressional leadership.

Hart may have picked up a few votes by promising to take a cut in pay if elected (Teno was being criticized for favoring federal pay raises). The Keep Teno in Congress Committee reported receipts of $87,675.43 and expenditures of $89,833.41. The Hart Committee reported receipts of $29,675.32 and expenditures of the same amount. Teno buzzed across the great open spaces at the controls of his own plane, Larry Hart, at the wheel of his highway travel trailer. Teno got there first, with a majority of 19,700 votes.

In the summer of 1977 politically conscious Wyomingites were speculating whether Teno would seek another term in the House or try for the Senate seat made available by Cliff Hansen's retirement. In September, 1977, Teno, who was sixty-one, announced that he planned to retire from politics at the expiration of his term in January, 1979. For a Wyoming senator and a Wyoming congressman to retire at the same time was unprecedented. Congressmen had sometimes given up their seats to try for a place in the Senate, and O'Mahoney and Simpson had retired, but it was the usual practice to hang on until defeat. The two vacancies in Washington justified the prediction that the primary election in September, 1978, would be more interesting than usual.

CHAPTER 19

Postwar Society and Culture

WYOMING RESIDENTS have often proclaimed that they are different. A Lost Cabin sheepman, P. H. Shallenberger, for example, told the Wyoming Wool Growers in 1927 that Wyoming with its "open ranges and outdoor life can never have the same ideas or ideals as those of states . . . where the entire population has been lambed in sheds." Struthers Burt wrote in *Powder River* (1938) that "Wyoming is more of a secret society than a state, where everyone knows everyone else, at least by reputation, and there is a special handshake and an implicit acknowledgment." Agnes Wright Spring, at about the same time, wrote in the W.P.A. Writers' Project book *Wyoming* that "Wyoming for many years resembled a huge family; everyone of importance seemed to be

581

personally known through the State." The Cheyenne newspapers, she added, carried statewide personal columns.

Later, two well-qualified visiting observers pointed to other distinctions. John Gunther in his book *Inside U.S.A.* (1947) described Wyoming as the friendliest and most unspoiled state he had ever visited. Its people were open and unsophisticated, and almost everyone had a nickname, he asserted. Another visitor, Neil Morgan, in *Westward Tilt* (1963) reported much the same. He found the people friendly, leisurely, and remote. He contrasted Wyoming with the faster-growing states to the south and west, and concluded that "except for Alaska, there is no American state on which the passage of time and man has left so small an imprint as Wyoming."

Gunther and Pearce did not explain what made Wyoming people so friendly. Were they friendly because two big-city reporters had come to write what they hoped would be favorable comments about the state? Or were they merely repeating what everyone knows, that small-town folks, unlike people in crowded cities, will recognize one another, speak, and even use nicknames? Struthers Burt did not describe the "special handshake" nor tell how many people outside of Jackson Hole used it. Mrs. Spring did not say how many people were not important enough to belong to the "huge family."

Thousands of acquaintances scattered all over the state used nicknames or given names in referring to a few prominent people. Dutch, Ev, and Tracy were sufficient greeting or identification for the very successful basketball coaches Willard Witte and Everett Shelton and the eminent publisher Tracy McCraken.[1] Also, there was Ralph McWhinnie who during his forty-five years in the University of Wyoming Admissions Office (1918–1963) reputedly could recognize and call by name everyone who had ever registered during those years, as well as all Masons, Rotarians, Episcopalians, and stray Sigma

---

[1] Before his death in 1960 at the age of sixty-six, publisher Tracy S. McCraken of Cheyenne was a phenomenon in Wyoming journalism. For many years he controlled seven of the state's ten daily newspapers (all except two in Casper and one in Sheridan). He was Democratic national committeeman, 1942–1960, but did not use his press control for partisan purposes. In Cheyenne a Democratic editor ran the morning *Wyoming Eagle*, while a Republican editor ran the evening *Wyoming State Tribune*. The same policy was applied in Laramie. When the two Laramie papers were combined, the successor paper was declared to be "unpolitical." Similarly, McCraken's single papers in Rawlins, Rock Springs, and Worland were not partisan. McCraken was a conservative Democrat who exerted his considerable political influence behind the scenes. *Time* magazine in 1954 described him as "Wyoming's Mr. Big." His son Robert managed the newspaper chain after 1960.

Nu's from other states. In 1977 at age seventy-nine he still knew almost everyone.

Nonetheless, isolation, parochialism, and sectionalism obtained in prewar Wyoming. Great distances, long work days, prolonged winters, and poverty restricted intercommunication. Most people read no common newspaper, listened to no common radio station. Besides their local paper, they read, each according to his section, a Denver, Salt Lake City, Billings, or Rapid City paper. They knew more about their neighboring state than they knew about their own.

Hard times abetted competition for county seat designation and land offices, sharpened rivalry between communities, and set upstate people to scheming how they might move the College of Agriculture from Laramie or state government agencies from Cheyenne. But as they prospered after the war, citizens turned more to building their own communities from within without cannibalizing others.

In the 1950's better automobiles, a splendid network of asphalt roads, and enough wealth to make longer trips feasible enabled most of the people to become familiar with their state and its many interesting communities for the first time. Also, in the 1970's, for the first time, the state had a newspaper which was circulated all over the state on the morning it was published. Trucks radiated from centrally located Casper after midnight and delivered the *Casper Star-Tribune* in most cities and towns before breakfast. The paper featured investigative reporting, as well as full-state coverage by its many local correspondents. Phil McAuley, hard-driving managing editor, relished controversy, stepped on toes occasionally, and made his paper required reading for all who wanted to know what was going on in the state.

The *Star-Tribune*'s certified circulation in 1976 was 30,312, compared with 10,520 for its closest competitor, the *Wyoming State Tribune* (Cheyenne).

In 1977 there were nine dailies, twenty-six weeklies, and three semiweekly papers (Lander, Powell, and Torrington). Only Cheyenne had two dailies, both owned by the McCraken family. Six of the dailies called themselves Independent; one identified itself as Democratic, one as Republican, and one as Independent-Democratic.[2]

Three cities had television stations, Casper (KTWO), Cheyenne (KYCU), and Thermopolis (KWRB). In 1976, KTWO had a net

[2] The Casper, Laramie, Rawlins, Riverton, Sheridan, and Worland papers were Independent; the Cheyenne morning paper was Democratic, Cheyenne evening paper, Republican, and Rock Springs paper, Independent-Democratic.

weekly circulation of 72,000 homes; KYCU, 58,000, partly in Colorado
and Nebraska; and KWRB, 9,000.[3] Like the Casper newspaper, the
Casper TV station aggressively expressed opinions on controversial
issues. Jack Rosenthal, a Buffalo, Wyoming, native and graduate of the
University of Wyoming, was the principal developer of KTWO after
1964.[4] In addition to the three TV stations, the state had thirty-eight
radio stations. Casper's central location made it possible for its 50,000-
watt, clear-channel KTWO radio station to be heard almost from
border to border.

The changes wrought by television and radio in Wyoming life cannot
be measured precisely. Certainly the broadcast media delivered entertainment, news, and public affairs programs to tens of thousands of
homes where, before World War II, local weekly newspapers had been
the principal contacts with the outside world. No doubt the broadcast media made the people of Wyoming better informed than
ever before, and more like people in other parts of the nation and the
world.

SORTING OUT THE RESIDENTS BECOMES MORE COMPLEX

Wyoming and its people were harder to pigeonhole in postwar years
than before. Universal public education, mobility, the media, chain
stores and other forms of commercial enterprise, and federal aid in its
many forms had erased some of the differences which used to distinguish
Americans from state to state and city to city.

Frontier godlessness had become less obvious. As reported above
(pp. 221–225 and 446), Wyoming ranked low among the states in percentage of church memberships. Many men and quite a few women
quit going to church when they went west, partly because of the great
distances and the sparsity of population, and partly because they could
not find the denominations to which they had formerly belonged. More
choices were available in the 1970's, yet church attendance still lagged
behind that of the Middle West. In 1977, Wyoming had about 50,000
Roman Catholics, 30,000 Mormons, 3,000 Eastern Orthodox, a few

---

[3] The circulation figures come from a November, 1976, audience survey conducted
by the American Research Bureau, a division of Control Data.

[4] Jack Rosenthal resided in Casper but spent much of his time elsewhere, carrying
out his duties as president of the Broadcast Division of Harriscope Broadcasting
Corporation, Los Angeles. Rosenthal was responsible for all of the broadcast operations
of Harriscope, which owned six television stations—in Chicago, Albuquerque, Bakers-
field, Billings, Great Falls, and Casper.

hundred Jews, and 250,000 Protestants, many of whom did not attend church services regularly.

Ninety-eight per cent of the people in 1970 were white. The other 2 per cent included about 3,000 Arapaho Indians, 2,000 Shoshoni Indians, 2,500 blacks, 400 Japanese, 125 Chinese, and a few Koreans, Filipinos, and Vietnamese.[5] The foreign-born totaled 6,980. Illiteracy was rare, the level of education high. Except for the paucity of blacks, the Wyoming population was fairly representative of American people in general.

Forty-four per cent of the residents in 1970 were Wyoming natives. Most of the others had been born in the Middle West or in Colorado, Utah, or Montana. Most of the people were descendants of the "old" immigration which had come from the British Isles, Germany, and Scandinavia. Small waves of a "new" immigation had come from Austria, Greece, and Italy, most of them in the first decade of the twentieth century. These twentieth-century immigrants from south-eastern Europe were not numerous enough to take away northwestern Europe's dominance. About 1,200 Japanese and 1,400 Russian Germans also arrived after 1900.[6] Mexican Americans constituted the largest visible minority. They had come north from time to time to work for sugarbeet farmers or the Union Pacific Railroad. The 1970 census reported 13,894 persons of Spanish origin or descent (mostly Mexican Americans).[7]

Acculturation came quickly for the European immigrants who settled in Wyoming. The "old" immigrants were already quite well assimilated when the "new" immigrants arrived in small numbers in the 1890's, in greater numbers in the first decade of the twentieth century, and in small numbers again thereafter. Acculturation was somewhat slower for the "new" immigrants (Slavs, Greeks, Basques, Poles, Italians,

[5] The Indians were almost all on the Wind River Reservation. Laramie County had 1,481 blacks; Natrona, 410; Sweetwater, 236; and Albany, 179.

[6] The number of Wyoming's natives of Austria jumped from 1,132 in 1900 to 3,966 in 1910; of natives of Greece, from 230 in 1900 to 1,915 in 1910; of natives of Italy, from 781 in 1900 to 1,961 in 1910. It should be noted, however, that "Austrians" in 1910 and before included many persons who would be counted as natives of Italy, Yugoslavia, or Czechoslovakia after the partition of Austria consequent to World War I.
The number of Japanese increased from 397 in 1900 to 1,575 in 1910; of Russians, mostly of German stock, from 119 in 1900 to 763 in 1910, and to 1,482 in 1920.

[7] The Mexican Americans resided (in descending order) in Laramie, Carbon, Albany, Natrona, Fremont, Goshen, Park, and Washakie counties. The 1970 census offers overlapping data: 18,551 persons of Spanish language; 12,408 U.S. natives whose mother tongue is Spanish; 857 foreign-born whose mother tongue is Spanish.

Russian Germans, Czechs), yet they too were assimilated quite rapidly. Their concentrations were so small that, as a rule, they did not establish separate schools and churches. The Greeks were exceptional in that they organized Eastern Orthodox churches in Cheyenne and Rock Springs. Most of the Japanese settled in Sweetwater and Carbon counties, where they worked in the coal mines and on railroad sections. Most of them stayed in Wyoming only a few years.

Three exceptions marred the picture of general acceptance of the Europeans. (1) The legislature in 1895 petitioned Congress to restrict immigration to the United States. (2) During World War I, Germans were abused and ordered to speak only English, "the language of your country." (3) In the early 1920's the Ku Klux Klan organized a few units in the Big Horn Basin and in Cheyenne. They burned crosses and painted the letters KKK on front porches to intimidate primarily Roman Catholics, foreign-born and native, and secondarily, blacks and Jews.

Appreciation of different cultures grew after World War II. In the 1970's foreign languages could be used, without fear of ridicule, by the few who could speak them. Ethnic and racist jokes became very rare. Foreign foods, music, dancing, and customs gained favor, as fewer people really knew much about them. So thorough had been the acculturation that Rock Springs, the state's most international city, and Buffalo, the center of Basque culture, could not, by most visitors, be distinguished from other cities of similar size.

Nonetheless, black Americans, Native Americans, Mexican Americans, and Oriental Americans were still not accepted as equals by many European Americans. Perhaps it was a good portent, however, that almost everyone would either deny that he had prejudice or would say that he was trying to overcome his prejudice.

Sixty per cent of the people in 1970 lived in cities (2,500 population or more), the largest being Cheyenne (40,892), followed by Casper (39,397), Laramie, 23,100; Rock Springs, 11,674; and Sheridan, 10,856. All five of these cities grew in the 1970's until Cheyenne and Casper approached 48,000 in 1977; Laramie, 25,000; Rock Springs, 20,000; and Sheridan, 13,000. Gillette and Green River each had about 12,000. The state's population was estimated at 400,000 in the summer of 1977. The new residents, many of them transient single men, came from all directions, and especially from neighboring states. Part of the increase resulted because natives who in the past had been forced to leave in search of work were finding jobs at home.

Although the 1970 census omitted such data, the censuses of 1950 and 1960 showed that Nebraska was the birthplace of more Wyoming residents than any other state except Wyoming. Following Nebraska as states of origin came, in descending order, Colorado, Missouri, Iowa, Kansas, South Dakota, Montana, Oklahoma, Utah, and Texas. These were generally conservative states, politically, and election returns in the 1970's suggested that additions to the electorate were coming from conservative states as in the past. The Middle West had supplied most of the state's political leaders, although a number of natives such as Robert Carey, Milward Simpson, Joe Hickey, Cliff Hansen, Jim Griffith, and Keith and Thyra Thomson had been elected to high office.

The state's traditional man's-world reputation might end when the inrush of transient single men stopped. In 1970 there were 166,717 males and 165,699 females. For a century the females had gained on the males in every decade.

The median age in 1970 was 27.2, compared with 28.1 for the nation. Three counties had exceptional concentrations of older people; Niobrara County had the highest median age, 37.5, Sheridan, 36.8, and Hot Springs, 36.5. At the other extreme, university students accounted for Albany County's median age of 23.2, and young workers for Campbell County's 23.4.

Since the days of the mountain men, Wyoming had always had more than its share of transients. In the three decades between 1940 and 1970 for the first time more people had migrated out of state than into it; yet the traffic had not been all one-way. Even in the decade 1960–1970, when the population increased only 2,350, the state had 31,901 residents in 1970 who had resided in other states five years earlier. In the slow-growth 1960's there must have been an exodus of more than 50,000, considering that there was an excess of births over deaths.

Mobility was a national characteristic, and a good one if not over-done, but Wyoming parents would have been happier had their children found better employment opportunities at home. Although more than 75 per cent of the University of Wyoming's living alumni had enrolled from Wyoming, only 60 per cent of them were still in the state in 1976. This situation had improved in the 1970's; only 43 per cent of the alumni had been located in the state in 1964.

THE SCHOOLS

The postwar years brought greater changes than ever before to education at all levels. Of major importance was the Foundation

Program, which was approved by the legislature in 1955. All school districts were assured a minimum level of educational services. The Foundation Program had been foreshadowed by the adoption of an equalization fund in 1935 when the Great Depression threatened to close some schools entirely. The equalization fund, however, had always been very small. In 1955 the legislature provided that every district should have for general operation expense a sum of money equal to $5,500 times the number of classroom units. The $5,500 allowance per classroom unit set in 1955 grew thereafter, reaching $20,300 in 1977. The amount of money to be distributed to each district from the foundation fund was determined by subtracting the sum of the local district resources from the total amount of the Foundation Program. In short, the districts with low assessed valuation would get more state aid than high-valuation districts, some of which would get no state aid. Inequities remained, with the result that some legislators in 1977 argued that there would not be truly equal education until mineral evaluation had been transferred to the state level. State sources were providing only 37 per cent of the funding for school districts in 1977.

Two constitutional amendments helped with the financing of public school education. One, approved by the electorate in 1948, provided state support in the form of a permissive six-mill levy on the assessed valuation of property. The second amendment, adopted in 1966, provided for a mandatory twelve-mill levy in each county for the support and maintenance of the public schools. Meanwhile, increasing minerals production and federal royalties meant more money available for public schools since they received 50 per cent of the federal royalties returned to the state and distributed according to a formula set by the 1923 legislature.

Because it was thought better to have fewer and larger schools, consolidation had been attempted from time to time, with small success. There were more than 400 school districts in 1920, and 399 in 1933. A school district reorganization law was enacted in 1947, permitting county committees to redistrict. Since this was not mandatory, it took much negotiating by State Superintendent Velma Linford to get the number below 200 before she left office in 1963. Five years later the number had been cut to 165.

The legislature in 1969 codified all public elementary and secondary education statutes, and included provision for further unification. County planning committees were required to submit county plans to a state committee on school district reorganization. The number of districts was forced down to 42 in 1973, then was allowed to rise to 53 in 1977. Dissatisfied with state plans for them, school boards in Big Horn and Fremont counties brought lawsuits against the state reorganization committee.

The 1969 education code abolished the century-old office of county superintendent, which had been occupied almost always by women since the 1880's. Most of the one-room schools (1,226 in 1926), which the county superintendents had supervised, were closed by consolidation. Rural coordinators on the staffs of unified districts took charge of the one-room schools that survived.

Federal aid played an important and controversial role in bringing changes. Some of the regulations and paper work that accompanied federal funds exasperated school boards and administrators. Yet no doubt Wyoming youth had access to more educational programs, better equipment and facilities, better testing and counseling services, and more sophisticated teachers in the 1970's than ever before. In a quality-of-life survey in 1973, based on 1970 data, the Midwest Research Institute of Kansas City, Missouri, had rated the quality of Wyoming public schools second only to those of Iowa among the fifty states. Nevertheless, many citizens were not completely satisfied, one persistent cry being "Back to the Basics."

Court decisions and statutes encouraged teachers to discard their usual humble demeanor. They were no longer sheep obsequiously following their administrators without questions. Sydney Spiegel, a brilliant and popular social studies teacher in Cheyenne East High School, for example, dared to organize a chapter of the American Federation of Teachers, and to argue with administrators about policies and practices. He even proposed that principals be rated by teachers, be required to do some teaching, and stop interrupting his classes. After tolerating Spiegel for nineteen years, the board voted unanimously to fire him in June, 1973. They alleged that he differed from them in teaching philosophy and had an "adverse effect on . . . stability, discipline, cooperative attitude, civic responsibility, loyalty, maturity of judgment, personality and character of the students in his classes."

After a three-year battle in the state's district and supreme courts, Spiegel won reinstatement. A few months later he sued in federal and state courts, asking damages in excess of $350,000. Federal District Judge Ewing T. Kerr, Cheyenne, ruled that the statute of limitations had run out on his claims, leaving him only the state courts for potential redress.

Several other teachers followed Spiegel's example with so-so success. They learned that dismissed teachers seeking reinstatement could expect interminable delays and expensive litigation, which few teachers could afford. The average salary of Wyoming public school teachers in the 1976–1977 school year was $12,778, about $1,500 below the national average. Beginning salaries ranged from $8,400 to $10,300 in 1976, and maximum salaries from $13,500 to $20,000.

Concluding that a teacher could not deal with his employers very effectively as an individual, the Wyoming Education Association followed the lead of its national counter part and took on the role of advocacy for teacher rights and benefits. More than half of the states in 1977 allowed collective bargaining by public employees, but Wyoming did not.

The tradition that state superintendents of public instruction should always be women ended with Velma Linford's defeat in 1962. With only one exception (Jack Gage, 1935–1939), women occupied the office from 1911 to 1963. Thereafter three men, Cecil Shaw, Harry Roberts, and Robert Schrader, headed the State Department of Education.

HIGHER EDUCATION

After World War II higher education expanded remarkably. In Wyoming ten times as many students registered in the fall of 1977 as had ever done so in any fall before the war. Before 1945 the land-grant University of Wyoming at Laramie, founded in 1886, had been the only institution of higher education in the state; it had about two thousand students in 1940 and 1941. Thereafter, seven two-year colleges were added: Casper College (1945), Northwest Community College at Powell (1946), Northern Wyoming College at Sheridan (1948), Eastern Wyoming College in Torrington (1948), Western Wyoming College at Rock Springs (1959), Central Wyoming College at Riverton (1966), and Laramie County Community College at Cheyenne (1968). The seven colleges received varying amounts of state aid, depending on enrollment and availability of local resources, as determined by the Community College Commission, a coordinating agency created by the legislature in 1971.

Many more parents were sending their sons and daughters to college after the war. Also, returning veterans, subsidized by the G.I. Bill, pushed enrollments upward in the late 1940's. Expansion slowed in the 1950's as veterans completed their programs and the small crop of babies born in the Great Depression reached college age. Then the high birth rate of the 1940's caused enrollments to rise sharply in the 1960's before leveling off in the 1970's. In the fall of 1977 about 9,000 students registered at the university and 17,728 at the seven community colleges. In terms of full-time equivalents (twelve credit hours) the university had about 10,200 and the community colleges 8,843, because the colleges had so many evening students taking only one or two courses.

The university's financial support, physical plant, and programs grew spectacularly. The 9 per cent of federal oil and gas royalty money assigned to the university for capital improvements by the 1923 legislature paid for some of the buildings. As the state's only four-year school, the university had certain advantages. Every community had many alumni and many students. Usually more than half of the members of the legislature were alumni of the university. The absence of other four-year competitors for state appropriations kept critical scrutiny and hostile publicity at a minimum. To operate the university for the biennium, the legislature in 1976 appropriated $63,077,229 from the general fund. At the same time the Community College Commission received $20,527,263 for distribution to the seven colleges.

Heroic infusions of federal money for the sciences followed the announcement in 1957 that the USSR had launched an artificial earth satellite (sputnik) before the United States had done so. Not without misgivings about the future, when federal support might decline, the legislature supplied matching funds which made possible the construction, equipping, and manning of the university's magnificent G. D. Humphrey Science Center.

Several other programs received special emphasis as an "islands of excellence" policy was adopted. Since Wyoming could not compete with more populous and wealthy states in all fields, money was poured into a few departments while others suffered from relative neglect.

Board of trustees president Milward Simpson and university president G. D. Humphrey obtained several million dollars from William Robertson Coe of Cody, Wyoming, and Oyster Bay, Long Island, with which to build the William Robertson Coe Library and endow the School of American Studies. The American Studies program achieved national recognition before most of its endowment income was diverted to help support the far-ranging activities of the Western History Research Center.

Intercollegiate football received major attention, thanks to two forceful alumni, Tracy McCraken and Milward Simpson, who dominated the board of trustees in the 1940's and 1950's. If Ev Shelton, using mainly Wyoming boys, could win the national championship in basketball, as he did in 1943, why couldn't the heights be stormed in football? When President J. L. Morrill moved to the University of Minnesota in 1945, the trustees selected for their new president George Duke Humphrey, who had established a successful football program at Mississippi State during his ten years as president there.

Duke Humphrey and Glenn "Red" Jacoby, new director of athletics, with the enthusiastic support of the trustees, soon had a winning program at Wyoming. The university's football teams, which had never before been invited to play in even a minor bowl, began playing in the major ones and won four of five bowl games. Good coaches used Wyoming as a launching pad, Bowden Wyatt jumping to Arkansas, Phil Dickens to Indiana, and Bob Devaney to Nebraska. Wyoming, which could pay competitive salaries, could not match television contracts and other perquisites.

Duke Humphrey insisted that the emphasis on football was necessary to unify the state and get full support for the university as a whole. He argued that all state universities played football, a sizable budget was required whether you won or lost, and the deficit would be smaller with a winning team. The War Memorial Stadium and Field House were built in 1949, partly with funds obtained in a public subscription drive and partly with state appropriations. Several thousand fans bought season tickets, all students were required to do so, and several thousand fans appeared intermittently, sometimes filling the 18,000-capacity stadium. Most of the spectators lived in Laramie and Cheyenne. Many thousands of other fans heard the play-by-play radio reports, glowed with pride, and thought better of the university. As long as McCraken, Simpson, Humphrey, and Jacoby stood shoulder to shoulder, one triumph led to another. They were Wyoming's Four Horsemen. But Simpson left the board of trustees when his term as governor ended in 1959, McCraken died in 1960, and President Humphrey retired in 1964. With the momentum they had generated, Lloyd Eaton, a very capable head coach, kept the machine rolling. His teams won the Western Athletic Conference (WAC) title in 1966 and 1967, and played in the Sugar Bowl on January 1, 1968 (losing to Louisiana State University 20–13). His team won the conference title again in 1968 and was well on the way to another title in 1969 when something happened that would have been unlikely had the Four Horsemen been intact.

On Thursday morning, October 16, 1969, Willie S. Black, chancellor of the Black Student Alliance (BSA), hand delivered identical letters to President William Carlson and Coach Eaton asking that the university and other WAC schools not schedule games with Brigham Young University (BYU) so long as the Mormon church continued its alleged racist policies. The letters also suggested that black athletes should protest "inhuman and racist" policies and should wear black armbands in the BYU contests already scheduled. The BSA was only one of many groups that in 1969 were trying to persuade Mormon church leaders to change the church's teaching that no black person could become a priest in the church. Black armbands were being worn extensively at the time to protest against American involvement in the Vietnam War. The U.S. Supreme Court had recently ruled that school children in Des Moines might wear black armbands to school in protest against the war, despite a school board order not to wear them. Wearing armbands was a legal exercise of freedom of expression, said the Court.

Following football practice on the afternoon of the day on which he had received the letter from the BSA, Coach Eaton spoke with tri-captain Joe Williams, a member of the BSA, and reminded him of a coaching rule which prohibited player participation in protests or demonstrations. The next morning (Friday) at 9:30 A.M. fourteen black football players in street clothes, all members of the BSA, entered Eaton's office in a group wearing black armbands. They sought permission to wear the armbands in a game to be played with BYU the following day. The confrontation was brief, no more than ten minutes at the most. One of the blacks, Jerry Berry, told a news reporter later that day, "As soon as we went into the office, Eaton said he could save us a lot of words. He told us we had made our bid, and from now on we were off the team." [8]

Coach Eaton told the Black Fourteen that their football scholarships were canceled, and that they were through playing for Wyoming because they had violated the coaching rule which they had accepted without protest at the beginning of the season, i.e., that they would not participate in any demonstrations. They had violated that rule when they wore the armbands into his office. He dismissed the Black Fourteen and advised university president Carlson of his action.

[8] *Laramie Boomerang*, October 19, 1969.

President Carlson, Governor Stan Hathaway, Red Jacoby, and five trustees spent most of that cold, snowy night in Old Main trying desperately to achieve a compromise. Five other trustees participated by telephone. Coach Eaton was adamant. He had been named United Press International's man of the year for Wyoming in 1967, and the state's broadcasters and news writers would repeat the honor in 1969, soon after his dismissal of the Black Fourteen. He was the most popular man in the state. The black players, who might have been persuaded to give up their armbands had they been allowed to discuss the issue at length before the ultimatum, were less tractable that night. Some of them said they would not play unless they could wear the armbands; others said they would never play as long as Eaton was the head coach.

The next morning (Saturday) the trustees announced their full support of Coach Eaton except for one detail; although the Black Fourteen were no longer members of the football team, they could continue in school and receive board and room, subject to later review. Most of the black players left the university. Aided by the National Association for the Advancement of Colored People (NAACP) they filed a $1.1 million civil suit in federal district court. Their attorneys asked for a temporary restraining order and for the convening of a three-judge federal panel. Judge Ewing T. Kerr, Federal District Court judge, Cheyenne, rejected the request for a restraining order and a three-judge panel. Instead he took under consideration a motion from the defendants to dismiss the suit.

A year later, with most of the plaintiffs absent (only one was a Wyoming resident), Judge Kerr dismissed the suit on several grounds. The U.S. circuit court, Denver, on appeal affirmed Judge Kerr's ruling that the Black Fourteen could not sue the state without its permission and could not collect monetary damages against state officers. But the appeals court also ordered Judge Kerr to hold a full hearing on disputed facts bearing on the constitutional civil rights issues: "We cannot agree that the making of findings and the dismissal . . . was proper. . . . We do not feel that the present record supported a summary disposition. . . . such close and delicate constitutional questions should be decided when the facts are fully developed at trial." [9]

Judge Kerr's full hearing occurred two years after the Black Fourteen's dismissal. Three of the original plaintiffs had withdrawn from the

[9] The record of the litigation may be found in 310 Federal Supplement 1342–1353 (1970), 443 Federal Reporter 2d 422–434 (1971), 333 Federal Supplement 107–115 (1971), and 468 Federal Reporter 2d 1079–1084 (1972).

action. Ten other plaintiffs failed to appear in support of their claims. Only Melvin R. Hamilton was present; the others were scattered all over the country.

In the full hearing it was Mel Hamilton and his attorney, Weston W. Reeves, against defendants Lloyd Eaton, Clifford E. "Jerry" Hollon, Alfred M. Pence, and William D. Carlson and their legal counsel, Clarence A. Brimmer, attorney general, and William Kallal and Fred Reed, assistant attorneys general. The defendants prevailed. Judge Kerr in October, 1971, held that Hamilton's right to freedom of speech by the First Amendment could not be held paramount to the Mormon church's right to practice its religion free from state-supported protest. Finally, in May, 1972, the appeals court let Judge Kerr's second dismissal stand, concluding that the findings of the district court "are not clearly erroneous. . . . We feel that the Trustees' decision was a proper means of respecting the rights of others to their beliefs, in accordance with this policy of religious neutrality." Mel Hamilton and the NAACP decided not to carry a costly appeal to the U.S. Supreme Court.

During the three years the judges were contemplating the issues, Coach Eaton's peremptory dismissal of the Black Fourteen had triggered all manner of repercussions. Several issues emerged: discipline, freedom of speech, freedom of religion, racism, the contractual obligation to give the Black Fourteen an education, the limits of a coach's authority, the place of football in a university, and how soon it becomes politically possible to fire a Sugar Bowl coach after he begins to lose games.

Had there been a state referendum within two weeks after the dismissal of the blacks, Eaton would have been supported by a majority of the electorate. Ardent and vocal football fans defended the coach vehemently. At the BYU game they chanted in unison, "We love Eaton." The Alumni Association's directors supported him unanimously. Only the Student Senate, the Faculty Senate, and the faculty of the College of Arts and Sciences complained. After Eaton refused to discuss the issue with them, the Student Senate by a vote of 17–1 "expressed shock at the callous, insensitive treatment afforded 14 black athletes who acted on a matter of conscience with restraint, with moderation, and with responsibility." After Eaton also refused to discuss the matter with the Faculty Senate, that body by a vote of 37–1 adopted a resolution asking that the dismissal be changed to a temporary suspension pending an investigation by an ad hoc faculty-student committee. Eaton and the trustees ignored the suggestion. The faculty of the College of Arts and Sciences voted overwhelmingly to censure the coach.

The faculty and staff of the College of Agriculture, almost unanimously, signed a petition supporting the coach and trustees. The faculties of other parts of the university were more evenly divided and took no action. The Episcopal church's bishop of Wyoming, whose flock became embroiled, recalled later that "the affair . . . revealed deep racial prejudice . . . where it was unsuspected. People were as much incensed because they were black as they were because they broke the discipline."

The major news services made the Black Fourteen famous nationally and followed with more interest than usual the fortunes of the decimated University of Wyoming football team. In 1969 the remnants of the undefeated team, which had won its first four games before the blacks were dismissed, also defeated Brigham Young and San Jose State but lost its last four games. Thereafter recruiting, especially of black players, became exceedingly difficult. After his team won only one of ten games in 1970, Eaton at age fifty-three retired as coach and accepted an appointment as assistant athletic director, a new position with unspecified duties. Early in September, 1971, he resigned to take a position as an area scout for four professional football teams, work in which discipline and dealing with blacks would not be a factor.

Lloyd Eaton's departure brought no joy to the football fans. The football teams continued to lose, year after year. The stadium, to which 7,000 seats had been added in 1970, making its total capacity 25,000, was rarely more than half full.

After seven lean years the storm clouds finally dissolved as the combination of Coach Fred Akers, team spirit, the renewed involvement of talented black players, and luck brought a conference co-championship and a bowl bid in 1976. The trustees were so overjoyed that they immediately voted $62,000 in bonuses, apparently on the recommendation of athletic director George McCarty—$10,000 to McCarty, $10,000 to head coach Akers, and somewhat smaller sums to the other coaches. A few days later, with two games remaining, Akers accepted the head coaching position at the University of Texas. Thereafter his Wyoming coaching suffered. The team lost its last game of the regular season to a nonconference foe, the Air Force Academy, 41–21, and the Fiesta Bowl game to Oklahoma, 41–7. Finding the bowl game receipts insufficient, the trustees had to dip into the university's unrestricted gifts to pay the bonuses. The chairman of the board conceded to the legislative appropriations committee two months later that, after seven lean years, the bowl bid caused such euphoria that the trustees made a mistake.

The departure of Fred Akers gave the trustees temporary relief from the pressure he had applied on them to cover the football stadium with a plastic dome. Akers maintained that it would be impossible to recruit top-drawer players without a dome and other new facilities. To make a covered stadium more appealing it was described as an "All Events Center," in which citizens from the four corners of the state could assemble for all kinds of activities, day and night. The center, which would cost upwards of $20 million, was rejected by the legislature in 1975 and 1976. The 1977, legislature, however, authorized the expenditure of $2,559,000 for a 7,000-seat addition to the stadium and $770,000 for the acquisition of designs and construction specifications for future improvements to the field house.

The All Events Center, like the Black Fourteen incident, caused much controversy and raised doubts about the doctrine that emphasis on football would unify the state. If booby trapped, the paths leading to great football teams could cause as much disunity and grief as football de-emphasis. Yet very few football fans wanted de-emphasis. That would mean depending on Wyoming boys and playing Montana, Idaho, North Dakota, and South Dakota schools, which were comparable to the University of Wyoming in size. The fans preferred the Western Athletic Conference, in which all the schools except Wyoming were much larger.

It appeared to some people that since 1948 the university trustees had devoted more time and thought to football than to any other aspect of university business. Some faculty members thought this was salutary because as long as they were occupied, the trustees found little time for mischief. Once in 1947, for example, when they had time on their hands, they disrupted the education processes for three months by ordering what appeared to most of the faculty to be a useless, not to say pernicious, textbook probe. At the time the cold war between the U.S. and the USSR had caused fear among conservatives that "un-American" and "subversive" ideas might be taught in the schools.

Wyoming would be one of the last places one would expect to find dangerous subversive activities in 1947. Yet the board of trustees on October 24, 1947, directed President Humphrey to appoint a special committee to examine all textbooks used in the social science departments of the university, including the university high school and elementary school. The faculty learned about the probe from a streamer headline in the *Laramie Daily Bulletin* on October 25. Faculty members thought there already were adequate safeguards in supervision by deans and department heads and in the annual evaluation reports all students submitted to the deans about their instructors. Many faculty members considered the action an infringement on academic freedom. They had never heard of such an investigation at any other university. Resolutions condemning the probe and asking an explanation were passed by the Student Senate, Mortar Board, university Veterans' Club, and Associated Independent Students. After three weeks of mounting apprehension among faculty and students, President Humphrey appointed three deans and four senior faculty members not identified with the social sciences to read the sixty-four books. Then the faculty in its regular December meeting voted 123–24 to elect a committee of fifteen, and elected the committee, with instructions to ask the board of trustees for a hearing regarding the investigation.

Later in December reporters from the *New York Herald-Tribune* and *Denver Post* turned up and filed stories. The *Herald-Tribune* story reported that "the state and the university are as conservative bodies as could be found," and that neither the faculty nor the student body "has ever shown any tendency toward radicalism." One trustee was quoted as having said that the trustees would check the textbooks "every year from now on until the crack of doom." Another was reported to have scoffed at "all this bunk about academic freedom."

After a preliminary difficulty in defining "un-American" and "subversive," the seven book readers completed their assignment in two months. How many pages they actually read has never been revealed. They failed, they said, to find any material that fell under the denomination of subversive or un-American. This report enabled the trustees and the Committee of Fifteen to reconcile their differences and reach a general agreement on January 24, 1948. The faculty conceded that the board had the right to prescribe textbooks (an old state law gave the board that right). The faculty also dropped a request that the board "rescind the original action and thus neutralize the widespread opinion that free inquiry is threatened at the University." The Committee of Fifteen had no hope of getting this recision, which had been proposed in a petition signed by 103 faculty members, including a number of staunch conservatives. On the other hand, the board agreed that "except upon extraordinary occasions now unforeseen, it will be unnecessary to deviate from the traditional procedure of textbook selection." If an examination should be thought desirable in the future, the board would first confer "with the President and the deans and the department heads concerned." The board also reaffirmed its adherence to academic freedom "as defined by the joint statement of the American Association of Colleges and the American Association of University Professors," and laid down several other principles with which the Committee of Fifteen took no exception: "Sound instruction requires honest and objective presentation of both fact and theory. In the final analysis, the loyalty, integrity, and intellectual honesty of instructors must and should be relied upon to prevent the infiltration of subversive and un-American doctrines into University classrooms. Complete freedom of discussion of pertinent issues and ideas, however controversial, should be encouraged." No further textbook probes were suggested in the next thirty years.

Like their parents and the faculty, the students at the university have always been remarkably cautious and conservative. True, they had gone out on strike in 1931 when President A. G. Crane insulted some of the coeds, and they had joined the protest against the textbook probe in 1947. Except for the Student Senate's criticism of Eaton, the students had been divided and indecisive with respect to the Black Fourteen and Dome controversies. And they showed more restraint than students at most other state universities during the Vietnam War.

ANOTHER FOUR-YEAR SCHOOL?

Unsuccessful attempts were made in the legislature in 1971, 1973, and 1975 to make Casper College a four-year school. The proposal lost in the Senate 19–11 in 1973, and 20–10 in 1975. In its latest form the proposal asked for authority to grant two degrees, a Bachelor of Science in applied studies (applied business, public service, and industrial technology) and a Bachelor of Arts in general studies (an interdisciplinary program with no discipline major except "general studies," mainly in the social sciences and humanities).

Four members of Natrona County's legislative delegation (Representatives Warren Morton, Jack Sidi, and Diemer True, and Senator Dick Sadler) withdrew their support for the proposed four-year program after the defeat in 1975. Warren Morton said that the proposal had become a political liability for Casper, Natrona County, and the college's two-year program. Senator Dick Sadler explained that most of the opposition came from the other community colleges. "These schools," he said, "have the same fear as the University—the loss of students and competition for the almighty buck." Morton suggested a new approach; for example, offerings of third-year and fourth-year courses by the University of Wyoming on the Casper College campus. This suggestion was implemented a year later, at the instigation of Natrona County's Representative Russ Donley, in the 1976 budget session of the legislature. After a one-year trial, however, the Casper College board of trustees announced in June, 1977, that it was withdrawing its support and the university would have to find facilities off the Casper College campus if it decided to continue its extension courses after May, 1978.

Casper College's four-year proposal was certainly not dead. The legislature would have to deal with it again sooner or later, because many Casper people were determined to have a four-year school.

THE COLLEGE OF HUMAN MEDICINE

Meanwhile, another expansion of educational services, the university's new College of Human Medicine was maturing. Promoted primarily by a group of physicians, it was designed to train up to 120 family-practice doctors at a time, graduating 30 each year. Small towns were having trouble getting doctors. For many years the university had offered premedical training and had paid medical schools in other states, usually through the Western Interstate Commission for Higher Education (WICHE), to accept Wyoming students. When it became more difficult to get Wyoming students admitted to medical schools, and when more than 75 per cent of the Wyoming students who were graduated from such schools chose to practice in other states, it was decided to start the College of Human Medicine. Several years of planning preceded the official creation of the college on July 1, 1976.

The immense cost of traditional medical schools was to be avoided by having no university hospital. The students would spend two years at the university beyond their premedical training, and a third year in specialized training in family practice residency centers in Casper and Cheyenne, or in a few of the state's largest hospitals. They would spend their fourth year primarily in small-town doctors' offices. Thereafter they would enter residency programs, some in Wyoming, some elsewhere.

As the College of Human Medicine prepared to accept its first students in 1980, some people became apprehensive about cost projections, what the new competition for appropriations would do to their pet projects, the quality of the new program, and the possibility that graduates would be no more inclined to practice in Wyoming than graduates under the old WICHE program. It had been announced that the College of Human Medicine would need $17.4 million for a building on the university campus and annual appropriations of $5.9 million to operate the college.

The college's $1.5 million residency center at Casper was completed in 1977 and construction was about to begin on a comparable facility in Cheyenne. Several administrators were on the payroll in Laramie. Nevertheless, critics in 1977 suggested scrapping the whole program. The issue probably would be decided by the legislature in 1978.

OPEN SEASON ON ADMINISTRATORS

The prestige of administrators in education declined in the 1960's and 1970's. Some principals and superintendents and administrators in higher education were looked upon as illustrations of the Peter Principle. Critics said that they may have been good coaches, teachers, or researchers at one time, but in administrative positions they had risen to the level of their incompetence. Policy making, personnel decisions, and paper shuffling were outside their area of expertise. Yet much depended on their leadership. Decisions made by school boards and boards of trustees could be little better than the information and suggestions advanced by the administrators.

Many professors thought that a university should be a cooperative enterprise, with students, faculty, administrators, and taxpayers sharing in decision making. All too often in Wyoming, adversary relationships developed, which professors attributed to excessively close-to-the-vest, unilateral administrative decisions. Many crises at the University of Wyoming in postwar years could have been avoided or mitigated had there been better communication between faculty and administration. The legislature in 1969 made the president of the Associated Students a member, ex officio, of the board of trustees, but no such communications link was established for the faculty. The university Faculty Senate, a representative, elective body of about fifty-five members, failed in several attempts to obtain a position, without vote, for its president on the board of trustees.

Disturbed by several developments, the Faculty Senate in January, 1977, polled 751 of the 770 members of the faculty, and asked the question, "Do you think President Carlson is administering the University of Wyoming in a manner that best serves the interests of

Wyoming, the university, the students, and the faculty?" Of the 464 who responded to that question, 319 gave the president an unsatisfactory rating and 145 rated him satisfactory.

Two months later, in March, 1977, the 150-member University Faculty Association, under the supervision of the National Education Association, conducted a faculty satisfaction survey that elicited 511 responses and the following opinions:

74% of 484 agreed with the statement "Trustees spend too much time on athletics."

82% of 481 agreed that "faculty are kept 'in the dark' about many things they should know."

83% of 477 agreed that "many misunderstandings result from poor communications."

Never before in the university's ninety-year history had faculty and administration been so at odds.

THE ARTS AND HUMANITIES

Art in Wyoming has spanned centuries, ranging from relatively simple Native American pictographs (painted) and petroglyphs (carved) on cliff and cave walls to a profusion of more elaborate modern works displayed in almost every community.

Alfred Jacob Miller was the first of many transient nineteenth-century artists who sketched and painted Wyoming scenes during brief visits. A Scotsman, William Drummond Stewart, employed Miller in New Orleans to accompany him to the Green River rendezvous in 1837. Later, in Stewart's castle in Scotland, Miller transferred details of his sketches to oil paintings. Several of Miller's paintings came to the University of Wyoming as gifts in the 1970's through the enterprise of Professor Robert C. Warner of the Journalism Department. Other famous transient artists who painted Wyoming scenes in the nineteenth century were Albert Bierstadt and Thomas Moran. A host of less well known itinerant artists left drawings and paintings of greater documentary than artistic value.[10]

One of the very first resident artists was Merritt Dana Houghton,

---

[10] For more details on this subject, see James H. Nottage, "A Centennial History of Artist Activities in Wyoming, 1837–1937," *Annals of Wyoming*, XLVIII, 1 (Spring 1976), 77–100.

whom many ranch and mine owners hired to paint pictures of their properties in Albany and Carbon counties beginning in 1875. Two Sheridan County artists, E. W. "Bill" Gollings (the "Cowboy Artist"), and Hans Kleiber, renowned for his superb etchings, began their distinguished careers in the first decade of the twentieth century. Amy Gardner at the University of Wyoming brought traveling exhibits and artists to Laramie in the 1920's.

During the Great Depression, substantial federal aid gave significant impetus to artistic endeavors. Several artists received small commissions to paint murals in the Capitol, public schools, and in the post offices at Greybull, Kemmerer, Powell, Riverton, and Worland. A Denver artist carved two limestone grizzly bear cubs which were placed in front of the post office at Mammoth in Yellowstone Park. Although the postmaster at Mammoth welcomed the cubs, he wrote later that their "resemblance to real bears is rather vague."[11]

Paintings by other WPA "work-relief" artists were loaned or donated to government-supported galleries in Casper, Evanston, Lander, Laramie, Newcastle, Rawlins, Riverton, Rock Springs, Sheridan, and Torrington. The University of Wyoming and many schools and libraries received gifts of paintings by WPA artists active in other states. The most noteworthy permanent collection resulting from the New Deal's support of art is the one adjacent to the Rock Springs Public Library. Elmer Halseth did much of the work connected with assembling and preserving the Rock Springs collection.

An art colony formed around Edward T. Grigware and Stan Kershaw at Cody in 1937. Other artists active in the 1930's and early 1940's were Raphael Lilywhite, Evelyn C. Hill, E. E. Lowry, and J. B. Smith in Laramie; Fern Lord Herring and Frederic H. Porter in Cheyenne; Joy and Lin Hopkins, Charles Anda, and Mrs. F. C. Nicolaysen in Casper; and Elizabeth Neal Forsling of Casper Mountain. The famous abstract painter Jackson Pollock (1912–1956) is sometimes claimed by Wyoming because he was born on a farm near Cody; but he left the state as a small boy, so he must be shared with Arizona, California, and New York.

The tenfold increase in university and college students in postwar years meant that many more young people than formerly were exposed to works of art and received art instruction. The $4 million Fine Arts

[11] H. R. Dieterich and Jacqueline Petravage, "New Deal Art in Wyoming: Some Case Studies," *Annals of Wyoming*, XLV, 1 (Spring 1973), 53–67.

Center at the university gave a great boost not only to art, but also to dance, drama, and music.

Another noteworthy development was the creation of the National Foundation on the Arts and Humanities by Congress in 1965. Soon two derivative organizations appeared, the National Foundation on the Arts and the National Foundation for the Humanities. The Arts Foundation quickly moved into the states; the Wyoming legislature established and partially funded the Wyoming Council on the Arts in 1967. National Arts Foundation funds, distributed by the Wyoming Arts Council, facilitated the stimulation and upgrading of art, music, theater, dance, and creative writing in many communities during the next ten years.

Pioneers in the Arts Council movement were Professor James M. Boyle of the University of Wyoming, Ruth Loomis of Cheyenne, Ruth Davis of Riverton, Elmer Halseth of Rock Springs, and George Hufsmith of Jackson. Governor Cliff Hansen appointed them to an Interim Committee on the Arts in 1966, and they prepared the way for the legislation of 1967. Beginning in 1967, a ten-member council, appointed by Governor Stan Hathaway, made annual grants to assist communities in developing the arts. Mrs. Stan (Bobbie) Hathaway, a great booster of the arts, was reported to have said that she wanted to place a paintbrush in everyone's hands.

Paintbrushes were already much more numerous than before World War II. Conrad Schwiering was a pioneer in the growing art colony of Jackson Hole, which included such notables as Grant Hagen, Archie Teater, and John Clymer. They and others in the colony found a ready market among tourists for their scenic, wildlife, and cowboy art. Other colonies with similar interests developed in Cody, where Nick Eggenhofer and James Bama stood out. Richard Hutt and Carleen Williams were leaders in Cheyenne; Joe and Mary Back, in Dubois; and Harry Jackson, in Lysite.

At the university, James Boyle, Robert Russin, Joe Deaderick, Richard Evans, and Victor Flach trained students in the use of various media and found time to exhibit from coast to coast. Russin placed much sculpture on the university campus and in Casper and Cheyenne, and major works in Los Angeles, Kansas City, and Santo Domingo. Hundreds of thousands of people each year stopped to admire his twelve-foot bronze bust of Abraham Lincoln on a thirty-foot base at a rest stop along Interstate Highway 80 on the summit of the Laramie Mountains ten miles east of Laramie. James T. Forrest taught art history and was director of the university's art museum. Ed Gothberg and James L. Gaither built an excellent department at Casper College. Artists at the university, Casper College, and the other community colleges mingled avant-garde experimentation with Western art. Several professional and many amateur artists could be found around each of the state's higher education institutions.

Most of the state's public schools had competent art teachers who practiced what they taught. To name and rank the several hundred skillful Wyoming artists and identify all the galleries and art guilds are tasks beyond the scope of this book.

Major art museums were the Whitney Gallery of Western Art in the Buffalo Bill Historical Center in Cody and the University of Wyoming Art Gallery in Laramie. Smaller galleries of note were the Bradford Brinton at Big Horn near Sheridan and the one in the State Historical Museum in Cheyenne. The Whitney Gallery, build in 1958 under the direction of Dr. Harold McCracken, had one of the finest collections of Western art in the world, including many works by Alfred Jacob Miller, George Catlin, Albert Bierstadt, Charles M. Russell, and Frederic Remington.

In music, Allan Willman built a superior reputation as pianist, composer, and administrator at the university. The department he headed maintained a symphony orchestra, string quartet, renowned Western Arts Trio (Brian Hanly, David Tomatz, and Werner Rose), and chorus. More than two hundred public musical performances were offered in Laramie and throughout the state each year. Casper had its symphony orchestra, organized by Blaine Coolbaugh in the 1940's and Cheyenne had its civic symphony and community chorus. The Grand Teton Music Festival, directed several years by Ernest Hagen and later by Ling Tung, presented varied programs every summer at Jackson Lake Lodge, Jackson, and Teton Village. David Tomatz in 1977 published a booklet, *Wyoming Composers*, in which he discussed the compositions of more than ninety past and present composers.

Wyoming was one of only two states whose Bicentennial Commissions sponsored operas to be performed in 1976. George Hufsmith's creation, *The Lynching on the Sweetwater*, dealt with conflict between big cattlemen and homesteaders in territorial Wyoming, culminating in the lynching of Ella Watson and James Averell. With singers and musicians mostly from the University of Wyoming music and drama departments, the opera was presented in Laramie, Rawlins, Riverton, Powell, Casper, and Lusk in March, 1976.

Almost every community had its high school or community band and chorus. The Casper Troopers, an oustanding drum and bugle corps directed by Jim Jones for many years, won numerous honors all over the nation and thrilled many home-state spectators.

An important artistic and cultural acquisition was the German-built pipe organ located in the concert hall of the university's Fine Arts Center. Each of the more than three thousand pipes was handcrafted by the E. F. Walcker firm and designed specifically for the university's concert hall. The organ's installation in 1972 was supervised by the Professor of Music and university organist Arthur Birkby, an internationally recognized recitalist, author, lecturer, and composer.

The National Endowment for the Humanities in 1970 followed the lead of its sister organization, the National Endowment on the Arts, and instigated the formation of six experimental state-based programs in Maine, Georgia, Oklahoma, Missouri, Oregon, and Wyoming. Unlike the Wyoming Council on the Arts, the Wyoming Council for the Humanities sought no state funding. Not being a state agency, the council experimented with various types of organization. In 1977 for the first time Governor Ed Herschler was asked to appoint two of the eighteen members of the council, without any state obligation being entailed.

The Humanities Council has distributed federal matching funds in support of local lectures, panels, debates, and television, radio, and film programs. It has emphasized audience participation in the discussion of public policy decisions. Humanists, for example, have brought their cultural traditions to bear on foreign policy questions, problems of the environment, the implications of technology, women's rights issues, pop culture, and social problems.

The council's primary target has been out-of-school adults, yet students have been permitted to participate. The council has avoided advocacy and action programs, preferring the discussion of issues from all points of view. The successful completion of the experimental programs in Wyoming and five other states in 1970 and 1971 persuaded the National Endowment for the Humanities to establish state-based organizations in all of the fifty states in later years.

Writers were as plentiful as artists, although not as conspicuous. Those who could not get their writings published filed them away instead of displaying them at local art exhibits or on walls of their homes, as artists could do with their creations.

The Easterners who visited Wyoming in the nineteenth century wrote much about the mountain men, Indians, travel on the trails, military affairs, cattlemen, cowboys, and the Union Pacific Railroad. The cowboys became more popular in the early twentieth century, thanks partly to Owen Wister, who spent part of many summers between 1885 and 1902 in Wyoming and published his famous novel, *The Virginian*, in 1902. The popular novelist Mary Roberts Rinehart, beginning in 1915, was often a guest at Eaton's dude ranch at Wolf near Sheridan. Ernest Hemingway did some writing in a northern Wyoming cabin. It seems far-fetched, however, to list Wister, Rinehart, Hemingway, and a host of other visitors as Wyoming authors.

On the other hand, Bill Nye, who spent more than half of his short life in Wisconsin, will always be identified with Wyoming because he established his reputation as a humorist while living in Laramie, 1876–1883. His best humor may be found in *Bill Nye and Boomerang* (1881), *Forty Liars and Other Lies* (1882), *Baled Hay* (1884), and *Remarks* (1887).

Among twentieth-century Wyoming authors, probably Struthers Burt and his wife, Katherine Newlin Burt, achieved the greatest fame. Easterners by birth and schooling, they called the Three Rivers Ranch in Jackson Hole home for more than forty years, beginning just before World War I. Mrs. Burt published twenty-five novels, her husband, seventeen volumes of assorted fiction, nonfiction, and verse. Two volumes by Struthers Burt, *Diary of a Dude Wrangler* (1924) and *Powder River, Let 'er Buck* (1938), appealed to many Wyomingites. Katherine Burt in late years was fiction editor for the *Ladies' Home Journal*.

Laramie's native son Thurman W. Arnold published two books while he was a law professor at Yale University, *The Symbols of Government* (1935) and *The Folklore of Capitalism* (1937). The latter, which became a national best seller, satirized some of the hallowed myths with which conservatives in general and economists in particular had blocked humanitarian reforms. In 1940, when he had become chief trust buster for the New Deal, he published a third book, *Bottlenecks of Business*, in which he criticized obstructions to fair competition. Toward the end of a successful legal career in Washington, D.C., he published another well-received volume, *Fair Fights and Foul: A Dissenting Lawyer's Life* (1965). In one of his celebrated legal battles he had defended Owen Lattimore successfully.

Many faculty members of the University of Wyoming published scholarly books and articles which were well known primarily to specialists in academic disciplines. Their total output might equal in bulk that of all other Wyoming authors. The publish-or-perish rule,

which was enforced ever more strictly in the College of Arts and
Sciences, assured a steady flow of ink to paper. No attempt will be
made here to evaluate the academic flood.

A unique niche was occupied, however, by Wilson O. Clough, who
was a great teacher and critic at the university for almost forty years
before he retired in 1961. As professor emeritus of English and American
studies he wrote more than he had been able to do when administration, committee work, and teaching took so much of his time. At age
eighty-three in 1977 he was still confronting his typewriter six days a
week. Clough's name appears on thirteen admirable books: two gram-
mar texts, published in 1942 and 1947; three volumes of poetry, *We,
Borne Along* (1949), *Brief Oasis* (1954), and *Past's Persisting* (1972); a
gathering of essays, *Academic and Otherwise* (1969); a study of the influence of the frontier experience on American literature, *The Necessary
Earth: Nature and Solitude in American Literature* (1964); *A History of the
University of Wyoming, 1887–1964* (1965, originally published in three
parts); an edition of *Intellectual Origins of American National Thought* (a
1961 revision of *Our Long Heritage: Pages from the Books Our Founding
Fathers Read*, published in 1955); three translations of French books into
English, Arthur Honegger's *I Am a Composer*, in collaboration with
Allan A. Willman (1966), Louis Laurent Simonin's *The Rocky Mountain
West in 1867* (1966), and Charles Morazé's *The Logic of History* (1976);
and a genealogical study of the Clow (Clough) family, *Dutch Uncles
and New England Cousins* (1976).

Other major Wyoming poets besides Clough are James Cole, Peggy
Simson Curry, Stephen W. Downey, Joe Langland, Ted Olson,
Robert A. Roripaugh, Alan Swallow, and Ann Winslow.

A list of important contributors to published prose must include
Olga Moore Arnold, William F. Bragg, Sr., William F. Bragg, Jr.,
Mabel Brown, Ruth Southworth Brown, Robert H. Burns, Elsa Spear
Byron, Maurine Carley, Roberta Cheney, Peggy Simson Curry,
Vaughan Elston, Marie H. Erwin, Hal Evarts, Rachel Ann Fish, Paul
Frison, Jack Gage, Doris Garst, Katherine Gress, Grace Raymond
Hebard, Lola Homsher, Charles King, Dee Linford, Velma Linford,
Caroline Lockhart, Harold McCracken, Gale W. McGee, Emmie D.
Mygatt, A. J. Mokler, Rebecca Northen, Mary O'Hara, Ted Olson,
Nancy Burrage Owen, Lorene Pearson, Mary Lou Pence, G. Edward
Pendray, Robert A. Roripaugh, Agnes Wright Spring, Elinore Stewart,
Betty Thorpe, Virginia Cole Trenholm, Mae and Jerry Urbanek,
David Wasden, Clarice Whittenburg, Charles E. Winter, and L.
Milton Woods.

No attempt will be made here to evaluate the vast outpouring of short stories in pulp magazines, the countless "formula" Western novels, and the "true West" accounts of semi-picaresque characters such as George Leroy Parker (Butch Cassidy) and Bill Carlisle. Trying to separate fact from fiction in the careers of the outlaw Parker and his "Wild Bunch" or "Hole-in-the-Wall Gang" has occupied many writers in Wyoming, Idaho, Utah, and Colorado. Carlisle's career as a train robber, penitentiary inmate, and legitimate businessman in Laramie has been quite well documented in his autobiography.

The Hole-in-the-Wall country west of Kaycee has fascinated many writers, not because it can be established that many outlaws ever went there but because fiction writers think it was an ideal setting for them. As Johnson County native Thelma Gatchell Condit explained in the *Annals of Wyoming* (Volume XXIX, p. 163):

Regardless of the magnification of reports and rumors . . . never was there a more perfect setting for an outlaw gang . . . full of box and blind canyons for hiding animals; plenty of easy escapes and high places for seeing all the surrounding country. [Outlaws] . . . would have missed an ideal opportunity had they failed to make use of such a place.

The statement offered in the Wyoming Writers' Project volume *Wyoming* in 1941 was still valid in 1977: "No Cather or Sandoz has yet told the story of Wyoming." Ruth Hudson noted in 1956 that Western writers generally were preoccupied with place and space, to the annoyance of Eastern critics. Wilson Clough commented later that Wyoming writers of fiction who had not experienced the tensions of contemporary big-city life seemed unable to provide novels with the conflict demanded by Eastern critics.

SOPHISTICATION, DEMOCRACY, AND EQUALITY

Wyoming people became more democratic, tolerant, and sophisticated after World War II. "White trade only" signs which were displayed in some restaurant windows before and during the war to exclude blacks, Mexican-Americans, and Indians disappeared thereafter. Upward-mobility opportunities improved for minorities. The textbook probe and the Black Fourteen episode made many people re-examine their beliefs about individual rights and responsibilities. The continuing emphasis on football brought many more blacks, both men and women, from other sections of the country to the university, just as emphasis on basketball brought them in smaller numbers to the university and the community colleges. The number of foreign students multiplied until there were 439 at the university in 1977 and many at the community colleges. The greatest attraction for the foreign students was the university's petroleum engineering program. Before World War II there might have been one or two black students and a dozen foreign students at the university at any one time.

In 1977 about one-third of the state's college-bound high school graduates attended out-of-state colleges and universities and about one-third of the University of Wyoming's students were nonresidents. The exchange contributed to Wyoming's sophistication. So did World War II, the Korean War, and the Vietnam conflict. Returning veterans brought new ideas which were sometimes at odds with those of their parents.

The legislature created a Commission on the Status of Women in 1965. In its 1972 report the commission stated that "although our state is known as the 'Equality State' . . . sex discrimination does exist and, in many cases, is accepted as normal. . . . Employment opportunities for women are curtailed sharply by sex discrimination." In 1973 the legislature ratified the Equal Rights Amendment (ERA), most of the opposition arising in the Senate, where the vote was 17–12. Selia Ribeiro and Julia Yelvington led an ERA coalition formed by many women's organizations. Governor Stan Hathaway and Secretary of State Thyra Thomson supported the coalition's lobbying efforts, which were necessary because many letters were written to legislators by women who maintained that they had all the rights they wanted.

Only seven of the ninety-two members of the legislature in 1977 were women, six in the House and one in the Senate. A great Women's Conference met in Casper in June, with Pat Duncombe presiding, to discuss the contemporary status of women. The *Casper Star-Tribune* praised the conference and described women's liberation as "one of the most significant movements in history. . . . It is the freeing of women from being drudges and an assertion of their individuality and a demand that they be treated similarly to any male and their talents be recognized."

THE BICENTENNIAL CELEBRATION, 1976

The character and interests of rank-and-file Wyoming people were illustrated by the nature of their participation in the nation's Bicentennial celebration. There had been no Wyoming (except Wyoming Valley

in Pennsylvania) in 1776. And the favorite pastime of Wyoming politicians and editorial writers in the 1970's was criticizing the federal
government. Yet the Wyoming people observed the Bicentennial with
as much wholehearted enthusiasm as could be found in any other state.

Governor Stan Hathaway in 1972 named a Bicentennial Commission
of twenty-one citizens to prepare for and supervise the state's part in the
national celebration.[12] Governor Hathaway urged the commission at
its organizational meeting to make the establishment of a state park at
Independence Rock its number one project. In the previous half
century there had been several attempts to acquire state control of the
famous granite landmark on the Oregon Trail fifty-five miles west of
Casper. The renewed interest in the 1970's was kindled by the ARBA's
attempt to get a large congressional appropriation for a Bicentennial
Park in each state, The Wyoming Bicentennial Commission chose
Independence Rock as the site for its Bicentennial Park, and proceeded
with its plan despite the failure of Congress to fund the national plan.
Title to the twenty-five-acre rock and land surrounding it was finally
acquired in 1977. The state legislature, which had earmarked $40,000
of Recreation Commission appropriations for land acquisition at
Independence Rock, would be asked to create the park within a year
or two.

Jack Rosenthal and Tom Stroock of Casper joined the commission
in funding a project by Robert Russin, University of Wyoming sculptor,
to cast and place near Independence Rock twelve-foot bronze statues

---

[12] The original twenty-one members were J. Reuel Armstrong, Mrs. Mabel E.
Brown, Lee R. Call, Peggy Simson Curry, George F. Guy, Mrs. Sylvia Hansen, Mary
Helen Hendry, T. A. Larson, Mrs. John U. Loomis, Charles Margolf, Mrs. Percy
Metz, Frank Norris, Jr., Helen L. Reynolds, Tom Shakespeare, Charles Sharp,
Darwin St. Clair, Mrs. Nels Smith, Sr., William R. Taliaferro, Randall Wagner, Paul
Westedt, and William H. Williams. The commission elected Peggy Simson Curry
chairman, T. A. Larson vice chairman, and Mary Helen Hendry secretary-treasurer.
Later Mrs. Nora Reimer replaced Mrs. Nels Smith and Glenn Sweem replaced
Charles Margolf. The commission chose Charles "Pat" Hall as its executive director,
and Selia Ribeiro as its administrative officer. After Selia Ribeiro resigned, Paulette
Weiser and Susan Sharp handled the administrative details.

The State Bicentennial Commission financed its activities mainly with $542,000
received from the American Revolution Bicentennial Administration (ARBA), of
which $377,500 had been appropriated by Congress and $164,500 had come from the
sale of official ARBA medallions struck by the U.S. Mint. The state legislature provided
$66,652 in appropriated funds. The State Commission also realized close to $100,000
in profits from its sales desk. Of these profits, $28,000 was returned to the general fund.
Local Bicentennial Committees had to match 50–50 the money they received from the
State Commission. The State Commission spent $244,152 for administration and paid
out $436,500 for projects from 1972 to 1977.

of an Indian and a mountain man exchanging friendly greetings. Because of delay in acquiring Independence Rock, the statues in 1976 were placed temporarily in front of the Travel Commission's headquarters near Cheyenne.

The State Bicentennial Commission used as its logo a bucking horse with a rider clad in colonial costume. Many natives disliked the logo, considering it to be a desecration of the state's bucking horse and cowboy symbol. The commission published a large book, *Documents of Wyoming Heritage*, containing reproductions of significant documents of the territory and state. The documents had been selected and annotated by a subcommittee of the commission and its executive director, Charles "Pat" Hall. Philatelic projects received much attention. The commission also subsidized the production of a twenty-eight-minute film, *Wyoming from the Beginning*, for use in schools, and a three-act opera, *Lynching on the Sweetwater*, which has been discussed above.

In another one of its major projects the Bicentennial Commission sponsored pens of liberty kits, developed by Susan Schank Fawcett of Casper. The kits included quill pens, inkwells, ruffled cuffs, cravats, and booklets which enabled elementary and intermediate school students in many parts of the state to re-enact scenes of the Revolutionary War period. Students using the kits played the parts of the Founding Fathers, debated issues, and concluded the exercise by signing the names of the men they represented below the Declaration of Independence.

The Bicentennial Commission, in addition to its own projects, funded and supervised projects of all kinds which were proposed and managed by local Bicentennial committees. Seventy-six communities completed almost 150 projects. Two of them involved the construction of new buildings, a civic center in Hulett and a mountain man museum in Pinedale. Many more projects involved the restoration of old structures for use as museums or other purposes. Three communities, Centennial, Riverton, and Torrington, acquired and renovated abandoned railway depots. Three other communities, Laramie, Lusk, and Rawlins, moved, restored, and furnished old log schoolhouses for use as museums. Sheridan renovated, for display, an old street car which had carried passengers on Sheridan streets early in the century, and a tiny pioneer post office. Encampment chose to restore an opera house and a two-story outhouse which had been used in the Sierra Madre where snowdrifts sometimes engulfed the first story. Big Horn restored a Bozeman Trail blacksmith shop; Lovell, a 1917 railroad caboose; Green River, the Expedition Island Pavillion; and Recluse, its log community hall.

Douglas built a memorial fountain at its county courthouse. Sinclair restored the Kistler Memorial Fountain in the Spanish-style Sinclair Hotel, which was being refurbished after a decade of disuse. Sheridan used a twelve-thousand-dollar grant to pay off a mortgage on its Trail End Museum (Kendrick mansion).

Jim Baker, a famous mountain man who had been inducted into the fur trade by Jim Bridger, built a two-story fortlike cabin near Savery in his declining years. In 1917, nineteen years after Baker's death, the cabin was moved two hundred miles over three mountain ranges to Frontier Park in Cheyenne, to add to the attractions there. As their Bicentennial project, the people of Savery brought the cabin back to Savery and rededicated it with appropriate speeches in the presence of Baker's descendants and other admirers, at least one score of whom were attired in mountain man regalia.

Another cabin, which Owen Wister had built in the 1920's in Jackson Hole, was trundled even farther, more than three-hundred miles, to Medicine Bow. Since the Jackson Hole folks no longer appreciated the cabin, the people of Medicine Bow claimed it. Wister had made their town famous by having some of the incidents in his novel *The Virginian* occur there.

Other communities for their Bicentennial observances engaged in pageantry, planted trees, presented assorted exhibitions, cleaned up their streets, established youth centers, sent Indian boys and girls on tour to Washington, D.C., presented dramas for young and old, helped with Indian powwows, promoted Mexican folk dancing, created parks, gathered oral history, sponsored youth camps, put on youth musicals and dance festivals, and sponsored the study and publication of local history.

Most communities celebrated the Fourth of July in 1976 with a little more seriousness than usual. The British Broadcasting Company filmed a sixty-minute documentary recording the 1976 observances at Lost Springs (population, 7) and Cody (population, 6,000). Both had parades and rodeos. The BBC showed the one thousand people who gathered at Lost Springs behaving with more dignity and sobriety than the larger crowd at Cody.

For one of its projects the University of Wyoming endorsed a powwow for its Indian students; for another, it dedicated a Bicentennial Park at the east end of the campus and planted a circle of thirteen pine trees, one for each of the original states of the Union.

Centennial (population 100), a town which had been founded in

1876, gave more time and thought to its Bicentennial celebration than any other community in the state. The townspeople on July 4, 1977, concluded their many activities with the burial of a time capsule in front of the old railway depot which had been converted into a museum. The small group in attendance at 11:00 A.M., the scheduled time that morning, would not soon forget the ceremony because almost all the able-bodied men of the community could be seen four-hundred yards away, fighting a fire which was destroying the sawmill where many of them were employed. The capsule was to be opened on July 10, 1990, when Wyoming would be celebrating its centennial of statehood.

Another time capsule, donated by the Reynolds Aluminum Company, was buried in front of the Supreme Court Building in Cheyenne. It was to be opened on July 4, 2076. Both of the time capsules contained memorabilia identified with the state's celebration of the nation's Bicentennial.

RECREATION

Opportunities for recreation multiplied in the postwar period. Affluence and new reservoirs contributed to a tremendous expansion of water sports. Who would have thought in the 1930's that eighty-nine sailboats would be participating in a regatta on Alcova Reservoir in 1977? There really weren't many more than eighty-nine sailboats in the state, but everyone who could afford it had to own a motorboat and a trailer with which to deliver it to water where there might be trout. Low water temperatures discouraged but did not prevent considerable outdoor swimming and water skiing.

Who could have foreseen in the 1930's the infestation of snowmobiles in the national forests which, to environmentalists, was as devastating as the pine bark beetle? Their noise frightened wild animals, disrupted their migration patterns, and ran some of them to death. A 1977 recreation survey conducted by University of Wyoming professor Don Warder in southwestern Wyoming indicated that the majority of the snowmobiles were owned by people with no more than a high school education. Unquestionably, people with four-wheel-drive pickups and recreational vehicles in summer, and snowmobiles in winter, cruised through the woods in far greater numbers than ever before, to the great annoyance of hikers and persons on skis and snowshoes.

Who would have anticipated in the 1930's that low-interest federal loans and grants would put golf courses with grass greens and commodious clubhouses near every city of any size? And swimming pools? And tennis courts? True, climate and weather restricted some types of development. The short summers and the wind, for example, sometimes inhibited baseball, tennis, swimming, and golf. Nonetheless, all four activities flourished to a greater extent than might be expected. Most high schools had indoor swimming pools, and the University of Wyoming, Casper, and Jackson had indoor tennis courts.

Wyomingites engaged in hundreds of recreational activities common elsewhere in America. They added a few exotic types such as horse-drawn chariot and cutter races, which had started in Star Valley in the 1920's and spread to Jackson and other towns after World War II.

Insufficient snow and lack of water for artificial snow sometimes limited activity at the state's twelve ski developments. Wyoming, a semiarid state, did not have nearly as much snow as many Easterners thought. There was very little ice skating because of the wind, rough ice, alternation of cold and warm days, and the danger of falling through thin ice on rivers and reservoirs.

Contrary to what might be expected, not more than 5 per cent of the Cowboy State's residents rode horses except on rare occasions. Boys preferred sports cars and pickups, while girls were denied horse ownership because of the high cost of feed and stabling.

The prevalence of outdoor living has been given credit for the excellent physical fitness of Wyoming's young men who were examined for military duty during World War II (see above, pp. 475–476). Yet in postwar years not one-half of the residents were outdoor types. Most of the residents spent very little time outdoors, and limited their interest in sports to watching others.

Using a random-sampling system believed to give results approximately 95 per cent representative of the Albany County residents, the university's Department of Recreation and Park Administration found in 1975 that the ten most popular recreation activities were, in descending order, listening to music, watching television, reading for pleasure, attending movies, attending parties, picnicking, playing card games, fishing, attending concerts and plays, and attending football games. Partying, which ranked fifth, included considerable private and public consumption of alcohol. The report noted that "the least engaged in recreational activity category was that of outdoor recreation. . . . In essence, the more sedentary the activity, the more popular the activity." This report would have distressed but not left speechless the Lost Cabin sheepman who told the Wool Growers convention in 1927

that Wyoming with its "open ranges and outdoor life, can never have
the same ideas or ideals as those of the states . . . where the entire
population has been lambed in sheds."

It should be remarked that there is a difference between how people
spend their time (listed above) and how they would spend their time if
they had the opportunity. Many Albany County people would give top
priority to watching a University of Wyoming football game, but they
cannot give much time in a year to doing that when there are only four
or five home games.

Devotees of outdoor recreation were much concerned about the
impact of the state's population growth on established patterns.
Residents were already distressed by the flood of weekend fishermen
and campers from Colorado and Utah. The new workers and their
families moving into the state would add to the pressure on fish,
wildlife, and camping areas, and would clutter up the national forests
worse than ever with four-wheel-drive vehicles and snowmobiles.

QUALITY OF LIFE

A quality-of-life study by the Midwest Research Institute of Kansas
City, Missouri, based on 1970 data, in 1973 ranked Wyoming sixth
among the fifty states, behind California, Colorado, Connecticut,
Washington, and Oregon. The six leaders were the only ones rated
excellent. Such ratings must be partly subjective; one man's meat is
another man's poison.

Moreover, Wyoming changed so much in the 1970's that the study
could not be considered valid for the later years of the decade. Observers in 1977 differed sharply in their opinions. On the plus side were
economic status, education, technology, low taxes, concern for senior
citizens, diminishing racism and inequality, efficient state and local
governments, state revenues, parks, open space, wildlife, better than
average hunting and fishing. On the minus side were crime rates,
divorce rate, increasing child abuse, excessive alcoholism, slaughter on
the highways, lack of adequate medical and dental care, deteriorating
hunting and fishing, longer lines, crowded parks, more highway con-
gestion, substandard welfare and retirement benefits, too high a ratio
of trailer housing to traditional housing, a great increase in dust
resulting from extensive disturbance of ground cover, rapidly rising
utility bills and other living costs, serious water supply problems, and
poor public transportation.

Environmentalists were fearful about the future. Mike Leon, *Sheridan Press* columnist, wrote that "within 20 years the Wyoming we once knew will have become unrecognizable. In less than a generation it will have been degraded from a leading example of environmental quality to one of the worst." Leon suggested that a united front between labor and agriculture was essential but "would never happen." Ted Olsen, retired diplomat, lamented that "the strip miners are at work only a hundred miles north of Laramie. Their monster mandibles are gnawing away the tender pelt of the prairie to gouge coal for our insatiable generators. When they move on they leave desolation, hideous and complete."[13]

Most residents were not so disturbed by strip mining, which appeared to be less of a threat than the proliferation of large industrial plants. State and federal law required that the surface be restored after strip mining. Land-management experts at the University of Wyoming, after several years of experimentation, advised that strip-mined land could be rehabilitated so that it would produce more feed than before, although not with precisely the same plants. Most of the land involved had never sustained more than one cow per forty acres and the total acreage to be mined in the foreseeable future was small.

Whether they wanted to block entirely or merely restrict strip mining, environmentalists performed a valuable service by insisting that developers adhere strictly to the law and by making citizens think about what limits ought to be put on development. Probably the next generation will honor Wyoming's environmentalists of the 1970's. Tom Bell (who left in 1974), Mike Leon, Bart Koehler, Colleen Kelly, Laney Hicks, Bruce Hamilton, Lynn Dickey, Leslie Peterson, Keith Becker, Hank Phibbs, and others, for very little pay, devoted their lives to preserving Wyoming's streams, fish, wildlife, forests, clean air, pure water, and uncluttered countryside. They were catching less abuse in 1977 than in previous years, as more people became aware of their fundamental idealism. They would lose some battles, but probably not as many as Mike Leon thought they would. Not all of their adversaries were nineteenth-century robber barons. Some of them made possible the comment by L. G. Rawl, senior vice-president of Exxon Corporation, in 1976: "One [hopeful] sign is a continued growth in the professional manager's sense of responsibility. The days are long past when he considers himself responsible to stockholders and no one else."

[13] *Ranch on the Laramie* (Boston: Little, Brown and Company, 1973), p. 237.

In 1977 Governor Ed Herschler's efforts to strike a balance between growth and preservation were very encouraging. With a growing understanding of Wyoming's assets and liabilities, the residents might be able to preserve the best of their heritage. As the citizens became more sophisticated and the corporate executives more responsible, together they could build a better Wyoming.

Appendix I

DECENNIAL RATE OF INCREASE IN POPULATION FOR THE UNITED STATES AND WYOMING, 1870–1970

	POPULATION			RATE OF INCREASE	
	U.S.	*Wyoming*		*U.S.* %	*Wyoming* %
1870	39,818,449	9,118			
1880	50,155,783	20,789	1870 to 1880	30.1	128.0
1890	62,947,714	62,555	1880 to 1890	25.5	200.9
1900	75,994,575	92,531	1890 to 1900	20.7	47.9
1910	91,972,266	145,965	1900 to 1910	21.0	57.7
1920	105,710,620	194,965	1910 to 1920	15.0	33.2
1930	122,775,046	225,565	1920 to 1930	16.2	16.0
1940	131,669,275	250,742	1930 to 1940	7.3	11.2
1950	150,697,361	290,529	1940 to 1950	14.5	15.9
1960	179,323,175	330,066	1950 to 1960	18.5	13.6
1970	203,184,772	332,416	1960 to 1970	13.6	0.7

Sources: *1960 U.S. Census of Population*, Vol. I, *Characteristics of the Population*, Part 1, "United States Summary," pp. 1-16, 1-18, 1-145; *1970 U.S. Census of Population*, Vol. I, Part 1, "United States Summary," pp. 1-261, and Part 52, "Wyoming," p. 7.

Appendix II

GOVERNORS OF THE TERRITORY OF WYOMING, 1869–1890

NAME	TERM OF OFFICE
John A. Campbell (R)	Apr. 15, 1869 to Mar. 1, 1875
John M. Thayer (R)	Mar. 1, 1875 to May 29, 1878
John W. Hoyt (R)	May 29, 1878 to Aug. 22, 1882
William Hale (R)	Aug. 22, 1882 to Jan. 13, 1885
E. S. N. Morgan (R) (Acting)	Jan. 13, 1885 to Feb. 28, 1885
Francis E. Warren (R)	Feb. 28, 1885 to Nov. 11, 1886
George W. Baxter (D)	Nov. 11, 1886 to Dec. 20, 1886
E. S. N. Morgan (R) (Acting)	Dec. 20, 1886 to Jan. 24, 1887
Thomas Moonlight (D)	Jan. 24, 1887 to Apr. 9, 1889
Francis E. Warren (R)	Apr. 9, 1889 to Oct. 11, 1890

Appendix III

GOVERNORS OF THE STATE OF WYOMING, 1890–1978

NAME	TERM OF OFFICE
Francis E. Warren (R)	Oct. 11, 1890 to Nov. 24, 1890
Amos W. Barber (R) (Acting)	Nov. 24, 1890 to Jan. 2, 1893
John E. Osborne (D)	Jan. 2, 1893 to Jan. 7, 1895
William A. Richards (R)	Jan. 7, 1895 to Jan. 2, 1899
DeForest Richards (R)	Jan. 2, 1899 to Apr. 28, 1903
Fenimore Chatterton (R) (Acting)	Apr. 28, 1903 to Jan. 2, 1905
Bryant B. Brooks (R)	Jan. 2, 1905 to Jan. 2, 1911
Joseph M. Carey (D)	Jan. 2, 1911 to Jan. 4, 1915
John B. Kendrick (D)	Jan. 4, 1915 to Feb. 26, 1917
Frank Houx (D) (Acting)	Feb. 26, 1917 to Jan. 6, 1919
Robert D. Carey (R)	Jan. 6, 1919 to Jan. 1, 1923
William B. Ross (D)	Jan. 1, 1923 to Oct. 2, 1924
Frank Lucas (R) (Acting)	Oct. 2, 1924 to Jan. 5, 1925
Nellie Tayloe Ross (D)	Jan. 5, 1925 to Jan. 3, 1927
Frank C. Emerson (R)	Jan. 3, 1927 to Feb. 18, 1931
Alonzo M. Clark (R) (Acting)	Feb. 18, 1931 to Jan. 2, 1933
Leslie A. Miller (D)	Jan. 2, 1933 to Jan. 2, 1939
Nels H. Smith (R)	Jan. 2, 1939 to Jan. 4, 1943
Lester C. Hunt (D)	Jan. 4, 1943 to Jan. 3, 1949
Arthur G. Crane (R) (Acting)	Jan. 3, 1949 to Jan. 1, 1951
Frank A. Barrett (R)	Jan. 1, 1951 to Jan. 3, 1953
C. J. "Doc" Rogers (R) (Acting)	Jan. 3, 1953 to Jan. 3, 1955
Milward L. Simpson (R)	Jan. 3, 1955 to Jan. 5, 1959
J. J. (Joe) Hickey (D)	Jan. 5, 1959 to Jan. 2, 1961
Jack R. Gage (D) (Acting)	Jan. 2, 1961 to Jan. 8, 1963
Clifford P. Hansen (R)	Jan. 8, 1963 to Jan. 2, 1967
Stanley K. Hathaway (R)	Jan. 2, 1967 to Jan. 6, 1975
Ed Herschler (D)	Jan. 6, 1975—

Sources

See page 639 for a discussion of significant new sources that became available during the years 1965–1977.
The William Robertson Coe Library, Science Library, and Geology Library at the University of Wyoming offer the best opportunities for studying Wyoming history. They have standard bibliographical aids, printed sources, a considerable quantity of manuscripts, and many rolls of microfilm copies of materials preserved elsewhere.

Outside the University of Wyoming Library, the most helpful source materials have been found in the Wyoming State Archives and Historical Department, Cheyenne; the National Archives, Washington, D.C.; the Bancroft Library in Berkeley, California; and the Henry E. Huntington Library in San Marino, California.

Not many general histories of Wyoming have been written. Hubert Howe Bancroft's *History of Nevada, Colorado, and Wyoming, 1540–1888* (San Francisco: The History Co., 1890) does not offer much of value in the 148 pages devoted to Wyoming. According to John W. Caughey, *Hubert Howe Bancroft, Historian of the West* (Berkeley and Los Angeles: University of California Press, 1946), Mrs. Frances Fuller Victor wrote sixteen-seventeenths of the Wyoming account and H. H. Bancroft one-seventeenth. H. H. Bancroft's nephew, Ashley Bancroft, and George H. Morrison in 1885 interviewed eighty-four leading citizens of Wyoming Territory and had ten others fill out questionnaires in their quest for information. The data they gathered are preserved in the Bancroft Library (with microfilm copies in the University of Wyoming Library), and have been helpful, especially for study of the cattle industry.

C. G. Coutant, Wyoming newspaperman, in the 1890's planned to publish a three-volume history of Wyoming, but was able to complete only the first part, *The History of Wyoming*, Volume I (Laramie: Chaplin, Spafford & Mathison, 1899). Unreliable and including nothing beyond 1869, Coutant's volume has been of limited value, and the same may be said of notes which Coutant made in preparing for further publication, which never came. These notes are filed in the Wyoming State Archives and Historical Department, Cheyenne.

More important are two three-volume works, I. S. Bartlett, *History of Wyoming* (Chicago: S. J. Clarke Publishing Co., 1918), and Frances B. Beard (ed.), *Wyoming from Territorial Days to the Present* (Chicago: American Historical Society, 1933). Each has one volume of narrative history and two volumes containing portraits and biographies

622

of persons who were willing to pay for the privilege of being included. The two works offer quite a bit of helpful information, though both fall short of being scholarly, critical histories.˙

A poorer example of the "mug book" type is Thomas S. Chamblin (ed.), *Historical Encyclopedia of Wyoming*, a two-volume work published in 1954 by the Wyoming Historical Institute (address unknown). Chamber of commerce secretaries and others supplied 150 pages of narrative history, while more than five hundred individuals, mostly from rural areas, paid generously for the privilege of having their biographies and portraits included. Chamblin's *Historical Encyclopedia* offers little sustenance for the serious student of Wyoming history.

One of the best-known books about the state is *Wyoming: A Guide to Its History, Highways, and People* (New York: Oxford University Press, 1941). Compiled in a W.P.A. project during the Great Depression, it was well edited by Agnes Wright Spring and Dee Linford. Though badly out of date, and never intended to be a comprehensive history, it is nevertheless a useful volume, especially for details of local history which can be found in the fine print of the "Tours" section.

Grace Raymond Hebard's *History and Government of Wyoming* (first published under the title *The Government of Wyoming: The History, Constitution and Administration of Affairs*), which appeared in eleven editions, the first in 1904, long blanketed the public schools of the state, but it is badly out of date and has been used little since Miss Hebard died in 1936. Much the same may be said of her *Pathbreakers from River to Ocean*, which was published in six editions.

Velma Linford's *Wyoming: Frontier State* (Denver: The Old West Publishing Co., 1947) was prepared for use as an eighth-grade textbook, as was the volume by Virginia Cole Trenholm and Maurine Carley, *Wyoming Pageant* (Casper: Prairie Publishing Co., 1946), but both books can be read with profit by many adults.

Clarice Whittenburg's *Wyoming People* (Denver: The Old West Publishing Co., 1958), though designed to be a fourth-grade textbook, likewise has been enjoyed by many adults.

Mae Urbanek's *Wyoming Wonderland* (Denver: Sage Books, 1964) is a brief historical survey in the romantic tradition, with many illustrations.

Marie H. Erwin's *Wyoming Historical Blue Book: A Legal and Political History of Wyoming, 1868–1943* (Denver: Bradford-Robson Printing Co., 1946) has been invaluable as a reference work, since it provides election returns for a 75-year period, in addition to much documentary and biographical material. Mrs. Erwin's original 1,471-page *Blue Book* has been reprinted in Virginia Cole Trenholm (ed.), *Wyoming Blue Book* (3 vols.; Cheyenne: Wyoming State Archives and Historical Department, 1974). Mrs. Erwin's work makes up the first two volumes, and the third volume contains election returns and other political data, portraits and biographies, and many essays by various authorities dealing with all phases of Wyoming state government, 1943–1974. Thus Mrs. Erwin's magnificent contribution to Wyoming history, which ended in 1943, has been brought down to 1974.

Cora M. Beach's *Women of Wyoming* (2 vols.; Casper: S. E. Boyer & Co., 1927–1929) contains much interesting biographical material, not only about Wyoming women, but also about their husbands. Of similar value is the large volume *Progressive Men of the State of Wyoming* (Chicago: A. W. Bowen and Co., 1903), prepared, it is thought, by C. G. Coutant.

Since 1936, I have supervised the writing of about eighty M.A. theses and five Ph.D. dissertations dealing with Wyoming-history topics.

Noteworthy also are Charles Lindsay, *The Big Horn Basin*, University of Nebraska Studies, Vols. XXVIII–XXIX (Lincoln: University of Nebraska, 1932); Alfred J. Mokler, *History of Natrona County, Wyoming, 1888–1922* (Chicago: R. R. Donnelley & Sons, 1923); Elizabeth Arnold Stone, *Uinta County: Its Place in History* (Laramie: The

Laramie Printing Co., 1924); Charles A. Welch, *History of the Big Horn Basin* (Salt Lake City: Printed by the Deseret News Press, 1940); and the anonymous volume *History of the Union Pacific Coal Mines, 1868 to 1940* (Omaha: The Colonial Press, 1940). The many works of Dr. Grace Raymond Hebard have been discussed in my article, "The Writings of Grace Raymond Hebard," *Annals of Wyoming*, X, 4 (October 1938), 151–154. Of special note are *Washakie* (Cleveland: Arthur H. Clark Co., 1930), *Sacajawea* (Glendale: Arthur H. Clark Co., 1933), and the two-volume work *The Bozeman Trail* (Cleveland: Arthur H. Clark Co., 1922). For *The Bozeman Trail*, Miss Hebard shared authorship with E. A. Brininstool. Miss Hebard's career is treated sympathetically in Janell A. Wenzel, "Dr. Grace Raymond Hebard as Western Historian" (Unpublished M.A. thesis, University of Wyoming, 1960). Miss Hebard was active in several capacities at the University of Wyoming for forty-five years (1891–1936). Lacking much training for historical research and writing, nevertheless she possessed tremendous drive and enthusiasm.

Hundreds of volumes have been published about limited aspects of nineteenth-century Wyoming history. Many of them are listed in Rose Mary Malone, *Wyomingana: Two Bibliographies* (Denver: Denver University Press, 1950); Harriett Knight Orr, *Bibliography for the History of Wyoming*, University of Wyoming Publications, XII, 1 (September 15, 1946), 1–51; and Eva Floy Wheeler, *Wyoming Writers* (Douglas, Wyo.: The Douglas Enterprise Co., 1940).

As a federal depository, the University of Wyoming Library has hundreds of thousands of government documents, many thousands of which relate to Wyoming, and at least one thousand of them have contributed directly to this study. Helpful in locating Wyoming materials in the documents has been a typescript "Index of the Historical Material Concerning the State of Wyoming as Found in the Congressional Documents, 1803–1936," 800 pages in length, compiled by John Montgomery in 1937 and edited by Marie H. Erwin. It was prepared in a WPA project. Only three copies of the index are known to exist. One is in the State Library in Cheyenne, one is in the University of Wyoming Library, and I have the third, which was presented to me by Mrs. Erwin.

The University of Wyoming Library has the publications of the Wyoming State Historical Department, which include the *Miscellaneous Historical Collections* of 1897, 1920, and 1922; the *Miscellanies* of 1919; the *Quarterly Bulletin*, 1923–1925; and the *Annals of Wyoming* since 1925. The Wyoming State Historical Department in 1943 issued an *Index* covering publications through 1942, and in 1961 issued Volume II of the *Index*, covering the years 1943–1959.

While the federal-government documents and general collections of the University of Wyoming Library have been indispensable, most of the source material I have used in preparing this *History of Wyoming* is kept in that part of the library known as the Western History Research Center, which is presided over by Dr. Gene M. Gressley. Here are found virtually all published state records. I have read the House and Senate journals and sessions laws, for example, from 1869 to the present, and I have drawn information from many other series, such as messages of the governors and annual or biennial reports of the several state officials, departments, boards, and commissions. As the state government has expanded, its publications have become correspondingly voluminous.

In Dr. Gressley's domain also are many manuscript collections, the best known, and most useful for this study, being the Wyoming Stock Growers Association records and the Francis E. Warren Collection. Many scholars have tapped but not exhausted the research wealth available in the incomparable cattle history materials assembled by the Wyoming Stock Growers Association (1873—). Only a few scholars have exploited the equally rich collection left by Francis E. Warren, extraordinary merchant prince, stockman, governor, and United States senator. His collection extends from 1867 to

1929 and includes 183 letterbooks, besides many account books, scrapbooks, and assorted papers. Duane Rose, a graduate student at the University of Illinois, is using the collection in preparing a life of Warren as his doctoral dissertation. I have found the Warren Collection to be of great help, especially in my study of the 1880's and 1890's.

Despite their well-known shortcomings as sources, I have used newspapers extensively. Without the newspapers I would have known nothing about large areas of Wyoming life. As one phase of my work, I have read at least one newspaper (often more) for every week, and more often for every day, from September, 1867, to November, 1977. Cheyenne newspapers have been used more than others, but many other papers have been exploited also.

Directors and department heads of the State Archives and Historical Department, Cheyenne, have placed their collections at my disposal without restriction. They have custody of certain state records and manuscripts not available at the university and of a much larger newspaper collection than the university affords.

A chapter-by-chapter discussion of sources follows.

CHAPTER 1

THE NATURAL SETTING AND FIRST VISITORS

Many University of Wyoming faculty members, and others, have been helpful in supplying basic information for use in this introductory chapter. Dr. S. H. Knight's essay in *Wyoming: A Guide to Its History, Highways, and People* is the best short treatment of the state's geology and paleontology. Dr. T. J. Dunnewald discusses soils in *Wyoming Soils and Soils Materials* (Bulletin 349, University of Wyoming Agricultural Experiment Station, April, 1957). Dr. C. L. Porter has provided information on vegetation zones, Dr. A. A. Beetle on sagebrush, Dr. George T. Baxter on wild life and fish.

The Wyoming climate is described in *Climates of the States: Wyoming* (Washington: U.S. Government Printing Office, 1960), a United States Weather Bureau publication, and Harold Eppson, head of the university's weather station, has contributed further data. University of Wyoming Agricultural Experiment Station bulletins by Clarence F. Becker and John D. Alyea, *Temperature Probabilities in Wyoming* (Bulletin 415, June, 1964) and *Precipitation Probabilities in Wyoming* (Bulletin 416, June, 1964), offer detailed data.

Anthropological data have been taken from H. M. Wormington, *Ancient Man in North America* (4th ed.; Denver: Denver Museum of Natural History, 1957), and William T. Mulloy, *A Preliminary Historical Outline for the Northwestern Plains* (Laramie: University of Wyoming, 1958). Mae Urbanek describes the Spanish Diggings in "Stone Age Industry in Wyoming," *Annals of Wyoming*, XXVIII, 2 (October 1956), 119–126. The Great Medicine Wheel is discussed in "Wyoming Archaeological Notes," *Annals of Wyoming*, XXXI, 1 (April 1959), 94–100.

A translation of the journal of the Chevalier de La Verendrye by Anne H. Blegen is available in the *Oregon Historical Society Quarterly*, XXVI, 2 (June 1925), 116–129.

For the John Colter story, one may turn conveniently to Burton Harris, *John Colter: His Years in the Rockies* (New York: Scribner, 1952). Robert Stuart's narrative is available in P. A. Rollins (ed.), *The Discovery of the Oregon Trail* (New York: C. Scribner's Sons, 1935), and Kenneth A. Spaulding (ed.), *On the Oregon Trail: Robert Stuart's Journey of Discovery* (Norman: University of Oklahoma Press, 1953). Wilson Price Hunt's diary is included in the Rollins volume.

The best fur-trade volume for Wyoming students is Dale L. Morgan, *Jedediah Smith and the Opening of the West* (Indianapolis: Bobbs-Merrill Co., 1953). Valuable also are H. M. Chittenden, *The American Fur Trade of the Far West* (3 vols.; New York: Francis P. Harper, 1902; later issued in 2 vols.); Paul C. Phillips, *The Fur Trade* (2 vols.;

Norman: University of Oklahoma Press, 1961); and Dale L. Morgan (ed.), *The West of William H. Ashley* (Denver: The Old West Publishing Co., 1964).

For trails history, quite indispensable are the introductions and notes provided by Dale L. Morgan in *The Overland Diary of James A. Pritchard from Kentucky to California in 1849* (Denver: The Old West Publishing Co., 1959) and *Overland in 1846* (2 vols.; Georgetown, Calif.: Talisman Press, 1963). Morgan has dealt with ferries along the trails in the *Annals of Wyoming*, Volumes XXI, 2–3 (1949), XXXI, 1–2 (1959), and XXXII, 1–2 (1960). The student of the trails should see also V. E. Geiger and W. Bryarly, *Trail to California*, ed. David M. Potter (New Haven: Yale University Press, 1945); William H. Goetzmann, *Army Explorations in the American West, 1803–1863* (New Haven: Yale University Press, 1959); Paul C. Henderson, *Landmarks on the Oregon Trail* (New York: Published by Peter Decker for the Westerners, 1953); W. Turrentine Jackson, *Wagon Roads West: A Study of Federal Road Surveys and Construction in the Trans-Mississippi West, 1846–1869* (Berkeley and Los Angeles: University of California Press, 1952); David Lavender, *Westward Vision: The Story of the Oregon Trail* (New York: McGraw-Hill, 1963); Irene D. Paden, *Wake of the Prairie Schooner* (New York: Macmillan, 1947); Georgia Willis Read and Ruth Gaines (eds.), *Gold Rush: The Journals, Drawings, and Other Papers of J. Goldsborough Bruff* (New York: Columbia University Press, 1949); Wallace Stegner, *The Gathering of Zion: The Story of the Mormon Trail* (New York: McGraw-Hill, 1964); and George R. Stewart, *The California Trail* (New York: McGraw-Hill, 1962).

A seminal study, full of provocative ideas regarding several aspects dealt with in this introductory chapter, and including an extensive bibliography, is James C. Malin, *The Grassland of North America: Prolegomena to Its History with Addenda* (Lawrence: James C. Malin, 1956). W. P. Webb, *The Great Plains* (Boston: Ginn and Co., 1931), is a minor classic, with definite merits and defects which can be best appreciated if supplementary reading is done in Fred A. Shannon's appraisal of it in *Critiques of Research in the Social Sciences: III* (New York: Social Science Research Council, 1940) and in the chapter "Webb and Regionalism," pp. 259–277, in Malin's book named above.

CHAPTER 2

THE INDIANS

Several works which I have used in preparing this chapter are William T. Hagan, *American Indians* (Chicago: University of Chicago Press, 1961); F. W. Hodge (ed.), *Handbook of American Indians North of Mexico* (2 vols.; Washington: U.S. Government Printing Office, 1907–1910); Charles J. Kappler (ed.), *Indian Affairs: Laws and Treaties* (2 vols.; Washington: U.S. Government Printing Office, 1904); Robert H. Lowie, *Indians of the Plains* (New York: Published for the American Museum of Natural History by McGraw-Hill, 1954); and John R. Swanton, *The Indian Tribes of North America* (Washington: U.S. Government Printing Office, 1953).

Reports of the Commissioner of Indian Affairs to the Secretary of the Interior for the years 1851–1877 and the *Second Annual Report of the Board of Indian Commissioners for the Year 1870* (*Executive Document 39* [Serial 1440], 41 Cong., 3 Sess.) have been indispensable.

Significant correspondence concerning Colonel Moonlight's difficulties at Fort Laramie is preserved in *War of the Rebellion: Official Records of the Union and Confederate Armies* (Serial 101), Series 1, Vol. XLVIII, Part 1, pp. 276–277. Colonel Carrington's report on the Fetterman Massacre appears in *Senate Executive Document 33* (Serial 2504), 50 Cong., 1 Sess. Many other House and Senate executive and miscellaneous documents have been used, with the assistance of Marie H. Erwin's "Index," mentioned above.

I have drawn upon the following works, among others: Robert G. Athearn, *High*

Country Empire (New York: McGraw-Hill, 1960) and *William Tecumseh Sherman and the Settlement of the West* (Norman: University of Oklahoma Press, 1956); George Bird Grinnell, *The Cheyenne Indians* (New Haven: Yale University Press, 1923) and *The Fighting Cheyennes* (Norman: University of Oklahoma Press, 1956); LeRoy R. Hafen and Ann W. Hafen (eds.), *Powder River Campaigns and Sawyers Expedition of 1865* (Glendale: Arthur H. Clark Co., 1961); LeRoy R. Hafen and F. M. Young, *Fort Laramie and the Pageant of the West, 1834–1890* (Glendale: Arthur H. Clark Co., 1938); George E. Hyde, *A Sioux Chronicle* (Norman: University of Oklahoma Press, 1956), *Red Cloud's Folk: A History of the Oglala Sioux Indians* (Norman: University of Oklahoma Press, 1937), and *Spotted Tail's Folk: A History of the Brulé Sioux* (Norman: University of Oklahoma Press, 1961); Merrill J. Mattes, *Indians, Infants and Infantry* (Denver: The Old West Publishing Co., 1960); Doane Robinson, *A History of the Dakota or Sioux Indians* (Minneapolis: Ross and Haines, 1956); Edgar I. Stewart, *Custer's Luck* (Norman: University of Oklahoma Press, 1955); and Lodisa C. Watson, "Fort Laramie, 1849–1869" (Unpublished M.A. thesis, University of Wyoming, 1963).

Dale L. Morgan has published many documents dealing with the Shoshonis in the *Annals of Wyoming*, Volumes XXV–XXX (1953–1958). Of some use has been Roger D. Siebert, "A History of the Shoshoni Indians of Wyoming" (Unpublished M.A. thesis, University of Wyoming, 1961), and a volume which should become the standard work on the subject, Virginia Cole Trenholm and Maurine Carley, *The Shoshonis: Sentinels of the Rockies* (Norman: University of Oklahoma Press, 1964).

The belief that the Shoshoni woman of the Lewis and Clark Expedition died on the Wind River Reservation in 1884 rather than in South Dakota in 1812 is refuted by Irving Anderson, "Probing the Riddle of the Bird Woman," *Montana: The Magazine of Western History*, XXIII (October 1973), 2–17, and Harold P. Howard, *Sacajawea* (Norman: University of Oklahoma Press, 1971).

CHAPTER 3

THE COMING OF THE UNION PACIFIC

Two excellent books of many about the U.P. are Barry B. Combs, *Westward to Promontory: Building the Union Pacific across the Plains and Mountains* (Palo Alto: American West Publishing Co., 1969), and Robert G. Athearn, *Union Pacific Country* (New York: Rand-McNally, 1971). Dr. Wallace Farnham has published three important articles: "The Pacific Railroad Act of 1862," *Nebraska History*, XLIII, 3 (September 1962), 141–167; "'The Weakened Spring of Government': A Study in Nineteenth-Century American History," *American Historical Review*, LXVIII, 3 (April 1963), 662–680; and "Grenville Dodge and the Union Pacific: A Study of Historical Legends," *Journal of American History*, LI, 4 (March 1965), 632–650. In my own study of Union Pacific history I have treasured *Senate Executive Document 69* (Serial 2336), 47 Cong., 1 Sess., which in 252 pages of fine print provides all reports made by the government directors of the Union Pacific Railroad Company from 1864 to 1885.

The following works have also been helpful: Emmett D. Chisum, "The Construction of the Union Pacific Railroad Through Wyoming, 1867–1869" (Unpublished M.A. thesis, University of Wyoming, 1953); John P. Davis, *The Union Pacific Railway* (Chicago: S. C. Griggs and Co., 1894); Grenville M. Dodge, *How We Built the Union Pacific Railway* (*Senate Document 447*, 61 Cong., 2 Sess.); Robert W. Fogel, *The Union Pacific Railroad: A Case in Premature Enterprise* (Baltimore: Johns Hopkins Press, 1960); Marie Milligan Frazer, "Some Phases of the History of the Union Pacific Railroad" (Unpublished M.S. thesis, University of Wyoming, 1927); J. D. Galloway, *The First Transcontinental Railroad* (New York: Simmons-Boardman, 1950); Wesley S. Griswold, *A Work of Giants: Building the First Transcontinental Railroad* (New York: McGraw-Hill, 1962); J. R. Perkins, *Trails, Rails and War* (Indianapolis: Bobbs-Merrill Co., 1929);

Nelson Trottman, *History of the Union Pacific* (New York: The Ronald Press Co., 1923); and W. H. Wroten, Jr., "The Railroad Tie Industry in the Central Rocky Mountains, 1867–1900" (Unpublished doctoral dissertation, University of Colorado, 1956).

A major source has been the *Cheyenne Leader*. The University of Wyoming has microfilm copies of this newspaper, the original files of which are preserved in the Wyoming State Archives and Historical Department, Cheyenne. Drawn upon also have been University of Wyoming microfilm copies of the *Frontier Index* and the *Sweetwater Mines*, the originals of which are in the Bancroft Library, Berkeley, California.

Other information incorporated into this chapter has come from such diverse sources as H. H. Bancroft, *Popular Tribunals* (2 vols.; San Francisco: The History Co., 1887); C. Stanley Gustafson, "History of Vigilante and Mob Activity in Wyoming" (Unpublished M.A. thesis, University of Wyoming, 1961); Lola M. Homsher (ed.) *South Pass, 1868: James Chisholm's Journal of the Wyoming Gold Rush* (Lincoln: University of Nebraska Press, 1960); Ray Revere, "A History of Fort Sanders, Wyoming" (Unpublished M.A. thesis, University of Wyoming, 1960); Louis Laurent Simonin, *La Grand-Ouest des Etats Unis* (Paris: Charpentier, 1869); Elizabeth Arnold Stone, *Uinta County: Its Place in History* (Laramie: The Laramie Printing Co., 1924); J. H. Triggs, *History and Directory of Laramie City* (Laramie: Daily Sentinel Print., 1875); and United States War Department, *Reports of Explorations and Surveys to Ascertain the Most Practicable and Economical Route for a Railroad from the Mississippi River to the Pacific Ocean, 1853–1858* (11 vols.; Washington: A. O. P. Nicholson, Printer, 1855–1859; Serials 791–801).

CHAPTER 4

ORGANIZATION OF WYOMING TERRITORY AND
ADOPTION OF WOMAN SUFFRAGE

Excellent background reading for study of Wyoming territorial organization is found in Earl S. Pomeroy, *The Territories and the United States, 1861–1890* (Philadelphia: University of Pennsylvania Press, 1947); Howard R. Lamar, *Dakota Territory, 1861–1889: A Study of Frontier Politics* (New Haven: Yale University Press, 1956); and Herbert S. Schell, *History of South Dakota* (Lincoln: University of Nebraska Press, 1961).

I have found fundamental data for use in this chapter in the Wyoming territorial records preserved in the National Archives; the *Congressional Globe*; the journals of the Wyoming House and Council; *The Laws of Wyoming, 1869*; Marie H. Erwin, *Wyoming Historical Blue Book* (cited above); Governor John A. Campbell's diary, 1869–1875, published in the *Annals of Wyoming*, Volume X, Nos. 1, 2, 3, and 4 (1938); a typed copy of the complete 1870 census returns preserved in the University of Wyoming Library; and the files of three newspapers, the *Cheyenne Leader*, the *Wyoming Tribune*, and the *Laramie Sentinel*. Also, not to be overlooked is Peter K. Simpson's "History of the First Wyoming Legislature" (Unpublished M.A. thesis, University of Wyoming, 1962).

Further documentation and additional details of the woman suffrage story as presented in this chapter may be found in T. A. Larson's article, "Dolls, Vassals, and Drudges—Pioneer Women in the West," *The Western Historical Quarterly*, III, 1 (January 1972), 5–16, and in T. A. Larson, *Wyoming: A History* (New York: W. W. Norton and Co., 1977), pp. 76–107. A number of newspapers, particularly the *Cheyenne Leader*, the *Wyoming Tribune*, and the *Laramie Sentinel*, have supplied many of the suffrage-story details. Other significant sources include the Hebard files at the University of Wyoming; the Wyoming House and Senate journals; the six-volume *History of Woman Suffrage*, ed. Elizabeth Cady Stanton, Susan B. Anthony, Mathilda Joslyn Gage, and Ida Husted Harper (Rochester and New York: Fowler & Wells, etc., 1881–1922);

Eleanor Flexner, *Century of Struggle: The Woman's Rights Movement in the United States* (Cambridge: Belknap Press of Harvard University Press, 1959); an anonymous twelve-page pamphlet, "Nine Years' Experience of Woman Suffrage in Wyoming" (Boston: W. K. Moody, Printer, 1879), a copy of which is in the possession of Mr. and Mrs. Jack Meldrum, Buffalo, Wyoming; and records in the Wyoming State Archives, particularly the *Letterpress Book, Secretary of State, Wyoming, May 25, 1869–October 11, 1872* and microfilm of Commissioners' Records A, Sweetwater County, 1870–1875.

CHAPTER 5

THE 1870's—A TROUBLED DECADE

In preparing this chapter I have leaned heavily on the Wyoming territorial papers in the National Archives; printed federal-government documents, particularly annual reports of the Commissioner of Indian Affairs and annual reports of the Secretary of the Interior; Wyoming House and Council journals and session laws; and Cheyenne and Laramie newspapers.

I have gone a second time to the Indian volumes listed for Chapter 2 and the Union Pacific volumes listed for Chapter 3.

I have also used the following: Leonard J. Arrington, *The Changing Economic Structure of the Mountain West, 1850–1950* (Logan: Utah State University Press, 1963); Joe DeBarthe, *Life and Adventures of Frank Grouard*, ed. Edgar I. Stewart (Norman: University of Oklahoma Press, 1958); Governor John A. Campbell's diary (cited for Chapter 4); Marie H. Erwin, *Wyoming Historical Blue Book*; Volumes I–III of L. G. (Pat) Flannery (ed.), *John Hunton's Diary, 1873–1884* (5 vols.; Lingle, Wyo.: Lingle Guide-Review, 1956–1964); Lola M. Homsher (ed.), *South Pass, 1868* (cited for Chapter 3); Charles King, *Campaigning with Crook and Stories of Army Life* (New York: Harper & Brothers, 1890); *Report of the Auditor of Railroad Accounts (Executive Documents, 46 Cong., 3 Sess., 1880–1881, Vol. X)*; reports of government directors of the Union Pacific Railroad for various years; Agnes Wright Spring, *The Cheyenne and Black Hills Stage and Express Routes* (Glendale: Arthur H. Clark Co., 1949); Edgar I. Stewart, *Custer's Luck* (cited for Chapter 2); Robert E. Strahorn, *The Handbook of Wyoming* (Cheyenne [Chicago: Knight & Leonard, Printers], 1877); J. W. Vaughn, *With Crook at the Rosebud* (Harrisburg: Stackpole Co., 1956) and *The Reynolds Campaign on Powder River* (Norman: University of Oklahoma Press, 1961); James H. Wilkins (ed.), *The Great Diamond Hoax and Other Stirring Incidents in the Life of Asbury Harpending* (Norman: University of Oklahoma Press, 1958); and Thurman Wilkins, *Clarence King* (New York: Macmillan, 1958).

Readers who would know more about Bill Nye are referred to my introductory essay in T. A. Larson (ed.), *Bill Nye's Western Humor* (Lincoln: University of Nebraska Press, 1968) and to the book by Frank Wilson Nye, *Bill Nye: His Own Life Story* (New York: The Century Co., 1926).

CHAPTER 6

PROGRESS UNDER DIVERSE LEADERS, 1879–1889

Especially important in the preparation of this chapter have been the Wyoming territorial papers in the National Archives; the annual reports of the Secretary of the Interior; Wyoming House and Council journals and session laws; files of several Wyoming newspapers; Francis E. Warren's letterbooks in the University of Wyoming Library; and an article by Henry J. Peterson, "John Wesley Hoyt," *Annals of Wyoming*, XXII, 1 (January 1950), 3–68.

Stephen W. Downey's poem, "The Immortals," appears in the *Congressional Record*, 46 Cong., 2 Sess., Vol. 10, Part V and Appendix, pp. 337–352.

W. Turrentine Jackson deals with Governor Moonlight in "Administration of Thomas Moonlight, 1887–89," *Annals of Wyoming*, XVIII, 2 (July 1946), 139–162.

Arguments in the case *United States* v. *The Douglas-Willan, Sartoris Company*, regarding the fencing of the public domain, can be found in *Wyoming Reports*, Vol. III, Cols. 287–310.

Other helpful volumes are Leonard J. Arrington, *The Changing Economic Structure of the Mountain West, 1850–1950* (cited for Chapter 5); Marie H. Erwin's *Wyoming Historical Blue Book* (cited above); Charles A. Guernsey, *Wyoming Cowboy Days* (New York: G. P. Putnam's Sons, 1936); and Michael E. Varney, "The History of the Chicago and North Western Railway's Black Hills Division" (Unpublished M.A. thesis, University of Wyoming, 1963).

CHAPTER 7

BOOM AND BUST IN CATTLE

Twice told are the tales of the cattle business in territorial Wyoming. Basic works (several of which include extensive bibliographies) are John Clay, *My Life on the Range* (Chicago: Privately printed, 1924); Marion Clawson, *The Western Range Livestock Industry* (New York: McGraw-Hill, 1950); Maurice Frink, *Cow Country Cavalcade* (Denver: The Old West Publishing Co., 1954); Maurice Frink, W. Turrentine Jackson, and Agnes Wright Spring, *When Grass Was King* (Boulder: University of Colorado Press, 1956); E. S. Osgood, *The Day of the Cattleman* (Minneapolis: University of Minnesota Press, 1929 and 1954); Louis Pelzer, *The Cattlemen's Frontier* (Glendale: Arthur H. Clark Co., 1936); and Agnes Wright Spring, *Seventy Years* (Gillette, Wyo.: Wyoming Stock Growers Association, 1942).

Land questions are handled in Marion Clawson, *Uncle Sam's Acres* (New York: Dodd, Mead, 1951); B. H. Hibbard, *History of the Public Land Policies* (New York: Macmillan, 1924); R. M. Robbins, *Our Landed Heritage: The Public Domain, 1776–1936* (Princeton: Princeton University Press, 1942); and W. P. Webb, *The Great Plains* (cited for Chapter 1).

Two relevant case studies of land acquisition are unpublished M.A. theses at the University of Wyoming by Z. L. Boughn, "Disposal of the Public Domain in Albany County, Wyoming, 1869–1890" (1964), and Davis J. Law, "The Application of Federal Land Laws to Thomas County, Nebraska" (1960).

Primary source materials used include, most important, the records of the Wyoming Stock Growers Association preserved in the University of Wyoming Library. Especially valuable have been two volumes of the proceedings of the association covering the period 1873–1899 and two volumes of executive-committee minutes covering the years 1881–1911.

Cheyenne and Laramie newspapers in particular, but several other newspapers as well, have proved useful. There is much about cattle in the interviews of Wyoming pioneers recorded by Ashley Bancroft and George A. Morrison in the spring of 1885. The original interview records are in the Bancroft Library, film copies in the University of Wyoming Library.

Government documents of special value include governors' reports in reports of the Secretary of the Interior; Thomas Donaldson, *The Public Domain with Statistics* (*House Miscellaneous Documents*, 47 Cong., 2 Sess., 1882–1883, Vol. XIX); *House Executive Documents*, 50 Cong., 1 Sess., 1887–1888, Vol. X (which contains much material on public lands); *Senate Documents*, 48 Cong., 1 Sess., 1883–1884, Vol. VI (which has *Senate Executive Document 127*, entitled *Unauthorized Fencing of Public Lands*); *House Executive Documents*, 46 Cong., 2 Sess., 1879–1880, Vol. XXII, pp. 544–547, where appears the report of the public-lands commission of 1879–1880; and *House Executive Document 267* (Serial 2304), 48 Cong., 2 Sess., which is the Nimmo Report.

Relevant articles are Gene M. Gressley, "The American Cattle Trust: A Study in Protest," *Pacific Historical Review*, XXX, 1 (February 1961), 61–77; W. Turrentine Jackson, "The Wyoming Stock Growers' Association: Its Years of Temporary Decline, 1886–1890," *Agricultural History*, XXII, 4 (October 1948), 260–270, and "The Wyoming Stock Growers' Association Political Power in Wyoming Territory, 1873–1890," *Mississippi Valley Historical Review*, XXXIII, 4 (March 1947), 571–594; T. A. Larson, "The Winter of 1886–87 in Wyoming," *Annals of Wyoming*, XIV, 1 (January 1942), 5–17; J. Orin Oliphant, "The Cattle Herds and Ranches of the Oregon Country, 1860–1890," *Agricultural History*, XXI, 4 (October 1947), 217–238; and William D. Zimmerman, "Live Cattle Export Trade Between United States and Great Britain," *Agricultural History*, XXXVI, 1 (January 1962), 46–52.

Further additions to the chapter have come from two rolls of microfilm of selected General Land Office records in the National Archives, filed (NIS 156) in the University of Wyoming Library; the typescript of a 1948 University of Wyoming M.A. thesis by Rebecca Williamson Carter Bailey, "Wyoming Stock Inspectors and Detectives, 1873–1890"; the *Sixth Annual Report* of James D. Hopkins, territorial veterinarian, December 12, 1887 (Cheyenne, 1888); and the typescript of a 1951 University of Utah doctoral dissertation by George W. Rollins, "The Struggle of the Cattleman, Sheepman and Settler for Control of Lands in Wyoming, 1867–1910."

CHAPTER 8

TERRITORIAL LIFE

Newspapers have been the most important sources for this chapter. Their contributions have been spliced at many points by threads chosen from the following: the two anonymous volumes *History of the Union Pacific Coal Mines, 1868–1940* (Omaha: The Colonial Press, 1940) and *Pioneer People of Douglas and Converse County, Wyoming, 1886* (Douglas, Wyo.: Privately published, 1962); J. H. Beadle, *Western Wilds and the Men Who Redeem Them* (Cincinnati: Jones Brothers & Co., 1881); Campton Bell, "The Early Theatres, Cheyenne, Wyoming, 1867–1881," *Annals of Wyoming*, XXV, 1 (January 1953), 3–21; Mabel E. Brown and Elizabeth J. Thorpe, *And Then There Was One: The Story of Cambria, Tubb Town and Newcastle* (Newcastle, Wyo.: Privately published, 1962); R. H. Burns, A. S. Gillespie, and W. G. Richardson, *Wyoming's Pioneer Ranches* (Laramie: Top-of-the-World Press, 1955)—dealing mainly with Laramie Plains ranches; Lorah B. Chaffin, *Sons of the West* (Caldwell: The Caxton Printers, Ltd., 1941); E. E. Dale, "The Cow Country in Transition," *Mississippi Valley Historical Review*, XXIV, 1 (June 1937), 3–20; W. R. Dubois III, "A Social History of Cheyenne, Wyoming, 1875–1885" (Unpublished M.A. thesis, University of Wyoming, 1963); L. G. (Pat) Flannery (ed.), *John Hunton's Diary, 1873–1884* (cited for Chapter 5); John J. Fox, "The Far West in the 80's," ed. T. A. Larson, *Annals of Wyoming*, XXI, 1 (January 1949), 3–87; T. D. Fromong, "The Development of Public Elementary and Secondary Education in Wyoming, 1869–1917" (Unpublished doctoral dissertation, University of Wyoming, 1962); Charles A. Guernsey, *Wyoming Cowboy Days* (cited for Chapter 6); Julius J. Humphrey, "The Political and Social Influences of Freemasonry in Territorial Wyoming, 1870–1885" (Unpublished M.A. thesis, University of Wyoming, 1964); Elizabeth Keen, "The Frontier Press," in Ruth Hudson (ed.), *Literature of the West* (Laramie: University of Wyoming, 1956), pp. 75–100; Laramie County Historical Society, *Early Cheyenne Homes, 1880–1890* (Cheyenne: Pioneer Printing Co., 1962); Velma Linford, *Wyoming: Frontier State* (Denver: The Old West Publishing Co., 1947); Martha Ferguson McKeown, *Them Was the Days* (New York: Macmillan, 1950); Woods Hocker Manley, *The Doctor's Wyoming Children* (New York:

Exposition Press, 1953)—about growing up in Evanston; Frank W. Mondell, *My Story*, published serially in the *Wyoming State Tribune* (Cheyenne) from August 1, 1935, to February 4, 1936; W. O. Owen's memoirs in typescript at the University of Wyoming Library; Mary Lou Pence and Lola M. Homsher, *Ghost Towns of Wyoming* (New York: Hastings House, 1956); Louise Pound, "Old Nebraska Folk Customs," *Nebraska History*, XXVIII, 1 (January–March 1947), 3–31; Elizabeth Arnold Stone, *Uinta County: Its Place in History* (Laramie: The Laramie Printing Co., 1924); John Charles Thompson, "In Old Wyoming," an editor's column which ran irregularly in the *Wyoming State Tribune* (Cheyenne) in the 1930's and 1940's; Virginia Cole Trenholm, *Footprints on the Frontier* (Douglas, Wyo.: Printed by Douglas Enterprise Co., 1945); Charles S. Washbaugh, "Recollections," *Buffalo Bulletin*, July 2, 1959; Walker D. Wyman, *Nothing But Prairie and Sky* (Norman: University of Oklahoma Press, 1954)—the story of Dakota cowboy Bruce Siberts, but it has relevance for Wyoming.

The story of church organization and life has been found in C. Rankin Barnes, *Ethelbert Talbot, 1848–1928* (Philadelphia: Church Historical Society, 1955); *Diary and Letters of the Reverend Joseph W. Cook, Missionary to Cheyenne*, arranged by Bishop N. S. Thomas (Laramie: The Laramie Printing Co., 1919); Patrick A. McGovern, *History of the Diocese of Cheyenne* (Cheyenne: Wyoming Labor Journal, 1941); Austin L. Moore (ed.), *Souls and Saddlebags: The Diaries and Correspondence of Frank L. Moore, Western Missionary, 1888–1896* (Denver: Big Mountain Press, 1962); Ethelbert Talbot, *My People of the Plains* (New York: Harper & Brothers, 1906).

CHAPTER 9

STATEHOOD

For events leading up to statehood, I have depended upon Wyoming territorial papers in the National Archives; Cheyenne newspapers; Marie H. Erwin's *Wyoming Historical Blue Book*; Governor Warren's report to the Secretary of the Interior, October 15, 1889, in *House Executive Documents*, 51 Cong., 1 Sess., 1889–1890, Vol. XIII (Serial 2726), pp. 561–705; the Wyoming House and Council journals; and the Wyoming Constitution and sessions laws. Of interest also are two articles by W. Turrentine Jackson: "Administration of Thomas Moonlight, 1887–89," *Annals of Wyoming*, XVIII, 2 (July 1946), 139–162, and "The Wyoming Stock Growers' Association Political Power in Wyoming Territory, 1873–1890," *Mississippi Valley Historical Review*, XXXIII, 4 (March 1947), 571–594. Brief surveys of the background of statehood are available in I. S. Bartlett, *History of Wyoming* (Chicago: S. J. Clarke Publishing Co., 1918), I, 185–190, and in Frances B. Beard (ed.), *Wyoming from Territorial Days to the Present* (Chicago: American Historical Society, 1933), I, 427–431.

For the constitutional convention and the constitution, the major source is the *Journal and Debates of the Constitutional Convention of the State of Wyoming* (Cheyenne: The Daily Sun, 1893). The chairman of the convention, M. C. Brown, discussed its work in "Constitution Making," in *Proceedings and Collections of the Wyoming State Historical Department, 1919–1920*, pp. 96–108. Another member of the convention, W. E. Chaplin, commented on its work in the *Wyoming State Tribune* (Cheyenne), August 26, 1934 (sec. 1, p. 2), and July 23, 1940 (sec. 3, p. 8). Two authors listed above, Bartlett and Beard, also discuss the convention and constitution, as does H. J. Peterson, *The Constitutional Convention of Wyoming* (Laramie: University of Wyoming, 1940). R. K. Prien reported on a painstaking comparison of the Wyoming Constitution with other state constitutions in "The Background of the Wyoming Constitution" (Unpublished M.A. thesis, University of Wyoming, 1956).

Marie H. Erwin includes pictures and brief biographies of the forty-nine men who attended the convention in her *Wyoming Historical Blue Book*, pp. 631–647.

John D. Hicks, *The Constitutions of the Northwest States*, University of Nebraska Studies,

XXIII, 1–2 (January–April 1923), focuses on Idaho, Montana, North Dakota, South Dakota, Washington, and Wyoming and makes some interesting comparisons.

Water rights and water law, and Wyoming's contributions to them, are discussed in Robert Dunbar's two articles "The Origin of the Colorado System of Water-Right Control," *Colorado Magazine,* XXVII (October 1950), 241–262, and "The Search for a Stable Water Right in Montana," *Agricultural History,* XXVIII, 4 (October 1954), 139–149; Wells A. Hutchins, *Selected Problems in the Law of Water Rights in the West* (Washington: U.S. Government Printing Office, 1942); Elwood Mead, *Irrigation Institutions* (New York: Macmillan, 1903); and William E. Smythe, *Conquest of Arid America* (New York: Harper & Brothers, 1900 and 1905). W. P. Webb offers a popular treatment of western water-law development in *The Great Plains* (cited for Chapter 1), pp. 431–452.

CHAPTER 10

YEARS OF STRUGGLE, 1890–1897

Many newspapers have contributed to this chapter, with those in Cheyenne and Laramie, the principal centers of population in the period, being the mainstays. Annual or biennial reports of state departments have supplied information, as have House and Senate journals and session laws. I have found the Warren letterbooks to be very rich for these years.

A useful survey of the national economy is Charles Hoffman, "The Depression of the Nineties", *Journal of Economic History,* XVI, 2 (June 1956), 137–164.

Pertinent are three unpublished University of Wyoming M.A. theses: Thomas A. Krueger, "Populism in Wyoming" (1960); George A. Paulson, "The Congressional Career of Joseph Maull Carey" (1962); and John K. Yoshida, "The Wyoming Election of 1892" (1956).

Perhaps too much has already been written about the Johnson County War, but the Wyoming historian cannot ignore an affair which is so celebrated in the state. Robert B. David is one of the few apologists for the Invaders in *Malcolm Campbell, Sheriff* (Casper: Wyomingana, Inc., 1931). Maurice Frink, in *Cow Country Cavalcade* (Denver: The Old West Publishing Co., 1954), tries hard to be impartial but tends to lean toward the Invaders.

Helena Huntington Smith's *The War on Powder River* (New York: McGraw-Hill, 1966) is the best study of the Invasion. The following books, however, are also significant: D. F. Baber, *The Longest Rope* (Caldwell: The Caxton Printers, Ltd., 1947); S. T. Clover, *On Special Assignment* (Boston: Lothrop Publishing Co., 1930); A. S. Mercer, *The Banditti of the Plains* (Norman: University of Oklahoma Press, 1954, and several previous editions elsewhere); N. O. Rush, *Mercer's Banditti of the Plains* (Tallahassee: Florida State University Library, 1961); Mari Sandoz, *The Cattlemen* (New York: Hastings House, 1958); and Lois Van Valkenburgh's 1939 University of Wyoming M.A. thesis, a really important contribution, "The Johnson County War: The Papers of Charles Bingham Penrose in the Library of the University of Wyoming with Introduction and Notes." Of value also are Charles H. Burritt's letters in the University of Wyoming Library, published in the *Buffalo Bulletin,* August 17, 1961; Struthers Burt, *Powder River Let 'er Buck* (New York: Farrar & Rinehart, 1938), pp. 267–307; Joe DeBarthe's editorials in the *Buffalo Bulletin,* December, 1891–March, 1892; O. H. "Jack" Flagg's editorials and news stories in the *Buffalo Bulletin,* May, 1892; and eight Francis E. Warren letterbooks which cover the period from June 3, 1891, to June 30, 1893.

Other passages in this chapter have been enriched by renewed reference to previously mentioned works by Leonard Arrington, I. S. Bartlett, Frances B. Beard, John

Clay, Marie H. Erwin, Charles A. Guernsey, Charles Lindsay, Frank W. Mondell, and Austin L. Moore. The *Congressional Record*, the United States Census returns, and Wyoming Stock Growers Association records have been consulted. Significant assistance has been obtained from the following: Roy E. Huffman, *Irrigation Development and Public Water Policy* (New York: The Ronald Press Co., 1953); Harold D. Roberts, *Salt Creek, Wyoming: The Story of a Great Oil Field* (Denver: Midwest Oil Corporation, 1956); George W. Rollins, "The Struggle of the Cattleman, Sheepman and Settler for Control of Lands in Wyoming, 1867–1910" (Unpublished doctoral dissertation, University of Utah, 1951); Clark L. Spence, "Melbourne, the Australian Rain Wizard," *Annals of Wyoming*, XXXIII, 1 (April 1961), 5–18; Sublette County Artists' Guild, *Tales of the Seeds-Ke-Dee* (Denver: Big Mountain Press, 1963); and Owen Wister's diary, 1885–1900 (fifteen manuscript volumes in the University of Wyoming Library.) About one-third of Wister's diary entries have been published in Fanny Kemble Wister (ed.), *Owen Wister Out West: His Journals and Letters* (Chicago: University of Chicago Press, 1958).

Social life of the 1890's is presented charmingly in Will Frackleton and Herman Seely, *Sagebrush Dentist* (Chicago: A. C. McClurg & Co., 1941, and Pasadena: Trail's End Publishing Co., 1947), and Woods Hocker Manley, *The Doctor's Wyoming Children* (New York: Exposition Press, 1953).

CHAPTER 11

INTO THE TWENTIETH CENTURY

Sources mined with the best results in preparing this chapter are reports of various state departments; journals of the Wyoming House and Senate; assorted newspapers; the ever indispensable *Wyoming Historical Blue Book*; Frank W. and Doris B. Osterwald, "Wyoming Mineral Resources," *Geological Survey of Wyoming*, Bulletin 45 (June 1952); and seven University of Wyoming M.A. theses (all in typescript) written under my supervision: Anne Carolyn Hansen, "The Congressional Career of Senator Francis E. Warren from 1890 to 1902" (1942); Robert F. Jones, "The Political Career of Senator Francis E. Warren, 1902–1912" (1949); Wesley D. Bowen, "The Congressional Career of Senator Francis E. Warren, 1912–1920" (1949); Albert G. Anderson, Jr., "The Political Career of Senator Clarence D. Clark" (1953); Jo Ann Fley, "John B. Kendrick's Career in the U.S. Senate" (1953); William T. Sullins, "The History of the Salt Creek Oil Field" (1954); D. H. Wernimont, "Frank W. Mondell as a Congressman" (1956); and M. V. Lewellyn, "John Kendrick and the Revival of the Democratic Party in Wyoming, 1910–1914" (1975). See also Betsy Ross Peters, "Joseph M. Carey and the Progressive Movement in Wyoming" (Ph.D. dissertation, University of Wyoming, 1971).

1958), tells the story of the cowboy volunteers of 1898. For copper-mining history, the following have been tapped: Henry G. Fisk, "Past Copper Mining in Southern Wyoming" (Typescript, University of Wyoming Library); Velma Linford, "The Grand Encampment," *The Westerners Brand Book*, III (Denver, 1949), 1–25; and occasional issues of the *Grand Encampment Herald* in the University of Wyoming's collections.

Railroad history has been strengthened by reference to Robert J. Casey and W. A. S. Douglas, *Pioneer Railroad: The Story of the Chicago and North Western System* (New York: Whittlesey House, 1948), and two works by Richard C. Overton, *Burlington West* (Cambridge: Harvard University Press, 1941) and *Gulf to Rockies* (Austin: University of Texas Press, 1953).

Noteworthy, too, have been the contributions of Leslie A. Miller's memoirs (in typescript at the University of Wyoming Library).

CHAPTER 12

HUGGERMUGGER ON THE RANGE, 1898–1914

George E. Mowry, *The Era of Theodore Roosevelt, 1900–1912* (New York: Harper, 1958), as in Chapter 11, supplies a national backdrop for Wyoming events. So do general studies such as Robert G. Athearn, *High Country Empire* (New York: McGraw-Hill, 1960); Marion Clawson, *Uncle Sam's Acres* (New York: Dodd, Mead, 1951); Phillip O. Foss, *Politics and Grass: The Administration of Grazing on the Public Domain* (Seattle: University of Washington Press, 1960); B. J. Hibbard, *A History of the Public Land Policies* (New York: Macmillan, 1924); Roy E. Huffman, *Irrigation Development and Public Water Policy* (New York: The Ronald Press Co., 1953); James C. Malin, *The Grassland of North America: Prolegomena to Its History with Addenda* (Lawrence: James C. Malin, 1956); E. Louise Peffer, *The Closing of the Public Domain* (Stanford: Stanford University Press, 1951); Gifford Pinchot, *Breaking New Ground* (New York: Harcourt, Brace, 1947); Elmo Richardson, *The Politics of Conservation: Crusades and Controversies, 1897–1913* (Berkeley: University of California Press, 1962); Roy M. Robbins, *Our Landed Heritage* (Princeton: Princeton University Press, 1942); and W. P. Webb, *The Great Plains* (Boston: Ginn and Co., 1931).

Primary source materials have been quarried from reports of the Commissioner of the General Land Office in reports of the Secretary of the Interior; annual and biennial reports of various state boards, commissions, and departments; Wyoming House and Senate journals; the *Congressional Record*; and Marie H. Erwin, *Wyoming Historical Blue Book*.

Occasional use has been made of Harold E. Briggs, *Frontiers of the Northwest* (New York: D. Appleton-Century Co., 1950); Robert K. Bruce, "History of the Medicine Bow National Forest" (Unpublished M.A. thesis, University of Wyoming, 1959); Fenimore C. Chatterton, *Yesterday's Wyoming* (Aurora, Colo.: Powder River Publishers, 1957); Mary Wilma M. Hargreaves, *Dry Farming in the Northern Great Plains, 1900–1925* (Cambridge: Harvard University Press, 1957); the George W. Rollins dissertation listed above for Chapter 10; Henry Trautwein, "History of the Wyoming Wool Growers Association" (Unpublished M.A. thesis, University of Wyoming, 1964); the seven M.A. theses listed above for Chapter 11; Edward N. Wentworth's admirable *America's Sheep Trails* (Ames: Iowa State College Press, 1948); and the remarkable *Report in the Matter of the Investigation of Charges that the Interior Department Permitted the Unlawful Fencing and Inclosure of Certain Lands of the Public Domain in the States of Colorado and Wyoming, and More Particularly the Fencing and Inclosure of 46,330 Acres of Public Lands in Wyoming and 1,120 Acres in Colorado by the Warren Live Stock Company* (Washington: U.S. Government Printing Office, 1913), which is *House Report 1335* (Serial 6334), 62 Cong., 3 Sess.

CHAPTER 13

THE FIRST WORLD WAR

A stimulating background volume for this chapter and the next two is W. E. Leuchtenburg, *The Perils of Prosperity, 1914–32* (Chicago: University of Chicago Press, 1958).

Source materials for this chapter include many newspapers, Wyoming session laws and House and Senate journals; quite a number of Wyoming board, commission, and department biennial reports, but especially those of the state commissioner of labor and statistics; *Hearings before the Committee on the Public Lands, U.S. House of Representatives, 65th Congress, 2d Session, on H.R. 3233, A Bill to Authorize Exploration for and Disposition of Coal, Phosphate, Oil, Gas, Potassium, or Sodium and S. 2812, An Act to Encourage and Promote the Mining of Coal, Phosphate, Oil, Gas, and Sodium on the Public Domain*

(Washington: U.S. Government Printing Office, 1918); and Marie H. Erwin, *Wyoming Historical Blue Book*.

Of some help have been Bartlett, Beard, and Mondell (all mentioned previously); the Anderson, Bowen, Fley, Sullins, and Wernimont theses listed above for Chapter 11; T. Blake Kennedy's memoirs and Leslie A. Miller's memoirs (both in typescript at the University of Wyoming Library); Leonard P. Ayres, *The War with Germany: A Statistical Summary* (Washington: U.S. Government Printing Office, 1919); J. Leonard Bates, "The Midwest Decision, 1915," *Pacific Northwest Quarterly*, LI, 1 (January 1960), 26–34, and *The Origins of Teapot Dome: Progressives, Parties, and Petroleum, 1909–1921* (Urbana: University of Illinois Press, 1963); Mary Basler Dahlgren, "Fifty Years of Service: History of the Wyoming Federation of Women's Clubs 1904 to 1954" (Unpublished M.A. thesis, University of Wyoming, 1956); Edmund L. Escolas, "Wyoming's Workmen's Compensation System, 1915–1960" *Wyoming Trade Winds*, IV, 10 (December 1961); A. B. Genung, "Agriculture in the World War Period," in United States Department of Agriculture, *Year Book of Agriculture, 1940* (Washington: U.S. Government Printing Office, 1941), pp. 277–295; Lloyd P. Jorgenson, "Agricultural Expansion into the Semiarid Lands of the West North Central States during the First World War," *Agricultural History*, XXIII, 1 (January 1949), 30–41; A. J. Mokler, *History of Natrona County, Wyoming, 1888–1922* (Chicago: R. R. Donnelley & Sons, 1923); Harold D. Roberts, *Salt Creek, Wyoming* (cited for Chapter 10); and Agnes Wright Spring, *William Chapin Deming of Wyoming* (Glendale, Calif.: Privately printed in a limited edition by the Arthur H. Clark Co., 1944).

CHAPTERS 14 AND 15

DEPRESSION YEARS, 1920–1939 *and* POLITICS AND
GOVERNMENT, 1920–1940

The bibliographies for these two chapters largely overlap. Excellent background reading is available in such works as Irving Bernstein, *The Lean Years: A History of the American Worker, 1920–1933* (Boston: Houghton Mifflin, 1960); John D. Hicks, *The Republican Ascendancy, 1921–1933* (New York: Harper, 1960); W. E. Leuchtenburg, *The Perils of Prosperity, 1914–1932* (Chicago: University of Chicago Press, 1958) and *Franklin D. Roosevelt and the New Deal, 1932–1940* (New York: Harper & Row, 1963); and three volumes by A. M. Schlesinger Jr., *The Crisis of the Old Order* (Boston: Houghton Mifflin, 1957), *The Coming of the New Deal* (Boston: Houghton Mifflin, 1958), and *The Politics of Upheaval* (Boston: Houghton Mifflin, 1960).

As usual, newspapers have been used extensively. So have state publications: session laws, House and Senate journals, and reports of many state departments, boards, and commissions—such as the Departments of Agriculture, Education, Highway, Law Enforcement, and Public Health; the Board of Equalization; the Board of Immigration; the Commissioner of Labor and Statistics; and the Commissioner of Public Lands and Farm Loans.

Pertinent typescript M.A. theses at the University of Wyoming are Barbara Jean Aslakson, "Nellie T. Ross: First Woman Governor" (1960); James P. Blaisdell, "A History of the Conservation Effort in Wyoming and the Wyoming Game and Fish Commission to 1950" (1964); Jo Ann Fley, "John B. Kendrick's Career in the U.S. Senate" (1953); Paul A. Hassler, "Some Effects of the Great Depression on the State of Wyoming, 1929–1934" (1957); Larry J. Krysl, "The Effects of the Great Depression on the State of Wyoming, 1935–1940" (1960); and Walter L. Samson, Jr., "The Political Career of Senator Francis E. Warren, 1920–1929" (1951).

Relevant publications include R. H. Burns, A. S. Gillespie, and W. G. Richardson, *Wyoming's Pioneer Ranches* (Laramie: Top-of-the-World Press, 1955); Wesley C. Calef, *Private Grazing and Public Lands* (Chicago: University of Chicago Press, 1960); Thomas

C. Donnelly (ed.), *Rocky Mountain Politics* (Albuquerque: University of New Mexico Press, 1940); Marie H. Erwin, *Wyoming Historical Blue Book* (Denver: Bradford-Robinson Printing Co., 1946); Maurice Frink, *Cow Country Cavalcade* (Denver: The Old West Publishing Co., 1954); Griffenhagen and Associates, *Report Made to the Special Legislative Committee on Organization and Revenue* (2 vols.; Vol. I, Cheyenne, 1933; Vol. II, Casper, 1933); Earl Lloyd and Paul A. Rechard, *Documents on the Use and Control of Wyoming Interstate Streams* (Cheyenne: State of Wyoming, 1957); James C. Malin, *The Grassland of North America* (cited for Chapter 12); Charles E. Winter, *Four Hundred Million Acres: The Public Lands and Resources* (Casper: Overland Publishing Co., 1932); and *Wyoming: A Guide to Its History, Highways, and People* (New York: Oxford University Press, 1941).

The Teapot Dome affair is treated in J. Leonard Bates, *The Origins of Teapot Dome: Progressives, Parties, and Petroleum, 1909–1921* (Urbana: University of Illinois Press, 1963); Burl Noggle, *Teapot Dome: Oil and Politics in the 1920's* (Baton Rouge: Louisiana State University Press, 1962); and M. R. Werner, *Teapot Dome* (New York: Viking Press, 1959). A source for other oil history is the *Midwest Review* (11 vols., 1920–1930), edited by Dan Greenburg in Casper.

Federal-government publications consulted in these chapters include: United States Department of Commerce, Bureau of the Census, *Religious Bodies: 1926* (2 vols.; Washington: U.S. Government Printing Office, 1930) and *Religious Bodies: 1936* (2 vols.; Washington: U.S. Government Printing Office, 1941); United States Department of the Interior, Bureau of Land Management, *Homesteads* (Washington: U.S. Government Printing Office, 1962); and Commissioner of the General Land Office reports in the annual reports of the Secretary of the Interior.

Finally, it needs to be stated that I have resided in Wyoming most of the time since 1936, have become acquainted with many state leaders, and have discussed developments of the 1920's and 1930's with them.

CHAPTER 16

THE SECOND WORLD WAR

This chapter is a condensation of my book *Wyoming's War Years, 1941–1945*, printed by Stanford University Press for the University of Wyoming in 1954. Although the book is out of print, copies can be found in many libraries.

CHAPTERS 17 AND 18

THE POSTWAR ECONOMY and POSTWAR
POLITICS AND GOVERNMENT

One who wants to accumulate a library dealing with current economic and political affairs in Wyoming needs only to get elected to the state legislature. Thereafter, he will receive pertinent material from public and private sources in every mail.

In preparing Chapters 17 and 18, session laws, House and Senate journals, Governors' messages, official directories of electoral returns, reports of many state departments and commissions, and newspapers have been indispensable. Interviews with many of the persons discussed have been helpful.

The periodicals *Cow Country* (Cheyenne), *Wyoming Stockman-Farmer* (Cheyenne), and *Wyoming Wool Grower* (Casper) mirror rural attitudes and contain useful data. The *Wyoming Labor Journal* (Cheyenne) changed its name to *Wyoming-Utah Labor Journal* in 1945 and then expired in 1949, leaving organized labor without a dependable editorial voice in the state. The periodicals *High Country News* (Lander), *In Wyoming* (Casper), *Wyoming News* (Cody), and *Wyoming Wildlife* are zestful and informative.

Economic developments are discussed in the Wyoming Employment Security

Commission's *Wyoming Labor Force Trends* and *Wyoming Employment Outlook*, both published in Casper. Other economic information is available in *Wyoming Progress Reports* of the Wyoming Department of Economic Planning and Development and various publications of the University of Wyoming's Institute for Policy Research. Research journals are published regularly by the Agricultural Experiment Station at the University of Wyoming. Minerals developments are well covered by the *Casper Star-Tribune*, the *Riverton Ranger*, the Wyoming Geological Survey (Laramie), U.S. Geological Survey (Laramie Office), Laramie Energy Research Center (LERC) in Laramie, and in the annual *Wyoming Mineral Yearbooks* of the Mineral Division, State Department of Planning and Development (Cheyenne). Water matters are discussed in publications of the Water Resources Research Institute at the University of Wyoming, the State Engineer's Office, and the Wyoming Water Development Association (Laramie).

Relevant M.A. theses available in typescript at the University of Wyoming are John T. Hinckley, "Public Land and the Public Interest," (Department of Political Science, 1949); John E. Hornoff, "The Political Career of Senator Edward V. Robertson" (1959); Kathleen M. Karpan, "A Political History of Jack Gage" (1975); and R. Jerome Woody, "The United States Senate Career of Lester C. Hunt" (1964). Karpan's study of Jack Gage was published in the *Annals of Wyoming*, XLVIII, 2 (Fall 1976), 167–252.

Analyses of Wyoming elections by political scientists such as H. H. Trachsel, Charles "Mike" Beall, Ralph Wade, John T. Hinckley, and John B. Richard appeared regularly in *The Western Political Quarterly* (Salt Lake City) for many years in the March, June, or September issues following the elections. No essays were published for the 1974 and 1976 elections.

Other relevant publications are Leonard J. Arrington, *The Changing Economic Structure of the Mountain West, 1850–1950* (cited for Chapter 5); Robert G. Athearn, *High Country Empire* (cited for Chapter 2); John R. Burroughs, *Guardian of the Grasslands: The First Hundred Years of the Wyoming Stock Grower's Association* (Cheyenne: Pioneer Printing, 1971); Winifred Galloway, "The History of Uranium in Wyoming" (A.B. honors thesis in American studies, University of Wyoming, 1961); Morris Garnsey, *America's New Frontier: The Mountain West* (New York: Knopf, 1950); Karl F. Kraenzel, *The Great Plains in Transition* (Norman: University of Oklahoma Press, 1955); I. M. Labowitz, *Federal Revenues and Expenditures in the Several States: Averages for the Fiscal Years 1959–1961* (Washington: U.S. Government Printing Office, 1962); T. A. Larson, *Wyoming: A History* (New York: W. W. Norton and Co., 1977), especially Chapters 4 and 5; Gerald D. Nash, *The American West in the Twentieth Century* (Englewood Cliffs, N.J.: Prentice-Hall, 1973); and John B. Richard, *Government and Politics of Wyoming* (3d ed.; Dubuque, Iowa: Kendall/Hunt Publishing Co., 1974).

Mineral taxation, which Wyoming legislators postponed from session to session and decade to decade because they lacked information on which to act, received much attention in the 1970's. Legislators can no longer use this excuse. Among recent studies are three by Leonard D. Bronder, research economist, for the Western Governors' Regional Energy Policy Office, Denver: "Taxation of Coal Mining: Review with Recommendations" (January, 1976), "Taxation of Surface and Underground Coal Mining in Western States" (August 1976); and "Severance Tax Comparisons among Western Governors' Regional Energy Policy Office States" (June 2, 1977). Another study is by Thomas F. Stinson, *State Taxation of Mineral Deposits and Production* (Interagency Energy-Environment Research and Development Program Report, U.S. Department of Agriculture and U.S. Environmental Protection Agency, Washington, D.C., January 1977).

CHAPTER 19

POSTWAR SOCIETY AND CULTURE

This chapter is a distillation of personal reflections based on almost fifty years of living in the state. Four summers, 1931–1934, in Yellowstone National Park gave me a chance to appreciate Wyoming's splendid scenery, wildlife, air, water, and light, and to recognize the state's responsibility to share the wealth with residents of less favored parts of the world. A one-year supply instructorship in the History Department at the University of Wyoming, 1936–1937, stretched into a lifetime career, during which I had unprecedented opportunities to study the state and its people.

Struthers Burt, John Gunther, Neal Peirce, Agnes Wright Spring, and many others, including the 16,000 students it was my privilege to teach and to be taught by at the University of Wyoming, have shaped my opinions. U.S. census reports provided some of the information I have used in this chapter. Newspapers, especially those of Laramie, Cheyenne, Casper, Sheridan, and Riverton, have been invaluable.

Personal files of the textbook probe, in which I was chairman of the Committee of Fifteen; of the Black Fourteen incident, in which I was one of ten faculty members who sponsored a resolution adopted by the Arts and Sciences faculty; of the state's Council for the Humanities, of which I was first state chairman; and of the state's Bicentennial Commission, of which I was vice chairman, provided insights helpful in the discussion of those topics.

The decision of the Albany County voters at the general election in 1976 to include one retired professor of history in the county's delegation to the state legislature opened many doors. That decision retreaded the professor and made me more of a student than a professor. It gave me fresh opportunities to study my favorite state and people. Some of the resulting reflections appear in Chapter 19.

SELECTED REFERENCES

(Additions, 1965–1977, to books about Wyoming.)

The presses were busier than ever before in the dozen years after the first edition of this *History of Wyoming* came out in 1965. Two members of the University of Wyoming English department, Richard F. Fleck and Robert A. Campbell, assembled "A Selective Literary Bibliography of Wyoming," which was published in the *Annals of Wyoming*, XLVI, 1 (Spring 1974), 75–112. A one-page supplement by Fleck appeared on p. 234 of the *Annals* (Fall 1975). Fleck and Campbell organized their bibliography under five headings: "Wyoming Authors on Wyoming," "American Authors on Wyoming," "Continental European Authors on Wyoming," "British Authors on Wyoming," and "A Bibliography of Bibliographies." Two other bibliographies which appeared in the period surveyed are Lola M. Homsher, *Wyoming: A Student's Guide to Localized History* (New York: Columbia University Teachers College Press, 1966) and Mae and Jerry Urbanek, *Know Wyoming: A Guide to Its Literature* (Boulder: Johnson Publishing Co., 1969).

No doubt the costliest publication project of the period was the recompilation and publishing of the Wyoming statutes. The legislature in 1977 appropriated $502,500 for this work which would replace the ten-volume *Wyoming Statutes* of 1957 and its many supplements. The Michie Company of Charlottesville, Virginia, was scheduled to have the new set ready for use by the legislature in February, 1978.

The romantic mountain man period of Wyoming history received a major addition to its literature in LeRoy R. Hafen (ed.), *Mountain Men and the Fur Trade of the Far West* (10 vols.; Glendale, Calif.: Arthur H. Clark Co., 1965–1972). Many authorities contributed to this compilation of 292 biographies of mountain men. Other additions are a revised edition of J. Cecil Alter, *James Bridger* (Westport, Conn.: Greenwood

Book Co., 1971); William Marshall Anderson, *The Rocky Mountain Journals of William Marshall Anderson: The West in 1834*, edited by Dale L. Morgan and Eleanor Towles Harris (San Marino, Calif.: The Huntington Library, 1967); Fred R. Gowans and Eugene E. Campbell, *Fort Bridger: Island in the Wilderness* (Provo: Brigham Young University Press, 1975); David Muench, *Rendezvous Country* (Palo Alto: American West Publishing Co., 1975); Carl P. Russell, *Firearms, Traps and Tools of the Mountain Men* (New York: Knopf, 1967); and Osborne Russell, *Journal of a Trapper* (Lincoln: University of Nebraska Press, 1965). Standard works on the fur trade published before 1965 are listed above among the sources for Chapter 1. I have devoted thirty pages to Wyoming's fur trade history in my book *Wyoming: A History* (New York: W. W. Norton and Co., 1977).

Standard works on Wyoming's trails history are listed above among the sources for Chapter 1. Important additions to that list are Gregory M. Franzwa, *The Oregon Trail Revisited* (St. Louis: Patrice Press, 1972); William H. Goetzmann, *Exploration and Empire: The Explorer and the Scientist in the Winning of the American West* (New York: Knopf, 1966); a revised edition of LeRoy R. Hafen, *Broken Hand: The life of Thomas Fitzpatrick, Mountain Man, Guide, and Indian Agent* (Denver: Old West Publishing Co., 1973); Donald Jackson and Mary Lee Spence (ed.), *The Expeditions of John Charles Fremont*, Vol. 1, including his expeditions through Wyoming in 1842 and 1843 (Urbana: University of Illinois Press, 1970); William E. Lass, *From the Missouri to the Great Salt Lake*, an account of overland freighting (Lincoln: Nebraska State Historical Society, 1972); Merrill J. Mattes, *The Great Platte River Road* (Lincoln: Nebraska State Historical Society, 1969); and Robert L. Munkres, *Saleratus and Sagebrush: The Oregon Trail through Wyoming* (Cheyenne: State Archives and Historical Department, 1974), Also, I devote thirty-five pages to trails history in the book mentioned above, *Wyoming: A History*.

Among other more or less noteworthy publications in the post-1965 years are these: a reprint edition (1977) by the Sweetwater County chapter, State Historical Society, of the anonymous *History of Union Pacific Coal Mines, 1868–1940*, originally published in 1940 by the Colonial Press, Omaha; Ellis L. Armstrong, Michael C. Robinson, and Suellen M. Hoy (ed.), *History of Public Works in the United States, 1776–1976* (Chicago: American Public Works Association, 1976); Robert G. Athearn, *Union Pacific Country* (New York: Rand-McNally, 1971; rptd. Lincoln: University of Nebraska Press, 1976); Glen Barrett, *Kemmerer, Wyoming, the Founding of an Independent Coal Town, 1897–1902* (Kemmerer: Quealy Services, Inc., 1972); Charles B. Beck, . . . *the damned elk et my broom!* (Cheyenne: privately printed, 1968); Lulu Parker Betenson, as told to Dora Flack, *Butch Cassidy, My Brother* (Provo: Brigham Young University Press, 1974); Orrin H. Bonney, *Battle Drums and Geysers: The Life and Journals of Lt. Gustavus Cheyney Doane, Soldier and Explorer of the Yellowstone and Snake River Regions* (Chicago: Sage Books, 1970); Bill Bragg, *Wyoming's Wealth: A History of Wyoming* (Basin: Big Horn Publishers, 1976); Mabel E. Brown and Elizabeth J. Thorpe, *Jubilee Memories* (Newcastle: Newcastle News Letter Journal, 1965); Elsa Spear Byron (ed.), *Bozeman Trail Scrapbook* (Sheridan: Mills Co., 1967); Otis Carney, *New Lease on Life: The Story of a City Family Who Quit the Rat Race and Moved to a Ranch in Wyoming* (New York: Random House, 1971); Centennial Historical Commission, *The Magic City of the Plains, 1867–1967* (Cheyenne: Cheyenne Centennial Committee, 1967); J. E. Chamberlain, *The Harrowing of Eden: White Attitudes toward Native Americans* (New York: Seabury Press, 1975); Roberta C. Cheney and Emmie D. Mygatt (eds.), *This is Wyoming . . . Listen* (Basin: Big Horn Books, 1977); Cleo Christiansen, *Sagebrush Settlements* (Lovell: Mountain States Printing, 1967); Wilson O. Clough, *A History of the University of Wyoming, 1887–1964* (Laramie: University of Wyoming, 1965); Barry B. Combs, *Westward to Promontory: Building the Union Pacific across the Plains and Mountains* (Palo Alto: American West Publishing Co., 1969); Roger B. Daniels, *Concentration Camps*

USA: Japanese Americans and World War II (New York: Holt, Rinehart and Winston, 1971); Everett Dick, *Conquering the Great American Desert* (Lincoln: Nebraska State Historical Society, 1975); Arthur F. Duntsch (ed.), *Crossroads of the West: A Pictorial History of Fremont County* (Riverton: Crossroads of the West, Inc., 1965); L. G. Flannery (ed.), *John Hunton's Diary*, Vol. 6, the last volume published (Glendale, Calif.; Arthur H. Clark Co., 1970); Shirley E. Flynn, *Our Heritage, 100 Years at St. Marks* (Cheyenne: Pioneer Printing Co., 1968); George C. Frison (ed.), *The Casper Site: A Hell Gap Bison Kill on the High Plains* (New York: Academic Press, 1974); Paul Frison, three small books by the Worland Press, *First White Woman in the Big Horn Basin* (1969), *The Apache Slave* (1969), and *Under the Ten Sleep Rim: An Autobiography* (1972); Jack R. Gage, *Wyoming Afoot and Horseback* (Cheyenne: Flintlock Publishing Co., 1966); Bertha Chambers Gillette, *Homesteading with the Elk: A Story of Frontier Life in Jackson Hole, Wyoming* (Idaho Falls: Mer-Jons Publishing Co., 1967); Lewis L. Gould, *Wyoming: A Political History, 1868–1896* (New Haven: Yale University Press, 1968); Fred R. Gowans, *Rocky Mountain Rendezvous: A History of the Fur Trade Rendezvous, 1825–1840* (Provo, Utah: Brigham Young University Press, 1976); Gene M. Gressley, *Bankers and Cattlemen* (New York: Knopf, 1966; rptd. Lincoln: University of Nebraska Press, 1971); Gene M. Gressley, *The Twentieth-Century American West: A Potpourri* (Columbia, Mo., University of Missouri Press, 1977); H. Duane Hampton, *How the U.S. Cavalry Saved Our National Parks* (Bloomington: Indiana University Press, 1971); Robert D. Hanesworth, *Daddy of 'em All: The Story of Cheyenne Frontier Days* (Cheyenne: Flintlock Publishing Co., 1967); James A. Hanson, *Metal Weapons, Tools, and Ornaments of the Teton Dakota Indians* (Lincoln: University of Nebraska Press, 1975); Robert V. Hine, *The American West: An Interpretive History* (Boston: Little Brown, 1973); William E. Hollon, *The Great American Desert: Then and Now* (Lincoln: University of Nebraska Press, 1975); Norris Hundley, Jr., *Water and the West: The Colorado River Compact and the Politics of Water in the American West* (Berkeley: University of California Press, 1975); Peggy Kirkbride, *From These Roots* (Cheyenne: Pioneer Printing and Stationery Co., 1972); Url Lanham, *The Bone Hunters* (New York: Columbia University Press, 1973); T. A. Larson (ed.), *Bill Nye's Western Humor* (Lincoln: University of Nebraska Press, 1968); Laramie County Chapter, Wyoming State Historical Society, *Cheyenne Landmarks* (Cheyenne: Pioneer Printing and Stationery Co., 1976); Sar A. Levitan and Barbara Hetrick, *Big Brother's Indian Programs— With Reservations* (New York: McGraw-Hill, 1971); J. D. Love and John C. Reed, Jr., *Creation of the Teton Landscape* (Jackson: Grand Teton Natural History Association, 1968); Harold McCracken, Richard I. Frost, Leo Platteter, and Don Hedgpeth, *The West of Buffalo Bill*, frontier art, Indian crafts, memorabilia from the Buffalo Bill Historical Center (New York: H. N. Abrams, 1974); R. E. McWhinnie (ed.), *Those Good Years at Wyoming University* (Laramie: University of Wyoming, 1965); Donald A. Messerschmidt (ed.), *The Grand Encampment* (Encampment: The Grand Encampment Museum, 1976); Harmon R. Mothershead, *The Swan Land and Cattle Co., Ltd.* (Norman: University of Oklahoma Press, 1971); Margaret E. and Olaus Murie, *Wapiti Wilderness* (New York: Knopf, 1966); Robert A. Murray, *Military Posts in the Powder River Country of Wyoming, 1865–1894* (Lincoln: University of Nebraska Press, 1968); Robert A. Murray, *Military Posts of Wyoming* (Fort Collins: The Old Army Press, 1974); Douglas W. Nelson, *Heart Mountain: The History of an American Concentration Camp* (Madison: State Historical Society, for the Department of History, University of Wisconsin, 1976); James C. Olson, *Red Cloud and the Sioux Problem* (Lincoln: University of Nebraska Press, 1965); Theodore B. Olson, *Ranch on the Laramie* (Boston: Little, Brown, 1973); Richard C. Overton, *Burlington Route* (New York: Knopf, 1965); Lucille Nichols Patrick, *The Best Little Town by a Dam Site* (Cheyenne: Flintlock Publishing Co., 1968); Lucille Nichols Patrick, *The Candy Kid: James Calvin "Kid" Nichols, 1883–1962* (Cheyenne: Flintlock Publishing Co., 1969); Mary Lou Pence, *The Laramie Story* (privately printed, 1968); Joseph M. Petulla, *American Environmental History and Conservation of Natural Resources* (San Francisco: Boyd and Fraser, 1977); John F. Reiger, *American Sportsmen and the Origins of Conservation* (New York: Winchester Press, 1975); Richard Reinhardt, *Out West on the Overland Train* (Secaurus, N.J.: Castle Books, 1967); W. S. Reese, *Six Score: The 120 Best Books on the Range Cattle Industry* (Austin: Kenkins Publishing Co., 1976); W. Sherman Savage, *Blacks in the West* (Westport, Conn.: Greenwood Press, 1977); David J. Saylor, *Jackson Hole, Wyoming: In the Shadows of the Tetons* (Norman: University of Oklahoma Press, 1971); Tom Shakespeare, *The Sky People* (New York: The Vantage Press, 1971); Louis L. Simonin, *The Rocky Mountain West in 1867*, translated from the French and edited by Wilson O. Clough (Lincoln: University of Nebraska Press, 1966); Charles Floyd Spencer, *Wyoming Homestead Heritage* (Hicksville, N.Y.: Exposition Press, 1975); Virginia Cole Trenholm, *The Arapahoes, Our People* (Norman: University of Oklahoma Press, 1970); Mae Urbanek, *Wyoming Place Names* (Boulder: Johnson Publishing Co., 1967); Robert M. Utley, *Frontier Regulars: The U.S. Army and the Indians, 1866–1891* (New York: Macmillan, 1974); Robert M. Utley, *Frontiersmen in Blue: The U.S. Army and the Indian, 1848–1865* (New York: Macmillan, 1967); J. W. Vaughn, *Indian Fights: New Facts on Seven Encounters* (Norman: University of Oklahoma Press, 1966); Robert Wakefield, *Schwiering and the West* (Aberdeen, S.D.: North Plains Press, 1973); David J. Wasden, *From Beaver to Oil: A Century in the Development of Wyoming's Big Horn Basin* (Cheyenne: Pioneer Printing and Stationery Co., 1973); L. Milton Woods, *Wyoming Country before Statehood* (Worland: Worland Press, 1971); Wyoming Recreation Commission, *Wyoming: A Guide to Historic Sites* (Basin: Big Horn Book Co., 1977); and Otis E. Young, Jr., *Black Powder and Hard Steel: Miners and Machines on the Old Western Frontier* (Norman: University of Oklahoma Press, 1976).

Four M.A. theses completed in 1977 in the University of Wyoming History Department merit attention: Eugene T. Carroll, "John Benjamin Kendrick, Western Senator: An Examination of Kendrick's Attitudes and Votes on Selected Western Conservation Measures"; John A. Fribley, "Bishop Ethelbert Talbot and the Missionary Experience on the Rocky Mountain Frontier, 1875–1900"; Gregg Kendrick, "An Environmental Spokesman: Olaus J. Murie and a Democratic Defense of Wilderness"; and Warren Onken, Jr., "Pioneer Missionary: The Life of John Roberts, 1853–1949."

Finally, just at press time, the Wyoming State Archives and Historical Department, Cheyenne, published two significant volumes: (1) Gordon Olaf Hendrickson, comp., *Wyoming Works Projects Administration Federal Writers' Project Collection Inventory* (Cheyenne, 1977). This inventory will save much time for scholars searching the voluminous records gathered by the Wyoming Writers' Project during the years 1936–1941. (2) Gordon Olaf Hendrickson, ed., *Peopling the High Plains: Wyoming's European Heritage* (Cheyenne, 1977). With a grant from the National Endowment for the Humanities, five research teams collected data on British, Italian, German, Greek, Basque, and Eastern European immigration to Wyoming. Dr. Hendrickson supervised the research teams, which were led by David Cookson, Don Hodgson, David Kathka, John C. Paige, and Earl P. Stinneford.

Acknowledgment

In the Preface and in the "Sources" section I have already expressed
appreciation for help many persons have given me in the preparation
of this *History of Wyoming*. Now as I pause at the end of my labors I
wish to pay my respects to one other—the late William Robertson Coe,
1869–1955, whose magnificent gift made possible construction of the
University of Wyoming Library, which is named for him. Mr. Coe also
endowed the university's School of American Studies. The library and
the special expenditures for books and research materials made possible
by the American Studies endowment have facilitated research and
writing not only for me but for many others as well. Each year the list
of persons who are indebted to Mr. Coe lengthens remarkably, and his
good works multiply.

Index

A

Abbott, George E., 315
Absaroka, state of, 471–472
Adams, Robert (Bob), 516
Adams, Thomas B., 153, 154, 185, 257
Administration and Fiscal Control, Department of (DAFC), 564
Afton, 291
Agriculture, 347, 359–365, 412, 416, 417; in 1880's, 162; during World War I, 396–397; during World War II, 487–489; after 1945, 523–528. *See also* Cattle industry, Dry farming, Reclamation, Sheep industry
Air age, begins, 425
Air Quality Act, 539–540, 562
Akers, Fred, 596, 597
Albany, 340
Albany County Stock Growers Association, 171
Albright, Horace M., 500
Alger Light Artillery, 311
All-American Indian Days, 532
Allemand, Joe, 371
All events center, 568, 597
Allied Chemical Company, 513
Almy (ghost town), 113, 142, 147, 298
Alsop, Thomas, 169
Alston, Felix, 371
Altitude, 1
Ambrose, Fred, 470
American Cattle Trust, 192–193

American Legion, 476, 481
American Studies, School of, 591
Ames brothers, Oakes and Oliver, 40, 62–63, 113–114
Ames monument, 62–63
Ancient man, 7
Anderson, A. A., 377–378
Anderson, Esther L., 468, 495, 502
Anderson, George D., 351
Angus, Red, 277
Animal life, 4
Anorthosite clay, 522
Anselmi, Don, 453
Anselmi, Rudolph, 551
Anthony, Susan B., 78, 83–84, 87
Anti-Saloon League, 408–409
Apportionment, legislative, 250, 251, 267, 289, 323, 393–394, 453, 463, 558, 565; and U.S. Supreme Court decision of 1964, 558
Appropriations, legislative, 1890–1897, 296; 1908–1924, 453–454; in 1929, 464; 1931, 464; 1933, 464; 1935, 469n; 1937, 469n; 1939, 469n; 1943, 497; 1945, 497; 1947, 545; 1949, 546; 1951 and 1953, 548; 1955, 549; 1957, 551; 1959, 552; 1961, 554; 1963, 556; 1965, 560; 1967, 562; 1969, 563; 1971, 564; 1973, 565; 1975 and 1976, 568
Arapaho Indians: frighten Robert Stuart, 8; activities to 1851, 12–15; and Colorado gold rush, 18–20; in Battle

645

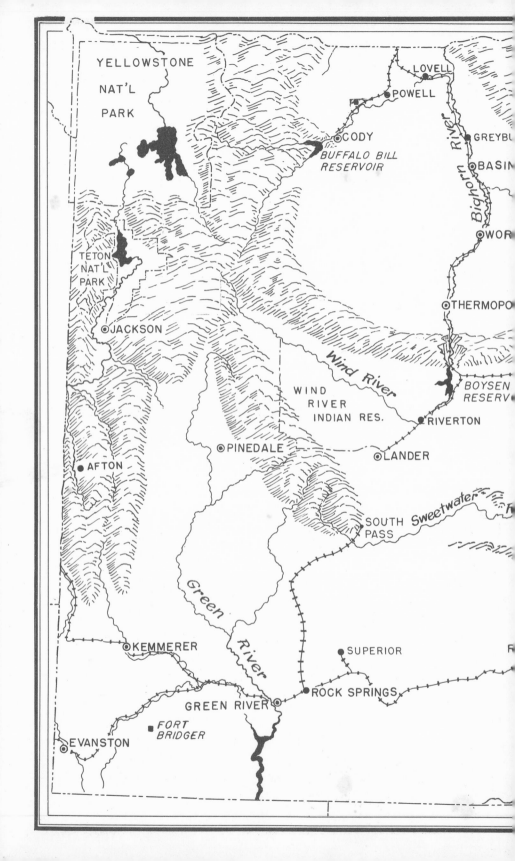